Management of the sales force

Management of the sales force

William J. Stanton
Professor of Marketing
University of Colorado

Richard H. Buskirk
Professor of Marketing
Southern Methodist University

Fifth edition   1978

RICHARD D. IRWIN, INC.   *Homewood, Illinois   60430*
IRWIN-DORSEY LIMITED   *Georgetown, Ontario   L7G 4B3*

ISBN 0-256-02046-9
Library of Congress Catalog Card No. 77–088288

Printed in the United States of America

6 7 8 9 0 MP 5 4 3 2 1 0

To Betty and Barbara

Preface

When the first edition of this book was published in 1959, our economic growth rate was strong and jobs for college graduates were plentiful. This new edition (the 5th) comes out in a quite different socioeconomic setting. Our economic growth rate and the birth rate both have slowed down considerably. Energy costs are soaring, high inflation is a persistent threat, and government regulation is increasing. Some industries face intensive foreign competition, and others periodically have to contend with shortages. People's values are changing. There is a demand for a better quality of life—and a better social and physical environment.

In response to this changing socioeconomic environment, the nature of the outside sales job has changed rather dramatically. A new kind of sales person has been developing—a more professional sales representative, a profit manager of a territory. These changes, in turn, have called for a substantial upgrading of the sales force executive's job. In the past the job often involved little more than being a field supervisor of the sales force. These managers often were little more than supersales persons. Today, in contrast, the job of a sales executive involves planning and evaluating sales force activities, as well as operating a sales force.

In this fifth edition of *Management of the Sales Force*, we have attempted to reflect these changing conditions in all parts of the book. At the same time, those who are familiar with the earlier editions will find that the basic scope, approach, and organization have been retained. This book is still concerned specifically with the management of an outside sales force and its activities. Outside sales people, those who go to the customers, are distinguished here from over-the-counter salespersons to whom the customers come. Therefore the book deals almost entirely with the management of sales forces of manufacturers and wholesaling middlemen.

In this edition all material has been updated, and several new concepts are introduced. Several chapters, including the one on ethical and social responsibilities of sales executives, have been substantially rewritten. Twenty-seven of the 44 cases are new. We also have added a series of 12 day-to-day operating problems of the sort typically faced by sales managers. These problems, located where appropriate within various chapters, are built around one firm—the Majestic Glass Company. They were written by Prof. Phillip McVey of the University of Nebraska—Lincoln.

The text has been shortened by reducing the depth of detail in many sections, and by reducing the number of chapters from 26 to 24. The former two chapters on sales organization have been combined into one. The former four chapters on recruiting and selection have been reduced to three, largely by condensing our discussion of psychological testing. The book has been redesigned physically, and the average length of sentences has been shortened to make the book a more effective learning tool. The careful editing in this edition also reflects the fact that outside sales forces now include women and members of minority groups. A female or black sales rep (representative) calling on an industrial purchasing agent no longer is a rarity. Consequently, in the relatively few instances that masculine pronouns are used in this book, they are used in a generic sense.

It seems appropriate that special attention should be devoted to the management of the sales force. This field should not be neglected by administrators in their preoccupation with marketing management. The sales people in the field have the task of properly carrying out the sales plan. In the final analysis, it is this group which brings in the revenue, and there is a direct relationship between company profits and the management of the sales force. Furthermore, the cost of administering and operating a sales force usually is by far the largest single marketing expense in a company.

The contents of this book can be valuable to student readers because their use of the knowledge can be fairly immediate. Few of them will become marketing managers very soon after graduation. Within a very few years, however, they may well be some type of sales force managers, perhaps at a district level. Even as sales people, they may be called upon to use material covered in this book. The year following their graduation they may come back to their alma mater as members of their firm's employee recruiting team. Or they may be called upon for suggestions regarding a proposed compensation, expense, or quota plan.

The text is divided into five main parts:

1. Introduction. In Chapter 2 we cast sales managers in their true role—that of an administrator. Also in the same chapter on adminis-

tration, we set forth a basic managerial philosophy which permeates the entire book. We believe that staffing—the selection of personnel at any level from top to bottom in an organization—is the most important function of administrators. It is not their *only* job, but it is the *most important* one.

2. Sales operations. This part, on operating a sales force, includes such topics as selecting, training, compensating, supervising, and stimulating sales people.

3. Sales planning. Part Three covers sales force activities and operations, including such tasks as determining sales and market potentials, forecasting sales, preparing sales department budgets, and establishing territories and quotas.

4. Sales analysis and evaluation. Part Four deals with analysis of sales operations and evaluation of sales people's productivity or effectiveness.

5. A look-ahead. Part Five includes chapters on the ethical problems and social responsibilities facing sales managers, and on career opportunities in sales management.

A question which may arise concerns the reason for putting sales planning and performance evaluation in a book which deals with sales force management. Today, most administrators of sales forces realize they cannot do an adequate job of managing their people without some planning and evaluation. Usually the people need guidance in the form of carefully designed districts and quotas, which in turn are based on forecasts, potentials, and budgets. The reason for including performance evaluation is much the same. Sales planning precedes the sales work, and evaluation should be done after the sales have been made for a period. After the results are in, management should analyze sales and costs by territories, products, or customer groups. This helps determine where there is need for change in territorial boundaries, quotas, compensation programs, training programs, or supervisory methods.

To help students understand and apply the material in the book, special attention has been given to the preparation of the discussion questions and the cases found at the end of the chapters. Generally the questions cannot be answered "straight out of the book." Instead, they are intended to be thought provoking and an aid in using the ideas set forth in the chapter. Many of the cases are intentionally designed as short examples of specific issues related to the topic covered in the chapter. In addition, in response to requests from many professors, we also have introduced some longer, more complex cases.

Directly and indirectly, many businessmen, publishers, present and past colleagues, and other professors have contributed greatly to the completion of this book. Many of these debts are acknowledged in footnotes and other references throughout the text. We particularly want to thank Professors Gary M. Armstrong, University of North Carolina at Chapel Hill, Phillip McVey, University of Nebraska-Lincoln, and Richard Nelson, San Francisco State University, for reviewing the entire manuscript and offering suggestions for its improvement.

January 1978   WILLIAM J. STANTON
                                                  RICHARD H. BUSKIRK

Contents

Part two   SALES OPERATIONS

Part four   SALES ANALYSIS AND EVALUATION

20   Analysis of sales volume   533

Introduction to sales analysis. Sales analysis and misdirected marketing effort. Problems involved in analysis of sales volume. Bases for
analyzing sales volume. Use of computers in sales analysis.

21   Marketing cost analysis   557

Nature and scope of marketing cost analysis. Problems involved in
marketing cost analysis. Types of marketing cost analysis. Use of findings from cost analysis. Return on investment.

22   Evaluating sales force performance   591

Nature and importance of performance evaluation. Program for
evaluating performance. Using evaluation data: An example.

Part five   A FORWARD LOOK

23   Ethical and social responsibilities of sales
executives   617

Business ethics and sales management. What is social responsibility?
Public regulation and sales managers.

24   Careers in sales management   650

The challenge. The wide variety of sales management positions. The life of a sales executive. The rewards of a sales management job. What it takes to be a successful sales manager. Women in selling.

CASES

Index   671

Part one

INTRODUCTION

The field of sales management

Nothing happens until somebody sells something.

ARTHUR H. MOTLEY

Like the song writers say, "Then was then and now is now," and "The times, they are a-changing." The 1970s saw the end of the post–World War II era—an era during which we experienced unparalleled economic prosperity, a high rate of economic growth, and a population boom. We also experienced an unpopular war, and dissenting movements among students, consumers, environmentalists, and civil rights advocates. The end of the era was characterized by price inflation, a severe recession, and an energy crisis.

As we prepare for the 1980s, new social and economic goals are being shaped by the realization that:

- Our birth rate is declining.
- The cost of energy is soaring.
- The rate of economic growth is slowing down, and the specter of inflation continues to haunt us.
- We no longer can afford the luxury of a socioeconomic philosophy based on a "cowboy frontier" economy of unlimited, low-cost resources. Instead, we live in a "spaceship" economy of limited, irreplaceable resources.
- We are developing a different set of social values which calls for a better quality of life and a pollution-free environment.
- We expect higher standards of social responsibility from business leaders.

These factors will present an interesting set of challenges to business management, and in particular to marketing and sales executives, in the 1980s. The success to be enjoyed by sales executives in the next decade will depend to a great extent upon their ability to meet these challenges. Sales force management activities must be attuned to this changing social, economic, and political environment.[1]

To introduce the study of sales force management, let's first review the nature and scope of marketing in the economy. Then let's see where the management of a sales force fits into a company's marketing program.

MARKETING IN OUR ECONOMY

Marketing is not solely a business activity. It has a broader, societal perspective which is more meaningful and truly descriptive of marketing today.

Societal dimensions of marketing

Any interpersonal or interorganizational relationship involving an exchange (a transaction) is marketing. That is, *the essence of marketing is a transaction—an exchange—intended to satisfy human needs or wants.* (In this book, the terms *needs* and *wants* are used interchangeably.) Consequently, marketing occurs any time one social unit strives to exchange something of value with another social unit. Marketing consists of all the activities designed to facilitate that exchange.[2]

Within this societal perspective then (1) the marketers (2) what they are marketing, and (3) their potential or target markets all assume broad dimensions. The category of *marketers* might include, in addition to business firms, such diverse social units as:

- A political party trying to market its candidate to the public.
- The director of an art museum providing new exhibits to generate greater attendance and financial support.
- A labor union marketing its ideas to its members and to company management.

---

[1] See Neil H. Jacoby, "Six Challenges to Business Management," *Business Horizons*, Autumn 1976, pp. 29–37; Alfred L. Seelye, "Societal Change and Business-Government Relationships," *MSU Business Topics*, Autumn 1975, pp. 5–11.

[2] See Philip Kotler, "A Generic Concept of Marketing," *Journal of Marketing*, April 1972, pp. 49–54; also see Philip Kotler and Sydney J. Levy, "Broadening the Concept of Marketing," *Journal of Marketing*, January 1969, pp. 10–15.

Professors are doing a marketing job when they try to make their courses interesting for their students. Anytime you try to persuade somebody to do something—donate to the Red Cross, do not litter the highways, save energy, accept a social date with you (or maybe marry you)—you are engaging in marketing.

In addition to the range of items normally considered as products and services, in a broader sense *what is being marketed* might include *ideas,* such as reducing air pollution or stopping smoking, or *people,* such as a new football coach or a political candidate.

In a broad sense, *target markets* include more than the direct consumers of products, services, and ideas. A state university's market includes the legislators who provide funds, the citizens living near the university who may be affected by its activities, and the alumni, as well as the faculty and students.

Business dimensions of marketing

But this is a book about managing a sales force primarily in a business setting. So let's see what marketing looks like in a business context. Marketing is a total system of business action designed to create and deliver a standard of living for consumers. Marketing involves:

Finding out what the consumers want,

> then planning and developing a product or service that will satisfy those wants,

>> and then determining the best way to price, promote, and distribute that product or service.

Stated more formally, marketing is *a total system of business activities designed to plan, price, promote, and distribute want-satisfying goods and services to present and potential customers.*

Marketing is:	
A system:	of business activities
Designed to:	plan, price, promote, and distribute
Something of value:	want-satisfying goods and services
To the benefit of:	the market—present and potential house-hold consumers or industrial users.

This definition has several significant implications:

First, it is a managerial systems definition.

Second, the entire system of business action should be market or customer oriented. Customers' wants must be recognized and satisfied effectively.

Third, marketing is a dynamic business procedure—a total, integrated process—rather than a fragmented assortment of institutions and functions. Marketing is not any one activity nor is it exactly the sum of several; rather, it is the result of the interaction of many activities.

Fourth, the marketing program starts with the germ of a product idea and does not end until the customers' wants are completely satisfied, which may be sometime after sales are made.

Fifth, to be successful, marketing must maximize profitable sales over the *long run*. Customers must be satisfied if a company is to get the repeat business which is ordinarily vital to success.

Current importance of marketing

Today most nations, regardless of their stage of economic development or their political philosophy, are recognizing the importance of marketing. Economic growth in developing nations depends upon their ability to develop effective distribution systems to handle their raw materials and their agricultural output. Countries with major state-owned industries (such as Great Britain, Sweden, and Italy) are looking to modern marketing practices as a way to improve their economic health. Even communist countries (Russia and other Eastern European nations) are beginning to use advertising and other marketing activities.

In the American economic system.   It is in the United States that marketing has been developed to its highest level. Creative marketing practices have been largely responsible for the high material standard of living in America. Today, through mass, low-cost marketing, we enjoy products which once were considered luxuries, and which still are so classified in many foreign countries.

Since about 1920, except for the World War II years, a strong buyers' market has existed in this country. That is, the available supply of products and services has far surpassed the effective demand for them. There has been relatively little difficulty in producing most of these goods; the real problem has been in selling them. During recession periods, people soon realize that it is a slowdown in marketing activity which is forcing cutbacks in production. It becomes evident that "nothing happens until somebody sells something."

Let's look at some quantitative measures which indicate the importance of marketing. Between one fourth and one third of the civilian labor force is engaged in marketing activities. This includes all employees in retailing, wholesaling, transportation, warehousing, and the communications industries. It also includes people employed in marketing departments of manufacturers, as well as those engaged in marketing activities for financial, service, agricultural, mining, and other so-called nonmarketing industries. Over the past century, jobs in marketing have increased at a much more rapid rate than jobs in production have. The great increase in the number of people in marketing is a reflection of its expanded role in the economy and the increased demand for marketing services.

Another measure of marketing's importance is its cost. On the average, about 50 cents of each dollar we spend at the retail level goes to cover marketing costs. These costs should not be confused with marketing *profits*, however, nor should it be assumed that products and services would cost less if there were no marketing activities.

An economy of abundance.   The type of economy we have in the United States largely explains why marketing is so much an American phenomenon. Unlike economies elsewhere in the world, ours is an economy of abundance. This means that as a nation we produce far beyond our subsistence needs. We have an adequate national disposable income and considerable discretionary purchasing power. Marketing is especially important for successful business performance in a highly competitive economy of abundance.

Marketing in an era of shortages.   In the 1970s many industries in the United States were faced rather abruptly with an economic situation which was quite new to management—there were shortages of materials with which to make their products and operate their factories, stores, and other institutions. Students of the situation have been advancing the idea that the United States has reached the end of an era characterized by economist Kenneth Boulding as a "cowboy economy"—an era which reflected the frontier philosophy of unlimited resources where a person could use products and waste them as he pleased.

We have said that there is little difficulty in producing goods—that the real problem is in selling them. In some industries today, this statement should be modified. Management is worried about how to *make* the products. At the same time, in most of these industries, management still has to worry about how to sell them. Shortages of some materials and the soaring cost of energy are causing substantial changes in the marketing programs of many companies. In an abrupt about-face from the product-line strategy of the 1950s and 1960s, many firms today are slimming down their product mix by eliminating low-profit items.

In sales force management, new strategies are needed in an era of shortages. For example, selecting and training sales people are different where the sales job is to service existing accounts and to allocate a scarce supply than when the job consists of creative selling to develop new accounts.[3]

The publicity devoted to shortages can be misleading, however. Essentially, the United States still has an economy of abundance, and consumers still have considerable disposable income. It is just that the priorities are changing, and management must recognize and adapt to the changes. Industries faced with shortages will *not* find marketing task easier, even though some executives have the shortsighted attitude: "Why spend money on marketing when we can sell all we can produce?" Most firms still face substantial challenges in marketing; competition within industries and between industries is still intense in most cases.

Nevertheless, environmental forces such as inflation and shortages are changing the life-style of U.S. consumers. These changes have significant implications for the marketing programs in many firms.

In the individual firm.   In many firms today, marketing considerations are the most critical factors in planning and decision making. In the past, unfortunately, a production orientation often permeated much of American business. Products have been designed by engineers, manufactured by production men, priced by accountants, and then given to sales managers to sell. Just *making* a good product will not ensure a company's success, nor will it have much bearing on consumer welfare. The product must be *marketed* to consumers before its full value can be realized.

Many organizational departments in a company are essential to its growth, but marketing is still the sole revenue-producing activity. Marketing generates the revenues that the financial people manage and the production people use in making products and services.

MARKETING MANAGEMENT AND ITS EVOLUTION

As business people have begun to recognize that marketing is vitally important to the success of a firm, an entirely new way of business thinking—a new philosophy—has evolved. This is called the *marketing concept.* For a business enterprise to realize the full benefits of the marketing concept, the philosophy must be translated into action. *Marketing management is the marketing concept in action.*

---

[3] See Michael B. Rothfeld, "A New Kind of Challenge for Salesmen," *Fortune,* April 1974, pp. 156–160 ff.; "Shortages Expand the Salesman's Role," *Industry Week,* March 18, 1974, p. 19; *Sales Management,* January 21, 1974, entire issue devoted to "How Can I Keep My Sales Force Running in a Crunch Economy?"

The marketing concept

This philosophy of business is based on three fundamental beliefs.

1. All company planning and operations should be *customer oriented.*
2. *Profitable sales volume* over the long run should be the goal of the firm, and not just volume for the sake of volume alone.
3. All marketing activities in a firm should be *organizationally coordinated.*

These three foundations of the marketing concept are diagrammed in Figure 1–1.

FIGURE 1–1
The marketing concept's three foundation stones

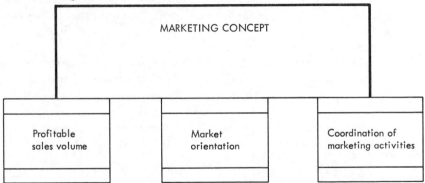

In its fullest sense, the marketing concept is a philosophy of business which states that the customers' want satisfaction is the economic and social justification for the firm's existence. Consequently, all company activities must be devoted to finding out what the customers want and then satisfying those wants, while making a profit over the long run.

Four-stage evolution of marketing management

Since the Industrial Revolution, marketing management in American business has evolved through three stages of development, and a fourth one is emerging. However, many companies are still in one of the earlier stages. Also, only a few firms as yet exhibit the managerial philosophies and practices which are characteristic of the most advanced developmental period. The four stages in the evolution of marketing management are diagramed below:

Production-orientation stage. During the first stage a company typically is production oriented. The executives in production and engineering shape the company's objectives and planning. The function of the sales department is simply to sell the production output, and at a price set by production and financial executives. This is the "build a better mousetrap" stage. The underlying assumption is that marketing effort is not needed to get people to buy a product which is well made and reasonably priced.

During this period, manufacturers have sales departments (marketing is not yet recognized), headed by a sales manager whose main job is to operate a sales force. As markets expand, separate organizational divisions are sometimes established for specialized marketing activities such as advertising or marketing research. This form of organizational pattern predominated in the United States until about the start of the Great Depression in the 1930s.

Sales-orientation stage. The depression made it quite clear that the main problem in our economy no longer was being able to make or grow enough products. Rather, the problem was selling this output. Just producing a better mousetrap was no assurance of market success. The product had to be sold, and this called for a substantial amount of promotional effort. Thus we entered a period during which selling and sales executives were given new respect and responsibilities by company management.

Unfortunately, also during this period selling acquired much of its bad reputation. This was the age of the "hard sell." The image of selling often reflected the tactics of the used-car or door-to-door encyclopedia salesman. Even today many organizations—both in business and nonbusiness settings—still believe they must operate with a sales-stage (that is, a hard-sell) philosophy in order to survive and prosper. Many home repair "services" and other door-to-door sales people still operate in this fashion, and charities often use hard-sell techniques to solicit contributions. The idea of first finding out what the consumer wants does not often enter the thinking of organizations operating in the sales stage. As long as there are companies operating with a sales-stage philosophy, there will be continued (and justified, in our opinion) criticism of selling and marketing.

Two significant organizational changes typically occur during the sales stage. First, all marketing activities, such as advertising and marketing research, are grouped under one executive, typically called a sales manager or the vice president of sales. Second, activities such as sales training or sales analysis, which formerly were located in departments outside of sales, are put in the sales department. The sales-orientation era generally extended from the 1930s well into the 1950s, although no specific dates sharply define any of the four stages.[4]

Marketing-orientation stage. In the third stage, companies embrace the concept of coordinated marketing management, directed toward the twin goals of customer satisfaction and *profitable* sales volume. Attention is focused on marketing rather than on selling, and the top executive is called a marketing manager or the vice president of marketing. In this stage, several activities which traditionally were the province of the production manager or other executives become the responsibility of the marketing manager (see Figure 1–2). For instance, inventory control, warehousing, and aspects of product planning are often turned over to the marketing manager. When a firm adopts the marketing concept and appoints a marketing manager, the position of the chief sales force executive (general sales manager, for example) drops down one level in the executive echelons.

The function of the marketing manager, according to General Electric, should be introduced at the beginning, rather than the end of the production cycle. In this way marketing can be integrated into each stage of the operations and can influence all short-term and long-range company policies.

Business is now in the third stage in the evolution of marketing management. The marketing concept has generally been adopted by both large and medium-sized companies. The president of Burroughs Corporation caught the spirit of firms which have fully embraced the marketing concept when he said, "Any company is nothing but a marketing organization." And the president of Pepsi-Cola has said, "Our business is the business of marketing."

---

[4] The conceptual foundations for scientific sales management and modern marketing management actually were laid in the literature of the 1920s and earlier, where we find a direct application of Frederick W. Taylor's scientific management concepts to early sales management. See Bernard J. LaLonde and Edward J. Morrison, "Marketing Management Concepts Yesterday and Today," *Journal of Marketing,* January 1967, pp. 9–13.

FIGURE 1–2
Company organization chart embracing the concept of marketing management

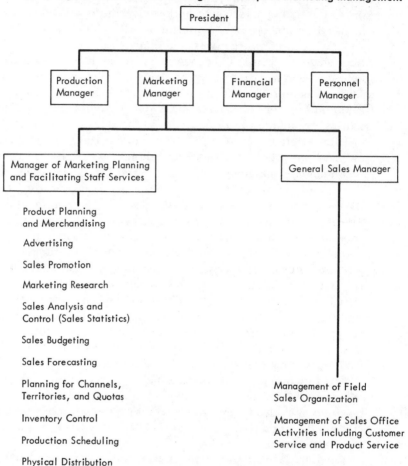

At this point all marketing activities have been integrated under a single marketing manager. Organizationally, the company has adopted the marketing concept.

The key to implementing the marketing concept successfully is a favorable attitude on the part of top management. As an executive at the Chase Manhattan Bank stated: "Marketing begins with top management. Only top management can provide the climate, the discipline, and the leadership required for a successful marketing program." A top marketing executive at International Minerals and Chemical Corporation warned:

But a company cannot become customer-conscious by edict. Since all organizations tend to emulate their leader, it is most important that the head of the business be thoroughly customer-conscious. . . . He can develop a mood, an atmosphere, and an esprit de corps reflecting the preeminence of the customer that permeates every nook and corner of the company.[5]

We are *not* saying that marketing executives should hold the top positions in a company. The marketing concept does *not* imply that the president of a firm must come up through the marketing department, or that other departments will wither on the organizational vine. But we *are* saying that the president must be marketing oriented, and *marketing thinking must pervade the entire organization.*

How well many companies have actually implemented the marketing concept, however, is still a moot point. There are many forms and degrees of market orientation. Probably many companies, although using the appropriately fashionable titles and other external trappings, are still paying little more than lip service to the concept. In many instances, unfortunately, the misunderstanding endures that marketing is merely a fancy name for selling.

The wave of consumer protests which has been called consumerism is an indicator to some people that there has been a failure to implement the marketing concept.[6] Others go so far as to suggest that the traditional marketing concept is an operational philosophy which conflicts with a company's social responsibility to its consumers.[7]

Social responsibility and human–orientation stage.   Social and economic conditions in the 1970s led to the fourth stage in the evolution of marketing management—a period characterized by a societal orientation. It is becoming increasingly obvious that marketing executives must act in a socially responsible manner if they wish to succeed, or even survive, in this era. External pressures—consumer discontent, a concern for environmental problems, and political-legal forces—are influencing marketing programs in countless firms.

Profit making will continue as a key goal in marketing management. However, in this fourth stage we can expect to see executives more concerned with long-run, rather than short-run, profit goals. Also, the

---

[5] Anthony E. Cascino, "Organizational Implications of the Marketing Concept," in Eugene J. Kelley and William Lazer (eds.), *Managerial Marketing: Perspectives and Viewpoints,* 3d ed. (Homewood, Ill.: Richard D. Irwin, Inc., 1967), p. 346.

[6] See Hiram C. Barksdale and Bill Darden, "Marketers' Attitudes toward the Marketing Concept," *Journal of Marketing,* October 1971, pp. 29–36.

[7] Martin L. Bell and C. William Emory, "The Faltering Marketing Concept," *Journal of Marketing,* October 1971, pp. 37–42. Peter Drucker (a professor and management consultant, and one who is certainly not unfriendly toward business) has referred to consumerism as "the shame of the total marketing concept."

concepts of social profit and social auditing will influence marketing managers.

This fourth stage also may be viewed more broadly as a human-orientation period, in which there will be a growing concern for the management of human resources in marketing. One mark of an affluent, economically well-developed society is a shift in consumption from products to services, and a shift in cultural emphasis from things to people. In this stage, marketing management must be concerned with creating and delivering a better quality of *life*, rather than with only a material standard of *living*.[8]

SALES FORCE MANAGEMENT AND THE TOTAL MARKETING PROGRAM

So far we have been discussing marketing and marketing management. But this is a book about the management of a sales force—that is, the management of the personal selling effort of a firm. So now let's consider the relationship between sales force management and marketing—and the place of personal selling in a company's total marketing program.

A company must operate its marketing system within a framework of forces which constitute the system's environment. Two sets of these forces are external to the company, and another two sets are internal.

External environment

Six macroenvironmental forces impinge considerably on any company's marketing system, yet they generally are *not* controllable by management. This set of forces includes:

1. Demography
2. Economic conditions
3. Sociocultural factors
4. Political-legal factors
5. Technology
6. Competition

In addition, a company faces a set of three forces which are also external but are *directly* a part of the firm's marketing system. These are the company's market, its suppliers, and marketing intermediaries (primarily middlemen). Figure 1–3 illustrates these external sets of forces. While generally classed as uncontrollable, these three elements are susceptible to a greater degree of company influence than

---

[8] See Leslie M. Dawson, "The Human Concept: New Philosophy for Business," *Business Horizons*, December 1969, pp. 29–38; Leonard L. Berry, "Marketing Challenges in the Age of People," *MSU Business Topics*, Winter 1972, pp. 7–13.

the others are. Note the two-way flows between the company and these three external elements in Figure 1–3. The company receives products and promotional messages from its suppliers. In return, the company sends payments and marketing information. The same types of exchanges occur between the company and its market. Any of these exchanges can go through one or more middlemen.

FIGURE 1–3
External environment of a company's marketing system

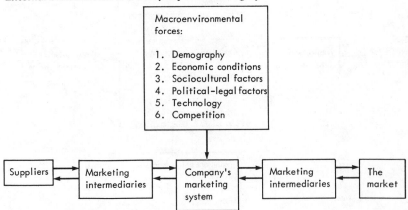

Six uncontrollable macroenvironmental forces impinge upon a company's marketing system. Three other external forces also tend to shape this system, but the company can influence these forces to some degree.

Internal variables in marketing systems

To reach its marketing goals, management has at its disposal two sets of internal, controllable forces: (1) the company's resources in nonmarketing areas and (2) the components of its *marketing mix*—its product, price structure, promotional activities, and distribution system. Figure 1–4 shows these internal forces combined with the forces in the external environment illustrated in Figure 1–3. The result is the company's total marketing system, set within its environment.

The *marketing mix* is the term used to describe the combination of the four "ingredients" which constitute the core of a company's marketing system. When these four—product, price, distribution, and promotion—are effectively blended, they form a marketing program designed to provide want-satisfying goods and services to the company's market.

FIGURE 1-4

A company's complete marketing system: A framework of internal resources operating within a set of external forces

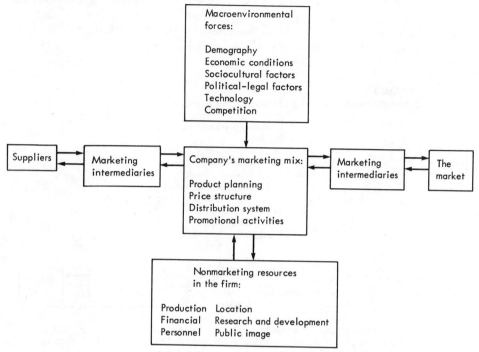

Promotional activities form a separate submix we call the *promotional mix* or the *communications mix* in the company's marketing program. The major elements in the promotional mix are the company's advertising, sales promotion, and personal selling effort. In the American economy the most important of these three, by any measure—people employed, dollars spent, sales generated—is the

FIGURE 1-5

The place of sales force management in a company's marketing management decision mix

A company's marketing mix:

Product planning
Price structure
Distribution system
Promotional activities

Personal selling ⟶ Management of the sales force

Advertising

Sales promotion

personal selling effort. It is the management of that personal selling effort—the management of the sales force—that is the topic of this book (see Figure 1–5).

NATURE AND IMPORTANCE OF SALES MANAGEMENT

Sales management (or sales force management) is the management of the personal selling component of a company's marketing program. During the early stages of the evolution of marketing management, sales management was viewed quite narrowly. Generally it was limited to such tasks as recruiting and selecting a sales force, and then training, compensating, supervising, and motivating these sales people. Today selling and sales management have taken on new dimensions. Furthermore, we are recognizing that the sales person's and the sales executive's jobs are different from other jobs.

New dimensions of sales management and selling

As marketing management has evolved, the concepts of sales management and selling have assumed significantly broader dimensions. Today's top sales force managers are involved more in setting sales goals, planning a program to reach these goals, and evaluating the results. Their job is to coordinate the field selling with the other elements in their company's total marketing program. They are more of planning executives and less operations managers, although they still are responsible for the general administration of sales force activities. Today less of their time is spent in daily routine contacts with sales people.

In a similarly broad vein, today's sales representatives are managers of a market area—their territories. Often they are assigned a profit responsibility in those markets. In line with the marketing concept, the sales reps are trained to identify customers' wants and to help solve customers' problems. They must organize much of their own time and effort. They may participate in recruiting, market planning in their territories, and other managerial activities.[9]

The societal dimension which characterizes the emergent fourth stage of marketing management has considerable influence on the nature and scope of sales management and on the jobs of sales people

---

[9] The term *sales rep* will be used frequently throughout this book as a short form of *sales representative*. Sales rep is commonly used in business, and it parallels such titles as factory rep or manufacturers' rep. We are using rep as synonymous with sales person, saleswoman, or salesman.

and sales executives. Table 1–1 illustrates the changing emphasis in sales management over the years, paralleling the four-stage evolution of marketing management.

TABLE 1–1
Changing emphasis in sales management

	1900–1920	1930–1940	1950–1960	1970–1980
Business response to perceived dominant environmental conditions	Production orientation	Sales orientation	Marketing orientation	Human orientation
Emphasis in management's conception of sales job	Personality, art	Scientific salesmanship	Professionalism	Personal fulfillment
Emphasis in sales management	Tight supervision and control	Broadened responsibilities	Strategies and profits	Total human resource development

Source: Leslie M. Dawson, "Toward a New Concept of Sales Management," *Journal of Marketing,* April 1970, p. 37.

How sales jobs differ from other jobs

Why is it useful to study the management of a sales force separately from the management of other classes of business personnel? Why are there no courses in the management of accountants or finance personnel? Separate treatment for sales people is warranted largely because the sales job is so different from other jobs and so important to a company's financial well-being.

Sales people represent their company to customers and to society in general. Opinions of the firm and its products are formed on the basis of impressions left by these people in their work and outside activities. The public ordinarily does not judge a company by its factory or office workers. But because sales reps are so visible and available, they are often blamed for mistakes made elsewhere in the firm.

Typically, a factory or office employee works under the close supervisory control of a foreman or office manager, whereas sales reps operate with little or no direct supervision. Compared with a sales person, most other employee groups can perform successfully with relatively little stimulation. For success in many selling tasks, however, a sales rep must work hard physically and mentally, be creative and persistent, and show great initiative—and this requires a high degree of motivation.

A sales person needs more tact and social intelligence than other employees on the same level in the organization. Many sales jobs require the rep to mix socially with customers, who frequently are people of high rank in their companies. Considerable social intelligence may be needed in dealing with difficult buyers.

Sales people are among the few employees authorized to spend company funds. They have the responsibility for the proper use of money for entertainment, room, food, transportation, and other business expenses. Their effectiveness in discharging this responsibility can have a significant influence on marketing costs and profits.

Sales jobs frequently require considerable traveling and demand much time away from home and family. Being in the field puts sales people in enemy territory, where they must deal with an apparently endless stream of customers who may seem determined not to buy their products. Mental stresses and disappointments, coupled with the physical demands of long hours, much traveling, strange beds and food, and perhaps heavy sample cases or catalogs, combine to require a degree of mental toughness and physical stamina that is rarely demanded in other types of jobs. Selling is hard work!

How sales management jobs differ from other management jobs

Some of the factors which make sales jobs different also affect the sales manager's job, which differs from other management jobs in several respects. A key point is that the geographical deployment of the sales force means that the sales manager cannot directly oversee the work, nor can the manager control the environment in which this work is done. Other aspects of jobs and careers in sales management are discussed in more detail in Chapter 24.

Importance of management of the sales force

The attention devoted to marketing management in many businesses today should in no way lessen the importance of sales force management. In fact, top administrators should be careful not to neglect the management of their sales forces in their preoccupation with marketing management.

When marketing management is stressed in a firm, executive attention is devoted to sales and market planning. Such emphasis may be well placed, but ordinarily it takes the sales force in the field to carry out the sales plan. No plan is of much value until it is executed properly. If sales people cannot successfully sell their product because they are improperly selected, trained, or compensated, the efforts devoted to product planning or sales planning are of little value. About the only exceptions are in firms that do not rely on their own sales force but instead primarily use advertising or agent middlemen, such as brokers, to move the products. Since the sales force is critical to the success of a concern's marketing venture, the sound management of these representatives is of obvious importance.

The cost of managing and operating a sales force typically is the largest single operating expense for most firms. While it is marketing's responsibility to generate sales volume revenues, these revenues are valuable only if sales expenses incurred in getting the volume are reasonable. The public's attention and criticism are most often directed at advertising and the amounts a firm spends for television or magazine exposure. Yet the firm's total advertising expenditures may be only 3 or 4 percent of net sales, while the total expenses related to sales people may be 15 or 20 percent of net sales.

In the administrative structure of most firms, many executive echelons are involved in sales force management. The term *sales manager* may be applied to any of the following:

- The top marketing executive.
- The head of the field sales force.
- A divisional manager responsible for several districts.
- The manager of any one of those districts.
- An administrator in charge of the people who sell only one of the company's product lines.

In contrast, when we speak of executives in advertising or marketing research, we are speaking of relatively few people.

For students there is an added dimension to the study of sales force management, because you soon may make contact with these activities. Within a year or two after graduation, you may well be serving as a sales supervisor or a district sales manager. Even as a sales person, you may engage in managerial activities such as visiting your alma mater to do employee recruiting. You may be asked to do some sales forecasting for your territory or to offer suggestions regarding a proposed compensation or quota plan.

QUESTIONS AND PROBLEMS

1. For each of the following organizations, describe what is being marketed, and what the target market is.
   a. Green Bay Packers professional football team.
   b. United Automobile Workers labor union.
   c. Professor teaching a freshman sociology course.

d. Resort hotel in Catskill Mountains (New York).

e. Police department in your city.

2. The number of people engaged in marketing activities has increased twelvefold between 1870 and 1950, while the number of production workers increased only threefold. How do you account for this fact? Does it indicate economic waste and relative inefficiency in marketing?

3. What is the marketing concept?

4. Explain the differences between the production stage and the sales stage in the evolution of marketing management.

5. Carefully distinguish between the sales stage and the marketing stage in the evolution of marketing management.

6. Name some companies you believe are still in the production stage. In the sales stage. Explain your reasoning in each example.

7. The president of Pepsi-Cola Company has said, "Our business is the business of marketing." How would you explain this idea to a student majoring in accounting, finance, or production management?

8. The quotation at the beginning of the chapter is "Nothing happens until somebody sells something." How would you convince a lawyer, production manager, farmer, banker, or aerospace engineer that the statement is true?

9. Explain how the six macroenvironmental forces listed in Figure 1–3 might influence a company's marketing program.

10. Explain the concept of the marketing mix and its relation to the management of a sales force.

11. Do you agree that "A sales job requires a degree of mental toughness and physical stamina rarely demanded in other types of jobs"? Discuss.

12. Explain why sales force management should continue to receive executive attention in a firm, even after the company adopts the marketing management concept.

2

The sales manager
as an administrator

The first impression that one gets of a ruler and of his
brains is from seeing the men that he has about him.
MACHIAVELLI

One of the ironies of sales management is that the person in charge usually acquires the position on the basis of selling talent but succeeds or fails in it because of administrative skills. These skills may or may not have been developed on the way up. In this chapter we explore the administrative aspects of the sales manager's job.

ADMINISTRATION: A DISTINCT SKILL

Administration has only recently been recognized as a separate body of knowledge, as the concept of managing people has become acceptable.[1] Perhaps our reluctance to acknowledge it stems from our cultural distaste for the idea of manipulating people by any means to do what needs to be done. Call it what you want, but this is management. Few things would happen in this world without it, and it is emphasized in our present socioeconomic system.

Technical ability not sufficient

Although many people with outstanding technical abilities do make good administrators, there is considerable evidence that the possession of technical talent alone does not necessarily make a good

---

[1] One early (1530) writer on administration, Niccolo Machiavelli, consistently has been criticized for his observations on the art of administering the activities of other people, even though his book *The Prince* has endured through the ages.

manager. (Witness the sports world, where many successful coaches—administrators—were only average players.) In the sales field, it is widely recognized that the best sales person may not make the best sales manager. The very factors that create an outstanding sales person can also cause failure as an administrator. For example, most highly successful sales people like extensive personal contact with customers in the field. The successful sales manager, however, must attend to a considerable amount of paper work—planning, controlling, and evaluating—in the home office. And, while many successful sales representatives have strong, aggressive personalities, this characteristic can be a liability to administrators who must work closely with superiors, equals, and subordinates.

While possession of technical skills does not necessarily make a good administrator, some degree of proficiency is needed. It would be difficult to envision a successful sales manager who had little knowledge of selling. First, a sales manager planning to hire sales people must know what attributes to look for. Second, the manager who lacks technical skills is continually at the mercy of subordinates. He cannot evaluate their competency or the soundness of their recommendations or methods of operation. Third, the sales manager must make the sales force confident that he can lead them, and his own successful sales experience can inspire such confidence. Finally, a person who is not fairly successful in selling may never get the chance to become a sales manager, no matter how good an administrator he may be potentially.

Universality of management principles

Most of the activities people engage in (such as war, business, sports) are goal directed—the participants seek to achieve something. Groups of individuals join together in the belief that they have the same goals and they are more likely to achieve them as a group. If any semblance of efficiency and orderly progress toward the goals is to be realized, the groups' activities must be managed—that is, planned, organized, and controlled.

The fundamental principles underlying success in administering all types of behavior are essentially the same. The memoirs of military leaders and sports coaches reveal that the basic principles underlying their success were no different than those business leaders have adopted. Gen. U.S. Grant was far more concerned with the qualities of his subordinates than with military strategy and tactics. Coaches attribute their success to subordinates, training programs, recruiting and selection procedures, and team morale.

It is this universality of management principles that allows the executive to transfer administrative abilities from one job to another with ease. The existence of these management principles makes administration a distinct skill separate from technical abilities.

Management can be learned

One top executive of a vigorously growing company, a leader in the Young Presidents' Organization, confessed to a group of business students that in his first job he discovered he was a terrible manager. He set out to rectify this deficiency by volunteering for charitable work. In this way he learned how to organize people and get them to work together. It was slow going, but he claimed it was well worth the effort.

Another young president reported he had learned a great deal about administration by studying executives and how they behaved in managing their enterprises. Observing the tactical behavior of both successful and unsuccessful managers helped him form some ideas on what and what not to do in managing people.

The moral of these tales is that you can learn to manage by managing. There is no inborn managerial trait.

WHAT A SALES MANAGER DOES

A glance at the table of contents of this book will provide some idea of the general scope of the sales manager's duties. Chapter 24, "Careers in Sales Managment," gives a detailed, personal view of the job.

First, the sales manager is responsible for hiring the sales force, arranging it in some meaningful organizational structure, and deploying it geographically. These activities are focused on maintaining a group of people in the field to sell the company's products and services. But that is only the beginning. Sales people need training, supervision, and motivation. These are the tasks devoted to improving performance of the sales force. The sales people must be compensated by some meaningful scheme, and the expenses they incur in pursuing the company's business must be reimbursed.

Planning is well recognized as one of management's main functions. The sales manager must analyze markets, develop sales forecasts, formulate budgets, set quotas, establish territories, and plot operational plans. And the manager who did not analyze and evaluate sales performance with an eye to improving it would be negligent. These are the obvious activities of the sales manager.

Sales managers also perform numerous tasks which cannot be classified so easily. Perhaps troubleshooting would best describe these activities. Customer relations figure largely in the sales manager's day: Things go wrong. Orders are late or incomplete. The wrong goods are sent. The goods are not what was ordered or are not of the expected quality. The credit department is giving a slow-paying customer a bad time. The list could go on.

The sales manager must also handle the competition, which seldom does what the company would like them to do. They cut prices, invade markets, bring out new products, hire away sales people, and steal accounts or dealers. And they can get rough and use unethical, even illegal, tactics to gain an increased share of the market. The sales manager is expected to handle such competitive developments and prevent the firm from being hurt by them.

Even within the organization the sales manager must cope with problems. The accountant questions expense accounts and can see no reason why the sales department needs more funds. Production is not making the right products; the customers want one model but the production planners produce more of another. The personnel manager insists that the sales department must hire more people from minority groups.

The sales manager's schedule is subject to constant interruption. In the morning mail there is a letter from the Federal Trade Commission accusing the company's sales force of misrepresentation. The manager will have to spend a great deal of time with the firm's lawyers to answer the charge. A college student majoring in marketing appears at the door and asks for an interview. The student's sales management professor has assigned a term paper in which a sales manager must be interviewed. There goes another afternoon. The phone rings, and the president's secretary asks if the sales manager will fill in for him at a trade association conference on industry standards. The manager looks at the schedule and sees that it will be necessary to cancel a speech before the local sales executive club. The manager's secretary ushers in a sales representative who has hopes of selling a data information system to the firm. The sales manager will be the ultimate decision maker because it will be paid for out of the sales department's budget.

Such activities, and many of the things sales managers do, could be classified as fighting fires. Sometimes they have little time left to devote to the basic things they should be doing, such as the topics covered in this book. They usually want to spend more time with the sales force and regret the amount of time they must spend on other things.

POLICY[2]

The word *policy* has been so widely used for a variety of concepts that it has lost precise meaning. It is applied to such statements as "It

---

[2] The material in this section is adapted from Richard H. Buskirk, *Business and Administrative Policy* (New York: John Wiley & Sons, Inc., 1971), pp. 145–50.

is the *policy* of this company to give Christmas bonuses." There are
many levels of policies, some being no more than work rules, but they
all play a role in the management of an enterprise. Indeed, it could be
maintained that routine day-to-day business is largely managed by
policy, and most decisions are made by reference to it. Thus the manager must devote time and thought to policy making and the handling
of exceptional circumstances.

The role of policy

Managers must appreciate that policies are not only necessary in
the management of an organization, they actually make the job easier.
Moreover, policies perform several definite functions for management.
They provide for uniform behavior, continuity of decisions, communications, automatic decision making, and protection from expediency.

Uniformity of behavior within the organization. Particularly in large
organizations, management must try to coordinate the behavior of all
work groups to minimize friction within the organization and outside
it. If one branch manager followed the practice of giving customers
expensive gifts for Christmas while other managers did not do so, for
example, it would only be a matter of time before some neglected
customer reacted adversely to this discrimination. Similarly, it would
be unwise to allow one plant manager complete freedom in purchasing while making all other plant managers use central purchasing.
Uniformity of organizational behavior avoids resentment over special
treatment. People want to be treated equally, and most resent
favoritism.

Continuity of decisions. There is also a need for uniformity of decisions over a period of time. Customers and employees alike expect to
be treated in the same manner each time they interact with a company; discontent can result from unexpected changes of policy.
Policies also bridge the gap between changes of management and
prevent inadvertent interruptions in successful operating procedures.
In General Motors, for example, the basic operating policies remain
essentially the same, despite changes in management. Each succeeding manager has been well schooled in the company's policies, so
leadership can be assumed with little noticeable change.

This continuity of decisions does not imply that policies do not
change over time. They most certainly must be altered to fit the changing realities of the situations to which they apply. However, policy
provides stability in the organization's behavior until it is altered.

A communication system. Written or stated policies are one means by
which management communicates its decisions to all levels of the
organization. Policy statements let everyone know what is expected.

They are particularly useful for for helping new employees quickly grasp what is expected of them and what they can expect from management.

An automatic decision maker.   One of the more important functions of policy is as an aid in decision making. A policy is a previously made decision. Once management has formulated a policy, it expects it to be applied to the proper problems without any time being wasted pondering them. In one company a customer who demands an advertising allowance puts the sales rep on the spot: Should such an allowance be granted or not? The problem goes to the sales manager and on up to higher echelons for decision. But in another company, which has a policy that under no circumstances will advertising allowances be given, the sales force has a predetermined answer which can immediately be given to their customers. They know what the established policy is.

The bulk of routine problems in any organizations should be handled through the application of policy. Thereby, the manager has time to deal with more crucial problems and need not be bogged down with ordinary matters.

The automatic decision-making function of policy, however, bothers many critics. It seems to imply that all matters can be settled by simply sorting through to find the proper policy to apply to a situation. If nothing exactly fits, the manager must find something close and force its application. Nothing could be further from the truth. Policy should never be blindly applied without the use of judgment. There are always exceptions, and managers and employees must be trained to recognize when it is not appropriate to apply a stated policy. But that is just the point—by applying policies whenever possible, thereby expediting the making of decisions, the administrator has more time to deal with the exceptions.

Protection from the pressures of expediency.   To most people, the most pressing problems are those that are immediately in front of them. The seriousness with which a problem is considered is often a direct function of its proximity in time. People tend to discount future problems, though they know this can lead to difficulties when they look at things in perspective.

The sales executive or administrator is strongly tempted to take the route of expediency in handling problems at hand, even though a dear price will later have to be paid for weak behavior. Established policies can keep managers from making ill-advised decisions based on immediate circumstances, to the detriment of the long-run best interests of the organization.

A top executive for the Florsheim Shoe Company related the following example as an illustration of the use of policy:

When DuPont was introducing Corfam, its marketing organization placed extreme pressure on quality shoe manufacturers, such as us, to incorporate the plastic material into our lines. This was a key factor in marketing strategy for Corfam: Get the material associated with quality before trading down to popular priced lines. All types of pressure and persuasion were employed to try to get us (Florsheim) to make some Corfam shoes. But our policy to make only quality *leather* shoes automatically made our decision for us in spite of the heavy pressure on us to change it. In this case we are quite glad to note that we escaped the problems that our competitors encountered with the material.

Policies that have been thought out carefully, without the pressures of expediency, are a far better basis for making decisions than are the factors perceived under pressure to make an immediate decision. The executive who chooses the route of expediency usually overlooks most of the long-run implications of the decision for the sake of short-run comfort.

The success of most organizations is due to a set of proven policies. This is not to say that any policy is superior to no policy. There are bad policies; companies that follow them fail. And some policies that have been sound in the past can become ill advised through changes in the environment of the firm. Sound management is continually alert to the need for policy revisions but does not make changes without conclusive proof of their advisability. Responsible management is reluctant to abandon a policy that has been sound over a period of time in favor of untried or unproven alternatives.

Types of policies

Organizational policies can be characterized along several dimensions. They may be strategic or operational, stated or unstated, covert or overt, and implicit or explicit.

Strategic versus operational. Top management makes strategic policies that guide the entire enterprise along selected routes. Florsheim, for example, in addition to its strategic policy of making only high-quality leather shoes, also has been pursuing a policy of expanding sales volume and profits by opening its own retail outlets in regional shopping centers. In sales management policy, some firms have the strategic policy of relying on personal selling for the back-bone of their promotion, while others believe in spending most of their promotional money on advertising. Avon is an example of the former, while Revlon is an example of the latter.

Operational policies are the guideposts that are established to carry out strategic policies. Many times they take on the appearance of work rules. In the typical organization, they are far more numerous than strategic policies.

Stated versus unstated. In certain instances, either stated or unstated policies are advisable. To improve morale and provide incentive, the firm might want to state openly its policy to promote from within. Only a stated policy could achieve the desired result in this case. There are other times, however, when it may be wise not to state a policy that nevertheless is operative, as in a firm with the policy of going outside to hire top executives. While some may detect the policy from the firm's actions, many cannot be sure of it.

An administrator should not be devious about company policies, however. Most management literature acknowledges the need to be honest and straightforward with people. Unstated policies, while not honest and forthright, are less devious than covert policies.

Covert versus overt. While a policy may not be stated, it may still be obvious because of management's overt actions and behavior. Indeed, the policies of most concerns can be detected from their actions. It is the policy of IBM to depend on inexperienced recent college graduates for sales recruits; its overt hiring behavior makes this quite clear.

There are times when management does not want certain parties to know the actual policy on a given matter. Perhaps the law is involved, or it is a matter involving the competition. Or management may try to conceal policy to protect its self-interests. The manager who regularly lets old salesmen go when they start to slack off would want to keep such a policy secret.

One large farm equipment manufacturer has a covert policy that its district managers must be promoted to regional manager by a certain age or be dismissed. They do not want their people to know of this policy, for obvious reasons. However, there are some sound reasons for such an up-or-out policy.

Implicit versus explicit. Management explicitly establishes many policies with thought and premeditation. Other policies are established through practice without an explicit decision being made. The salesmen for a large flooring manufacturer all wear conservative suits. This has never been a policy decision by management; it just has developed that way. Now it is an implicit policy.

OBJECTIVES

Objectives are necessary in planning operations—a plan needs goals. Without them, it is impossible to create a purposeful design. Texas Instruments has as one of its goals to reach $10 billion in sales by 1980, and its management really means it. This goal significantly affects most decisions made in the sales department. The company's marketing policies are aggressive because it insists on attaining a large share of the markets it enters. Another electronics firm is more interested in profits—rate of return on investment. It does not sell goods unless the price is right, and it does not go into markets that are relatively unprofitable. Its sales force seeks customers willing to pay a premium price for its goods. Such objectives have a profound impact upon a wide range of business decisions.

Another Texas Instruments objective states: Standard parts will be used as much as possible, variations will be minimized. This production-oriented policy, designed to minimize production costs and investments in dies and tooling, played havoc with the marketing program for home and office electronic calculators. The home market was covered by department stores and mass merchandisers, and the office market by business equipment dealers. While the office equipment dealers needed a 40 percent gross margin, the mass merchandisers cut prices to increase sales volume. This price discrepancy forced the company to offer two lines of calculators, one for each market segment, so that different price structures could be maintained.

Here the goal of using standard parts as much as possible entered the picture. As a result of this policy, the only difference between the two lines of calculators was cosmetic, which fooled few customers and even fewer dealers. Customers would not buy essentially the same machines for a higher price at the business equipment dealers, so that channel was lost for the most part to Texas Instruments. In this case the goal of minimizing parts differences conflicted with the goal of maximizing market share. After much managerial thought, the market-share goal dominated, and the line was redesigned to offer equipment dealers different machines.

Levels of objectives

Objectives vary in their levels of abstraction. There are broad overall objectives, such as making a certain level of profit or sales. Below this broad level, objectives may aim at obtaining a given share of the market or successfully introducing a new product or opening up a new channel of distribution. Beneath this level may be a multitude of specific objectives, such as obtaining 100 new dealers during the coming fiscal period, lowering selling costs by 2 percent, or establishing four new distribution centers. The manager of a new distribution center might have several more specific objectives, such as the hiring of five representatives by May 1, having the center in operation by June 1, and meeting all budgets. Both general and specific objectives are needed for planning.

The need for specific, written objectives

In the hurry and confusion of routine business operations, it is easy to lose sight of the purpose of activities. Yet, if they are not in alignment with the organization's objectives, they may be wasted effort. Even worse, they may be counterproductive if they move the group away from its goals. It helps the organization keep its objectives in mind if they are in written form. Then everyone should know them and be able to refer to them.

The tendency for statements of objectives to be little more than platitudes should be resisted vigorously. Such mouthings as "We should be of service to our customers and treat our employees fairly" are only hazy guideposts for making business decisions. To be useful, objectives must be sufficiently specific that the executive cannot read into them justification for whatever decision he or she might want to make.

Alignment of objectives and decisions

Once the firm's objectives have been agreed upon, all decisions should be in alignment with them. Decisions that are incompatible with objectives serve only to deter the realization of those goals.

This alignment seems simple and obvious, but it is not easy to achieve. All objectives are not compatible with one another. The example of how Texas Instruments' market objectives clashed with its production objectives is a case in point.

If a firm aims for a 15 percent return on investment and also wants a 10 percent annual growth rate, these two objectives will eventually clash. Heublein, Inc., encountered this difficulty in acquiring Hamms beer. Heublein had as one of its objectives a 15 percent rate of return on its investment. It also had ambitious growth objectives. Heublein management had the opportunity to buy Hamms, whose large sales volume nicely fit the company's growth objective. However, profits in the beer business are far less than 15 percent; Hamms was making about a 5 percent return on investment. If Heublein tried to satisfy the growth objective, the profit objective would have to be sacrificed. A few years later Heublein sold Hamms at a loss.

A priority of objectives is necessary to guide managers in making decisions that conflict with one or more objectives while fulfilling others. The more objectives management establishes, the more conflicts it will have to resolve. Given too many objectives, managers may become lost in a sea of goals, throw up their hands, and make their decisions solely on the basis of personal judgment. The objectives of some firms are so prolific and conflicting that clever executives can usually find some goal with which to justify whatever decisions are made.

Management by objectives[3]

In recent years, considerable interest has developed in a managerial philosophy called *management by objectives* (MBO). This is a healthy development, since it focuses the manager's attention on accomplishments rather than processes.

To understand the essence of this new managerial system, it is first necessary to understand the existing system. Traditional management essentially monitors what people do: Do they come to work on time? Do they turn in their paper work? Do they make their calls? The monitoring system can become quite complex, as management strives to make certain that everyone is doing what it wants them to do. The theory is that if everyone does what management tells them to do, the desired results will be forthcoming. The organization's goals will be achieved.

Management by objectives maintains that management should not care about the processes through which people work but only about the results—the objectives—they achieve. If a saleswoman achieves her sales quotas and meets her expense budgets, why should management care whether she works five days a week or two?

The manager practicing this new philosophy agrees with the subordinate on a series of very specific objectives to be achieved during a coming period. At the end of this period, the employee is evaluated on how well these objectives have been achieved.

While this theory has much philosophical virtue, it also has some operating flaws. First, it can be difficult to fix an employee's objectives in sufficient detail to cover all aspects of the job. How does one quantify a sales person's need for servicing previous sales? Second, management may want the employee to do something other than what was agreed upon. Conditions change rapidly in business, and the manager cannot continually approach the employee to renegotiate the agreement and still have the system mean much. Finally, much damage may be done before it is time to evaluate the employee's performance. The theory of the existing monitoring system is that management quickly detects deviant behavior or an inoperative plan and acts accordingly, and thus damage is minimized. If management waits until the end of the planning period to assess employee performance, it may be too late to avoid the consequences.

---

[3] See Donald W. Jackson, Jr., and Ramon J. Aldag, "Managing the Sales Force by Objectives," *MSU Business Topics*, Spring 1974, pp. 53–59.

Few managements endorse the MBO philosophy completely. Rather they combine it with monitoring to ensure that not only are employees achieving the desired results, they are doing so the way management wants.

STRATEGIES

The words *objectives, strategies,* and *tactics* take precise meaning only after the level of objectives has been established.[4] What may be an objective to a manager of one product may be only part of the strategy of the president of the company. For instance, the product manager may be given the dictate to achieve a certain dollar volume of sales in a coming period. He proceeds to form strategies and tactics to accomplish this goal. However, this sales volume may be only one small portion of the operating strategy of top management, whose *objective* may be the realization of a certain amount of profit or a certain level of operations for the period. No matter what the objective may be, the strategy is the plan of action by which the administrator hopes to achieve it, and the *tactics* are the details that activate the plan.

FIGURE 2–1
Relationships of objectives,
strategies, and tactics

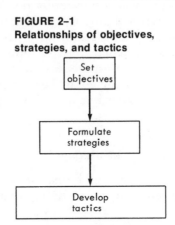

Every organization must have some plan of action—a strategy to be used—whether it is recognized or unrecognized. If the executive allows the strategy to go unrecognized, a dangerous situation may arise. An unrecognized plan of action cannot be evaluated or altered to meet

[4] See Lawrence Jacobs, "The Meaning of Goals," *Business Horizons,* Winter 1967, pp. 59–60, for an attempt to differentiate such terms as *goals, objectives, quotas, forecasts,* and *targets.*

conditions as they are encountered. The plan must be brought out into the open before the leaders can obtain maximum use of it. If the strategy is not recognized, probably it will be implemented with the wrong tactics.

To be effective, a strategy must be accompanied by the use of the proper tactics. Suppose a sales manager has been told to increase sales for the coming year by 10 percent—the goal has been given. After some thought the manager concludes that the best way to reach that goal would be to stress opening new accounts rather than trying to sell more goods to old accounts—the strategy would be to seek new customers. Now it is one thing to say to the sales force, "Go after new customers," but it is another thing to have them do it successfully. Therefore tactics are needed. One sales manager facing such a situation was able to provide the tactics and tools needed to get the job done by developing a special "initial stock" deal that was sufficiently attractive to entice new dealers to buy the firm's products.

The strategies chosen should be followed with some degree of perseverance. The manager who continually changes strategies never gives any of them time to work. Some strategies require time to be effective. A manager must be patient.

Many managers who are eager for results lack the patience needed to allow certain types of programs to bear fruit. New products are often taken off the market before they have had a fair chance to develop a following. One sales manager fired a representative who had been sent to open up a new territory because dealers were not flocking to the product as fast as the manager had expected. The fault was not that the salesman was inefficient but rather that the manager had unrealistic expectations.

Some common basic strategies

Underlying practically all human activities are certain fundamental strategies that can apply to any group endeavor. These strategies are not mutually exclusive, since they can overlap considerably, and they are certainly not exhaustive. They are principally concerned with numbers, speed, perfection, intellect, and surprise.

Strategy of numbers. "If you can't outthink or outrun them, then overwhelm them" is one way of stating the numbers strategy. In war, the superiority of numbers is well recognized. The forces that are inferior numerically must compensate by the use of other strategies. However, if the opponent is able to match these plans of action as well, numbers will win out in the end.

In business, the strategy of numbers also applies. Many individual grocery stores are run more efficiently and with better management than any of the stores of some large chains. Nevertheless, the chain's numbers may make it a bigger success. Similarly, a sales manager may recruit a small but highly competent sales force that can really sell, whereas some larger competitive firm will recruit anyone who wants to try to sell. A poor sales rep may sell only half as much as a good one. But the larger firm may have three times as many representatives who can be everywhere in the territory and make frequent calls.

This strategy is not generally recommended, because in many situations it does not work. Nevertheless, in some circumstances the strategy of numbers is sound. Business places no particular restriction on how many people can play on a team. The pep talk in which the coach tells his players that the opponents can have only an equal number on the field does not apply in selling.

Perhaps the best illustration of this strategy now in use is the multilevel distributive systems that have been set up by such organizations as Amway, Avon, Mary Kay, and Tupperware. They overwhelm the market with a horde of part-time representatives—sheer numbers.

Strategy of speed.   One classical answer to numbers in military and sporting endeavors has been speed. Smaller but faster groups often win out over larger but less mobile adversaries. Speed is of some use in marketing also, but it should not be overrated; it can be a very bad strategy.

The difference between selling activities and war or sporting events in this respect is that in a battle of either a military or sporting nature some time limit is established. The activity does not go on and on, and speed can be of great use in the short run. Its costs to the participants in weariness are not tallied until after the battle is over. In business, however, the battle is seldom over; it goes on day in and day out, year in and year out. Participants cannot maintain speed indefinitely with no effect on their performance. Also, as they get older, they may tend to slow down. Unless the leader is willing to adopt a policy whereby all personnel are expendable, eventually speed in selling activities can hurt the organization.

In some matters, speed is patently a bad strategy. Countless executives, in their hurry to market a new product or build a new plant, have made unwise decisions. Several years ago, a large manufacturer of aircraft heaters planned to market a new home heater and was anxious to distribute it as soon as possible. After testing six laboratory units in homes, top management wanted to sell the product the following year. The sales executives wanted to do more testing and marketing research work, but top management overruled them. The company entered the Dallas market and sold some 200 units. Complaints were numerous, and much trouble was caused by faulty production units. The firm also encountered installation problems that were new to them. Plumbing and heating contractors did not know how to install the product properly. Market experience indicated that the very delicate control mechanism was impractical for the furnace market. This sad experience could have been avoided had management not been in such a hurry.

The benefits of speed in business are much exaggerated. Manufacturers usually want to be the first in the market with a product. However, though Maytag entered the automatic washer industry late, this had little apparent effect on its ultimate success. Speed by itself may be a poor business strategy, and it frequently negates many other superior strategies. It it difficult to maintain a strategy of perfection along with one of speed, for example.

Strategy of perfection.   It is seldom wise to sacrifice perfection for speed or numbers. In war, neither is of much use against an army that executes its tactics with perfection, fights with know-how, and is proficient in its use of arms and ordnance. Similarly, perfection in product, personnel, or performance is much to be desired in business. Whatever is done should be done right.

In the management of a sales force, perfection should be a basic strategy in most instances. It makes no sense to make the effort to call on a prospect and botch the sale with inept selling techniques.

Strategy of intellect.   The strategy of intellect is not a pure one in that all strategies must make use of it. Some degree of intellect must be present to carry out any strategy, but some organizations place a premium on intelligence. Evidence of this strategy in action is an emphasis on both technical and marketing research. The executive who employs intellect as a basic strategy may think something like this: "Maybe we are small in number, and we do not execute plans as well as they might be, but at least we will be in the right market at the right time with the right product."

The difference between the strategy of intellect and a strategy of perfection in marketing is that often the smart action is to be something less than perfect. Perfection may cost more than the market will pay. In other activities, the executive hopes to solve problems with applied intelligence. This is a good strategy, one that cannot be ignored by any manager.

Strategy of surprise.   Surprise can be of tremendous advantage in the military and sporting worlds, but it is of little use in business. It is difficult to surprise the competition, since industrial security is almost impossible to maintain. Even if tight security is possible concerning some move, not much is usually gained by attempts to surprise the competition.

What real benefit do automobile manufacturers get from their efforts to keep the appearance of new models secret before a given date?

Competitors could not alter their products in time to copy them, since their designs have been set months previously, and most consumers do not care about the precise date the new models appear.

Nevertheless, there is often a need for secrecy about business decisions and contemplated actions. A firm's plans are one of its most vital assets. The intent may not be to surprise but to maintain an advantage.

TACTICS

The importance of tactics

Many fine strategies with highly desirable goals have failed for want of proper tactics. A sales manager formulated a new compensation plan designed to increase both sales and sales people's earnings—worthy goals. But he gave no thought to tactics, and when he tried a direct frontal attack, he was soundly defeated by the sales people, who were afraid of the new plan. Other tactics could have carried the day.

Indeed, many ill-advised strategies have been successful due to the use of excellent tactics. For example, a college administrator had developed an organizational plan he wished to have adopted. Unfortunately, it was a very bad plan, as subsequent events made obvious. Through expert tactical moves, he overcame the opposition that would have easily sidetracked the plan under more normal circumstances.

It may be that the successful execution of plans depends more on the tactics employed than upon their intrinsic soundness. Therefore the developer of a sound plan should be tactically adept, so that the good plans can compete successfully with their inferiors. Many talented young executives are thwarted in their ambitions because they operate under the naive assumption that right is might. Frequently, they are done in by people of lesser talents who are more proficient in the use of tactics. It is not enough to devise wise strategies; they must be implemented with the proper tactics.

Little has been written about administrative tactics, and the reason is apparent. We do not like the idea of tactics, because in our society it is not acceptable to appear as if we are manipulating people, and most tactics focus on manipulating people or structuring situations. Moreover, many tactics, when improperly applied, are considered unethical. Some administrators probably would be more willing to talk about their private lives than about the tactics they use in reaching their goals, and for good reason. It is usually best for other people to remain unaware of the tactics being used on them.

Therefore, learning about administrative tactics is up to the individual. You must learn about them through experience, on your own.

This is one reason the development of good administrators is relatively slow.

A noted writer on management recently said, "Tactics bore me. I'm only interested in strategy. That's the determinant of success!" Observation, experience, and logic indicate otherwise, however.

Suppose a sales manager has been told to cut sales costs by 10 percent. There are many different plans that could be adopted to achieve that objective. Some admittedly are more likely to reach the goal than others, and some are more difficult to institute than others. But it is the tactics the manager chooses to achieve the plan that will determine whether or not it works.

Tactics are the tools of the administrator, the tools used to carry out the firm's strategies or plans. A masterful administrator not only possesses a wide range of tactics but knows when and how to use them.

Proper use of tactics

Tactics themselves are amoral—they are neither good nor bad. They are simply behavior.

Whether or not a given tactic is correct in a certain situation depends upon many factors. There are no perfect tactics, and in any situation there is no one *best* tactic that can be used. Many tactics may work, some better than others. Many others may fail, some more surely than others.

Many administrators mistakenly use the same tactics repeatedly, regardless of the circumstances. They develop such habits because the favored tactics have worked for them previously. Success reinforces the habit of using a tactic. But success can be lulling. There comes a time when the tactic will not work, and that is usually a most critical time.

The classic example of administrative inability to vary tactics is the forceful, hard-hitting executive who uses strong, authoritarian tactics to climb through the ranks. Such an executive will discover that at the top such tactics are not effective in dealing with others of equal ability. New tactics are needed for the new environment. The manager who is unable to make the necessary tactical adjustments fails.

As tools of the administrator, tactics can be used as a hammer is—to pound nails or to smash thumbs. In themselves, the tools are neither good nor bad. It is up to the manager to learn how to use them properly.

Tactical evaluation of the situation

Tactical evaluation involves deciding which tactics to use in a situation. In making this decision the manager must decide how to confront the other party in the situation, whether peers, subordinates, customers, or competitors.

An executive faces a number of considerations when deciding upon a tactical plan or course of action. Some of the more critical elements in this tactical model are discussed below.

Stakes. How much money is involved? If the stakes are high, more forceful tactics may be needed than if the matter is inconsequential. On minor issues, many managers might choose to ignore the adversary in the matter.

Personalities. People react to situations in different ways. Some adversaries are belligerent and combative. Any direct action that would antagonize them might prod them into doing exactly what the manager does not want them to do. In such cases it would be better to use various indirect tactics. Other people are more passive and less apt to take offense at tactical actions. The relative belligerency of the other person's personality is only one of a multitude of character traits to be considered in making tactical decisions.

One's own personality characteristics also must be recognized. It is folly to try to bluff if one cannot carry through on the acting skills necessary to make the bluff believeable to the other party. Some managers find that their personalities are better suited for dealing with other people on a one-to-one basis rather than in groups. In their tactical maneuvering, they try to avoid group meetings and confrontations.

Power bases. The power held or perceived to be held by both parties plays a pivotal role in tactical selection. The manager who has a strong power base, an unassailable one, can make more forceful tactical moves. Managers who do not have the right to fire subordinates for example, must use other tactics.

The other party's power base also is critical. The tactic "Never wound a king" reflects the danger to the manager who undertakes to overrule or threaten anyone with more power.

As a general rule, managers have less power than they think they do, when the going gets rough. Power is also elusive. One may have it one day and not the next.

Future relationships. The manager cannot treat a customer that the firm hopes to do business with again in the future the same way as one who will be served only once. And the firm might be willing to take an errant supplier to court to satisfy a contract but would never do so with a good customer.

Censure. Certain tactics, if their use is publicly known, can result in censure by others. Tactics rarely remain secret, so those used should be able to bear up under scrutiny. Some managers mistakenly believe that the opinions of subordinates are not important. However, in any such conflict, it may be easier for the firm to fire a manager than a whole sales force.

Retaliation capabilities.   It makes sense to treat people carefully if they are in a position to retaliate. Taxpayers instinctively know they should not give the Internal Revenue Service a bad time, and who would anger a traffic officer?

Urgency.   The time dimensions of the matter must be appraised. If quick action is needed, direct, forceful tactics may have to be used. If there is enough time, more indirect, persuasive tactics may be in order.

Probability of success.   Tactics have different likelihoods of success in different situations. Some managers become so enchanted with a certain tactic they try to use it in situations in which it will not work. A football coach may favor a power running attack so much he insists on it even when passing tactics are clearly called for. A manager may enjoy communicating with the sales force informally, but may use the tactic when it is inappropriate.

Efforts required.   Some tactics require more managerial effort than others. Often the matter is not worth the effort it would take to handle it a certain way. A customer balks at paying a $2 late charge; merchandise arrives with slight damages costing about $5 to repair. Many managers ignore such issues, since the effort to handle them exceeds the gain to be realized.

Personal skills.   Some people can do certain things easily, others cannot. The manager who finds it difficult to fire people develops other ways of accomplishing the same task. The person who does not talk well resorts to written communications. Managers should use tactics at which they are adept.

Legal considerations.   Some issues are loaded with potential legal liability. If the firm could end up in court on the matter, the selection of tactics should be made carefully. There should be no reason to question their legality. One tactic would be to get the other party to commit itself on paper and to prepare appropriate documents for the firm.

Values.   The manager's personal values should play a key role in tactical selection. You should not do things that you don't feel right about. There are managers who will not fire a subordinate. They go out of their way to find some useful place for the person in the organization. Lying is a tactic many people use, to one degree or another. For others, any untruth violates their personal values.

Impact on others.   While the manager may intend for a tactic to be directed at a particular person, often it affects others. One manager hoped to drive out a subordinate with whom he clashed personally by harassing and insulting him. But the subordinate would have none of it; he fought back. The resulting conflict tore apart a previously united organization. The manager had not only badly misjudged his adversary, but he overlooked the impact of the conflict upon the organization.

In conclusion, the manager has many things to consider in selecting the tactics to use in a certain situation. The greater the issue, the more carefully these factors should be weighed.

An example of tactical decision making

The preceding discussion of tactics has been abstract; we have not defined specific tactics, which are innumerable. An example of tactical decision making will provide a more concrete idea of what tactics are and do. This is an example of an alcoholic salesman.

Bill Griff had been one of the company's leading salesmen for more than a decade, but his performance was steadily declining because he resorted to alcohol to console himself over his marital difficulties. Since Griff's territory had become a weak spot in the firm's distributive system, Henry Ewald, the sales manager, decided it had to be brought back to its former sales level—the goal was set. Ewald correctly perceived the problem: the territory's salesman was not doing the job properly. Something would have to be done regarding Griff.

Thus Ewald had to make a critical strategic decision—either dismiss Griff or reform him. Since a sober Griff was a proven performer with a great deal of value to the company, Ewald decided to first try to help Griff refrain from drinking. The plan was to keep Griff sober.

The manager mulled over the multitude of tactics open to him but settled on a direct, no-nonsense approach. Past experience had indicated that unless the alcoholic sincerely regretted his situation and desperately wanted to remedy it, there was no hope. So he flew out to talk with Griff. Note that the manager went to see the salesman rather than having the man come to see him—a deliberate tactic selected because Ewald wanted to investigate Griff's home situation and examine his present relationships with a few key accounts.

It soon became apparent that Griff was not likely to change. "I can handle my liquor. . . . It's just that competition is tougher these days. . . . I'm just as good as ever!" were the alibis and excuses Griff offered.

Ewald knew he should move fast to minimize the damage, since he saw little but grief in Griff's future. While he would have preferred to discharge Griff, to do so might have created some problems in the home office if Griff were to complain to top management about his sudden dismissal.

Ewald decided he would have to let Griff hang himself (a tactic). He furnished the rope (a tactic) by sending Griff a long letter relating his sales history and clearly telling him that henceforth if he did not meet all quotas he would be dismissed. Then the manager touched all bases (a tactic) by informing his superiors of the situation. As a bonus, he projected an image to the sales force (news of such situations al-

Introduction to

MAJESTIC GLASS COMPANY

A series of day-to-day operating problems facing a sales manager

Clyde D. Brion, general sales manager for the Majestic Glass Company, directed 18 sales people, each based in a different city. The company's factory, located in eastern Ohio, manufactured glass bottles, jars, and other glass containers. Bottles for cosmetics and toiletries accounted for the bulk of the sales volume, but containers for beer, soft drinks, shoe polish, milk, food products, and medicine were also important in the Majestic line.

Orders from large and regular customers were shipped direct from the Majestic factory to users' plants by rail. For smaller and infrequent buyers, stocks of standard bottles and jars were maintained in warehouses owned by public warehouse companies. The warehouse companies leased space to producers and distributors of many types of goods, billing each occupant monthly for the space actually used. Brion also rented desk space for each of his sales representatives at these warehouses. Telephone and basic secretarial services were also available, and this arrangement provided Majestic with regional sales branches, with stocks in 18 cities.

Rivalry was keen in the container industry. More than a dozen large firms were engaged in the manufacture of glass bottles and jars. Increasing competition was also provided by containers made of plastic, metal, and paper. It was especially important that the Majestic sales force be alert to new business possibilities, that they follow up leads and market tips quickly, and that they offer maximum service. It was Majestic's policy to meet competitor's prices, but not to undercut a competitor wilfully in order to steal business. Instead, the company relied on various original features of its containers to outsell competitors.

Each sales person was paid a commission of 10 percent on all sales in the territory in which he was located. He received an additional 5 percent on orders from new customers, provided the order was larger than a specified minimum quantity. A sales person could also draw on anticipated commissions, up to a limit determined by Brion. Usually this equaled the sales representative's average commission earnings for a good month's business in his territory.

At the time you are studying this case, Brion faced several problems in the operation of his sales force. He was anxious to solve each problem correctly, and at the same time to establish safeguards against a recurrence of the same problem if possible. If recurrence was thought to be probable, he wanted to establish a workable policy for dealing with the problem in the future.

Twelve of these operating problems facing Brion appear at various places in this text. In each instance, the particular problem is located at a relevant place in the chapter. The first in the series is a problem in managerial tactics, and it follows right after this introduction.

Note: This series of problems was written by Professor Phillip McVey, University of Nebraska at Lincoln. Reproduced with permission.

A day-to-day operating problem in the

MAJESTIC GLASS COMPANY (A)
Location of authority

Clyde Brion, General Sales Manager of the Majestic Glass Company, received the following letter from Centra Wineries, Inc., a San Francisco firm which had bought standard-line Majestic bottles for many years:

April 9

Mr. Clyde D. Brion
General Sales Manager
Majestic Glass Company
Lancaster, Ohio 43130

Dear Mr. Brion:

We have decided reluctantly that we must remove your company from our list of acceptable container vendors unless you can provide sales service more in keeping with our needs.

Please understand that this action in no way implies dissatisfaction with Majestic bottles or with your San Francisco representative, Mr. Harlow Britt.

As you know, the domestic wine industry is a fiercely competitive, fast-moving, low-margin business. Since we operate on a system of guaranteed resale prices to our distributors and dealers, any competitive price-cutting pressures must be met by trimming our costs. Such a small saving as 3 cents per unfilled bottle may on occasion make the difference between profitable and unprofitable business for us.

Similarly, to escape storage costs we never stock more than our immediate requirements of unfilled bottles. We depend upon bottle manufacturers to provide guaranteed deliveries to us on very short notice—never more than ten days.

While Mr. Britt is very helpful, we find that he lacks authority to adjust your prices to meet our needs, or to guarantee on-time deliveries to us at your risk. He tells us that he must have your written approval on these questions, and the time required to obtain it may be 24 to 72 hours.

We hope you can give Mr. Britt the authority he needs to retain our patronage.

Yours truly,
V. Collasini
Centra Wineries, Inc.

Brion checked his records on this customer and learned that the average elapsed time from order date to delivery date was 19 days. On orders which Britt had marked "*rush*" and Brion had expedited, the average elapsed time had been nine days. No deliveries had been guaranteed.

Question

Now what does Clyde Brion do? Answer the letter.

ways gets around) of being a fair man: "Ewald gave Griff every chance!" Moreover, he bought some time to locate a replacement for Griff.

Had Griff straightened himself out, the problem would have been solved. When his performance continued to be unsatisfactory, however, he was fired. There were no repercussions; everyone understood. In this case we will never know what the outcome would have been had Griff been fired right after Ewald's visit. It might have been uneventful, but this is not likely, because firing a formerly good salesman of long standing is not to be done casually.

THE SIX RELATIONSHIPS OF THE SALES EXECUTIVE

The sales manager must be able to handle relationships with numerous other people. In their transactions with the manager these people may be:

- Superiors.
- Equals.
- Subordinates.

- Competitors.
- Members of the community.
- Customers.

Superiors, equals, and subordinates may be people in the manager's own organization or in those of customers or competitors.

Each of these six relationships requires different applications of strategy and tactics. It is a mistake for an administrator to think that everyone can be handled in the same manner. Obviously, the same approach cannot be used on both superiors and subordinates, nor can the same strategies be used in dealing with competitors and customers. Deception may achieve the results desired when used with a rival, but it can be disastrous if applied to customer relations. Where presenting a fait accompli, without allowing further consideration, might be the correct tactic for use within an organization, the community could get incensed over its use in some matter involving social welfare.

RESPONSIBILITY OF THE ADMINISTRATOR

> The fundamental responsibility of the administrator is to staff the organization with the right people.

This statement expresses the basic philosophy of this book regarding the problem of managing people. Above all else, the administrator's basic duty and function in an organization is to staff it properly.

If the right people have been hired, even bad plans may be successful. But more importantly, the right people will not make bad plans. They eliminate or considerably lessen most of the manager's problems. With competent individuals, training is easier and more effective, compensation plans work as intended, minimum supervision and stimulation are required, and control of efforts poses fewer problems. In short, if competent individuals are hired, life is easier for the manager.

This is particularly important in sales management because marketing is an art of execution. The success of most marketing plans rests not so much with the plan as with the aptness with which it is carried out. Actually, devising proper marketing strategies is not at all difficult. Most of the time, the necessary actions are quite obvious. The success of the endeavor depends on the execution of the plan: how well the advertising is done, how well the sales force does its job, and how well the product is made.

If people are hired who are not able to execute the plans successfully, they can ruin the best of plans. If the right person is not hired for a sales job, training is a major problem, and supervision and stimulation problems that would otherwise be avoided might arise. A below-par sales rep requires constant attention and stimulation, and even then may not be able to perform satisfactorily. Morale of the sales force is a critical factor when poorly placed individuals convey their discontent to their fellow workers.

Immediate subordinates

The sales manager is most concerned with immediate subordinates. If you do a good job in picking your subordinates, they will in turn select the right people to serve below them. With the right subordinates, an executive may succeed in spite of himself.

Executives who cannot delegate responsibility and authority to their subordinates are not really administrators; they are just highly paid workers. No organization can grow with one person running it. The capacity of a single individual is too limited. Sooner or later the individual must give way, and when that happens the firm is in trouble if no provision has been made for a successor. Unless they have been prepared, subordinates will expect to continue being told what to do and when to do it. They will not be able to step in and take over.

Thus the manager must be prepared to devote whatever time and effort are needed to find the right person for any vacancy, particularly among immediate subordinates. Nothing the administrator does is more important than to give his full attention to the proper selection of subordinates.

QUESTIONS AND PROBLEMS

1. Should you alter your philosophies of management to fit a particular situation, or should you select your job to fit your philosophies of management?
2. What does it take to be a good leader?
3. Can leadership be learned? If so, how do you go about learning it?
4. Suppose you are a sales person. What traits should a sales manager have to manage you successfully?
5. Some observers have not been overly impressed with the transferability of administrative talents between significantly different organizations. They point to the difficulties many high-ranking military officers have upon retiring in trying to move into corporate management. What are the barriers to moving into management from the government or the armed forces?
6. Why do emotions interfere with good managerial judgment?
7. Are covert policies unethical?
8. In what way is the existence of a sales force the reflection of a strategy?
9. Why are executives strongly inclined to abide by the company's policies?
10. Why do many successful sales people fail to become good managers?

Case 2–1
PETER NALLEY
Star salesman, promoted, becomes
poor manager

The western regional sales manager in the Tape division of the Franklin Pennsylvania Corporation (FPC), Oscar Burrell, was wondering what to recommend in a situation involving Peter Nalley, formerly the top salesman in the Tape division. Nalley had recently been promoted to the position of district sales manager, but something happened. Nalley started drinking heavily, to the point where Burrell and other executives had to correct the situation.

FPC was a large, multinational, widely diversified company with manufacturing facilities in several states and eight foreign countries. Annual corporate sales were close to $750 million. Separate divisions of the company produced and marketed a variety of unrelated products, including luggage, sound and videotape recorders, adhesives, abrasives, chemicals, and plastics.

The Tape division was a major division in FPC, accounting for about 10 percent of the company's total sales volume and an even larger share of profits. This division produced over 200 different types of tape for industrial, commercial, and consumer markets. The product line included textile tapes, shoe tapes, lead and aluminum foil tapes, and electrical tapes. FPC's pressure-sensitive tapes and the filament, masking, and foam tapes were well accepted in industrial markets for a wide range of applications. FPC's cellulose tape competed with the "Scotch" and "Magic" brands marketed by the 3M Company (Minnesota Mining and Manufacturing). FPC also was testing a surgical tape to compete with a 3M product.

The 3M Company was the dominant firm in the tape industry. Other competition with FPC faced in its Tape division came from the Mystic Tape Corporation (a subsidiary of the Borden Company) and Permacel Tape Corporation (a division of Johnson & Johnson).

A little over a year ago, a vacancy in field sales management at the district level opened up in Burrell's western region of the Tape division. As far as Burrell was concerned, there was little doubt who the candidate for promotion should be. Peter Nalley had been the top salesman in the entire division for many years. He was the winner of every contest the company set up and regularly commuted to Bermuda as a reward for his prowess in the field. In every respect, he was a professional salesman. Hence when the opening for a field supervisory position occurred, Burrell and other sales management personnel readily agreed that Nalley was the outstanding candidate for the position. He was an arts and sciences major in college and had had a better than average grade point average. Management felt that he could handle the job, despite his apparent lack of business management training and background.

At the start of his new assignment, Nalley did a great job. Everyone liked him; his enthusiasm was quickly caught by everybody in his unit, and they were off to a fine start. First and second quarter industrial tape sales (his area of emphasis) were way above quota, and everything was apparently working smoothly. Management was content that they had made the right decision.

Six months later an adverse reaction began to set in. Morale began to sag. Nalley's men began to complain that he did not answer their questions or do anything about their problems. New recruits received little or no field training, and it was becoming increasingly apparent

that Nalley was slumping in his important supervisory responsibilities. Because he wanted each of his men to be fond of him personally, he was very reluctant to administer discipline, even for of-
fenses obvious to everyone. Before long it was rumored among his
subordinates that he had formed a group of favorites who were given
the best assignments.

In the meantime Nalley was working night and day to increase
sales. He knew that for some reason sales were not reaching the quota,
as they had when he first started in his new position. He felt that he
had to work extra hard to make up for whatever it was that was holding
them back. As a superlative salesman, he did this the only way he
knew how. He used his men as bird dogs and tried to close every major
sale himself, but to no avail. Morale slumped further, and so did sales.

Nalley was accustomed to taking an occasional drink. During his
years as a salesman, he drank moderately in the course of entertaining
customers. Now his use of alcohol increased, paralleling the increase
in anxieties and tensions in his new managerial position. Soon his
dependency on alcohol seemed to be out of control.

The end was quite abrupt. One day Nalley came to a sales meeting
with Burrell and some of his other superiors in an advanced stage of
intoxication. The executives were shocked at his condition and immediately sent him home. Burrell then suggested that they have a conference the following day to discuss what to do.

At this meeting, the executives were sitting around the table pondering the various proposals. Most of them indicated they thought
Nalley should be fired immediately. They felt the incident was inex-
cusable and unjustifiable under any circumstances. Some of the more
sympathetic members of the group, including Burrell, felt that the
problem was one they themselves had brought on. They realized that
in recruiting Nalley for the position they had failed to perceive that
selling and managing are two very different activities, qualitatively.
Success in one does not necessarily guarantee success in the other. In
fact, the reverse was true in Nalley's case. His major weakness was
that, as a personal salesman, he had never learned to work through his
subordinates. Being a gregarious type, he could not bear to take action
which might forfeit the affection (and support) of his men. All he knew
was how to do the job himself. This was sufficient in selling, but quite
inadequate in a managerial position.

In view of this, these executives felt Nalley should be dealt with in
a less severe manner than firing. Some felt that he could be given
another chance in perhaps a new territory or a new division, being
demoted to salesman again. Other sympathetic members of management who knew him better and liked him felt that perhaps it would be
enough to just warn him that such an occurrence had better not be

repeated. Someone suggested that perhaps they ought to indirectly encourage Nalley to quit his job with FPC and seek employment elsewhere.

Question

1. What action should FPC management take in the case of Peter Nalley?

3

Sales force organization

Order is a lovely thing.
ANNA BRANCH

In the management process, first you decide where you want to go and then you figure out how to get there. In more formal terms, management first should establish its objectives, and then plan the appropriate strategies and tactics to reach those goals. To implement this planning, the activities and people must be properly arranged and effectively coordinated. This is where the concept of organization comes in. The fundamentals of organization are essentially the same, whether we are talking about organizing a sales force, a production department, a football team, an army, or any other group involved in a common effort.

NATURE OF SALES ORGANIZATION

The concept of organization may beem nebulous or abstract. It will be helpful if we differentiate between:

Organization—as the end product or end result.
Organizing—as the process, or the means to the end result.

As the end product, an organization is simply an arrangement—a working structure—of activities (functions) involving a group of people. The goal is to arrange these functions so that the people involved can act *together* better than they can *individually*.

Organizational changes have occurred in companies' sales and marketing efforts as firms have found their existing structures were inappropriate to implement the marketing concept. As we noted in Figure 1–1 (Chapter 1), one foundation stone underlying the marketing concept is that all marketing activities should be organizationally integrated and coordinated. That is, all a firm's marketing activities should be centralized in one department. Then this department's plans and efforts must be organizationally coordinated with those of the other major departments, such as production and finance. Next, all the activities *within* the marketing system must be coordinated. That is, management should integrate all planning and operational policies that involve the personal-selling effort, the advertising program, product development, marketing research, relations with dealers and distributors, and so on.

PERTINENT CONCEPTS IN ORGANIZATION THEORY

If sales executives are familiar with some of the conceptual foundations in organization theory, perhaps they can better understand the organizational relationships and problems in their firms. Let's consider three of these concepts at this point.

The human factor in organization

Consideration of the human factor in administration has experienced some pendulumlike swings in American industry during the 20th century. Early in this century, organizational theory was influenced heavily by Frederick W. Taylor and others who developed their concepts in a mechanistic setting in factories and offices. Work standards and performance quotas were established rationally on the basis of time and motion studies. The emphasis was on the machine—on the task—and not on the individual human being.

The influence of these concepts is reflected in classical organizational theory. Organizational structures were highly formalized, highly authoritarian, and highly centralized. Workers were considered as inanimate objects to be ordered around and discarded when useless. In effect, a worker was just another machine. Sales departments were not immune to this type of organizational thinking. Salesmen were impersonally treated as little more than pins on a sales map.

In reaction to the impersonal treatment of workers, the thinking in organizational theory swung to the other extreme in the 1930s and 1940s, and the concept of human relations became quite fashionable. Writers stressed the importance of interpersonal relationships and the motivation of workers, including sales people. Management became less authoritarian and more participative. Sales executives began to realize that sales people are individuals with emotions, personalities, expectations, and self-concepts.

Current thinking in organizational theory recognizes that neither of these two extremes is effective in optimizing worker productivity and profitability. Today we seek a balance between the formalized, impersonal organizational structure and the human relations approach to administration. An organization is regarded as a total system, and decision-making theory is stressed.

Centralized versus decentralized organization

During the past three decades or so there has been a noticeable shift toward decentralized structure in sales and marketing organization—and in other divisions of the firm, also. The emergent organizational pattern is marketing oriented and externally directed, in contrast to the traditional production-oriented and internally directed structure.

Internal system versus external results. The production-oriented sales organization model is highly formalized and generally inflexible. Much emphasis is placed on the internal system and on procedures. Sales people and field sales managers are expected to follow established procedures. Management seems to be more concerned with the job and the system than with the results the system is supposed to produce. Thus the system becomes an end in itself rather than a means to an end.

The decentralized sales organization model is a less formal, more flexible structure. Management relies more on the people—their motivations, personalities, and general knowledge—than on the technical systems and procedures. The system is subordinated to the overall results. *How* you get the job done is not nearly so important as *did* you get it done. A word of caution is in order, however. Experience in large organizations suggests that decentralization must be accompanied by timely reporting and controls. A good marketing information system is essential.

Authority and control. In the traditional sales organization, full authority for all sales force management activities—selection, training, supervision, setting quotas, and so on—is centralized in the home office. Centralized authority requires close, tight control over the sales force and field sales managers to ensure that the one best system is being followed. In the newer type of sales organization, much of the authority and decision making regarding sales force activities is decentralized.

The degree of decentralization is related to the span of executive control. (By *span of executive control,* we mean the number of subordinates who report directly to one executive.) A highly centralized organization requires a *short* span of control. The reason for this is that if management is to maintain close and detailed control over a work force, the group must be small.

A direct relationship exists between the span of control and the number of executive levels in a company. The shorter the span of control, the greater the number of layers or echelons of supervision.

The relationship between span of control and number of executive levels has irreconcilable consequences. A company that can keep its span of control short is inevitably plagued with the problems that stem from multiple layers of supervision. Every time another level is added, the cost of executive overhead increases. Going through channels becomes slow and full of red tape. Furthermore, the channels of communication get clogged more easily. The more levels (links) there are between the decision maker and the operator carrying out the decision, the greater are chances for misunderstanding and mistakes in executing the decision. Information is misinterpreted as it passes through the channels, *if* it passes through.

In the decentralized model of sales organization, more authority is delegated to the field sales executives. There is a broader span of control. Because they are allowed to develop their own procedures, they can be more responsive to customers' wants and local competitive situations. See Figure 3–1.

FIGURE 3–1
Summary of contrasts between traditional and current models in organization theory

Traditional	Current
1. More likely to be production oriented.	1. More likely to be marketing oriented.
2. Internally oriented.	2. Oriented toward external environment.
3. Highly formalized and inflexible.	3. Less formalized; more flexible.
4. Centralized authority.	4. Decentralized authority.
5. More levels of supervision and shorter span of control.	5. Fewer levels of supervision and broader span of control.
6. Major concern is toward the system; system becomes an end in itself.	6. Management relies on the workers rather than on the system; system is only a means to an end.
7. Orientation is toward *how* the job is done.	7. Results oriented: *did* you get the job done.

Role of the informal organization

A healthy organization is a self-adjusting one. Through its own devices, it finds ways to get a job done with a minimum of effort. A formal organization's well-being is maintained by the system known as the *informal organization structure*. This structure represents how things *really* get done in a company, not how they are supposed to be done according to a formal plan. Most firms rely heavily on their informal structures to get the work done efficiently.

Here is one example of how an informal organization may actually work. The sales manager's secretary opens a letter from a customer who complains that he was overcharged on an order. If the lines of the formal organization chart were followed, the secretary would refer the letter to her boss, the sales manager. He in turn would relay the message up through executive echelons, until ultimately it reached the administrator who is over the chief executives in sales and accounting. This top administrator would forward the complaint down through channels in the accounting department to the appropriate person of responsibility in the billing division. The answer would follow the reverse path up and down through channels until the sales manager's secretary received it and could notify the customer. Such procedures are rather ridiculous, and most organizations would not follow them. Instead, the informal structure would be used. The sales manager's secretary would simply telephone or walk over to see a clerk in the billing department to find out what happened to the customer's order.

The informal organization also gives richer meaning to some of the time-honored principles of organization. For instance, a person should have only one boss. Fundamentally, this is a sound generalization. Yet, the informal structure adds dimensions of practicality and flexibility to this principle. Actually, we all have many bosses, each being granted authority over different activities. Consider the above example of the mistake in billing. When the sales manager's secretary telephoned the billing department, the people in that department granted her a certain amount of authority in that, on her request, they investigated the overcharged order. They realized this was the most efficient way of getting the job done. The sales secretary herself recognizes more than one boss, as witness a situation even so simple as complying with a janitor's request to close the windows at night.

CHARACTERISTICS OF A GOOD ORGANIZATION

In this section we will review six generalizations which typically characterize a good organization. These fundamentals are useful in designing a new organization or revising an existing one.

Organizational structure should reflect market orientation

Traditionally, in designing a sales organization a company would start with the president's office, the sales and marketing activities in the central office, and the other headquarter executives. By working from the top down, eventually the sales force and the field-selling operation would be structed. Today, we realize that exactly the opposite procedure should be employed. Management should focus attention first on the market and the sales force. Executives should consider the selling and marketing tasks necessary to capitalize on the market demand and to serve the firm's customers. From there, they can work back to the top marketing executive in the central office. En route they can provide the necessary structure, involving supervision of sales people, branch offices, and supportive marketing staff services.

Activities, not people, should be organized

The major sales activities are sales planning, sales operations, and sales performance evaluation. The organization should be built around these activities (or functions), and not around the people participating in them. Naturally, workers perform the activities, but ideally these people should be placed *after* the basic duties have been arranged.

In many respects, this generalization is most difficult to put into operation. From a practical standpoint, it is almost impossible to avoid organizing around people to some extent. Often, about all a company can realistically hope for is to organize its major activities without being unduly influenced by the people involved. However, within a given area it may be necessary to recognize the human factor and make corresponding organizational adjustments. Sometimes the vitality and effectiveness of an organization can be increased by adapting the structure to take advantage of available people's strengths. The managerial trick is to know how far to go when making these "people adaptations."

Responsibility and authority should be related properly

Misunderstandings often occur because someone did not know he was supposed to do a given job or, he was not granted adequate authority to fulfill the responsibility. Responsibility for each activity should be clearly spelled out (preferably in writing) and assigned to some individual. Then the necessary authority should be delegated to that person. If you are going to give a person a job to do, then give him the tools to do it. If branch managers are assigned a sales volume quota (the responsibility), they should be allowed to select their sales forces (the authority). Suppose a sales representative is given the responsibility for developing a new territory where competition is strong. The rep who cannot quote varying prices to meet this competition or approve a credit sale without first getting home-office sanction probably does not have enough authority to complement the responsibility.

Matching authority and responsibility, however, is usually easier said than done. For our branch managers to produce the assigned results—their responsibility—they would be given authority to set prices, select dealers, recruit and train sales reps, and so on. Yet it is unrealistic and uneconomical to delegate authority for these tasks. Even in selection and training, authority for certain functions may well be handled more effectively in some centralized manner, rather than letting each branch set up and operate its own program.

Span of executive control should be reasonable

An executive must have adequate time to spend with each of his subordinates—guiding their efforts, counseling with them, evaluating their results, and so on—in addition to performing other administrative tasks. Just what constitutes a reasonable span of executive control depends on many variables. It is generally recognized, however, that the number should be small—usually not more than six or eight persons or, in rare situations, perhaps ten.

There are a few guidelines for determining the appropriate number. If the subordinates' work is similar or their duties are routine, the span can be relatively wider. And the higher the ability levels of the executive and the subordinates, the greater can be the span of control.

Organization should be stable, but flexible

A good organization will be stable but flexible, like a tree. A tree has to be firmly and deeply rooted to withstand extreme blows, but above ground it must be able to give with the wind or it will snap off at its base.

The factor of *stability* in an organization means that the company has built a structure that can stand losses of managerial personnel at any level and still maintain peak efficiency. The company has trained replacements available. In athletics, the concept is referred to as depth in all positions. A stable organization also can take in stride any long-range expansion or contraction of its business.

The concept of *flexibility* in an organization refers more to short-run situations. A flexible structure, for example, will be able to adjust to seasonal fluctuations in needs for workers, or to counter the moves of a competitor who brings out a new product or goes into a new territory. Flexibility can be built into an organization by effective scheduling of executive duties or by subcontracting some of the work. An advertising department, for instance, might lease out the job of preparing the Christmas catalog.

Activities should be balanced and coordinated

A well-organized company keeps a good *balance* among all its divisions. That is, management does not let any unit become *unduly* more important than another. In an athletic situation where a team stresses either the offense or the defense to the neglect of the other, we say that team is basically unsound because the organization lacks balance. The ancient Greek adage "In all things, moderation" certainly is applicable to organization—in athletics, business, or any other group effort.

Sales department activities are tied in with virtually every other major function in business. Consequently, effective *coordination* is needed (1) between sales and nonmarketing departments, as well as (2) between sales and other marketing units.

Sales and nonmarketing activities.   Here are a few examples of how sales and nonmarketing departments can help each other.

Sales←——→production. The sales department can help the production people by:

- Furnishing an accurate, detailed sales forecast.
- Relaying customers' (and other field sources') ideas for new products.
- Relaying ideas regarding color, design, and packaging.

Production, in turn, can provide:

- Dependable production schedules to provide the right quantity and quality of goods at the right time.
- Products at a cost that will allow a competitive price.
- Technical product information.

Sales←——→finance and accounting.   These two groups can collaborate in controlling selling costs and in setting credit policies. In addition, the sales department can:

- Provide short-run sales forecasts as a basis for company budgeting.
- Supply a long-range forecast for capital expenditure planning.
- From sources in the field, provide current credit information about customers.

The finance and accounting people can help by:

- Providing information for setting quotas and designing pay plans.
- Preparing marketing cost analyses as bases for pricing and discounts.
- Supplying credit information on a customer prior to a sales call.

Sales←——→*personnel.* These two departments can work together in selecting and training sales people. They can cooperate in preparing selection forms (job description, application blanks, interview forms). Together they can develop and conduct sales training programs. Some companies rely heavily on the personnel department to do the selection and training. In other firms, most of this work is done by sales departments, perhaps using personnel's materials and facilities.

Sales←——→*legal.* Coordination with the legal department is essential because so much legislation directly affects marketing and sales activities. The legal division can offer interpretation of laws. A sales executive may propose some policy and want an opinion of its legality before putting it into operation. In some firms the legal department and the sales training department have joined forces to educate the field sales force regarding the Sherman, Clayton, Robinson-Patman, and other major laws related to sales force activities.

Sales and other marketing activities. Advertising is the major marketing activity to be coordinated with personal selling. Together, they constitute the main parts of the selling function in a company. Sales force executives also should work closely with the people in sales promotion and in the marketing information system (marketing research).

Sales←——→*advertising.* Even though this is an obvious area for a closely integrated effort, many firms have serious problems in coordinating their personal selling and advertising efforts. Often there is conflict between sales and advertising executives. Sales managers want such things as advertising campaigns designed to meet sales goals, more effective sales support, and advertisements the sales people can talk about. Advertising executives want a major role in marketing planning, more protection in size and allocation of the advertising appropriation, and a more secure place on the team of marketing executives.

Advertising and sales departments should collaborate, from the early stages of product planning all the way through to the final sale. Sales managers may discuss with advertising managers such topics as competition, problems in some territory, and selling points of various products. In this way, sales can help advertising direct its message more effectively at a given market. In return, advertising may help by informing sales about the advertising appeal, theme, and copy so that the sales force will be able to capitalize on the advertising by telling the same story.

Sales people in the field can help the advertising department by working with retailers to get the most effective use of vertical, cooperative advertising. The reps can report up-to-the-minute data regarding advertising done by competitors, especially at the local or retail level. Sales people also can supply the type of data that helps the manufacturer or its agency do a better job of creating and placing local advertising.

At the same time, advertising can be of direct help to the sales force in the field. It can pave the way for a call on a prospect by providing some information in advance and generally acquainting the prospect with the product. This service is particularly valuable when a sales person is calling on a prospect for the first time. Anything that helps to open a customer's door and mind to a sales rep is bound to increase that rep's morale and effectiveness.

BASIC TYPES OF ORGANIZATION

After looking at the sales organization charts in a large number of companies, you might get the idea that there are many different types of organizations. Actually, however, most organizations essentially can be classified in one of the following three basic categories:

1. The line organization.
2. The line-and-staff organization.
3. The functional organization.

Usually, most medium- and large-sized firms find it advantageous to expand their basic organization in some specialized fashion to enable the sales force to perform more effectively. This specialization ordinarily is modeled on one or a combination of the following bases:

1. Geographical territory.
2. Product line.
3. Type of customer.

The line organization

Nature and use. A line organization is the simplest form of organizational structure. Authority flows directly from the chief executive to the first subordinate, from the first to the second subordinate, and so on down the line. In its pure form, a line organization has no specialists or advisers. Planning is not separated from operating, and authority is highly centralized. In the most rudimentary form of line structure, the chief executive does all the planning and is in charge of all the operations, whether they are in production, sales, finance, or any other area in the company.

This form of organization can well be used by a very small firm. For example, a person who owns and operates a small wholesaling company may have six employees, none of whom has any supervisory duties. This organization chart would look like the one in Figure 3–2.

As this firm grows, the owner-president probably will not be able to continue to run the whole show alone and still do an effective job.

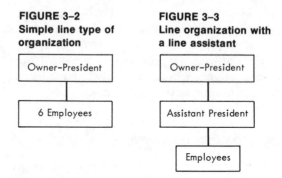

FIGURE 3–2
Simple line type of
organization

Owner–President

6 Employees

FIGURE 3–3
Line organization with
a line assistant

Owner–President

Assistant President

Employees

Therefore a line assistant is hired. There is no one best pattern for splitting the duties between these two. Usually the president still oversees all the functional areas of the business but handles only the broader aspects, such as establishing policies and planning the operation. The assistant sees that the plans are put into effect by the employees. The line of authority now flows from the president through the assistant to the employees, as shown in Figure 3–3.

It is possible for a company of fairly large size to have a complex organizational structure for the entire firm, while at the same time it has a simple line organization in the sales department.

Relative merits. A line type of sales organization is a simple structure. It usually is a low-cost operation, because it has few executives. It should ensure quick decision making and speedy action in putting policies into operation. Because of its highly centralized authority and responsibility, there probably is a minimum of buck-passing in the organization.

A line organization also has some severe limitations, especially if it is used in medium-sized or large companies. One drawback is the lack of managerial specialization. One person cannot be an expert in all phases of a business. And, even if he were, there would not be enough hours in the day to do all the jobs well.

Typically, a line organization, especially in a small company, lacks stability because it does not provide for replacement executives. Furthermore, the extreme centralization of authority generally retards the development of subordinate executives. Another problem occurs as the company expands—namely, the number of *levels* of subordinates increases. This in turn leads to clogged channels of communication, with all the evils attendant on delay, misunderstanding, and failure to receive information.

The line and staff organization

Nature and use. As the marketing operation in a company grows in size and complexity, it soon becomes apparent that a simple line type of organization is not sufficient for effective operation. The top marketing executive realizes a need for some staff assistants who are specialists in various areas of marketing, such as advertising or marketing research. In addition, there is a need for an assistant executive whose job it is to manage the sales force. The resultant structure is a line-and-staff type of organization, as depicted in Figure 3–4.

FIGURE 3–4
Line-and-staff sales organization

In this type of organization, authority flows from the chief marketing executive through the field sales manager to the sales force. The middle vertical segment of Figure 3–4 is much like a line organization. The chief marketing executive is the line officer ultimately responsible for developing all sales plans and for the success of sales operations. However, now this executive has staff assistants to aid in these tasks.

The job of a staff executive is to help the top marketing manager. Each staff manager is also responsible for all planning connected with his specialized activity. The staff executives have no authority over the sales force. These executives can only *advise* the sales reps' boss, the field sales manager.

The line and staff is probably the most widely used basic form of organization in sales departments today. It is likely to be used when any of the following conditions exists for a company:

- The sales force is large in number.
- The market is regional or national.
- The line of products is varied.
- The number of customers is large.
- The company wants to put increased emphasis on sales planning in relation to sales operations.

Line authority and staff authority held by same executive. In most firms the staff managers have under them some subexecutives or nonsupervisory employees. In this organizational structure, the head of the specialized activity is a line officer in some situations and a staff officer in others. The advertising manager, for example, has line authority over the people in his department. However, he still is in a staff capacity to the chief marketing manager, to other staff executives, and to the sales force.

In a different set of circumstances, a staff manager also may be given line authority. Consider a sales training director who is instructed to prepare a program emphasizing service and missionary selling. He can only make recommendations. He has no authority to put his program into effect. Theoretically, every time he wants to instruct a sales person he must go through the field sales manager. A system of this nature often can be slow and inefficient. To improve the situation, the field sales manager may give the training executive line authority to deal directly with the sales force.

The practice of giving staff officers line authority under temporary and limited conditions is quite prevalent, and from a realistic standpoint it makes sense. Even so, built into the practice are all the dangers attendant on a person's having more than one boss.

Relative merits. The line-and-staff form of organization enables a company to enjoy the benefits of division of labor. Planning and operating can be separated, and planning can be done by an expert in each field. This not only ensures better planning in each area but also relieves the chief sales executive of much work. He is free to devote his talents to top-level planning, to line responsibilities, and to other general administrative matters.

A line-and-staff organizational structure does have some limitations for a company, regardless of its size. The total executive cost can be high because additional specialists must be hired, and many of these staff executives have departments of their own. This form of organization also makes for a slower mode of operation. When a problem arises, it usually is assigned to a staff person for study and recommendation. Of course, it is presumed that the more careful and expert consideration of problems is well worth the price of a slower pace. Another potential limitation is in the responsibility-authority relationships.

Strong staff executives may try to take on line authority instead of staying in the role of adviser. Another problem lies with the line executive who either completely bypasses the staff departments or consistently ignores their advice.

It should be noted that many of these limitations are not inherent disadvantages of a line-and-staff organization. Instead, they are manifestations of poor administration.

Functional organization

Nature and use.   The functional type of organization is a step beyond the line-and-staff form, even though at first glance the two may look alike. In both types, the activities of the marketing department are separated into groups, and a functional specialist is put in charge of each group. Thus a firm may have an advertising manager, a field sales manager, and a marketing research manager under either of the two forms. Here the similarity ends. In a functional organization, each of the specialized executives has *line* authority over his particular activity, whereas in a line-and-staff structure these executives have only *advisory* authority.

In a functional organization, it is not at all unusual for a number of executives to be giving orders to the sales force. The sales promotion manager for a manufacturer may want the sales force to make a list of all the window displays secured by competitors. The credit manager might like the sales people to make collections on delinquent accounts. In a line-and-staff structure, these staff executives could only *recommend* to the field sales manager that the sales reps perform the duties. Under a functional plan, both would have line authority to *order* the sales people to do the jobs or to *order* the assistant sales manager to see that the jobs were done. In Figure 3–5, the functional authority is flowing directly to the sales force from these two managers.

A functional organization ordinarily is found in conjunction with a line-and-staff or territorial or product type of structure. This type of authority is best fitted to a situation in which the number of executives who may use it is limited. The greater the number of executives with functional authority over the operating people, the greater the opportunity for trouble.

Relative merits.   A major drawback to the functional plan obviously is that some of the line officers or sales people get orders from more than one person, thus violating a basic tenet of good organization. The practice also involves the risk of overloading these or of giving them conflicting orders. Furthermore, the line executives who are consistently bypassed soon find their own influence and importance reduced. Theoretically, of course, some top manager coordinates this type of

FIGURE 3–5
Functional sales organization

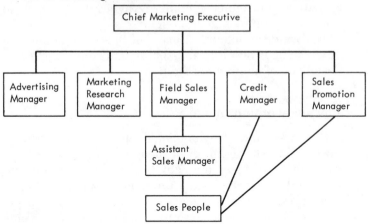

organization, but from a practical standpoint, effective coordination is very difficult.

For a company that can successfully use a functional organization, this form has all the advantages that result from specialization of labor, because each function gets expert supervision and control. In contrast to a line-and-staff organization, there is little risk that plans formulated by functional executives will not be placed in operation. The functional officers can *order* that their plans be carried out. They are not in the position of having to *advise* that this be done, and then leaving it up to a line officer to determine *whether* it is done.

SPECIALIZATION WITHIN THE SALES DEPARTMENT

In the organizational examples considered above, the sales force has not been split on any basis. It has reported directly to the chief marketing executive or an assistant or to the field sales manager. With a larger sales force, however, the job of the line executive charged with its administration is more difficult. The number and complexity of a company's products and markets may also require some organizational division if the sales effort is to be effective.

The most common way to divide the responsibilities in a sales department is to split the sales force on some basis of sales specialization. The most frequently used bases are by:

1. Geographical territories.
2. Types of products sold.

3. Classes of customers.
4. Some combination of these three categories.

Specialization by products or market really is a specialization of knowledge. Another basis is specialization by *task*.[1] In most firms and for most products, field sales reps have two very different jobs—*sales development* and *sales maintenance*. They continually must generate a stream of new customers, while at the same time providing full service for existing accounts. The satisfactory performance of each of these jobs requires different techniques and qualifications. The task of sales development usually is the more difficult of the two, and, it tends to be neglected. One remedy for this situation is to reorganize the field sales force so the sales people are assigned either development or maintenance work, but not both.

Of course, there are some problems in this type of organizational specialization. The costs are high. Sometimes management is unable to relieve sales reps from account maintenance tasks so they can concentrate on development selling. Also, there is a scarcity of people who can qualify for the development sales jobs.

Geographical territories

Probably the most widely used system for dividing responsibility and line authority over sales operations is to organize the sales force on the basis of geographical territories. In this type of structure, each sales person is assigned a separate geographical area, called a *territory,* in which to sell. A reasonable number of sales people representing contiguous territories are placed under a territorial executive who reports to the field sales manager. The territorial sales executive is typically called a regional, divisional, or district sales manager. In companies with large sales forces, it is not unusual to find two or three levels of territorial sales executives (see Figure 3–6).

Some form of territorial organization is probably used by the great majority of companies that have grown beyond the stage of small business and sell in a market broader than a local one. A territorial organization is best suited for a company that sells closely related products. Otherwise, the sales department is likely to be organized on the combined bases of territories and products.

Territorial sales executives usually have complete authority over their own geographical areas. In some respects, it is almost as if they were running their own businesses. In fact, many firms encourage this attitude by preparing profit and loss statements for the areas. Each

---

[1] George N. Kahn and Abraham Schuchman, "Specialize Your Salesmen!" *Harvard Business Review*, January–February 1961, pp. 90–98.

FIGURE 3-6
Territorial sales organization

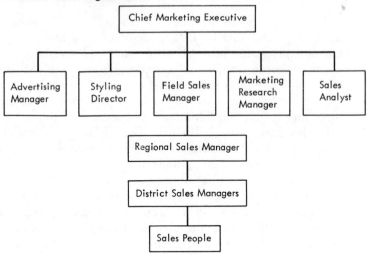

area is treated as a separate profit center, and some type of profit accountability is placed on the territorial manager.

A firm can derive many benefits by dividing the line authority in its sales department on the basis of geographical territories. The plan usually ensures better coverage of the entire market, as well as better control over the sales force and sales operations. A second benefit is that the company is in a better position to meet local competition by having an executive responsible for a limited segment of the market. Local management also can act more rapidly in servicing customers and in handling problems. Line authority at the local level means there is no need to check with headquarters every time a decision must be made on some territorial issue. A territorial organization also is more flexible; it can adapt to individual regional needs and conditions.

Territorial specialization by function typically is lacking in an organization, and this is a drawback. Each district manager, for instance, may have to do a small amount of work in advertising, sales analysis, and credits and collections, in addition to managing a sales force. Another limiting factor is expense. As more levels of territorial executives are established, the company increases its overhead cost of management.

Product specialization

The type of product sold is another frequently used basis for dividing the responsibilities and activities within a sales department. Product specialization may be employed in a number of different forms: (1) the sales force and the line authority in sales force management may be separated into product groups, (2) the supporting functional staff activities may be specialized by product line, or (3) line selling and staff support may both be divided by products.

   Product-operating specialization. In the company whose organization chart is given in Figure 3–7, products have been separated into

FIGURE 3–7
Sales organization with product-operating specialization

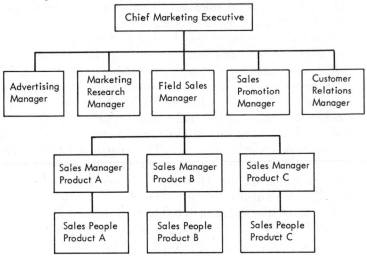

three lines. One group of sales reps sells only the products included in line A. All sales people in group A report directly to the sales manager of product line A, who in turn is responsible to the field sales manager. As far as sales operations are concerned, each product division is completely separate and autonomous. To simplify this illustration, it is assumed that there is no territorial structure, otherwise the basis of organization would be a combination plan. The three product sales managers are strictly operating executives; they have no staff assistants. The staff executives in advertising, marketing research, sales promotion, and customer relations all are centralized in the home office and are not specialized by product line.

   A product-operating type of organization is likely to be used when the company is selling:

   • A variety of complex, technical products—as in the chemicals or electronics field.

- Many thousands of products—a hardware wholesaler, for example. The products are not necessarily technical; there simply are too many items for one sales person to handle.
- Very dissimilar, unrelated products—a rubber company may use three sales forces to sell (a) truck and auto tires, (b) rubber footware, and (c) industrial rubber products, such as belts, bushings, and insulating materials.

The major advantage of this form of organization is the specialized attention each product line gets from the sales force. Also, each line gets more executive attention because one person is specifically responsible for a particular product group.

Probably the biggest drawback is that in many instances more than one sales person from a company calls on the same customer. Not only is this duplication of coverage expensive, it also can create ill will on the part of the customers. In addition, much overlapping in territorial coverage occurs even when no overlapping among customers does. Another weakness is the increase in the cost of executive personnel that results from adding product sales managers, many of whom need an assistant or small office staff. This structure has the same weakness as the territorial-operating type in that the product sales managers have no staff assistants. Therefore, functional specialization by product line is lacking at this executive level.

Functional specialization by product.   Several different sales organizational structures are available to a company which intends to make use of staff assistants who specialize by product line. Figures 3–8 and 3–9 illustrate two of these alternatives.

FIGURE 3–8
Sales organization illustrating use of product-staff specialization

The company charted in Figure 3–8 has three staff executives, called product managers, each bearing the responsibility for planning and developing a marketing program for a separate group of products. These people have no line authority over the sales force or the sales force managers. They can only advise and make recommendations to the line officers. The sales force is not specialized by products. Instead, each sales person sells the products of all three product managers. Each product manager works with other functional specialists in planning the advertising, packaging, and personal selling effort related to his group of products. The product manager concept is discussed in more detail in the next section.

A company can use a product-staff structure, as in Figure 3–8, when it wants some of the advantages of specialization by product line at the planning level, but at the same time does not need the specialization at the selling level. Thus, in one stroke the product-staff organization corrects two of the weaknesses in a product-operating structure—the problems of duplicate calls on a customer and the lack of specialization in planning the functional activities. Of course, a product-staff organization loses any advantage of having sales people specialize in a limited line of goods. Otherwise, the relative merits of the two structures are about the same.

Some very large companies prefer to use what amounts to a functional organization based on product divisions (see Figure 3–9). In such a structure, under the chief marketing executive are the usual

FIGURE 3–9
Sales organization with product-functional specialization

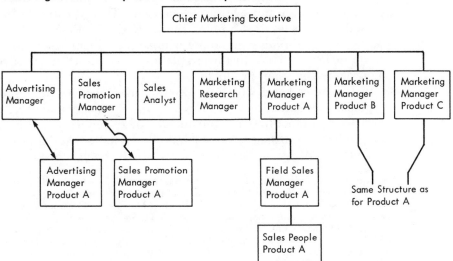

assistants in charge of specialized activities. In addition, there are separate product marketing managers, each with a sales force and a staff of functional assistants. The staff executives are under the *line* authority of the product marketing manager and under the *functional* authority of the corresponding executive in the home office. In Figure 3–9, for example, under the line direction of each of the three product marketing managers is an advertising manager whose energies are devoted to one line of products. At the same time, there is a general advertising manager in the home office who coordinates all company advertising and has functional authority over each product advertising manager. In effect, each product-staff officer has two bosses. This, of course, is a major drawback to the plan.

The product manager.   The concept of the product manager (also called a brand manager or a merchandise manager), while widely used, is controversial. A large number of firms have adopted the product manager concept over the past 20 to 30 years. During the past decade, however, some name companies (Pepsi-Cola, Eastman Kodak, and Levi Strauss, for example) either have abandoned the system or have made major changes in it. Use of this concept is under pressure, and important structural changes in it seem inevitable.[2]

There are two basic product manager structures. In one, the product managers are *staff* executives responsible for planning and developing a complete marketing program for one line of products. They forecast sales, plan marketing strategy, plan the advertising and personal-selling programs, and generally are concerned with the market growth and profitability of their products. However, this type of executive has no line authority over the field sales force. They can only advise, not order, sales people and sales force managers. This type of organization is used by Procter & Gamble, Kimberly-Clark (Kleenex, Delsey), Clairol, Lever Brothers, and other companies. The product managers' efforts are oriented heavily toward planning and directing the advertising programs for their products.

In the other basic structure, product managers have far broader responsibility and authority. They are, in effect, the marketing managers for a product line, or "presidents" of a "company." The Nestlé Corporation, for instance, has separate divisional marketing managers for coffee products and for chocolate products. Each is responsible for

---

[2] See, for example, Richard M. Clewett and Stanley F. Stasch, "Shifting Role of the Product Manager," *Harvard Business Review*, January–February 1975, pp. 65–73; Victor P. Buell, "The Changing Role of the Product Manager in Consumer Goods Companies," *Journal of Marketing*, July 1975, pp. 3–11; Stephens Dietz, "Get More Out of Your Brand Management," *Harvard Business Review*, July–August 1973, pp. 127–36; B. Charles Ames, "Dilemma of Product/Market Management," *Harvard Business Review*, March–April 1971, pp. 66–74; and "The Brand Manager: No Longer King," *Business Week*, June 9, 1973, p. 58.

advertising, marketing research, and product planning, and each has a separate sales force.

Actually, the product manager is not a new organizational concept. For years, it has been used in department stores where there is a departmental buyer system and each merchandise manager has complete responsibilities for a limited line of products. In the manufacturing field, Procter & Gamble and Johnson & Johnson have used the brand manager system for a half century with considerable success.

For most firms, however, the product manager is a relatively new specialist in marketing organizations. Companies are using product managers as a form of organizational decentralization to cope with the growing numbers of products and markets, as well as the increasing complexities of modern marketing. The use of product managers brings the benefits of specialization to each product line or market segment. Coordination among products and among marketing functions should also be improved. A long-range benefit that both the executive and the company derive is that the product manager system is an excellent training ground for future top marketing executives. The job of product manager usually involves all major areas of a company's operation—finance, production, and marketing.

The product-manager system does have some problems, however. Frequently, personnel conflicts and frustrations enter the system when a product manager must work through or around people in an attempt to fulfill large responsibilities without having much real authority.

Companies that use the product manager system generally have an authority-responsibility problem. Most of these firms assign profit responsibility to a brand manager without giving this executive commensurate authority and control over prices and costs—the major factors affecting profits.[3]

Type of customer

Many companies have divided the line authority in their sales departments on the basis of type of customer, classed by either type of industry or channel of distribution. The customer basis of organization is closely related to the product-operating plan. In fact, some firms have split their sales forces by product line because each product goes

[3] For some illustrations of how various forms of interpersonal influence are exerted by product managers in the absence of formal authority, see Gary R. Gemmill and David L. Wilemon, "The Product Manager as an Influence Agent," *Journal of Marketing*, January 1972, pp. 26–30; Alladi Venkatesh and David L. Wilemon, "Interpersonal Influence in Product Management," *Journal of Marketing*, October 1976, pp. 33–40; and Roger A. Kerin and James T. Rothe, "Personal Influence in Product Management: An Empirical Study," in Barnett A. Greenberg (ed.), *1974 Proceedings, Southern Marketing Association*, 1975, pp. 117–19.

to a different customer group. (You can see this similarity in Figure 3–10.) The sales managers in charge of each industry group are purely line operating executives responsible to the field sales manager and with authority over one group of sales people. These executives have

FIGURE 3–10
Sales organization specialized by type of customer

no staff assistants under them. Each sales rep sells the full line of products used by the customer group.

Customer-group specialization in the sales force is likely to increase in usage as more companies fully implement the marketing concept. Certainly this basis of specialization is consistent with the customer-oriented philosophy which underlies the marketing concept. The emphasis is on markets rather than on products or production processes. Among the companies that already have made the market-specialization move in their sales organizations are such well-known names as Xerox, IBM, Gulf Oil, NCR, Hewlett-Packard, General Foods, and General Electric.[4]

A company is especially likely to organize its sales force on a customer-group basis when:

- Each customer group has individualized needs, and selling to these groups requires specialized knowledge of the given industry. In the data processing division of IBM, for example, one group of

---

[4] See Mack Hanan, "Reorganize Your Company around Its Markets," *Harvard Business Review*, November-December 1974, pp. 63–74; "NCR's Radical Shift in Marketing Tactics," *Business Week*, December 8, 1973, p. 102; and "Specialist Selling Makes New Converts," *Business Week*, July 28, 1973, p. 44.

sales people sells to the financial industry, another unit sells to aircraft and missile manufacturers, a third sales force sells to textile producers, and so on.

- There is a reasonable geographic concentration within each customer group.
- Management wants to separate its channels of distribution as much as possible in order to minimize friction among them. Consequently, different sales forces are used for each major channel.

Although it overcomes some of the disadvantages of product specialization and conflict of interest between channels, the customer type of organization does have some limitations. It makes for overlapping of territorial coverage and, in this respect it is costly. As with the other divisions of line authority, it also increases the executive overhead expense. Finally, unless separating the sales force by markets also results in some product specialization, the customer-based organization is subject to the disadvantages of full-line selling.

Combination of organization bases

In the examples of organizational bases given above, it has been assumed that when a company divides its sales force it is done on only one basis, such as territory, product, or customer. Actually, many firms use some combination drawn from the several structures already discussed. The number of possible combinations is obviously quite large. As one example, a firm may combine territorial-operating with product-staff specializations (through the use of product managers). Or a sales force may combine customer specialization with territorial specialization.

QUESTIONS AND PROBLEMS

1. In relation to management's treatment of workers, contrast the classical organization theory approach and the human relations approach. Which approach should be adopted in the organization of a sales force?
2. Explain the relationship between the degree of centralization and the span of executive control in a sales organization.
3. Some executives are hesitant to delegate authority and responsibility, even though they recognize that delegation is desirable. One writer offered the following reasons why these managers may be reluctant to delegate:
    a. The executive gets trapped in the "I can do it better myself" fallacy.
    b. Lack of ability to communicate what is to be done.
    c. Lack of confidence in subordinates.

  d. Being handicapped by an aversion to taking a chance.

  What are some ways in which each of these obstacles may be overcome?

4. An authority in the field of management has stated the following reasons why subordinates avoid accepting responsibility:

  a. Subordinate finds it easier to ask the boss rather than decide for self how to deal with the problem.

  b. Fear of criticism for mistakes.

  c. Subordinate already has more work than he can do.

  d. Subordinate feels he lacks necessary information and resources to do a good job.

  Suggest ways in which each of these points may be successfully counteracted by management.

5. Explain how coordination can be effectively secured between the sales department and each of the following departments: production, engineering and design, personnel, finance, export sales.

6. *a.* What are the reasons for the lack of coordination that sometimes exists between advertising executives and field sales managers?

  b. What are some proposals for developing better coordination between these two groups?

7. The choice of organizational structure is influenced by factors such as:

  a. Size of the company.

  b. Nature of the products.

  c. Nature and density of the market.

  d. Ability of executives.

  e. Financial condition of the company.

  Explain how each of these conditions may affect the choice of structure.

8. In your opinion, what are the best policies or procedures for solving the following problems, which often are found in a line and staff organization?

  a. A strong-willed staff executive tries to take on line authority instead of remaining as an adviser.

  b. A line executive consistently bypasses or ignores advice from staff departments.

  c. The rate of executive decision making is slowed down.

  d. Empire-building is encouraged or facilitated.

  e. A staff executive, such as the training director or marketing research manager, is given line authority in a temporary situation and then tries to keep or expand this authority.

9. Sales development and sales maintenance were described in the text as two very different jobs. The satisfactory performance of each requires different qualifications. In what ways may the personnel requirements for these two jobs be different?

10. Do you recommend that the management in the following companies develop a centralized or decentralized organizational structure? Explain your position in each case.

  a. Manufacturer of high-quality women's ready-to-wear. Has 100 sales people selling to department stores and specialty stores throughout the nation.

b. Hardware wholesaler covering the southeast quarter of the country with 50 sales people.

c. Manufacturer of chemicals used in fertilizers. Has 35 sales people and sells to 500 accounts located throughout the country.

d. Manufacturer of office machines with 1,000 sales people.

11. What are the limitations and problems typically encountered when line authority is decentralized? What can management do to offset these difficulties?

12. A regional hardware wholesaler located in Detroit, Michigan, employed 20 sales people, each of whom sold the full line of products. It was becoming apparent that the list of products was simply too long for one person to sell effectively. The company felt it had a choice of (a) reorganizing the sales force by product lines or (b) adding more representatives, reducing each person's territory but still having each one carry the full line. What is your recommendation?

13. What organizational problems may occur when a company adopts some form of product manager organizational structure in its marketing department?

Case 3–1
CATTLEMEN'S MUTUAL INSURANCE COMPANY
Reorganizing sales force after adding new product

The Cattlemen's Mutual Insurance Company was a large company which, until a few years ago, specialized in fire, casualty, and auto insurance. Almost since its start the company has had a satisfactory financial performance. It was currently rated A+ (excellent) by the Alfred M. Best Company, a recognized and respected independent organization which rates insurance companies. Last year the premium income from fire, casualty, and auto policies was $52 million, and profit after payment of dividends to policy holders was about $700,000. However, the times were changing. The company was faced with (a) shrinking profit margins in the fire-casualty-auto field plus (b) the public's seeming preference to do its insurance business with as few companies as possible.

In light of these two factors, management in Cattlemen's Mutual recently decided to enter the field of life insurance. After deciding to add life insurance to its product line, the next big managerial problem was whether the life policies should be sold through the existing sales force or whether a separate sales force should be established.

Cattlemen's Mutual was started over 60 years ago in Omaha, Nebraska. Its founders perceived a need on the part of ranchers, farmers, and small businessmen for lower cost insurance than they were able to buy at that time from other companies. Through the years Cattlemen's Mutual broadened its market coverage considerably, reaching urban as well as rural residents and small businessmen with an extensive line of fire, casualty, auto, and, now, life insurance policies. The policy line included homeowners' policies (fire, theft, personal liability), workmen's compensation, inland marine insurance, group accident and health coverage, complete auto coverage, and life insurance (term, whole life, endowment, annuity, group life).

The insurance industry is regulated to a considerable extent by state insurance commissions. The industry—whether it be fire, casualty, auto, or life insurance—is highly competitive. Most firms generally compete on a service basis, however, rather than engaging in price competition. These companies price their policies on the basis of standard rates established by the rating bureaus to which the firms belong. Nevertheless, Cattlemen's Mutual had been able to price its policies, especially its fire, casualty, and auto insurance, below the level of many competitors by virtue of selling only to highly preferred risks. The company sold to drivers who had been accident-free for a period of years, or to homeowners and businessmen located in neighborhoods not likely to be plagued with rioting, burning, or looting.

Even with their strategy of marketing to preferred risks, Cattlemen's Mutual was faced with shrinking profits, especially in the auto insurance part of their business. The entire auto insurance industry has been caught in a profit squeeze during the past several years. The industry found it quite difficult to get state insurance departments to approve premium increases which would be large enough to match the rapid rise in repair costs and claims. The increased frequency and costs of auto accidents raised the insurance companies' costs to the point where industrywide losses, or extremely small profits, occurred in the late 1960s and the 1970s.

The situation was not quite so severe in the fire and casualty fields. Nevertheless, the effects of inflation and the high losses in crime-ridden urban areas served to reduce profits to dangerously low levels.

All these conditions served to make life insurance a highly attractive field to fire-casualty-auto underwriters. The risks were more predictable because actuarial studies on life expectancies were quite accurate. The field was reasonably profitable and the potential almost unlimited. People can carry as much life insurance as they desire and can pay for. Because practically no one has fully insured the discounted value of total future income, most people are underinsured and thus are prospective buyers.

Cattlemen's Mutual added a full line of life insurance policies, believing that this new field would bring the desired stability and added profits to the corporate structure. Management also believed that life insurance would be less vulnerable to government regulation. Management further felt that the company had the human talent necessary to handle the new line. On the inside of the company there were actuaries and systems people. On the outside there was an established sales force who could use their present fire-casualty-auto customers as a starting list of prospects for life insurance.

Cattlemen's Mutual had a sales force of about 450 sales agents supervised by 40 district sales managers. Providing "professional insurance counselors," as the company preferred to call them, was in contrast to most competitive fire and casualty firms, which sold through independent insurance brokers.

During their first year with the firm, the sales reps for Cattlemen's Mutual were paid a guaranteed drawing account of $9,000–$10,000, depending upon whether they were assigned to rural or urban territories. After the first year, they were paid on a straight commission basis. They received a large share of the premium on a new fire, casualty, or auto policy, and then received a commission of 10–15 percent of the premiums on renewal policies.

Like most insurance firms, Cattlemen's found it very difficult to recruit and keep good sales people. College graduates rarely want to be career sales reps, but prefer to get into management training programs. Other sources of sales agents have proven to be equally poor in supplying large quantities of good prospects. Cattlemen's management understood that the life insurance industry suffers a 95 percent turnover in the sales force during a five-year period.

Mr. Kenneth Fedders, a sales executive who had been with the company for many years after starting out as a salesman, voiced the opinion that Cattlemen's Mutual should use its existing sales force to sell the new life insurance line. Fedders said his decision was influenced by two compelling factors. First was his belief that many of the company's present customers were good prospects for life insurance, and management did not want two sales reps from the same firm calling on a given customer. The other factor was the time, cost, and difficulty of recruiting and training a new sales force. He realized, of course, that more sales people would eventually be needed, whether or not separate sales forces were used. However, the new agents could be added more slowly if the existing sales force was used to sell life policies.

One of the marketing executives in the home office, ·Ms. Barbara Krause, argued that Cattlemen's should establish a new and separate sales force to sell the line of life insurance policies. As Ms. Krause viewed the situation, to use the existing fire-casualty-auto insurance sales people would pose monumental motivation problems. She believed that many of the older, established insurance agents (sales people) considered themselves as fire-casualty-auto insurance agents first and foremost. That is what they were originally hired and trained to do. Krause felt that it would be virtually impossible to change the habits of these older agents—that is, to get them to switch over and give a balanced treatment to life insurance.

Krause also believed (although some of the other executives disagreed with her) that the two sales jobs—fire-casualty-auto insurance and life insurance—were really quite different in several respects. Finally, Krause reminded her colleagues that some of Cattlemen's largest competitors—Travelers, Aetna, and Insurance Company of North America, for example—had set up separate sales forces to handle life insurance.

At this point the vice president of sales, Mr. L. R. Gerrard, was trying to determine which sales force organizational structure the company should adopt. If he decided to use his existing sales force, then he would have to figure out how his district sales managers might redirect the selling efforts of their agents and motivate them to do a productive, effective job of selling life insurance.

Question

1. Should Cattlemen's Mutual use its existing sales force to sell the new line of life insurance policies, or should a separate sales force be established?

Case 3–2

KIMBERLY MANUFACTURING COMPANY
Sales organization for new products and markets

The power tool division of the Kimberly Manufacturing Company was planning to introduce soon two new products, one for the consumer market and one for industrial users. Sales volume in power tools

and the number of sales calls on industrial users had been declining
during the past two years. Consequently, the field sales manager of the
power tool division, Mr. Glenn Abbott, was wondering whether the
present organizational structure in his sales force was the best arrangement for both meeting competition and for capitalizing on the
expanded market opportunities made possible by the expanded product lines.

The Kimberly Manufacturing Company was a large manufacturer of
a widely diversified assortment of products, most of which were sold to
the industrial market. Except for power tools, the company, had no
experience with consumer products. Kimberly had diversified both by
acquiring existing companies and by expanding its own product line.
Sales last year were $225 million. In addition to power tools, the com-
pany made and marketed such products as meters and valves for the
gas, oil, and water industries. They also made taxi meters, parking
meters, pumps, plastic molds, iron and steel castings, and sewer cleaning equipment. Its home offices were in Cleveland, Ohio, and the
company operated manufacturing facilities in 11 states and five
foreign countries.

Kimberly marketed electrical and pneumatic power tools, both portable and stationary models. These products were sold to both consumer and industrial markets. Separate Kimberly-owned brands were
used to differentiate the portable tools from the stationary models. In
addition, the firm manufactured power tools under retailers' brands,
such as Sears, Roebuck's Craftsman label. Sales last year in the power
tool division totaled $20 million.

Competitive gaps existed in the product assortment that reached
each of these markets, but the two new product lines were intended to
fill these gaps. In the consumer market, a new low-priced line was
intended to complement the product group that had consisted only of
higher priced units. A new line of portable tools, designed primarily
for industrial users, was intended to round out the product assortment.
While sales declined in 1976 and 1977, management, in its long-range
planning, was anticipating that the company's sales volume of power
tools would double in the next seven years. Major competition was
expected to continue from such companies as Black and Decker, Stanley, Rockwell Manufacturing Company, and the producers of Skil
power tools.

As field sales manager in the power tool division, Mr. Abbott was
responsible for reaching the national sales volume goals set for power
tools *sold through distributors* (wholesalers) in the United States. (A
separate sales organization was used to sell directly to private brand
customers and to large chain store organizations and discount retailers.) Reporting to Mr. Abbott were ten regional sales managers,

covering approximately 100 territories. The sales force under each regional manager was divided into two groups on the basis of brands (product lines)—portable or stationary tools.

Both groups of sales people called on many different types of wholesalers. These reps sold to automotive wholesalers, hardware wholesalers, builders' supply houses, machine tool distributors, and any other type of industrial distributor or consumer goods wholesaler whose customers could constitute a reasonably sized market for Kimberly power tools. People in either sales force also might call on retail dealers in a promotional or missionary capacity. The sales reps might perform such assignments as demonstrating the proper tool for a given job, setting up in-store promotions, arranging for the dealers to participate in Kimberly's cooperative television and newspaper advertising programs, or training dealer salesmen to sell Kimberly tools more effectively.

Several factors prompted Abbott to review his sales organizational structure. With its ambitious new-product program to round out its line, the company was in effect expanding both its consumer and industrial markets. The broader product assortment, however, made each member of the sales forces less specialized than before. This was occurring at the same time that Kimberly's competitors were moving toward a more specialized type of sales organization. Only recently Kimberly's biggest competitor—in fact, the largest company in the industry—had divided its sales force into four specialized groups. Other smaller competitors marketed only a limited line of power tools, so their sales force efforts had automatically become more specialized than Kimberly's. The decline in sales volume was another factor stimulating Abbott, although he recognized that the organizational structure may have had no relation to the drop-off volume. Abbott also was sensitive to a common drawback to a product-type sales organization—namely, two sales people, each with a separate product line, may be calling on the same customer. There also were instances of conflicts and lack of coordination between portable-tool salesmen and stationary-tool salesmen in setting up cooperative advertising and other promotional programs with some retail accounts.

To get more specialized selling effort, Abbott was considering an organizational structure in which each of the existing sales forces would be divided into two groups, according to class of customer. Thus, Kimberly would have four sales forces, the same as its biggest competitor. Existing and potential accounts would be analyzed to determine whether in the main they served an industrial or a consumer market. Then they would be divided accordingly and separate sales forces would be assigned to each customer group. Each industrial account, to illustrate, would be called on by an industrial portable-tool sales rep and an industrial stationary-tool sales rep.

Abbott realized that this four-way division of the sales force would mean adding more sales reps. Such a structure might also entail a different supervisory arrangement at the regional manager level. The increased specialization of effort would be a definite plus factor. Interviews with the sales people showed that most of them preferred to work in one market or the other. That is, they preferred to do industrial selling or to do the type of sales and promotional work involved with wholesalers and retailers in the consumer market. Rarely did the interview uncover a person who liked both types of selling equally well.

Another alternative being considered was to stay with the double sales force structure but divide the reps on a customer basis rather than by products. That is, one sales group would sell both portable and stationary power tools, but only to industrial accounts. In this arrangement, Kimberly would hope to develop account specialists and, at the same time, have only one person call on a given account. Organizing the sales force by customer group meant, nevertheless, that each sales rep would cease to be a product specialist. People now selling only portable tools, for example, would have to broaden their product base to include product knowledge and uses in the stationary-tool line. Analyses had shown, however, that specialization by market would also be accompanied to some degree by specialization by product. That is, sales to the industrial accounts tended to fall into certain product patterns that were different from the product mix sold to consumer market accounts.

Mr. Abbott also was considering other organizational arrangements. One suggestion was to continue with the existing structure but to supplement it with better programs for motivating and supervising the sales force. The sales manager in the Chicago regional office, Mr. Charles Webster, had proposed quite differently that the company abandon its specialized sales forces. Instead, he would give each sales rep a smaller geographic territory in which to sell both portable and stationary tools to all classes of customers. Mr. Webster argued that neither the customer groups nor the product lines were sufficiently different to warrant the costs and problems that accrue from specialization.

Regardless of the type of sales organization finally selected—but assuming Kimberly continued with more than one sales force, whether it was specialized by customer, product, or some other basis—there would still be an organizational question involving the regional managers. Abbott was wondering whether to continue with one regional manager over all groups of sales people in a given region or to establish separate managers for each group of sales people in a region. If the sales force were further specialized, this would put increased responsibility on the regional managers under the present system. Furthermore, Kimberly's major competitor was using specialized managers along with its more specialized sales force.

The fundamental problem was simply this: At what level should the organization be divided, on whatever basis is selected? At the level of sales reps only? At the regional manager level? Or conceivably at the field sales manager level, with a separate field sales manager for each major group of sales reps? Abbott also was considering the possibility of using product managers or customer-group managers in a staff capacity to plan merchandising and promotional programs and to otherwise support the field selling effort.

Questions

1. What type of sales force organization should the Kimberly Company adopt?
2. Should the company continue with its existing regional manager structure?

Case 3–3

UNIVERSAL METALS, INC.
Need for reorganization

"Perhaps a bit of history regarding our sales organization will help you in your coming weeks as our new sales manager," said Don Lopez, president of Universal Metals, Inc., to Bud Marti, the new sales manager. Mr. Lopez added, "It seems as if our sales force has been in a constant state of upheaval for the past five years. A year hasn't gone by but what we have reorganized it in some way or other. But nothing seems to work."

"Let me go back to 1972 and trace our troubles for you," Mr. Lopez continued. "Our growth had been great and we were making plenty of money, sold everything in the place with no trouble. Then suddenly we were hit with a recession. Sales dropped 40 percent and profits turned to losses. We at first thought that it was happening to everyone, but soon we discovered that our competitors were not being hit as hard as we were. Their sales people seemed to be able to sell goods into accounts where our people couldn't.

"We became most unhappy with our sales organization, which at the time consisted of 25 men who reported to one sales manager. We fired the sales manager and brought in a man from one of our most successful competitors. It cost some money to get him, but we were willing to pay it.

Well, right off the bat this bozo wants to hire three assistant sales managers to supervise the sales force, a sales training director to train them, a sales analyst for the home office, and a home office sales engineer to back up the field sales force technically."

"That's a lot of money," commented Mr. Marti when Lopez paused, "How did he justify it to you?"

"I remember it well because it scared me to death," Lopez said. "He said that if we wanted to be a big-time company we would have to do things the way the big boys do them. He insisted that the key to success was to back up the field people with tremendous support from the home office and supervise them closely in the field."

"Well, how did it work out?"

"Need you ask? Sales stayed about the same but our costs skyrocketed. We lost our shirts. I never saw such confusion. No one seemed to know what he was supposed to do. So we fired the sales manager and promoted one of the sales reps to the job. He immediately cleaned out all of the staff the other fellow had hired so we were back to go. But not quite."

"Oh, did the new manager make some changes?" Marti asked.

"He felt that our real problem was that the reps couldn't sell to all types of customers, so he divided them into two groups. The first bunch of ten reps was to sell to the large manufacturers, where there was a lot of engineering work to be done with the customer's people. The second group was to cover the small metal fabricators, where engineering was not so important, where you dealt with the owner directly," Lopez explained.

"What happened?"

"More confusion. The reps didn't want to give up their customers, so they held onto them as long as they could. And it didn't seem to help sales. We didn't sell any more large accounts than we were previously selling. That sales manager got tired of managing and asked to go back into the field where he felt he knew what to do.

"The next sales manager was selected with more care," Lopez continued. "We interviewed more than 20 people until we found this fellow who had a terrific record over at National Casting. We thought we had a barn burner in him. He came in, surveyed the situation, and wrote a report for me on what he had to do."

"You're shaking your head. What went wrong?," Marti inquired.

"He insisted that he had personally spent a day with each sales representative to diagnose what was wrong with the operation," said Lopez. "On the basis of his judgment, 16 of our sales reps were incompetent, with no hope of ever becoming the type of sales rep he thought was needed to do the job. He planned to fire them immediately. Then he would call in the remaining nine reps for an intensive training session to teach them how to sell the way he wanted them to. I remember vividly how he leaned over my desk with his fists clenched and sternly said 'My sales force will sell the way I want them to sell or they won't be around.'

"Well, we had some words over that report," Lopez said. "I just could not let him fire 16 people who had been with us from the beginning and who had helped build us. I wanted him to train all of them, but he said it couldn't be done. They just weren't his 'type of people.' That kind of talk really gets my dander up. He was putting these people down like they were dirt, and I told him so. Well, one thing led to another, and there went our sales manager."

"And you had no inkling of this aspect of his personality before hiring him?" asked Marti.

Lopez drew a deep breath and confessed, "I must say that we did. His boss described him as one tough driving guy who was hard to live with but who really got results. I guess all we wanted to hear was that he got results. We didn't stop to think about how he got them."

"And so here we are," Marti summarized. "You want to know what I have found out and what I intend to do about it."

"That's it!" said Lopez. "Have you anything yet?"

"It's a bit premature now to lay out a program for you," Marti replied, "but the seeds of it are in everything that has happened previously. I'll be ready next Friday for a report on my proposed program."

"Fair enough," said Lopez.

Marti had already made up his mind about what needed to be done, but he did not want to reveal his thinking until he had figured out how to go about it best. He had quickly related to everything that had been told him. The sales manager who had wanted to reorganize for some staff support was right. The span of control had been ridiculous, and the reps were getting no support from the home office. The second manager had been right in seeing that the reps could not sell to all types of customer equally effectively. The third manager was certainly correct in that this sales force had on it some people with most mediocre talents. For the most part, they were a seedy crew.

But Bud realized that there would be little he could do directly about this immediately. It would be a problem that would have to be worked on. For the time being he had to develop a means for working with these people, and that seemed to call for some sort of reorganization.

Question

1. What organizational changes should Bud Marti recommend?

Part two

SALES OPERATIONS

Part Two

SALES OPERATIONS

4

Selecting the sales force— Determining the kind of people wanted

So very difficult a matter is it to trace and find out the truth of anything by history.
PLUTARCH

A time-honored recipe for rabbit stew begins: "First catch a rabbit." Similarly, the first step in operating a sales force is to select the sales people. One indication of the difficulty and importance of the sales selection function is that three chapters in this book are devoted to the problem.

NATURE OF THE SALES JOB

Not only does the sales job differ from nonselling jobs, as noted in Chapter 1, but the sales job of today is quite different from that of yesteryear. The old type of salesman—the drummer, the Willy Loman of *Death of a Salesman*—generally is gone, and his talents are not especially sought after in the present economy. True, aggressive, hard-hitting sales people still exist and may always have a role in some fields, but they are no longer typical. Instead, with the acceptance of the marketing concept by a firm, a new type of sales person is emerging—a territorial marketing manager. Rather than simply pushing whatever products the factory gives them to sell, the new breed is concerned with relaying consumer wants back to the firm so that appropriate products may be developed. They engage in a *total* selling job—missionary selling, servicing customers, selling the full line of products, and training customers' sales people. They also serve as territorial profit managers and act as a mirror of the market by feeding back marketing intelligence.

In this new position, the sales person occupies many roles with many divergent role partners, and heavy emotional demands are placed on him.[1] Among the roles he fills are persuader, serviceman, information gatherer, expediter, coordinator, problem definer, traveler, display arranger, and customer ego builder. He operates socially, psychologically, and physically independent of the usual worker-boss relationship. In his performance, the sales representative must cope with role conflicts of identification and advocacy. He must identify alternately with the company and with the customer. In so doing, there may be conflicts regarding whose position—the company's or the customer's—he is advocating. The several groups with whom he interacts often have differing and conflicting expectations of the sales rep.

The sales person's job thus involves a wide range of behaviors. The emotional demands on sales people are great because of the high level of role conflict, and because they must handle the behavioral ambiguities pretty much on their own. If management can determine the emotional and interactional demands of a given sales job, and then weave these into job descriptions and selection devices, the results of the selection effort should be successful.

Wide variety of sales jobs

No two selling jobs are alike. The types of jobs and the requirements needed to fill them cover a very wide spectrum. The job of a soft drink driver–sales person who calls in routine fashion on a group of retail stores is in another world from that of the computer sales person who sells a system for retrieving and disseminating information to an automobile manufacturer. Similarly, a sales person for a cosmetics manufacturer selling door to door has a job only remotely related to that of an airplane manufacturer selling a fleet of executive-type aircraft to large firms.

One useful way to classify the many different types of sales jobs is to array them on the basis of the creative skills required in the job. An

---

[1] This and the following paragraph are adapted from James A. Belasco, "The Salesman's Role Revisited," *Journal of Marketing*, April 1966, pp. 6–11.

example which moves from the very simple to the highly complex is the following list of positions:[2]

1. Positions in which the salesjob is primarily to deliver the product—e.g., driver–sales person for soft drinks, milk, or fuel oil. The selling responsibilities are secondary. Good service and a pleasant personality may lead to more sales, but few of these people originate many sales.

2. Positions in which the sales person is primarily an *inside* order taker—e.g., the retail clerk standing behind a counter. The customers come to the sales person. Most of them have already decided to buy; the sales person only serves them. The sales rep may use suggestion selling but ordinarily cannot do much more.

3. Positions in which the sales person is primarily an *outside* order taker, going to the customer in the field—e.g., a packing house, soap, or spice sales person who calls on retail food stores. They do little creative selling. In contacts with chain store personnel, these reps actually may be discouraged from doing any hard selling. That task is left to executives higher in the organization.

4. Positions in which the sales person is not expected or permitted to solicit an order. The job is to build goodwill, perform promotional activities, or provide services for the customers. This is the missionary sales person for a distiller, or the detail sales rep for an ethical pharmaceutical manufacturer.

5. Positions in which the major emphasis is placed on technical product knowledge—e.g., the sales engineer.

6. Positions which demand creative selling of tangible products, such as vacuum cleaners, airplanes, encyclopedias, or oil well drilling equipment. Here, the sales job often is more difficult because the customers may not be aware of their need for the product. Or, they may not realize how new products can satisfy their wants better than those they are presently using. When the product is of a technical nature, this category may overlap that of the sales engineer.

7. Positions which require creative selling of intangibles, such as insurance, advertising services, consulting services, or communications systems. Intangibles typically are more difficult to sell because they are less readily demonstrated.

IMPORTANCE OF A GOOD SELECTION PROGRAM

A firm's selection program has societal implications, such as the need for efficient utilization of manpower and the recognition of the

---

[2] Adapted from Robert N. McMurry, "The Mystique of Super-Salesmanship," *Harvard Business Review*, March–April 1961, p. 114.

waste of human and material resources that may result from poor selection. But it also is of vital importance to the continued well-being of the firm itself.

Problem of getting good sales people

A sound selection program is essential because of the scarcity of qualified sales people and recruits. Even in a firm where production lines are closing down for one day a week, the sales department may still be looking for able representatives. In fact, if the concern had an adequate number of qualified sales reps, it might not be necessary to curtail production, because top-notch sales people might be able to sell the factory output.

Qualified sales people and interested prospects are in short supply for several reasons. One is that selling as a career does not have the prestige attached to some other callings. This judgment is made even though a sales career offers opportunities for much greater financial rewards than generally are available in other fields. Another problem is that many young men and women are not aware of the excellent opportunities provided by sales jobs, especially in industrial sales. They may consider selling synonymous with clerking in a retail store.

But perhaps the biggest obstacle to finding good prospects is the fact that most people do not have the ability to be successful in selling. The jobs are hard work. They require considerable physical stamina and mental toughness. The results are easily measurable, and people fear proven failure. Many people lack the inner security and self-confidence to take on the challenge of a sales job.

Sales managers are no better than their sales forces

Within limits, a sales manager is no better than the people working under him, so it pays to select subordinates as wisely as possible. Generally, a sales executive is judged on the basis of how his sales force performs. Ordinarily, no administrator who has incapable people under him can go very far. Under comparable product and market conditions, a slightly inferior sales force may outperform a better one because it has a much more able manager. An executive with a very poor sales force, however, cannot surpass a competitor who has much better qualified sales people, no matter how good the first executive may be.

Good selection job eases other managerial tasks

For any executive, doing a good job of selecting people to work for him simplifies his other administrative problems. Conversely, selection mistakes compound his problems in other areas. Sometimes, sales managers debate the relative importance of selection versus training, supervision, or some other managerial activity. Proper training, compensation, supervision, and stimulation are all vitally important to the successful management of a sales force. *However, the thesis of this book is that the proper selection of sales people is the key activity in the management of a sales force.* If a company selects the right people for the sales job, training them is easier, less supervision is required, motivation is less difficult, and control of the sales force is not a major problem.

Direct cost savings from good selection

A good selection job undoubtedly reduces the rate of turnover in a sales force. This in turn results in direct cost savings, which can be quite substantial. A beginning sales person may cost the company as high as $50,000 before reaching a productive status. Average costs of $20,000–25,000 are quite common in many industries. These figures include recruiting and selection costs, the sales person's salary and travel expenses, and a pro rata share of the training and supervision costs.

Other benefits from good selection

A well-selected sales force should be more productive than a poorly chosen one. Consequently, with proper selection management should be able to minimize the difficult-to-measure indirect expense of lost sales—sales that would have been made if the representatives had been better selected. Sound selection also can be a factor in building good customer relations. Long tenure in a territory can help a sales rep build goodwill. He becomes well acquainted with the customers' needs and problems, and they place their confidence in him. On the other hand, a procession of new reps probably cannot be very well informed about the product and its uses, the territory and its particular requirements, or the customers and their behavior.

REASONS FOR POOR SELECTION

Many of the reasons given for the poor job of hiring done by some sales managers can be grouped under one broad point—namely, the lack of a scientific attitude and method. A corollary factor has been management's refusal to take the necessary time for good selection and the reluctance to give the activity its proper recognition in administration.

Many executives have not prepared detailed descriptions of the sales job. As a result, they do not know what qualities to look for in a recruit. Poor selection is also caused by failure to use an adequate number of the tools available. Firms may hire a person without doing enough interviewing, for example.

Often executives do not know what characteristics make a good sales person. Consequently, selection is made on the basis of a single outstanding physical or personality trait which the executive considers important. Even if they do know some specific qualification, such as a personality trait, it is questionable whether the tools are available to determine to what extent the individual prospect possesses that trait. As a result of this basic weakness, many personal prejudices are found in selection. Some sales administrators have biases concerning certain physical or personality characteristics. Sales managers are apt to claim, "I know a good man when I see one." This is often the same sort of administrator who believes that "Salesmen are born, not made," and "A good salesman can sell anything."

RESPONSIBILITY FOR SELECTION

In larger firms that have many sales people and branches, the responsibility for selection is delegated in various ways. Controlling factors are top management's philosophies regarding centralization versus decentralization of authority. In most large companies, some sales executive still retains the responsibility of final approval in hiring sales people. Very often, the personnel department helps the sales department by doing much of the organized recruiting or by preparing selection tools such as application blanks and patterned interview forms. Often personnel does the initial screening of applicants. However, the final authority for hiring usually rests in the sales department.

The question of who in the sales department will make the final decision regarding the applicant is apt to arise particularly in companies that operate with a branch organization. In some concerns, territorial executives are given full authority to hire people in their regions. When selection is decentralized, the home office should do all it can to establish guides for the territorial executives to follow. Even though selection may be entirely decentralized, a home-office sales administrator usually has veto power over any selection choice of the field executive. This executive should use the veto infrequently, however, to avoid undermining the morale and confidence of the field managers.

Far more common than complete decentralization of the sales selection function is the practice for managers in territorial offices to do much of the preliminary work and leave the final hiring decision up to sales executives in the home office.

THE LAW AND SALES FORCE SELECTION

The legislation of the 1960s and 1970s providing for civil rights has had a major impact on the employment practices (recruiting, selection, compensation, promotion, termination, etc.) of business and nonbusiness organizations in the United States. This broad coverage includes the recruiting and selection of sales personnel. The particular laws and other regulations which are directly related to sales force selection are:[3]

1. *Title VII of the Civil Rights Act of 1964, as amended.* In any employment activity, an organization may *not* discriminate on the basis of race, color, religion, nationality, or sex. The Equal Employment Opportunity Commission (EEOC) was established under this law to administer its provisions.

2. *Office of Federal Contract Compliance (OFCC) regulations.* This office in the Department of Labor has established affirmative action regulations and guidelines in employment practices which must be complied with by any organization holding a federal contract.

3. *The Age Discrimination in Employment Act of 1967.* This law applies essentially to the 40–65 age group. An organization cannot discriminate in its hiring or termination practices because of a person's age.

These laws and related regulatory guidelines emphasize two concepts of employment: *nondiscrimination* and *affirmative action. Nondiscrimination* requires elimination of all existing discriminatory conditions, whether purposeful or inadvertent. *Affirmative action* requires the employer to do more than ensure neutrality with regard to race, color, religion, sex, and national origin. It requires the employer *to make additional efforts* to recruit, employ, and promote qualified members of groups formerly excluded, even if that exclusion cannot be traced to discriminatory actions of the employer.[4]

In general, these laws and regulations prohibit a sales executive from discriminating on the basis of race, religion, color, age, sex, or nationality in the course of recruiting and selecting sales people. EEOC regulations apply to organizations with 25 or more employees. The OFCC requirements apply to firms with 50 or more workers. In addition, the OFCC requires companies to submit in writing their programs for complying with affirmative action guidelines. Either

---

[3] For an excellent review of these laws and regulations designed to prevent discrimination in employment, see Ruth G. Shaeffer, *Nondiscrimination in Employment: Changing Perspectives, 1963–1972,* The Conference Board, Report 589 (New York, 1973), and Shaeffer, *Nondiscrimination in Employment, 1973–1975: A Broadening and Deepening National Effort,* The Conference Board, Report 677 (New York, 1975).

[4] See Executive Order 11246, as amended by Executive Order 11375, U.S. Department of Health, Education, and Welfare, 1972.

A day-to-day operating problem in the

MAJESTIC GLASS COMPANY (B)
Adding blacks to the sales force

There were seldom any vacancies on the Majestic Glass Company sales force and Mr. Clyde Brion, general sales manager, was proud of that fact. He had several applications from available recruits on an informal waiting list, and he tried to keep the facts on these applicants up to date. Occasionally unsolicited applications were received, and some were from unusual types of applicants. For example, Brion had once been urged to hire an ex-convict. On more than one occasion he had been asked to explain why there were no women on the force. When such requests were endorsed by other Majestic executives, by customers, or by public officials, Brion believed he could not ignore them.

One after noon he was asked to come to the office of the company president, Mr. Boyd Russell. He found himself in a conference with Russell, several other department heads, and two black men who were introduced as representatives of the Affirmative Action Program in the Department of Health, Education, and Welfare.

The visitors explained that the Majestic Glass Company had been loyally served for many years by blacks who worked in the factory, on the custodial staff, and in a few cases in clerical jobs. However, there were no blacks holding supervisory, sales, or managerial jobs. There followed a direct request that the company place some blacks in each of these categories or suffer censure through national publicity. When asked if qualified blacks could be found, the visitors displayed well-prepared dossiers on several men. As nearly as Brion could judge during a quick examination of these files, the men easily met the minimum standards he had maintained in sales force recruiting.

The meeting continued after the visitors had left. Brion said that a black man would find "rough sledding" on the sales force, because of the probable resentment toward him by some customers, and the uncertainty of getting hotel accommodations and service in restaurants, especially when entertaining customers and prospects. Brion also pointed out that there were no openings on the sales force now or in the near future. To accommodate a black, he would be forced either to discharge a salesman now at work or to create a new and unnecessary territory.

In closing the meeting, Russell said, "We'll have to look at this thing positively, men. Life could get mighty unpleasant for us if we don't!"

Question

What action should Clyde Brion take in this situation?

Note: See the introduction to this series of problems in Chapter 2 for the necessary background on the company, its market, and its competition.

agency may conduct an audit of a firm to determine whether the company is in compliance with the regulations.

The guidelines set by both these agencies cover the full scope of sales force selection activities—setting hiring specifications, recruiting applicants, and processing these applicants. Prescribed limits are set regarding the use of various tools in the selection procedure, such as application blanks, interviews, and tests.

Possibly the biggest problem these agencies pose for sales executives is that the burden of proof generally rests with the company to show that it is complying with the regulations. That is, the firm must be able to demonstrate that its recruiting and selection processes are not discriminatory. Management must be able to validate (if called upon to do so) any of its selection requirements, sources, or tools. For example, assume that a firm uses a formal list of questions in an interview or some kind of psychological or intelligence test. Then the company must be able to demonstrate that these interview questions or the test scores are predictive of success in a given sales job. That is, the test results or interview answers must be correlated with job performance. And such validation is no easy task!

A company is very likely to be considered in noncompliance—at least on a prima facie basis—when its work force does not include a significant number of women, or when its racial or ethnic composition is out of proportion to the ratios of the population in that part of the country. Historically, outside sales forces have been composed almost entirely of white males. It is true that today in many industries, black or female sales representatives calling on customers are no longer a rarity. At the same time, however, most firms have some distance to go before they truly can say there is equality in their sales force in terms of female or minority representation. The main problem is finding sufficient numbers of qualified and interested applicants. Consequently, the factor of complying with nondiscrimination regulations poses important and expensive problems for most sales executives today.

SCOPE OF THE SALES SELECTION PROGRAM

The scope of sales selection includes three major activities, each of which may be further subdivided.

1. *Determine the number and type of sales people wanted.* This involves analysis of the job and preparation of a written job description. It also entails a determination of the qualifications necessary to fill the job.

2. *Recruit a number of applicants.* This step includes locating

good sources of sales people, contacting the recruits, and maintaining a close relationship with the sources.

3. *Process the recruits and select the qualified sales people.* The final part of the selection function has two phases. First, it is necessary to establish a procedure for measuring the recruits (from step 2) against the predetermined standards (from step 1). Second, the system must be placed into actual operation in order to select the necessary number of people who have the proper qualifications.

The first step is the topic of the remainder of this chapter. Step 2, recruiting applicants, is discussed in Chapter 5, and Step 3, processing applicants, in Chapter 6.

DETERMINING THE NUMBER AND TYPE OF PEOPLE WANTED

A good purchasing agent must determine both the quantitative and qualitative specifications for a product or service before ordering it. Even if the order is for nothing more complicated than lead pencils, the purchasing agent must state the quantity needed. Regarding quality, it may be essential to specify hardness of lead, color of lead, color of outer wood, diameter of pencil, type of eraser, and any printing that may be desired on the pencil.

In similar fashion, a sales manager needs detailed specifications when selecting sales people. Otherwise he cannot know what to look for. Certainly, a company should be as careful in buying the services of men and women as it is in buying the products used or sold by these people.

Number of sales people needed

A company should figure as closely as possible how many sales reps it needs and then hire only that number. It should not employ more than are really needed with the intent of weeding out some as time goes by. This practice indicates that the firm has no faith in its selection system and is using actual performance on the job as an additional selection tool.

Sales personnel needs should be forecast well in advance of the time the people will actually be employed. This policy not only forces the various sales units to plan in a systematic fashion, it also allows for better programming of recruiting, interviewing, and other steps in the selection procedure. Foresight in estimating needs for workers provides a pool of trained people when the need arises and enables the company to avoid a crash hiring program.

Management can estimate the number of sales people to be needed in a given future period by considering such factors as (1) expected losses from present sales force; (2) sales forecast for coming period; (3) proposed changes in product line, geographic scope of market, and intensity of market coverage; and (4) competition. Assume, as an example, that a company with 100 sales people is selling in the eastern half of the country. The executives concerned with staffing the sales force can plan for the coming year along the following lines. Records show that five people will retire. Past experience indicates that an average turnover of 10 percent may be expected because of resignations and discharges; this is another 10 people. Plans call for 15 to be promoted out of the sales force. The total needs so far are 30 people. According to estimates, another 15 will be needed in order to cover the Illinois-Indiana market more intensively to meet local competition, and to enable the company to complete its plans to expand into the Oklahoma-Texas-Louisiana market. Thus, a total of 45 new sales representatives must be hired within the next year.

Some authorities contend that the present methods used in most companies to determine the number of sales reps needed are highly unsophisticated. Executive judgment is heavily relied on. The result often is that many firms do not employ the optimum number of sales people in terms of profit maximization. In the above illustration, for instance, these writers might ask: How did management select 15 as the number of additional sales reps needed for more intensive coverage of the Illinois-Indiana market and for expansion into the Southwest? Past trial-and-error experience probably was an influencing factor. Past sales and selling expense ratios may rigidly determine future planning. Even if a careful analysis once was made to determine how many were needed to cover given accounts, the results may not be applicable in the present, since changes have occurred in the firm's markets and in its mix of promotional methods.

The basic reason for the imprecise approach is that management does not know how much to spend on the personal-selling ingredient in its promotional mix. Furthermore, once having decided on an expenditure level, management does not know what sales volume should result, or whether a similar expenditure for an alternative marketing effort (advertising, sales promotion) would have resulted in a better volume and profit position.

We have not yet developed a generally workable technique for determining by quantitative methods the optimum number of sales people a firm should have.[5] Mathematical models can simulate the

---

[5] The remainder of this section is adapted from Zarrel V. Lambert, "Determining the Number of Salesmen to Employ: An Empirical Study" (unpublished doctoral dissertation, Pennsylvania State University, 1966), especially pp. 12–37. Also see Lambert and Fred W. Kniffin, "Response Functions and Their Application in Sales Force Management," *Southern Journal of Business*, January 1970, pp. 1–11; and Marvin A. Jolson, "How Important Is Sales Force Size?" *Business Studies*, Spring 1971, pp. 31–40.

optimum number of sales people and their deployment throughout the company's market. These models are based on the logic of marginal analysis and the principle of diminishing sales returns. That is, a company should continue to add sales people up to the point where the marginal (incremental) cost of selecting and maintaining them is equal to the marginal revenues they generate.[6] It is assumed, further, that the cost of getting additional customers or units of volume increases with each succeeding unit. To use these models, however, management must be able to predict how sales volume will respond to *changes* in the size of the sales force. Apparently, the models have not yet been able to do this in a realistic, generally applicable manner. One problem is that typically they have too many limiting assumptions, and another drawback is the lack of sufficient empirical testing.

Job analysis and description

Preparing a job analysis is the first major step involved in finding out what type of person is wanted to fill the position. It is a careful study made in detail in order to identify clearly every aspect of the position.

Three terms related to this topic are:

- *Job analysis* is the actual task of determining what constitutes a given job.
- *Job description* is the document that sets forth in writing the findings in the job analysis.
- *Job qualifications* (sometimes called hiring specifications) are the several specific, personal qualifications and characteristics that applicants should have in order to be selected for the given job.

We should not combine the analysis of a sales position with a determination of qualifications needed to fill the job. For two reasons we note that these are separate and distinct activities, and we consider them in separate sections. First, in some writing on the topic the two activities are grouped so that each does not stand out as a separate activity. Second, it is customary for some companies to include in their printed job descriptions a list of job qualifications. Certainly, no harm is done if a company wants to combine the two for publication purposes, just so it is recognized that the one printed statement is the result of two separate analyses.

---

[6] The marginal approach assumes the firm's goal is to maximize net profits rather than to maximize sales volume or share of market, or to minimize selling costs. Also, while the theoretical model concentrates on personal selling, to be generally applicable the model must consider the interrelationships between personal selling, other promotional methods, and other ingredients (price, product, and so on) in the marketing mix.

There are big differences among the many types of sales positions, and management should certainly prepare a separate analysis for each one. A firm ordinarily would not use the same analysis for the jobs of file clerk and typist just because they both are office jobs. Nor would it be satisfied with the same description for the jobs of turret lathe operator and drill press operator, even though they both are production jobs. By the same token, it should not accept the same analysis for missionary sales people and for senior product sales people, although both are sales jobs.

Once the job is analyzed, the resultant description should be put in writing. To be satisfactory, the job analysis and subsequent written description must be done in great detail. It is not enough to say that the sales person is supposed to sell the product, call on the customers, or build goodwill toward the company. Points such as these may make good section headings, but a complete job description lists many duties under each. Unless the position is described in detail, the executives doing the sales selection cannot know what to look for among the applicants, nor will the prospects really know what they are applying for. In fact, a too brief description may be worse than none at all. A firm that has no written job descriptions should at least know it is ignorant regarding what to look for in recruits. However, a company with very short job descriptions may be operating under the delusion that it has done a good job and is in a position to do well in selecting its sales people.

Figure 4–1 is an example of a job description used by the Armstrong Cork Company for a sales job in the company's Floor Products Division. This position—entitled marketing representative—involves selling to wholesalers a wide range of resilient flooring products, including sheet flooring, resilient tile, and adhesives.

A longer form, illustrated in Figure 4–2, is used by a manufacturer of health-care products (hospital, surgical specialties, and patient-care items) for its field sales representatives.

Uses of job description. A job description is invaluable in all stages of the hiring process. Recruiters cannot talk very intelligently to prospective applicants if they do not know in detail what constitutes the job. A firm cannot develop application blanks, psychological tests, and other tools if it has not first analyzed the job.

However, hiring is only one of the many uses for a job description. *It is probably the most important single tool used in the operation of a sales force.*

A job analysis can be the foundation of a sales training program. By studying the description, the executive in charge of sales training knows in detail what the sales people's duties are, what they must learn, and possibly even the difficulty of the various tasks. As a result, a

FIGURE 4 –1
Job description—marketing representative

ARMSTRONG CORK COMPANY, FLOOR PRODUCTS DIVISION

JOB FUNCTION

Under general supervision of the District Manager or Assistant District Manager, this position is responsible for developing and achieving maximum profitable sales volume of Division products in an assigned territory.

DIMENSIONS

Sales volume—ranges from $__–$__ million.
Territory—the District is typically divided into geographic areas with this position responsible for one of those areas; additionally, the position will be given direct responsibility for 1–4 Armstrong wholesalers.
Product Line—consists of a wide range of resilient flooring products including: Corlon and Solarian sheet flooring; resilient tile; roto-vinyl sheet flooring; and adhesives and sundries.
Distribution—is achieved by sales to wholesalers who in turn sell to flooring specialty stores, flooring contractors, specialty stores, furniture stores, department stores and building supply dealers.
Major Emphasis—is directed toward developing and improving the wholesalers in all their functions through such means as training and assisting wholesaler salesman, helping these people make specific sales, developing new business, and generally contributing to the effectiveness of their operations.

ORGANIZATION SUPERVISED

None

PRINCIPAL ACTIVITIES

1. Develops and achieves maximum sales volume consistent with realistic sales projections within assigned territory. Controls expenditures within approved expense budget.
2. Develops and maintains favorable wholesale distribution of entire Division line within assigned territory. Recommends on the addition or termination of wholesalers. Develops thorough familiarity with wholesaler's business, sales activity, potentials and requirements.
3. Closely oversees operations of assigned wholesaler. Advises or assists them in such areas as inventory selection and control, service to customers, profit opportunities and ratios, etc. Investigates and corrects problem situations such as duplication of orders, receipt of poor quality goods, etc. Draws upon Armstrong staff services as special assistance is indicated.

FIGURE 4 –1 (continued)

4. Promotes Armstrong product line and its features and sales points, and an understanding of Armstrong policies and procedures, among the entire wholesaler organization. Keeps personnel informed of new products, price changes, and related concerns. Adapts Lancaster promotional services to local needs and conducts sales meetings to explain same; follows through on all promotions.
5. Assists wholesalers sales personnel in concerned territory in their selling efforts, and trains same through promotional meetings, traveling with each person on a regular basis, helping in making specific sales, and developing new business.
6. Plans territory coverage. Regularly calls upon key retail accounts (current and prospective). Takes orders; promotes the marketing and display of Armstrong products; encourages dealer to capitalize on Armstrong's advertising and promotional efforts; introduces new materials; trains counter personnel; provides literature and samples.
7. Investigates and evaluates field complaints; recommends disposition of complaints accordingly.
8. Keeps District Manager's Office and Lancaster advised on matters of specific business interest such as market conditions, competitive situations, product needs, etc. Consults with District Manager's Office concerning matters of policy, unusual situations, pricing, etc.

Note: This description is written primarily for position evaluation purposes. It describes duties and responsibilities which are representative of the nature and level of work assigned to the position. The principal activities are representative and not necessarily all-inclusive.

training program can be geared to their needs. If the job calls for promotional work, the training program may include instructions on dressing windows or making product demonstrations, for example.

Job descriptions are also used in developing compensation plans; the type of job determines to a great extent the type of pay plan used. If management does not have a clear idea about what the sales force is supposed to do, it is difficult to design a sound compensation structure.

Sales supervision and motivation are other sales management tasks in which the job analysis can be used extensively. By knowing the details of the job, supervisors are in a position to do a superior job of guiding sales people.

Often a job description is an official document which is part of the contract between management and a salesmen's union. In connection with the evaluation of a sales person's efforts, if a company designs a merit rating sheet that includes many of the detailed aspects of the sales job, periodic performance ratings should be easier and more meaningful.

FIGURE 4–2
Job description—Field sales representative
C. R. BARD, INC.—Murray Hill, N.J.

I. PRODUCTS SOLD
  A. Hospital, surgical specialties, and patient-care items. All of the products sold are utilized in the diagnostic phase, in actual surgical procedures, or in the general pre- and post-operative care of the hospital patient. A portion of the product line is devoted to patient prostheses and appliances.

II. CALLS ON CUSTOMERS
  A. Type of customers called on:
    1. Recognized surgical supply distributors, who stock a wide range of hospital, physician, and laity supplies. The distributor maintains an active sales force of his own and covers a representative area which includes numerous hospital and physician accounts.
    2. General and specialized hospitals which care for the ill.
    3. Physicians who specialize in the practice of urology and other specialized branches of surgery, particularly anesthesiology and cardiovascular surgery.
  B. Frequency of calls (minimums expected)
    1. Surgical supply distributors—as often as necessary, depending upon volume realized and cooperation received.
    2. Hospitals, under 50 beds—whenever practical (no schedule)

        50–99 beds— 2 calls per year
        100–245 beds— 6 calls per year
        250 and over—12 calls per year

    3. Physicians (specialized)—recognized urologists should be called on in their offices a minimum of twice per year. Urological residents should be called on each time a call is made at the hospital where they are in attendance. (It is suggested that a minimum of one physician call per day be made; more if time permits.)
  C. Personnel to be called on:
    1. Surgical supply distributors—all personnel including owners, management, purchasing, sales management, inventory control, and all stock and order department people. In addition, the Bard representative is expected to know outside sales personnel of his distributors, and distributor sales personnel who work in his area but are associated with important customers outside his area.
    2. Hospitals
        a. 100 beds and over—Administrator or Assistant, Purchasing Personnel, Operating Room Supervisor,

FIGURE 4–2 *(continued)*

Obstetrics Supervisor, Pediatric Nursing Supervisor, Cysto Supervisor, Central Supply Room Supervisor, Director of Nurses and/or Director of Nursing Services and Education, Anesthesiologist, I.V. therapists, chest surgeons, all urologists and urological residents, and the Chief of Staff.

  b. Under 100 beds—Administrator, Purchasing Personnel, Operating Room Supervisor, Central Supply Room Supervisor, Cysto Supervisor, Director of Nursing, Anesthesiologist, all urologists, chest surgeon, if available.

 3. Physicians (specialized)—As outlined under frequency of calls.

 4. Using market potentials provided to plan work in the areas where maximum return may be expected.

 D. Type of selling required:

  1. Creative selling—placing sales emphasis on the needs of the buyer. Promotion of items that benefit the hospital and patient, with better patient care the end result.

  2. Missionary selling—introducing new items to hospitals, distributors and physicians. Calling on prospects previously never contacted.

  3. Follow up calls on accounts who have accepted new products or the general line for first time to ensure continued business. Plan and hold a sales.meeting at least once a year with all dealers doing annual volume of $15,000 per year. Unless specifically directed, sales meetings with dealers having less volume is optional.

  4. Promoting the established general line to all established accounts both hospital, doctor and distributor in an effort to increase the volume of items purchased.

  5. Distributor calls—introduction of new items to surgical distributors. Conduct dealer sales meetings to stimulate their sales force to promote your product line. Call and procure stock orders regularly from distributors after establishing reasonable inventory levels on your merchandise.

 III. OTHER PROMOTIONAL WORK REQUIRED

  A. Conduct meetings at the hospital level when necessary to indoctrinate nursing personnel on new techniques, and new products.

  B. Teach dealer salesmen how to sell new items and the standard product line with emphasis on exclusive features and advantages not offered by the competition.

  C. Conduct market surveys and assist in market testing new items when or if requested by marketing department.

FIGURE 4–2 (continued)

D. Initiate and conduct Concept Procedural Studies in hospitals (outlined in Concept Selling Brochure).

IV. CLERICAL WORK REQUIRED
A. Daily call reports. During the month of January each year, the salesman should fill out and send to the home office and divisional managers, a Call Report on all his hospitals listing by name and title all the people to be called on at each institution.
B. Weekly summary of calls.
C. Weekly expense report. Traveletter.
D. Filing of above forms in own file.
E. Writing up dealer stock and turnover orders on company forms.
F. Requests for samples.
G. Memos to home office and divisional managers requesting or conveying information.
H. Itinerary, advance cards, and miscellaneous records.
I. Send copies of all correspondence and reports to divisional managers.

V. RESPONSIBILITY TO IMMEDIATE SUPERVISOR
A. Every sales representative is assigned to a division which incorporates several sales territories.
B. Each division is managed by a divisional manager who is responsible for all of the sales representatives and territories in his division.
C. All territory sales representatives are under the supervision of and accountable to the divisional manager of his division.
D. The sales representative carries out all instructions and performs all duties assigned to him by his divisional manager. He is under the supervision of his manager on all matters pertaining to the sales operation of his territory.
E. It is the responsibility of the sales representative to know and be able to advise his divisional manager what hospitals in his area are using comparable products of another manufacturer. He is expected to dispatch competitive product and price information to his manager as he learns it.
F. He should know product usage in his territory and the percentage of business by product line which he controls.
G. It is the responsibility of the sales representative to recommend to his divisional manager the addition or deletion of distributors in his territory.

VI. PERSONALITY AND PHYSICAL CHARACTERISTICS REQUIRED
A. Applicant must have the highest character evidenced by sincere, honest, and ethical behavior.

FIGURE 4–2 *(concluded)*

> B. Well-groomed, neat appearance.
> C. Good posture, sales bearing.
> D. Must be in good health, able to travel by all forms of transportation.
> E. Demonstrate skills of persuasion.
> F. Affable, personable, and enthusiastic.
> G. High degree of self-discipline and motivation.
> H. Good organizer, with qualities of leadership.
> I. Persistent and able to follow directions.
>
> VII. MINIMUM REQUIREMENTS AS TO EDUCATION AND PRODUCT OR SPECIAL KNOWLEDGE
> A. College degree preferred, but not mandatory if comparable experience or knowledge is evidenced.
> B. No technical education required, but strong interest in the sale of technical items used in the hospital industry is an asset.
> C. Persons with successful sales records and background in any area of marketing will be extended preference.
> D. Applicants with no sales background, but exhibiting strong sales desire will be interviewed and tested for sales aptitude.
> E. All applicants will be personally interviewed and tested by professional testing agency examination forms.
>
> VIII. TRAVEL REQUIRED
> A. Representative must be able and willing to routinely travel extensively within the confines of his assigned territory, remaining away from home overnight when necessary. In addition, representative will be required to travel outside of his own territory when his attendance at conventions, meetings, conferences, and so on is required.

Finally, when a job analysis is finished and written up in detail, management is in a position to determine whether each sales person has a reasonable work load. In some cases, after the executive has had chance to look at what the rep is being asked to do, duties may be reassigned or the work load lightened to make it more realistic. Sales managers are often surprised when they see in print how much they are expecting from the sales force.

Scope of job description. In most well-prepared job descriptions there are basic similarities in the items of information included (see Figures 4–1 and 4–2 above). The following points typically are covered:

1. Title of job, in sufficient description so there is no vagueness, especially in a company that has several different types of sales jobs.
2. Organizational relationships—to whom do the sales people report?
3. Duties and responsibilities related to the job—planning activities, actual selling activities, customer servicing tasks, clerical duties, and self-management responsibilities.
4. Hiring specifications. While job qualifications technically are not part of a job analysis, there is merit in presenting the job duties and the job qualifications in one document.

In addition, a good job description should include a minimum of two types of information.

1. The technical requirements of the job:
    a. What sales people must know relative to their products and services.
    b. What they must know in order to offer effective marketing and other business consulting services to customers.
2. The demands of the job—that is, the amount of autonomy given the sales people and the pressure they must work under.

Qualifications needed to fill the job

Most difficult part of selection function.   The next step in a selection program—determining which qualifications are needed to fill the job—is probably the most difficult one in the entire selection process. One reason is that management is dealing with human beings, and this means that a multitude of subjective and very complex characteristics is involved. Some of the qualifications that make a good sales person are not separable from those needed in some other vocation. It is generally believed that a sales person should be in good health, but than so should a soldier, football player, or ditchdigger. The ability to meet people is a quality that good sales people share with good morticians, politicians, and bus drivers.

Another problem is that management must determine the degree to which each trait must be possessed. It is not enough to say that a sales person must be self-confident, persuasive, and ambitious. The question is *how* persuasive or *how* ambitious. It is not a case of a person's being self-confident or not; it is not a yes or no situation. Many degrees exist within the extremes. For many traits, particularly those dealing with personality, management has not been able to quantify the degree to which they are possessed by an individual.

A corollary requirement is to determine how essential each quality s, and also the extent to which the absence of one trait, or a low score in it, can be offset by a high score on another factor. A firm may state that a person must be a college graduate with three years' business experience before he will be hired as a sales rep. Are these two requirements absolutely essential, just as stated, or is some substitution permissible? Would the firm hire a person with only three years of college and five years' experience?

Further difficulty may arise in recognizing which of the desired traits are innate and which may be acquired through good training. A firm may make a mistake in turning down potential sales reps because they speak too softly or they have no experience in selling the company's product. These are traits that probably can be developed in a good training program. On the other hand, when a person's history shows a lack of ambition, resourcefulness, and industriousness, it is probably a mistake to hire that applicant in the fond hope that these attributes can be acquired during training sessions.

Importance of individualized standards.   All types of sales work do not require the same characteristics. The traits found in successful sales engineers, for instance, are not the same as those possessed by missionary sales people. Consequently, the qualifications needed to fill each sales job should be determined on an individualized basis.

The standards of success used by one business are not necessarily valid for others, even in the same industry. Enterprises that sell virtually identical products may require different qualities in their sales forces because of differences in the methods of selling or promotional mix in the companies. A firm that sells vacuum cleaners or brushes by the door-to-door method probably looks for different traits in its sales force than does a company that sells the same products to wholesalers and large retailers.

A sales rep who fails in *one* company or territory may not necessarily fail in *all* companies or territories. Many people have become successful with one firm after being something of a failure in an earlier environment. Even within a given firm, sales people sometimes have performed poorly in one territory (because of social, religious, or other environmental factors) but have been successful after transfer to another region. Sometimes, these factors make it necessary to establish different qualifications for two reps who hold the same type of job in a company.

While establishing individual standards, sales executives should remember three points. The first is the potential danger that job requirements are set too high. The second point is that management should be scientifically objective in setting hiring standards. For many sales executives, this means disregarding old, unscientifically founded ideas on what makes a good sales person. Finally, a firm must be careful not to establish qualifications bounded by unnecessarily narrow limits that not only hamper selection but may cause the company to miss some potentially excellent reps.

Are there generally desirable characteristics for sales people? While the need for individualized job descriptions and hiring qualifications is recognized, there still may be some basic characteristics that are generally desirable for sales people. An appropriate answer to the question whether there are such characteristics is a qualified yes—a "yes, but" sort of reply. One reason for the hesitancy is that such lists are extremely risky. Some expert has his list published, and immediately sales executives adopt it, to a far greater degree than was ever intended.

Another reason for the qualified answer is that lists of characteristics are often so vague and general as to be of little value for any given company or job. A typical list may include such requirements as good health, mental ability, persuasiveness, tact, self-confidence, industriousness, enthusiasm, and emotional stability. Usually, no attempt is made to rate these traits in relative importance, nor is there any recognition of the degree of attainment desired for a characteristic. There are degrees of enthusiasm, for example, and it is impossible to generalize meaningfully on how much is needed in selling.

In identifying the mystique which distinguishes many outstanding salesmen from the merely good or mediocre ones, Robert McMurry observed that supersalesmen have a "natural facility as 'wooers.' These are persons who have an inherent flair for winning the acceptance of others."[7] At the same time, he noted, many of these "wooers" have what psychologists would call infantile or pathological personalities. These salesmen have failed to grow up emotionally. As children, they never felt wanted by anyone. Now, to compensate, they have a compulsive need to win—to gain the acceptance and affection of others. McMurry identified the following six attributes as being exhibited by successful salesmen:

- A high level of energy.
- Abounding self-confidence.
- A value system marked by a chronic hunger for money, an improved standard of living, and more status and prestige.
- An established habit of working hard and without close supervision.
- A habit of perseverance.
- A natural tendency to be competitive.

---

[7] Robert N. McMurry and James S. Arnold, *How to Build a Dynamic Sales Organization* (New York: McGraw-Hill Co., 1968), p. 3; also see McMurry, "The Mystique of Super-Salesmanship."

In an even shorter list, two industrial psychologists contended that to be successful a salesman must possess at least two basic personality qualities:

Empathy—the ability to identify with another person's wants, problems, situation, and so on.

Ego drive—the desire to compete, to persuade, to convince, and to win in face-to-face sales situations.[8]

Rather than try to develop a list of generally wanted traits, we suggest the following set of major categories. The individual company can fill in the details to suit its own needs.

1. Mental (intelligence, planning ability).
2. Physical (age, appearance, health, speaking abilities).[9]
3. Experience (education, sales experience, other business experience).
4. Environmental (membership in organizations, amount of insurance owned, marital status, number of dependents, own or rent a home, length of residence in community, religion, race, family and social background).[10]
5. Personality (ambition, interest, enthusiasm, tact, resourcefulness, emotional stability, persuasiveness, dominance, self-confidence, self-reliance, initiative).

In companies that are subject to EEOC and OFCC guidelines, many hiring qualifications that were traditionally used to screen sales force applicants no longer can be used, unless the company can show that they are "bona fide occupational qualifications" (BFOQ). For example, a dishonorable military discharge or an arrest (or even a conviction) now cannot be used to screen out an applicant, unless the company can demonstrate the validity of the qualification. Otherwise, an interviewer cannot even ask "Have you ever been arrested?" or "Have you ever been convicted of a felony?"

---

[8] David Mayer and Herbert M. Greenberg, "What Makes a Good Salesman" *Harvard Business Review*, July–August 1964, pp. 119–25. For a fine overview of other personal selling research pertaining to predictors of successful sales performance, see James C. Cotham III, "Selecting Salesmen: Approaches and Problems," *MSU Business Topics*, Winter 1970, pp. 64–72.

[9] Regardless of whether there is a valid relationship between the physical characteristics of salesmen and their degree of success in selling, research evidence suggests that many sales managers continue to consider physical appearance and stature as important hiring qualifications. See David L. Kurtz, "Physical Appearance and Stature: Important Variables in Sales Recruiting," *Personnel Journal*, December 1969, pp. 981–83.

[10] When dealing with age, sex, race, or religion, care must be taken to comply with laws regarding nondiscrimination in employment.

Methods of determining qualifications.   We simply do not have a general method that is satisfactory for every company to use in determining the qualifications needed in its sales force. Several different procedures currently are being used. Some are adaptable for companies that have large sales forces and have been in business for some time, so that recorded histories of background and performance are available. Other methods may be used by large or small, and old or new firms. The five methods discussed in this section are study of the job description, an analysis of personal histories, failure analysis, analysis of exit interviews, and outside sources of information.

Study of job description.   If management has prepared a good job description, many of the hiring specifications can be deduced from a careful study of that document. From job description statements about the degree of sales supervision, for instance, management can decide to what extent the sales person should have the imagination and re- sourcefulness to work alone, undirected by field supervisors. State- ments about product knowledge requirements and the nature of the product, viewed in light of the company's training program, indicate something about the desired technical background or experience qualifications.

Analysis of personal histories.   A company in business for several years and with a large sales force can determine its job qualifications by analyzing the personal histories of its present and past sales people. The age and size requirements for the data are necessary to get a sample of histories large enough so that the findings are reasonably reliable. The basic theory underlying the method is that by analyzing various characteristics of good and poor sales reps, it is possible to discover certain traits present in the good reps and absent in the poor ones. It is presumed, then, that these traits are some of the ones re- quired for success in the given job, and they would be listed as essen- tial qualifications.

The first step in this analysis is to get a list of all present and past sales people, along with their *selection* records (application blanks, patterned interviews, and so on) and their *performance* records (merit rating forms, sales results, quotas, and job evaluations).

The next step is to divide the sales force into two or three groups, depending on management's judgment of their present and potential sales effectiveness. In our example here, the reps can be divided into two groups, based on a good-poor classification. Obviously, sound ex- ecutive judgment is needed in deciding to which group a particular sales person should be assigned. Some possible criteria are sales volume, percentage of sales quota attained, gross margin, net profit, ratio of expenses to sales, and performance in missionary selling jobs.

TABLE 4-1
Sales people's age at time of hiring
COMPANY A

Age bracket	No. of good reps	No. of poor reps	Total reps	Percentage of good reps
Under 25	30	70	100	30
25–35	180	20	200	90
36–45	100	50	150	66⅔
46–55	40	60	100	40
Over 55	10	40	50	20
Total	360	240	600	

The third step is time-consuming and must be done in careful detail. For each characteristic that might have a bearing on success in selling, the sales executive determines whether there is any significant difference in the extent to which the trait is possessed by the good sales people as contrasted to the poor ones. Some characteristics are much easier to determine than others. It is reasonably simple to ascertain differences between good and poor performers in such qualifications as age at time of hiring, previous sales experience, or amount of insurance owned. However, it is much more difficult to measure differences in personality traits possessed by the two groups.

Age at time of hiring and amount of education are two characteristics used here to illustrate how personal histories can be studied. Tables 4–1 and 4–2 show the results of the hypothetical case. Of 600 past and present sales people included in the sample, 360 were considered good—not a very high average, incidentally. Age brackets were estab-

TABLE 4-2
Amount of previous education of sales people
COMPANY A

Amount of education	No. of good reps	No. of poor reps	Total reps	Percentage of good reps
Less than four years high school	30	70	100	30
High school graduate	250	25	275	91
Some college	20	80	100	20
College graduate	55	45	100	55
Postgraduate study	5	20	25	20
Total	360	240	600	

lished, and the 600 were placed in the bracket that represented each rep's age when hired. From an analysis of Table 4–1, it is apparent that the sales people most apt to succeed in company A were between 25 and 35 years of age when selected. Of those in that age group when hired, 90 percent turned out to be good sales reps. Under 25 or over 55 seem to be the poorest ages for hiring.

Table 4–2 shows that graduation from high school seems to be the ideal amount of education needed for future success in the job. A person who started high school or college but did not graduate seems to be a particularly poor risk. From the findings on age and education, it is probable that some years of business experience are necessary in companyA. If 18 is the average age of students graduating from high school and 25 to 35 is the best hiring age range, some years in between have to be accounted for.

Essentially similar analyses may be made for any other trait suspected of influencing success in selling in a given company. The firm could study environmental and experience factors in much the same manner as age and education. Mental abilities may be quantified by means of intelligence tests. General physical condition could be measured by giving the person a score on a physical examination or a rating on general appearance and fluency of speech. Personality traits are the one category that is extremely difficult to measure objectively or quantitatively. Many firms use personality tests for this purpose, but their real value in selection is open to considerable question. In the final analysis, most firms probably must rely on executive judgment in determining which personality characteristics are present in good sales people and absent in poor ones.

After a complete analysis of personal-history records, a company should be able to describe the ideal qualifications for a specific job. The list probably will be quite long. However, a business must know how much less than the ideal it can take and still be reasonably assured of hiring a potentially successful sales representative. In Table 4–1, for example, 25 to 35 was found to be the ideal age range for hiring. The question is whether it is the *only* bracket to be considered, or whether the firm could hire someone in the 36 to 45 range if the applicant were outstanding in many other characteristics.

For quantitatively measurable traits, there is one possible solution to this problem. First, management would select what it considers to be the critical characteristics, say 10 to 20 of them. Then, gradations or subdivisions would be set up for each selected qualification. Examples are given at the left in Tables 4–1 and 4–2, where age brackets and varying amounts of education are established. After the personal-history analysis is completed, a score or rating may be attached to each subdivision.

This raises the problem of rating or scoring the relative importance of each characteristic and each gradation within the item. A careful study of the findings of the personal-history analysis usually shows that the various success factors are not of equal importance. Therefore, the company should assign different weights to each item and to the divisions within each one. For example, the maximum weight given to previous business experience may be 12, but the top possible score in educational background may be only 8. The scores assigned to grades within each qualification may be as follows:

Business experience		Education	
None	0	Less than high school	2
Less than 1 year	2	High school graduate	8
1–2 years	6	Some college	3
3–4 years	8	College graduate	5
5–7 years	12	Postgraduate work	3
8–10 years	10	Graduate degree	2
Over 10 years	4		

The implication is that business experience as a general qualification at best is about 50 percent more important than the educational background of a recruit (a maximum weight of 12 compared to one of 8). Also, five to seven years of business work is twice as valuable as one or two years (12 v. 6). Being a high school graduate with no additional schooling is worth about the same as three or four years of business experience (8 v. 8).

After points are assigned to each division of the selected qualifications, then all the sales people studied in the personal-history analysis could be graded on these traits. Assume that 15 factors were selected, with the top possible score totaling 150. Probably no one would achieve a perfect score. However, the company can determine the minimum number of points that a person should get in order to have a reasonable chance for success. Company A (from Tables 4–1 and 4–2) may find, for example, that the minimum score achieved among the 360 good sales people was 110 out of the 150 points.

Some firms slightly modify the above procedure to take into account the age of the applicant, because the age at the time of hiring affects the score received on several other items. Compare two people, one hired at age 30 and the other at age 40. The older person probably belongs to more clubs, owns more insurance, and has more business experience. As a result, his total score is higher. In the long run, however, the younger person may turn out to be the more successful sales rep. To adjust for the age factor, some firms use it as the main control item rather than as an individual qualification to be scored along with the others. Each of the 360 sales reps in company A would be graded on the same basis, but the grades would be interpreted differently to account for the age at the time of hiring. The minimum score for those in the 25–35 age bracket might be 95. In the 36–45 group it could be 110, and in the 46-and-over division, 125 might be the lowest acceptable score.

There are some limitations in the personal-history analysis technique. One was implied earlier—relatively few companies have the data base needed to operate this analysis. Another is that the "good" and "poor" classifications refer only to the people actually hired by this firm. The good sales people were not necessarily the best that could have been hired. Furthermore, the analysis is historical. That is, it shows what qualifications were desirable in the past, but it does not allow for changing times and requirements.

Failure analysis: Knockout factors.   A by-product of a personal-history analysis is a list of the characteristics that a sales person should *not* have. That is, they are predictive of failure in the sales job. Although this is a negative approach to the problem of determining hiring specifications, it may be effective. One company, for example, identified the following knockout factors:

- Instability of residence.
- Failure in business within past two years.
- Divorce or separation within past two years.
- Excessive personal indebtedness—debts cannot be met within two years from earnings on the new job.
- A previous standard of living that was too high.
- Unexplained gaps in employment record.

An applicant who possessed any of these characteristics would *not* be hired. The company believed this applicant would *not* be successful in the sales job.

In view of current legal implications, a company has to be very careful in using the concept of failure analysis. Before the executives establish any knockout factor, such as divorce or instability of residence, they had better be sure they can validate that factor as a negative hiring qualification. That is, they must be able to prove that any given factor truly is indicative of failure in a particular sales job.

Analysis of exit interviews.   Many firms follow a practice of interviewing people who are leaving the sales force for any reason. An analysis of these exit interviews may tell the organization something about the qualifications needed for the job.

Theoretically, an exit interview would seem to be a good method of getting valuable information. When sales reps are about to leave a company, it might seem that they will be honest and forthright about their reasons for doing so. However, realistically, the exit interview usually is less than valuable and may even be misleading. Few give the real reason they are leaving, particularly if it reflects badly on the organization or any one in it. In the future these people may want a recommendation from the company, and they do not want to risk antagonizing anyone when they leave.

Sources of information outside the firm. For companies too new or too small to get any value out of analyses of personal histories, an outside source may help in establishing job qualifications. One external source is a consulting firm that specializes in personnel selection. A company could also seek information from a similar but noncompeting firm. The use of outside sources seems to violate an earlier stated generalization that a concern should develop its own individual job qualifications. From a practical standpoint, however, sometimes outside help is needed for a firm to get started in developing a good selection system.

QUESTIONS AND PROBLEMS

1. Referring to the seven-way classification of sales jobs found early in this chapter, answer these questions:
   a. In which types of jobs is the sales rep most free from close supervision?
   b. Which types are likely to be the highest paid?
   c. Which groups are likely to involve the most traveling?
   d. For which groups is a high degree of motivation most necessary?
   Explain your reasoning in each case.
2. "Careful selection is important, but not essential, in building an effective sales force. Improper selection of sales people can be overcome by a good training program, sound supervision, or an excellent compensation program." Do you agree? Discuss.
3. "Salesmen are born, not made." Do you agree? If so, why does a firm need a training program or sales supervisors? If you do not agree—that is, you believe sales reps are made, not born—then why is so much stress placed on the importance of good selection? Perhaps a firm should spend far less time and money on selection and instead place the effort in a thorough training program.
4. In the following companies, who should have the responsibility for selecting the sales force? Should it be the president, chief sales force executive, district sales manager, or someone in the personnel department?
   a. International Harvester Company.
   b. Large distributor of home appliances.
   c. Automobile dealer in St. Louis, Missouri.
   d. Furniture manufacturer in Grand Rapids, Michigan.

5. "A good salesman can sell anything." Do you agree? What evidence do you have to support your opinion?

6. If a person wants to be a top-notch professional career sales rep and has no interest in being a manager, is a college education necessary? Discuss. If your answer is yes, what courses should be required? If your answer is no, why do so many firms recruit sales people from colleges, and why is a college education so often listed in the qualifications for a sales job?

7. When a company wants to hire a sales engineer—that is, fill a position where the major emphasis is placed on technical product knowledge— should this firm recruit engineers and train them to sell, or recruit sales reps and teach them the necessary technical information and abilities?

8. When selecting a sales force, many companies have adopted the policy of hiring only experienced sales people, and preferably those who have had experience selling similar or directly competitive products. Under what conditions, if any, may this be a sound policy?

9. After interviewing some of the sales force and/or the appropriate executives, prepare a detailed job description for one of the following jobs.
    a. Automobile dealer sales person.
    b. Driver–sales person for local soft drink bottler.
    c. Missionary sales person for a manufacturer.
    d. Sales person for some type of wholesaler.

10. Prepare a list of qualifications needed to fill each job you analyzed and described in the preceding problem.

11. Prepare a list of the qualifications you feel are necessary to fill the sales job described in Figure 4–1. Do the same for the job outlined in Figure 4–2.

Case 4–1
THE VALLEY FARMS
Change in sales force selection policy

The Valley Farms was a marketing cooperative representing the growers of fresh vegetables in a famous valley in California. The products were strictly graded and controlled by the coop, and it maintained sales representatives in each of the nation's major fresh vegetable markets. These reps called on and worked closely with the produce buyers for the chain grocery stores. The system had been most successful for more than 40 years.

As Ms. Roberta Kovatto, the elected president of the cooperative, looked over the sales force that had assembled at one of the coop's national conventions, she was struck by the thought that they all looked alike: All were white males about 50 years old of larger than average physical proportions.

She asked Mr. Albert Mendez, the general manager, for a summary of the sales forces members' backgrounds. It was even more startling to discover that most of them had graduated from one of three universities in the West. The exceptions had been hired on the basis of their outstanding sales records for some produce middleman.

Kovatto did not hesitate to let Mendez know how she felt about the matter. While the issue of discrimination in the hiring of sales reps had never arisen, if it ever did she was sure that the organization would not have a leg to stand on. She asked for an explanation.

Mendez replied, "I hope you realize that we don't lose anyone from our sales force. These men have been with us for years, long before all this equal opportunity business came about. We just don't have any openings. When the last one occurred, we had 11 applicants on our doorstep the next day, all of whom we considered excellent prospects. As for the concentration of men from those schools, I understand the reason is buried back in our early days. The manager just went down to the nearest aggie schools and recruited. He got all the bodies he wanted there so he saw no reason to go elsewhere. Since that time, the sales force has perpetuated itself. When an opening does occur, one of the sales reps always has a good man for the job. And that man seems to be someone from his old school or circle of friends. Since these guys have done a great job for us over the years, no one has seen any reason to change how we've been doing things."

Kovatto nodded and said, "Well, I think we're going to have to do something about this. There is no reason at all why women can't sell produce as well as men. I think you had better develop some sort of plan to take care of this problem."

Mendez listened and then reminded Kovatto that she had no direct authority over him. He took his orders from the board of directors as a whole and not from any one or few individuals on it. He suggested that she take the matter up with the board. "It is not my job to tell the board whom to hire," he said. "I just manage operations."

Kovatto knew that Mendez was correct. It was a matter for the board.

Questions

1. What should Roberta Kovatto do about the situation?
2. Evaluate the coop's position.
3. Why hasn't a discrimination suit been filed against the coop?

Case 4–2

TEXAS REFINERY CORPORATION
Hiring only men over 40 for sales force

As board chairman and president of the Fort Worth–based Texas Refinery Corporation (TRC), co-founded by his father 50 years ago, A. M. Pate, Jr., employs 6,000 full- and part-time salesmen. Their average age is 55, and more than 400 of them are at least 65 years old. But there is nothing charitable about Pate's predilection for older salesmen; he says it is just good business. "We try not to hire a man under 40 for our sales force," Pate explains. "Older men do a better selling job for us, and we find they are more serious about their work."

Indeed, the company's own point system for evaluating prospective salesmen clearly discriminates against junior citizens—and big city slickers. An applicant must amass 21 points to qualify, but he automatically loses 5 points if he is under 40 and gains 5 points if he is from a city with a population under 25,000. Since TRC's customers for its line of lubricants and roofing compounds are mostly small-town businessmen, a folksy, low-key approach used by older salesmen seems to work best. "What's more," Pate says, "the oldsters are less likely to steal or perpetrate fraudulent sales. TRC, in fact, has even stopped running credit checks on applicants for selling jobs."

TRC salesmen are paid on a commission basis, and while many of the over-65s seem content simply to supplement their social security benefits, some hard drivers earn substantial incomes. Even though he took off ten weeks, as he does each year, to fish the lakes near his home in Baraboo, Wis., Al Cornelius, 65, still earned nearly $26,000 in 1970. Harbaugh, slower pace and all, has managed to put 50,000 miles on his car since 1969 and earned more than $8,000 last year. Al Wilhelmi, 67, of Upper Sandusky, Ohio, received nearly $40,000 in commissions and won a new Cadillac for his outstanding performance. "I'm really a young fellow," he chuckles. "I'm disgustingly healthy. My bones and muscles creak a bit, but what the heck."

"I'm convinced that older people have more imagination and ability than younger ones," Pate says. "We'll always have room for a man in his 50s, 60s, 70s or older—provided he has some sales ability. These salesmen frequently tell me, 'I'd rather wear out than rust out.' And their wives are delighted to have them out of the house sometimes."

Note: Adapted from "Social-Security Swinger," *Newsweek*, January 3, 1972, pp. 37–38. Copyright Newsweek, Inc. Reproduced with permission.

Question

1. Evaluate TRC's policy of hiring only men over 40 for the sales force.
    a. Why do you think the policy has been successful for TRC?
    b. To what extent do you think other companies could adopt this policy?

5

Selecting the sales force— Recruiting applicants

Leave no stone unturned.
EURIPIDES

After determining the number and type of sales people wanted, the next major step in selecting a sales force is to recruit several applicants for the position to be filled. Recruiting is defined here as including all activities involved in securing individuals who will apply for the job. The concept does not include any of the actual processing of the people by means of interviews, tests, or other hiring tools; this step is the topic of Chapter 6.

IMPORTANCE OF PLANNED RECRUITING

A sound selection program cannot exist without a well-planned and well-operated system for recruiting applicants. If recruiting is done on a haphazard basis, a company runs the risk of entirely overlooking, or losing contact with, good sources of prospective sales people. Poor recruiting practices may also force an organization to hire people it really does not want, simply because some sales representatives are needed and the firm must select immediately from the available applicants.

A well-planned and efficiently operated recruiting program also is needed because it is so difficult to attract good prospects to the sales field. The demand for trained people in other occupations, coupled with the general lack of interest and prestige in selling, have done much to cut into potential sales personnel. At the same time, the need for good sales people probably will continue to increase into the 1980s.

The high rate of turnover experienced in many sales forces means that these firms should be doing a continual recruiting job. The turnover factor is related in some respects to the tight labor market for sales people. When good people are in short supply, they receive and accept for employment more frequently, and turnover increases.[1]

The importance of recruiting grows in relation to increases in the costs of selecting sales people and maintaining them in the field. Certainly, the direct costs of recruiting are increasing—costs such as the expenses of maintaining recruiting teams and placing recruiting advertisements. But more important than the *direct* costs of recruiting is the effect that recruiting may have on the *total* costs of selection and training. For example, it may be desirable to increase the cost of the recruiting activity if it results in finding a better quality of applicants. Management should view the selection process as a subsystem in sales force management and use a *total* cost approach to this subsystem. Thus, the recruiting activity should be optimized so as to reduce the *total* costs of selecting and developing new sales people to the point where their productivity is profitable.

Need for many recruits

A philosophy to follow in recruiting is to get a sufficient number of qualified applicants to put through the selection process in order to maximize the chances of finding the right person for a job. The laws of probability support this policy. The shortage of qualified sales representatives makes it more imperative for a business to screen several people for each opening.

Recruiting is a screening device

A recruiting program serves as an automatic screening device in sales selection. Therefore management must make sure it does not bypass potentially successful sales people through the recruiting procedures that are used. Recruiters who interview college students, for

---

[1] $\text{Turnover} = \dfrac{\text{Number of people hired}}{\text{Average size of sales force}}$. A 100 percent turnover does not necessarily mean that the entire sales force has been replaced. In a staff of 500, half may have stayed the entire year, while the other 250 were replaced twice. All together 500 were hired in a year, so a 100 percent turnover is said to result.

example, should be careful not to screen out good prospects in the interviewing process. There is also a screening factor in the recruiting sources used, such as the choice of colleges visited or the selection of newspapers in which advertisements are placed. An advertisement in *The Wall Street Journal*, for instance, attracts a different type of recruit than does an ad in a metropolitan daily.

Factors influencing the importance of recruiting

Recruiting is not equally important or extensive in all firms. The quality of sales people needed, the rate of turnover among the sales force, and the firm's financial condition are just three of the factors that account for this difference. Another influencing factor—the number of people needed—was discussed in the preceding chapter.

Ordinarily, the higher the caliber of sales person needed, the greater is the number of applicants that must be screened before finding one who meets the hiring specifications. Also, the difficulty of getting an adequate number of desirable recruits increases as the quality requirements increase.

Continual recruiting is essential in firms with a high rate of turnover in the sales force. This situation is frequently found, for example, among firms that sell directly to the consumer on a door-to-door basis or through party-plan selling (Avon Products, Stanley Home Products). In direct selling organizations, it is not unusual to find an annual turnover ratio of 100 percent in the sales force.[2]

Financial resources in a firm can influence the extent of recruiting done and the methods used. Companies that do not feel a financial strain may be able to employ traveling recruiting teams, whereas less fortunate firms must rely more on advertisements and correspondence.

The law and sales force recruiting

The civil rights laws and regulations referred to in the preceding chapter are applicable to a company's recruiting efforts. Management cannot discriminate on the basis of race, color, religion, nationality, age, or sex in its recruiting activities—in its choice of sources, for example. The affirmative action guidelines issued by the Office of Federal Contract Compliance (OFCC) state that management must take affirmative action to notify women and minority groups when there is a vacancy in

---

[2] In contrast, the findings from a study of 665 large manufacturers showed that the median rate of resignations plus discharges totaled only 4 percent of the sales force. See David A. Weeks, "Turnover Rates for Salesmen," *Conference Board Record*, April 1966, pp. 18–22.

the sales force. This means, for example, that the company must advertise in newspapers and magazines likely to be read by these groups. And the advertisements should state that the company is an "Equal Opportunity Employer M/F."

SOURCES OF SALES REPRESENTATIVES

Find and maintain good sources

Most firms actively recruit sales reps from multiple sources. To determine the best sources, a recruiter could first find out where the company's best sales people came from in the past, assuming there has been no substantial change in the job description or job qualifications for a given job.

To determine these sources, an executive may use the essence of the method suggested in Chapter 4 for analyzing personal histories in order to establish hiring specifications (qualifications). All present and past sales people can be separated into two or three groups, according to their all-around sales ability. Then a careful study can be made to determine where the top performers came from and if there is any significant difference in these sources as contrasted to the sources of the people rated in the lower group.

An examination of the job analysis and hiring specifications will reveal other factors that affect a recruiter's choice of sources of prospects. The educational qualifications for the job, for example, may indicate whether colleges are potential producers of recruits.

Once satisfactory sources are located, management should maintain a continuing relationship with them, even during periods when no hiring is being done. Firms that want college graduates often find they can build goodwill during the off hiring season by keeping in touch with individual professors who have furnished assistance in the past. Customers who supplied leads to good people in the past should be reminded periodically of the company's gratitude and encouraged to suggest more prospects.

If a firm must do any significant amount of recruiting, it should be done on a continuing basis. Even when no immediate need for replacements or additions to the sales force exists, this firm should be developing lists of future prospects and, if possible, be contacting and screening them. Of course, a company ordinarily cannot screen a group of applicants and then expect them to wait an indefinite period for a vacancy to occur. However, the company at least can provide itself with lists of potential recruits so that a reservoir of leads is available when needed.

Some frequently used sources of sales representatives or sources of leads to them are as follows:

- Within the company.
- Other companies (competitors, customers, noncompetitors).
- Educational institutions.
- Advertisements.
- Employment agencies.
- Voluntary applicants.
- Women, minorities, and other underemployed groups.

Within the company

Present sales force. A company's sales force is an excellent source of leads to new recruits. Present sales people should know what sort of person the firm is seeking. They know the job and company well, and, if they are satisfied, they can do much to sell the opportunities to prospective applicants. Also, prospects get to know something of the job and its problems just from knowing the sales reps.

As a firm's sales people meet representatives from other companies and make contacts through social, athletic, fraternal, and business clubs, they are in a good position to know when a person is interested in changing jobs. Often they are well acquainted with the general qualifications of some of the prospects. Furthermore, sales people frequently have a self-interest in recruiting their co-workers.

In using its own sales people, the firm may be encouraging them to become recruiters at the expense of time they should be spending with customers. There is also the risk that sales reps may recommend friends or business associates on the basis of personal feelings rather than an impartial evaluation of the prospect's qualifications. The advantages of using the sales force for leads, however, far outweigh the drawbacks. Even if some unqualified people are recruited, the firm should be able to weed them out through its selection process.

Factory or office employees. Some companies recruit their sales force from among workers in their production plants or offices. The chances of finding good sales people should be increased, because management has been able to observe these people and evaluate their potential as sales reps. These workers, particularly plant employees, are acquainted with the technical aspects of the product and are indoctrinated in company philosophies, policies, and programs. Thus, the need for some of the training is eliminated. In fact, some firms start all new sales people in the office or plant so they can become acquainted with company procedures, customer lists, and product lines before joining the field sales force. Hiring sales people from within the company can be a great morale booster, because most plant and office workers consider transfer to the sales department as a promotion.

Recruiting from within the organization has some limitations. It is risky to take workers who have proven themselves to be outstanding performers in the office or factory and transfer them to a sales job where they may not have the same success. In some cases, antagonism can build among plant or office supervisors who feel their workers are being pirated by the sales department.

Other companies: Competitors, customers, noncompetitors

The controversial question of whether to hire competitors' sales people is argued on ethical grounds and from an economic standpoint. The ethical aspects of the problem generally depend on who made the employment overture. If a sales person from company A seeks employment and is hired by company B, a competitor, probably no question of ethics is involved. The reason is that the sales person, not company B, made the overture. On the other hand, some people feel it would be unethical for company B to raid A's sales force by actively recruiting its reps. One may wonder whether attempting to take a competitor's best sales people is basically any different from trying to take its best markets or customers. While the first practice is considered unethical, the second is called competition. Some companies refuse to hire competitors' sales people. Whether the policy stems from high ethical standards or fear of retaliation is an interesting point to consider.

From an economic point of view, there also are mixed feelings regarding the recruiting of competitors' sales people. On one hand, they know the product and the market very well. They also are experienced sellers and therefore require less training. On the other, it may be harder for these people to unlearn old practices and make the adjustment to a new environment than it would be for recruits from other sources. In other cases, a company hires a competitor's sales person with the expectation that he will switch his customers to the new business. If he is unable to do so, his new employer is disappointed.

A firm may seek sales recruits or leads to prospects from its customers. Purchasing agents often are good sources of names. They know what impresses them in a sales rep, and they know reasonably well the abilities of the sales reps who call on them.

Customers' employees themselves may be a source of sales people.

Often, retail clerks make good sales people for wholesalers and manufacturers. These clerks are acquainted with the product and they also know something of the behavior of the retailers—the market to which the hiring firm sells. Furthermore, good retail clerks are not totally lacking in sales ability, so the task of training them is lightened a bit.

Sales reps working for noncompeting companies are another source, particularly if they are selling products related to those sold by the recruiting firm or are selling to the same market. Recruits from this source presumably have some sales ability and need less training. Sometimes, sales managers of other companies may be willing to furnish names of applicants they have discovered but cannot use at the moment.

Recruiting from other firms raises some questions. Hiring the good employees of a customer obviously has drawbacks. The task must be handled very diplomatically if the customer is not to be lost forever. People hired from other companies may not have the same degree of loyalty as recruits promoted from within. The outsiders are more mobile, as evidenced by their willingness to change employers. A concern that hires from the outside should be especially careful to determine why the applicants are interested in changing jobs and why they want to work for the hiring company. It may be that they are ambitious and figure that the quickest way to move up is to move from one company to another.

Educational institutions

Colleges and universities are sometimes used as sources of recruits for career sales jobs. More often, however, companies using college recruiting are hiring graduating college students for eventual management positions. The sales job is merely the first step on the career ladder. It is doubtful that colleges are a good recruiting source for *career* sales jobs. Unless the job involves creative selling, carries social prestige, and offers a great challenge and opportunity, the better-than-average college graduate will not be attracted by it.

Graduates of high schools or vocational schools may be fine prospects for selling careers, especially if the job is routine in nature and does not require much technical training or college-developed abilities. Junior college graduates may be a good recruiting source for the company that prefers its sales reps to have some college work but does not require a four-year degree.

If the sales job is adequately demanding and carries enough compensation in dollars and other benefits, qualified college graduates may prove to be a fine source of applicants. Generally, these people are more easily adaptable than their more experienced counterparts.

They have developed no loyalties to a firm or industry, and they probably have not acquired many bad work habits. Usually, they have acquired certain social graces. They often are more poised and mature than a person of the same age without college training. Good students usually have developed their ability to think logically and to express themselves reasonably well. Ordinarily they do a good job of budgeting their time and managing their daily activities. The very fact that they have been graduated is generally indicative of a degree of perseverance. Finally, some of the training of many students has been sufficiently technical in nature so that they are well grounded in the principles applicable to a given field.

A major drawback to university graduates as sales recruits is that usually they are inexperienced in selling or in business generally. Another criticism is that they are jobhoppers and will not stay with one company very long. It is not known whether college graduates are significantly different from any other group of young people in this respect.

Undoubtedly, the biggest single problem in locating prospects from college sources is the extremely unfavorable impression students have regarding the field of selling. It is particularly distressing that many students sneer at selling not from knowledge or experience in the field, but because of gross misconceptions about what is involved in most sales jobs. Their understanding of selling often is limited largely to door-to-door and retail-store types. Selling has a bad image with college students and teachers. It is associated with job insecurity, insincerity, low status, and lack of creativity.

Through advertisements

Advertisements are both a *source* of leads to sales recruits and a *method* of reaching them. Newspapers and trade journals are the most widely used media, although others have also been used. Some companies use advertisements to recruit high-caliber sales people for particularly challenging jobs. However, most often firms that use advertising—particularly in newspapers—are trying to fill the less attractive type of sales job, such as door-to-door selling, clerking in a retail store, or driver route selling. Many businesses use advertisements only after they have exhausted other sources.

Advertisements ordinarily produce a large quantity of applicants, but the average quality of the applicants is questionable. The cost of reaching these recruits is low. However, an additional burden is placed on the subsequent phases of the selection system if little screening was done in the advertising copy.

The quality of prospects recruited by advertisements may be increased by careful selection of media and by proper statements of information placed in the copy. For example, by buying space in a trade journal rather than in a daily newspaper, a firm is automatically more selective in its search. The more information given in the notice, the more it serves as a qualitative screening device.

To be effective, a recruiting ad must *attract attention* and *have credibility*. An advertisement that does not get read, or one that is read but is not considered believable and sincere, is a waste of effort.

Now, what information should be included in a recruiting advertisement? Here are some points to consider:

1. *Company name.* The answer is, "it all depends." By placing their names in their ads, well-known firms may attract applicants who otherwise would not answer a blind ad. But companies which have a poor public image (such as door-to-door sellers) often must hide their identities in an ad in order to attract prospects. People may not even nibble at an invitation if they know in advance the name of the advertiser.

2. *Product.* Usually "yes," unless it is a product (gravestones and cemetery lots, perhaps) that is likely to turn away prospects who otherwise might get interested once they learned more about the company and the job opportunities.

3. *Territory.* Yes, especially if it is *not* in the area where the ad is run.

4. *Hiring qualifications.* Include enough of them so the ad serves as a useful screening device. But keep in mind the legal guidelines when stating any hiring requirements. For example, it is illegal to specify an age or sex requirement, unless you can prove it is a bona fide occupational qualification. As a general rule, all ads should carry the "Equal Opportunity Employer M/F" line.

5. *Compensation plan, expense plan, and fringe benefits.* Include some information in these areas, especially if it is a strong point. A company paying straight salary is more likely to mention this point than is one that pays straight commission.

6. *How to contact the employer.* The ad must have a phone number, a mailing address, or a time and place for personal interviews.

Management must also decide which day of the week to insert the advertisement, where to locate it in the media, and what size it should be. Sunday papers are read more leisurely and thoroughly, but in a weekday edition one company's advertisement stands out more because there are fewer such ads. People seriously looking for jobs read the want ads every day.

Some organizations do no recruitment advertising. Instead they answer situation-wanted advertisements placed by people who are looking for sales jobs. These firms are interested in people who show enough initiative to seek out a job rather than waiting for one to come to them.

Voluntary applicants

The counterpart of the person who places an ad in the situation-wanted section of a newspaper is the one who walks in the front door and says, "I want a job selling for your company." Voluntary applicants are an excellent source of sales recruits, although usually there are not enough of them. These applicants certainly are interested in the firm. Furthermore, it is likely that they have done some investigating to determine whether they would like the job. They probably possess a high degree of initiative, self-confidence, and self-reliance.

Employment agencies

Agencies that place sales people are fine sources of retail sales clerks, part-time sales people, or door-to-door sellers. Agencies that specialize in placing executive personnel may also be a source of high-caliber, creative sales recruits. Federal and state employment services usually are not considered good sources, because the better prospects probably do not register at these offices.

If the agency is carefully selected and good relations are established with it, the dividends can be satisfying. The agency can do some of the initial screening, because presumably it will abide by the job specifications given it. Agencies where the fee is paid by the employer probably will attract a better quality of sales recruit. The cost to the employer for the agency's fee may well be offset by the savings in advertising and initial screening activities it performs.

Women, minorities, and other underemployed groups

As sources of sales recruits, many companies rely heavily on groups available for part-time work—such as teachers, students, housewives, and members of military forces. Door-to-door selling firms in cosmetics, silverware, or cooking utensils frequently use students or housewives as sales people. Firms that sell encyclopedias often bolster their sales force during the summer by hiring teachers. As a group, the underemployed labor pools lend themselves nicely to sales work in many situations. They are easy to contact, readily available, and usually have flexible hours during which they can work. Some of the most difficult personnel problems faced by sales executives, however, are connected with the management of a parttime sales force. It offers real challenges in training, compensation, and supervision of personnel.

Minority groups. Nonwhites, particularly blacks, constitute a major underemployed labor force from which management has not aggressively recruited sales people in the past, but to which increasing attention is being devoted. The 1964 Civil Rights Act, of course, is one politico-legal impetus moving management in this direction. In fear of an economic backlash, the sales force typically has the lowest percentage of black employees of any department in a company. One reason management has hesitated is fear that customers will react unfavorably to black sales reps.

Companies have reported mixed results in their efforts to recruit sales and marketing employees from minority groups.[3] Where good or excellent progress has been reported in recruiting, it most likely is for nonselling jobs in the marketing department, or for inside sales work. Many executives have reported only limited success in attracting minority groups into outside sales jobs—that is, jobs where the sales people go to the customers. A company seriously interested in recruiting blacks, for example, is likely to encounter two problems—the shortage of experienced applicants, and lack of interest in industrial selling. Nevertheless, the need for good sales people is likely to increase rather than decline. Consequently, economic, political, and social pressures undoubtedly will continue to stimulate sales executives to intensify their recruiting efforts among minority groups.

Women. The same economic, social, and legal pressures are stimulating sales executives to recruit women for outside sales forces. For many years women have outnumbered men in retail, in-store sales jobs. Women have also played important roles in advertising and marketing research. It has only been in recent years, however, that businesses have hired women for nonretail, outside sales jobs.[4] In the early 1970s, several major companies (Dow Chemical, Texaco, Xerox, for example) for the first time either recruited women for outside industrial selling jobs, or promoted female sales representatives into sales management positions.

Sales executives have discovered that, given a chance, qualified women often equaled or surpassed their male peers in sales ability. When dealing with buyers, female sales reps have three advantages over salesmen, according to some sales managers. First, the buyer will nearly always see a saleswoman, even one who has consistently refused to see male representatives from the same company.

---

[3] See David L. Hurwood, "More Blacks and Women in Sales and Marketing?" *Conference Board Record*, February 1973, pp. 38–44.

[4] This section is adapted from Sally Scanlon, "Women in Sales: Ms. Is a Hit!" *Sales Management*, February 5, 1973, p. 22; also see *Women in Selling: The Problems and the Promise* (New York: Research Institute of America, Inc., New York, 1974).

Second, because female sales reps are easily remembered, their companies and product lines tend to stick in a buyer's mind. And, third, women tend to be better listeners, so buyers will openly discuss their problems. This gives the female sales rep a better chance to learn about the buyers' needs and then explain how her products can satisfy them.

Management's initially favorable reaction to the hiring of saleswomen in many firms is not limited to consumer products companies or service industries. Women also are performing well as sales recruits in industrial sales jobs. Possible contributing factors to this high-level performance are the facts that whenever a minority group enters a new field, (1) the most highly motivated people enter first, and (2) they tend to be bright, well-educated, and especially hard workers.

Some sales executives are reluctant to hire women for outside selling jobs because of two traditional points of concern. One is fear of possible romantic involvements with buyers or fellow salesmen. The other is the belief that turnover rates may be increased because of marriage, pregnancy, or husbands being transferred to another city. In firms which have seriously recruited and used women in outside selling, these problems apparently have not been significant. Turnover rates for saleswomen have not been appreciably different from those of salesmen. Moreover, there seems to be an increasing acceptance of women as sales reps by both salesmen and sales managers. In one opinion poll, a sample of New York sales executives rated women against men on several factors involved in selling. The results were favorable (see Table 5–1).

TABLE 5–1
Sales executives' ratings of women against men in selling

Characteristics	No. of replies	Women better	Same as men	Women not as good as men
Selling ability	72	8.3%	73.6%	18.1%
Earnings	73	5.5	69.9	24.7
Ability to follow through	71	31.0	63.4	5.6
General attitude toward job	71	28.1	60.6	12.7
Creativity	78	21.8	59.0	19.2
Reliability	72	29.2	56.9	13.9
Longevity	64	10.9	53.1	32.8
Ability to "take the knocks"	73	8.2	49.3	42.5
Ability to travel	72	0	48.6	51.4
Promotability	66	7.6	43.9	48.5

Source: Sales Executives Club of New York, as reported in *Sales Management*, February 5, 1973, p. 27.

FACTORS INFLUENCING CHOICE OF RECRUITING SOURCES

Throughout our discussion of recruiting sources, we cited examples showing when a given source might be used. In each instance, certain factors influenced management's decision. At this point, we shall summarize some of the factors management should consider when deciding which sources to use for recruiting sales people.

1. *Nature of the product.* If the product is highly technical, the firm will recruit sales people experienced in that field, or prospects with appropriate technical background. The firm may look in its own production department.

2. *Nature of the market.* To deal with knowledgeable purchasing agents, the firm may prefer to recruit experienced sales people. If long-standing buyer-seller relationships are important, it must recruit people experienced in that field. Ethnic customer groups may require sales people to speak a foreign language.

3. *Policy on promoting from within the company.* When this policy exists, recruiters know where to look first.

4. *Sales training provided by company.* A company that can train its new sales people can recruit from colleges and sources of un-trained, inexperienced people. Otherwise, it must recruit experienced sales representatives.

5. *Is the company hiring career sales people?* Is the job a stepping-stone to management positions? For career jobs, a firm probably will *not* recruit seniors in colleges and universities.

6. *Sources of successful recruits in the past.* Sources which supplied most successful recruits for a position in the past can be consulted, provided there have been no substantial changes in the job.

7. *Money available for recruiting.* Limited recruiting funds force a firm to limit its recruiting sources and methods.

8. *Legal considerations.* Civil rights laws and federal agency regulations must be considered in deciding where to look for sales force recruits.

QUESTIONS AND PROBLEMS

1. Is it ethical for a sales manager to directly approach a competitor's sales person with an outright offer of a better job?
2. How would the sources and methods of recruiting sales people *differ* among the following firms?
   a. A company selling precision instruments to the petroleum industry.
   b. A coffee roaster and canner in Denver selling to wholesalers and retailers in the Southwest and the Rocky Mountain regions.

    c. A national firm selling kitchenware by the door-to-door method.

    d. A luggage manufacturer selling a high-grade product nationally through selected retail outlets.

3. The following firms want to hire sales people, and as recruiting sources the executives are considering *(a)* other divisions of the company, *(b)* competitors' sales forces, and *(c)* colleges and universities. Evaluate each of these three as sources of sales people for each company.

    a. Manufacturer of paper and paper products.

    b. Manufacturer of breakfast cereals.

    c. Manufacturer of dictating machines and transcribing equipment.

4. One manufacturer of dictating machines recruits only experienced people and does no recruiting among graduating college students. A competitor recruits extensively among colleges in its search for sales people. How do you account for the difference in sources used by virtually identical firms?

5. How do you account for the fact that college students have a very low regard for selling, even though the job of sales person can offer tremendous challenge and can be one of the highest paying jobs in the country?

6. What methods and sources should a firm use to recruit women for its sales force?

7. Should the salary or probable amount of commission be stated in a recruiting advertisement?

8. The following companies are looking for product sales people and decide to use advertising to recruit applicants. For each firm, you are asked to select the specific advertising media and to write a recruiting advertisement for one of those media. You may supply or assume whatever additional facts you need.

    a. Manufacturers' agent handling lighting fixtures for both the industrial and consumer markets.

    b. Manufacturer of outboard motors.

    c. Wholesaler of lumber and building materials.

9. What sources should be used to recruit sales reps to fill the job described in Figure 4–1? In Figure 4–2?

10. Evaluate the recruiting advertisements for sales people shown in the accompanying illustration.

a.

b.

c.

d.

e.

Case 5–1

CERAMIC ARTWORKS COMPANY
Recruiting a sales representative

Mr. Hans Dietrich and his two sons were in some disagreement regarding what sources should be used to recruit one or two sales people for the Ceramic Artworks Company, a firm Dietrich had just started. Dietrich was a computer systems analyst and mathematician on the verge of retirement from an electronics firm in Colorado Springs, Colorado. In his spare time through the years, he had experimented with photography, ceramics, and portrait painting. He had $6,000 which he used to set up the new company, with production facilities in his basement. He hoped to build this business slowly, steadily, and solidly, without going too far into debt or using too much of his savings.

The Ceramic Artworks Company produced only one product— ceramic portrait cameos. The cameo was a three-dimensional, sculptured bust profile of a person (see Exhibit 1). Cameos could be made of any object of reasonable size, but Dietrich was interested in making cameos only of people's profiles. He said, "My cameos are a combination of photography and art on ceramics. A cameo is quite different from a photograph or an oil painting. Besides being three-dimensional, a cameo has the added attraction of timelessness and classic beauty."

EXHIBIT 1
Picture of a Ceramic Artworks cameo

The best profile in a Ceramic cameo usually was white or gray in color. This profile was mounted on an oval frame which was trimmed rather ornately in gold or bronze. The background was a pastel color (magenta, lime green, or peacock blue) to contrast with the white head. Typically a cameo would be hung on a wall in home or office.

Ceramic Artworks planned to sell its cameos through department stores. An agreement would be signed with each store, spelling out the suggested price, the promotional arrangements, and any exclusive territorial rights for the store. Ceramic Artworks would furnish the photographic apparatus and train a store employee in its use. This apparatus consisted of three cameras placed in a triangular setting around the person to be photographed. Ceramic planned to sell each finished cameo to the store for $27.50 and intended that the store sell it to the customer for $49.95. Thus the store would enjoy a 45 percent markup on its selling price.

As far as Dietrich knew, no other company in the United States provided a personal cameo portrait service similar to the Ceramic Artworks product. The nearest competitors were: "shadow portraits" (usually simple, blackpaper reproductions); sculptors and stone masons who did bust sculptures of the rich or famous; portrait photographers; and portrait painters.

Dietrich realized that the planned price of his product was considerably higher than that usually charged by commercial photographers—his major competition. He felt that with proper promotion, however, no other type of portrait could compete with the nature and quality of his cameo reproductions.

Ceramic's major target market was the middle-income market, and within that broad group, several different market segments seemed to offer especially attractive possibilities. Grandparents and parents were seen as a major potential market segment, as they were attracted to cameos of their children, much as they now bought photographic or oil portraits. Sweethearts and spouses were two other potential segments. Each of the large market segments would be reached by a modest promotional program, geared to particular geographic areas and feast days such as Christmas, graduation, or Mother's Day.

Ceramic Artworks planned to employ one, or possibly two, sales people in the initial stages of the firm's operations. Initially, the sales person's main task would be to call on department stores and sell them on the idea of carrying Ceramic's product. Later, after successfully contracting with a number of stores, the sales representative would have the dual responsibilities of servicing existing accounts and seeking new ones.

The sales person would be provided with a sales kit which included samples of cameos and their photographic models, promotional tools and examples, photographic apparatus information, and information on the terms of the contracts. The kit was small enough to carry in a car or plane.

Dietrich was well aware that the sales person would be a key factor in determining the success or failure of the venture. He said, "Department stores will be hard to sell. In all likelihood they will be hesitant to engage in this new and unique venture. Consequently, the sales person's sales ability, personality, and technical know-how could prove to be deciding factors in persuading a department store to take us on."

The sales representative was to be paid a straight commission of 10 percent of sales. With the current production capacity, the sales rep could earn about $5,000 a month or $60,000 a year as a maximum. So Dietrich felt the new rep would have adequate incentive and potential. Because of the company's limited financial situation, the sales person was expected to pay his own travel expenses. However, these expenses were expected to be minimal in the beginning. The sales rep was expected to concentrate efforts in the narrow band of cities along the east slope of the Rocky Mountains in Colorado, ranging from Ft. Collins and Greeley in the north, down through the Denver and Colorado Springs metropolitan areas, to Pueblo in the south.

The new sales person would need some reserve funds to cover his business and personal living expenses during this introductory period. Once the cameo product passed the introductory stage, Dietrich expected that a sales person's commissions would rise rapidly. When that time arrived, Mr. Dietrich felt that production facilities and market opportunities would expand. He mentioned the possibility of selling in the ski resorts of Colorado where there were many expensive gift shops. He spoke of selling in the metropolitan areas of neighboring states—Albuquerque, Santa Fe, Omaha, Lincoln, Wichita, Kansas City, and Oklahoma City.

Ceramic Artworks had no facilities or personnel to train a sales rep, other than to explain the production process. Yet this new sales representative had to be convinced that the product had real sales potential and that the company was a sound business venture. He was risking the loss of his time and business-expense investment if the company was not successful.

Dietrich realized he had to select this new sales person rather quickly, because the company was about ready to produce cameos. All they needed was customer-subjects to be photographed and "cameoized." However, Dietrich was uncertain about where he should look to recruit this person, so he first discussed the problem with his two sons. Being college educated, they felt that college graduates had a definite advantage as sales people. They also knew, however, that the title "salesman" does not have the prestigious position in society that college graduates desire. Consequently, these people would be difficult to recruit. Nevertheless, they still preferred to recruit college graduates.

Dietrich strongly disagreed with his sons. Having been an insurance agent before he went into data processing, he believed that education was not needed to become a good sales rep. He put more weight on training and experience. "You can't learn the 'salesman's touch' from a book," he said. "I would much rather find an older, established person with a good sales delivery—one who has become polished over the years through trial and error."

Other people also made suggestions. Some felt that experienced people in the photographic or art industries were good prospects. Others said that good sales people working for large department stores (Sears, Penney's) were best qualified. Other suggestions included manufacturers' agents, certain employees of Ceramic Artworks, and even Dietrich himself.

So Dietrich was left to consider the diverse suggestions from his employees, his sons' approach, and his own "gut feelings." Though uncertainty haunted him at night, one thing he was sure of—that the new sales person could make or break his first attempt at his own business.

Question

1. What recruiting sources should Ceramic Artworks Company use?

Case 5–2
CAROL ANN, INC.
Recruiting door-to-door representatives

After five years of successful regional distribution, the management of Carol Ann, Inc., felt it was time to expand the geographical scope of its operations to the west.

Carol Ann, Inc., had been formed in 1972 by Carol Ann Katz to manufacture and distribute a line of household pet supplies directly to their owners. She copied the proven sales plans of such firms as Mary Kay Cosmetics, Sarah Coventry, and Tupperware. Under these selling programs each sales rep was an independent contractor who bought goods from the company and resold them to the customers.

Orders for the pet supplies were taken by the reps at small social gatherings in the homes of hostesses who were interested in the gifts and commissions given those who gave the parties. The sales rep purchased the goods for discounts from the list price of 40 to 50 percent, depending upon the quantities purchased. The rep paid the hostess a minimum of 10 percent commission on all goods sold at her "show." If the rep was able to book two or more future "shows" to be given by the people attending a show, the hostess received a 20 percent commission on the business written at her show. Each show was limited to five people plus the hostess.

During the company's growth in the Southeast region, new sales people were recruited by the existing reps. The senior rep was then paid a 4 percent commission (override) on all subsequent business written by the new rep, so long as the recruiter was with the company. This system had been most satisfactory for the normal growth that was enjoyed from the Atlanta distribution base.

However, Katz realized that initially some other recruiting system would have to be used if the new Los Angeles distribution center were to have sufficient sales volume quickly enough to be economically feasible.

At a meeting on the problem, her sales manager, Mr. Al Dogue, proposed taking a full page ad in the *Los Angeles Times* to explain the Carol Ann sales opportunity. The ad would invite everyone interested to attend a meeting at the Century Plaza Hotel at which time a complete presentation would be made. Those people still interested would be interviewed later. He saw a need to hold such meetings each week at different locations—such as Long Beach, Santa Ana, San Diego, Riverside, Santa Barbara, and Pasadena.

Ms. Fran Fish, the controller, objected to the costs of such a recruiting program. "A full page ad in the *Los Angeles Times* would cost at least $5,000 and that's nonsense. Find a cheaper way to get your people."

Mr. Jack Bird, vice president of operations, countered, "It would only be expensive if the plan didn't produce enough sales reps."

Ms. Nancy Rock, vice president of personnel, ventured, "It would seem to me that we could enter that market with less of a splash. If things don't go right at the meeting, we could walk away with egg on our face. It is embarrassing to throw a party and have no one show up. Perhaps a less conspicious beginning would be wiser. Let's advertise modestly for recruits, and then send some people out to interview them to get things rolling."

Katz listened to their discussion of these viewpoints but noticed that one director who was sitting in on the meeting had not said anything. She asked, "What do you make of this, Dr. Hays?"

He replied, "Who is to be in charge of the L.A. operation?"

"Helen Booker, one of our sales directors," answered Dogue.

"Is she any good?"

"We obviously think so," was the quick retort.

"I was under the impression that the Los Angeles operation was to be an independent profit center," Dr. Hays stated.

"It is!" Fish emphasized.

"Then why are we talking about this problem? It's not ours. It belongs to Mrs. Booker. Let her figure out how to build her sales force. Give her a budget and turn her loose.

"But she will still need a lot of help and guidance from us," insisted Dogue. "And some sort of recruiting program must be developed. It seems reasonable to me that we provide her with our thinking on this matter."

"It's late. The meeting's adjourned. Thank you for your thoughts," Katz concluded. She had some thinking to do.

Question

1. What would you recommend be done in this situation?

6

Selecting the sales force— Processing applicants

A liar should have a good memory.
QUINTILIAN

Once the number and type of sales people needed have been determined, and applicants for the job have been recruited, management is ready for the third and final stage in the sales selection function. This step involves (1) the development of a system for measuring the applicants against the predetermined requirements, (2) a critical evaluation of the tools and procedures to be used, and (3) the actual use of these tools to select the sales people. The major selection tools are:

- Application blanks.
- Personal interviews.
- References and credit reports.
- Tests.
- Physical examinations.
- Rating sheets.

The sequence in which selection tools are used varies among companies. Initial screening (beyond that done by the recruiting) may start with an application blank, an interview, or some form of test. The purpose of the initial screen is to eliminate, as soon and as inexpensively as possible, the obviously undesirable recruits. Therefore, no matter which technique is used first it usually is brief—a short application blank, an interview of only a few minutes, or a simple test that can be administered and interpreted easily and quickly. This procedure is in line with the general idea that the *least costly selection tools should be used first.*

No single selection tool is adequate by itself. A series of them should be used for a careful determination of an applicant's qualifications. In many cases, one tool complements another or can be used to verify information derived from another. Some pertinent data ordinarily come only through an interview, while other traits may be discernible only by testing.

The tools a company uses to process its sales recruits should be designed to fit the particular needs of the firm. Standardized forms (application blanks, interview forms, and so on) prepared for general use are typically less effective than those a company develops on its own.

These tools and procedures are only aids to sound executive judgment and not substitutes for it. The performance of prevailing selection systems has been considerably less than ideal. They can eliminate obviously unqualified candidates and generally spot extremely capable individuals. However, for the mass of recruits who normally fall between these extremes, the tools currently used can only predict, but not guarantee, those who will be successful in the job. As a result, generous quantities of executive judgment still are essential in selecting sales representatives.

LEGAL CONSIDERATIONS

The traditional use of several of the hiring tools has been considerably limited by EEOC and OFCC rulings. For companies subject to Affirmative Action guidelines, it is essential to keep an "applicant flow chart," which lists the processed applicants by sex and ethnic group. If there is a disproportionately high rate of rejection of women or minority applicants, each step in the hiring process (application blanks, interviews, tests, rating sheets, etc.) may be reviewed to determine which tool is producing this result. When the particular tool is identified, it must undergo a complicated, expensive validation procedure, if management wants to continue using it. If no disproportionate rejection of women or minorities in the selection process has been found, there is no validation requirement.

Many questions traditionally asked on application blanks and interviews either are no longer allowable, or they must be handled very carefully. Sometimes questions in sensitive areas are asked *after* the person is hired—as in the case of age and marital status for insurance purposes. Questions in sensitive areas may be asked *during* these interviews, however, if they relate to bona fide occupational qualifications (BFOQ). Age and sex may be BFOQs, for example, if the sales job calls for a woman to model the line of apparel she is selling, or a man must read a particular TV commercial. If a certain ethnic background and ability to speak a certain foreign language are BFOQs, then obviously questions pertaining to these factors are perfectly okay.

APPLICATION BLANKS

Reasons for using application blanks

The application blank, or personal-history record, as it is sometimes called, is one of the two most widely used selection tools. (The other is the interview.) Sometimes a firm uses two blanks—a short one and a longer, more detailed one.

The short one ordinarily is used only as an initial screening device. No executive's time need be taken to administer or interpret this form. Instead, an office employee can give the applicant the short blank to fill out and then can do the initial interpreting. If, for example, a certain amount of education or number of years of business experience is stated as a requirement for the job, the employee can check the completed blank to determine whether the applicant has these minimum qualifications.

A longer blank may be used as an initial screen or for other purposes. The facts stated on the form can be the basis for probing in an interview—for instance, asking several questions relating to the job experience as stated on the blank. In the future the data on the blank may be used to reevaluate the characteristics needed for the job. As discussed in Chapter 4, application blanks are one of the main sources of information used by a firm to study the backgrounds of its good and poor sales people, and to establish scores and weights on specific requirements for sales positions.

Information sought on application blanks

Seek pertinent information only. The company ordinarily should ask only for information it intends to use now or later. Unless a question relates to some standard or job qualification, its presence on the blank is debatable. It may be that the question is needed to complete personal records of some sort. For instance, the causes of the parents' death may be required for company insurance programs. However, items of this nature may well be recorded elsewhere, so the blank can be left free to carry only those questions that have been proven significantly indicative of potential success or failure.

A number of factors affect the type and amount of information requested on an application blank. One is the objective the company has in using the blank. If it serves as an initial screen or as an application for an interview, it probably is shorter than one that will be a complete personal-history record.

The other selection tools and records used often influence the design of the application blank. The company may want to omit questions that are answered by other tools. Use of a patterned interview with recorded answers, for instance, may enable a concern to shorten its blank. On the other hand, a company may want to duplicate its questions in order to check on applicants' honesty by seeing if their answers on the blank coincide with those obtained from other sources.

Job qualifications usually influence the questions on application blanks. A firm trying to hire people with five to ten years of sales experience, for example, is not so concerned about a recruit's activity in college organizations as is the company that is hiring recent college graduates. The longer a person has been out of school, the more a firm can look at things other than university activities as indicators of abilities.

Another factor is the degree to which the selection function is decentralized. If home-office executives take part in the hiring, the application blank probably is detailed. These executives may have to do much of the screening without having an opportunity to interview the applicants. But if territorial managers do the hiring, the blank may be shorter because other tools—especially the interview—can be used more extensively.

Information typically requested.   In Chapter 4 we proposed a five-part classification of sales job qualifications—mental, physical, experience, environmental, and personality. An application blank is an excellent tool for getting significant information in three of these categories—physical, experience, and environmental. In addition, carefully phrased and interpreted questions often can shed some light even on the mental abilities and personality traits of the recruits.

Assuming that a certain physical condition is a bona fide occupational qualification, a company might ask such questions as:

What is your height? Your weight?

What is your general physical condition?

What defects do you have in speech? Hearing? Sight? Have you ever had any trouble with your feet? Hernia?

Date of last physical examination? Reason for it?

Have you ever been rejected for life insurance? Reason?

What has been the total medical expense during the last three years for yourself?

Are you willing to take a physical examination now at company expense?

On an application blank, experience requirements are usually divided into two groups—educational background and work experience. Regarding educational training, applicants typically are asked a series of questions about each stage of schooling, starting with grade school or high school and carrying on through college or other types of institutions, such as vocational schools.

Questions about educational background are asked because companies believe that applicants' activities and performance in school tell something about their mental abilities and personality traits. Anyone who was graduated from high school or college (depending on the firm's requirements) is presumed to have the necessary basic intelligence. A course of study indicates much about a person's interests. Students who concentrated in foreign languages or fine arts have different interests and aptitudes than accounting majors do, for example. Having graduated suggests a degree of perseverance. Having worked one's way, at least partially, through school may indicate self-reliance and industry. Further, holding office in school organizations may provide some evidence of leadership qualities.

Most application blanks ask for information about the candidate's employment history, including an accounting for periods of unemployment. If a company has certain experience qualifications, the application blank is a good tool for determining the extent to which a candidate fulfills the requirements. People's business backgrounds also often tell much about their talents and interests. The hiring firm probably is interested in how the applicant has progressed over the years. For instance, has each move resulted in a better job with more pay, added responsibility, or greater opportunity? Companies usually also are interested in the reasons a person gives for leaving each job. If possible, a prospective employer should check on this point with someone other than the applicant in order to get as complete a story as possible.

Companies ordinarily are interested in the environmental qualifications of prospective employees. Usually the first part of an application blank seeks such factual information as name, address, date of birth, marital status, home and business phone numbers, and social security number. Then questions are asked on such significant topics as the following:

Amount of life insurance carried.

Financial condition—savings, investments, and so on.

Membership in social, service, and business organizations.

Offices held in organizations.

Outside interests—hobbies, athletic endeavors, and others.

Length of residence at each address for past five to ten years.

Information on the prospect's environment can be extremely helpful because it çan indicate a good deal about the person's interests, capabilities, and personality. Active participation in organizations may be evidence of an ability to meet and mix with people, and holding office may imply leadership traits and administrative abilities. Carrying adequate life insurance suggests that the applicant is stable, interested in security, and responsible.

Another group of useful questions on a blank pertains directly to the job for which application is being made. These include:

Why do you want this job?

Why do you want to change jobs?

What minimum income do you require?

What do you want to be doing 10 years from now?

Are you willing to travel? To be transferred?

Can you drive? Do you have a driver's license?

Has your driver's license ever been revoked? Why?

Do you own an automobile?

Are you willing to use your own car for business?

Scored or weighted application blanks

One method we have suggested for determining the qualifications needed to fill a given position is to analyze the personal histories of past and present sales people. A detailed example of weighting and scoring personal history records was given in Chapter 4.

The application blank is an excellent tool for finding the extent to which a recruit possesses the traits that have been shown to be significant by the personal-history analysis. Questions can be placed on the blank and the answers scored in accordance with the predetermined standards. An applicant who scores higher than an established minimum number of points is moved on to the next step in the hiring-screening process. One who fails to attain the minimum score usually is rejected from further consideration at that point. It is possible, of course, that an applicant with a low score on the blank could turn out to be a successful sales person. However, the chances are not favorable, and a company ordinarily should not risk hiring such an applicant.

PERSONAL INTERVIEWS

Nature and purpose

Virtually no sales person is ever hired without a personal interview, and there are no satisfactory substitutes for this procedure. Much has been written about the use of weighted application blanks, various kinds of tests, and other aids in hiring, but none of these tools completely takes the place of getting to know the applicants personally by talking to them. It was said several years ago, and is still true today, that "The answer to better selection of salesmen is to be found in the mastery of a technique of planned interviewing, probably the most important technique for any executive to know because it helps not only in appraising but in understanding a man in such a way that you can supervise and motivate him better."[1] Furthermore, the interview can be used in any size company. Firms that are too new or too small to use weighted application blanks or psychological tests can use any type of interview.

Reasons for interviewing recruits.   In selection, the personal interview is used fundamentally to help determine a person's fitness for the job. The tool may be employed as the initial screening device, and it also usually plays a part in some subsequent stage of the hiring process.

A series of personal interviews also serves to determine characteristics that are not always observable by other means. An interview is probably the best way to find out something about the recruits' conversational ability, speaking voice, and intelligence. By seeing the applicant in person, an executive can appraise physical characteristics such as general appearance and care given to clothes. Certain personality traits may also be observed to some degree. The applicant's poise under the strain of an interview may be noted, along with any ability to dominate or lead a conversation.

Another purpose in interviewing is to verify and interpret facts stated on the application blank. For example, the applicant may have stated that he was a district manager in some previous job. The prospective employer may ask what were his responsibilities, how many employees did he supervise, and what were his administrative duties. It is possible to check on a person's truthfulness by repeating some of the questions asked on the personal-history record.

It is important that the interview serves as a two-way channel of communication. The interview not only is a means by which a company determines an applicant's fitness for a job. It also offers an employer an opportunity to answer the recruit's questions about the com-

---

[1] Jack H. McQuaig, "The Selection of Star Salesmen," *Sales/Marketing Today*, July 1965, p. 20.

pany and the position. The applicant can be told about such things as the nature of the job, the compensation, the type of training and supervision provided, and the opportunities for the future.

Applicants should be told the truth in all respects. To mislead or oversell them regarding the position only creates future problems. They need sufficient information so that they can decide whether they really want the job, or whether they would accept it only until something better comes along. Actually, applicants can save a firm a considerable sum in the long run by turning down offers that they know are not what they want.

Information wanted and questions asked.   Fundamentally, all the questions asked during an interview are aimed at determining four points regarding an applicant:

1.   Is he qualified for the job?
2.   How badly does he want or need the job?
3.   Can the company furnish him with the success he wants? That is, will the job help him realize his goals?
4.   Will he achieve the level of work his capacity will allow? That is, will he strive to produce to his fullest ability?

A list of the detailed questions that could be asked on the above four major points might run for pages. Even then, each firm would have to select the questions judiciously; different queries would be pertinent for different firms. In general, the inquiries are mainly of the type intended to examine the applicants' past behavior, experiences, environment, and motivation. What a person has been and has done in the past is indicative of what that person probably will be and do in the future. Certain types of questions regarding the future ordinarily are also included: "What would you like to be doing five years from now? How much do you hope to be earning in three years? Where do you want this job to lead?"

Bases for classifying personal interviews.   Four bases may be used to categorize selection interviews:

1.   *Degree to which interviews are preplanned.* The questioning may be done in a formally patterned, guided manner, or in an informal, nondirected fashion.
2.   *Timing of interview.* There may be a brief interview as part of the initial screening, or there may be longer ones in subsequent stages of the selection process.
3.   *Persons interviewed.* The company may also want to talk with the applicant's spouse and family.
4.   *Applicant's awareness of being interviewed.* The firm may or may not want prospective employees to be conscious of the fact that they are being interviewed.

Patterned versus nondirected interviews

Selection interviews can differ, depending upon the extent to which the questions are detailed in advance and the conversation is guided by the interviewer. At one end of the scale is the totally patterned or guided interview, and at the other end is the informal, nondirected type.

In a patterned interview, the procedure is highly standardized. The interviewers for a firm all use the same guide sheet on which is listed a series of questions. Each person interviewed is asked these questions in the order listed on the sheet. The standard form also has a place for the interviewer to record the applicant's answer to each question. The notations may be made in the presence of the interviewer, after making a proper explanatory statement, or the replies may be noted immediately after the conversation is ended.

Patterned interviews. The patterned or guided interview is designed to overcome problems encountered in using personal interviews as a selection technique. Many sales executives engaged in selection activities do not know what questions to ask. They may know what qualifications are necessary for the job, but they do not know what questions will bring forth the information about the applicant's possession of these characteristics.

Another common problem is the interviewer's unfamiliarity with the job description or application blank. The interviewer who does not know in detail what the job entails and what the necessary qualifications cannot do a good interviewing job.

A third problem is that most interviewers are unable to interpret the answers to many of their questions. Qualified personnel have no opportunity to assist in the interpretation of answers to queries in the nonpatterned type of interview, because the applicants' comments are not recorded.

The guided interview has been developed to help solve these three problems. First, the interviewer is furnished with the questions to be asked. These have been carefully designed to help determine the applicant's fitness for the job. The skills of many people may be brought to bear in formulating the questions, rather than placing the entire burden on a lone interviewer. Use of the standardized list also means that more than one person can do the interviewing and the results still will be comparable.

Second, the interviewer must write down the answers. This furnishes a permanent record, with all its advantages. An applicant's shortcomings noted on the patterned interview report can serve as subjects to be covered in training and supervision. As long as the results of the interview are in writing, several people may evaluate the recruit's qualifications. Persons more qualified than the interviewer may have a part in the appraisal. In a company where the final selection is made in the home office (after the preliminary screening is done in the branches), the guided interview records are especially important.

Some people criticize the patterned interview as being inflexible. When interviewers are given a standard list of questions, with instructions not to deviate, they are unable to use their own judgment to modify the interview to meet particular conditions that may come up during the conversation. Actually, a patterned interview need not be as inflexible as these critics imply. Trained interviewers can use their own judgment and can make slight modifications without detracting at all from the full value of the guided form.

Other critics object to the interviewer's writing answers in front of the applicant. They believe that just being interviewed places the applicant under much strain. An alternative is to make the notes after the interview is ended, but this is something less than ideal. After a lengthy conversation, it is questionable whether the interviewer can recall the exact answers to each question.

Nondirected interviews.   At the end of the scale opposite the patterned interview is the informal, nondirected one. The applicant is urged to talk freely on any subject. Ordinarily, the interviewer asks a few questions to get the applicant talking on certain subjects, such as his business experiences, home life, and school activities. The interviewer does very little talking—just enough to keep the conversation rolling. The theory in this type of interview is that significant characteristics come to light if the applicant is encouraged to speak freely.

The major problem with the nondirected interview is that much time may be consumed in unearthing little information. Some of what is said by an applicant may be irrelevant or incapable of being appraised. This type of interview requires far more interpretive skill on the part of the interviewer than is true of the patterned form. There is no written record that can be passed on to someone else for appraisal. In some cases, a tape recording of the interview may be made without the recruit's knowledge. Also, the values of standardization are lost in the nondirected type.

Most firms today use an interview format that falls somewhere between the two extremes of the patterned and the nondirected interview. Usually, the interviewers have in mind a few topics they want to cover in the talks. They probably do very little writing in the presence of the applicants. Even in the same firm, interviewers vary considerably in regard to content of interview and techniques used in interviewing. There seems to be a definite trend, however, toward the use of a more patterned or guided form of interview.

Timing of the interview

During initial screening. Companies often use an interview instead of an application blank as the initial screening device. For example, when recruiting teams visit college campuses or meet the people who are responding to an advertisement, one or more members of the team may interview the prospect very briefly to determine only whether the person should be considered further. Initial screening interviews should be short—possibly only 15 or 20 minutes.

Because interviewing takes the valuable time of executives, the interviewer should find out as soon as possible if the recruit is obviously uninterested or unqualified. The necessary information may be determined first by giving a brief description of the job and, second, by asking a few direct questions to ascertain whether the recruit meets the minimum requirements. Some prospects may disqualify themselves once they find out something about the job, and another segment may be eliminated for failing to meet the basic requirements.

At later stages. Firms that do a thorough selection job ordinarily interview applicants several times before they are hired. After applicants pass through the initial screen, but before a final decision can be reached, much remains to be learned about them. In turn, they must be told many things about the job.

A sound generalization regarding interviewing techniques is that a company should not depend on a single interview, a single interviewer, or a single place for the interviewing. These ideas are built on the principle that the more time spent with the prospective recruit and the more people who talk with him, the greater is the opportunity to get to know him and his qualifications. It is usually a mistake to hire a person after only one interview.

When more than one person does the interviewing, they can compare notes on a recruit and thus reduce the chance that unfair bias will creep into their individual evaluations. Conducting the conversations in different settings makes it easier to bring up certain topics. Taking applicants out to dinner for an interview, for example, makes it easier to determine something of their social traits and their opinions on entertaining and drinking.

Interviewing the spouse and family

For many years management has been aware of how important an executive's spouse is to that executive's progress in the company. Sales managers also recognize the influence a sales *person's* spouse can have on that rep's performance. Unless the spouse and family of the sales representative are satisfied and proud of the rep's job, the representative probably will not give his best performance.

Consequently, it is becoming a common practice to interview the recruit's spouse before a hiring decision is made. These interviews may be conducted with the couple in an office meeting, during a social engagement such as dinner, or, preferably, in the couple's home. By visiting the recruit's home, the interviewer also can appraise the home environment and meet the rest of the family.

To simplify this section, let's assume that the company is hiring a salesman. However, the points developed here are equally applicable when a firm is hiring a saleswoman. In that case, management should interview her husband to determine if he is supportive of her taking the selling job. In either hiring situation (man or woman), an interviewer also should try to talk with teen-age children who are living at home.

During an interview with the wife of a prospective salesman, management can get the wife's opinion on specific topics, such as the people her husband will meet, the problem of being away from home so much, the reputation of the company, the nature of the product, and the type of sales job. Many stories have been told about traveling salesmen, but they are not particularly funny to their wives. There may be a question of the prestige connected with the work. If a man is to sell a product about which there may be a social question (for example, ladies' lingerie or alcoholic beverages), a firm should know the wife's attitude toward it. Another purpose served by the interview is that it gives management a chance to sell the recruit's wife and family on the job and its opportunities.

Applicant's awareness of interview

In most interviews, the applicants are well aware that they are being interviewed. Realizing this, companies sometimes wonder how much they are really finding out about applicants. A person who is at all perceptive, has a high degree of social intelligence, and wants the job is very apt, in replying to many questions, to give answers that he thinks will leave a favorable impression. These replies may not necessarily be the full truth, but then the full truth may not get him the job.

It is possible that a good interviewer can get honest answers to the questions asked. It is also possible to verify the answers given to some queries by resorting to other selection tools. However, the applicant wants to put his best foot forward, assuming that he wants the job. Therefore, the main factor being measured is one aspect of the person's social intelligence—his ability to make the proper responses. A person would have to be very unperceptive not to realize that he is supposed to get along with his fellow workers and should have a good reason for leaving his former job. He knows it is better to have left a position for greater opportunity in a new one rather than because he felt his boss was incompetent and played favorites.

There is no questioning the importance of social intelligence in selling. It is also encouraging that a recruit has knowledge of the proper way to act in an interview. Probably, those lacking in these abilities should be eliminated. However, the prospective employer still must find out everything possible about the applicant.

An important type of interview is one during which the company hopes the applicant will forget or not realize he is being interviewed. The purpose is to get him off guard or away from his "interviewing manners," and then talk with him when he is more his natural self. Ordinarily an interview of this nature is not held on company premises. It may be possible to determine something about a person's emotional stability by observing him under the stress of a golf match, a football or baseball game, or a cocktail party. Some firms conduct these interviews in a cocktail lounge. A sales person may be called on frequently to entertain customers, so the company wants to be certain no liquor problems will arise. Another reason is that a man is apt to relax and say what he really thinks in such an informal setting.

In these situations, a leading statement in the form of a complaint from the interviewer may encourage the prospective recruit to speak more freely. During a golf game, for example, the interviewer may criticize the poor condition of the greens or complain about the way the club is operated. While watching a football game, the interviewer may criticize the officials or the coaches' choice of plays. The recruit may start to speak his mind in these unguarded moments. Sometimes, a chronic complainer just needs someone to get him started, and he will be critical of many things. He may even tell what he really thought of his former job and employer. Care must be taken to differentiate between the person who is complaining just to agree with the interviewer and the one who is a habitual complainer, a basically unhappy person.

In interviews where the applicant does not realize he is being interviewed, the interviewer has a greater responsibility to interpret the person's behavior and remarks correctly. Notes may be made at the conclusion of the interview, but there is no standard list of questions. The interviewer's own judgment and ingenuity must be used during the encounter.

REFERENCES AND OTHER OUTSIDE SOURCES

When processing applicants for sales jobs, an administrator can get help from two general sources of information outside the company. In the first, the applicant furnishes the leads; this is typically called a reference. In the other, the company solicits information on its own initiative; this source includes credit or insurance reports.

The typical procedure is for the prospective employer to check by personal visit, telephone, or letter with the people listed by the applicant as references. Whichever method is selected, it should be used preferably *after* the recruit fills out an application blank, but *before* a lengthy interview. In this manner, various statements made on the blank may be verified. If there still is some question, the interview offers an opportunity to investigate further.

A personal visit or telephone call to a reference is usually a better method than a letter. However, none of the three is without some significant weakness. Use of the telephone or a personal visit has the advantage that the statements the person makes are not in writing. While a telephone call is a fast way of contacting the reference, it also can be an expensive one, particularly if a long-distance call is involved. Also, some companies do not supply information to a stranger who calls on the telephone. While a personal visit is generally recommended, it may take much time and is not practical unless the reference is located near the future employer. A letter is probably used more frequently than the other two methods but often it is of little real value. Firms hesitate to put in writing anything that is seriously derogatory.

Who is a valuable reference from the prospective employer's viewpoint? No simple generalization can be made about the value of former employers as references. In some cases, they can be excellent sources of information. They may know the applicant well and be willing to give an honest appraisal. If a present employer wants to get rid of or, for that matter, wants to keep the employee, it is doubtful whether such a reference can be of much help to the hiring firm. If the prospect has been a salesman, it may be a good idea to talk to some of his customers. They know something of his sales ability, personal habits, and personality traits. It is especially helpful if the prospective employer is personally acquainted with the individual listed as a reference by an applicant.

When talking with an applicant's former employers, probably the key question to ask is: "Would you rehire him?" Other questions may determine facts and opinions about dates of employment, attendance record, nature of duties, ability to get along with people, and reason for leaving.

Prospective employers usually can learn much more by soliciting information through their own connections than they can from names given by applicants. Representatives from the hiring firm may talk to a former professor not listed as a reference by the applicant, for ex-

A day-to-day operating problem in the

MAJESTIC GLASS COMPANY (C)

Request to rehire former salesman, now in penitentiary

Mr. Clyde Brion, general sales manager for Majestic Glass Company, was visited in his office by Mrs. Edgar Jenner, a pale, sick-looking woman, accompanied by a man who identified himself as parole officer of the Ohio State Department of Correction. As Brion knew, Mrs. Jenner was the wife of a former Majestic salesman based in Detroit. At this time Jenner was in the Ohio Penitentiary, serving the third year of a seven-year sentence for manslaughter committed while driving a car under the influence of liquor. The case had attracted much newspaper attention because the victim was a pretty teen-age daughter of a U.S. senator, struck down crossing a quiet street on her way to a church where she was to have been a bridesmaid at the wedding of another senator's daughter.

Except for an attempt to escape custody during his trial, Jenner had been a docile prisoner. The parole officer described him as remorseful, morose, and worried about his wife as well as about his own future. A doctor at the penitentiary had found him free of any addiction to alcohol and had recommended that he be freed if he could return to his regular work in familiar surroundings. Mrs. Jenner asked Brion to rehire her husband.

Until his conviction, Jenner had been a satisfactory, though not an outstanding, salesman for Majestic. In sales volume, his territory had never ranked higher than ninth among the 18 territories, despite his six years on the sales force. The Detroit area was believed to have considerably more potential than he was able to tap. Jenner had used his drawing account regularly, saying that he needed extra money to pay medical bills on his wife's long illness.

The Detroit territory had not been permanently filled since Jenner had left it. Because it was relatively close to the Majestic home offices, Brion had preferred to use it as a training territory for new salesmen, supervised by himself.

Question

Should Clyde Brion rehire Edgar Jenner?

Note: See the introduction to this series of problems in Chapter 2 for the necessary background on the company, its market, and its competition.

ample. Or someone in the company may be acquainted with a former employer.

On balance, the merit of the reference as a selection tool is questionable. Yet, management really dare not bypass the use of this selection tool. If only one significant fact is uncovered, it makes the effort worthwhile. Handled carefully and intelligently, references may be valuable, but unfortunately, most are worth very little. The use of references requires special caution in one respect. A person who is a success or failure in one job will not necessarily repeat the same performance in the next one. There may have been a good reason for doing poorly in one position, and this may well have been the fault of the employer.

A special source of outside information is the credit report, or a report from some other type of investigating agency. These agencies specialize in preemployment investigative interviews with former employees, co-workers, sales managers, neighbors, and creditors. Reports from local credit bureaus through their affiliation with their national association can provide a wealth of information on a prospective sales person. Often, former employers and other references give information to a credit bureau that they would not divulge to a prospective employer. These reports touch on many phases of a person's background, such as his habits, home life, and financial condition. Even such points as domestic problems, bill-paying practices, and current indebtedness are related in a credit report, as well as the standard facts on educational and business background.

PSYCHOLOGICAL TESTING

Psychological testing is another major tool often used in the sales selection process. Typically a company uses a *battery* of these tests— that is, several different tests—rather than a *single* test. Over the years, psychological testing undoubtedly has been the most controversial of all the selection tools. Today the added question of the legality of testing has increased the complexity and the controversy surrounding its use.

The five types of tests commonly used in selection of sales personnel are:

1. Intelligence tests. These are intended to measure native intelligence or IQ (intelligence quotient).
2. Knowledge tests. Designed to measure what the applicant knows about some product, service, market, and so on.
3. Aptitude tests. Designed to measure aptitude for selling.

4. Interests tests.
5. Personality tests.

Legal aspects of testing

There is some confusion and misunderstanding regarding the use of tests in the personnel selection process. Some court cases and compliance agency rulings have left many executives with the idea that it is illegal to use testing in the selection process. *Testing is not illegal.* Many companies which are audited by compliance agencies are using tests. In fact, a testing and selection order issued by the OFCC (Office of Federal Contract Compliance) says that "properly validated and standardized employee selection procedures can significantly contribute to the implementation of non-discriminatory personnel policies" and that "professionally developed tests . . . may significantly aid in the development and maintenance of an efficient work force."

The key phrases in the above quotation are "properly validated" and "professionally developed." A firm should use either professional in-house psychologists or a competent outside consultant. The sales executives should *not* be the people who are selecting the tests to be used.

In our earlier discussion of application blanks and interviews, we observed that the questions asked must be relevant to the job being filled. Furthermore, if a compliance agency questions a company about relevance, the burden of proof is on the company to show that its questions and procedures are relevant. That same situation prevails regarding the use of tests. The test questions must be demonstrably relevant to the job. For this reason it usually is advisable for a company to develop its own test specifically designed for its own jobs. These tailor-made tests are in contrast to general-use tests such as the Otis Self-Administering Test of Mental Ability, the Bernreuter Personality Inventory, and the Strong Vocational Interest Blank, which are used in a wide variety of situations.

Validation can be a complex, time-consuming, expensive process. However, proof of validation of tests is *not* required by compliance agencies *unless* there is a disproportionately large rejection of women or minorities in the selection process.

To summarize the legal situation, testing is perfectly acceptable if done correctly. A company should use a battery of tests designed by a professional to meet the needs of the particular job. The company should keep records to show that the tests and test questions are relevant, and that the tests do not screen out a disproportionately large number of women or minorities.

Reasons for using psychological tests

Fundamentally, sales executives use testing in sales force selection to increase their chances of selecting good sales people. Now let's elaborate on that generalization.

Tests are used to identify more accurately the various traits and qualifications that usually cannot be measured by other selection tools, such as application blanks or interviews. These traits may be grouped, as tests are, into five categories: (1) intelligence, (2) achievement, (3) aptitude, (4) interests, and (5) personality.

Another purpose for using tests is that they can provide a basis for interviewing. Any questionable points spotted in the test results may be probed more deeply by interviewers.

As a company's sales force grows larger, management may need a more formalized selection program. Procedures that were satisfactory when hiring only one or two sales people in a year may not work with larger numbers. Then more people are involved in the selection process, and the company needs a more structured hiring program. A program of applicant testing—*properly administered and interpreted* —can be an effective part of a formal, research-based sales force selection program.

Another reason for using testing relates to the costs of hiring and training sales people. These costs are already high and are still rising. Any selection tool is highly desirable if it can reduce sales force turnover and increase sales productivity by doing an effective selection job. A properly administered testing program can help to offset these high costs by increasing the chances of selecting effective sales people. The added costs of testing are relatively small when compared with the losses than can result from poor selection.

Dangers and problems in testing

Most testing procedures generate the concept of an average or normal type of employee. The implication is that this person is the best type to hire for a given job. The danger is that a potentially successful sales representative may be screened out simply because he does not fit the stereotype. Testing may eliminate the truly creative person, who may not fall in the average or normal range in testing. At the same time, creativity may be the very trait that would make him an outstanding sales representative.

Another problem with testing is that it may be used as a managerial buck-passing technique. If a new sales recruit does not perform successfully, a sales executive can say: "It isn't my fault. The tests predicted that he would succeed."

A related danger is that tests may be used as the sole deciding knockout factor. An applicant may look good based on interviews, the application blanks, and reference checks. But if his test scores are especially low, management is scared off and will not hire him. Thus the tests are not always used only as *one aid* in hiring. They can become the deciding factor—the sole determinant—in the hiring decision, especially when scores are low.

In some cases tests are misused because executives fail to apply the concept of a *range* of scores. These managers believe that the highest score on a test indicates the best prospective sales person. For many kinds of tests, psychologists agree, a *range* of scores is acceptable. All who fall within that range should be judged as equally qualified for the job. Unfortunately, most people—perhaps because of their schooling—tend to feel that a person scoring near the high end of the acceptable range is a better prospect than one scoring in the middle or lower part of that range.

Another factor to watch for in testing is that applicants can fake the answers on some tests, especially on some personality or interest tests. The reasonably intelligent applicants for a sales job realize that they should indicate a preference for mixing with people, in contrast to staying home and reading a good book.

Cultural bias is another situation that can creep into tests. A person may score poorly—not because of a lack of interest, aptitude, or native intelligence—but only because the test included questions which assumed a certain cultural background.

Finally, testing is affected by some of the problems we discussed in Chapter 4 in connection with determining hiring specifications. We cannot isolate the traits needed for success in a particular sales job. Some of the traits that make a good sales representative also might make a good lawyer, actor, or bus driver. A test may indicate that an applicant has these traits. But you don't know whether that person will turn out to be a good sales representative or a good bus driver. Furthermore, in sales selection we need to know the extent to which each trait is needed for sales success, and the extent to which one trait can be substituted for another. So far, we have been largely unsuccessful in our attempts to quantitatively measure these traits by testing or by other means.

Conditions in which testing is most effective

A program for testing in sales selection is more likely to be successful and effective when any of the following conditions exist:

- The firm hires a relatively large number of sales people, and management realizes that its existing selection system is poor.

- The company is hiring young, inexperienced people about whom little is known. If experienced representatives are being selected, their performance records rather than test results should be the criterion.
- The personnel being selected are not likely to be "test-wise," so the danger of faking (intentionally answering incorrectly) is minimized.
- The executives responsible for interviewing the recruits are not adept at discovering personality traits and selling aptitudes. Normally, executives with a great deal of experience in hiring do a much better job of interviewing than an administrator who is new at the job.
- In companies where the cost of failure is high, the expense of testing may be considered a small insurance premium to make certain that no one slips through the selection screen. If the testing procedure catches just one failure a year who would otherwise have been hired, the costs of the testing may be justified.
- The executives are competent to interpret the psychologist's recommendations properly, and they feel free to act on their own judgment regardless of the tests.
- The firm is willing to undertake a program of test development and validation which may be expensive and take a considerable period of time.

Conclusions on testing

We are very cautious about recommending the use of psychological tests to hire sales people. We feel that effective interviewing is still the best selection tool among those commonly used today. Of course, we recognize that testing can be effective, and we support its use if two conditions exist. First, the tests should be tailor-made by a qualified person for a specific job in a given company. Second, the tests should be used *only* as an *aid* in the selection process, not as the sole factor determining whether an applicant will be hired.

Unfortunately, these two conditions often are not present when testing is used. Too many sales executives have adopted the "patent medicine" of general-use tests without understanding the implicit assumptions and limitations of these remedies. Furthermore, in too many instances tests have been used as the sole knockout factor— disqualifying an applicant who otherwise looked good in interviews and reference checks. At the other extreme, it is also a mistake to use tests as the actual or final determining factor in deciding to hire an applicant.

PHYSICAL EXAMINATIONS

A physical examination is virtually a necessity in selecting recruits for many jobs that require the same degree of physical activity and create the same tensions that selling does. While poor physical condition may enable a person to perform satisfactorily at some jobs, it will not do for selling. The sales recruit should appreciate the opportunity to get a complete physical checkup, and the company should insist on it. It is not enough merely to ask questions about the applicant's physical condition and medical history on an application blank or during an interview. The examination given during the course of the hiring process should be very thorough, and the results must be interpreted properly. Ordinarily, the interpretation can be done by a doctor in consultation with the sales executives concerned.

RATING SHEETS

As a selection device, rating sheets may be used in conjunction with another tool, such as an application blank or an interview, or they may be used to reflect the composite findings gathered from several sources. A place on the application blank labeled "not to be filled in by applicant" may be used to evaluate or score the responses on the form.

The use of an *interview* rating sheet is a common practice. The rating sheet may be part of the patterned interview form or a separate one to be filled out after the interview is finished.

A rating sheet that is a result of composite information gathered from many tools and sources is particularly valuable in summing up what is known about an applicant. Any rating sheet has the advantage of furnishing a written record of someone's impression of the prospective employee. These records may be kept permanently and referred to later in connection with training, supervision, discipline, or promotion. It is a method of comparing applicants and of comparing opinions of the people who do the rating.

COMING TO A CONCLUSION ABOUT AN APPLICANT

When all other steps have been completed in the selection process, one thing remains to be done. The company must make a decision on whether or not to hire each applicant. This involves a review of everything known about the prospect. What detailed impressions has he made? What are his qualifications from the past, and what is his potential? What does he want, and what can the firm offer him? The last point is far broader than just the monetary aspects of his desires in relation to the firm's offer. Involved are all his hopes, dreams, and ambitions, as matched against the present and future opportunities, challenges, and other types of rewards offered by the job and the company.

If the decision is to hire the person, the next step is to make a formal offer. The conditions and details of the offer probably have been spelled out earlier. There should be no surprises in the formal offer. It is possible that some details of the job will not be known until after the induction training period. For example, the recruit may be told when hired that on completion of his training he will be assigned to one of three given branches, and the final decision on the assignment can be delayed. In all cases, the terms of the offer should be set down in writing for the protection of both the recruit and the firm. Many companies have contracts that must be signed by all new sales people. These documents spell out in considerable detail all the facts pertaining to territories, compensation, expenses, and other important information.

QUESTIONS AND PROBLEMS

1. One sales executive claims he "knows a good man when he sees one," and therefore he does not like to be bothered by so-called scientific selection processes. What can you offer to refute this claim? Would your answer be any different if you knew that the sales manager who made the statement had a low rate of turnover in his sales force and was running a highly profitable operation?

2. In the "Application for Sales Position" form that an Aptitude Testing firm has prepared, the following questions are asked. In each case, what do you think the questions are designed to find out?
    a. What is the most monotonous task you ever did?
    b. In people you like, what do you like about them?
    c. What kind of a job do you think your spouse would like to see you have?
    d. What has been your outstanding disappointment in life?
    e. What is your spouse's (or family's) criticism of you?
    f. What type of selling do you think gives sales people the greatest satisfaction—frequent small successes, or many turndowns followed by one big success?

3. Many firms request interested applicants to send in a letter of application in their own handwriting. What is the purpose of this request? Is this selection method basically any different from using palmistry or astrology as selection aids? Under what conditions would a firm be wise to employ these tools?

4. How may the limitations of the interview be eliminated, reduced, or counterbalanced?

5. When interviewing an applicant for a sales job, management ordinarily should be vitally interested in complete answers to the following three points:

   a. How badly does the applicant want or need the job?
   b. Can the job furnish him with the success he wants or offer him the opportunity to realize his goals in life?
   c. Will he strive to achieve the level of work his capacity will allow?

   Prepare a series of questions an interviewer might ask with respect to each of these three points.

6. What type of questions should an interviewer ask to determine if an applicant possesses the following traits:

   a. Ability to define a problem.
   b. Ability to analyze logically.
   c. Ability to make a decision.
   d. Dependability.
   e. Self-confidence.
   f. Initiative.
   g. Resourcefulness and imagination.
   h. Perseverence.

7. Soon many of you will be interviewed by companies who recruit graduating students. Some questions an interviewer may ask are listed below. What is each question trying to determine, and how would you answer it?

   a. Why do you want to work for this company?
   b. Why should we hire you?
   c. How much do you hope to be earning in three years?
   d. If you come to work for us, what kind of a job do you expect to have with us in three years?
   e. What do you expect out of this job? Or this firm?

8. Can you eliminate the personal biases and prejudices of interviewers so they will conduct an interview impartially?

9. A series of traits generally considered undesirable in a sales person are listed below. What tools can management use to determine whether an applicant possesses any of these characteristics? If you feel that an interview or application blank can be used in this case, what questions should be asked?

   a. Failed in a business.
   b. Has a history of not staying in one job very long.
   c. Spouse or family is not sold on the job.
   d. Was not able to pass an insurance physical examination.
   e. Has domestic problems.
   f. Has financial problems.
   g. Does not get along well with other people; is the lone-wolf type.

10. The text rated the reference as a not very helpful selection tool. Do you

agree with this appraisal? If so, why do you think it continues to be used by virtually every firm that is hiring sales people or other employees?

11.   Under what conditions would you recommend that a company use a battery of tests as part of its procedures for selecting sales people?

12.   What are some of the problems or dangers in using tests as part of the sales force selection process?

13.   Many sales managers claim that the real factor that determines whether people will be a success in selling is their motivation to work hard. Where is this motivational factor measured in psychological testing? Can it be measured? How should sales managers determine a person's motivation to do a good job?

14.   We generally are cautious about supporting testing as part of the selection process. Assuming that you are a strong advocate of testing for this purpose, what points would you bring forth to counter the authors' caution and to support the use of testing?

Case 6–1
AIR SYSTEMS, INC.
Hiring a new sales engineer

Brock Newman, sales manager for Air Systems, Inc., sank back in the easy chair in a corner of his library to ponder some problems that could not be left behind at the office. The bustle there precluded much contemplation of important issues in favor of "fighting fires." He opened his briefcase and pulled out a folder which contained the records of three men who were being considered to fill an opening in the Chicago branch to replace a sales engineer who had retired.

Air Systems, Inc., designed and installed heating, cooling, and air treatment systems for large commercial buildings. The average sale was $200,000, with some projects running as high as $10 million. Sales of $1 million to $3 million were not unusual. Each system required custom design and close work with the mechanical contractor on the job and the architect. The owner of the building often played a key role in the buying decision because of the importance of the air systems to the occupants' satisfaction. If the owner planned on selling the building in the near future, then the project was not considered to be a good prospect for Air Systems equipment, which was premium priced, quality goods.

After screening more than 30 people for the job and advertising the opening in the proper trade journals, the search had narrowed down to three outstanding recruits. Now a decision had to be made about which one to hire. Newman reviewed the information that had been gathered on each man.

Tim Kennedy. Age 36, married, graduated from an air conditioning trade school. He had a good credit report, and references gave strong recommendations. Born and raised in the Chicago area, Kennedy had started working for a large air conditioning contractor 15 years previously as an installer. He had been promoted to foreman but asked for an assignment in sales after two years as project foreman. Because of his personality and the employer's need for sales people, Kennedy was given some selling assignments, which he carried out with great success. For the past five years he had been the firm's leading salesman. People to whom he sold spoke highly of him. While he was happy with his job, his earnings were limited by the size of the projects the company sold. His earnings could double with Air Systems, as the company's average sales engineer earned $48,000 in 1977. Throughout the years Kennedy had continually studied heating and cooling engineering. Air Systems engineers approved of his technical competence for the job.

All personal interviews were favorable. Kennedy was a most personable, impressive individual. The general consensus of all interviewers was that Tim would do a good job of selling but that he lacked the background and polish for advancement into management. One interviewer had written a comment on the bottom of the rating sheet that the company should hire Kennedy, since the bowling team needed his 205 average.

Bob Kane. Age 41, married, three children, graduate engineer from Drexel Institute. All field investigations were positive. He was born in Trenton, N.J., educated in Philadelphia, and had lived in Chicago since graduation from college. Kane was currently employed as a design engineer for one of Air System's major suppliers of equipment. He had developed numerous technical advances in air treatment equipment and was highly regarded in the industry as one who could develop unusual solutions to particularly difficult problems. His work had exposed him to considerable customer contact throughout the years. The people who worked with him reported that he was easy to work with and most cooperative.

The company's interviews all gave Kane strong hire recommendations. They commented on his brilliance, knowledge of the industry, and maturity. One rater said, "I think this man has great potential. He should be able to immediately capture the confidence of the people to whom we sell." Newman noted that Kane's hobby was model railroading. He mused, "That's a new one. I don't think I've ever known a salesman who was a model railroader."

Howard Rowe. Age 50, married, children grown, born and raised in Chicago. After graduating from Northwestern in architectural engineering, Rowe had worked for five years for one of the city's most prestigious architectural firms, with good results. He left to form his own architectual practice, which specialized in commercial buildings. All reports indicated that the practice flourished, and Rowe prospered. He had sold his practice and retired two years previously. He had applied for a job with Air Systems because, "I found out I couldn't retire. I loved what I was doing. I like building things and miss it dreadfully. I want to get back into the game, but I don't want any more of my own business. It's too much hassle and worry. I want out in the field where the action is."

Rowe had provided outstanding references from the city's leading architects and mechanical engineers. It was clear that he was well known and well respected in the Chicago construction industry. He also had entree into the Chicago and North Shore social circles from his numerous club memberships in various prestigious organizations.

The interviewers were all most impressed with Rowe. The general tenor of their comments was that he was an industry statesman who was well connected with all the right people. They felt he could do the company a lot of good in places where the existing sales force was having trouble even getting to see the right people.

Newman shook his head. He wondered if he could hire all three of the men, but he knew that it would not be possible. The budget allowed only one of them to be hired. He had talked with all three of the individuals and after each interview was convinced that the person with whom he had just talked was the person to hire. He took out a pad of paper and began listing for each person the advantages and the risks involved if that man were hired.

Questions

1. Make such a list for each of the three recruits.
2. Whom would you hire?

Case 6–2
ACME LINEN COMPANY
Selecting a sales representative

Last year both sales and profits declined in the Western Division of the Acme Linen Company, and about three months ago Mr. A. K. Gambrell, the sales manager of that division, resigned because of failing health. Mr. Oswald Briggs, who replaced Gambrell, was given the responsibility for rebuilding and expanding the sales of the Western Division. Briggs's most immediate problem was to hire a sales representative for the Arizona–New Mexico territory. About a year ago Mr. Ed Carney, the salesman who had covered that territory for Acme and who had been doing an excellent job, left the company to accept a job with a major competitor. Carney also persuaded several good Acme customers to transfer their business to his new employer.

Mr. Frank Stiles, who replaced Carney, had not performed satisfactorily. His sales volume for the year was $100,000, as compared to Carney's annual average volume of $500,000. Soon after taking over as divisional sales manager, Briggs recognized he had to do something about Stiles. Briggs realized that Stiles was relatively new on the job and that Carney had taken many of Acme's best accounts in that territory. However, after considering the relative merits of the options open to him, Briggs decided to discharge Stiles and had done so two months ago. Since then, of course, the territory had been virtually uncovered. In the meantime Briggs was aggressively recruiting and had located four good prospects. Now he had to decide which one to hire.

Acme Linen Company was an institutional wholesaler of textile products such as sheets, pillowcases, towels, washcloths, bath mats, blankets, bedspreads, pillows, shower curtains, and draperies. The company sold to institutions such as hotels, motels, hospitals, nursing homes, and universities. The products were packaged in large lots (e.g., ten *dozen* sheets in one package), and the products were more durable than similar items sold to consumers in retail stores.

There was no major difference between the products sold by the various institutional wholesalers. They all bought similar products from the same mills. Typically, Acme would buy 3,000 dozen sheets from a mill and leave them stored at the mill. When an order would come in, Acme would then have the mill put the Acme label on the product and ship it directly to the customer. Sometimes Acme would buy the entire stock of a product being closed out by a mill. Then when the Acme label was placed on this product, customers could not easily make price comparisons with competitive goods. This practice proved to be a major competitive advantage for Acme salesmen.

Last year (1977), Acme's Western Division sales were $2.7 million and profits were $150,000. This was down from 1976 sales of $3 million and profits of $300,000. In contrast, total company sales were $12 million in 1977 and $10.5 million in 1976. Profits were $1,200,000 in 1977 and $1,050,000 in 1976.

Briggs estimated that Acme, along with three other institutional wholesalers, accounted for about 50 percent of institutional sales. Two

of these three competitors had been founded by former Acme salesmen who took some Acme customers with them. Retailers and large
manufacturers accounted for about 30 percent, and American Hospital
Supply and Will-Ross made up the rest of the market. One interesting
aspect of the competitive situation was the fact that several of Acme's
manufacturer-suppliers (e.g., Fieldcrest, Cannon, Burlington, Jones
and Bates, and Pearl Pillow Co.) competed with Acme by selling directly to institutional users.

Acme planned to expand its Western Division's sales. The company
currently had no coverage in California, Oregon, or Washington. Management also expected that some of its major customer groups, such as
colleges, hospitals, and the travel industry, would expand faster than
the average growth rate for American industry.

In the course of recruiting a new sales person for the Arizona–New
Mexico territory, Briggs developed a job description, the main points
of which were as follows:

1. The general duties of the sales person were to increase sales
over a long-range period in the area, in a profitable manner. The rep
would answer directly to the divisional sales manager. The territory
included all of Arizona and New Mexico, and in Texas, a 30-mile
radius around El Paso.

2. The sales person was to coordinate with the sales manager all
bid work to be done in the territory; all delivery schedules; all credit
problems or approval; all convention scheduling; all sales samples
needed; and all office supplies needed.

3. The sales person would communicate and coordinate with the
treasurer of Acme Linen Co. any matters concerning collection of
past-due accounts, all expense vouchers, and unusual expenses incurred in his territory. And, the treasurer was to receive a copy of the
sales reports and memos concerning questions or problems with sales
commissions received.

4. The sales person was to communicate to the Acme buyer all
trends in the territory, new products introduced by the competition,
and any long-range contracts negotiated with customers.

5. The sales person also had to communicate with the sales manager concerning any secretarial work needed in order to keep paper
work at a minimum. And, the sales person was to communicate to
Acme's president any other problems.

6. It was expected that the sales person would telephone the divisional main office at least once a week to receive any home-office
messages.

7. The sales person's main responsibility was to increase sales in a
profitable manner. His sales quota was to be set by the sales manager.

He was to be responsible for arranging delivery schedules for his customers; allowing for warehousing, transportation, and timing of delivery. He was responsible for scheduling his own itinerary and maintaining the company car, keeping track of travel and entertainment expenses, and reporting them weekly to the office manager. It was his duty to furnish samples and gifts to his customers. Samples were to be carried in his car.

8.   Complaints were to be handled by the sales person in such a way as to develop long-range goodwill for the company. His stock book was to be kept up to date, and copies of all orders were to be sent to the sales manager. The sales person was required to have a sales conference with the vice president in charge of the Western Division every three months. And, he was to have a personal conference in Cleveland (home office) once a year. The sales person was required to attend all company sales or training conferences.

9.   The sales person would be paid a commission of 10 percent of the gross margin earned on each sale. A beginning sales person was placed on a guaranteed drawing account during his first year with the company. The company provided a new car every two years and an expense account.

10.   The sales person could take up to four weeks' vacation, but there were no paid vacations. The company provided a group health insurance and life insurance plan. The company provided a profit-sharing plan and paid in 5 percent of the sales person's net compensation. The sales person could match that amount if he wished. Finally, a sales person could buy products at company cost.

Acme's compensation plan and pricing policy were somewhat different from other companies in the field. Acme furnished each sales rep with a price book which stated the costs of all products from the various suppliers. This price book also stated suggested list prices. Prices then were set by the sales rep and were based on what the market would bear. For example, if in order to establish a new account, a sales rep had to sell at cost (make no gross margin and thus no commission), then he could do this. Or, if he could sell at a 50–60 percent gross margin, this too was acceptable. The average gross margin was about 30 percent. Because a sales person's commission was based on his actual gross margin and not the margin derived from the list prices, management hoped that the sales person's self-interest would stimulate him to sell at highly profitable prices. (This pricing policy had some interesting implications in relation to the Robinson-Patman Act.) A fair sales person usually produced about $300,000 a year in sales volume. Top sales people reached $500,000–$800,000 in volume. Sales people's earnings ranged from $7,000 to $35,000 last year.

Following is a summary of the qualifications of each of the four prospects whom Briggs considered to be the best of the applicants he had screened.

1. *Joseph Schurz.*   He is married, has one child, and is in his early forties. He is a high school graduate, lives in Phoenix, Arizona, and has been a Will-Ross Company salesman for 10 years. He has an excellent record in sales—annual volume is $1 million, including $200,000 in textiles. He knows the textile business and currently sells in a territory which includes New Mexico, Phoenix, and San Diego, California. He would require a minimum income of $20,000 during his first year with Acme. Currently he is earning $26,000 a year. Schurz currently sells out of a catalog, i.e., each item has one price only. He has stated that if he takes the job, he would expect to be earning $50,000 by the end of the fifth year. He said he wanted the position because it was a challenge. And, he could see that institutional wholesalers were gaining a greater share of the market each year.

2. *Conrad Hanson.*   He is in his early thirties, married, with three children. He has worked for a family-owned laundry in Phoenix for the past three years. The laundry specializes in institutional service. He has been successful in selling for the laundry, earning $18,000 last year. He has a good knowledge of bedding, but not of the other items sold by Acme. He would require $18,000 for at least the first year. He left the laundry because he was not a family member, and this factor limited his chances for a management or ownership position. He seemed very enthusiastic about the Acme job and said that it offered him opportunities for growth.

3. *Anne Waller.*   She is in her early thirties, married, with no children. She had one year of college. She is currently finishing her third year as a sales rep in the Denver, Colorado, area for the Powell Linen Company, a major competitor of Acme. Her annual volume is $300,000 and she has an excellent knowledge of the products sold by Acme Company. She would require an income of $12,000 a year for the first two years with Acme. Waller said she was not happy in her position with the Powell Company because that firm was poorly managed. Also, Powell's lack of a warehouse in the Denver area led to problems with some of Waller's customers and contributed to her relatively low sales volume. (The Denver area Acme salesman had an annual volume of $700,000.)

4. *Edward Torres.*   He is a recent college graduate in business from the University of Colorado, with an excellent college record. He is a native of Colorado and has recently been married. He has a good record of part-time and summer selling on the retail level. He stated that he had liked what selling he had done. He had very little knowledge of selling industrial textiles. He was very outgoing and energetic

and seemed to want the job badly. He would require an income of $8,500 for the first year.

In the process of deciding which person to hire, Briggs realized there were additional factors he should consider. He was concerned with the ethical and business implications if he hired a sales person away from a large, powerful competitor such as Powell Company. In the past when Acme lost key salesmen who started their own competitive firms, Acme's management contacted manufacturer-suppliers and got some of them to agree not to sell to those new firms. That arrangement lasted for about a year. Currently, however, all the major wholesalers were on good terms, and Briggs wondered if he would awaken old hostilities if he were to hire a Powell Company saleswoman.

It took a long time to build up a territory. Two factors—(a) Carney's leaving and taking some good customers with him, and (b) the absence of an Acme sales rep in the Arizona–New Mexico territory since Stiles was fired—meant that a new sales rep would have to start from scratch, almost as if a new territory were being opened.

Also, the job had very little status. It was difficult, day-to-day, selling of industrial products that were far from glamorous. Most of the best sales people had no college background. Some had less than high school educations. The industry relied on high earnings and titles to compensate the reps for their low status positions.

However, Briggs believed the situation was changing. More buyers for hospitals and larger institutions had college backgrounds. He believed that in the future the sales people would have to be more sophisticated and better educated. A sales rep who had an obvious lack of education or sophistication might be a bad choice for the future.

If a sales person had to be relocated, it would be costly. There was also the possibility that a person from the Rocky Mountain area would not adjust to the warmer Southwest. In addition, there was no guarantee that a person who was not doing well in one area would become successful if moved to a new environment.

If a rep who did not have a good knowledge of the business were hired, he would have to be trained. Briggs estimated that training costs, in addition to salary, for a new sales rep would amount to about $4,000.

Question

1. Whom should Mr. Briggs hire as a sales representative in the Arizona–New Mexico territory?

7

Assimilating new sales people into the organization

A bad beginning makes a bad ending.
EURIPIDES

The selection efforts made in the costly process of hiring people, no matter how excellently executed, can be nullified completely if the new recruit is not properly integrated into the organization. This chapter covers the introduction of the new person into the work group. Recognizing that people may be basically motivated more by social than by economic forces, we will show how this orientation affects their reactions to their initial relationships with superiors and fellow workers.

INITIAL INDOCTRINATION

Most firms start indoctrinating the recruit the minute initial contact is made. Booklets describe the operations of the company and tell what a distinctive organization it is. These publications are part of the recruiting process described in Chapter 5. Further introductory work is done in the selection interviews (Chapter 6). The sales executive describes many aspects of the company's operations and answers questions the recruit may pose. If these activities are properly performed, trainees will not come into the organization without some information about it.

Some firms prepare detailed booklets about the company's history, the executives, the product line, and the various financial, health, and recreational programs available through the company. If such a publication is presented to the recruit upon hiring, there is an opportunity to absorb its contents before reporting for work. Immediately on reporting for work, the trainee should be allowed to ask questions concerning the job or the company.

The assimilation of a new sales rep who is thrust into a sales territory right from the start with no home-office training is especially difficult. Such situations offer little opportunity for the new person to become integrated with the work group. In such situations, socalled "lone wolves" are born. While many sales managers complain that their sales people are not "team players," little has been done to make them part of a team.

After an initial descriptive introduction to the business, the home-office trainee usually begins a program of familiarization with the actual operations of the firm. This is the initial stage of training, which is discussed in Chapter 8.

DETAILS OF THE JOB

In the employee introduction program, the details of the job, the company, and compensation are "the little things that count."

Parking

All employees are concerned with the accommodations for their autos. Many firms find it advisable to supervise the distribution of such status symbols closely, in order to avoid seeming inequities. Parking is of special interest to sales people who must come and go from the office or plant several times a day.

If sales people are unable to find convenient parking when on calls, considerable selling time may be lost. In metropolitan areas where downtown parking space is scarce, the sales manager may investigate the possibility of providing the sales force with commercial licenses which allow parking in loading zones.

Eating

If the company maintains dining facilities, their use must be fully explained to the new employee. Use of the executive dining room for entertaining customers should be explained. Some firms have arrangements with outside restaurants to accommodate the sales force and their customers, with the bill forwarded directly to the firm. Such arrangements also should be explained.

Office practices

Office facilities and supplies for the new rep should be checked to see that he or she has everything needed and knows where to get supplies.

Some office practices and policies do not have official sanction but nevertheless have considerable force. Most groups have informal policies on such things as gift funds, betting, parties, and other activities incidental to the job. The new employee should be briefed on these by a fellow worker. If the manager did this, it might seem to give official sanction to these activities. When the boss explains the football pool, for example, it is as if the employee is being told to participate in it.

The paycheck

The pocketbook is a quick way to a good attitude. Misunderstandings concerning the paycheck can make anyone suspicious. It is most discouraging for a sales trainee who knows he is earning $1,200 per month to receive a check for $870. He realizes that some income tax and social security tax must come out of the $1,200, but he thinks, "There must be some error; taxes wouldn't be that much." The trainee should be told when and how he will be paid, and all deductions should be itemized so that he will know exactly what to expect.

If a drawing account is provided, it is particularly important to explain it in detail. Some of the pertinent problems are:

- What happens if the rep gets too far in debt?
- What happens if the person leaves the company and still owes on the drawing account?
- Just how are commissions used to offset the advanced money?

The expense account

Many misunderstandings arise over expense accounts. The new sales rep must be told precisely what can and cannot be put on the expense sheet and in what manner the expense money will be paid—whether it can be drawn prior to incurring the expenses or will be paid after filing the report.

If certain tacit limitations are placed on various items, these should be made clear. It is far better for the manager to tell the new person about any under-the-table arrangements than to have the other sales people do it. For instance, one organization permits its employees to spend any amount necessary on entertainment. The total is left to the discretion of the sales person. However, if a considerable sum is spent on any one night, they want it distributed over several nights so as not to arouse suspicion in the accounting office. The sales manager unofficially tells the sales force of these practices.

The manager also tells new employees how to recover money spent on marginal selling expenses. These are expenses that do not clearly fall in allowable categories, but nevertheless would not have been incurred had the person not been working for the firm.

MEETING FELLOW WORKERS

The new employee and present employees are both uncertain of the new person's exact status in the organization. This must be made clear to all, to avoid misunderstandings. Some firms send an information sheet on each new employee to all interested personnel which tells what he or she will be doing with the company.

The new rep needs to know exactly from whom he takes orders. The entire organizational plan should be explained so he knows (a) his relationship to others, (b) who else reports to his immediate boss, (c) and who are the boss's superiors in the department and the company. Other employees need to know how the new employee fits into the organization. Secretaries must be informed of their relationship to him. Those who report to the same boss must be made acquainted with their workmate, and other employees also should be informed about the position he occupies.

Introductions are a two-way street—the new sales person is eager to meet fellow employees, and they want to meet him or her. However, a short formal introduction does not fill the need. The introductory ceremony should be so arranged that the parties involved have enough time to do more than just say hello. A short chat with each person is a great aid. It allows individuals to get more than an instantaneous impression of one another, and it helps them to remember one another's names. Present employees should be given background information on the new sales person, so that they will be able to converse on some common ground. The new rep should be briefed on the people to be met—who they are, what they do, and what their interests are.

The administrator must keep in mind that the manner in which the group treats the new worker will reflect management's treatment. If the sales manager does not show him respect and consideration, probably the other employees will not do so either. In a sense, the manager's attitude establishes the individual's informal status in the group.

Consider the case of a new sales recruit who is young and just out of school. Such a sales person would not be accomplished but would require considerable training and experience. The sales manager's most idle remark, such as, "Oh, he will be okay in time, but right now he is just a green kid," can set the key for the rep's treatment by other employees: "He's just a green kid, that's what the boss said and he should know." The individual is pegged as incompetent, and from then on may have a difficult time with the group. For some, this person will never live down that initial unflattering stereotype.

If the manager should mention that a new sales rep is a top-notch prospect with a great potential, he will be looked on in a different light. Of course, such compliments must be handled judiciously so that other employees do not become jealous.

The initial introduction of the person to the work group is particularly critical in the hiring of women sales representatives. The reception, status, and initial relationships of the sales woman will depend to a large extent upon how management regards her, and how the work group perceives management as regarding her. If she has been hired as a token observance of equal rights rulings, that attitude will probably be communicated to the other members of the work group. This would be a poor basis for good working relationships.

NEED FOR EFFECTIVE COMMUNICATION

For some years now, the importance of effective communication has been stressed in management theory. Effective communication is especially relevant when new reps join a sales force.

Vertical channels of communication

The first weeks on the job are difficult for all. The new recruit has innumerable questions, uncertainties, and insecurities. The manager must do extra work to get the recruit started. Fellow employees may have to make some allowances for the new employee's lack of experience. These added tasks are necessary if the recruit is to be made part of the work group.

The first few days are particularly trying, since the new person has not had time to develop communications with other members of the organization and must look to the manager for answers. The manager should give as much time as possible to getting the trainee started in the right direction. A good technique is to have a regular conference with the new employee at the beginning of each day, for a time, to answer questions and present new material.

New sales reps appreciate this attention. It makes them feel wanted and valued by the company—something most individuals earnestly seek. One of the quickest ways to affect a person's attitude adversely is to ignore him. New reps may interpret this lack of attention as meaning that the sales manager does not care about them, whereas the truth probably is that the executive is just preoccupied with operational problems. It comes as quite a blow to new workers to encounter such apparent disinterest, since while they were being interviewed they were given so much attention. Then suddenly the honeymoon is over. They now think it was just sales talk, and they should have known better than to be taken in by it. The wise sales manager will try to prolong the honeymoon for awhile until the new people can take their place in the organization.

A classic example of the impact of the first few days on a new employee is this account by a college graduate who went to work for a large manufacturer of industrial products:

> On my first day at work I knew nobody except my boss and his assistant. I was given a little glass-enclosed office along the same line as some other such offices. People were working all over the place but I didn't know who they were or what they were doing. I had been introduced to my boss's secretary and was told she would take care of me. I wasn't quite sure what he meant by that and I discovered that she didn't either, for she was of no assistance. I could not get a letter typed by her. Later I made friends with another secretary who was new on the job and in the same position I was. She typed all my stuff and really looked after me. She would come in and dust off my desk and generally be my secretary. I am certain that she was supposed to be doing something else, but no one seemed to know what was going on and I had no objection to having a secretary, so that was that. I guess we had been shoved together because of the complete indifference of everybody to our plight.
>
> I tried to look busy and kept reading all sorts of reports that were stacked around, but I had been given little direction. The boss had said upon my reporting for work, "Here is a marketing consultant's report on a new product we are thinking of making. Read it and give me your impressions." That was the last I saw of him for three weeks, since he had to go out of town. I completed the report in two days. I really went over it and did some outside investigation on my own. But there was a limit to what I could do with it. So I quickly ran out of work to do.
>
> Then I hit upon doing library research on the subject and started going down to the city library. It was a good place to loaf, and I enjoyed getting into a lot of books which I had never realized existed. It was quite an education but it came to and end in time, and still I had no work to do or anyone to tell me to do something.
>
> I started to go to the show in the afternoon, getting back just in time to

punch out on the clock. Can you imagine that; all of us had to punch in and out on a time clock. It was ridiculous, since it accomplished nothing. I felt rather guilty about going to the show in the afternoons, but it was better than sitting around that office and having everyone look at you and wondering what you were supposed to be doing.

The secretary of my boss's boss was an old hen who thought she ran the place. She really gave me a bad time when she saw me goofing off. Boy, those icy stares of hers were enough to freeze the devil himself. I tried to get to see the top boss about my plight, but she would not let me near him. He was always in a conference or out of town or something like that. I knew that they were lies because I had seen him cutting it up a bit on several occasions in there, but what could I do? The old battleaxe controlled the door to his office, and we didn't meet anywhere. I had to eat in the cafeteria while he was in the big shot's dining room. We couldn't even use the same rest rooms. Boy, was he ever guarded!

Well, to make a long story short, it did not take me long to decide that I would quit at the end of summer and go back to graduate school. I made up my mind in late June and told them the first of August that I thought I needed more schooling. They gave me an exit interview and the personnel man asked me how I liked the company and all that stuff. I kept my tongue and told him that it was fine and that I had learned a lot, but that I felt incompetent and wanted to know more about marketing since I had majored in another subject in school. He said that he was sorry to see me go and that he thought I had a good future with the firm and all that bunk. Even my boss never tumbled to the real reason why I quit. It never dawned on him that he had not said over one hundred words to me during the whole three months I was under him. To top it off, I had not moved to town yet but was commuting 100 miles a day to work and they did not even know it. The boss was surprised when I told him the commuting problem was getting me down. Well, there were a lot more little things, but that is the basic story of what actually happened to me.

This actual case history is indicative of what happens when the sales manager is not aware of the needs of a new representative. If the new sales rep is not closely supervised and trained during the first few weeks on the job, he may become discouraged and quit. Although it might seem that new employees would enjoy "working" without supervision, such is not the case. They are eager to learn the profession and get into the field, so they can find a place in the organization.

Horizontal channels of communication

It is a serious mistake for the sales manager to force trainees to rely on the grapevine to find out what is going on in the organization and what is expected of them. However, they have no alternative if they are not provided with proper communication channels. Instead of being able to use vertical communication channels, they are forced to use horizontal ones. That is, they seek information from other personnel on their own level in the organization. In the example of the college graduate who went to work for the manufacturer, there was a lack of contact between subordinates and superiors. It had gone so far that the boss had surrounded himself with barriers to keep his subordinates away from him.

When new people are forced to go to unofficial sources for instruction, not only does the executive run the risk that wrong or undesirable information will be given to them, but their allegiance can become divided. The informant in effect assumes some managerial functions, and the recruit comes to rely on this source of information. For instance, in the example cited above, the secretary came to the new employee for work instructions; in fact, he became her manager. Her allegiance was transferred in part to her source of guidance.

The problem is further complicated because frequently those employees who actively solicit listeners for their information may not be the ones with whom it is wise for the recruit to become associated. Often, it is the malcontents, the office politicians, and the downright incompetents who are excessively interested in that type of activity. Information should come from management; moreover, it should come promptly and completely.

MEETING SOCIAL AND PSYCHOLOGICAL NEEDS

An individual's assimilation into the organization involves considerably more than just getting started on the job. He or she should be socially integrated into the new environment. The administrator who forgets that people are essentially social animals is destined for some rather disappointing results. For many people, their social and psychological needs overrule their economic requirements. There are innumerable instances of employees who could considerably better themselves by changing positions or moving to another location. However, they are content to remain where they are, because they are happily integrated into the social structure around them. Individuals like to be among friends and familiar faces. It makes them feel as though they belong to something, and they feel more secure.

However, people often must pull up their roots and leave their home and friends. They are thrust into a strange city with a tired spouse, upset children, and a home in transition. It is a wonder that they can work with any degree of efficiency under such conditions. For this reason, many managers have a policy of hiring only local people for a territory. They do not want to force employees to move from their environment, feeling that people are far more effictive if left among their friends and in their areas of acquaintance. However, this policy may be difficult to maintain. In many instances a firm may be forced to hire someone of a lower caliber than desired just to satisfy the location requirement.

The sales manager is in a position to cushion the shock of social uprooting. Some social activities and contacts should be provided in a new location. This means more than just inviting people to a party. Most college administrators, for example, are aware of this problem for new faculty members and have organized newcomers' clubs. The new faculty family is considered a newcomer for two years before it is expected to have formed its own social contacts. Even after the families leave the newcomers' club they tend to stick together and do not really integrate into the major group. Hence, true assimilation of the family into the organization is not accomplished even by this plan. However, it is successful in that some social contacts are provided for a new family.

The manager should take positive steps to see that the family gets into activities in which they are interested. The golfer should be worked into a foursome, and the bridge player invited to join some group. However, this is not always easy to do. The foursomes are already set up, so until some break occurs the new family may be left out, and it is not always possible to create a new foursome.

A vice president of marketing for a sizable consumer goods concern was elated when he persuaded a nationally prominent market research expert to join his staff. Two years later the boss was hurt and bewildered when the man resigned to go with a competitor. "They bought him from us," was his rationalization. The market researcher's version, however, was as follows:

> He was the weirdest boss I've ever had. When he hired me you'd have thought we were really going to do some great things together. Then every time I tried to get approval for some project, he'd throw cold water on it. I had no social and precious little professional contact with the man during my two years with him. We had him and his wife over twice for some parties, but you know, I don't even know where he lives or what his home phone number is. I can't work for a guy like that. I need good, close relationships with my boss to do my job as I want to do it.

The researcher never really felt that he was a part of the team.

LIVING ACCOMMODATIONS

A sales representative whose home life is in a state of confusion or who is unhappy about living in accommodations cannot perform the job well. For that reason, sales executives in recent years have formalized company policies on aiding new employees in moving and getting established in a home.

Employee mobility has caused many businesses to provide allowances to alleviate some of the inconveniences of moving. Most have adopted plans for defraying the moving expenses of personnel, such as paying for a first-class carrier which furnishes all services. However, many firms do not compensate employees for the incidental expenses of moving that are inescapable. It is usually necessary to buy new drapes, rugs, furniture, and other items to fit a new house, and many houses require a considerable investment for renovation. Families in the military service insist that it costs them a full $1,000 over and above the amount the government pays each time they move. Thus moving is not a minor matter, either economically or psychologically.

Most large companies usually pay for the following moving expenses when they transfer employees:

- Packing and moving of all household furnishings and equipment, with insurance to cover any damage.
- Meals, lodgings, and first-class transportation by land or air for the entire family and for family pets.
- Broker's commissions and legal fees for buying or selling homes.
- Entire expense of putting up the employee and family in a hotel for several weeks after arrival, and thereafter the difference between charges for hotel rooms and normal rental costs if other living space has not been found.
- Installation of appliances in the new home and allowances toward refitting draperies, carpeting, and blinds.
- A reasonable number of personal trips between the new and old location when the employee is separated from the family for a long time.
- A trip for the spouse to visit the new location to look for a new house, and expenses while house hunting.

Many people arrive on the job financially embarrassed and in need of money on which to live. They greatly appreciate receiving their expenses as promptly as possible. Some firms find that they must advance funds for support until payday. Some college graduates have not taken the jobs they wanted because they lacked funds to get to the location. They had to accept positions with locally situated firms. It is easy for the executive to forget that a great number of families have no surplus funds. A proud person in this position—and there are quite a few of them—will not tell a prospective employer the real reason why a job offer is rejected.

Money is not the only factor involved in making a move; time also is important. A manufacturer of heavy equipment for oil field, mining, and construction work has a policy for employee moves that seems to work well. First, all moving expenses are paid at the first-class tariff rate *in advance,* and they are paid on a generous weight. Many of the college graduates whose first jobs are with this concern move themselves in a trailer and keep the cash realized. Next, all expenses are paid for the family to live in a hotel or motel while looking for an apartment or house. No limit is set, but most people spend about two weeks under such an arrangement.

The purpose of this policy, from the company's point of view, is to allow new employees enough time to find suitable living accommodations. They do not want to force the family to move into anything that happens to be vacant. Such vacancies are usually marginal properties; that is why they are not occupied. It takes time to find what is wanted. By providing enough time the company makes sure the employee will be satisfied and will not have to make a second move soon. People who have enjoyed the benefits of this policy say that it allows them to stay solvent. They are not forced to pay rent in advance of receiving any salary, and company support of the family keeps them from going into debt right at the start. Little money has to be spent before receiving the first paycheck.

A new trainee may need some assistance in locating a home, although this must be handled with tact and offered on a strictly voluntary basis. The sales manager is in a position to know the real estate market in the city considerably better than the newcomer. If new employees make a serious mistake in their purchase of a home, it can considerably injure their morale and effectiveness, in addition to damaging their financial status.

Experience indicates that people become better integrated into the community if they purchase a home rather than renting one. The renter always considers the home temporary, whereas the homeowner feels established and takes a more active part in civic activities. Because of its social responsibilities to its employees and the community, the company should do all in its power to encourage homeownership. Some firms loan their employees down payments for homes and otherwise assist them financially. Many have insuring devices by which they encourage their mobile employees to buy homes. They will guarantee the worker against loss on his house if he is forced to sell because of a move dictated by the company. With that guarantee, most employees do not hesitate about buying a house.

QUESTIONS AND PROBLEMS

1. The statement was made that a manager may find it advisable to supervise distribution of status symbols. What are some of these status symbols, and why should the manager be concerned with them?

2. In the story related by a college graduate about his first few days at work,

one sales manager commented that the man was just a spoiled brat who simply was not capable of doing an honest day's work, and that the firm was fortunate in getting rid of him. He said that, after all, the sales manager cannot wetnurse each employee. A person must be able to come into a job and work without all the coddling sometimes recommended. Does this chapter distort the actual need for introductory activities out of proportion to the real problem in industry? Why not adopt a sink-or-swim philosophy on the matter? If a person is really good, why is all of this attention needed?

3. What are some of the actions a sales manager can take to provide new employees with social contacts and activities?

4. Why should sales managers encourage their people to own *nice* homes?

5. Should the sales manager attempt to warn the trainee about listening to or being influenced by certain other people in the organization for whom the manager has particularly low regard?

6. With the introduction of more women to sales positions, what special problems might arise in assimilating them into an all-male sales force?

7. To what extent can members of the peer group facilitate a trainee's assimilation into the work group? How could management encourage such efforts?

8. One manager maintained, "You can always spot the malcontents in our organization—just watch to see who runs to befriend the new person." Evaluate that statement. If it is true, of what significance is it to the person?

9. What difference does the size of the organization make in the assimilation of the individual into the work group?

10. How long should it take for a new person to become well integrated into the work situation?

Case 7-1
TERRY AND THE BOSS
Personal adjustment to the job

Terry Tanner, a promising college graduate who had gone to work for the Decormate Corporation in Los Angeles as a sales trainee a year previously, had been mulling over for some time the thought of leaving his job to return to his home town. As he sat in his boss's outer office awaiting a final interview with him, he recalled the history of his year in the big city.

He and his wife had arrived bright-eyed and eager for an exciting career, fresh from the small-town life which they had found to be so boring, or so they had thought at the time. The company had offered him an attractive proposition and he was eager to get at the world. Now, one year later, he felt beaten. Things had not gone as they had expected.

They were used to a social life with several rather close friends with whom they had grown up. They had not been able to make such friends in Los Angeles. The few acquaintances with whom they had done anything socially did not really appeal to them. It seemed as if all they wanted to do was get drunk, and neither Terry nor his wife cared much for that. Their social life had been confined largely to going alone to movies and football games.

They lived in an apartment in West Los Angeles from which it was only a 20-minute drive to Decormate's home office. Terry's wife had found employment as a receptionist for a local doctor. They both felt that prices were much too high. Their rent for the two-bedroom apartment was $250 a month. They could have rented a much nicer house in their home town for considerably less money.

"Come on in, Terry," the boss said. "I want very much to talk to you. I think you are making a bad mistake leaving us and I intend to do everything I can to talk you out of it."

Terry did not know what to reply to this approach, since he had not expected it. An exit interview was supposed to be a rather routine affair, or so he had been taught in college. Both parties were to say nice things, tell some lies, and part friends.

"What are your plans?" the boss asked, sparing Terry the need to reply to his first remark.

Terry sat down, drew a deep breath, and started talking, "We don't really have any firm plans except to go back home. The big city just isn't for us. We haven't seemed to be able to make the friends we want in L.A."

The boss nodded, indicating that Terry should proceed.

"And things are so expensive around here We just barely keep our heads above water with both of us working. I don't see how we could ever really save some money," Terry said.

"You want to make some real money? Is that it?"

"Yes! I think I am able to do it."

"Is there anything else that bothers you, Terry?"

Terry hesitated for a moment, but then blurted out something he had not planned on divulging, "Well, as a matter of fact, there is. I have not found my life on the job to be as satisfying as I had thought it would be. I have always liked to work closely with other people and form close friendships with my associates. It hasn't happened here. I work largely by myself in the field and hardly know anyone in the company. I don't even know anyone well enough that I feel I should say goodbye to them!"

The boss frowned, but Terry continued, "I am sorry, sir, but you asked me. I don't mean it personally, but only as the way I feel about things on the job. I know that a sales trainee isn't going to work with a lot of other people, but I have been in the field selling almost every day except for the few days I was training."

"Do you like your work?" the boss inquired.

"Definitely, sir. I really enjoy selling furniture to our dealers."

"That's important, Terry."

The boss then said nothing; neither did Terry. Silence controlled the situation for a short time, as if each were waiting for the other to commit his forces to the argument. Finally the boss said in measured tones, "Terry, grow up! You're a big boy now, but you're running home to mamma. Go home and you're a quitter. L.A. has whipped you. You can't compete in the big time so you're going home where the folks will protect you, is that it? If your performance this last year had not proved to me that you have great ability, I would be led to believe you don't have the stuff to be a winner. But we know you have, don't we, Terry?"

Terry was shocked and angered at what he considered to be an unfair attack on his character. He fought back. "A man's got to go where he is happy, and we're not happy here."

" 'We're not' or your wife's not? Which is it, Terry? Let's get it on the table where we can see it. You love going to all the games here in L.A. I know you've said how much action there is in this town. Something to do all the time. You saw the Lakers-Knicks the other night and loved it. It's not you who wants to go home, but your wife, isn't it?"

Terry did not like this flung in his face. There were many aspects of L.A. life that did appeal to him, but he countered, "Perhaps, but the cost of living is still a problem that can't be overcome. I don't see how we can ever really live the way we want to around here."

"Good grief, man! How in the world can you say that? If you can't make it here, you can't make it anywhere. There is more opportunity here than anywhere on earth. Look around you. People are making money, living well!"

Terry recognized that the boomerang had been used on him and he knew it was true that much money was to be made in Los Angeles. Opportunities were abundant.

"And how do you propose to make a living in your home town, go to work for your old man?"

"No, he works for the power company. I was thinking of working for the bank."

"Perhaps you'd better. Goodbye and good luck, Terry. You really have the makings of a great furniture man, but there is nothing I can do to change your wife's mind if she is calling the shots on your career. If she wants you safe and sound in the bank, well . . . that's your affair."

Terry burned. He did not like this talk at all. He fought back, "Perhaps, but we are still greatly disappointed in our relationships within the company. I have never had a single social contact with you, sir. Down home the boss always has several parties for his people each year. It is the thing to do. I just don't feel that I have enjoyed working for you. I want more from my job than just work and pay!"

The boss nodded. "I am sorry that you feel that way. We assume that since this is such a big city, all our people will find their own diversions. This is the place where we make the money that buys all the things we want." The boss paused, then continued, "Let's call off the war. I know you're a good man and want to keep you very much. Go home and really give it some thought. And . . . oh yes, to complicate things for you, let's raise your pay . . . say another $400 a month. Give me your answer at 10 tomorrow morning."

Terry walked slowly out the door. And he thought it would be so easy to quit!

Questions

1. Make an outsider's appraisal of this situation.
2. Where does the fault lie in this matter?

8

Content of sales training programs

Practice is the best of all instructors.
SYRUS

The essential content of sales training programs is salesmanship. It would be difficult to plan and conduct a sales training program without knowing something about how to sell. Instruction in the skills of personal selling is vanishing in higher education, however, so the survey of the field presented in this chapter provides an overview of the art. Extension of your study of selling beyond the material presented here should convince you of the need for a sales manager to be a competent persuader.

ATTITUDES AND PHILOSOPHIES ABOUT SELLING

Before instruction on the techniques of salesmanship is begun, trainees should be properly prepared psychologically. Several factors other than mastery of the persuasion process can have a strong effect on success or failure in selling. The first is proper orientation of the trainees' attitudes and philosophies toward the job and the selling profession. Unless this is accomplished, the trainer is wasting time trying to perfect their sales techniques. They are largely unreceptive because certain myths block their learning. We will state the most prevalent of these myths and comment on why they have been proven false.

> *Myth no. 1.*   Sales people are born—not made.

Probably nothing has so hindered the acceptance of sales training as this erroneous cliché. Even today many people, including some sales managers, still believe that great persuaders are born with sales ability—they cannot be trained. This simply is not true.

One of the first attitudes to instill in sales trainees is the value of sales training. They should accept the idea that, given the appropriate aptitudes and qualifications, by proper training a raw recruit can be developed into an excellent sales person. For trainees who do not accept this proposition, the rest of the training program will be ineffective.

The idea that properly qualified people can be trained to sell is not an easy one to instill. To get the idea across, the trainer can use case histories of successful sales reps who entered the company's training program as anything but "born salesmen." They also can relate the successful experience of well-known firms in such industries or office machines, chemicals, and building materials which have devoted considerable resources to the intensive training of inexperienced recruits with no particular flair for selling.

> *Myth no. 2.*   Sales people must be good talkers.

Nonsense! Good sales people are good *listeners.* They learn that most useful talent is asking the right questions to get the prospect to talk about what the sales rep wants to hear.

The sales person never learns much while talking. The prospect has information the rep needs, and he will have to ask the right questions to learn it. He also must learn to listen to the prospects' answers.

> *Myth no. 3.*   Selling is a matter of knowing the right techniques or tricks.

People have always sought a magic way to solve all their problems instantly, but history has yet to record anyone finding such a wondrous procedure. Neither have sales people discovered any "magic" selling techniques. Granted there are certain methods that seem to work for some people, but sales success clearly does not depend upon them. Successful sales people use a wide variety of selling techniques, and many sales people who try to use the tactics that work for others fail in the process.

Success in selling is not merely a matter of mastering techniques. Rather it is a result of several potent factors, such as work habits, attitudes, products sold, and markets covered.

> *Myth no. 4.*   A good sales rep can sell anything.

Not so! Many successful sales people were failures earlier in their careers when they tried to sell some product that was not suited to their talents. A successful sales career results when the individual is joined with the "right" product made by the "right" company and sold to the "right" people. But this does not mean there is only one right situation for a person. That would pose an impossible problem. Rather, there are a substantial number of sales jobs in which any one sales person can prosper. However, a sales rep who is great at selling widgets for World Wide Widgets should not expect to succeed in selling everything.

> *Myth no. 5.*   A good sales person can sell ice to an eskimo.

A good sales person would never think of trying to sell ice to an Eskimo. Instead, the professional persuader would try to find someone who needed the ice and had the money to buy it.

Selling is not a sport in which one tries to unload unwanted goods on an unwilling buyer who is unable to pay for them. Good selling starts by finding someone who needs the product and can afford it.

THE PURPOSE OF SELLING AND THE PEOPLE WHO DO IT

A good training program should instill in trainees a thorough understanding of their role and importance in our socioeconomic system. People must appreciate the value of their contribution to enhance their sense of well-being. In selling, morale is a key factor in determining success. An understanding of the social and economic purpose of selling should help trainees to counter the critics of selling and the generally poor image of sales people in our society.

Specifically, a training program should acquaint trainees with their role in such activities as:

• Introducing innovation to markets.
• Conveying information to customers.
• Facilitating consumption.
• Serving as a channel of communication between the company and its markets.
• Solving problems for customers.

It also should show how the position can aid the employee's self-development.

Introducing innovation to markets.

Compared with the past or with many other nations, the rate of product innovation in this country today is staggering. The life cycle of products seems to grow shorter. As soon as one new item reaches the market, two newer ones are being developed in laboratories. But innovation is of little social or economic value until it is brought out of the laboratory. The task of introducing these new articles is the function of personal selling and advertising.

How can the accountant know about all the innovations in data processing? How can the electronics engineer keep abreast of the availability of the latest developments in various components? How can a physician keep up with the latest available drugs? The answer to all these questions is the same. Sales reps in these fields bear a large measure of the responsibility for bringing new products and services to the attention of potential buyers. The detailer for the pharmaceutical manufacturer calls on physicians to inform them of new developments in drugs. The busy M.D. depends to a great extent on these visits to keep abreast of drugs as they are developed, and their characteristics and side effects. Computer sales engineers call on accountants and executives to inform them of recent developments in data processing.

Without sales reps the introduction of innovations would be impeded, because people have neither the time nor the inclination to be continually seeking out the newest developments in their fields.

Conveying information

Professional sales representatives are experts in their fields who should know more about their products and the problems they solve than any other person. This product-knowledge function is so important that a large segment of most training programs is devoted to it. The sales rep is a consultant to customers when they have technical problems. If he were not available, the customer would have to hire the same talents elsewhere. For the firm to eliminate sales people might not lower costs but could decrease sales, since the customer might not be able to obtain the necessary technical assistance elsewhere.

Facilitating the consumption process

People want all sorts of goods and services which inertia may keep them from buying. If goods and services are not bought in sufficient volume, production processes slow down and economic activity tends to lag. In effect, consumption creates employment.

Sales efforts stimulate the consumption process by reducing people's inherent reluctance to make purchase decisions. Not only do persuasive activities attempt to overcome such inertia and encourage people to buy what they want, they also make it easier to do so.

Acting as intelligence agent and communication channel

One of the growing problems in operating a complex society such as ours is maintaining communications between producers and their markets. Formerly the tailor, for example, was personally acquainted with his customers, who told him exactly what to make for them. Today, various middlemen have been inserted between the manufacturer and the consumer. Yet, the basic problem of communicating the consumers' desires to the manufacturer still exists.

The essential communication function is now performed largely by the sales force. A manufacturer of men's slacks for the collegiate market was caught napping one year when styles changed slightly. College men were wearing slacks with distinctly tapered legs; he was producing them with a fuller dimension. His salesmen discovered the trend when retailers told them of it. Adjustments in patterns were made immediately in the factory.

Firms without sales reps may not know what is happening in the market. One firm selling supplies to floral wholesalers was being undercut by a competitor who was giving an additional 10 percent free-goods deal under the table to key wholesalers who agreed to handle the line exclusively. Management in the first firm knew that its sales were dropping but did not know why. It was fortunate that a good customer eventually told them of the competitor's practice, and they were able to counter it before losses became too large. However, this delay in meeting competition seriously injured the firm. A good sales rep would have quickly discovered the competitor's practice.

Nothing is gained and much is lost by selling goods but not being paid for them. Some customers are bad credit risks, many are poor business people, and some are swindlers who seek to defraud the seller. An alert sales rep in contact with those potential customers should be able to detect when it is unwise to accept an order. There are prospects to whom it is unwise to sell. The training program should prepare sales people to recognize them.

Helping solve customers' problems

Good sales people know that when they get an order they have just started to work for the customer. They also perform many services for prospects before they get an order. If customers do not get service from a supplier, they will seek other sources of supply.

After selling an electronic computer, for example, the sales engineer must make certain that it is operating properly, that the customer's personnel know how to operate it, and that the programming satisfactorily resolves the customer's problems. One Remington-Rand office machines salesman whose only account is a large bank in New York has spent numerous nights at the bank helping to solve the bank's problems. A sportswear saleswoman called on a small apparel dealer who had a serious overstock of outerwear, which reduced her open-to-buy budget. The saleswoman did not try to sell her line but rather spent hours planning a promotion that would reduce the dealer's overstock. Thereby she created a loyal customer.

There is no shortage of problems to solve. The sales person who seeks a sale has only to look for one and solve it.

Self-development

A good training program reinforces the attitude that a professional sales person can never achieve perfection. Consequently, he or she should continually seek self-improvement.

Being an avid reader, particularly on topics of salesmanship, pays off. It is important to learn everything new in the art of persuasion. It is also important to learn everything possible about new products in the field, new uses for these products, and emerging problems in the industry. Just one new idea from these sources can pay handsome rewards.

It takes time to develop selling talents. And the primary responsibility for this development rests on the sales person. Trainers, teachers, superiors, and peers can help, but the main thrust, the inner drive and determination needed to develop skills must be provided by the individual.

PRODUCT KNOWLEDGE AND APPLICATIONS

In selling, sales people not only must know about the products they sell but also must believe in their merits. A large part of most training programs is devoted to providing knowledge about the products and services to be sold and their applications. The amount of product training ordinarily varies according to its technical complexity. Such firms as IBM and Xerox spend a large portion of their sales training efforts on product knowledge and applications.

Methods of teaching product knowledge

Several methods have been successfully used in teaching product knowledge. The key is to let trainees work with the products and learn how to operate them. Lectures are of little value by themselves. In the introductory phases, however, they are useful to familiarize trainees with the product in general. Good visuals greatly increase effectiveness of a lecture.

A large hardware wholesaler, Belknap Hardware of Louisville, Kentucky, started sales trainees in the warehouse to acquaint them with the entire product line. The South Wind Division of the Stewart-Warner Company started its trainees in the technical service department, where each person learned to tear down and repair the products. They become intimately familiar with the workings of the items and were able to perform any repair job that might arise. The trainee learned to take apart and reassemble each of the products and had to pass a written test on them.

Some companies believe that sales trainees should spend some time on the production line and in various jobs throughout the plant to learn how the product is made and to appreciate the quality that goes into it. Such training provides a sound foundation for selling.

Customers can readily detect the sales rep's expertise or lack of it. They appreciate a knowledgeable rep. If you were sick, you would want the services of the best, most knowledgeable doctor in town. Similarly, a customer with a "sick" oil well or production process wants the best, most expert sales engineers.

Applications of product knowledge

Trainees who have learned about the product's technical aspects must also know how they can be applied to customers' problems. It is one thing to know products; it is another to be able to apply this information in the field. One of the big advantages of organizing a sales force along customer-class lines is that it greatly simplifies the teaching of product uses. A trainee who will call on only one type of customer needs to learn only the product-use problems in that industry.

Trainees should be taken into the field to study and observe the firm's product in actual use. There is, however, ample room for classroom study of product applications. Sometimes actual case problems can be used to project the trainee into commonly encountered situations. Laboratory exercises are useful in showing how the firm's product can be employed to solve a customer's problem. *Application engineering* is a term frequently applied to this aspect of selling. Xerox has prepared a large manual for its sales trainees which contains case histories of how its copying machines have been used in specific applications.

Knowledge of competitive products

Sales people should know their competitors' products almost as well as their own, because they are called on to sell against them. A sales rep who is not familiar with competitors' goods cannot compare his line with theirs. He will also be unable to correct inaccurate statements a prospect may make about a competitor's product. Often prospects either have been given incorrect information or have erroneously assumed things about a competitor's product that are not so. Such misconceptions can seriously affect the outcome of a sale.

Detailed knowledge of competing products allows the sales rep to design a presentation to stress the advantages of his product over the competitive item. Every product has some competitive deficiencies. Once the sales rep determines what his major competition is, he can sell against it intelligently without actually mentioning the competitor's name. He merely stresses that the product he is selling does not have the deficiencies the competitors' item has.

Continuation of product training

Product training is a continuing function. Every time new models are brought out or new competitive developments appear, the sales force must be trained to handle them. Retraining on existing products also is frequently necessary, as sales people become forgetful or careless about technical knowledge.

Much of this continuous training is done through product bulletins sent to the sales force to keep them abreast of product developments. As the home office learns of difficulties with a product and develops ways of handling them, the sales force should be given this information in order to head off possible trouble in the field.

KNOWLEDGE ABOUT THE COMPANY

All trainees need a certain amount of information about the company's history and organization and policies. It is also important that the training program include an explanation of company policies and procedures and the reasons for them. When a sales representative can answer a customer's complaint about a company policy by explaining the reasons for it, this not only may retain the customer, it also boosts the rep's morale.

Company knowledge is not difficult to teach. The lecture method can be used extensively, combined with printed materials covering the information. A common weakness in training programs is that an inordinately long period of time often is devoted to company knowledge. In this, a little bit goes a long way.

It is more important for trainees to be shown how to relate to the corporate operating system—whom to contact to get certain things done, how the system operates, and why the system is so constructed. New employees for the huge corporate giants, in particular, may be in awe of the organizational monster with which they have become associated, despite the fact that usually they will be concerned with only a small subsystem.

THE SELLING PROCESS

After the requisite background information has been given trainees, they should be introduced to the selling process and the techniques that have proven effective in selling the company's products. A company sales trainer can be far more effective in teaching sales techniques for a particular firm than someone else teaching a general-purpose salesmanship course. The sales trainer is able to incorporate the firm's experiences into the training program and to focus efforts entirely on the specific products to be sold.

One of the first ideas to be communicated to trainees is that there are no magic sales techniques. There is no one method that can be used to close every sale. It must be stressed that the techniques recommended are simply those that experience has indicated seem to work better than others in most cases.

The actual selling process can be likened to a chain, each link of which must be closed successfully if the chain is to be usable. If each of the steps in the process is not culminated successfully, the seller will fail to get the order. However, each step overlaps others, and their sequence is sometimes altered to meet the situation at hand. For example, objections usually are answered after the presentation, but often objections must be handled as they arise throughout the presentation. Closing frequently is interwoven into the presentation, because many good sales reps like to try a close early in a presentation to see if the prospect is ready to buy.

The eight steps in the selling process to be discussed in this section are:

1. Prospecting.
2. The preapproach.
3. The approach.
4. The presentation.

5. The trial close.
6. Meeting objections.
7. The closing.
8. Follow-up.

Prospecting

A prospect can be defined as someone who needs the product offered and is able to buy it. Successful sales people do not waste their time calling on people who are not prospects. They have a limited amount of time for selling, and it must not be wasted on those who either have no need for the product or cannot afford to buy it.

After trainees have learned the importance of calling only on good prospects, they must be shown how to develop a system by which the names and addresses of good prospects will flow steadily to them. The trainer should focus on prospecting systems that have proven successful for the firm. There is little need to discuss systems used for other types of products. Instruction on prospecting can be provided by a combination lecture and case-history method. Sales people for the firm who are particularly adept at prospecting may be brought in to discuss their systems.

Names and addresses of good prospects can be obtained in a number of ways. A sales manager may prepare a list for each sales representative. Customers can suggest new leads, and present users may want new or different models of the product. Many sales executives believe that a firm's best prospects are its own present customers. They reason: These people know us and our wares; if they are satisfied customers, they will most likely prefer buying from us again in preference to a seller with whom they have no experience. A competitor's customers also can be good prospects. A saleswoman for a new copier sought out firms that were using IBM copying machines. She reasoned that these concerns had already shown they recognized a need for a copier, and her machine could offset the disadvantages of the IBM model. Announcements of engagements, weddings, or births can furnish leads to the sale of many products. Regularly published lists of building permits issued can provide leads for sales of home furnishings, insurance, and related products.

A day-to-day operating problem in

THE MAJESTIC GLASS COMPANY (D)

Handling leads

Inquiries were frequently received at Mr. Clyde Brion's office from prospective customers in response to the companys' advertising in business periodicals. Brion's usual procedure was to write a letter to the inquirer immediately, offering as much information as possible, and stating that the "Majestic representative in your area will call on you within a few days." He then would send a copy of the inquiry to the salesman in whose territory the prospect was located, requesting that a follow-up call be made and that a report be submitted to him.

Often there was no immediate response from the salesman. Brion reasoned that he might be away from his office or busy on other calls. Therefore he took no immediate action except to watch the weekly activity reports submitted by the salesman, to see if the name of the inquirer appeared in the list of calls made. When it did not, as was true in a large number of instances, Brion wrote to the salesman again, asking for an explanation. Common replies were that the salesman had overlooked the inquiry, had responded with a telephone call rather than a visit, had checked on the prospect in local directories and decided against a follow-up, or had sufficient personal information to know that a call would not be fruitful.

Brion believed that some of his salesmen discounted the value of advertising inquiries. He thought that substantial amounts of business might be lost in this way, and without good follow-up the advertising of the company was largely wasted.

Question

What should Clyde Brion do?

Note: See the introduction to this series of problems in Chapter 2 for the necessary background on the company, its market, and its competition.

When the sales rep first uncovers the name of a likely customer it is merely a lead to a prospect—a "suspect." The name must be qualified as to the person's needs and ability to buy before it can be considered a prospect. The qualification of suspects is one of the functions of the next step in the selling process—the preapproach.

The preapproach

Four functions of the preapproach should be described for trainees. First, it should qualify the lead, or disclose the party's needs and ability to buy. Second, it should provide information that will enable the seller to tailor the presentation especially for the prospect. Third, it should provide information that may keep the sales rep from making serious tactical errors during the presentation. Finally, a good preapproach increases the sales rep's confidence and makes him feel able to handle whatever may arise during the sale.

Trainees should be told the type of preapproach information that will be most helpful. The first thing most sales reps would like to know, of course, is whether or not the suspect has a need for the product. It may be that the person has just purchased one and is not in the market. Next, they want to know whether or not the person has the ability to buy the product. This information is called "qualifying" information in that it qualifies the person as either a prospect or a nonprospect. Then, sales reps want to know as much as possible about the environment in which the product is to be used. There are some situations in which the product would not be adequate for the job. It is not good salesmanship to sell a product that will fail to serve the buyer well. If the product will not solve the prospect's problem, it should not be sold. The sales rep will never build a loyal following of customers by selling them goods that will not do the job.

If the prospect is an industrial firm, the sales rep should learn everything possible about its business, its size, its present purchasing practices, the location of its plants, the names of its executives, the names of people who influence the purchase, and other related data. If the prospective buyer has been having problems, the seller should become familiar with them. Many times, such information is available from the prospect's competitors or from other sales people who call on the account.

Before calling on anyone, the rep should know the correct spelling and pronunciation of the person's name and exact title in the firm. Knowledge of the prospect's educational background, experience in the company, age, fraternal affiliations, marital status, family, religion, and any other facts available concerning the person's personal habits and beliefs is also helpful. The purpose of obtaining such personal background material is twofold: to keep from making serious social blunders, and to locate some common interests between the prospect and the sales person. For example, perhaps the sales person and the prospect went to the same university, or they are members of the same fraternity or were raised in the same home town. Anything that the two have in common facilitates the presentation and makes the prospect more friendly.

Even sales people who regularly call on the same accounts, preapproach information is vital. Card systems are developed so that the sales representative can review information about the customer which has been gathered over a period of time. As the customer is called on year after year, the rep gets to know more and more about the account. Information such as birthdays and anniversary dates of customers is useful if it is acceptable in the industry to send token gifts on these occasions. While it might seem difficult to get such information, it is amazing what can be learned about customers. In industrial selling, the people inside the company who are interested in having the company buy the product will often provide a great deal of personal information about the firm's decision makers. Personal information also can be uncovered in directories and biographical publications such as *Who's Who in America*. Even such a simple tactic as driving by the prospect's home or place of business can disclose much about the person. When a sale is of critical importance, some firms order a credit investigation of the account.

The approach

When the sales representative has the name of a prospect and adequate preapproach information, the next step is the actual approach. This is usually the first minute or so of a sale. It frequently makes or breaks the entire presentation. If the approach fails, the sales person often does not get a chance to give one.

Trainees should be informed that a good approach does three things: It gets the prospect's attention, immediately inspires interest in hearing more about the proposition, and makes an easy transition into the presentation. One textbook in the field of salesmanship lists ten methods that can be used in approaching a prospect.[1] For a sales training program, only four basic approaches need be considered: (1) the introductory approach, (2) the product approach, (3) the consumer-benefit approach, and (4) the referral approach.

---

[1] Frederic A. Russell, Frank Beach, and Richard H. Buskirk, *Textbook of Salesmanship*, 10th ed. (New York: McGraw-Hill Book Co., Inc., 1977), ch. 8.

Introductory approach. In the introductory approach, the sales person introduces himself to the prospect and states what company he represents. While this approach is by far the most frequently used, it is also probably the weakest because it does very little to further the sale. Frequently, there is a necessity to use another approach immediately after the introduction. This approach gains little attention, and the prospect's interest is minimal unless the representative has been expected.

Product approach. The product approach consists of handing the product to the prospect, with little or no conversation. One salesman selling costume jewelry to department store buyers would walk up to the buyer and lay his leading designs on the desk, saying absolutely nothing. Almost inevitably, the buyer would look over the merchandise and say something like, "OK, where is the rest of the line, and what's the story?" If the buyer had no use for this type and quality of merchandise, the salesman immediately knew, and little effort was lost. The product approach can be used most effectively when the product is unique and creates interest on sight.

Consumer-benefit approach. The sales person starts the sale in a consumer-benefit approach by informing the prospect of what the firm can provide in benefits. Then he asks if the prospect would be interested in obtaining those benefits. The consumer-benefit approach directs the prospect's attention toward the benefits the firm has to deliver.

One life insurance agent would begin a conversation with a prospect by asking, "How would you like to receive $1,000 a month each month on retirement?" If the prospect allowed that such a sum would be attractive, the agent would reply, "If you will answer a few questions for me, I would like to draw up a plan that would give you just that. But, first, I must have some information about your personal circumstances."

Similarly, many industrial sales reps use the consumer-benefit approach when they start by asking the purchasing agent if the company would like to save a certain amount on a certain process during the coming year. From the information gathered in the preapproach the seller should be able to pinpoint the benefit most likely sought by the potential buyer and use that appeal as the opening for the sale. One saleswoman would prepare three consumer-benefit approaches so that two could be held in reserve in case the first one failed to elicit a positive response from the prospect.

Referral approach. Often the referral approach is successful in getting an audience with a prospect. It consists of obtaining the permission of a past or present customer to use its name as a reference in meeting a new prospect. A satisfied customer may even write a short note to a friend who is a prospect, introducing the sales rep. This approach works well because the prospect has an immediate bond of friendship with the seller and, out of courtesy to the friend, will hear what the sales rep has to say. A referral will get a hearing, but some other approach must be used to make the transition into the presentation.

The presentation

The presentation is the main body of the sale, in which the product or proposition is presented and the prospect is shown the benefits that await the buyer. Trainees should know the characteristics of a good sales presentation. It is built around a forceful demonstration of the article, during which all selling points are visualized and buying motives are dramatized to arouse the interest and desire of the prospect to buy the item. The necessity for demonstrating everything possible during the presentation cannot be emphasized too strongly for trainees. If it is feasible, the prospect should participate actively in the demonstration. It is far better for a prospect to drive a new automobile than just be taken for a ride in it by the sales person, for example.

The advisability of using a prepared sales presentation, better known as a canned sales talk, is a matter of considerable controversy. Without doubt, a prepared presentation done poorly and without feeling will be a dismal experience. However, many firms use them with successful results. The prepared presentation has several advantages:

- It gives new sales people confidence.
- It can utilize tested sales techniques that have proved effective.
- It gives some assurance that the complete story will be told.
- It greatly simplifies sales training.

The use of a prepared presentation does *not* mean that the sales person cannot use his or her own words. In many instances, in fact, individual thoughts are encouraged. Above all, the sales person's own feeling and personality should be evident in the presentation.

The heart of teaching salesmanship lies in the trainer's ability to provide trainees with the demonstration techniques and visual aids that have proven most effective for the firm. Trainees must be impressed with the importance of the presentation to a successful sale.

Essentially, some claims are made during the presentation, claims that are aimed at the prospect's likely buying motives. Then by the use of various techniques the sales representative endeavors to prove the truth of those claims. If the prospect does not believe the claims made for the product, a sale is not likely. Thus the key to an effective presentation is believability.

The trial close

Throughout the presentation, the sales rep makes trial closes in order to determine whether the customer is ready to buy. The prospect may be ready to buy before the presentation is started; the product may have been shopped for many months, and a decision to purchase it may already have been made. In such a case, all that must be done is to make the transaction.

Some prospects know early in the sale that they want to buy, whereas others may remain unconvinced for some time. Trainees should be taught how the trial close is used to ascertain just how favorable the prospect is toward the proposition. This can be done by asking such questions as:

Which of these models do you think you would like best?

Which color do you prefer?

How would you like to pay for this—by cash or on terms?

Now just exactly when would you need this article?

If you owned this, would you really use it?

Don't you think this feature would be of great assistance to you?

The person who is ready to buy answers such statements readily and positively. A prospect who is not convinced either avoids answering the questions or denies an interest in buying the item. If all goes well in the trial close, the sales representative goes right on into an assumptive close and wraps up the sale. If one encounters obstacles, however, and detects an unconvinced attitude on the part of the prospect, the next phase of selling must be undertaken.

Meeting objections

Objections are encountered in practically every sale. They should be welcomed, because they indicate that the prospect has some interest in the proposition. A prospect who is not interested in buying seldom raises any objections. She or he can go along with the presentation silently, but say at the end, "I'm not interested in your deal." The person who objects to the seller's claims and asks questions obviously has some interest in the product. If his objections can be met satisfactorily, he will buy.

Stated and hidden objections. Objections can be classified as stated or hidden. Prospects may state their objections to a proposition openly and give the sales person a chance to answer them. This is an ideal circumstance, because everything is out in the open and the sales person does not need to read the prospect's mind. Unfortunately, in many instances prospects hide their real reasons for not buying. Besides having hidden objections, their stated objections may be phony. A woman may say that she does not like the looks of your product, when she really thinks your price is too high. Another prospect may complain about the price, when what he is really thinking is that he does not trust your service or ability to perform according to contract. Unless the real barrier to the sale can be determined, it cannot be overcome.

Trainees should know the two major techniques for discovering hidden objections. One is to keep the prospect talking by asking questions that probe his thinking. The other is to use insights gained through experience in selling the product, combined with a knowledge of the proposition's weaknesses and the prospect's situation, to perceive the hidden objection.

However, some sales people have developed special methods for getting the prospect to disclose what is blocking the sale. One saleswoman uses what she calls her "appeal for honesty" tactic. In essence she says to the reluctant prospect, "You expect me to be honest with you, as you should. But haven't I the same right—to expect you to be honest with me? Now honestly, what is bothering you about the proposition?"

Objections to price and product. There are objections to price, product, and timing of purchase. Timing objections are called procrastinations. Objections on price can be in one of two categories. Either the prospect is saying that he feels he cannot afford the price being asked, or he may be saying that he feels the price is too high for what is being offered. Each requires a different approach in answering.

Product objections can be answered best when the sales person has extensive product knowledge of both the item being sold and competitive products. Without product knowledge such as that provided for trainees, the rep may be lost in answering such objections. All products have advantages and disadvantages. In answering product objections, normally the sales rep hopes to show how the product's advantages will compensate for its disadvantages, in comparison with competing items.

The prospect may be misinformed or may not understand some of the technical aspects of the proposition. In this case, additional information along these lines should be provided. There are instances in which the prospect's objections to the product can be met simply and effectively by altering the product to suit the customer. A man looking at some long-sleeve dress shirts with a neck size of 19 objected, "But I hate long sleeves, and these shirts are always far too big around the body." The salesman replied, "No problem. We'll cut off the sleeves and take in the body without charge." The customer was so pleased he bought several shirts, and a $66 sale was transacted.

Procrastinating objections.   Procrastinating objections can be difficult to overcome. Such objections as:

Let me think about it awhile.

I have to talk it over with my family.

I have to wait until next month's paycheck.

I want to look around some more.

are all used by the procrastinating prospect as excuses for not acting on a proposition immediately.

Experience has shown that the sales person who can be put off with procrastinating objections will lose far too many sales. In reality, the prospect is just vacillating. If the sale is not closed immediately, it will be lost to a competitor who is more perceptive. A real estate broker tells of the time he allowed a good prospect to think about a house over the weekend. When the broker called on Monday morning, he discovered that another agent had sold his prospect a house on Saturday night.

In door-to-door selling, usually a sale that cannot be closed on one call has little chance of completion. In many industrial sales, however, the prospect cannot be pushed into a sale without creating considerable ill will. Also, the amount of aggressiveness must be modified to fit the prospect and the situation. In some situations, the sales rep must be patient or lose the sale. Some people will not be pushed or rushed.

The general strategy in handling most objections is to avoid arguments at any cost. The trainee should be taught to ask questions that help the prospect to clarify his thinking instead. This provides insights into the precise obstacles that are hindering the sale. The best sales people usually are the ones who have developed to a fine degree the art of asking questions and thus getting the prospect to talk. Even if the prospect is dead wrong, care must be taken to offer no offense. A sales rep can win an argument only to lose the sale.

The closing

To this point in the selling process, everything has had only one goal—to get the order. If the representative fails to close the presentation properly by asking for the order, all is for naught. Trainees might consider the close the easiest part of the sale to remember. In fact, however, many sales people do everything right until they get to the close, and then they fail to ask for the order. They seem to think the prospect will buy automatically. But often the prospect needs a little urging, and the close provides that impetus.

The assumptive close.   Most sales people rely on what is known as the assumptive close, or some variation of it, as their basic closing technique. In using the assumptive close, they merely assume that prospects are going to purchase the article and begin taking orders by asking such questions as:

> Now what size do you want?
>
> Do you spell your name with an *e* or an *i*?
>
> To what address do you want this delivered?
>
> When can we deliver this—today or tomorrow morning?
>
> Will three dozen be enough, or had I better send you four?
>
> When can our engineers talk with your machine operators?

If the prospect answers such questions on minor points, the closing is underway.

The assumptive close is the most natural thing in the world. For the sales person who starts with a good prospect, has done an excellent job of selling the product, and has met all the objections, what is there left to do but write the order?

The physical action close.   When the sales person is through with the presentation and feels it is time to close the deal, certain physical actions may suggest to the prospect that the time to sign has come. It could be as minor an act as handing the pen to the prospect. One carpet salesman had good success by pulling out a tape measure and beginning to measure up the premises for the precise fit. A saleswoman for automobiles would go get the keys to the car being considered and hand them to the prospect to signify "The car is yours now!" The assumptive close of starting to write up the order is in effect a physical action. The physical action close is merely a nonverbal extension.

Standing-room-only close.   The prospect who believes the product offered may be difficult to get may be encouraged to sign the order. If it is true that deliveries are delayed, or if supplies are scarce, or if for any other reason the seller may not be able to supply the needs of the buyer, the sales rep can do the prospect a favor by describing the situation.

The rep might say: "In all honesty I cannot guarantee you that we still have the model you want in stock. It is our most popular item and moves out rapidly. If you want it, I'll call the warehouse and see if we have it. OK?" Or, "We have a waiting list for this machine of two months and it gets longer every day. If you want to get this equipment on line as soon as possible, let me phone in the order right now."

While this closing tactic involves some degree of pressure, this is acceptable as long as they are the truth. The sales person often is unable to guarantee deliveries or does not have what is wanted. Prospects should always be informed of the supply situation.

The standing-room-only close is a good one to use to overcome procrastinating prospects. The message to them is, "If you wait, you may not be able to buy it."

Trap close. The prospect's objection can sometimes be used to close the sale. The prospect says, "I wouldn't pay more than $4,000 for that car," though it carries a $4,600 ticket. Knowing that the boss will take the $4,000 and be happy, the sales person can say, "That's an awfully low price for that car, but we have nothing to lose by writing up the deal for that amount and seeing if the boss will accept it." Note that the prospect had to agree to buy for $4,000 before the seller accepted the deal.

The trap close can sometimes be used in answering product objections which can be met by altering the product rather than the price. If a prospective homeowner did not like a house because it did not have a swimming pool, the contractors could quote a price which included a pool and give the buyer what she wanted.

Special-offer close. Some sales managers find it advantageous to furnish their sales force with a special deal to offer customers each time around the territory. The 3M Company's Scotch Tape division at one time used this closing tactic. If the special deal were a billfold, the sales rep might say, "If you put in this specially priced deal display today, we will include this billfold."

Frequently the special offer is a particularly attractive price deal that is good only for a short time. Sears uses this tactic in selling appliances on its "One Day Only" sales. The basic idea is to forestall and overcome the procrastinating objections of prospects.

Follow-up

Trainees should be taught that the sale is not over once the order is obtained. A good sales representative follows it up in various ways. Immediately after obtaining the order the rep usually reassures the buyer that a wise decision has been made. He makes certain that all questions have been answered and that the buyer understands the details of the contract. If the merchandise is to be delivered at a later date, the sales rep is usually wise either to be present at the time of delivery or to call soon after to ensure that the customer has been given satisfactory service and that everything is all right. At this time, he often can obtain leads on other good prospects known to the customer.

The training program should provide trainees with a specific follow-up system which is suited to the type of goods being sold. It is not enough to tell them that all sales should be properly followed up.

A good follow-up is the key to building a loyal clientele, which ultimately results in a handsome income for the sales person. Satisfied customers voluntarily provide more business. People truly appreciate being served by good sales people, and once they have located a person who has the knack of pleasing them they are not likely to forget that individual in the future.

One furniture salesman in a large department store built a tremendous following in his trading area through an excellent follow-up procedure. Immediately after obtaining an order, the salesman did everything he could to expedite delivery of the merchandise. He went into the warehouse and handpicked the pieces purchased to make certain the woods had beautiful grains and were not damaged. He made friends of the truck drivers, so they would take particular care with his orders to see that they were delivered on time and in perfect condition. Shortly after the furniture was delivered, he called to see if everything was all right or if anything should be returned because it was damaged or defective. He claimed that on four out of five of these calls he sold additional merchandise with little or no effort. The customer simply wanted something else and was so pleased with her treatment that she gave the order to him on the spot. The key to really great selling lies in delivering satisfaction and making sure that one's customers are absolutely pleased with their acquisitions.

QUESTIONS AND PROBLEMS

1. In what ways is company knowledge necessary? How would the lack of it hinder a sales person?

2. In what ways does the lack of product knowledge hinder a sales rep?

3. Why should the trainer place the subject of philosophies and attitudes before actual selling techniques in the program?

4. Develop a good prospecting system for a printing sales rep.

5. Outline the preapproach information you would try to get on a prospect to whom you were planning on selling a Dictaphone dictating system. Exactly where would you look for each bit of information?

6. If you were selling for a Chrysler dealer, how would you go about locating good prospects?

7. Develop some good approaches to use in selling your prospect for the dictating system.

8. What visuals would you develop in working up a presentation for selling a water softener to homeowners?

9. Develop some trial closes to be used in your presentation of the dictating system.

10. Develop the closes you would try to use in closing the sale of the dictating system.

11. What follow-up efforts would be required in the sale of a dictating system?

12. How would you handle the objection, "But my secretary takes dictation quite well, and I am sure she would not like this new dictating machine"?

13. How can the trainee best learn how to handle objections?

Case 8–1

MADISON PUBLISHING COMPANY
Continual sales training

Mr. Carl Timms, the new sales manager for the Madison Publishing Company, was planning the program for the forthcoming January sales meeting with his 120 college textbook sales people.

The Madison Publishing Company was one of the largest publishers of text and trade books in the world, but in recent years its profitability had left a great deal to be desired. Several management changes were made in hopes that a reversal of fortunes would result. Timms had been brought in from a competing firm as sales manager in the hope that he could straighten out the sales force, which was regarded by most informed observers in the industry as one of the worst. The reps did not seem to know how to sell books very well, at least not well enough to suit management.

Timms had made several immediate changes in sales management policies. One of the more significant was to abandon the standard salary compensation plans most publishers maintained. Instead, he substituted a plan that provided for considerable incentive. The experienced representatives would make significantly more money under the new plan, but the poorer ones would lose. They might even lose their jobs. Timms wanted sales reps who could sell with the best in the industry.

The college book sales reps called upon professors to acquaint them with the books in their respective fields that were published by Madison. Most of their efforts were focused on the new book list—books published in the current year. However, management had earmarked 50 books from the backlist—books published in previous years—that were big sellers and should be given special attention.

While the traveler called upon college professors to ask them to adopt the books, the actual order for the goods was not given by these prospects. The professors would notify the college bookstore of their choices of books for adoption for the courses they would be teaching. The bookstore would send the orders to the publisher.

Several classic problems faced college book sales reps:

- They had too many books to sell, about which they knew far too little.
- They had difficulty finding the right college professors, let alone influencing them.
- College professors as a general rule were not very cooperative. Relationships with them were rather unusual, to say the least.

- They did not have the product knowledge with which to meet some of the professor's product objections.

Consequently, a philosophy had developed among several collegiate sales forces that the sales rep's main function was to sample books—to see that professors were given those books that they could use in the classes they taught. This role was far more comfortable for them because they were now playing Santa Claus. They did not have to apply a bit of salesmanship to the professor.

Timms intended to change that philosophy for his sales people. He knew quite well that the successful firms in the industry had reps who really sold books. It had been proven many times over that a good rep could sell books to professors, despite the disclaimers made by the professors.

In particular, Timms was interested in getting his sales people to dig into objections and meet them. Seldom would a book rep be able to answer such standard objections as:

> The administration doesn't like us to change books.
> I have my course all worked up around this other book.
> It's not the approach I use.
> It's too high a level.
> It's too low a level.
> It's too long.
> It's too short.
> Let me think about it.
> We'll have to meet on it.
> It's too late to change adoptions.

Timms wanted the sales force to deal with the professors' objections and not back away. A bit of investigating uncovered the fact that most of them did not know how to go about handling objections, and even fewer knew how to uncover the professor's hidden objections. Timms decided that the coming meeting in January would be devoted in part to sessions with a sales expert on the handling of objections.

Questions

1. How should the topic of objections be handled?
2. How much time should be devoted to the subject?
3. Should the sales expert conducting the training sessions be familiar with the book business, or could he be from any industry?

Case 8–2
CERAMIC COOLING TOWER COMPANY
Making sales presentations more effective

The Ceramic Cooling Tower Company of Fort Worth, Texas, manufactured large installations for cooling liquids and gases to customer specifications. Its largest market was for the cooling equipment to air condition large industrial and commercial buildings. Transactions ranged from $100,000 to $10 million, and contracts for $1 and 2 million were not uncommon.

The company distributed directly to builders through a sales force of 52 sales engineers who are supervised by five regional managers. Many of these sales engineers were manufacturers' representatives who also handled other brands of cooling towers. The company did have its own full-time reps in many of the major markets. The sales force was paid on a straight commission basis. Regional managers received a good salary and a generous incentive bonus for the sales volume of the reps reporting to them. If a regional manager's rep sold $6 million worth of equipment, for example, the manager's total pay would be $135,000 for the year.

Management had not been overly pleased with sales results and intended to increase sales threefold over the next two years. Mr. Leonard Mann, the sales manager, has disgustedly pointed out that there were many reps who had not sold an installation in two years. Mann has just assumed the managership and has vowed that the situation will be considerably improved or some changes would be made.

Traditionally, the sales reps had worked directly with architects and mechanical contractors who install the air conditioning to try to persuade them to specify Ceramic's equipment. Cost objections were commonly encountered because a ceramic cooling tower is significantly more expensive initially than alternate cooling towers. However, savings in use more than offset the higher initial cost. The ceramic cooling tower maintains a higher efficiency over its lifetime, thus lowering energy costs. It also lasts much longer, thus lowering replacement and maintenance costs. Exhibit 1 is a cost comparison which is commonly shown to prospects. The sales issue is one of higher initial outlay versus lower long-run total costs.

Mann planned to institute a sales-support program designed to help sales reps and regional managers do a more effective job. One portion of this program was to have the regional managers give the sales engineers training in how to make their sales presentations more effective. Mann had hired an outside sales trainer, Jack Bird, to meet with the regional managers to help them prepare for this instruction.

EXHIBIT 1
20-year life cycle analysis: Cash flow comparison
CERAMIC COOLING TOWER COMPANY

	Ceramic cooling tower	Alternate cooling tower
Original cost	$ 72,200	$ 31,160
Interest	60,647	26,175
Electricity		
Tower fan	57,034	114,024
Water pumping	19,901	18,670
Increased electricity for total system due to loss of thermal performance	0	73,177
Total electricity	$ 76,935	$205,871
Maintenance costs	6,851	21,418
Replacement costs	0	24,431
Total	$216,633	$309,055

TOTAL SAVINGS ON CERAMIC TOWER, $92,422

A two-day meeting was scheduled at which the new sales-support program was to be introduced to the regional managers. The first day of the meeting was to be devoted to the sales trainer's presentation. Mr. Bird planned to focus on two aspects of the sales presentation:

- How to Make the Prospect Believe Our Claims
- How to Determine and Answer Objections

The first day had been divided into four sessions. At the first session, the entire sales-support program would be disclosed. Then Mr. Bird would present an overview of the persuasion process and discuss his ideas of how to train sales people. The second session would focus on making presentations more believable, and the third session would concentrate on objections. In the last session, a videotaped sales presentation made by the Dallas sales engineer would be shown, and the regional managers would be asked to evaluate it.

Some of the key thoughts that were to be advanced to the regional managers were:

- The firm is committed to decentralized sales management, which means that the burden of achieving the company's sales forecasts is on the regional managers. That is why they are paid so handsomely. If the burden for sales performance fell on the home office, there would be little need to pay the regional managers so well.

- Management means to make things happen. The firm's sales goal *will* be met. It is the regional managers' job to make this happen. The sales-support program is designed to help them do the job.
- They will be able to reach the goals only if they get better performances from their people.
- To do that they will have to train their people.

Mr. Bird was to meet management to outline his thoughts on how to make the company's sales presentations more effective. He had studied the materials sent him by the company. (Exhibits 2 and 3).

Questions

1. How can the sales engineers make the owners believe the firm's claims?
2. What objections can be expected from the air conditioning contractors? From the architects? From the owners?
3. How can each of these objections be met?

EXHIBIT 2
SALES PRESENTATION MATERIAL

WHY BUY PERMANENT CERAMIC COOLING TOWER?

The twenty-five year guarantee on the fill and fill support is offered *only* by Ceramic.

Lifetime thermal performance: With Ceramic's *structurally* supported fill, 100% thermal performance is maintained for the *life of the project*. Other fill types are suspended or spaced, allowing *sag and droop* with subsequent water channeling and thus reduced thermal performance.

Fill comparison: Ceramic's fill is *less than 3% hygro-scopic* in two-hour boil tests, as opposed to approximately 18–20% for asbestos cement board fill.

Heat-cold: Ceramic towers are in service to cool *over 170°F hot water*—a temperature *prohibitive* for wood or plastic fills. Ceramic Cooling Towers have been *FROZEN* into a solid cube of ice with no deterioration—a claim which *no* other manufacturer can make.

Drift loss: Conventional towers' stated drift loss of 0.2 of 1% is *four hundred percent* greater than that guaranteed by Ceramic.

Noise: Ceramics are *QUIET*—tests show an average of 10 db (90%) lower noise level than the reported for conventional cooling towers.

Reduced water treatment: With Ceramic's inert fill and a water distribution system shielded from the sun, water *treatment* requirements are *virtually none.*

Maintenance: There is absolutely *no* maintenance on the fill for the *life* of the project!

Exhibit 2 *(continued)*

C.T.I. rating: Ceramic Towers are certified by the Cooling Tower Institute in accordance with CTI Bulletin STD-201—an important *ASSURANCE* that you are buying a *one hundred percent capacity tower.* (Ask conventional cooling tower manufacturers to furnish this certificate.)

Installations: Ceramic's hundreds of installations reflect the *broadest experience* in the field of installing *PERMANENT* towers. Ceramic includes airports, universities, hospitals, office buildings, refineries, steel mills, foundries, chemical plants and other commercial and industrial installations.

Reliability: Ceramic Cooling Towers were chosen for a number of *Nuclear Power Plants' Emergency Core Cooling System.* This critical service requires the very best, Class 1, water cooling equipment.

Company: Ceramic Cooling Tower Company is an outgrowth of the Acme Brick Company, a Texas corporation established in 1891, having over 30 years' experience in building *permanent cooling towers.* It is a subsidiary of Justin Industries headquartered in Fort Worth, Texas. *CCT Export Corporation* is a subsidiary of *Ceramic Cooling Tower Company.*

EXHIBIT 3

CERAMIC COOLING TOWER COMPANY

LIFE CYCLE COST ANALYSIS DATA SHEET

Prepared for: Name: _____

                  Address: _____

        Project Name: _____

       Owner's Name: _____

1. *Basic Study Data*
   Number of years for life cycle study: _____ Years
   Study basis: Present worth _____ Annual cost _____
   Interest rate on borrowed capital: _____ Percent
   Inflation rate: Internals _____ Electricity _____ Maintenance _____
   Tons of air conditioning _____ Tons
   Estimated annual operating hours @ equivalent full load _____ Hours
   Current cost per KWH of electricity _____ Cents per KWH
   Number of ceramic cells _____
   Conventional tower description: Name _____
                               Model no. _____   No. cells _____

	Ceramic cooling tower	*Conventional cooling tower*
2. *Design Data*		
Total fan motor horsepower	_____	_____
Total pump head from tower basin curb	_____ ft.	_____ ft.
3. *Initial Cost*		
Internal components	_____	_____
Structure and basin	_____	_____
Architectural screening	not required	_____
Electrical equipment	_____	_____
Added piping costs	_____	_____
Fire protection costs	not required	_____
4. *Maintenance Cost*		
Annual percent of original cost re- quired for maintenance	_____	_____
5. *Replacement Cost*		
Estimated life of tower	25 years plus	_____
6. *Water Treatment Cost* (algaecide)	not required	_____

9

Developing and conducting a sales training program

A teacher affects eternity. He can never tell where his influence stops.

HENRY ADAMS

"Sales training? Who needs it? I hire proven producers and turn them loose." While numerous sales managers would echo the sentiments of the one who voiced this philosophy, there are a few flaws in its logic. First, the supply of proven sales people is so scant that only a few firms can follow such a policy. A great deal of sales training must be done to create an adequate supply of able sales representatives.

Second, top sales people do not come cheap. What a firm saves in training costs may be more than lost in higher wages.

Third, the sales results of firms that have developed sales training programs have been excellent. Simply stated, sales training pays off.

The sales manager devotes considerable effort and funds to selecting the sales force. These may be wasted if selection is not followed up with the proper training. The training program is a vital link in the process of converting the recruit into a full-fledged, productive member of the work group.

In this chapter we shall discuss the various aspects of developing and executing a sales training program. Each program must be tailor-made to accomplish the ends desired by management, because each firm's situation is unique, and the training plans of other firms are seldom applicable.

In developing a sales training program, the administrator should consider the problem areas discussed in this chapter. They pose such questions as:

- What are the objectives of the program?
- Who should be trained?
- How much training is needed?
- Who should do the training?
- When should the training take place?
- Where should it be done?
- What teaching methods should be used?
- How should the program be evaluated?

What should be taught in the program was covered in Chapter 8.

The four basic types of training programs are: (1) initial or indoctrination training; (2) refresher courses; (3) continuous training programs; (4) executive development programs. The answers to the above questions vary with the type of program being considered.

OBJECTIVES OF TRAINING

In addition to the obvious goal of increasing sales productivity, training programs have other objectives. Results usually expected include a lower turnover rate, better morale, control of the sales force, improved customer relations, lower selling costs, and better use of time.

Lower turnover

Good training programs lower job turnover because well-trained people are less likely to fail. There are numerous examples of firms which push new employees into the field without adequate training, only to have them quit when they fail. Their people do not have a chance when they must face customers without adequate product knowledge or sound selling techniques. New sales reps are apt to become discouraged when they fail to sell their first few customers. And once discouragement occurs, failure is not far behind. Few people relish being losers.

A well-thought-out training program will prepare the trainee for the realities of a life in sales. One of these is that discouragement and disappointment are to be expected early in a sales career. Being forewarned of these mental hurdles is the first step toward overcoming them. The trainee who is able to handle the early problems is less likely to become discouraged and quit.

Better morale

Closely tied to turnover is the matter of morale. People who are confident that they have been given the training they need have a much better attitude toward their job, the company, and life in general. Those who are thrust into the business world without proper preparation for what will be encountered are likely to suffer from poor morale.

Lack of purpose is one foundation of poor morale, and dissatisfaction with details is only part of its superstructure. Hence, one of the major objectives of a sales training program should be to give trainees some idea about their purpose in the company and in society. Those who have a purpose in life can tolerate many inconveniences, disappointments, and adverse events to reach what they believe to be a worthwhile goal.

Control of the sales force

The training program should establish the behavior expected of the sales force. Sales people should know and understand the control mechanisms management uses to ensure that the selling job is being properly performed. An important section of any program should be a discussion of the importance of the reports the sales force submits and the use management makes of them.

Trainees also should be taught how to control their own activities. Instruction should be provided on routing, the use of personal records, the apportionment of selling effort, and other self-management techniques.

Improved customer relations

A good training program shows trainees how to render service to their customers. They should learn how to avoid overselling, how to determine which products are needed, and how to adjust complaints. Moreover, they should become aware of the importance of establishing and maintaining good customer relations. Well-trained sales personnel have acquired the skills necessary to please their customers.

Lower selling costs

One goal of the training program should be to instruct trainees in the control and reduction of expenses. Thus the program can result in direct savings. Moreover, selling expenses as a percent of sales are lowered as the sales reps become more proficient in their selling skills. Suppose that the combined salary and expenses necessary to keep a representative in the field is $2,000 a month. If training increases the rep's productivity from $20,000 to $24,000 a month, for example, expenses would be lowered from 10 to 8.33 percent.

Better use of time

Management has become increasingly interested in how employees use their time. A growing realization that considerable time is wasted has led to study of how to increase productivity. The goal is to learn how to produce more output from the relatively few hours available for working.

Certainly, the sales trainee should be exposed to a serious discussion of how to use time and how to make the most from the time available. More will be said on this subject in Chapter 24, "Careers in Sales Management."

Need for specific objectives

After establishing the broad objectives of the program, such as those discussed above, the sales manager should set specific objectives for the training program. It is insufficient to say that the purpose of the program is to increase sales volume. This statement is so general that it serves only as a hazy guidepost for making decisions. The manager should break down the broad objectives into several specific goals, such as improving prospecting methods, handling objections, or strengthening closing techniques. Meeting these separate goals should result in achievement of the broad objectives.

NEED FOR TRAINING

All sales people need some training. Even accomplished professional salesmen who have been with the firm for years need training on new products and continual review and refinement of their selling techniques. New employees who have had a substantial amount of sales experience must be instructed in the company's products and its selling methods. Although basic selling ability is transferable to a large extent, they must be taught how to sell their new employer's products in the way the company wants them sold. The recruit with little or no selling experience must be schooled completely in selling techniques, along with all other aspects of the job.

It is better to overestimate the amount of training required than to underestimate it. Many trainees will have exaggerated their experience and abilities in order to convince the prospective employer that they should be hired. Most recruits who have had some saleswork still have an inadequate knowledge of selling techniques. Some may have considerable unlearning to do before they can get started properly, because they have acquired bad selling habits that need to be corrected.

The amount of training each person needs or receives depends on several factors, such as the nature of the product and the market, the amount of money the company is able and willing to invest in the program, and the general attitude of management toward sales training. Obviously, the need for training increases with the technical complexity of the product, variety of customer types, and intelligence and ability of the customers.

In establishing the need for training, it is usually advisable to perform a *difficulty analysis* of the sales job. In making such a study, the sales manager attempts to discover just what difficulties are encountered in the field so that proper training can be devised to help overcome those problems.

The difficulty analysis is usually made by going into the field and interviewing sales reps about the problems that are giving them the most trouble. Frequently the investigator goes over a series of calls in which the reps failed to get orders. In each instance, an attempt is made to discover just what caused the failure. If the analysis discloses that the rep is picking poor prospects, for example, additional training on prospecting would be required. If it shows the reps failed to get orders because the proposal did not meet the prospects' needs, additional training would be required in how to make the right application of the product to prospects' problems.

WHO SHOULD DO THE TRAINING

There are three basic sources of trainers: regular line executives, staff personnel, or outside specialists. Any one or a combination of these can be used successfully. It is not uncommon to find firms that use all three, each for different purposes.

Line personnel

Training by line personnel consists of instruction by such executives as senior sales representatives, field supervisors, territorial managers, or sales managers who are in direct command of the sales force.

Advantages. Line sales executives' words carry much more authority than those of staff people or outside specialists, since the trainees know that these people have had successful sales experience. When the boss does the training, a certain unity of action is achieved because there can be no mistaking what the supervisor expects. Further, recruits can be trained to sell the way the manager wants them to sell.

There may be considerable differences in the training techniques used by line managers and those used by staff personnel or outside specialists. Line executives who train their own sales people can evaluate each person's ability better than administrators who do not participate in the training program can. Also, better rapport can be obtained between the executive and the sales force, since training affords a wonderful opportunity to become acquainted.

Disadvantages. The disadvantages of using line personnel are lack of time and lack of teaching ability. The pressures of other activities force the manager to give, at best, only partial attention to the training program, and this can be harmful to trainee morale. If the line executive is to do the training, there must be adequate time to do it properly. It should not be added to the executive's other duties, as is usually the case.

A line executive may know a great deal about selling but be unable to teach others about it. As any college student can attest, many people who are experts in their fields are unable to communicate their knowledge to others. On the other hand, many great teachers are only average scholars. It is important to distinguish between the possession of knowledge, and the ability to impart it to others and thereby to affect their behavior.

It must be emphasized that neither of these disadvantages is drastic, and they can be remedied by proper managerial action. Line administrators can be given the necessary time for training. And teachers are not necessarily born; they also can be trained.

The line executive has a place in the training program. While line managers may not be able to bear the entire load, they should be used in selected circumstances. The day-to-day training, whether or not it is part of a training program, is always conducted by line supervisors such as sales managers. In small organizations, there is little choice. The sales manager must do the training, since the operation is not large enough to employ staff trainers.

Staff trainers

Staff trainers can be hired specifically to conduct a training program, or they can be staff people who hold other jobs in personnel, production, or office management. We will focus on the specially hired sales trainer, since use of other staff personnel ordinarily is not recommended. Members of the personnel department are seldom qualified to conduct a sales training program. They may be involved in certain phases of the instruction, such as furnishing company information or handling the physical arrangements of the program. However, it is usually unwise to entrust the technical details of the training program to them.

Often a staff trainer is maintained, even though the sales manager prefers to have the line executives do the actual training. In this capacity, the trainer sets up the program, teaches the line executives how to train, and prepares the materials needed for instruction. Staff trainers are more likely to be found in initial training programs than elsewhere.

Advantages. A trainer specifically hired to handle the training program can attend to all the details, prepare the many necessary materials, and give the trainee all the attention required. The ideal staff trainer would be an excellent teacher with a thorough understanding of the problems of educating people. Frequently it is less expensive to hire a specialized staff training officer than it is to add the line executives needed if sufficient time is to be allowed them for training activities.

A staff trainer can do far more than training the firm's sales force. The training department can conduct courses for distributors and dealers. It can also take the program into the field and conduct training sessions with a minimum of time lost to field personnel.

Disadvantages. In theory, the staff trainer lacks control over the trainees and does not speak with the authority of a line executive. However, in practice this is an academic point, since the trainees know that the trainer has the backing of the boss.

Additional cost is incurred in maintaining a separate training department. The median salary of the trainer alone will be about $20,000 per year, depending on his or her qualifications. This limits the size of the firm that can afford to hire a sales trainer; smaller concerns cannot afford the cost.

There is a danger that an ambitious staff trainer will institute far more training than is required. This is not an inherent disadvantage of staff training so much as it is an administrative weakness. Nevertheless, the danger of empire-building always exists when a staff activity is added.

Outside training specialists

In practically every large city there are firms that specialize in sales training. Their scope varies widely. Some will establish and administer an entire training program, while others specialize in teaching sales techniques. The latter leave the dissemination of product knowledge and company information to the firm's executives. Sometimes these training firms specialize in a very narrow field. There are organizations that do nothing but train real estate brokers or insurance agents or retail sales clerks.

There are also individual experts who consult on training problems. One source of such consultants is college professors who are skilled in teaching salesmanship. People who have become recognized authorities on various phases of selling often are inspiring speakers and put on a good show.

These consultants are ideal for smaller firms that cannot use a full-time training specialist but do need someone with training talents. By retaining a consultant, they can buy as much training as they need, with minimum cost. Even large organizations find use for outside specialists, as in spot assignments, brief refresher courses, or training sessions at conventions. They are frequently the mainstay of executive development programs.

WHEN TRAINING SHOULD TAKE PLACE

Some training must take place immediately after hiring. Basic product knowledge and company information are the minimum requirements for getting the new sales person started. How much more is needed or desirable depends on the particular sales manager.

There are two basic attitudes toward the timing of training. Some executives believe that no one should be placed in the field who is not fully trained, not only in product and company knowledge but also in selling techniques. Their training programs may last from a few weeks to as much as a year or more before sales people are sent into the field. They may have the trainee work for awhile in either production or service to acquire product knowledge.

Other managers want the recruit to exhibit a desire to sell before they invest in training that person. Some insurance companies require a new agent to sell a certain amount of life insurance before going to a sales school. The first training program is only a basic course, after which the agent must again go into the field and sell successfully before attending the more advanced schools for underwriters.

This philosophy has considerable educational and managerial

merit. From the educational point of view, it is much easier to train people who have had field experience than those who have not faced a prospect. People who have experience in facing problems are eager to get answers to them. They are in a better position to learn than inexperienced people, since they are emotionally involved in the learning process. If they have been told by many prospects that the price is too high, for example, they will be eager to find out how to cope with that objection. In college courses, students who have had any business experience are usually much more eager to learn.

From a managerial point of view, weak prospective sales people are usually eliminated if they must sell before being trained. By putting new employees in the field first, the manager also has the opportunity to determine how much and what type of training they really need. The only trouble is that many people may be eliminated by this "push them off the dock" method who might have been successful had they been given proper instruction.

About the only times delayed training should be used is in situations where product knowledge is easily acquired and the prospect does not require a polished selling approach. Delayed training is usually practiced by firms whose customers are sold only once, with each sale of little importance to total volume. If a sales rep botches a particular sale, the company is not seriously injured. Companies whose sales plans require the rep to call repeatedly on the same group of customers or on customers whose patronage is important usually insist that the representative be completely trained before approaching customers.

The need for training does not end with completion of the initial program. Sales people continually need refresher courses, but this type of training can lower morale if it is not done properly. The trainees must feel that they are getting something for their time and efforts. One question that arises is whether the refresher training will be done on company or employees' time. Some executives feel that after the initial training period the individual's own time should be used for such efforts, and some nights or days off should be devoted to self-improvement. Thus no time is lost on the job, and the individual's sincerity about desiring better performance is demonstrated.

From this point of view, off-duty training has merit. However, the effect on morale can be bad. Sales people usually have little enough time at home and begrudge additional intrusion on their free time. It is not unusual for employers to expect their employees to study while off duty even though they attend courses on company time. They feel that a salesman should show some evidence of good faith in wanting to better himself in return for the company's expenditures for his future.

The reaction of the sales rep to timing of the training program depends in large part on the purpose of training. If it benefits only the firm, the rep resents being forced to acquire it on his own time. However, if the nature of the course is to encourage self-improvment, rather than to deal with specific selling problems of the firm, the ambitious individual may not mind attending it after working hours.

WHERE TRAINING SHOULD TAKE PLACE

The basic problem in the location of the training program is determining the extent to which it should be centralized. Unless some reason can be found for centralizing all training in one location, it should be decentralized. Centralized training is usually more expensive and requires more organizational effort than training in the field. Small firms with all selling activities under the same roof have no decision to make on this matter, because all activities, including training, are centralized.

Decentralized training

Decentralized training can take one or a combination of several forms: (1) office instruction, (2) use of senior salesmen, (3) on-the-job tutoring, or (4) traveling sales clinics. There are many advantages to decentralized training. First, it is usually cheaper than centralized training. The trainee is left in the field to work while learning, and the substantial expenses of supporting both the trainee and a central school staff are avoided.

There are also some definite educational advantages to having training take place on the local level. Education is to some degree a matter of time. It has been proven that cram courses are inefficient, since much of what is learned initially is quickly forgotten. Centralized schools of necessity use intensified programs. If training takes place little by little over a period of time, as in decentralized programs, more learning eventually is realized. In decentralized programs, too, the trainee continually faces problems and is close to the scene of activity.

Considerable managerial benefits are realized in that the branch manager or an assistant usually is made directly responsible for decentralized training. The branch manager who does a good job can instill in the trainee confidence in his leadership. At the same time, the manager is provided with an excellent opportunity for evaluating the relative worth of the trainees.

The only weakness of decentralized training—and it is a big one—is that the branch manager may not be able to perform the training role properly. If the manager is not a good trainer or does not really care, the program will be a failure.

It is almost impossible to avoid some decentralized training. Although initial training and inspirational meetings can be held centrally, continual day-to-day training must be done at the local level.

Centralized training

Centralized training may be presented in the form of organized schools with planned programs or periodic conventions or sales meetings held in some central location, such as the home office or a large city or resort. Some sales schools operate virtually on a year-round basis, but most firms do not find such operations necessary. Only companies that continually hire new sales people and process a large number each year find it necessary to develop permanent training installations. Smaller concerns typically conduct one or two sales schools a year which last from two to four weeks. Such programs are usually conducted near the home office.

Strengths of centralized training. In centralized training, highly capable personnel, including skilled teachers, are usually readily available. Proximity to the plant or the home office allows the trainees to become acquainted with home-office personnel and manufacturing facilities. It is important for them to meet the top executives. Centralized training certainly saves executive time for instructing classes; there is no need for wasted travel time. Also, a centralized school normally has available more formal facilities for training than are available in the field. Necessary equipment and materials are handy for the instructor's use. Another significant advantage is that the trainees can get to know one another. An esprit de corps can develop among the members of any given class, and this is conducive to good morale.

From an educational standpoint, removing trainees from the home setting, where they are not subject to the distractions of home life and its daily problems, has some merit. Attention can be focused entirely on learning how to be a better sales person.

Weaknesses of centralized training. Centralized training has two main weaknesses. First, as noted, it is expensive to take people out of the field and support them while training. Contrasted with the relatively small cost incurred for most decentralized programs, the cost required to undertake a centralized program must be carefully considered.

Second, the amount of time a person can be kept at a central training location is limited, not only in the amount of money the firm can spend for it but in the time trainees will devote to training without becoming bored. When boredom sets in, education stops. Married people, particularly, seldom want to be away from their families more than a few weeks at a time.

Administrative problems. The sales manager must consider certain administrative problems when planning a central program. First, there is a delicate balance between how much free time the trainee should be allowed and how much class time should be required. If insufficient free time is allowed, the trainees will become restless and resentful. With too much freedom, however, the training program will degenerate into a party at the company's expense. In either case, morale will suffer. Serious trainees will become disgusted at having to spend their time away from home for a party, and all concerned will be unhappy if they are overworked.

Then there is a multitude of details to be taken care of—important details such as lodgings, meals, transportation, arranging the schedules for instructors, preparing materials, and arranging for entertainment. This is a full-time task for an assistant. A great amount of administrative time must be devoted to training programs if things are to go smoothly.

SOME FUNDAMENTALS OF TEACHING

The fundamental principles of teaching and learning apply in sales training programs. Some characteristics of the teaching situation which should particularly characterize these programs are discussed in this section.

Maximum participation

One goal of the teacher is to obtain maximum participation by students. This means not only that *all* students should be allowed to participate, but also that as much time as possible should be devoted to trainee participation. The best teaching methods all are basically dependent on this provision. It has been proven time and again that student participation in sales presentations is the most effective method for teaching selling techniques.

Attitude of teacher

Students are quick to detect any adverse attitudes of the teacher and to resent them. The trainer's attitude must be one of helpful assistance to the trainees and their problems. A trainer who is tempted to become impatient or sarcastic will lose rapport with the group. If he belittles or destructively criticizes the demonstration sales, for example, little learning from them will take place. Students do not like to be belittled for their ignorance. They rightly feel that this is the exact reason they are in class.

Enthusiasm

Enthusiasm is one of the most helpful personality traits the trainer can possess, and it is contagious. Students can hardly become enthusiastic about the material if the teacher acts as if it is boring. Sales trainees will not believe that selling can be fun, interesting, and challenging if the instructor does not act as though it is. Keeping the students interested is necessary if learning is to take place. Students who are mentally asleep learn little.

Confidence in the teacher

If learning is to be achieved, the students must have complete confidence in the ability and knowledge of the instructor. If the trainees do not believe what the trainer says, they may passively resist all the teacher's suggestions. Confidence cannot be attained easily; it is developed only through experience and ability. It is difficult for trainees to have confidence in anyone teaching selling techniques who has not had some firsthand selling experience in the field. Up to a point, the more experience, the better.

TECHNIQUES OF PRESENTATION

Techniques for presenting the material in a sales training program which have proved to be effective include the following:

Lectures.	Role playing.
Discussion.	Videotapes.
Demonstrations.	On-the-job training.

All methods of presenting material are not equally effective. However, often the instructor has little choice of methods because of the nature of the material to be presented. For instance, in teaching company information it is impossible to use the role-playing technique. The lecture method supplemented with visual aids is about the only reasonable choice for this material.

Lectures

The lecture method can present more information in a shorter period of time to a larger number of students than any of the other techniques. However, it is relatively ineffective for the presentation of much of the material on salesmanship. The temptation to lecture excessively must be fought vigorously, since it frequently represents the easiest path to follow.

A *limited* amount of lecturing has a place in most sales training programs. Although company information and some product knowledge can be presented in published material, some lecturing usually is required to explain it. Also, a lecture is frequently the best way to present a basic outline of a subject, and it can serve to stimulate, guide, and steer discussion and other teaching methods into the channels desired. Although selling techniques are best taught by participation methods, short lectures introducing the students to the problems and the principles underlying them can be extremely helpful. Just pushing the students into sales demonstrations without previous orientation to the subject can be quite confusing.

Lecturing is usually more effective if it is broken up into short sessions interspersed with other activities. Attention to a lecture usually can be sustained only for a relatively short time, and care must be taken to end it before attention wanders.

Lectures must be thoughtfully planned so that all the points are adequately covered. However, it is a serious mistake to give a lecture by reading from a detailed outline or from a completely written manuscript. The learning process often suffers, because it is very difficult to convey enthusiasm and rapport with a class while reading something to them. Extemporaneous speaking, properly done, adds much to any lecture.

Lecturing should be more prevalent in initial sales training programs than in refresher courses. Experienced sales people cannot benefit from this type of material nearly as much as new sales reps.

Discussion

Discussion can take several forms. Many are simply open talks on various topics between the teacher and the students, with the teacher's role being to control the discussion and stimulate it. However, some special devices have been developed to facilitate discussions.

Cases. One widely used technique for stimulating discussion and for providing students with a realistic learning experience is the case history method. Each student is furnished with a written case similar to those at the ends of the chapters in this book. Care must be taken to see that each case stimulates discussion in the specific areas the trainer wants to cover in a session.

A case gives students practice in solving actual selling problems. Suppose a case relates the story of one salesman's unsuccessful attempts at getting by secretaries in order to have sales interviews with their bosses. The trainees would be asked to analyze the man's difficulty and recommend what they would do to remedy the situation. Normally, each trainee has a slightly different view of the matter. In the ensuing discussion the students are encouraged to examine all aspects of the problem and challenge one another's opinions and statements.

Cases are widely used in executive development programs and in various supervisory training schools which currently are quite popular in industry. However, at present there is a shortage of suitable cases involving selling behavior. The sales trainer usually must collect and prepare the cases for use in the firm's own training program.

Round tables. This form of discussion usually consists of dividing a large group into smaller ones so that each person can participate more fully. If the class is over 15 or 20 members, it is usually difficult to get each person to participate fully in any discussion. A few dominating individuals usually take far more than their share of time. If the class is divided into groups of 7 to 10 persons, each member may be forced to carry a share of the discussion. In small groups, any one trainee's silence is immediately noticeable, whereas in a larger group this may not be true.

Panels. The panel is basically a round-table discussion performed before an audience—the class. Usually, a moderator puts questions to various members of the panel, and cross comments between the panel members are encouraged. Sometimes the panel answers questions submitted by members of the audience. This serves to stimulate the class, since they have an interest in the questions.

It is usually advisable to staff the panel with individuals who have some standing in the eyes of the students. Successful sales reps or executives of the firm often can serve well in this capacity if they are available.

Discussion should play a large role in any sales training program, since it gives the students opportunity to get their own problems discussed. It is the best method for making available to trainees the experiences of competent sales people. It also is the best method for providing experienced sales reps with a vehicle for exchanging thoughts and know-how. The choice between the use of cases, round tables, panels, or plain open discussion should be determined by the situation. If the class is large, it probably should be broken into small groups. If good cases are available, they probably should be used. If competent panel members are not available, it is unwise to attempt a panel discussion. Since each of the discussion techniques is good, sometimes the trainer finds it advisable to use all of them in one program just to provide a change of pace and varied learning experiences. Discussion is probably weakest in the initial training of green recruits, since they may not know enough to carry on an intelligent discussion.

Demonstrations

Demonstrations can be used to great advantage in teaching both product knowledge and selling techniques. What more effective way is there to teach how a product operates than to actually demonstrate it? Instead of just telling about the different types of closes that can be used in getting an order, for example, it is better to demonstrate each before the class. Innumerable situations in selling are difficult to describe, but the trainee can be shown how to handle them. It is a sound training practice to demonstrate everything possible, and the instructor should make certain to demonstrate each point possible for the trainees.

The educational theory supporting the use of demonstrations in training programs is twofold. First, it has been proven many times that the eye is a better path to the brain than the ear. The visualization of any point increases the likelihood of its being learned. Second, many subjects are so complex and have so many interrelationships that they can only be made clear if the students actually observe these relationships. It would be almost impossible to communicate to a trainee the operation of a Dictaphone by any other method, for example. The product must be demonstrated if the student is to learn how it operates and appreciate its finer points.

Role playing

In role playing, the trainee attempts to sell a product to a hypothetical prospect. If the role-playing method is to work effectively, care must be taken to make the prospect realistic.

This type of learning-by-doing education can be highly effective in the teaching of selling techniques, particularly in initial training programs. The trainees are placed in situations that subject them to some of the many unforeseen developments that always arise in selling. Besides the training in selling techniques it provides, role playing also allows the instructor to work with the trainee on such things as voice, poise, bearing, mannerisms, speech, and movements, which are all important.

Many things brought to light by role-playing situations would otherwise remain unknown. Ordinarily calm and collected students have broken down in an actual sale from nervousness or lack of confidence. There is no question that role playing is the best method yet developed for convincing the student of the validity of certain principles. The instructor can stress the necessity for product information. But let a trainee come before the class in a role-playing situation who does not adequately know the product, and the ridiculousness of the situation is brought to the class's attention in an unforgettable manner. In one instance, a student was to sell Pyrex glass cooking ware to a hardware store owner. Thinking that the "unbreakable" feature of the product meant that it was literally unbreakable, the student's approach consisted of coming in the door and deliberately dropping a set of Pyrex ware onto the floor. He had hoped to demonstrate forcibly to the merchant his product's major selling point. This could have been an excellent approach. Unfortunately, as he swept up the broken glass he succeeded only in convincing everyone that he did not know his product—the "unbreakable" feature he had been told about referred only to the application of heat. This demonstration was indelibly etched into the memory of the students. To this day when members of the class see the teacher they laugh about the incident, and many have related just how it taught them an unforgettable lesson. They said they resolved never to be caught in the same position as that student standing there, embarrassed, sweeping up a pile of broken glass.

Role playing also shows the student in a most convincing fashion that *knowing* what to do is one thing, but *doing* it is another. One of the major weaknesses of most salesmanship courses is that they only teach the student *about* selling, not *how* to sell. Many students can recite all the various methods of approaching prospects, answering objections, and closing the sale. However, they are shocked to learn how much of this knowledge they can forget in the emotional involvement of a sales situation.

In any sales training program designed to teach recruits selling techniques, extensive use should be made of role playing. It takes practice to perfect a sales presentation; one or two attempts are inadequate. Although there is no established number of times each trainee should be placed into a role-playing situation, usually four or five times is the minimum.

Observers. Many trainers prefer to have each sales presentation performed before the entire class so all students can benefit from it. While this obviously reduces the number of presentations that can be made in a given length of time, it does have much to recommend it. First, often the students can see in the sale things that escape the teacher and can recommend actions that would otherwise go unmentioned. Second, possible resentment of criticism may be avoided by allowing the class to do the major criticizing. If the class members all say the same thing, the trainee is more likely to accept it as the truth. Third, while the person doing the role playing is learning, the class learns by watching. Often class members are deeply impressed and see things they resolve never to do.

Each presentation invariably gets better as the role-taking turns progress through the class, even though for each student the role may be a first sale. The first few presentations are usually very poor. The teacher must take care to inform the class and the person chosen to lead off the series that many mistakes will be made and things will not go smoothly. It should be pointed out to the students that they will learn best through making mistakes. Sometimes the instructor is wise to pick people with some apparent skill in verbal expression and selling to make the first few presentations. This can get the sessions off to a good start and give trainees who are completely inexperienced some idea about the process.

In handling the role-playing sessions, the trainer must convince the students of the importance of taking criticism in the right way. They must be convinced that it is meant to help them earn more money eventually, and nothing personal is meant by any criticism. The trainer should point out that there is no such thing as a perfect sale—all sales people make mistakes in almost every sale. They must realize that for many problems there are no cut and dried answers. Criticisms on these points are only designed to give them some ideas about other ways of handling the problems.

Role playing without criticism is of limited value, since the trainee has no way of determining what he may be doing wrong. Although practice without observers may aid the trainee to polish his delivery and mastery of the presentation, much more is accomplished when observers are present to give him their reactions to his performance.

An important fact frequently overlooked by many teachers of salesmanship is that the trainee should be commended on the good features of the sale. These can provide a learning experience as valuable as the mistakes. In one sale when the prospect was a blustering, loud individual who had strong opinions about the product being sold, the salesman spoke in a soft, calm voice and allowed the prospect to talk freely about his feelings. Certainly, the interview took more time than usual, but the salesman was able to shape his presentation to fit the man's stated desires and dislikes. Also, the class observed how the prospect quieted down as the salesman got calmer, in direct contrast to a previous sale presentation when the salesman made the mistake of getting loud right along with the prospect, until they were yelling at each other.

Frequently, the trainer is tempted to concentrate too much on the small details at the expense of ignoring the larger factors involved. One of the first questions the instructor should put to the class is: "Just why did Joan fail to make the sale?" or "Just why did Joe get the order?" It is important for the students to acquire an ability to see just where a sale was made or lost. Frequently, one major reason or event decided the affair. For instance, one trainee did a rather poor job in making her presentation and in attempting to close, but she got the order anyway. It was easy to point out the many mistakes, but much more was learned by indicating the basic reason why the order was obtained. In this case, it was because the saleswoman had taken the trouble to locate an excellent prospect and had allowed him to do all the talking. She just let the man talk himself into the sale, which is good selling in many circumstances. This one factor overrode all the small errors the saleswoman had made.

Videotapes

Modern technology has made possible the audiovisual recording of role-playing sales presentations. Thus trainees can see themselves in action, and the instructor can make comments at the proper moments.

A great deal of instructional material can be put on videotapes so trainees can study them at their own convenience. A tape of the company's leading sales producer in action could serve a good purpose. All that is needed are a television camera, a video recorder, and some viewing sets. The cost of this equipment—approximately $2,500—is relatively small in relation to the benefits that can be derived.

On-the-job training

On-the-job sales training places the student in a more realistic situation than any of the other techniques discussed here. Usually this method is used as the final stage of the trainee's sales education.

Actual supervision of on-the-job training can take several forms. The sales supervisor, the trainer, or a senior salesman may go along with a new sales person on the first few calls to observe him in action and to provide some suggestions on how to improve his performance. A few of these check rides are often included in a sales training program for the purpose of appraising how well the trainee has learned his lessons and to find out if additional training is required. In situations where it is awkward for a second person to accompany the sales rep into the prospect's office, the trainer must talk over each sale with the trainee afterward. Together they analyze the entire presentation to determine what was done right and what was done wrong.

Some selling situations allow the trainee to gain initial experience in selling to customers who come to the company's offices. In these cases it may be possible to set up facilities for observation of the sales trainee in action.

The amount of on-the-job training that can be done economically is limited, since it is rather time-consuming for both the trainee and the trainer. The educational benefits of training while actually selling rapidly diminish after a few calls. Consequently, the trainer cannot make this method a major portion of the initial training program, but it is widely used in continuous programs.

COMMON MISTAKES IN TRAINING

We can summarize this chapter by outlining many of the common mistakes made in planning and executing a sales training program. Probably the greatest mistake most managers make is not planning the program properly. They seem to think it unnecessary to give much thought to training, feeling that they need only pass on the wisdom they have acquired over their many years in the selling profession. Such training efforts are little more than friendly talks, and neither the manager nor the trainee knows exactly what is being learned. There is little likelihood that the trainee will obtain the necessary skills by this type of training.

Another all too common error is including boring speakers in the program. No student can learn while mentally fighting the instructor. Although the teacher may have something worthwhile to say, the students will never hear it if their attention has been focused on the manner of delivery or other aspects of the presentation. The teacher must have the confidence of the students and must immediately gain rapport with them to communicate the knowledge effectively.

Many managers try to do too much at one session. In their eagerness to complete the training program, they overwhelm the student with far more information than can be possibly absorbed. For instance, it is possible to present a rough framework of the entire selling process in two or three hours of lecturing. If a test is then given to determine how much students have learned in such a session, the results may shock the instructor. The material comes too fast for comprehension.

Unrealistic sales demonstrations plague many training programs. Often, they are so obviously structured that the students become disgusted at the oversimplification of the selling process. When the trainer points out that many of these sales demonstrations are typical of what they will be facing, they find it difficult to believe, and little learning takes place.

Training programs often do not provide for sufficient recognition of trainees. The basic principle on which sales training programs should be built is maximum participation by students. Through discussion techniques, role playing, and on-the-job training, the trainee must be incorporated into the program, not only mentally but physically. This can only occur if the size of the class is small enough. It is a mistake to allow a sales training class to include more than 20 or 30 persons.

Many firms fail to establish specific objectives for their training efforts. As a result, there is a temptation to include in the program far too much product knowledge, company information, and sales psychology. Instead, the trainees may really need such specific instruction as how to plan a week's activity, how to determine prospects' needs, how to figure the trade-in value of an old machine, or how to get good preapproach information on a prospect.

Finally, many managements fail to budget sufficient funds for adequate training. Training costs money; good training costs even more. To the budget-conscious executive, training costs seem expendable during lean times, something that can be postponed until the larder is full. But experience indicates that for successful firms, training is a matter of basic policy. They recognize it as the foundation of a successful sales force.

QUESTIONS AND PROBLEMS

1. "I don't have any training program. I just hire salesmen who have already proven successful for other companies, and turn them loose. I let the big corporations do all my training for me and then just hire away their best people." This was the attitude expressed by the sales manager of one relatively small office machines agency. Is this a sound policy? What are some of the strengths and weaknesses of this position?

2. "Salesmen are born, not made. It's futile to try to train a man to be a salesman, so I don't." How would you answer a sales manager who said this to you if you were trying to get him to hire you as a sales trainer?

3. "The school of hard knocks is the best training school for salesmen. I just shove them off the dock. Those that have it in them will learn selling on their own, and those who don't have it in them, well, we don't want them around the company anyway." How would you answer a manager who said this?

4. How can the sales manager keep top-notch sales reps interested in continual training programs?

5. You have been made sales trainer for a firm with 125 sales people. How would you determine their specific training needs?

6. How can the sales manager determine the excellence of the various instructors in the firm's training program?

7. In what ways can a teacher unknowingly belittle students?

8. What are the attributes of a good teacher? A poor one?

9. What would be the differences in the methodology used for training new sales people and conducting a refresher training course for experienced ones?

10. How should the sales trainer go about establishing the agenda or curriculum for a refresher course?

11. What are some of the pitfalls of on-the-job training?

Case 9-1

GRANITE CITY COMPANY
Developing a sales training program

Harvey Jenkins, president of Granite City Machine Tool Sales Company, had for some time been concerned with the selling skills of his 11-man sales force. During the previous two years he had tried to indirectly encourage his sales manager, Harry Snow, to propose some sort of a continual training program for the sales force, but he had met with no success. Either Snow had not understood his suggestions, or he was deliberately ignoring them in the hope that Jenkins would forget all about them. Each time Jenkins heard of some sales atrocity committed by one of the sales people which would have been avoided even with a minimal training program, he again would resolve that something must be done.

In a specially called meeting, Jenkins had been able to get Snow's attention by saying, "Harry, for two years I've been after you to develop a sales training program, with no results. Now I'm to the point where either we're going to have a new sales training program or a new sales manager. It's your choice, Harry." Snow got the message. He replied, "I know, boss, but I've just been so busy dealing with all the emergencies that seem to come up everyday that I haven't had time to do much about it."

Jenkins retorted, "Harry, that's just the point. If we had a decent training program there wouldn't be so many emergencies. Our sales engineers would know how to handle these sales problems and would not keep running to you every time they have trouble. Now I want on my desk, one week from today, a concrete plan of what you propose to do about it."

Snow left the boss's office more than a bit shaken and uncertain about how to proceed with his task. He really didn't know much about sales training programs. He had gravitated into his job when it opened up through the death of the previous sales manager. Snow had been Granite City's outstanding sales engineer, a feat he had accomplished without the benefit of any formal sales training program. He had been heard to comment, "I don't see why we should provide sales training for our people. If they can't do the job then we'll clear them out and bring in somebody who can. The only way to learn how to sell machine tools is to get out into the field, keep your eyes and ears open, and learn from your mistakes."

The Granite City Machine Tool Sales Company was distributor for most of the leading machine tool makers in the country, and featured such leading brand names as Cincinnati Milling Machine, Ingersoll, and Milliken. It sold these brands exclusively in a 50-mile area around Granite City's huge industrial district. Granite City, population 1 million, was one of the Midwest's leading diversified manufacturing centers. Thus the potential volume for machine tool sales was substantial. The sales company had been formed at the turn of the century by Jenkins's grandfather and was wholly owned by the family. It was considered a good place to work by its employees; employee turnover was almost negligible. The sales engineers were paid on a straight salary basis and frequently worked closely with one another in developing proposals for prospective customers of machine tools. The firm's sales volume in 1977 was $23 million. The average sales engineer made $22,000 per year and had been with the firm, on the average, for 11 years.

Harry Snow had started with the company as a high school dropout, age 14, by working in the service department as a stock boy. He had worked diligently while taking additional course work at a local night school to acquire the knowledge about engineering that was needed for the sales job. When he was 25 years old, he got his first opportunity to sell, being assigned a territory that had suddenly opened up through death of a sales engineer. For 20 years Snow had been one of the firm's outstanding producers and was rewarded with the sales managership in 1974.

Now Snow felt he needed some guidance on the training program and sought out Curt Ryan, an officer for the American Machine Tool Distributors Association. He had heard Ryan speak several times at meetings about the need for sales training and describe what help the association was providing for its member firms. So Snow flew to Pittsburgh for a conference. During the meeting he learned of the association's intentions to offer a two-day session on sales techniques to the sales engineers of member firms. These sessions were to be conducted by outside sales training experts with whom the association had been working closely. The cost was to be $300 per person.

Snow left his conference with Ryan convinced that the association's program was the answer to his prayer. He could have the association do the sales training job for him. Upon returning to Granite City, he disclosed his thoughts to his assistant sales manager, Madge Evans. Then he asked her what she thought of the plan.

She asked, "You really want to know, or do you want me to say something that you want to hear?"

"No, no, give it to me straight. What's wrong with it?" Snow replied.

"Harry, I really don't think that's what Mr. Jenkins is looking for. Is a two-day session on sales techniques really going to satisfy him? Is it going to take care of our problems with our sales engineers?"

Snow was sorry he had asked Evans, so he grumbled something that sounded like "Thanks" and retreated to his office. There he was disturbed by a telephone call from Abe Simon, a sales engineer who thought he had a big problem. Simon wasn't sure what kind of machine a long-time customer really needed, or what to do with the customer's used equipment. The customer had demanded that Granite City dispose of the old equipment, but the company strongly preferred not to handle trade-ins. That was left to firms that specialized in resale of used equipment.

After a 15-minute talk with Simon, Snow called Evans into the office. He had decided to delegate his own problem. Snow said, "Okay, since you think we need a different training program, the job's yours. You develop it. Have it on my desk by Friday morning." Snow was smug about how cleverly he had handled the problem. He chortled, "Now you can understand what they mean by delegation. It's a great opportunity for you to grow and develop, Madge."

Evans did not appreciate Snow's delight. She spent the week before the deadline studying all the materials she could find on sales training in the local library. On Friday morning she laid on Snow's desk the basic outline of a sales training program (Exhibit 1). He looked over the outline of her program and asked its costs. She handed him the budget for the program (Exhibit 2). He whistled and said, "That's way too much. Harv will never pop for that much money."

Evans said, "Well, we won't know if we don't ask, will we? He wanted a sales training program and here it is. He didn't say anything about price." Snow said, "Let me study this, Madge. I'll be back with you." He thought he had best find comfort on the golf course. However, his search for a game was terminated by Sam Kane, a sales engineer who had another "big problem."

That night Snow worried about the situation into which he had gotten himself. If he took Evans's proposal to the boss intact and it was accepted, even with some modifications, it might make him look bad

EXHIBIT 1
Sales training program

GRANITE CITY MACHINE TOOL SALES COMPANY

On the second and fourth Fridays each month the sales force will meet in the home office for the entire day. The morning sessions will focus on product knowledge and applications of the machine tools to the customer's problems. We will rely heavily on technical support from the manufacturers. Each Friday will feature one particular machine, and its maker is expected to conduct the meeting. The reason for this emphasis is that it is obvious that our sales engineers have much to learn about the goods we sell. Moreover, there are continual new developments which need to be introduced.

The afternoon sessions will focus on selling techniques. We will start at the beginning, and each session will cover one topic. The first six sessions will cover the following topics:

Prospecting
Developing a Prospect's Profile and Planning the Sale
Approaching the Prospect
Making Your Claims Believable
Handling Objections
Closing the Sale

After that we will continually dig into each topic but will change teaching methodology to deal with the engineers' problems in selling to specific prospects.

for not doing it himself. On the other hand, if he revised the program slightly and left her authorship off it, the truth would undoubtedly get out, and he would look like a glory-seeking male chauvinist. If he didn't show the boss anything, just sat on the report, he would be in trouble Monday morning. If he developed his own sales training program, significantly different from the one Evans had developed, it would do little to foster good relationships in the office. Moreover, he

EXHIBIT 2
Budget for sales training program for 1978

GRANITE CITY MACHINE TOOL SALES COMPANY

We will have to develop materials, particularly visuals, to support the classroom efforts	$ 4,000
We will have to bring in outside experts to instruct on many phases of salesmanship	5,000
Maintenance cost for meals, etc.	2,500
Total	$11,500

wasn't certain how he would go about changing her program in any meaningful way that would stand up under the boss's cross-examination. Snow just wasn't sure what to do come Monday morning.

Questions

1. What errors in managerial tactics has Harry Snow made?
2. What would you advise Snow to do?

10

Compensating the sales force

*How little you know about the age you live in if you
fancy that honey is sweeter than cash in hand.*

OVID

The structure for sales force compensation looks something like
this:

Financial compensation.
  Direct payment of money.
  Indirect payment—paid vacations or company-financed insurance
    programs, for example.
Nonfinancial compensation.
  Opportunity to advance in the job.
  Recognition inside and outside the firm.
  Self-respect.
  Other intangible benefits.

Most of our discussion in this and the next chapter will deal with
direct payments of *financial* compensation.

The compensation problem is twofold. A company must determine
both the *level* of earnings and the *method* of paying its sales force.

> *Level of earnings.* The total dollar income paid to each sales repre-
> sentative for a given period of time.
>
> *Method of compensation.* The plan by which the workers earn or
> reach the intended level. One company may use a straight salary
> method of payment, for instance, while another may choose to
> pay a commission.

IMPORTANCE OF SALES FORCE COMPENSATION

A sales force cannot be considered soundly managed unless there is a well-developed and well-administered compensation plan. The pay plan is important because of its impact on the sales force, the company, and customer relations.

1. The sales force. A basic tenet of our economic system is that people should be justly compensated for their labors. A good compensation plan can do much to develop a highly productive sales force because it will help to instill a high degree of morale and industriousness. A poorly developed or administered plan also may be an open-door invitation for a union to attempt to organize the sales force.

2. The company. Management wants to keep its sales expenses as low as possible and at the same time encourage profitable operations by the sales force. The compensation plan can be used as a method of controlling the activities of the sales force. When a company is faced with rising break-even points, the situation generally calls for an increase in sales volume, a decrease in expenses, or both. Increased sales often can be stimulated by a properly designed compensation plan.

In regard to expenses, many firms feel, rightly or wrongly, that their production costs already are as low as is practical. The only other major area for expense reduction is in the marketing department, and there an easily noticed major item is the total cost of the sales force.

3. Customer relations and goodwill. If the compensation system encourages overselling customers, ill will toward the firm can result. Sales compensation has social implications because selling is so important in our economic system. The extent to which marketing can deliver a high standard of living to the people is greatly dependent on the methods used to pay one major group of deliverers—the sales people.

Most companies treat all personal-selling expenses—including sales force compensation—as current operating expense items. When the compensation expense is payment for efforts in *developing* a market, in contrast to payments for *maintenance selling* activities, however, the developmental compensation cost is better treated as a capital investment. This cost can be amortized over a period of years, and throughout this period the returns on the investment can be evaluated. Referring to the costs associated with a specialized development sales force, Kahn and Schuchman have made some persuasive comments:

> Maximum sales development simply cannot be obtained efficiently if management demands that income from it exceed its cost period by period. Development expenditure is not an operating cost, but a capital investment ranking among the most important that a firm can make. . . .

The most valuable asset of a firm is its pool of customers, and if development is to succeed, it must be viewed as a capital investment in developing this pool.

. . . Even more importantly, management must recognize that development selling cannot be expected to bear the immediate fruits of sales maintenance. It must come to recognize that expenditures for market development are the close and supporting kin to product development expenditures. Management must be ready to invest in the market in the same way as it invests in plant and equipment or research and development.[1]

If it uses the current period to evaluate compensation expenditures, management may decide to discontinue a seemingly unprofitable market venture. Yet, this same venture might have proven profitable if management had viewed it over a longer term, using the capital investment concept of compensation costs.

DETERMINING NEED FOR REVISION OF PRESENT PLAN

Most firms usually need to *revise* their present compensation plans rather than develop completely new ones. Before changing a plan, a company first should determine whether indications such as decreasing volume, increasing selling costs, fewer sales reps reaching their quotas, or increased turnover are evidence of weaknesses in the compensation system, or whether the fault lies elsewhere. If the results of this analysis indicate the compensation plan is at fault, the manager must determine *why* the present plan is not satisfactory. A list of key questions such as the following could be developed to help determine whether the plan needs to be changed:

- Are the sales people generally satisfied with the plan?
- Does it lead to the accomplishment of the objectives for which it was established?
- Does it encourage sales people to sell the profitable products and do the necessary missionary tasks?

If, after analyzing its situation, a firm gives answers of no to many questions of this nature, some modification of the compensation plan would seem to be needed.

The search for the most effective compensation plan may seem never-ending. Sales managers should realize there are inherent conflicts in the objectives of most compensation plans. They want a plan

---

[1] George N. Kahn and Abraham Schuchman, "Specialize Your Salesmen!" *Harvard Business Review*, January–February 1961, pp. 97–98.

that will maximize the sales reps' income and at the same time minimize the company's outlay, or they want one plan to give the sales force security and stability of income as well as much incentive. In each situation, the desires are diametrically opposite. About all a manager can do is adjust the pay plan until a reasonably satisfactory compromise is reached.

CONSIDERATIONS PRECEDING ACTUAL DESIGNING OF PLAN

The task of designing a compensation plan for sales people may be easier if management keeps in mind a few fundamental points. First, no single plan fits all situations. Consequently, a firm should have a plan tailor-made for its own specific objectives. There may be a marked similarity among the general features used by several firms, but the details should reflect the individual objectives of each company. Many companies also need more than one compensation plan because of differences in types of sales jobs, territories, products, or customers.

Sales compensation should be related to the general compensation structure of the company. Sometimes office or factory workers feel they are underpaid compared with sales people. Other workers may envy a person who does some traveling and is on an expense account. Sales people, on the other hand, sometimes look longingly at the gains made by the blue-collar worker. Production employees have achieved benefits through the efforts of their unions, and often similar benefits have not been given to the sales force or other white-collar workers in the same firm. To approach equality of compensation for all the major occupational groups in a firm, management should make use of the developments in job evaluation and salary and wage administration. Even then, it takes keen executive judgment to come anywhere near equating the various compensation structures.

From the practical standpoint of operating a sales force, however, it is far more important to achieve *external* consistency in sales people's earnings. If there is a choice to be made, management should pay its sales force at a level competitive with the income of similarly qualified sales people in other firms, rather than attempting to equate the earnings of the sales force with those of office or factory personnel within the firm.

At frequent stages during the development of a compensation plan, management should solicit suggestions from the sales force. Soliciting their opinions may uncover facets of the compensation problem that never would have occurred to management. It also is more likely to result in acceptance of the plan by sales people.

Broad objectives of a compensation plan

The broad, general objectives of a good compensation plan are not mutually exclusive. In some instances, various objectives set for the plan may conflict with one another.

To correlate efforts, results, and rewards.   One general objective is to correlate sales people's rewards with their results and efforts. That is, payment should be directly commensurate with productivity. This is an ideal that most companies constantly seek and seldom achieve, since it is virtually impossible to measure quantitatively what a person is worth to a company. For example, a given amount of effort on the part of salesman Bill Garner may result in $10,000 of sales. The same amount and quality of work put forth by Sue Anderson may not result in any sales. Instead, Sue is building the foundation for profitable future business with a customer. However, this relationship may not be reflected in sales until some months or even years later.

In another case, Joe Knight and Mary Swan are selling in separate territories or are selling different product lines. Each does the same quantity and quality of work. Yet, Joe's sales consistently run 40 percent higher than Mary's. The reason may be in the difference in territorial potentials or in the basic difficulty of selling the different products. However, if the company attempts to equalize territorial sales potentials, then some other factor becomes unequal. For instance, Joe's territory now may have a 40 percent larger potential than Mary's, but each can be covered in about the same time. If the districts were adjusted to have equal potential, then Mary would have to travel more and work harder to get the same amount of sales as Joe.

These examples illustrate the difficulty of equating results with rewards. Sometimes the goal may be reached by paying a commission based on net sales, *if* a firm wants only to stimulate sales and does not care to have its sales force do anything but sell. The rewards then may be related closely to the results.

To control and direct sales activities.   A good pay plan should act as an unseen supervisor of the sales force by enabling management to control and direct their activities. Often today, this means motivating the reps to ensure a *fully balanced selling effort.* As a business implements the marketing concept, its sales people tend to become territorial marketing managers. This, in turn, means that they must be motivated to do a *total* selling job. That is, the compensation plan must offer incentive sufficiently flexible to cover such varied tasks as full-line selling, missionary work, marketing intelligence feedback, training junior sales reps, or controlling selling expenses, whenever these tasks are applicable.

On the other hand, a business may not be interested in a balanced sales effort. Inventory problems may force a firm to put all its energies into selling a limited number of products. Or, entrance into new markets may call for considerable short-run emphasis on customer development, even at the expense of immediate volume.

To ensure proper treatment of customers.   Another goal of a good compensation plan is to encourage sales people to treat customers properly. This aim is in some respects a corollary of the goal of controlling and directing the sales force, because consideration of customer interests ordinarily is in line with company objectives. Improper treatment of customers is a sure way to lose them to competitors.

To attract, keep, and develop competent sales people.   A good pay plan aids in building the quality of sales force desired by the company. First a good compensation plan should assist in *attracting* the caliber of reps wanted. Both the level and the method of compensation are important in reaching this goal. Either factor by itself ordinarily is not enough. Many retail institutions, for example, have difficulty in attracting qualified college graduates because the level of pay is too low. It is true that a company may offset a slightly lower level by providing greater future opportunity or by virtue of its location in a desirable environment. However, there is a limit to how far a business can go in offering substitutes for a competitive level and an attractive method of compensation, and still attract the caliber of sales force it wants.

A sound plan should also help to *keep* the desirable people hired and eliminate those who prove to have been poorly selected. Because no foolproof hiring system has yet been devised, it is possible that a firm with a reasonably good selection system may still make mistakes in hiring. Some of these mistakes may survive the formal training period. Then the burden for discovering and eliminating them falls to other managerial tools, one of which is the compensation plan. Evidence of incompetency usually appears soon after some incentive method is employed. Incompetent reps cannot make their quotas, or they do not earn a sufficiently large commission or bonus.

The organization also should use its pay plan to encourage good sales people to stay with the firm and help develop a loyal, satisfied, hard-hitting sales force. Sometimes a concern exerts considerable effort to attract a sales recruits, and then they are forgotten in matters of salary adjustments or other compensation features.

Basic requirements of a sound plan

In order to have some chance of achieving general objectives such as the four stated above, certain requirements should be met by the compensation plan. There is no standard list of these points. In fact, no sharp dividing line exists between an *objective* and a *requirement* of a sound plan.

Provision for two types of income.   An ideal compensation plan for a sales force provides both a steady income and an incentive income. This represents another conflict in the goals of a compensation plan. It is not possible to design a workable system that offers the greatest degree of both security and incentive. The concepts are mutually incompatible. In practice, the company must develop a compromise structure.

1. *Steady income.*   Any plan should provide a regular income, at least at a minimum level. The principle behind this point is that sales reps should not have to worry about how they will meet bare living expenses. If they have a bad month, if they are in seasonal doldrums, or if they are sick and cannot work for a period, they should not be totally without income. An attempt also should be made to eliminate extreme fluctuations in their earnings from one period to another.

Management must establish the *level* of this regular income. The sales rep should be able to meet living expenses, but the level should not be so high it lessens the desire for incentive pay.

2. *Incentive income.*   Besides a regular income, a good pay plan should furnish an incentive to induce above-minimum performance. Most people do better when offered a reward for some specific action than when no incentive is involved.

Flexibility.   A good plan is sufficiently flexible to meet the needs of individual territories, products, sales people, and business conditions. Not all territories present the same opportunity. A representative in a developed territory where the company is the leader in its field ordinarily should not be compensated by the same method as the person just sent into a district where the company has never before been represented.

Flexibility is needed to adjust for differences in products. Some are easier to sell than others. Some are staple products and can be sold on an ordertaking basis with frequent repeat sales. Others are sold one to a customer. There are no reorders, and much creative selling is needed.

The variations in a sales person's performance should be reflected rapidly in earnings. Few things can ruin morale faster than for a sales person to do far more than is required and then be uncompensated for the extra effort because the pay plan is inflexible. A sound compensation system also is adjustable to changes in business conditions. It should be possible to alter the plan so the reps cannot loaf and still receive high incomes just because there is a strong seller's market and sales are easy to make. By the same token, when times are genuinely hard a firm should not risk losing its good sales people simply because an inflexible plan will not grant them additional income to tide them over until business is better.

Simplicity and ease of understanding.   Simplicity is a hallmark of a good compensation plan. Sales people should have no trouble at all in understanding it and being able to figure what their income will be. The plan also should provide for payment as soon as possible after income is earned. Delays in payments of commissions or bonuses tend to destroy any simplicity in the plan because the rep has trouble keeping track of what was earned during the period. Delays also remove much of the incentive of such payments, since immediate rewards are more motivating than delayed ones.

Economy and competitiveness.   From management's standpoint, a compensation plan should be economical to administer, in order to minimize the office expense connected with computing the payroll. Furthermore, a firm wants to keep its sales force expenses in line with those of its competition. Otherwise, either the price of the product must eventually be increased, to the detriment of the firm, or else the profit margin will be decreased.

Fairness.   A good compensation plan is fair to both the sales force and management. If the sales people are paid more on a basis of years of service than on how well they do their job, dissatisfaction undoubtedly will occur among the younger reps. One way to ensure fairness in a plan is to base it as much as possible on factors that are controllable by the sales force and are measurable. More is said on this point in the next section.

STEPS IN DESIGNING A PLAN

Review job analysis and description

The first step in the design of a new compensation plan or the revision of an established one is to review carefully the detailed job description that was developed as part of the selection program. This should disclose the exact nature, scope, and probable difficulty of the job. There should be a separate description for each selling position, such as sales engineer, regular product sales person, missionary sales person, or sales trainee. The job descriptions indicate what services and abilities the business is paying for.

Determine specific objectives of plan

Part of the job of designing a compensation plan is deciding specifically what it is intended to accomplish. It is not enough to say that the goal is to get an honest day's work for a day's pay, or to attract good people. These are examples of the broad, general type of objective referred to earlier—objectives every plan should attempt to reach. In addition, a firm should have more detailed, specific aims in mind for a given job or type of sales person. Some examples of specific objectives are cited below, along with suggestions for the compensation method which can accomplish them best.

1. *Increase volume of net sales.* Some form of incentive is usually necessary, such as a commission or a bonus. A commission with a progressive rate may serve well, that is, the more the person sells, the higher the rate of commission.

2. *Increase sales volume of a certain class of products or to certain classes of customers.* A higher rate of commission may be paid on sales of the high-margin items, or whichever line of goods the company is trying to push. A bonus or higher rate of commission may be paid on sales made to desirable customer groups.

3. *Obtain new accounts.* A bonus may be paid for every new account brought in, or this activity may be reflected in a higher salary.

4. *Stimulate missionary work.* This includes such activities as training dealer sales people, making demonstrations, building displays, or offering accounting advice to customers. Some of these efforts can be individually measured; if so, it is possible to pay some form of commission for their accomplishment. Efforts that cannot be measured easily may be rewarded by having the salary form the bulk of the total compensation.

5. *Minimize expenses.* A bonus may be based on how much a sales rep's expenses run below an expense quota or how much they decrease from one period to another.

6. *Develop a new territory.* Probably all the income could be in the form of a salary, at least in the earliest stages of development.

It is surprising how often a firm has a sales force compensation system that is at odds with management's stated goals. In one study among firms in the southern California area, for instance, 40 percent of the respondents wanted a compensation plan "that emphasizes profitability." Yet only 4 percent of them had a commission or bonus plan based on profitability of a sale, and only 13 percent had a plan that controlled selling expenses. Contrary to the stated objective, in a big 77 percent of the cases a commission or bonus was based on sales volume. Next to profitability, the most desired feature was "additional incentive for top performers." Yet not a single company reported having such a feature in their sales compensation system.[2]

---

[2] "Does Your Pay Plan Suit Company Goals?" *Salesweek*, July, 1961, p. 12.

Determine job elements controllable by sales force and objectively measurable

Compensation should be based only on those items that are controllable by sales people and that can be measured. However meritorious, this is an ideal which is virtually impossible to implement completely. Yet, effective management can move toward this ideal.

Most factors contributing to sales success are controllable by the sales force only partially or not at all. Sales people have some control over their sales volume, for instance, but this control is limited by product attributes and company pricing policies. The point is that a firm should base each sales person's compensation on factors over which he has a maximum of control. It should be based on his own sales volume, for instance, rather than on total company volume. Or it should be based on his profit after deducting his direct expenses rather than on the net profit of the branch out of which he operates.

Once the firm has isolated the factors over which the sales people have a reasonable degree of control, the next step is to give as much consideration as possible to the elements that can be measured objectively. For instance, sales, selling expense, calls made, new accounts brought in, displays set up, or gross margin contributed are all quantitatively measurable. In contrast, such factors as building goodwill, contributing new sales ideas, or training dealer sales people are not easily evaluated, even though they are largely controllable by the sales representatives. This is not to say that these factors should be ignored in compensation matters, but executive judgment must be applied to a far greater extent concerning them. When management must consider subjectively measured factors in its appraisal of a person's productivity and overall worth to the company, then we get variations in compensation levels that are sometimes hard to justify to the sales force.

Establish the level of compensation

Importance of level.   As noted at the beginning of this chapter, one of the two most important steps in designing a pay plan is to determine the *level* of compensation (the other is to develop the *method*). The level of pay means the average earnings of the sales people— the average cost to the company over a given time period. Usually a firm establishes the level of pay before determining the method of compensation. The method is the general means by which the desired level is reached. In many respects, the level is more important than the method. To the sales reps, the level is their average gross income. Regardless of whether they get it in the form of salary or commission, they are more interested in how much they have earned than in how they earned it. To the company, it is the level of income that is the direct sales cost.

Management is also interested in the level because it is the factor that basically attracts most sales people. If they believe they will not be able to earn as much as they would like, they will probably not be attracted to the job regardless of the method used. On the other hand, they may take a sales job that offers an opportunity for a high income, even though the firm may not offer the exact combination of salary, commission, and bonus they prefer. Even society should be concerned with the level of compensation, because in the final analysis it is the *amount* of the sales people's earnings rather than the *method* of pay that is reflected in the cost of the product.

In spite of the importance of the level of sales compensation, surprisingly little has been written on the subject. When compensation is discussed in articles or conferences, the greater part of the attention is devoted to *how* the sales force should be paid rather than *what* their pay should be.

Unless a firm gives adequate attention to pay levels, it may be *overcompensating* its sales people relative to competitor's sales forces. This unduly raises selling costs and reduces profits. Overcompensating the sales force can have a dual affect on management personnel problems. First, it may be difficult to fill management positions with sales reps because they are reluctant to leave the higher paying sales jobs. Second, the morale of management personnel is undermined if sales people's earnings far exceed theirs. It can be equally harmful to *underpay* the sales force in relation to competitive levels. Almost inevitably, underpayment results in attracting a lower quality of sales people, with the attendant losses from poor performance.

When compensation levels are established on a companywide basis in order to keep morale high among office and plant workers, sales people may receive less than they could in competitive firms. Sometimes management underestimates the competitive level because of a lack of market knowledge. Underpayment also may occur when management judges the market level only on the basis of direct monetary compensation, with no regard for indirect monetary factors such as paid vacations, retirement plans, and company-financed insurance programs which other firms may offer.

Factors influencing level of compensation.   How does a company decide what it should pay its sales people? Ordinarily, it would be expected that the going rate of pay for sales reps—that is, the competitive level—would be a major determinant. But there is no clearly prevailing rate of pay for a given sales job in the same sense that there is for a certain type of office or factory work. Compensation levels for sales people do vary considerably among the different industries. Table 10–1 shows some examples of this spread. For companies in the apparel manufacturing industry, the median earnings of their *highest paid* sales person were $35,000 in 1974. Among producers of stone, clay, or glass products, the comparable median pay of top performers was $19,000. The median compensation for the *lowest paid* sales person in firms that make food or lumber products was $12,000. In contrast, the lowest paid sales people in petroleum refining averaged $18,000. Similar spreads in pay levels were reported in several service industries, such as computer services and insurance.

TABLE 10–1
Examples of variations in sales compensation levels—Median compensation for highest and lowest paid sales persons in companies in selected industries, 1974

Highest paid sales persons		*Lowest paid sales persons*	
Manufacturing:		Manufacturing:	
Apparel	$35,000	Petroleum refining	$18,000
Furniture	32,500	Electrical machinery and	
Primary metals	23,000	equipment	16,000
Stone-clay-glass		Food	12,000
products	19,000	Lumber	12,000
Services:		Services:	
Computer services and		Computer servicing	
electronic data		and electronic	
processing	$30,100	data processing	$16,600
Insurance	22,400	Insurance	13,000

Source: "What Salesmen Earn," *Sales Management,* October 6, 1975, p. 55. Data from survey by Research Institute of America.

The wide range of levels indicates that it is not clear just what constitutes a competitive earnings figure for sales people. So management must consider other guidelines, such as the experience requirements, the caliber of the job, or how well the company and its products are known. The pay level usually must be higher in a firm that spends less for advertising or is less well known than other companies. The firm with an effective sales training program may pay at a lower level than the organization that has no such facilities but must hire experienced sales people from competitors or other industries.

The amount the firm can *afford* to pay is an influencing factor in some cases, whether or not this level is competitive. A weak financial position may force management to tie the sales representatives' earnings directly to their productivity by paying them a straight commission on sales or gross margin.

There are some correlative relationships that may be useful guides.

The level of sales compensation seems to be related closely to the (1) method of compensation, (2) the size of the company, and (3) the age of the sales people.

Typically, a sales force with some incentive features in its compensation plan has a higher average pay than a group on straight salary. A large percentage of the sales forces in the highest paying industries as reported in the Table 10–1 worked under a straight commission pay plan.

Smaller firms in an industry generally tend to pay their sales forces more than larger firms do.[3] This seems to be because the smaller firm usually is less known, spends less on advertising, and has yet to develop a reputation for its products. Management must rely heavily on personal selling and a competent sales force. Also, the smaller firm usually does not have a comprehensive training program and so must pay more to hire experienced people.

Sales people's earnings tend to be related to their age.[4] Up to a point this is understandable, because older representatives have more experience and have developed more skills, so their productivity should be higher. In some firms, however, the tendency is to increase the pay level of older sales representatives even after their productivity has stabilized or started to decline.

Placing limitations on earnings.   One controversial question is whether management should place a ceiling or a limitation of some sort on the earnings of sales people. The question is most likely to arise when some part or all of the compensation plan is a commission on sales. Under a commission plan, in contrast to other types, a sales person is more likely to benefit from a windfall sale. This is defined as a single large order or a large new account for which the sales person gets a substantial boost in earnings, even though he has put forth no special effort and has little or no control over the sale. The question of limitations may also arise when a sales person's earnings are exceptionally high because he is getting a good commission rate and is selling in a growth territory with a high market potential.

Executives responsible for managing sales compensation plans strongly believe that there should be a wide pay differential between a field sales manager and members of the sales force, according to a Conference Board study.[5] This study reported a median pay differen-

[3] Richard C. Smyth, "Financial Incentives for Salesmen," *Harvard Business Review*, January–February 1968, pp. 110–11, 113.

[4] Ibid., pp. 110–12.

[5] The Conference Board, *Compensating Field Sales Representatives*, Studies in Personnel Policy, No. 202 (New York, 1966), pp. 38–40. On the point of pay differential, this study covered 300 sales forces in widely varied industries—consumer goods and industrial products, technical and nontechnical.

tial of 30 percent between first-level field sales managers and their average experienced sales representatives. That is, the executives' earnings were 30 percent higher than their subordinates'. However, as the commission segment (in contrast to the salary segment) of total earnings increases, the earnings differential between sales person and manager decreases. Some of the reasons why a wide differential (in effect, a limitation on sales earnings) is favored are:

1. It reduces the chances that star sales representatives will earn more than their bosses, thus raising questions of the boss's managerial fitness and adversely affecting executive morale.

2. It encourages field executives to think of themselves as managers and not just advanced sales people.

3. A star sales person is not likely to turn down a promotion to manager if this means a raise in pay. Also, a newly promoted sales executive is unlikely to continue to spend too much time in personal selling.

4. In the case of windfall sales, the argument is that sales people should not receive financial benefit from circumstances over which they have had no influence.

5. A wide differential can facilitate many aspects of compensation administration. A firm has some room to make regional cost-of-living adjustments in salaries without upsetting the entire sales person–executive salary chain. Also, a wide differential can leave management with enough "running room" to preclude the need for a written statement setting maximum pay limits, thereby maintaining the impression of unlimited earnings for sales people.

The reasons for having no ceilings or limitations seem to outweigh the arguments favoring them. The more a sales person earns, the more the company makes, particularly if the earnings are in the form of a bonus or commission. The idea of a ceiling seems totally alien to the philosophy of selling. A firm ordinarily does not say that it wants to limit the sales of its products to x dollars a year. The company probably would admit it is ridiculous to discourage or even turn down business beyond a certain figure, assuming that plant capacity were available. Yet, placing limits on sales reps' incomes has the same effect as discouraging sales in many cases. One recognized way to deter sales of low-margin items is to pay a very low rate of commission on sales of these products. By the same token, one way to limit overall sales is to establish methods that slow down or stop a person's earnings after they reach a given point. Sales people do not earn incentive income unless they produce, and the more they produce, the better off the company usually is.

If management does decide to curb the earnings of its sales people, several methods are available. One direct attack is to establish a maximum amount—a ceiling—above which the company will not pay. Another approach is to reduce commissions or bonus payments on all sales. Or the firm may establish a system of regressive commission rates, whereby successively lower commission rates are paid as sales volume increases beyond a given level. Windfall accounts may be classified as house accounts. These accounts are turned over to the territorial sales manager, and the sales person receives no earnings credit for sales to them. Management may even take the rather drastic step of changing its basic compensation plan so that less emphasis is placed on the incentive features and more on the fixed element of salary.

QUESTIONS AND PROBLEMS

1. "The compensation plan is the most important influence on a sales person's morale, and it is the most effective of all managerial tools for controlling, directing, and stimulating a sales force." Discuss all aspects of this statement.

2. Give several specific examples of evidence that may indicate that a sales force compensation plan needs revision.

3. As stated in this chapter, two of the broad goals of a sound compensation plan are to control and direct sales force activities, and to ensure proper treatment of customers. Can these goals be reached by use of any managerial tool or activity other than a good pay plan?

4. When designing a compensation plan for sales people, of what use is the job description?

5. Study some companies located near your school to determine the extent to which their sales compensation plans actually are aligned with management's stated goals for these plans.

6. "If a sales rep is entirely satisfied with the *level* of income, it follows that the *method* of compensation is unimportant." Discuss.

7. Rank the following types of sales jobs by total earnings, showing which type you feel should have the highest level of compensation, which is second, and so on. Justify your rankings.
   a. Missionary sales for a large soap company.
   b. Sales for a steel manufacturer.
   c. Door-to-door brush sales.
   d. Sales for appliance wholesalers.
   e. Life insurance sales.
   f. Sales for a manufacturer of office machines.
   g. Sales for a manufacturer of children's clothes, calling on retail department and other clothing stores.
   h. Sales for a firm selling conveyor systems.

8. "If the level and method of compensation are entirely satisfactory, management need not fear that the sales force will succumb to unionization." Discuss.

9. "The level and method of compensation vitally affect the program for selecting, training, and supervising a sales force. However, the selection systems or the training and supervision have no bearing on the level or method of compensation." Do you agree? Discuss.

10. Should the level of sales compensation in a firm with a national market be affected by regional variations in the general wage scale and the cost of living? Will your decision be influenced by the firm's policy regarding geographical differentials for its plant and office employees?

11. In 1972, a firm hired several college graduates in sales jobs for a salary of $700 a month plus expenses. By 1977, most of these people were making a salary of $925 to $975 a month plus expenses. In 1977, the same company hired more graduates and paid them $900 a month plus expenses. This was a competitive salary for qualified college graduates in 1977. Thus, the people with no experience received about the same pay level as those with four years' experience. Discuss the problems involved in this situation and suggest remedies.

12. If sales people's earnings have no limit, and often a good sales rep in a given firm can earn more than some of the company's sales managers, what incentive does a sales person in this company have for wanting to move up into management? Especially consider the sales people for whom a promotion means a decrease in income.

11

Compensating
the sales force
(continued)

*There is nothing so degrading as the constant
anxiety about one's means of livelihood.*
MAUGHAM

Two steps will complete our job of designing a sales compensation plan, which we began in the preceding chapter. One step is to determine the *method* of compensation. The other step is a series of final activities such as pretesting the plan, getting the approval of management and the sales force, putting the plan into effect, and providing for its frequent review and evaluation.

The compensation *method* chosen by a firm should (1) enable the company to reach its specified objectives, (2) bring the average earnings of sales people to the desired level, while (3) meeting as many of the requirements of a sound plan as possible.

The building blocks which are available to management when constructing a sales compensation plan include:

Salaries.

Drawing accounts.

Commissions.

Bonuses.

Expenses.

Profit sharing.

Indirect monetary benefits (vacation, insurance, pensions, and so on).

Some of these components act as an incentive for the sales force; others offer stability and security in earnings; still others may help the firm to control its sales costs. The more elements used in building a plan, the more complex it is.

BASIC TYPES OF COMPENSATION PLANS

Fundamentally, there are only three widely used methods of compensating a sales force:

1. A straight salary—a fixed element related to a unit of time during which the sales person is working.
2. A straight commission—a variable element related to the performance of a specific unit of work.
3. Some combination of compensation elements.

Since the end of World War II, there has been a significant growth in some form of plan that combines salary with an incentive feature. This trend has been primarily at the expense of salary-only plans, although there also has been a decrease in the popularity of straight commission plans. Moreover, the incentive component of sales force compensation is increasing and is becoming a larger proportion of the total pay.

Several major studies of sales compensation methods bear out these observations. Comparison of the Conference Board's 1971 report of manufacturers' pay plans for salesmen with its similar studies in 1966 and 1946[1] indicates the following trends in use of the major types of plans:

	1971	1966	1946
Number of manufacturers	341	665	433
Type of plan:			
Straight salary	19%	22%	37%
Straight commission	11	11	15
Salary plus incentives	70	67	48
	100%	100%	100%

In its 1971 survey of 505 U.S. companies, the Dartnell Corporation reported that 68 percent of the firms were using some method of salary plus incentive compensation for their sales people. About 13 percent

---

[1] The Conference Board, *Salesmen's Compensation Plans,* Studies in Personnel Policy, No. 81 (New York, 1946), p. 13; Conference Board, *Compensating Field Sales Representatives,* Studies in Personnel Policy, No. 202 (New York, 1966), p. 19; Conference Board, *Compensating Salesmen and Sales Executives,* Report 579 (New York, 1972), p. 41.

paid straight salary, and 19 percent used a straight commission with or without a drawing account.[2]

These overall figures do not reveal the wide industry variations in compensation methods preferred for sales forces. Aerospace firms and petroleum products companies, for example, tend to prefer straight salary plans. At the other extreme, companies manufacturing leather products, furniture, or apparel have traditionally favored straight commission plans.

A Research Institute of America study surveyed the compensation practices of over 2,000 firms, including wholesalers, retailers, and marketers of services as well as manufacturers. In addition, the sales people in these industries were surveyed for their preferences.[3] The results indicated the following practices and preferences:

	Current company practices				Sales peoples' preferences
	Manu-fac-turers	Whole-salers	Re-tailers	Ser-vices	
Straight salary	22%	13%	11%	42%	6%
Straight commission (with or without drawing account)	12	32	15	8	18
Salary plus incentive	66	55	74	50	76
	100%	100%	100%	100%	100%

Note that wholesalers are heavy users of straight commission plans; service firms prefer straight salary more than is typical of other groups; and the sales people themselves strongly endorse some form of combination plan.

Emphasis shifting from volume to profits

Traditionally, sales compensation plans in general and the incentive features in particular have been geared to generate sales volume for a firm. For years, in textbooks and among business executives, gross margins and some forms of net profits have been recognized as sound bases on which to build incentives into these pay plans. Yet this rec-

[2] Dartnell Corporation, *Compensation of Salesmen* (Chicago, 1971), p. 14. For a study which compared compensation plans in 1970 and 1950 and reported the same general trends toward salary-plus combination plans, see Jack R. Dauner, "Salesmen Compensation: More!" *Sales Management*, December 13, 1971, p. 27.

[3] Research Institute of America, *Sales Compensation Practices* (New York, 1965), p. 3.

ognition was largely lip service as far as sales executives were concerned. In recent years, however, there has been a modest shift in emphasis away from sales volume *alone* as the incentive base in sales compensation, and toward *profitable* sales volume.

The rise of profit consciousness probably coincides with the increasing acceptance of the marketing concept and the profit squeeze faced by so many firms in recent years. Executives have seen that an *increase* in company sales often is accompanied by a *decrease* in company profits. Consequently, they are coming to realize that sales volume alone is a poor indicator of a sales person's value to his firm.

The attention to profits does not mean that management has abandoned sales volume as a basis for incentive pay—far from it, as a matter of fact. Surveys show that a great majority of firms still base their commission payments on sales volume. These summary figures sometimes hide a very important fact. That is, while based on sales volume, these commission plans often are structured so as to achieve desirable goals such as encouraging full-line selling, getting new accounts, stressing profitable products, or pushing new products.

When designing profit-stressing incentive plans, many firms adopt the gross margin approach. That is, the commission or other incentive is based on the gross margin (net sales less cost of goods sold) resulting from a sales rep's total sales. Different rates of commission may be paid for different product lines in order to encourage sales force efforts toward some products more than others. An alternative approach is the contribution-to-overhead method. Under this method, the incentive pay is based on the gross margin less all marketing costs that can be charged *directly* to a given sales person. The problem in most profit-based plans is to develop one that accomplishes management's goal while at the same time meeting the "simplicity" requirement of a good plan.[4]

STRAIGHT SALARY PLANS

A salary is a direct monetary reward paid for performing certain duties over a period of *time*. The amount of payment is related to a unit of time rather than to the work accomplished. A salary is a fixed element in a pay plan. That is, in each pay period, the same amount of money is paid to a sales rep, regardless of that person's sales, missionary efforts, or other measures of productivity.

---

[4] For a series of business-oriented articles discussing sales compensation plans in several individual companies, see "Sales Force Compensation," *Sales and Marketing Management* (Special Report), August 23, 1976.

Strengths of straight salary plans

The assured regularity of income that a straight salary provides should give the sales person a considerable degree of security. A salary plan also provides a large measure of stability in earnings, without the wide fluctuations often found in commission plans.

The assurance of a regular, stable income can do much to develop loyal, well-satisfied sales people. Sales forces on straight salary usually have lower rates of turnover than those on commission. Sales people on a salary are more likely to feel they are a part of the company rather than being in business for themselves.

A salary plan is a good one to use during the developmental stage of a job, territory, or product. New recruits are usually paid a salary while in a training program, and for a period thereafter, until they can earn a satisfactory income under another method. When opening up a new market, a company frequently will send in its best sales people. These reps may have been on some kind of commission plan. During the pioneering stage in the new market, however, they will be switched to a straight salary plan. This move accomplishes two things—the reps' income is maintained at a reasonable level; and they are likely to do a well-rounded market development job rather than limiting themselves to commission-producing activities.

Management can direct the sales force into a variety of activities more easily under a salary plan than under any other method of compensation. As long as sales people are on a salary, it probably does not matter to them what job assignments they receive, assuming that the performance evaluation they receive is correspondingly based on these assignments. People who are paid a commission on sales may understandably balk if they are asked to spend time doing missionary work. Such activities mean time away from selling and therefore a decrease in immediate income. Management can explain how sales and income will increase greatly in the future if they do extra missionary work now. But the chances are that most sales people are not impressed by this argument.

Because people on salary are less likely to be concerned with immediate sales volume, they can give proper consideration to the customers' interests. There is no need for high-pressure selling, and there is little danger of overstocking a customer. Customers often react more favorably to a sales person if they know he is on straight salary, because they feel he is more apt to consider their interests. Of course, if performance evaluation is based primarily on meeting a volume quota, the drive for sales volume exists, regardless of which pay plan is used.

Limitations and administrative problems in the plans

Often what are considered limitations of a straight salary plan are really not *inherent* weaknesses in the plan, but only a reflection of poor administration. A good example is the frequently stated objection that a salary plan provides no direct incentive to the sales force. Part of this failure to furnish incentive usually can be traced to the *frequency* and *bases* of adjustment, which are administrative matters. Theoretically, salaries could be revised daily, weekly, or monthly in relation to the sales person's performance, but from a practical standpoint this is ordinarily not done. If it were, it would void the advantages of simplicity of operation and stability of income which a straight salary plan offers. The practice often is to go to the other extreme and seldom revise salaries. Adjustment is not made often enough to encourage extra effort or to keep the plan flexible.

Many salary plans fail to provide adequate incentive because the bases of adjustment are not sound. People should get raises in pay periodically if their work is more than satisfactory. But often there is no clear-cut understanding of what constitutes satisfactory accomplishment. Salary administration seems to be on a basis of expediency or arbitrariness. A person who complains enough or threatens to quit may get a salary increase, or raises may be geared to seniority. Often, people with long service are paid too much in relation to their results, while high-producing younger reps are underpaid.

A salary plan basically does not offer a strong, direct incentive to better performance in the same way that a commission or a bonus does. However, this drawback is usually accentuated out of all proportion because of administrative weaknesses.

Another disadvantage of a straight salary is the fact that it is a fixed cost. There is no direct relationship between salary expense and sales volume. When sales are down, the fixed cost of compensation can be a burden on the firm. When a business expands into new geographical territories or when new recruits are being trained, the salary cost can loom very large in the financial picture, because there is low sales volume from these products or trainees.

Another administrative problem is related to an advantage of a salary plan—namely, that management is able to direct the activities of the sales force. This presupposes that the workers are adequately supervised and that management gives proper credit for the types of activities it wants to encourage. A salary plan has no automatic feature that will stimulate a sales person to contact new prospects or sell high-margin items just because an executive says to do it. There must be a supervisory system to properly instruct the reps and then check up to be certain the job was done. Suppose that management urges sales people to do nonselling missionary tasks and then judges them on the basis of sales volume. They soon observe the inconsistency and respond to no direction unless it involves selling the product.

When a straight salary plan is best

Generally speaking, a salary plan is best used when management wants a well-balanced sales job, and when the executives are able to supervise the reps in a way that they are stimulated. Some of the specific situations for which a straight salary is better suited are as follows:

1. Sales recruits are in training or are still so new on the job that they cannot sell enough under a commission to make a decent income.
2. The company wants to enter a new geographical territory or sell a new line of products.
3. Several reps must work together for long periods in order to sell one account.
4. Sales involve a technical product which requires lengthy presale and postsale service and negotiations.
5. The job entails only missionary sales activities.

STRAIGHT COMMISSION PLANS

The straight commission plan involves a regular payment for the performance of a *unit* of work. In contrast to the salary method, which is a fixed payment for a unit of time, the commission is related to a unit of accomplishment. It is usually based on factors that are largely controllable by the sales people. The commission plan consists of three items: (1) a base on which performance is measured and payment is made—for example, net sales in dollars or product units; (2) a rate, which is the amount paid for each unit of accomplishment—for example, if a firm pays a nickel in commission for each dollar of sales, the rate is 5 percent; (3) a point where commission payments will start. The straight commission method may or may not include a provision for advances against future earnings (a drawing account). Also, the business may pay the sales people's travel expenses separately, or the commission may be adjusted upward and the reps pay their own expenses.

In evaluating the commission method, the major advantages of a salary are usually limitations of a commission plan, and the strong points of a commission are generally the weak ones of a salary. Essentially, the two methods are diametrical opposites.

Advantages of straight commission plans

Probably the major advantage of the straight commission method of sales compensation is the terrific incentive it gives the sales force. Many firms have no ceiling on sales reps' commission earnings, so their opportunities are unlimited. On the average, sales people on commission have a higher level of earnings than those on salary, except under very poor business conditions. In many types of commission selling, the sales reps can see the immediate reward for their efforts. They need not wait for the next salary review. They know they get $5 on every $100 order, or $15 for each supermarket display. Commission payments are a strong motivating factor to get the reps to work hard. Typically, a sales person on commission averages more hours of work each week than one on salary does.

A corollary advantage from the sales force point of view is the freedom of operation enjoyed by reps on straight commission. In many respects, they are almost independent business people. They often set their own hours and their own work schedule. Of course, this very advantage to the sales force works in reverse for management. It tends to weaken management's control over sales reps.

Some sales managers believe that the combination of maximum incentive and freedom of operation attracts a better caliber of sales person. However, there are no acceptable statistics to support the claim that a commission plan, or any other pay plan, tends to attract superior sales people. It is probably true, however, that a commission plan does a better and faster job of weeding out misfits.

If they are compensated in direct relation to their productivity, the better sales people are not apt to charge that they are being underpaid or are subsidizing the less able ones. Furthermore, sales representatives generally feel the commission plan is a fair one, assuming that the base and rate are fair, because their earnings are related to their own results. No one else's judgment affects their income, as is true under a salary plan. When incomes from *commissions* decrease, not nearly so many complaints are apt to come from the men as when *salaries* must be revised downward, even though the reason may be the same in each case.

Another big advantage to the company is that selling costs are controllable in relation to sales or some other base. The violent fluctuations of selling expenses as a percentage of sales that often accompany salary plans usually do not occur when a commission plan is used. In some cases, a firm that is not strong financially must resort to a commission because it cannot risk lack of control over selling expenses, even though otherwise it might be better to pay the sales force a salary.

Disadvantages of the plans

Several often-cited limitations of the commission method of sales compensation can be summed up under one point: It is difficult to supervise and direct the activities of members of the sales force because they tend to think they are in business for themselves.

Under the usual commission structure based on sales volume, often the sales people's only concern is to sell more merchandise, without regard to the interests of the company or the customer. The reps concentrate on easy-to-sell items and frequently ignore those that are slow-moving. In an effort to increase volume, they may make price concessions even to the detriment of the employer. Customers may be overstocked or sold more expensive items than is necessary.

Sales representatives on commission often disregard any thought of a fully balanced sales job, and management cannot expect them to do missionary work. They are more likely to skim the cream off a territorial market than to work it intensively. This preoccupation with sales is especially true when the sale is a one-time venture and there is very little repeat business.

Management is not totally helpless to combat some of these problems. In fact, considerable control may be exercised through the judicious modification of commission rates and bases. For example, to deter the sale of easy-to-sell, low-margin items, a commission may be paid on gross profit. Use of the gross profit base also discourages price concessions. A lower commission rate on easy-to-sell products also lessens the attention they receive.

Another disadvantage of the commission method is that earnings may fluctuate widely for reasons not controllable by the sales reps. In boom times, they may have a very high level of earnings through no particular effort of their own. On the other hand, when business is bad, sales people's earnings may drop sharply, even though they are working harder than ever.

When a straight commission plan is best

Conditions under which the straight commission method is best can be summarized as follows:

1. A company is in a weak financial position and cannot risk any arrangement other than one in which selling costs can be related directly to sales.
2. Great incentive is needed to get adequate sales.

3. Very little nonselling, missionary work is needed.
4. Adequate field supervision is not possible or feasible, so the firm must rely on a commission to accomplish the desired sales objectives.
5. Business conditions are good, and the sales force as a group prefers to go on straight commission.
6. Part-time sales people or independent contractors are used.

Administrative problems with the commission method

Several administrative problems are involved in use of the commission method, whether it is the only element in a compensation plan or it is part of a combination plan.

Commission bases. Most bases are related to sales volume, profits, or, in some cases, nonselling activities. A commission may be paid on sales as measured in dollars or units of the product.

A company can encourage attention to expense reduction or greater profit by basing commissions on gross margin, or on gross margin minus direct sales expenses. In some firms, the commission ostensibly is based on sales volume, but by establishing different rates for different product lines the company, in effect, is stressing the profit feature. That is, higher commission rates are paid on the high-margin products to encourage their sales. Conversely, low rates are paid on sales of products that carry low margins.

Sometimes, payment depends on the performance of some task such as making demonstrations or calling on new prospects. To speak of paying a commission for each demonstration made is considered by some to be a questionable use of the term. Some executives prefer the word *bonus*. In this text we will continue to use the term *commission* in these cases, because it represents payment for the performance of regularly expected activities.

Rates of commission. Management must determine the rate of commission—that is, the amount paid for each unit of accomplishment. Rates vary among companies, and even within a given firm there may be rate differentials among the products or territories. The choice of rates may be affected by such factors as (1) the level of income desired for the sales force, (2) the profitability of given products, (3) difficulty in selling a product, (4) classes of customers, or (5) territorial problems.

Rates may be constant throughout all stages of sales volume, or they may be on a sliding scale, going upward or downward as sales volume increases or decreases. A *progressive* rate is one that increases as the volume increases. To illustrate, a business may pay 3 percent on sales up to $10,000 a month, 5 percent on the next $40,000 (sales from

$10,000 to $50,000), and 6 percent on everything over $50,000. A sales person who had sales of $65,000 for the month, would receive a commission of $3,200, computed as follows:

3% on first $10,000	$ 300
5% on $10,000–50,000	2,000
6% on $15,000 (amount over $50,000)	900
	$3,200

A progressive rate is intended to offer a great incentive to the reps in that the more they sell, the more they make on each sale. The company usually can afford to step up the rate because only the variable costs increase with each marginal dollar of volume. The larger the sales, the less the overhead charged to each unit of volume. A progressive rate is also justified if sales are increasingly difficult to make as volume goes up. A progressive rate requires careful administration to prevent reps from taking advantage of the system. They may postdate or predate orders so all fall in one period. Thus they artificially boost their volume during a given period and consequently qualify for a higher rate on the last orders turned in.

A *regressive* rate works in reverse. The concern may pay 7 percent on the first $20,000 of sales in a given period, 5 percent on the next $20,000, and 3 percent on all sales over $40,000. A regressive rate has some merit if it is hard to get the first order, but once it is signed the reorders come frequently and automatically. A regressive rate also may be used to even out the earnings of all sales people or to reduce the effect of windfall sales. A regressive rate requires careful administration to discourage a sales person from withholding orders at the end of a commission period when they would command a lower rate, and then turning them in at the start of the next period when these orders would result in a higher commission rate.

Drawing accounts. Administrators must determine whether or not a drawing account will be employed. A drawing account may be a fixed sum advanced to a sales person at regular time intervals, such as weekly or monthly. Or it may be a limited amount that a rep can draw against as wanted during the period, so long as the outstanding balance has not reached the predetermined limit. The amount drawn is paid back to the company out of the person's commission earnings during the same period.

A drawing account may or may not be guaranteed. Under a *nonguaranteed* plan, the advance is strictly a loan. If a sales person does not earn enough in commissions to pay back the advanced funds in one time period, then the balance of the debt is carried over to the next period. As an example, assume that a salesman has a draw of $400 a month and earns a commission of 5 percent on sales. If his sales were $10,000 in January, his total commissions would be $500, out of which the company would withhold $400 to cover the amount drawn he drew at the first of the month. If he sold only $6,000 in January, his commissions would total $300, all of which would be withheld to cover the advance draw. He would then be $100 in arrears, which would be carried over to February. If his sales in that month were $11,000, with commissions of $550, then he would receive only $50. The company would take $100 to cover the carry-over debt from January and $400 to pay for the February draw, leaving $50.

A *guaranteed* drawing account is operated in much the same fashion, with one big exception. At the end of a stated period, if a sales rep's commissions total less than his draw, the debt is canceled. It is not carried forward, and he starts with a clean slate. Thus a guaranteed draw is much like a salary.

Drawing accounts are used to offset some of the drawbacks of the straight commission plan in that they add a semblance of security and regularity of income. In businesses where sales fluctuate considerably on a seasonal basis, an advance can be very helpful to sales people. In effect, the company is taking over some of their budgeting problems. Assume a case in an industry where sales are high from October through December and April through June. Without a drawing account, the reps must make the high earnings of October–December stretch to cover the lean months of January–March, and many people cannot save or budget in this manner.

When a new sales person is put on a job or a new territory is opened, the company may use a drawing account for a period of time rather than change the compensation plan from commission to salary. This is particularly likely to happen if past experience shows that in a relatively short time the situation will correct itself. That is, in time the new sales people or those with new markets can do well on a commission and can easily repay their drawing accounts.

However, for many firms the operating and administrative problems far offset the possible advantages of drawing accounts. Clerical and bookkeeping work is increased to take care of the necessary computations. Also, drawing accounts do not furnish management with much opportunity to control the reps' activities. Unless a drawing account is carefully controlled, various abuses can arise. Sales people may come to think of the account as something that belongs to them as a salary, not as a loan. Some may run far in arrears until they see the situation is hopeless. Then, realizing they can never earn enough in commissions to pay back the debt, they quit their jobs. Because of the problems involved in drawing accounts relative to other methods, there has been a trend away from their use during the past several years. The tendency is, instead, to supplement a commission with a base salary.

Many of these abuses are not inherent weaknesses of the system but are simply evidences of poor management. Executives should be careful to point out to new reps that a drawing account is a loan and not a salary. It certainly is the fault of the administration when sales reps are allowed drawing accounts long after it is evident that they are not capable of producing effectively on the job. Once a person is far in arrears, it is wishful thinking to expect repayment in most cases. Management should not allow a long period of time to elapse before set-.tling up on drawing accounts. A quarterly or semiannual settlement period is frequently used as a reasonable length of time. Ordinarily, it is a mistake to let an account run as long as a year with no reconciliation.

Split commissions.   When two or more sales people work together on a sale, administrative provision must be made to split any commission or other credit given. Various situations can arise which call for a decision on the issue. It may take three people to complete a sale of some large, technical product. One may be the territorial sales rep, the second a sales engineer or service representative from the home office, and the third could be the district manager. If a commission or bonus is part of the compensation plan for each of these people, distribution of the credit is a problem.

Geographical location can also complicate the commission division. For example, a sales person in the Birmingham district may make a sale, but the order is placed through the buyer's home office in Atlanta. To further complicate matters, delivery may be made to plants in Nashville and New Orleans as well as to Birmingham. If each of the

---

A day-to-day operating problem in the

MAJESTIC GLASS COMPANY (E)

A split-commission situation in sales compensation

Several of Majestic's largest customers were huge nationwide corporations having plants and offices in several cities where members of the sales force were located. Some had numerous product divisions, and several executives might be involved in purchasing at different cities. Such complexities made it difficult for Clyde Brion, general sales manager, to decide which Majestic sales representative should receive the commission for a particular order. Often these orders were very large.

For example, the Cincinnati sales representative, Elton Boggess, had turned in an order for cosmetics bottles from the Mi Charmé Products Company in that city, totaling more than $200,000. Furthermore, Boggess had written *New Customer* across the face of the order, thus claiming the additional 5 percent commission on orders from new customers. The order clearly stated that the bottles were to be shipped to the Mi Charmé plant at Baltimore, Maryland. Baltimore customers were called on by James Woodall, Majestic's sales rep based in Washington, D.C.

Brion remembered having read in a recent issue of *The Wall Street Journal* that the Mi Charmé Products Company had been purchased by Elaine Marhman, Inc., of New York City. This firm was best known for its foods line. It had been a regular buyer of Majestic salad oil bottles through Majestic's New York City salesman, Bradley Norton.

To complicate the incident, Brion found in the same mail that had brought Boggess's order an identical order from Woodall, also claiming the extra commission for having sold a new customer. Had the duplication not been noticed, Majestic might have delivered a double amount of merchandise.

Brion tried to resolve the situation by telephoning the director of purchasing for Elaine Marhman, Inc. This official offered little help, saying that the firm's buying procedures for the "cosmetics division" were not yet formalized. However, he was familiar with the order in question and remembered having talked with Woodall about it while in Washington, D.C.

Brion then telephoned Norton, the New York City sales rep, who said that he was busily working on the Mi Charmé order but it had not yet been confirmed. He said that he did not intend to claim it as a new-customer order, nor did he know to what extent Boggess or Woodall had participated in the sale.

Brion asked, "Who should get the commission, then?" Norton laughed and replied, "I guess that's what we have a sales manager for, sir!"

Questions

How should the regular 10 percent commission be split in this situation?

Should this order qualify for the additional 5 percent paid on new-customer orders?

Note: See the introduction to this series of problems in Chapter 2 for the necessary background on the company, its market, and its competition.

four cities mentioned is in a different territory covered by separate sales reps, the sales manager has a real problem in splitting any commission involved. The Birmingham sales person may want to claim full credit, pointing out that the order basically originated in his territory and through his efforts. At the same time, the Atlanta rep may have been calling on the buyer's home office for some time. The problem of split commissions can be particularly nasty when central buying offices are concerned. Often, the sales people in the outlying territories feel that their efforts avail them little. They believe that the sales reps located in cities with many central offices are living parasitically off the hard workers in the hinterland.

No simple or generally accepted method exists for handling split credits. Instead, each firm must feel its own way, using executive judgment to arrive at a policy. Practices differ even in the same industry. As a rule of thumb, management should allow only a limited number of percentage splits, such as 50–50 or 75–25. Moreover, a sales person who really makes no contribution to the sale should not receive any commission credit, even though delivery is made into his territory.

House accounts.   House or no-commission accounts are customers serviced by the branch or home-office executives. Usually, no commission is given to sales people when sales are made to these accounts. Problems are minimized if management follows two policies. First, the number of house accounts must be severely limited. Second, all house or no-commission accounts must be clearly defined in advance of solicitation. House accounts may be justified when windfall commissions would otherwise result without commensurate effort, as with reorders from large national accounts or the federal government. House accounts also are in order when the efforts of one or more executives are required to make a sale. Abuses can creep into the system when management steps in too often or takes the good accounts, some of which have been developed by the sales force.

Commission pools.   In some instances, management can partially solve the problem of split commissions or excess house accounts by establishing a commission pool. Under a pool arrangement, all commissions on sales when more than one person is involved are placed in a common fund. Then, at the end of a given period, the total in the pool is distributed among the participating sales people, according to some predetermined basis. In regard to house accounts, some companies have agreed that when house sales reach a certain figure, all commissions on additional house sales are placed in a pool for later distribution among the sales force. The major administrative problems are to establish the basis for deciding what commissions will be pooled and then to determine how the accumulated funds will be divided.

Mail and telephone sales. An executive decision must be made on whether to pay a commission on an order mailed or telephoned in by the customer. Most firms pay a commission on such orders because, presumably, they came as a result of selling effort made at some time by the territorial representative. In fact, many companies urge small accounts to send in mail or telephone orders in an attempt to reduce the sales people's calls and the expense connected with such accounts.

Sales with trade-ins. A policy must be established for commission payments on sales made with a trade-in. Some firms pay the commission on the difference between the sales price of the product and the amount allowed on a trade-in. If the item sold for $1,000 and $300 was allowed on the used trade-in, the commission would be based on $700. Then, if the sales person later sells the item received on trade-in, the same procedure is followed. Other firms pay a commission on the full selling price of the product—$1,000 in the last example. Then another commission is paid when the traded-in item is resold. Another method is to pay on the "washout," or net profit made after both the new product and the traded-in items are sold. The following facts may be assumed in the sale of a new automobile, for example. The invoice cost plus freight on the new car is $3,200, and it is sold for $4,000. The amount allowed on the trade-in is $2,500; $300 is the cost to fix up the old car, and it is sold for $2,600. The company would pay a commission on the $600 it netted on the complete series.

Installment sales. On installment sales, some firms pay the full commission to the sales person when the sale is made, even though it will be some time before full payment is received. Even if the buyer defaults and the product is repossessed, no penalty is suffered by the sales person. In other cases, the sales person receives the commission piecemeal, as the installments are paid by the buyer. Basically, this is the system used by many life insurance companies. A sales person may get 30 percent of the first year's premium and 10 percent of each subsequent annual premium. If the policy is dropped, commission payments cease.

Bad debts. When sales people are paid by the commission method, policy must be set regarding who should bear the burden of loss from bad debts, particularly in sales when the merchandise cannot be repossessed. To a great extent, this depends on how much authority the sales force has in determining whether a given customer should be granted credit. Probably the most widely used practice is to pay full commission to the sales person, even though the customer later defaults in payments. This policy is usually adopted where the sales people have little or nothing to say about granting credit.

Sales returns. If a commission is based on sales, the usual practice is to pay on *net* sales—that is, gross sales minus returns and allowances.

Therefore, if a sale is made and the commission is paid, and then part of the order is returned, it is necessary to recoup from the sales person the commission paid on the return goods. It is true that the return may not have been caused by anything the sales person did. Possibly, the order was delivered late or a mistake was made in filling it, and as a result the buyer was angry and returned the merchandise. However, the principle behind the system is that the bulk of returns are the fault of the sales force because they oversell customers who later change their minds.

COMBINATION PLANS

Today, some form of combination plan is used in about two thirds of all sales forces. While the various compensation elements may be grouped in countless ways to form a pay system, most of the combined arrangements seem to fall within relatively few categories, such as:

Salary and commission.
Salary and bonus.
Salary, commission, and bonus.
Commission and guaranteed drawing account.
Commission and bonus.

The additional compensation elements of profit sharing and expenses may be worked into any of the above groupings. Or, they may be combined with either straight salary or straight commission.

Broadly speaking, the purpose of any combination plan is to overcome the weaknesses of a single method, such as straight salary or straight commission, while at the same time keeping its strong points. The degree to which a combination plan can be considered successful depends on management's ability to achieve the desired balance among the several elements used to build the plan.

What should be the respective proportions of the incentive and salary features in a compensation plan? One half of the sales people questioned in one study said the salary should be 75 percent or more; almost 9 out of 10 wanted at least 50 percent salary.[5] Another researcher observed that in more than half the industries he studied (where an incentive plan was used) the proportion of incentive compensation was simply too small to be an effective motivator. He concluded that the incentive as a minimum should be 25 percent of the total income.[6] The proportions of salary and incentive that should be

[5] Research Institute of America, *Sales Compensation Practices*, pp. 2–3.

[6] Richard C. Smyth, "Financial Incentives for Salesmen," *Harvard Business Review*, January–February 1968, pp. 114–15.

used depend on the nature of the selling tasks and the company's marketing goals. The incentive share should be larger or smaller in relation to the significance of the sales person's skill and persuasiveness in making the sale. The salary element is larger when management emphasizes customer servicing, a total selling effort, or team selling.

Additional components

Three components in combination plans have not yet been discussed. They are bonuses, profit sharing, and expenses.

Bonus. Nature and purpose. A *bonus* is probably the most loosely used word in the compensation vocabulary. As a result, sometimes it is difficult to assess accurately the extent to which it is used in pay plans. A bonus is a lump-sum payment for an above-normal performance. It is not related directly to the accomplishment of a *specific* unit of work as a commission is. Because of its nature, a bonus cannot be used alone but instead must always be combined with other methods such as a salary or commission.

Strictly speaking, neither the amount of the bonus nor the basis for distributing it need be announced in advance by management. In fact, management theoretically has no obligation to pay a bonus in any given year, even though one has been paid for several preceding years. Employees may know they will get a bonus, but they never know in advance how much it will be in total or how management will distribute it. Beyond these *narrowly defined* usages, however, there is a more realistic use of the term which considerably broadens its meaning. Most sales bonuses are intended to stimulate the sales force to perform certain tasks by offering an incentive. Unless the plan is explained fully in advance, management will gain nothing for the bonus given.

In practice it may be difficult to draw a clear line between a bonus and a commission. For instance, management agrees to pay a lump sum of $500 when a sales person's sales reach a quota. Many call this plan a bonus because it is a lump-sum payment not directly related to each sales dollar. Others say it is *not* a bonus because there was a previously established and announced agreement. Quite possibly the distinction is an academic matter to sales managers. The name given to a compensation element may not be important, just so they know what it accomplishes, how it operates, and what administrative problems are involved.

The most commonly used basis for paying a bonus is the measure of a sales person's performance against a quota—typically, a sales volume quota or an expense quota. A sales rep may get a cash bonus for reaching a sales quota or x dollars for going 10 percent over quota. To keep direct selling expenses within 8 percent of sales, at the end of the year a firm may pay to each rep a bonus equal to half the amount by which his expenses are under the 8 percent ratio. If his sales were $100,000 and expenses were $7,000 (7 percent), the bonus would be $500, or half the savings under the 8 percent ($8,000) expense quota.

Many other bonus payment bases, while used to a lesser extent, may serve management admirably in given situations. These bases include gross margin on sales, new accounts acquired, and profits earned by the entire company or by a geographical division. A bonus may be paid to an individual salesman or to a group of people.

Evaluation of bonuses. It is difficult to make a general evaluation of the bonus element in sales compensation because of the variety of payment bases and distribution methods used. The key to much of the success of a bonus lies in the method of its distribution. Unless a sales person can see that the bonus he receives is related to his results, much of the possible incentive is lost. In some cases, a bonus is distributed equally among all sales people. In other instances, it may be spread in proportion to each person's total earnings. These two methods are questionable if a firm wants to effectively stimulate its sales force. One person may work much harder than another, but the first can get a much smaller bonus simply because his salary is lower than that of the other sales reps.

A group bonus plan is subject to similar criticisms. One member of the group may not see how his efforts are receiving a proportionate reward. The better sales reps may feel they are carrying the poor ones. A sales person may even feel he gains more in a given sales situation by actually going against group interest. For instance, the commission he may make on a sale by cutting a price may more than offset the loss in his share of the group profit bonus on the sale. On the other hand, a group bonus certainly should encourage the teamwork which is so necessary in many types of industrial selling.

Probably the most effective use of a bonus is first to base the payments on some quantitative factor controllable by the sales force, such as reaching a sales or expense quota, rather than on net profits or some intangible, such as building goodwill. Then, the payments should be related to the performance of the activity. Actually, the nearer a firm reaches these two goals, the more the bonus becomes a commission. However, this is of no great moment if the goal of both is to stimulate the sales force to perform the activities management wants.

Of course, once a quantitative measure enters the picture, flexibility is reduced. Some sales managers prefer not to overformalize bonus plans. They feel that the salary and commission elements introduce enough rigidity into a pay plan, and they want to have the element of flexibility afforded by a subjectively distributed bonus. From a realistic standpoint, however, it is probably wishful thinking to believe that a considerable degree of flexibility can be practiced at the same time all the other goals of a bonus plan are achieved.

Profit sharing. Profit sharing is *not* widely used as a separate method of paying a sales force or as an important part of a combination plan. It would seem to be a serious mistake to make profit sharing a significant part of a compensation plan for sales people because they do not have sufficient control over profits. Inefficiencies in purchasing or production may raise costs to the point where profits are erased even though the sales force does a better than average job. The reverse may also be true; production cost savings, plus a sellers' market, may result in huge profits with little effort on the part of the sales force. Profit sharing offers no direct incentive for increasing sales or performing any task ordered by management.

Expenses. Ordinarily, reimbursement for travel and other sales expenses incurred by the sales force should be kept separate from their compensation. The two elements usually cause enough problems on their own without combining them, and their nature and purposes are entirely different. Even when handled separately, expense payments can result in a net addition or deduction from a person's earnings, so difficult is the problem of reimbursement. However, many companies do group the two by building a compensation plan under which the sales reps pay all their own expenses. The subject of sales force expenses is covered in the next chapter.

Salary-plus plans

Three commonly used combination plans involving salary are salary plus commission, salary plus bonus, and salary plus commission and bonus. In all three, sales reps usually are reimbursed separately for their expenses.

Salary plus commission. This plan is probably used more than any other type of compensation method, but no generally agreed-on percentage division prevails between the fixed and the variable elements. The salary-commission plan tends to enjoy the advantages of a salary plus the incentive and flexibility features of a commission. But this plan is more complex and costly to operate because of the increased number of elements involved. Also, the addition of incentive features at the expense of the salary can reduce the element of managerial control over the sales force. In the final analysis, as was mentioned earlier, the success of this plan—or of any combination plan, for that matter—depends largely on the balance achieved among the elements.

Salary plus bonus. For the company that essentially wants to control its sales force at all times and still offer some incentive, a salary plus bonus may be the answer. Usually, the salary element constitutes the major part of the total earnings—much more so than in a salary-commission plan. The salary plus bonus arrangement is excellent for the firm that wants some activity encouraged for a short period of time and then dropped so some other task can be emphasized. However, the incentive under a salary-bonus plan typically is not so strong as under a commission arrangement. In general, this plan enables management to control and direct sales force activities more than the straight salary plan does. All the control features of a straight salary are present, plus the opportunity for a special push behind some task the employer feels is particularly desirable.

Salary plus commission and bonus. This plan is likely to be used by firms which use a salary plus commission plan, but occasionally would like to stimulate some specific, extra nonselling effort. Management may want to get some new accounts or push the missionary work behind one product line. In situations of this nature, the bonus feature is an ideal addition to the pay plan. Use of all three elements—salary, commission, and bonus—can result in an excellent structure if properly administered. The salary gives the control and income security advantages; the commission furnishes regular incentives; and the bonus is available to stimulate trouble-shooting assignments.

Commission-plus plans

Two additional typical combination plans involve a commission but no salary. In one, a commission is combined with a guaranteed drawing account, and in the other with a bonus.

Commission plus guaranteed drawing account. As explained earlier, a guaranteed drawing account is an advance against commissions which must be paid back if commissions are large enough in a given period. However, any indebtedness at the end of the period is canceled.

From a mechanical standpoint, a guaranteed draw is much like a salary. The draw plus a commission is similar to a salary plus commission over quota. In this case, the quota would be the amount of the drawing account. For example, a rep who was paid a guaranteed draw of $600 a month plus a commission of 5 percent on net sales would start receiving a commission when his sales reached $12,000 a month. While this plan may be similar to salary plus commission from a computational viewpoint, it has significant psychological differences.

First, management probably can adjust the level of the drawing account much easier than the level of salary. Second, under a commission plus guaranteed drawing account plan the company has the fixed-cost weakness of the salary without the control advantages, because most sales people probably link the plan more to straight commission.

Commission plus bonus. Sometimes an organization wants to alleviate the ills of a straight commission plan without being restricted by a fixed-cost element such as a salary or guaranteed draw. The addition of a bonus structure may be a happy solution, particularly when the commission is paid on net sales starting at the zero point. When management wants to encourage sales of high-margin items, for example, a bonus may be paid for reaching a certain quota of sales of these products.

Point systems in compensation plans

In a point system for compensation, credit for performance of a task is recorded in points, and compensation is paid in proportion to the total points earned in a given period. The point system is not a separate basic compensation method. Instead, it is a distinct way of determining how much to pay a sales person under one of the plans discussed above. Under this system, management itemizes all the tasks it wants to encourage and then assigns point values to each in relation to the emphasis attached to the task.

To maximize the effects of the point system, the duties should be broken down into some detail. For example, instead of giving points for missionary work, that task may be divided into several units, such as training distributor sales people or calling on new accounts. Points may be established for advertising and promotional activities, such as building displays or persuading dealers to run cooperative advertisements. Different point values may be set for each dollar of sales of the various product lines in order to encourage the sales of high-margin items or seasonal goods that must be closed out.

The entire compensation plan or only a part of it may be related to a point system. For instance, under a straight commission plan a sales person may be paid a dollar for every 10 points accumulated, and the point values may be related to gross margin as follows:

1. Products with gross margin of 10–18 percent: 1 point for each $5 of sales.
2. Products with gross margin of 19–30 percent: 3 points for each $5 of sales.

3. Products with gross margin of over 30 percent: 5 points for each $5 of sales.

In addition, the firm may encourage a sales rep to pay attention to something other than sales volume by giving points for a small number of nonselling tasks, such as:

1. New prospect called on: 10 points.
2. Order from a new account: 25 points. (This is in addition to the points acquired in relation to the gross margin on the order.)
3. Display built: 20 points.

Probably the biggest advantage of a point system is its flexibility, which enables management to guide and control the sales force activities. Management can emphasize or deemphasize the performance of any given task simply by changing the point values for accomplishing it. A sales executive can broaden the base of a commission or bonus plan simply by assigning points to additional jobs. Furthermore, it usually is easier to change point values than to alter the base or rate for a commission.

A point system requires careful administration in establishing point values if the system is to result in the desired degree of managerial control. The goal of a well-rounded sales job can be thwarted if sales people try to accumulate points through one or two jobs. They may do this because these tasks come easy for them. Or, it may be that the points for each duty are out of balance. That is, a specific job carries far more credit than the effort or results warrant. Another administrative problem is the need to devise some method for checking on sales people's achievements to be certain they have properly performed the activities for which they have claimed points.

INDIRECT MONETARY COMPENSATION

In the past, sales managers typically felt that their responsibility for compensation of the sales force ended when the paychecks were tendered. If there were any additional financial benefits, such as vacations or insurance, management usually reserved them for office and factory workers. The sales force was considered a unit apart, frequently not even a member of the family of employees. The salesman was a lone wolf, a rugged individualist, and a traveling man.

Today, however, young people going into selling are more security conscious, and management is acquiring a sense of social responsibility. Sales executives are realizing that they owe their sales force members more than just a paycheck. Rewards are due in two other general areas. One is *nonfinancial compensation* in the form of honors, recognition, and opportunity. These features help sales people develop a sense of self-worth and of belonging to a group. The other type of reward is *indirect monetary payment* of items that have the same effect as money, though payment is in a less direct form than salary or commission. These items, which are also referred to as fringe benefits, include such things as retirement plans, vacations, and insurance. Management's handling of these two broad types of rewards can have as much effect on sales people's morale as any policy relating to a salary level or commission rate.

The trend toward the inclusion of indirect monetary payments in sales compensation plans began after World War II. Indeed, what is referred to as fringe benefits is better considered a part of the whole. Today, most sales people enjoy the same employee benefits (vacation, insurance, and so on) as do other employees in comparable positions in a company. This is especially true for sales people who have some element of salary in their compensation plans.

Most firms give their sales people paid holidays and provide paid vacations of varying lengths (usually two to three, or two to four weeks), depending upon the employees' length of service. Paid vacations present a managerial problem in connection with sales people who work partly or entirely on commission. They usually receive no vacation pay to represent the commission. Firms often give these reps their regular drawing accounts, which must be repaid from postvacation earnings. Also, many companies pay a commission to the reps on any sales that come in from their territories while they are on vacation. Most medium- and large-sized firms provide various insurance programs (group life, medical, hospitalization) for their sales force.

Outside sales people are covered under the federal Social Security Act. In addition, significant numbers of firms have included their sales forces under a company retirement plan that supplements the social security program. Only the smallest companies still seem to have no pension plans, but the sales force is not singled out. Generally no employees are covered by pensions in these firms.

The main argument against a retirement plan is its cost. Some companies finance the entire plan. However, the majority probably use a system in which both the employer and the sales people contribute. Sales people's participation may be based on their total earnings or only on the amount reflected in their salaries. Another popular method is for the employer to put a share of the profits into a pension fund.

As a summary comment regarding fringe benefits, sales people who are paid straight commissions usually do not fare quite so well as do those who receive salaries.

Indirect monetary benefits are proving to be important in attracting desirable sales applicants. Since these benefits are being given in so many competitive nonsales jobs, it has become almost a necessity to offer similar benefits in order to recruit qualified sales people. It is probable that these benefits give sales people a greater degree of security and make them more loyal and cooperative. These characteristics undoubtedly have some bearing on a reduction in the turnover rate. It also seems a reasonable conjecture that a good program of fringe benefits can be a strong deterrent to unionization of a sales force.

FACTORS INFLUENCING CHOICE OF PLAN

Throughout the discussion covering the major types of compensation plans, examples were cited of conditions under which a given plan would operate best. In each instance, one or more factors influenced the choice of a particular method of payment. Sales managers should consider these factors when selecting a compensation method. Some of the more important points to be taken into account are:

1. Nature of the market and channels of distribution.
2. Nature of the job.
3. Caliber of the sales people.
4. Financial condition of the company.
5. General business conditions.

FINAL STEPS IN DEVELOPMENT OF THE PLAN

Pretest the plan

After management has tentatively selected the method of compensation to be used, the next step is to pretest the entire compensation plan as much as possible. This involves determining how the proposed plan would have operated if it had been in effect during the past few years. Management can estimate what the cost to the company would have been and what income would have been earned by the reps. The study should help find out whether there would have been any undesirable windfall earnings or periods of abnormally low income for each sales person.

No amount of pretesting can answer all questions. If the new plan had been in effect, sales might have been quite different. The commission features of a plan are easier to pretest than is the salary element. If the base salary is adjusted 20 percent upward, it is hard to say how much more effective the missionary work will be or how much harder the sales force will work. However, several calculations can be made regarding the commission or bonus elements. By assuming various levels of sales for each line of products, management can compute what the compensation cost will be. Pretesting is time-consuming; it may be expensive and may require considerable clerical work.

Regardless of its limitations, pretesting is a necessity. After spending untold hours in developing a compensation plan, it is unthinkable that management would not attempt to see how it might operate before installing it formally.

Introduce plan to sales force

If the plan has been developed carefully, the sales people have been asked for their suggestions and criticisms. When the plan is ready to be installed, the sales force should again be consulted. Often, sales people believe that management is only trying to cut sales costs, and any adjustment in compensation must be intended to lower their earnings. The final plan should be introduced in small conference groups, so the reps have a chance to ask questions and management has the greatest possible opportunity to explain the system.

Install plan and evaluate it periodically

A compensation plan may be installed throughout the entire sales force, or it may be placed in only one or two territories as a form of test situation. If a company does not feel that a pretest can be conducted under realistic conditions, it may prefer to field test the plan in a few districts under actual selling conditions, in order to locate any weaknesses.

The final step in management of sales force compensation is to make certain the entire plan will be reappraised frequently to prevent it from becoming outmoded. A common mistake is to spend much time and money developing a good compensation system (or selection or training program) and then let the system become outdated. A person's job often changes over a period of time. Market and product conditions change. It is only sound management to keep a compensation plan in tune with the times.

QUESTIONS AND PROBLEMS

1. Following are three problems often faced by sales managers:
   a. Sales people tend to overemphasize the easy-to-sell parts of multiple

product lines in an effort to build sales volume; other more profitable lines are forced into the background.

b. Sales people need to spend more time developing new accounts.

c. In order to improve a company's long-term position, sales people should be doing more missionary work and developing long-term customers to meet expected competition, rather than just striving to meet this year's volume quota.

In each case suggest a specific type of compensation plan that may be used to solve these problems.

2. What is the economic justification underlying the progressive commission rate? Is there any economic justification for a regressive rate? Is a regressive rate psychologically sound? Which of the two rates is better for stimulating a sales force?

3. What factors determine the commission rate to be paid sales people for a manufacturer of portable power tools? What conditions may influence a sales manager to reduce the established rates?

4. When sales reps are paid a straight commission and they sell merchandise on credit, should delinquent and defaulted accounts be charged to them? Would your decision be different if they were under a salary-commission plan?

5. What plan do you recommend each of the following companies should use to handle split commissions?

a. Manufacturer of sheets, pillowcases, towels, and related items sells to a department store chain. The order is placed through the chain's buying offices in New York, and delivery is made to stores throughout the country on an order from the department manager in each store. The manufacturer's sales people call on the units of the chain located in their territories.

b. Manufacturer of oil well drilling equipment sells to main offices of drilling contractors, but delivery is made to field offices and drilling locations. Sales people in area where product is delivered must service the item.

6. What is the difference between a salary and a guaranteed drawing account?

7. If you were given a choice as a sales person would you prefer an increase in earnings in the form of some indirect monetary item, such as a company-financed annuity, or in the form of an equivalent increase in salary or commissions?

8. If all employees—sales and otherwise—in a company receive paid vacations, except the sales people on straight commission, should management establish a policy whereby these reps are given the same benefits? If so, how should management determine the amount to pay the commission men during their vacations?

9. If a commission or a bonus is an element in the sales compensation plan, explain how there may be seasonal fluctuations in earnings. How can management reduce or eliminate these fluctuations without changing the basic compensation plan?

10. In what respects would a compensation plan differ among sales people for the following firms?
    a. Manufacturer of small airplanes used by executives.
    b. Wholesaler of office equipment and supplies.
    c. Automobile dealer.

11. If management wants to reduce its sales reps' *level* of earnings, what *method* will have the least harmful effect on morale?

12. Give some specific examples of how each of the following factors can influence a company's choice of a compensation plan for its sales force.
    a. Caliber of the sales people.
    b. Nature of the job.
    c. Financial condition of the company.

13. Design a compensation plan for the job described in Figure 4–1 (Chapter 4). Do the same for the job outlined in Figure 4–2.

Case 11–1
ZACCONE BROS., INC.
Revising a sales force compensation plan

Vince and Phil Zaccone, co-owners of an International Harvester (I–H) dealership in central California, were concerned about the complaints being received from customers of long standing to the effect that Zaccone salesmen were high-pressuring them to buy larger and more expensive equipment than they really needed. Consequently, the two brothers were considering how they might change their sales compensation plan to restore a customer orientation for the salesmen.

The family-owned company had been established in 1926 as an International Harvester service center and parts dealer. Then, as a favorable growth pattern developed, the brothers expanded their product lines to include a reasonably complete assortment of I–H trucks, tractors, and farm equipment. A few years ago Zaccone Bros. began to order parts and offer service for other manufacturers' models of farm machinery and equipment. About that same time the company added a separate line of hardware goods consisting of paints and accessories, chain saws, ammunition, hydraulic hose products, and industrial V–belts for motors.

However, the main thrust of the company's effort still was to sell and service International–Harvester products, whether new or used, and to carry out fully all the warranty work. The parts department, for example, carried parts for every machine I–H made which was likely to be used in Zaccone's trading area.

By the mid–1970s Zaccone Bros. had become one of the largest I–H dealers in California north of Los Angeles. In 1977 the company had a net sales volume of $1,213,000, with net profits of $100,000 after taxes. 1977 was a particularly good year for this dealership; for several years previously profits had been around $80,000.

The market for International Harvester's trucks, tractors, and farm equipment was quite large and diversified. Consequently, Zaccone Bros. sold to a wide range of customers—individuals and businesses, small-order buyers and multiunit buyers. The bulk of the business, however, stemmed from farming or heavy industry. About half the trading area's population was involved in one or the other of these two broad industry classifications. These buyers generally were well informed about various competitive products, and they generally knew what products were best suited for their needs.

Competition from other dealers had increased considerably over the past 20 years. This competition came from other I–H dealers, as well as from dealers of other brands. The combination of well informed-buyers and increasing competition caused Zaccone Bros. to be sensitive to customers' complaints.

The organizational structure of the dealership was somewhat unusual in that the co-owners, Vince and Phil, each carried the title of president (see Exhibit 1). Vince was in charge of the parts department

EXHIBIT 1
ZACCONE BROS., INC.
Organization chart

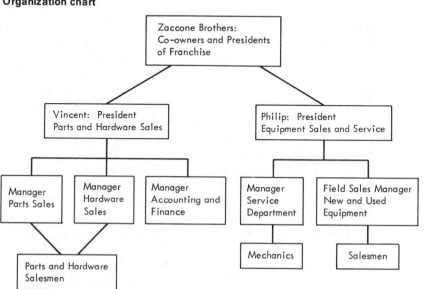

and the sale of hardware products. The manager of the accounting and finance department also reported directly to Vince. Each parts and hardware salesman was qualified to sell all parts which might be needed by a customer, and they also were qualified to give instructions on assembly and use of the parts.

Phil was in charge of the service department and all sales of new and used machinery and equipment (trucks, tractors, heavy farm equipment). Reporting to Phil was a service manager and the field sales manager who administered the activities of the five-man field sales force. The mechanics were qualified to work on all types and models of machinery and trucks. Each of the five salesmen sold the entire line of I–H trucks and equipment.

Vince and Phil were well acquainted with each other's departments and often helped out in one another's area. Each man also on occasion assisted in selling. All major decisions were a joint, mutual effort of the two brothers. The various departmental managers—parts, hardware, service, and field sales—were responsible for planning and developing the marketing programs for their individual departments. Then the two presidents would get together to integrate all the separate programs into one final company marketing plan.

During the past year Phil had been increasingly aware that many of the company's old customers were not returning to Zaccone for smaller, fill-in types of products. When both Phil and Vince became sufficiently concerned about this turn of events, they began to ask a few old customers what was the matter. That was when the brothers found out that the salesmen had been making some customers angry by often pushing a product which was larger or heavier duty (and thus more expensive) than the farmer or other industrial buyer actually needed. In this way the salesmen received higher commissions.

When the brothers started discussing how they might prevent the equipment salesmen from antagonizing customers, but still keep their competitive edge, Phil wondered if maybe their sales compensation plan should be revised. At that time the salesmen were paid a salary of $8,000 a year plus a commission of 2 percent on their sales of all machinery and equipment, both new and used. The field sales manager, who once was a salesman in the company, was paid a salary of $11,000 plus a commission of 1½ percent on total net sales of new and used equipment. Phil did observe that sales of heavy-construction tractors and the latest models of crop pickers were higher than he had originally forecasted. However, he had never attributed this to any unusual pressure from the salesmen in their sales presentations.

The field sales manager suggested that the two partner-presidents should call a meeting of the salesmen and tell them about the unfavorable customer reactions. Phil was reluctant to do this because such a meeting would point the finger at certain salesmen and lower their morale. At the same time the people who were not guilty of the pressure selling tactics might resent being included in the meeting, and thus their morale also would suffer. Phil was inclined to drop the commission element in the pay plan and increase the salary so that the level of salesmen's compensation would not drop.

Vince, on the other hand, doubted if the problem was so serious as to cause a revamping of the whole pay structure. Sales and profits had been increasing (in spite of any complaints), and he saw no significant weakness in the existing compensation plan.

Questions

1. Should Zaccone Bros. change its existing sales compensation plan?
2. If so, what changes would you recommend?

Case 11–2
CLEMSON MEAT COMPANY
Revising a sales force compensation plan

The Clemson Meat Company was a family-owned meat processing and packing company which sold high-quality perishable meat products directly to retail grocers and supermarkets. The company had been started in the 1930s, and the main processing plant was located in a large western city. Clemson also operated a hog-slaughtering plant in a small town about 100 miles from the main plant.

The company's sales volume, about $85 million a year, had been increasing about 10 to 12 percent a year and management expected this growth rate to continue.

However, like most meat packers, Clemson operated on a narrow net profit margin—1 percent of sales. In the previous year Clemson had incurred a small loss. The company had no control over the price of live hogs, its main raw material. Consequently, Mr. Peter Jauch, the vice president of sales, was looking for a way to cut sales operating expenses in the hopes of contributing to a profit. Particularly, some questionable sales practices had come to Mr. Jauch's attention which made him wonder if perhaps his sales force compensation plan might need some changes.

Clemson's 22 sales reps had a thorough knowledge of meats and the meat industry. They usually were hired from competitive firms. Most of these sales people were around 35–40 years of age and had been with Clemson at least ten years. Mr. Jauch believed that his firm had attracted some of the best sales reps in the business. He attributed this, in part, to the Clemson compensation plan. Most of the competitors paid their sales people a straight salary. Clemson paid a salary plus an incentive bonus which could run as high as 52 percent of the salary.

The Clemson products were divided into six categories. Each sales person sold the full line. The six product groups and their share of the company's sales were as follows:

Fresh pork	60%
Wieners	12
Bacon	12
Ham	6
Sausage	6
Lunch meats	4
	100%

Since meat products are perishable, orders had to be filled very quickly. Clemson's small size made it flexible enough to receive orders one day and ship them the next. Freshness is important; it increases salability and shelf life. Clemson had the most modern packaging equipment available. Consequently, the company could vacuum pack its products to ensure that freshness and quality were preserved as long as possible.

Clemson sold in 14 western states, including Hawaii. The company sold to some 3,500 accounts, but Mr. Jauch estimated that the potential in these states was about three times that number. Clemson sold primarily to retailers, although it did export some frozen meats to Japan. Each sales person handled 6 or 7 large accounts. In the Colorado market, for example, two retail supermarket chains—King Soopers and Safeway—accounted for about 85 percent of Clemson's sales. In general, the retail accounts had been decreasing in number but increasing in average size. Consequently, Mr. Jauch believed that the company could continue its growth without adding more sales people, at least for the next couple of years.

Clemson was one of the largest meat packing firms in the West, but they ranked well down the list among all U.S. packing companies. Clemson's two major competitors were Oscar Mayer and the Cudahy Bar-S brands. It was difficult to generalize on the market shares held by the major competitors. In some cities Oscar Mayer would be a strong leader, while in other cities Clemson was in the top spot. Recently, in one large western city, for example, a newspaper survey of brand preferences and market shares showed the results given in Exhibit 1.

EXHIBIT 1
Market shares, by company, for meat products

	Ham	Bacon	Lunch meat	Wieners	Sausage
Clemson	36%	18%	31%	37%	19%
Oscar Mayer		2	26	9	
Cudahy	31	22	3	17	2
Regional chain	4	11	11	6	10
Safeway	5	10	16	11	14
Others (Swift, Armour, Hormel, etc).	24	27	13	20	55*
Totals	100%	100%	100%	100%	100%

* Jimmy Dean brand = 25%.

Clemson's major competitive advantages were its flexibility and its modern production facilities. For example, the company operated a hot dog machine which manufactured 30,000 wieners per hour. The company's major limitation, as Mr. Jauch saw it, was that Clemson was too small to advertise as heavily as its major competitors.

Clemson's sales compensation plan essentially was a salary plus a bonus. Salaries ranged from $700 to $1,000 a month. The bonus, a percentage of salary, was based on how much a salesman exceeded his quota. Tonnage quotas in each of five categories of processed meats (fresh pork was not included) were assigned to each salesman. These quotas were based on past sales, as adjusted for current economic conditions and market outlook. The quotas and bonuses were computed quarterly.

The bonus was a certain amount paid for each ton of meat sold in excess of quota. To encourage a balanced selling job of all products, management set limits for the bonuses in each category of processed meats. For example, the total bonus paid for selling hot dogs could not exceed 12 percent of salary. These limits in each product category were as follows:

Wieners	12%
Hams	6
Sausage	12
Lunch meat	12
Bacon	10
Total	52%

Thus, a sales rep's total bonus for all products was limited to 52 percent of his salary.

The sales people were also provided with unlimited expense accounts but were required to submit itemized statements. Clemson allowed its sales force to grant an allowance or discount of 4 cents per pound as a concession to customers in special situations.

Recently, it has been brought to Mr. Jauch's attention that the sales of three sales reps were fluctuating about 500,000 pounds from one three-month period to the next. This represented 10 to 12 percent of the average 4 to 5 million pounds of meat sold by each salesman during a quarterly period. Apparently, in order to exceed their volume quotas, these salesmen were convincing some of their customers that they needed more meat than was actually the case. The retail buyers consequently would be overstocked one period and would underbuy the next period in order to balance things out. Fluctuations of this sort caused production inefficiencies, thus increasing costs.

Upon further investigation of past records, Mr. Jauch discovered that on virtually all of their orders, these same three salesmen were shaving 4 cents a pound from the list price. (This was the same 4 cents a pound the company allowed only as a special price concession.) Thus, Clemson was not realizing its planned profit margins in these territories. Moreover, sales on low-margin products far exceeded sales of high-margin items. As a final point, Mr. Jauch felt that the travel and business expenses of these salesmen were much too high.

Each of the three salesmen involved had been with Clemson for over ten years and was well established in his territory. Each handled a number of large accounts. These salesmen were very good—they knew meat and could sell it. They liked to write up big orders. They consistently won or came close to winning the annual sales contest for the greatest volume sold. They also had the highest earnings last year.

Mr. Jauch began to think that this situation might exist to a considerable extent throughout the sales force. He expressed the opinion that, if so, the compensation plan probably was contributing to this undesirable situation. He wondered what changes should be made in the compensation plan. He wanted to accomplish three objectives: (1) stimulate the sales force to be more profit oriented; (2) maintain production schedules at an even level; and (3) continue to enjoy a 10–12 percent increase in annual sales volume.

Question

1. What changes should be made in the sales compensation plan for Clemson Meat Company?

Case 11–3
STRYMARK COATINGS, INC.
Revising a sales force compensation plan

Top management in Strymark Coatings, Inc., had decided to make a major shift in the company's overall marketing goals and strategy. The vice president of sales, Mr. André Vimont, and the vice-president of marketing, Mr. Eugene Robinson, both were wondering what effect, if any, this change in marketing goals would have on the compensation plan now used for the Strymark sales force. Any significant shift in company objectives would require adjustments in many areas within the firm, but for the moment the sales and marketing executives were concerned with their sales force compensation plan.

Strymark was a profitable, medium-sized manufacturer of metal and wood finishes. Sales volume last year was $32 million, and it had been fluctuating around that figure for the past few years. The home office and main plant was located in Cleveland, Ohio, and there were branch plants in Los Angeles, Seattle, St. Louis, Jersey City, Boston, and High Point, North Carolina. A branch warehouse was maintained in Chicago. Strymark sold directly to its customers and did not use any kind of middlemen.

In addition to the vice presidents of sales and marketing, there was a vice president of research and development, and each branch plant also was headed by a vice president. These nine executives reported directly to Strymark's president. Any change in the sales force compensation plan would involve not only the two vice presidents of sales and marketing but also the president and the plant vice presidents. These officers were considered to be conservative, cost conscious, and slow to change, yet interested in new ideas. While they were receptive to innovation, they really had to be sold on it before making any changes.

Up to the present time the company's marketing goal was to concentrate on selective technical product areas in order to produce finishes for highly specialized products and customer needs. For the most part, these customers were small and medium-sized firms. When Strymark did sell to giant firms such as Anheuser-Busch (Budweiser) or IBM, the orders were relatively small and were for highly specialized products.

Management's new marketing goal for Strymark was to generate a substantial increase in sales volume, while still retaining its high rate of profit. The key strategy leading to this goal was to shift selling emphasis to the more complex, large, multiplant and multinational type of customers who typically ordered in large quantities.

The chief reason for these decisions was that Strymark needed more revenue to support its research and development efforts. To continue to meet the intense competition from large chemical companies and the technological changes demanded by the market, Strymark had to provide a high level of technical expertise. Such research cost a lot of money.

Generally Strymark was able to maintain a good profit margin on most of its products. There were two reasons for his happy situation. First, quite often Strymark was the only firm that produced a given product. Because it was much smaller than its major competitors, Strymark often would research, develop, and supply a product in response to a demand the large competitors felt was too small to bother with. The second reason Strymark maintained its profit margins was that the cost of its coatings usually was a very small part of the total cost of a completed product. Consequently in the eyes of its customers, the price of a Strymark finish was of secondary importance when compared with the factors of fast delivery, special attention, and the other services which Strymark provided.

Strymark's major competitors were large chemical companies such as Glidden, DuPont, Mobil, Inmont, and DeSoto. These larger companies, to some extent, were either unable or unwilling to spend research and development money on anything but large-volume business. What was considered small-volume business to them, however, often was large-volume business for Strymark. Consequently, Strymark often would do research on products the larger firms had no time for. Moreover, Strymark often could do these jobs faster and with less "red tape" than its larger competitors.

In the finishes and coatings industry, the firms competed on the basis of: (1) sales force ability, (2) technical expertise in the fields of research and development and quality control, (3) the ability to deliver the product quickly, (4) the follow-up technical service, and (5) the cost. Strymark's competitors were strongest in the areas of technical expertise and cost. Size was the basic factor here, since the competitors' huge research and development budgets enabled them to develop new basic materials far beyond Strymark's capabilities. Their larger size also enabled them to sell their products at a lower cost because of the higher volume.

Strymark's strongest competitive advantages were its ability to deliver a product quickly and its follow-up technical service. Strymark also emphasized the ability of its sales force, its high-quality products, and its flexibility in meeting the specialized needs of its customers.

Mr. Vimont estimated that the total market for all industrial finishes and coatings amounted to over $1 billion a year. Strymark had a very small share of this market. The company's capacity was several times larger than its present sales level.

The market for industrial coatings included a wide variety of firms—in fact, virtually any manufacturer of a metal or wood product that was painted, stained, or chemically coated. The market's breadth was illustrated by a sampling of Strymark's current customer groups: furniture (Drexel, Thomasville); business machines (IBM, Control Data); containers (Continental Can, American Can); architectural metals (Reynolds Aluminum, Armco Steel); plus a variety of appliance, automotive parts, and musical instrument companies.

In view of the company's decision to alter its marketing goals, Mr. Vimont and Mr. Robinson both realized that Strymark would have to change its customer mix. The firm's goal of generating a substantial increase in sales volume meant that it had to strive for larger customers: As a potential customer mix, Vimont cited such examples as Coors brewery (containers), Boeing (aircraft), Weyerhaeuser (prefinished paneling and exterior siding), General Electric (appliances). In cases where Strymark already was selling to very large firms (IBM, Continental Can, and Armco Steel, for example), Strymark would try to increase its average order size and total sales with these large buyers.

Strymark's 50 sales people were paid a straight commission on their net sales volume. They paid their own expenses and provided their own automobiles. The sales reps were not assigned a sales quota. The company had a rather flexible (Vimont called it "loose") territorial structure. Each sales person's specialty, or his area of product or customer interest, determined who would be assigned to a given account. Management did, however, try to keep the sales people's accounts geographically concentrated so, in effect, each had a territory. Some trading and reassignments of accounts did occur as a result of deaths, resignations, or sometimes a strong request from a sales person.

Commissions varied between 5 percent and 15 percent, depending upon the product. Before a product was priced, the sales rep and the assistant sales manager agreed upon the commission. Each product was then priced at the designated profit and commission level and was adjusted for competition, if necessary. This was done every time a new product was sold or an old product repriced. With most products, because they were so specialized, this procedure is done individually with each sales person. In the case of a product to be carried in stock for a period of time and sold by several sales people, the commission setting and the pricing were done at the annual sales meeting, with the salesmen as a group agreeing to the commission rate. There was no sliding commission scale—either progressive or regressive—based on the size of one sale or on a sales rep's total volume.

Strymark's sales force was pleased with the compensation plan. It provided them with a high degree of motivation, opportunity for technical specialization, independence, and flexibility. Their earnings generally were higher than the level of other sales people in the industry.

However, both Vimont and Robinson believed that the company's new marketing goals would suffer under the existing pay plan. The shift to the larger volume orders would mean a shift to multiplant and multinational accounts. Several sales people would be required to handle each account. Each one would no longer be working alone.

In these team-selling situations, Vimont said it would be difficult to measure objectively each person's efforts or contributions and also virtually impossible to apportion commission credit for results. Any system the company would set up for splitting the commissions, Vimont felt, would not please all of the sales people involved in that particular group sale.

Another problem Vimont anticipated was that, in most cases, it would take time to develop these larger accounts to the point where the sales people could earn good commissions. They would have to be motivated in some way so that they would spend the necessary time to develop these new accounts. The purpose and value of the new marketing goals could largely be negated if the sales force continued to concentrate on its former type of customers, only because that is where they had been earning good money.

Thus, Vimont and Robinson realized they were faced with a problem. They believed they needed to develop a new compensation plan which, on the one hand, would be adaptable to the new larger accounts and team-selling effort. Yet it should maintain the present incentive and high-level productivity on the part of the good sales reps, who were quite happy with the present commission plan. Vimont also reminded other executives that the shift of emphasis to the larger volume accounts did *not* mean that the present customers were to be dropped.

As one possibility for a new pay plan, Vimont thought that the company needed some type of split-commission arrangement which could be acceptable to the sales people involved in a given team-selling situation. Robinson suggested that maybe they should switch the sales force to a straight salary plan. He said this would encourage the salesmen to spend more time in carefully developing the new large accounts. One of the assistant sales managers said there was nothing wrong with the existing plan of straight commission. He said the reps liked it; they made good money under it, and the sales results were profitable for Strymark. He felt all these conditions would continue to exist if the company stayed with the present plan even when selling to the new accounts.

Another marketing executive proposed that the company split its sales force into two divisions—one would handle the smaller accounts, and the other would work only in teams, handling the new large, multiplant accounts. The first group would continue on straight commission, while the team sellers would be paid a straight salary. Both groups would have the same fringe benefits—insurance, pension plan, vacations, and so on.

Question

1. What sales compensation plan should Strymark adopt to enable it to handle both the large and the small accounts?

Case 11–4
NEBRASKA SUPPLY COMPANY
Establishing a sales compensation plan

The Nebraska Supply Company distributed a wide line of high-quality meat, fish, and poultry products to hotels, restaurants, and the institutional trade (colleges, hospitals, prisons, and so on). Top management in Nebraska Supply was planning to expand substantially its geographic market coverage and its sales force. In view of this proposed expansion, the company's sales manager, Mr. Glenn McVey, has decided this would be an appropriate time to review and evaluate the existing compensation plan for the salesmen. If this appraisal indicated that the pay plan should be revised, McVey felt it would be better to make any changes now before the company added new sales people and expanded its market.

Nebraska Supply Company was a major subsidiary of the Nebraska Land and Cattle Company, a diversified holding company. This holding company originally had owned and operated some huge cattle ranches in western Nebraska and Wyoming. Through the years the Nebraska Land and Cattle Co. had divested itself of these land holdings and broadened its investment base. In addition to Nebraska Supply (its meat distributor subsidiary), the holding company had two other large subsidiaries—the Ogallala Feed Lots Co. and the Cornhusker Packing Co. These three subsidiaries provided the parent holding company with a large degree of vertical integration in producing and marketing meat products. The holding company, in turn, provided the necessary central management and financing which were of considerable help to the subsidiaries.

Nebraska Supply marketed a full line of fresh meat, fish, and poultry products. The company also carried a variety of smoked meats, sausages, and canned meat items. The company sold meats in all sizes and shapes. The various cuts of meat ranged from specific weights and sizes of individual steaks up to hindquarters and loin ends. The product mix also included such items as portioned hamburgers, roast-sized cuts, and precut chops. Nebraska Supply also would fabricate meat products into custom-shaped items or portioned cuts to fill the standing special orders from large hotels or restaurants.

One of Nebraska Supply's competitive advantages was its efforts to give specialized service and products to its customers whenever possible. The company also tried to be alert to the changing needs of its customers as they reflected changes in the tastes of the ultimate consumers. Nebraska Supply procured most of its beef, lamb, and veal products from its subsidiary—the Cornhusker Packing Co. The other products—fresh pork, fish, poultry, most sausages, and canned meats—were purchased from a variety of sources. Nebraska Supply also did some of its own custom cutting or portioning. The company operated its own fleet of refrigerated trucks to supply its customers.

The geographic market of Nebraska Supply covered the western two thirds of Nebraska, northeast Colorado, and most of Wyoming. The company's proposed expansion would add the western half of South Dakota, eastern two thirds of Montana, and the rest of Colorado east of the Rocky Mountains. (See Exhibit 1.) As part of this expansion, Nebraska Supply planned to add a branch in northern Colorado and one in northern Wyoming.

The proposed market expansion by Nebraska Supply was motivated by the company's excellent sales history, the growing importance of the hotel-restaurant-institutional market, and the forecast for continued market growth. McVey indicated that there had been a fivefold increase in the company's sales over the past six years. Furthermore, he saw no reason why the company's sales should not continue to increase at a satisfactory rate. According to government figures, the per capita consumption of beef in the United States almost doubled from 1955 to 1970. The per capita consumption of beef was projected to reach 130 pounds by 1980. Further research published in the house magazine of the Monfort Company of Colorado, a major competitor of Nebraska Supply, indicated that about 40 percent of all domestically produced beef in the United States was marketed to hotels, restaurants, and institutions. "Certainly," observed McVey, "the combination of all these present and forecasted market indicators augurs well for the future growth and market expansion in the Nebraska Supply Company."

McVey also could see that *qualitative* changes were occurring in the market and the environment in which his firm operated. And he realized his company's production and marketing strategies and tac-

EXHIBIT 1
Geographic market
NEBRASKA SUPPLY COMPANY

tics were bound to be affected by these changes. McVey thought that Mr. Ken Monfort, president of Monfort of Colorado, had reflected the tenor of the times in a recent speech he had made to the Texas and Southwestern Meat Packers Association. Using the song title "Age of Aquarius," as the keynote for his speech, Monfort defined that age as:

> The age of the citizen, the age of the consumer, the age of the purist, and the age for those who would protect our environment. For the meat industry, it means:

- Adoption of a policy of far greater emphasis on sanitation and quality control.
- Strict labeling of products to include, for example, the amount of fat content in a hot dog and other items because the public has the right to know.
- That cheapness, efficiency, and ease of operation must give way to cleanliness, wholesomeness, and healthfulness.

• Accepting the responsibility "that is and should be ours" to make these changes.

In the course of appraising his sales compensation plan, McVey first reviewed some of the aspects of the sales job and some of the market conditions which were peculiar to the meat industry. Each of the sales reps traveled through an assigned geographical territory, servicing established accounts and attempting to develop new customers. These sales people procured orders from customers, made deliveries of small items, and paid particular attention to the importance of giving quick, frequent, and complete service to all customers, large and small. McVey believed that it was this high quality of missionary work which gave his Nebraska Supply sales force a differential advantage over the competition.

In addition to servicing all present and potential accounts, each sales person also was expected to do the necessary missionary work for all the large house accounts in his territory. While servicing these house accounts, it was not uncommon for sales people to take small orders.

In all of the territories, the sales to the various restaurant and hotel accounts fluctuated considerably from week to week, both in the assortment of cuts of meat ordered and in the total tonnage sold. In addition, the prices charged to Nebraska Supply for the different cuts of meat varied from week to week because of the fluctuating prices in the commodity markets from which Nebraska Supply and the Cornhusker Packing Company did their purchasing. Firms which distribute meats to the hotel, restaurant, and institutional trade typically operate on very small profit margins. These customer groups often order large quantities of low-profit meats. As a result of all these factors, Nebraska Supply not only had weekly fluctuations in the tonnage of meat sold but also had constantly changing prices and profits on the different cuts of meat.

The sales people were compensated on a straight salary basis, with a beginning salary of $700 a month. The sales people also had a limited expense account and were given a company car which they could use for their own personal purposes. The company provided a group life insurance policy and a major medical and hospitalization insurance policy, with all premiums being paid by the company. After the sales reps had completed the company training program and had attained some field selling experience, they usually were given a raise in salary. These advancements usually continued very rapidly and at the end of three years, a sales person usually participated in the company's profit sharing plan.

Executives in the parent holding company were constantly looking

for new programs and procedures which would improve product qual
ity and increase the benefits to employees, customers, and the com
pany. In line with this philosophy, McVey started thinking that i
Nebraska Supply switched from a straight salary to some kind of com
bination plan which included a commission, the new plan might resul
in larger sales volume, increased profits, and higher total income fo
the sales force. McVey recognized that the straight salary plan offerec
the sales force security and stability of earnings. As a result, the rep:
on salary would be more inclined to work for the firm and less inclinec
to feel that they were in business for themselves. McVey also recog
nized the following disadvantages of the straight salary plan: it lackec
sufficient incentive for the sales force, and there was no direct relation
ship between selling costs and sales volume.

In studying the advantages of a commission plan, McVey realizec
that the commission method would offer the sales reps a tremendou:
incentive to increase sales. He also found that, on the average, the
commission plan would give the sales force a higher level of earnings
Another advantage, from the sales people's point of view, would be
freedom of operation. On the other hand, under a commission plan the
sales force would be more difficult to supervise. They might fail to
perform a fully balanced sales job by reducing the amount of mission
ary work done.

McVey investigated the types of commission plans being used in
the meat industry and found two that might fit his company's needs
The first was one which based the commission on the tonnage of mea
sold. The second was one where the commission was a percentage
of the gross margin earned on the various cuts of meat sold. McVey
then asked his assistant manager to evaluate the present program in
relation to the two alternatives and to present a recommendation to
him at their next meeting.

Question

1. What compensation plan should Glenn McVey use for the sales force?

12

Sales force expenses and transportation

Our men give their talent to the company and their genius to their expense accounts.

LIFE MAGAZINE

One sales manager has observed that properly handled expense accounts are at best a nuisance, and improperly managed accounts amount to grand larceny. Granted that he may have had an unusually sour view of the situation, his opinion nevertheless points up the problem of controlling the travel and business expenses incurred by the sales force.[1]

INTERNAL REVENUE SERVICE REGULATIONS

Income tax laws affect how management can treat the travel, entertainment, and gift expenses of sales people. When Congress became convinced that substantial tax income was being lost because of the deductions being claimed for these items, it cracked down in the Revenue Act of 1962.

The law establishes stringent limitations on the deductibility of these expenses.[2] Clear and specific requirements are made for de-

---

[1] One survey of nearly 900 sales managers found that 77 percent felt that salesmen's expenses were higher than necessary, and 50 percent admitted they did not have the control they would like over these increasing expenses. See *Controlling Salesmen's Expenses*, File 32 (New York: Research Institute of America, 1970).

[2] See U.S. Treasury Department, Internal Revenue Service, *Rules for Deducting Travel, Entertainment, and Gift Expenses: New Recordkeeping Rules*, Document 5049, January 1963.

tailed substantiation of: (1) amount of the expense, (2) time and place of the expense, (3) business purpose of the expense, and (4) business relationship between the giver and the recipient of any entertainment or gifts. For entertainment, receipts are required for each separate expenditure of $25 or more. The company must state: (1) date, place, and type of entertainment, (2) business reason for the entertainment or the nature of the business benefit to be derived, and (3) names and titles of the persons entertained in order to establish the business relationship. Receipts are required for all transportation and lodging. Sales people must maintain an account book or daily diary. Records must show the date of departure, return, city of destination, number of days away from home, and the business reason for the trip. The use of yachts, lodges, or country clubs for business must be clearly documented. Such facilities must be used more than 50 percent of the time for business purposes, or all but actual out-of-pocket entertainment expenses are disallowed. If a sales manager uses a country club 100 days during the year, of which 75 are for business purposes, then 75 percent of the club dues would be deductible, plus the actual costs of the entertainment such as guest fees, food, or cart rentals. The deductible cost of gifts is limited to $25 a year per person.

LEGITIMATE TRAVEL AND BUSINESS EXPENSES

Management should identify in writing the expenses for which the company will pay—not only the broad expense categories, such as transportation or lodging, but also the details within each category. To say that transportation is a legitimate expense is not enough. In the case of air travel, to illustrate, management may reimburse only for air coach fare. Those who choose to travel first class, pay the difference. Specific guidelines should let sales reps know whether they must lease the cheapest rental car available. If they take a taxi from the airport rather than the less expensive bus, will the company pick up the tab? Such matters need clarification.

When determining allowable items, a good general policy is that the sales person should be reimbursed for business expenses incurred in connection with work, and for personal expenditures that were made while traveling on the job and that would not have been necessary otherwise. The first part of the policy statement provides for expenditures for entertainment, telegrams, office supplies, and transportation. Many of these expenses may be incurred either on the road or while selling in the home-office city. The second part of the statement refers to such items as overnight lodging, meals, and possibly laundry or valet service away from home. Sometimes it is difficult to draw a line between what a person spends on the road and what would have been spent for the same thing at home. One must eat whether at home or traveling, but it usually costs more to eat out than to eat at home. Rather than trying to determine the difference in the cost of meals at home and on the road, most firms pay all meal expenses while the employee is traveling away from home.

There may be no unanimous agreement on what constitutes a legitimate expense for reimbursement, but it is possible to generalize about major categories of expenses. In some compensation plans the sales reps pay their own expenses, and in these cases reimbursement by the company is not an issue.

Usually, all *transportation* costs incurred while on the job will be paid by the company. So will all *lodging* costs incurred while the rep is away from home overnight on business. Most firms require the overnight lodging to be in connection with an out-of-town trip. However, when sales people who live in the suburbs must stay in town late for meetings with customers, some companies permit them to stay at a downtown hotel at company expense. Some concerns limit the amount that will be allowed for a night's lodging. The cost of *meals* while traveling out of town also usually is paid by the company, although limits frequently are placed on the sums allowed.

Telephone, telegraph, and other *communication costs* are considered legitimate business expenses by the typical firm. Another business expense that ordinarily is allowable covers such items as *office supplies,* including notebooks and briefcases, and *stenographic service.*

Generally, there is less agreement on reimbursement for such borderline items as laundry, valet expenses, or personal telephone calls to home. A Dartnell study found that personal calls home were reimbursed by about half of the firms surveyed.[3] A common policy on laundry is to cover this expense only after the sales person has been away from home for some period such as a week. The reasoning is that such expenses would be incurred whether or not the person were at home. Because management wants to encourage sales people to make a good appearance and realizes that laundry costs more on the road than at home, a partial allowance is made by many organizations.

Undoubtedly, the most controversial of all expense categories is *entertainment* and *gifts.* A few firms allow no entertainment whatsoever, while others are at the opposite extreme. The prevailing practice seems to be to allow all necessary and reasonable entertainment

---

[3] *Compensation of Salesmen* (Chicago: Dartnell Corp., 1971).

expenses. There are limits in the form of per-person maximums on allowable items, such as meals and theater tickets, or the entertainment may be restricted to lunches or dinners. If a luncheon can be used as a quiet interlude with a customer away from the distractions and tensions of the office, or store, much can be gained by both the seller and buyer. Furthermore, allowing sales people to have entertainment expense accounts may mean they will work 14-hour days. Care must be taken not to become involved in an entertainment race with competitors, with each trying to win customers' business with lavish entertaining and gift giving rather than with the merits of product value and company service.

Giving business gifts is a practice of long standing. Now, however, many firms limit the practice to the Christmas season. Surveys show divided opinions on gift giving. Some firms do it because they like to; they would not care to stop. Other organizations would prefer to halt the practice but feel they would suffer competitively, so they continue. Limiting the tax deductibility of business gifts to $25 per year per recipient has altered the gift-giving practices of many companies.

CHARACTERISTICS OF A SOUND EXPENSE PLAN

An expense plan that is well conceived and executed has certain general characteristics which are discussed in this section.

No net gain or loss

The expense plan should be designed so that employees neither profit nor lose under it. A sales rep should net the same income working on the road as at home. Ideally, even when the rep pays his own expenses, the total sum allotted should be just enough to leave him with the same earnings after expenses as he would have had if the company paid the expenses separately. Admittedly, in practice this ideal is difficult to achieve.

While expense allowances should not be used in lieu of compensation, some firms intentionally follow this practice, with the approval of the sales force. The employee often prefers an increase in a nontaxable expense account to a raise in taxable salary or commissions.

The practice of compensating people by way of the expense account is wrong on at least two important counts. First, it is poor management because it tends to nullify the control feature of a good compensation plan. If a firm provides higher limits on an expense account in lieu of an increase in compensation, a sales rep's opportunity to increase his income is based more on his ability to pad his expense account than on his ability to do a better sales job. Second, the practice encourages people to violate the income tax law. An expense account is nontaxable only to the extent that it reimburses the employee for the legitimate business expenses incurred. If a sales person gets an increase in expense allowances and the total allowance exceeds total costs, the excess expense money is taxable.

Equitable treatment

Sales reps should be able to maintain approximately the same standard of living on the road as at home. They should not have to sacrifice comfort to stay within expense limits. Sales managers should recognize differences in travel expenses among the different territories. Costs are higher in an Atlantic Seaboard territory than in one in the Great Plains, for example. A plan should be flexible enough to reflect expense differentials caused by variations in types of customers, need for pioneering or prospecting a territory, and seasonal factors.

No curtailment of beneficial activities

A good expense plan should not hamper the performance of selling duties, nor should it curtail activities which may be beneficial to the company. A plan that attempts to set selling expenses as a percentage of sales may discourage a rep from developing a new territory. If expenses are limited to 1 percent of sales, for instance, no one would be anxious to go into a new territory, where expenses are often abnormally high in relation to volume in the beginning. If a company wants a rep to make demonstrations, train dealer sales people, and generally build goodwill by working with the customers, it would be a mistake to limit expenses to a certain percentage of sales or a certain dollar amount.

Simple and economical

A sound expense control plan should be simple and economical to administer. Clerical and administrative expenses should be minimized. Often too much unnecessary detail is required in expense reports. Some firms ask for information that could just as well be placed on other reports. In fact, the information required on the expense account may be duplicated elsewhere.

Avoidance of disputes

A good expense plan should prevent misunderstandings between management and the sales force. One way to reach this goal is to consult with the sales force when establishing or revising an expense control plan. The plan should be explained clearly, in detail, and in writing to the sales force before it is put into effect or before newly hired people are placed under it. The company should pay promptly or, better yet, make an advance payment available to those who need it.

Company control of expenses and elimination of padding

Under a good plan, no expense is allowed to get out of hand, and padding of expense accounts is curtailed. At the same time, control must not be considered synonymous with stinginess. A sales executive should be able to get all the benefits of control without damaging sales force morale by adopting a Scrooge-like approach.

Expense account padding is a problem faced at one time or another by most sales managers. Actually, it is more apt to be a *symptom* of a problem than a real problem. Often, good judgment in other areas will preclude sales reps' mistreatment of their expense accounts. Recognition of achievement, a good training program, and an adequate compensation plan are the sort of managerial practices that help eliminate expense account padding. The problem is minimized when rapport has been established with the sales people and they understand the expense account system and feel they are reimbursed fairly for all valid expenses.

Sales people should have some incentive to reduce their business expenses. However, it is difficult for management to implement this generalization. It is not wise to offer a bonus or other reward for reducing expenses from the level in some previous period. Such a reward may imply that the sales person has been padding expenses or spending more than is reasonable. Management therefore seems to be paying extra just to eliminate the padding—that is, paying the individual for telling the truth or doing what should have been done all along. In some firms, the reward for economizing on expenses takes the form of a higher merit rating, which should lead to a promotion or increase in salary. Expense plans under which firms offer the incentive of a commission or a bonus to those who keep their expenses below a certain figure are discussed later in the chapter.

METHODS OF CONTROLLING EXPENSES

One of the first managerial decisions to be made regarding the control of sales people's expenses is whether the company will pay these costs, or the reps will pay their own expenses out of their compensation.

If the firm decides to pay for expenses, three major types of plans are generally used. One is to allow unlimited payments for legitimate costs. The second is a system under which payments are limited by one method or another. The third plan uses some type of combination arrangement. About 70 percent of companies surveyed pay "all reasonable expenses," thus moving away from set allowances for items or time periods, according to a Dartnell study of 505 national and regional firms.[4]

The majority of firms pay for travel and business expenses incurred by their sales people. This practice is almost universally followed if salary is an element in the compensation plan. If the sales reps pay all their own expenses, the chances are that they are compensated by the straight commission method.

Sales people pay own expenses

Several arguments may be advanced in favor of having sales representatives pay their own expenses. They often prefer the plan because it gives them more freedom of operation. They need not account for their expenditures. Some also feel that it enables them to get a better break on their income taxes. They are able to charge off a greater percentage of their total income as business expenses than they could if the compensation and expense payments were carefully separated. From the company's standpoint, the plan is simple, and administrative costs are minimized.

When sales people pay their own expenses, however, management loses considerable control over their activities. A person spending his own funds will do so as he sees fit, not as management directs. While the wise sales rep will entertain modestly with his own money, when it is necessary to gain or keep an account, management cannot expect him to spend his own money on substantial entertainment that is not directly associated with getting an order. A sales rep paying his own expenses also could not be expected to travel some distance to take care of company business.

Sales people who are paid by a straight commission usually pay their own expenses for two reasons. First, management has decided that it is willing to pay a certain percentage of sales for the execution of the field sales function. They offer the total amount to the sales rep and say, in effect, "What's left over after you pay your costs is yours." Second, people being paid a straight commission might find the temptation to cheat on an expense account during periods of lean sales overwhelming. One of the considerations in having a straight commis-

---

[4] Ibid., p. 189.

sion plan in the first place is that it places the sales rep in the position of having to sell or starve. The polite term is *incentive,* but in reality it is sell or don't eat. Testimony from many successful sales people bears witness to the effectiveness of such plans.

Having the sales force pay its own expenses works well when the reps' expenses are predictable and relatively small, and entertainment is not needed. The management of a paper products wholesale house, for example, paid its people above-market wages and told them to pay their own expenses.

Unlimited-payment plans

The most widely used method of expense control is to reimburse sales representatives for all the legitimate business and travel costs they incur while on company business. There is no limit on total expenses or individual items, but the reps are required to submit itemized accounts of expenditures. Usually, the reports are turned in every week or two. If the system works well, reimbursement is prompt.

One of the prime advantages of the unlimited method of expense control is its flexibility. Cost differentials caused by variations in territories, jobs, or products present no problems under this plan. Flexibility also contributes to making the plan a fair one for both sales people and management, assuming that the former report their expenditures honestly and accurately. Furthermore, this plan gives management some control over the sales reps' activities. If sales executives want a new territory developed, new accounts called on in out-of-the-way places, or much entertainment money spent on a particular customer, the expense plan certainly is no deterrent.

On the other hand, unlimited method of controlling expenses may not allow management to forecast its direct selling costs accurately. The unlimited feature is an open invitation for some people to be extravagant or pad their expense accounts with unjustifiable items. Certainly, the plan offers no incentive for a sales person to economize.

It is questionable whether the unlimited expense plan creates more or fewer disputes between management and the sales force than is true of other expense-control systems. The unlimited feature should reduce the number of disagreements, but friction may arise if management questions items on the expense reports. Probably the major need in any unlimited-payment plan is to establish a successful method of controlling the expenses. The best general method may be to hire good people in the first place and then manage them so that they are not unreasonable in their use of expense accounts. More specifically, a good sales manager will analyze the reports to determine what is reasonable and practicable. When a rep's expenses get out of line, it probably will be apparent to his manager.

Limited-payment plans and flat allowances

Two other general methods of controlling expenses limit payment in some fashion. In one method, the allowable amount is limited for each item. For example, management may say it will pay a maximum of $20 for a motel or hotel room, $3 for breakfast, $5 for lunch, and $10 for the evening meal (or $18 each day for food), 12 cents a mile for automobile transportation, and so on for each expense item. In the other control plan, payment is limited by allowing a flat sum for a period of time, such as a day or a week. One company may pay $30 a day; another firm may set its allowance at $200 a week. Similar limits may be used throughout all territories, or separate ones may be established to take into account territorial cost differentials.

Limited-payment plans may be suitable when sales reps' activities are sufficiently regular so that expenses can be forecast. Some form of flat allowance plan may well be used when the sales job is routine and the travel plan is repetitive.

Probably the major problem involved in administering the limited-payment plan is to establish the limits for each item or time period. To do a thorough job may require considerable managerial time and clerical expense. Past reports may be studied to determine the mileage typically covered each day. Hotel and motel directories may be examined to establish limits on lodging. It is essential that a separate study be conducted for each territory to ensure that regional differentials do not creep in unnoticed. It is also important to bring the sales force into the deliberations and to get their opinions. Once the allowable limits are determined, the job is not finished. Periodic reexaminations are necessary to ensure that the limits are realistic.

There are advantages to some limitations on expense payments. Management can budget its expenses more accurately because a maximum can be reasonably forecast for each person. One claimed advantage of limited allowances is that it reduces expense account padding, although it is doubtful that this claim can be validated. Friction and disputes between management and the sales force should be reduced, particularly if the expense limits are fair. Moreover, the expense limits communicate to the sales force what is expected of them. When management sets a limit of $25 on what can be spent entertaining a customer on any one day, that gives the sales people a standard by which to gauge their entertainment efforts.

A flat allowance has several drawbacks. First, high-caliber sales people may object to such a plan; they may feel that the company cannot trust them under an unlimited method. Second, the system is inflexible. A sales rep may have some unusual expense, such as an entertainment item he could not escape without losing the account. If entertainment is not an allowable expense, he may not be reimbursed.

Some companies bypass the factor of inflexibility by allowing unusual expenses if they are reported separately with an explanatory note, and management approves the exception.

When limits are set for each item, the plan may be hard to control. For example, if a firm allows $4 for lunch and $10 for dinner, and a rep actually spends $4 for each meal, he can report the total expenditure on a $4–$10 division, but he is not telling the truth. It would be better for management to set a daily limit for the food and let the sales person distribute the amount as preferred. A sales rep may also run over the limit on food and under it on lodging, but still come out with the proper total. There is usually considerable switching of expenditures among expense items as attempts are made to recoup the money spent in excess of the limit for one item by padding the claim for some other item. When a rep spends over the limits for a day or a week, the excess may even be regained by filing for expenses on days not actually worked. When this practice was questioned by top management, one sales manager replied, "So what? We still have a lid on our sales costs, and those tricks just put some flexibility into the plan."

Another potential drawback to any limited-payment plan or flat allowance is that it may not be kept so current that it reflects the changing cost structures in a territory. If the plan is kept current, the firm must budget the additional administrative expense needed for a periodic review. Moreover, the plan is good only if the sales force believes the limits are equitable. And it cannot prevent a cheater from trying to economize on expenses and then padding the account up to the allowable limits.

Combination plans

The advantages of both the limited and unlimited plans can sometimes be realized by developing a control method that combines the two. Management may set limits on items such as food and lodging, for example, but place no ceiling on transportation.

Another combination method is an expense quota plan. Under this system, management sets a limit on the total allowable expense for a period of time, but the ceiling is related to some other item on the operating statement, such as net sales. For example, a quota of $400 may be set for a month because monthly sales are expected to be $10,000. Expenses can be tied to sales even more directly by allowing sales representatives a monthly expense account not to exceed 5 percent of their net sales. The compensation plan can play some part in this expense-control system in provisions to pay a bonus if the rep keeps expenses at some given amount under quota.

Expense quota plans do have the advantage of enabling management to relate sales force expenses to net sales, and in this method some degree of control may be exerted over this direct selling cost. Furthermore, the reps have some operating flexibility within the total expense budget. By making them expense conscious, they are not so apt to be wasteful.

The very fact that the reps are made expense conscious is one of the most severe limitations to the expense quota plan. Management should encourage its sales people to channel their thinking into methods of increasing sales volume and gross margin rather than decreasing their own travel and business expenses. Sales reps expenses should be related to net sales only over a long period of time and for the entire company.

FACTORS AFFECTING EXPENSE CONTROL PLAN

Various factors may affect the *level* of expense payment or the *method* of expense control a company decides to adopt.

Type of compensation plan

The method of compensation used may have some bearing on the type of expense plan adopted. It is not uncommon for reps on a straight commission to pay their own expenses. When sales people are operating under a straight salary plan, almost invariably the company pays the man's travel and business expenses. Sometimes, the expense quota plan is related to the bonus method of compensation.

Nature of territories

The size, density, and location of territories can have a considerable effect on the type of expense plan adopted by the company. A sales rep who covers the metropolitan Chicago district in an automobile should be reimbursed differently than a person who has the upper New England area. Furthermore, the stage of business development achieved by a company in a given territory can affect its expense plan. Ordinarily, to operate in a *new* territory, more expense money per dollar of sales is needed than is required to sell in an *established* district.

Method of transportation used

When the sales reps travel by automobile, the type of expense control plan must be different than when they use some other type of transportation. If a sales person uses his own car, management must establish an equitable method for reimbursing him. Obviously, none of these problems arise if the man travels by airplane.

Nature of job and its relation to products and customers

Three factors—job, product, and customers—each may influence the type of expense control plan used in an organization. To see the influence of the job alone, consider a soap manufacturer who sells to large retail chains. One group of sales people may sell the product to the home office of the chain and thus deal with high-level executives. These sales representatives probably require the flexibility of an unlimited plan. However, the manufacturer's missionary sales reps who visit the individual stores in the chain probably have a routine job with an established route list, and therefore some form of limited allowance plan is appropriate.

It may be that the nature of the product calls for differences in expense plans. A sales rep for a dress manufacturer calling on buyers for department and specialty stores probably would be under an unlimited plan, whereas the representative of a chewing gum manufacturer calling on drug and grocery stores would be reimbursed for expenses by a fixed sum method. Some products require the sales person to spend extensive periods of time in servicing the account before the sale can be consummated. After the sale is made, an additional period of servicing may be required. In situations of this nature, it is more difficult to forecast expense requirements; therefore, an element of flexibility must be introduced into the plan.

Caliber of sales people

An experienced, high-quality sales rep is more apt to be on an unlimited payment plan than is a new recruit. Closely supervised sales people frequently are placed on some form of a flat allowance or limited payment plan, while an unsupervised sales engineer is probably operating under an unlimited payment.

CONTROL OF SALES FORCE TRANSPORTATION

One significant sales expense in which there is little room for managerial discretion is the cost of transporting sales representatives to call on customers. Decisions regarding transportation expenses are usually rather clear-cut because they are based on costs and the precise nature of the selling environment. The rep who covers Manhattan must use taxis, buses, and the subway; a car would be next to useless. In Los Angeles without a car, the rep goes nowhere. The situation largely dictates the transportation requirement. Some aspects of it are open to managerial control, however.

Ownership of automobiles

Since most sales travel is done by automobile, a car has become an almost standard item of equipment for the sales representative. Management may provide company-owned cars, the vehicle may be leased from a rental agency, or sales people may use their own cars while traveling on company business. While all three methods are widely used, there has been a noticeable trend toward the leasing arrangement.

No one policy for automobile ownership is best under all conditions. The final decision rests on a consideration of several factors, some of which are discussed briefly in the following paragraphs.

1. *Size of sales force.*   With a small sales force, simplicity and economy are achieved either by having sales people own their automobiles or by leasing cars for them. Only with a large sales force does the company generally find it advantageous to own the automobiles. Unquestionably the easiest course of action is to let the sales force arrange for its own transportation, but other factors can override managerial convenience.

2. *Availability of centralized maintenance and storage facilities.*   If a company maintains centralized vehicle storage and repair facilities, it is in a good position to furnish the sales force with cars. A company which operates a fleet of trucks, for example, usually has garage and maintenance facilities available.

3. *Unusual design required.*   Some companies require the cars used by their sales people to be a special color, have a specially constructed body, or carry some form of company advertising. Sometimes the vehicle must double as a sales car and a delivery truck. In these situations, the company should furnish the cars.

4. *Control of car's operating condition.*   If the company furnishes the car, management is in a better position to demand that it be kept presentable. The company probably provides later model cars than the sales person's own car, which could be old enough to embarrass the company. However, a sales rep may take better care of the car if it is his own than if it is company owned or leased.

5. *Personal preferences.*   People may be financially able and willing to furnish their own cars for work. When they *must* provide the cars, however, management runs the risk of losing some good applicants for sales positions. Everyone will not want to drive their own automobiles for company business, or they may not have suitable cars.

6. Annual mileage.   The average annual mileage covered by representatives influences ownership of the automobile. The more mileage driven, the more advantageous it becomes for the company to own the cars. The point of indifference would vary depending upon the cars used and the company's auto expense allowances. Suppose the company pays a flat 15 cents per mile auto allowance and has calculated the cost of owning the preferred model to be $2,000 a year, plus 10 cents a mile. Under these circumstances the point of indifference would be 40,000 miles. If the sales people covered less than this mileage, management would probably encourage them to own the cars except in very unusual circumstances.

7. Operating cost.   It is hard to generalize on which of the three alternatives—employee owned, company owned, or leasing—offers the lowest operating cost to the company. The answer depends to a great extent on rental costs, number of miles driven, and method of reimbursing the sales force. It also is difficult to measure some of the indirect costs of company ownership, such as the administrative expense of operating the system.

8. Investments.   If the company is not in a strong financial position or for any other reason does not want to make the investment in automobiles, the alternative is to lease the cars or have the salesmen provide their own. If firms hire people who do not own a car suitable for the job or do not have the money to buy one, these firms may prefer to arrange financing for the purchaser rather than buying the cars outright.

9. Administrative problems.   One of the major administrative problems when the company furnishes cars is whether they can be used by sales people for their own personal use and, if so, to what extent. A general policy seems to be to allow them to use the company car for personal transportation. Management may or may not suggest some limits. If a no-limit policy is adopted, reps may not buy their own cars, or the company car can be one of two automobiles in the family. Use of the company car for private purposes can be an additional factor in a decision to accept a job with the organization. Such a benefit is another indirect monetary payment, the same as group insurance or a paid vacation.

There is no general policy on the payment of operating expenses for a company car used for private purposes. Some businesses ask the rep to pay for the gas when driving the car for personal use; others pay all expenses for both business and private use. Some ask that operating expenses be paid only on long personal trips such as vacations.

The strongest point in favor of leasing is not the economics of the situation but the convenience of management. Leasing is the easiest way to put the sales force on wheels. The marketing executive does not have to be a transportation expert, and problems of buying the car, maintaining it, and later reselling it are avoided.

Reimbursement plans

Sales people who must use their own automobiles on company business must be reimbursed for the cost. Three separate types of expenditures are involved in owning and operating a car. One is *variable costs*, which are generally related directly to the number of miles driven. Examples of these items are gasoline, oil, lubrication, tires, and normal service maintenance. A second class of expenditures is *fixed costs*, which tend to be related to periods of time rather than miles driven. These costs include depreciation, license fees (state, city, driver), and insurance (public liability, property damage, comprehensive, collision). A third group of *miscellaneous expenses* is difficult to standardize or budget in detail in advance. Typical items in this group are tolls (bridge, highway), parking and storage charges, and major repairs. Usually the third type of costs is not incorporated into one of the ordinary automobile expense control plans. These items are listed separately on the expense account.

Sales people may be reimbursed for using their cars on company business by some kind of a fixed allowance plan or by a flexible payment method.

Fixed-allowance plans. One general type of fixed-allowance plan is based on *mileage* and another is based on a period of *time*. Under the first, the employee is paid the same amount for each mile driven on company business. Today, a typical rate probably is between 12 and 16 cents a mile. The flat rate per mile is used by more companies than any other major plan, although there is a trend away from it toward some more flexible method. Under the other type of fixed-allowance system, a flat sum is paid for each period of time, such as a week or a month, regardless of the number of miles driven. The reimbursements cover both fixed and variable automobile costs.

The fixed-allowance plans have several advantages. They are generally simple and economical to administer. Sales people know in advance what they will be paid, and if payment is based on a flat allowance for a given period of time, the company can budget this expense in advance. People who drive many miles (20,000–30,000) prefer it because they can generally make money under such a plan.

The criticisms of fixed-allowance plans are so severe, however, that we wonder why they remain so popular. Generally speaking, the plans are inflexible and may be very unfair to the sales people. Some may benefit financially while others lose. The fixed sum for a given time period can be reasonably good only if all men travel in a routine fashion and costs are the same in each territory. Similarly, the flat mileage allowance is equitable only if all reps travel about the same number of miles in the same type of cars under the same operating conditions. These conditions are highly unlikely and unrealistic.

Consider the inequities introduced, for example, by variations in the number of miles driven. In the operation of an automobile, some costs are fixed regardless of the number of miles driven. Therefore, the greater amount of driving, the more miles over which to amortize the fixed costs. So the fixed costs per mile decrease as the total mileage increases. Under a fixed allowance per mile, every additional mile works to the financial benefit of the sales reps. An example is outlined in Table 12–1. Assuming annual fixed costs of $1,700, per mile variable costs of 6 cents, and a mileage allowance of 15 cents, the results are shown for various annual mileages. If a sales representative drives 5,000 miles per year, he receives $750 when his real costs are $2,000, so his earnings are reduced by $1,250. At the other extreme, a representative who drives 40,000 miles gets $6,000, which is a gain of $1,900 over his actual costs. If the representative were paid a fixed sum per month, similar inequities would result, but in reverse. That is, a payment of $200 a month would benefit the low-mileage traveler at the expense of the person who drove many miles in a year.

Operating costs for automobile travel vary by region, and typically a flat payment plan does not recognize this factor. Variable costs per mile are significantly higher in city driving than in a territory where longer distances are involved. Furthermore, not all cities of similar size have similar operating costs. The price of gasoline, for example, will vary among regions.

TABLE 12–1
Example of results of flat rate per mile plan under varying annual mileages

Annual mileage	Fixed cost	Variable costs at 6 cents per mile	Total costs	Per mile costs	Payment to representatives	Gain or loss to representatives
5,000	$1,700	$ 300	$2,000	$.40	$ 750	−$1,250
10,000	1,700	600	2,300	.23	1,500	− 800
20,000	1,700	1,200	2,900	.145	3,000	+ 100
30,000	1,700	1,800	3,500	.117	4,500	+ 1,000
40,000	1,700	2,400	4,100	.103	6,000	+ 1,900

Flexible allowance plans. To avoid the inherent weaknesses in a fixed allowance system, several flexible control plans have been developed.

1. *Graduated mileage rates.* One type of flexible plan pays a different allowance per mile depending on the total miles driven in a

time period. For example, one firm pays 15 cents a mile for the first 15,000 miles driven in a year and 10 cents a mile for those above 15,000. Another organization pays 14 cents a mile for the first 500 miles driven in a month and 8 cents on each mile over 500 a month. Mileage allowances are graduated downward to reflect the fact that total costs per mile decrease as mileage goes up. While a graduated plan corrects some of the faults of a flat-rate method, differences in territorial costs and types of automobiles generally are not considered.

2. *Combination of allowance per time period and mileage rate.* An improvement over the graduated mileage method of expense control is the combination system under which management figures automobile allowances in two parts. Thus the differences between fixed and variable costs of owning and operating a car are reflected in the payment. To cover fixed costs, a flat payment is made for each given time period, such as a week or a month. In addition, variable costs are reimbursed by mileage allowances which usually are flat rates although they could be graduated. For example, one company pays $100 a month plus 8 cents a mile; another pays $125 a month plus 10 cents a mile over 750 miles a month.

A widely recognized and respected plan was developed in 1933 by R. E. Runzheimer Sr., who founded an automobile management consulting firm now headquartered in Rochester, Wisconsin. In one study, the company divided the nation into 29 basic cost areas and computed the total amount of ownership and operating expenses for each of the regions. Table 12–2 shows the 1977 cost allowances. In some respects, the Runzheimer plan gives the same results as the graduated mileage system in that the more miles driven, the smaller is the per-mile allowance. However, the Runzheimer plan is much more accurate because payments reflect variations in types of cars, miles driven, and territorial operating costs. For an intermediate-size 1977 Chevrolet, Ford, or Plymouth, for instance, the annual fixed costs varied from about $2,260 in the San Francisco region down to a little under $1,500 in South Dakota and Maryland-Virginia. Mileage allowances, excluding Alaska, ranged from 6.6 cents around Reno, Nevada, down to 5.3 cents in northern Texas. In summary, a Runzheimer-type plan seems to be the most equitable and accurate method for paying sales people for the use of their automobiles.

MISCELLANEOUS METHODS OF EXPENSE CONTROL

Credit cards

Many firms are using credit cards to control various expense items. A growing number of services and products may be purchased through

TABLE 12–2
1977 automobile standard allowances

Cost area number	Basing point	Fixed ownership costs Annual	Fixed ownership costs Per day	Operating costs per mile
1	San Francisco, Calif.	$2,267	$6.21	6.3¢
2	Bakersfield, Calif.	1,869	5.12	6.5
3	Reno, Nev.	1,690	4.63	6.6
4	Denver, Colo.	1,697	4.65	6.2
5	Albuquerque, N.M.	1,708	4.68	6.2
6	Billings, Mont.	1,861	5.10	6.2
7	Sioux Fall, S.D.	1,489	4.08	6.0
8	Grand Island, Neb.	1,624	4.45	5.6
9	Springfield, Mo.............	1,649	4.52	5.5
10	Oklahoma City, Okla.	1,627	4.46	5.4
11	El Paso, Tex................	1,744	4.78	6.0
12	Dallas, Tex.	1,708	4.68	5.3
13	St. Paul, Minn.	1,697	4.65	6.1
14	Des Moines, Iowa	1,551	4.25	5.6
15	Evanston, Ill.	1,591	4.36	5.7
16	Ft. Smith, Ark.	1,540	4.22	6.0
17	Toledo, Ohio	1,566	4.29	5.6
18	Chester, W. Va.............	1,573	4.31	6.1
19	Mobile, Ala.................	1,653	4.53	6.2
20	Rutland, Vt.................	1,533	4.20	5.9
21	Brookline, Mass.	2,182	5.98	5.9
22	Mineola, N.Y.	1,865	5.11	5.6
23	Harrisburg, Pa.	1,525	4.18	6.0
24	Essex, Md.	1,478	4.05	5.6
25	Atlanta, Ga.................	1,686	4.62	6.1
26	Jacksonville, Fla............	1,511	4.14	5.5
27	Fairbanks, Alaska	2,044	5.60	7.9
28	Anchorage, Alaska	1,992	5.46	7.5
29	Honolulu, Hawaii	1,752	4.80	6.5

Cost figures represent an intermediate Chevrolet-Ford-Plymouth with a standard 8-cylinder engine, automatic transmission, power steering, power disc brakes, AM radio, and air conditioning.
All costs were based on an economic-use cycle of either 3 years or 60,000 miles, whichever comes first.
Source: with permission of Runzheimer & Co., Inc.

a credit card system. When management encourages or even requires its sales people to use a credit card system, they need to carry less money, and the risks of loss or theft are reduced. Credit cards are widely used for air travel and car rentals.

The expense bank account

In some instances an undue burden is placed on representatives who have to pay for their expenses and then wait for reimbursement. They may have to finance three of four weeks' expenses—$600 to $800. To avoid this, some firms place a certain sum, say $300, in a checking account for each representative. The rep pays expenses by drawing on that account. When the account needs replenishment, or at regular intervals, the rep files an expense report. Upon approval of the report, the amount accounted for is deposited in the checking account to bring it back up to the initial sum.

QUESTIONS AND PROBLEMS

1. "The expense-control plan should enable our representatives to maintain (at no extra cost to them) the same standard of living while on the road that they enjoy at home," said the sales manager of a metal products manufacturer. Discuss the implications in this statement.

2. When recruiting sales people, some firms offer as a lure an expense plan and the opportunity for net additional income through the plan. Evaluate this policy on economic, human relations, and ethical bases.

3. A petroleum firm operating in the Midwest with a sales force of 300 people planned to sell its fleet of company-owned automobiles and have the sales people henceforth furnish their own cars. What problems are involved in this change?

4. The oil company noted in question 3 was trying to decide which method should be used to reimburse the sales force for the use of their cars on business. Each rep traveled about 18,000 miles a year. The company was computing the costs on the assumption that they drove a Ford, Chevrolet, or Plymouth. The following payment methods were under consideration. What would be the total cost to the firm under each of the three proposals?
   a. A straight 15 cents a mile.
   b. $150 a month plus 8 cents a mile.
   c. The Runzheimer plan. Use Table 12–2 and assume that the 300-man sales force was equally divided among territories based around St. Paul, Chicago, and Toledo.

5. In lieu of a salary increase last year, a television manufacturer granted its sales force the privilege of using company cars for any personal purpose, and the company paid all expenses. Previously, the firm had strictly prohibited any personal use of these cars. Discuss all aspects of this policy decision.

6. One publisher was considering leasing small Chevrolet or Dodge cars instead of paying its present 15 cents per mile to them for using their private cars. Several of the reps were driving economy cars and were willing to take less than 15 cents per mile in order to keep from changing cars. What should the firm do?

7. What should management do if a particularly good salesman is padding his expense account?

Case 12–1
RUGG AND SONS
Change in expense account policy

Brad Nolan had assumed the sales managership of Rugg and Sons, a wholesaler of mining supplies and equipment, at the beginning of the week. On Wednesday, his secretary gave him the prior week's expense accounts for his eight salesmen. A brief glance quickly disclosed that they were outstanding works of fiction. Brad had been around enough to know a padded expense account when he saw one, and he was looking at eight of the most plushly lined examples he had ever seen. He was furious; a $7 breakfast insulted his intelligence. He picked up the phone to summon to his office whoever on the sales force was handy. Ed Topp was the unfortunate victim, once again proving the folly of a salesman spending too much time in the home office.

"Ed, what in blue blazes is this you turned in, the defense budget?" Brad yelled as he shoved Ed's expense account at him. While Ed looked a bit uncomfortable, he was also a bit peeved, for he felt he was being unduly singled out for a whipping boy. "Did you really think you could slip this nonsense by me?" Brad demanded.

Ed countered, "I think you better check with the boss on this. He forgot to tell you something about how we do things around here."

"What's that?"

"I'd rather he told you."

"You tell me!"

"That's how we get part of our pay around here," Topp said. "You can't really think that we would be working here for the low salaries the company pays, do you? You know the game. Everybody saves money this way."

Nolan thought a bit, then said, "Thank you for telling me. I think we will be having a meeting on this matter in the very near future." Nolan took the matter up with his boss and found that what Ed had told him was true. He was distressed; he did not approve of the practice in any respect. It was not only illegal, but he thought it to be poor management.

After a night's thought on the issue, Nolan resolved that things would be done his way or he would move on. He could not be a party to such fraud. It was a matter not only of ethics but also of intelligence. All he could do was lose under such an arrangement. When he told his boss this he was given the power to change the policy as he might desire. The boss had acquiesced so easily that Nolan was convinced he also wanted to be free of the practice and was happy to have someone do it for him.

Then Nolan wondered exactly how he should go about making the change and what the changes should be. He wanted honest expense reporting, but should it be an open expense system, or should he place limits on the various types of expenditures? And how should salaries be adjusted?

Questions

1. How should Brad Nolan proceed with the expense account matter administratively?
2. What type of expense account system should be adopted?

Case 12–2
GINNY'S TOGS
Mobile display rooms

Erma Kirk, sales manager for Ginny's Togs, a popular-priced line of women's clothes, had been aware for some time that several of her sales reps were unhappy with the company's arrangements for their transportation while on the job.

The company's sales force consisted of seven men who had a total of 142 years of sales experience in the women's wear industry, and nine women with a total of 33 years of sales experience in the business, reflecting their more recent acceptance as sales employees. The company furnished each of the reps a new leased Cadillac each year. The average mileage on the trade-in was 41,000. The lease payment was $216 a month in 1977. Operating costs, which were paid by the company, averaged 8.4 cents a mile.

Carol Hagan, sales rep for the states of Missouri, Kansas, Nebraska, and Iowa, was not happy with these travel arrangements because they placed what she believed was an unneeded physical burden on her 5 foot, 1 inch, 101-pound frame. Traditionally, sales reps carried the dress samples in large, bulky bags, each of which weighed about 35 pounds. These bags were carried in the trunk of the car and on the back seat. At each stop they had to be lifted out of the car and hung on a portable, collapsible hanging rack on rollers. When possible, this rack was rolled into the merchant's office. Many times parking was not convenient, and though some good customers would have a stock clerk help Carol with the task, she could not count on it.

Some of the men also complained of the onerous job of carrying the samples around, but they saw little they could do about it. Sometimes they were able to set up a showroom in a local motel and have the merchant "work the line" away from the store, but usually the motel's facilities were unsuitable for such use.

Carol had met a salesman for a competing line of sportswear who covered the same territory. This salesman had a motor home that had been specially fitted as a display room and entertainment center. The rep did not usually sleep in the motorized display room, but on occasion, he did live out of it. He told her that the rig had cost him $25,000, and the cost to drive it was about 13 cents a mile. He claimed it was an effective way to sell, and his own sales volume had increased 18 percent on the first trip around the territory in it.

Carol reported the information to management and asked to be provided with a similar motor home from which she could work. She felt it would solve several problems she had encountered: no more hauling the samples in and out of the car, no more living out of a suitcase, no more lack of space in which to show the line properly.

Kirk, the sales manager, had been aware of the use of motor homes as salesrooms but had received some mixed reports on them. Many sales reps who had tried them out had found them inconvenient or too expensive. Kirk pointed out to Carol that at 13 cents a mile it would cost $1,886 more a year just to drive the vehicles. Moreover, the $25,000 investment more than doubled the overhead costs. She told Hagan that considerable thought would have to be given to her request before any action could be taken.

Four months passed during which Carol heard no more about her request. When she pressed for an answer she was again stalled, and she finally realized that she was being stalled out of the picture. So she made a personal appeal for consideration to Kirk: "If you don't want to do it for the whole sales force, at least do it for me."

Kirk replied, "We can't do anything like that, Carol, it would be bad policy. Others on the sales force would want one just like yours, or better. There would be no end of trouble over it."

Hagan thought for a minute and then made another proposition: "Then let the company continue paying me exactly what it has been for the cars and mileage, and let my buy the motor home and pay for the difference from my own pocket."

"Let me take it up with top management before giving you an answer" was Kirk's reply.

Question

1. What should Erma Kirk, the sales manager, do?

13

Supervising the sales force

Many receive advice, few profit by it.
SYRUS

When the sales supervisor for a large food products company was asked to describe an average work week, he focused on the immediate working problem of his sales force. His week was described as follows:

> This week was rather typical. On Monday I rode all day with a new saleswoman who needs a lot of help. She has a lot to learn, and I'll have to spend a good deal of time with her this year to develop her potential.
>
> Tuesday morning I spent with a man whose performance has fallen off, to see what the trouble was. As I thought, he had been having problems with his wife. He'd been drinking, so she had locked him out of the house. We talked about it at some length. Finally I had to tell him that if he could not get control of his personal life I would have to recommend his termination.
>
> That afternoon I spent checking out the calls reportedly made by a salesman who isn't doing at all well. I am afraid he is through. He's been telling us some tales. He never made half of the calls he had reported. I suspect his expense accounts won't stand much scrutiny, either.
>
> Wednesday, I spent with Bob Conner, working on a very large potential account. He's a good man, but he needs help.
>
> Thursday I rode with two other reps, just checking them out.
>
> Friday I spent on paper work and planning next week. Wrote letters to all of the people who report to me.

Many managers use the word *supervision* with reference to all the activities of operating and controlling the efforts of the sales force. More strictly, it should refer only to direct working relationships between the sales person and superiors. The sales manager who checks with the sales people each morning to see what their plans are for the day is *directly* supervising their activities. Many other managerial actions constitute *indirect* supervision, such as auditing expense accounts or appraising sales performance.

REASONS FOR PROVIDING SUPERVISION

One significant reason for supervising the sales force is to give them more sales training. In many ways, the field supervisor is an on-the-job sales training executive. The most effective sales training takes place over a period of time, and it is best done in the field while sales reps are actually facing day-to-day problems. Good supervision can do much to develop an inexperienced recruit into a valuable employee.

In some selling situations, sales reps need technical help or other assistance in making sales. The supervisor is prepared to provide such help in many circumstances, such as assisting a sales engineer to make a presentation to a major prospective customer.

Supervision is frequently used as an enforcement tool to ensure that company policies and orders are being followed. In this role, the supervisor is working in much the same capacity as a foreman in the plant, with the purpose of making certain that the reps are doing their jobs properly. Jobs that call for little selling ability and consist mainly of repetitive, nonselling duties require rather close supervision to ensure that the tasks are actually carried out. The American Tobacco Company, for example, finds it necessary to maintain close supervision over promotional people who call on convenience outlets to install point-of-purchase displays and perform other merchandising tasks.

Some sales managers believe that direct supervision stimulates sales people to do better work. There is a limit to how much an employee can be prodded without becoming resentful, however.

Supervision can engender good morale. To some sales reps, the knowledge that someone in the organization cares about the work they do and gives them recognition for their activities is highly important. Just the fact that the supervisor is in personal contact should have a good effect on sales people's morale.

Ultimately, the basic reason for supervising the sales force is to make sure they are doing their jobs and to provide management with knowledge of what is going on in the field. The manager of a sales force whose members are not doing their jobs, and who does not know this is the case, will be judged to be inept. Experience garnered by generations of managers has shown that good management requires good supervision.

REASONS FOR NEGLECT OF SUPERVISION

Supervision seems to be a neglected phase of sales management. One could easily come to that conclusion by scanning the literature on the subject. Relatively little pertaining to supervision of the sales force appears in the trade journals. Several factors can account for the neglect of the topic.

Many sales managers feel that direct supervision costs more than it is worth. The field supervisor adds an additional level to the administrative pyramid in the organization, and it is difficult to prove whether that level produces sufficient additional profit to warrant its existence. One company with 30 sales people had four regional sales managers whose principal duties were to supervise the work of the sales force. When the company encountered financial difficulties, it fired ten ineffective salesmen and put the four regional managers back into territories as sales reps. Management could not justify their cost.

The sales manager seldom has sufficient time available to provide more than minimal supervision for sales people in the field. Many managers prefer to try to hire good people and then supervise them from headquarters. Management's inability to find enough time to give sales people the supervision they need is regretted often.

Another reason for the neglect of supervision is that frequently sales reps resent it. Many people go into selling to escape direct supervision. Psychologically, they thrive on being independent and free from control. They regard themselves as independent and view with suspicion any encroachment on their freedom. Some sales people welcome assistance by a *good* supervisor, however. They understand that the supervisor is there to help them to do a better job and to make more money.

The geographic dispersion of sales reps over wide areas makes close supervision difficult. Moreover, it costs a great deal to maintain supervision in the field.

Supervision may also be neglected because there are no magic rules or mathematical formulas for supervising human activities. It is not one of the more attractive areas of business administration. Little organized factual knowledge is available to the sales supervisor, yet he must be not only technically competent in the field of selling but also a master human relations practitioner. Since these are relatively intangible factors, there is little to guide a sales supervisor's behavior other than experience and wisdom.

AMOUNT OF SUPERVISION NEEDED

There are dangers in either over- or undersupervising the sales force. Supervision costs are considerable, and management does not want to spend more on it than is necessary to accomplish results.

Dangers of oversupervising

Oversupervising can hamper the performance of sales representatives. While one purpose of providing supervision is to improve morale, too much of it can have just the opposite effect. Able, independent sales reps resent managers who hold too tight a rein on them. Many people go into selling to escape such direct control.

Oversupervision also can mean wasted time for both the rep and the supervisor. The major function of sales is to sell merchandise, which cannot be accomplished if the sales people are overburdened with conferences and meetings with supervisors.

Providing any supervision entails some risks. A highly regarded large corporation lost a good salesman when, being transferred to a new region of his choice, he came under the direction of a supervisor with whom he had a serious personality conflict.

Dangers of undersupervising

The dangers of undersupervision are much the same as those of oversupervision. Morale can suffer and costs can rise as a result. A sales rep who is not getting the attention or supervision needed to do the job properly is likely to develop a poor attitude toward the job. He or she may feel that the boss does not know what is happening and does not particularly care. Without proper supervision to improve performance, such a rep may eventually be fired or quit. Another type of sales person may be a potentially good persuader but may have a few problems that are unknown to the home office. A good supervisor may be able to identify and handle such problems.

Too little supervision, also can result in high costs. A good supervisor can reduce sales expenses, increase production, and decrease turnover in the sales force.

Ignorance can be another penalty for insufficient supervision. Without the information that supervision can provide, a sales manager may not know what is happening in the field. Although he may receive sales reports at regular intervals, he may have no mechanism for determining their accuracy.

A day-to-day operating problem in the

MAJESTIC GLASS COMPANY (F)
A young salesman seems unable to make decisions

Watching an airport taxi discharge a passenger in the driveway of his home one Saturday morning, Mr. Clyde Brion, general sales manager for Majestic Glass Company, knew that he was about to receive another visit from his Atlanta salesman, Wilbur Devlin. Brion muttered to himself, "When will this kid ever stand on his own two feet?" and gave up his plans to work on his lawn.

At age 28, Devlin was one of the youngest people on the Majestic sales force. The Atlanta territory was his first assignment after completing the sales training course. He was known to take his work seriously, but he had displayed such a heavy dependence upon other people that at times it appeared no decision was small enough for him to make by himself. He was a handsome young man with a winning smile and an engaging personality, but these qualities may have merely increased the willingness of others to help him.

Devlin seized almost any pretext to telephone, telegraph, or visit Brion. Usually he sought help in solving some problem concerning one of his customers, such as which product to recommend for a particular use, how to handle breakage adjustments, or how to quote prices. After answering each question, Brion had pointed out that Devlin could have handled it himself by consulting the Majestic catalog or the company sales procedures manual, or by using his own judgment. Nevertheless, the requests for help continued, and Devlin did not appear to be embarrassed in asking for assistance.

Besides Brion, others were doing favors for Devlin that they were not asked for by other sales people. He had obtained help from the Majestic attorney in buying a home in Atlanta. One of the accounting department supervisors was found to be working on Devlin's personal income tax return.

Sales of the Atlanta territory had shown a modest increase since Devlin had been assigned there, but selling expenses in that territory were much higher than the company average. Brion believed that the expense ratio was being adversely affected by Devlin's requests for help and by the costs of his frequent trips to Ohio.

On this Saturday morning, after he had taken Devlin into his living room, Brion quickly discerned from the salesman's notes and remarks that the problem which had prompted him to fly to Lancaster involved a simple choice between two types of acid bottles for a small chemicals processor. He expected that the customer's requirements could be filled from warehouse stocks, and the estimated profit potential was less than the airline fare for Mr. Devlin's visit.

Question

What should Clyde Brion do to get Wilbur Devlin to stand on his own two feet—that is, to quit being so dependent on other people?

Note: See the introduction to this series of problems in Chapter 2 for the necessary background on the company, its market, and its competition.

Factors in determining how much supervision is needed

The foremost factor in determining how much supervision is required in a given situation is the quality of the sales force. If only topnotch recruits or sales people with proven results are hired, little supervision should be attempted. The training, enforcement, and stimulation that supervision can provide are usually not needed for those who are competent to do the job without prodding.

On the other end of the sales force scale are the newly hired individuals with below-average ability and no selling experience. It would be difficult to give such reps too much supervision. They need the sales training and assistance that a supervisor can provide. They also need constant stimulation and must be watched closely to see that they abide by company policies.

In between these two extremes of sales force quality there is an almost unlimited number of variations. In determining the proper amount of supervision to be provided, the sales manager must consider several other factors. The first is the importance of the sales job in the overall achievement of the organization's objectives. If the relative importance of any one rep's performance is large in the overall sales picture of the firm, it is good management to make certain that this rep does the job well. In such organizations as door-to-door selling firms and large concerns that hire people to do mainly sales promotional work, the importance of any one person to the overall success of the operation is almost negligible. Although some supervision is usually maintained in these instances, it is not vitally important.

The geographical distribution and concentration of the sales force should be considered in determining the degree of supervision, because they affect the costs of supervision. Firms with a few sales people, each responsible for a territory of several states, may find the job of maintaining close contact so costly and difficult as to be almost prohibitive. These firms usually hire able talent, thereby minimizing the amount of supervision required. Companies that sell in a small region, such as a metropolitan area or a small portion of a state, find close contact with their sales force relatively easy to maintain. The reps are frequently in the office and are working closely with the sales manager. Supervision in such circumstances poses no great problem, and its costs are minimized.

The size of the sales force also has an effect on the amount and type of supervision attempted by management. If the sales force is relatively small, many sales managers find that they can handle the job themselves, without supervisors. The larger the sales force, the more necessary it becomes to hire personnel to do nothing but direct sales people through formal supervisory activities. There are two reasons for this. First, the size of the organization prohibits the sales manager from knowing exactly what each sales rep is doing. Second, larger organizations pose greater morale problems, in general, than do smaller groups.

The compensation plan used and the existence of other control mechanisms can affect the amount of personal supervision needed. In general, management usually finds close supervision more necessary when the reps are being paid largely by salary. A strong, *properly designed* incentive system can provide many of the benefits of supervision, as can a detailed method for evaluating sales performances.

SUPERVISORY PERSONNEL

Three classifications of management personnel generally perform supervisory functions. They are: (1) the sales manager or assistants in the home office, (2) branch managers, or (3) field supervisors.

Note that all three categories consist of line executives. It would be unwise to allow staff personnel to assume regular supervisory activities over the sales force. The marketing research director, the advertising manager, or the credit manager must not be allowed to short-circuit the chain of command and directly supervise the sales force. The credit manager who wants to see whether the sales force is collecting credit information on various accounts should go through line channels. Otherwise, a sales rep who sees that the credit manager has direct authority may emphasize credit collection at the expense of other activities. The administrator in closest contact with the sales force gets its attention.

Home-office supervision

The majority of firms in the country probably provide only home-office supervision. They do not maintain field supervisors or have branch managers. Thus, in the study of sales management considerable attention should be given to home-office supervisory techniques. If the sales force is relatively small and consists of experienced sales people, the sales manager can personally supervise the group. As an organization grows in size, some separate provision must be made for supervision from the home office. Frequently management finds it advisable to employ an assistant to handle correspondence with the sales force and perform other supervisory duties such as publishing sales bulletins and sales manuals.

Branch managers

Most firms with branch offices use the branch managers as field supervisors. At this level in the organization the sales force is usually broken down into groups of relatively few reps, and the branch manager can give them adequate supervision. Further, geographical concentration makes it possible for branch managers to contact reps daily and to exercise considerable supervision with minimum effort. Nevertheless, supervision does not occur automatically in such cases. It must be made a specific part of the branch manager's job description. Moreover, the manager should be trained in supervisory techniques and problems.

Supervision usually is a large part of the branch manager's job. The magnitude of the branch manager's job may be so great, however, that there is little time for personal supervision of the sales force. The big weakness in using branch managers as supervisors is that often they cannot do the job properly and still administer the other activities of the branch.

Field supervisors

When the sales force requires more than minimum supervision and is so large the sales manager is unable to provide it, management thinks of ways to institute the supervision needed. One or two sales reps who have shown management potential may be made senior sales people and given some supervisory responsibilities.

Frequently, this is the first step up the company's managerial ladder. The field supervisor sometimes retains some selling duties in addition to the job of overseeing the activities of other reps. Usually the field supervisor is either a trainer or an inspector, depending on the situation. As a trainer, the person must be able to detect and rectify errors being made by members of the sales force and help them develop their selling skills.

TOOLS AND TECHNIQUES OF SUPERVISION

The tools and techniques used in supervising the sales force include: personal contact, correspondence and telephone contact, meetings and conventions, printed aids, and automatic supervisory aids provided by sales management practices. Another tool, sales reps' reports, is discussed in a separate section.

Personal contact

The topic of supervision usually conveys the idea of a field supervisor who is in personal contact with the sales force. While this is an important method of supervision, it is only one of several that are used. Typically, the supervisor visits sales reps on the job and tries to help them with whatever problems are evident. The range of activities is wide, from trying to help with personal problems to assisting in selling difficult customers or settling grievances. If the situation requires close supervision, personal contact undoubtedly is the best supervisory method.

Correspondence and telephone contact

Many sales executives try to supervise through the mails, but it is extremely difficult for one party to communicate complex matters to another in a letter. Sales managers can overcome this disadvantage to a degree by using the telephone to handle some matters, but even the telephone cannot establish the rapport obtained by face-to-face contact.

Long-distance telephone rates have dropped to the point that sales managers can talk with reps everywhere for a reasonable cost, particularly at night. A great deal of telephone time can be purchased for the price of an airline ticket to visit a rep in the field.

Meetings and conventions

Sales meetings provide an opportunity for the sales manager to come face to face with reps, and they can exchange bits of intelligence. Management is able to determine what the reps are doing to meet certain problems, and they have the opportunity to determine what management expects of them.

Some firms that sell in a limited area are able to hold daily meetings. One real estate firm has its agents meet each morning at 9 to plan each person's day and to bring to their attention new listings and special conditions. Companies whose sales forces are widely dispersed may find it difficult to meet more than a few times a year.

Printed aids

Sales manuals, bulletins, or company house organs can be of help in supervising the sales force. A good sales manual tells sales people what to do in various circumstances. Many of the answers to questions they raise can be given just as effectively in a publication as by personal supervision.

Automatic supervisory aids

Several other managerial tools which provide help with supervision can be called automatic supervisory techniques. These are sales management techniques which have inherent supervisory powers and work automatically toward their goals. These techniques can be exceptionally effective. Unlike the field supervisor or other supervisory methods, these automatic techniques travel with the reps everywhere, every minute of the day, and on every call they make. They constantly exert pressure to guide the individual in conforming to the overall sales plan.

Compensation plan. By far the most important automatic supervisory tool is the compensation plan. The details of the plan under which the sales people are paid encourage them to do certain things to maximize their earnings. If the job calls for an exceptionally high incentive to sell a large volume of goods, for example, a compensation plan designed to achieve such a goal is far more effective in supervising the rep's activities than is any other method of supervision.

Territories. Establishment of specific sales territories automatically supervises reps to some degree. It tells them what areas they are responsible for and where to seek orders. The size of the territory also can govern the rep's behavior. A sales person who is given far more territory than can possibly be covered is encouraged to skim the cream off the market. One who is given a too-small territory may be forced to seek out all potential buyers to make a quota.

Quotas. Sales quotas can serve as supervisory tool in addition to a method of stimulating performance. By setting quotas for various product lines or for certain classes of customers, the sales manager can guide the activities of the sales force into desired channels. This can be a particularly effective supervisory tool when combined with the compensation plan so that the achievement of a balanced sales effort is reflected in the rep's earnings.

Expense accounts. Policies on expenses automatically guide sales force behavior effectively as any personal supervision can. If the sales manager places a limit on the amount spent to entertain prospects, the sales rep will have to curtail such activities, for example.

Sales analysis procedures. The sales analysis procedures which are discussed in Part Four are also an aid to supervision. By evaluating the performance of each sales person on the basis of (1) sales volume for each product, or (2) various indexes of efficiency such as calls made, days worked, miles traveled, and orders taken, the sales manager can spot those who need help on certain points.

Often this analysis of performance can uncover sales reps' problems more quickly than personal supervision can. For instance, it may not be apparent to a field supervisor that a representative is having trouble closing sales. Yet an analysis of the orders taken in relation to the calls made by this rep can uncover the fact that a very low percentage of prospects is being closed. A field supervisor or a sales manager preparing to visit a sales rep should be armed with analysis figures on the rep's performance. Sales analysis merely identifies problems, however; it does not solve them.

SALES PEOPLE'S REPORTS

Sales reports can be a tool used in supervision, but they also serve other purposes. As a supervisory tool, the report is a silent enforcer of company policy. The rep who knows he must account for all his activities will feel more secure and comfortable if he stays within company policy.

Sales reports advise management what is happening in the field. Most sales managers expect sales people to report observations of competitive activities, reactions of customers to company policies and products, and other information management should know. Frequently, the sales manager has little contact with the marketplace other than through the sales reps.

Sales reports also provide records for evaluating individual sales reps' performance. Such information as the number of calls made, number of orders taken, miles traveled, days worked, new prospects called on, and new accounts sold is taken into account in the analyst's computations. The results of such calculations can be no better than the validity of the data on which they are based, so accurate reports are a necessity.

Another effect of sales reports is to help sales people plan their activities. When they know they will have to report what they did during the week, they have an incentive to organize their activities. A report that does not reflect sound, careful planning will not make a favorable impression. Reports should show, for example, that they are routing themselves properly, calling on the various classes of customers in the right ratio, and so forth.

Report forms provide a basis whereby management can evaluate reps as prospective managerial material. Promptness in filing reports, accuracy and completeness of data, and reporting format used can tell management many things about a rep's work habits and abilities. A favorable impression of the managerial talents of an individual who was unable to complete reports competently and promptly would be unlikely.

Items to be reported

Reports can be a great nuisance; they have been the bane of many a sales rep's existence. They must be filled out on the rep's own time, and often they are so detailed and complex they are aggravating. Sales managers should be careful not to burden the sales force with useless form-filling activities. Unless a given bit of information is definitely needed, it should not be requested.

Use of reports

Sales reports should not be used as a basis for censuring a sales person. They should be used only to obtain information and to supervise sales activities. If the sales manager censures reps for actions reported, they simply will not report them again. One salesman was reprimanded for reporting the *actual* time it took him to travel between Topeka and Kansas City. He reported four hours' traveling time, which was the truth. He had encountered a blinding blizzard all the way, but there was no place to report this on the form. He was sent a letter wanting to know what he did with the time he wasted on a normally one-hour trip. This was a misuse of the report form. Thereafter he reported only what was normal, so his reports were unreliable. The sales manager might like to know if someone does not work one day of the week. However, if he reprimands those who report the day off, they will not report it again. Many sales people have learned to apportion their calls over the entire work week in their reports, regardless of when they were actually made.

Having sales people file false information has no value. If the reports are being used as a basis for further analysis, untrue reports can cause considerable harm. For this reason many sales managers make it clear in initial sales training that complete honesty is expected in reporting, and any deviation is grounds for discharge. Once this dictate has been laid down, however, the sales manager should use judgment in reacting to the information the sales people provide. If in the long run they are doing the job adequately, possibly derogatory information they may reveal in the short run should perhaps be discounted. The manager should not let one or a few incidents distort the total picture but should get the whole story before taking any action on a reported incident.

SPAN OF CONTROL

How many sales representatives a manager can successfully supervise is always open to question. If the span of control is too large—that is, if too many reps report to the manager—many of the benefits of supervision are lost. It is impossible for the supervisor to give adequate time to any one person, and supervisory effectiveness is reduced.

Management is always tempted to place one more individual under the supervisor, since the span of control is directly related to the costs of supervision. If a sales force consists of 200 people and the established span of control is 10, it would be necessary to hire 20 supervisors. However, the sales manager might figure that if one more could be added under each supervisor, one supervisory position could be eliminated. So it goes, sometimes, until each supervisor has far too many reps under him to be effective with any of them.

A large span of control also has an impact on the morale of both the reps and the supervisors. The supervisors know that they cannot do a good job if they have too many reps under them, which hurts their morale. In turn, they are likely to pass on this attitude to their subordinates.

One way to figure the span of control uses the following method. First, management decides how frequently the supervisor should visit each rep—daily, weekly, or monthly. Next, it decides how much time the supervisor should spend with each of them—a full working day, or just a few hours? With these decisions established, computation of the span of control, and therefore of the number of supervisors required, is a matter of mathematics. Suppose the sales force consists of 250 people and the sales manager wants each of them to be contacted for one full day each month. Assuming there are 250 working days in the year and ignoring travel time, each supervisor can make 250 contacts. Therefore, there can be 20 or 21 reps under each supervisor, since each rep must be contacted 12 times a year.

In practice, some of the factors involved in the above calculations are variable. Therefore, determining the proper span of control in a given firm may require considerable detail work and executive judgment. Some allowance must be made for travel time; supervisors in more concentrated areas need not travel as much and should be able to contact more reps. Furthermore, the frequency with which the supervisor visits reps and the length of the visits may vary. A supervisor may have more frequent contact and spend more time per call with newer sales reps than with those who are more experienced.

In making judgments regarding the amount of supervision required by various reps, many factors must be considered. These include the rep's experience, personality, location, ability, and importance to the organization. It may be advisable to have some sales reps directly supervised, but not others. Also, it should not be inferred that each supervisor should have the same span of control. Supervisors' abilities, as well as their geographical locations, vary.

WORKING WITH SALES PEOPLE

The greatest need for supervising sales people is in firms that hire inexperienced people for sales jobs in which some degree of skill is necessary. A good supervisor can do a great deal to develop effective sales reps from people with the talent to acquire skills in the field.

Evaluation of the individual

The supervisor must first learn to evaluate the abilities of each sales person. Thomas Horton, a topflight sales manager, describes what he looks for when he rides with a sales rep:

> The first thing I look for is how well the man knows his way around his territory. Right after I took this job, I rode with a man in Boston who had been in the territory for three years but he couldn't find Boston University. It was obvious he hadn't been working the territory. I pinned him down and he finally admitted that he was holding down two jobs. Swindling us! The real salesman knows all the short cuts in his territory. He moves around fast.
>
> Next, I look for how well he knows the people upon whom we call. The good man is on a personal basis with them. You can tell if he has been calling on them.
>
> I always worry when the man climbs in the car, starts the motor, then asks me, "Where should I go?" He should have a plan. He should know where he is going, why he is going there, and what he is going to do when we get there. He should know what he wants to accomplish during each call. I fear for the man who makes courtesy calls. He's just making a nuisance of himself while wasting our money.
>
> I like to see records of the call and see them used before making a call. He should study each call and refresh his memory of previous contacts by using the records.
>
> When we get into the call I like to see a man who knows how to dig in after a sale when the going gets rough. The guy who folds up when the customer says "no" needs a great deal of help. He may even need another line of work.
>
> While we are riding between calls, I pump him for his philosophies of selling and his aspirations. I want to know his values. Above all, I am trying to get a good line on his intelligence, his wits.
>
> Every now and then one of the more clever men will try to sandbag me by only calling on good friends. I guard against this by always dictating a few calls of my own.
>
> Then there are those glib-tongued rascals who talk a good game but can't deliver the goods. They can fool you for awhile, but if you keep your eye on results and close your ears to alibis, you can quickly detect the feather merchants.
>
> Finally, I like to see a man who loves the business and knows what it is all about. I fear for the man who is not well wired into the industry. The guy who is working for us just because it's a job has no future. He's not much use to us nor even to himself.[1]

---

[1] From a speech by Thomas Horton, formerly vice president, Litton Industries, now president, Thomas Horton and Daughters.

Another sales manager developed a checklist for supervisors to use in pinpointing the areas in which the individual sales person needs help. The form presented in Figure 13–1 is an example of a supervisory checklist.

FIGURE 13–1
Evaluation of performance

	Satisfactory	Needs Help
Personal appearance		
Organization of sales material		
Knowledge of product line		
Knowledge of individual products		
Knowledge of customer's problems		
Spends time with right people		
Personal relationships with accounts		
Persuasive skills		
Knows how to handle objections		
Pushes for the order		
Knows how to handle complaints		
Manages time properly		

Development of the individual

Once a sales person's weaknesses have been pinpointed, the supervisor should develop a plan for remedying them. Some are simple to handle, while others are impossible. The rep who does not know the product line merely needs to spend some time studying the company's products. If he will not exert the necessary effort, he evidently does not care for the job. The person who lacks persuasive skills or who is lazy, however, may pose serious problems for the supervisor.

Most remedial efforts begin with the supervisor talking with the individual about the problem and offering guidance. Most problems can be handled in this manner, but occasionally additional efforts must be made. Sales people who have difficulty with presentations may be enrolled in a public speaking course. Those who need more training in sales techniques may be sent to sales training schools. Those who are unaware of customers' applications may be provided some training in them. Solution of these types of problems is simply a matter of logic.

Common problems encountered

Certain supervisory problems are almost universally encountered by sales managers. These include laziness, alcoholism, expense account misuse, and other personal problems.

Laziness.   The largest single reason people fail in selling is that they will not work hard enough. Many sales jobs attract people with easygoing personalities because lack of close supervision allows them to work whenever they please. Unfortunately, they do not want to work often or hard enough to get the job done. The bill of particulars against the lazy sales rep is familiar to any experienced sales manager:

- Does not start making calls until late morning.
- Takes long lunch hours.
- Will not make late afternoon calls.
- Does not work at all when there is something else to do—golf, a ballgame, skiing.

It would be nice to be able to suggest some ways of dealing with the lazy sales person. However, there is little the manager can do but fire him. Some lazy people do change character when they discover a reason for working, but this must come from within the individual. They must develop goals that can only be achieved by hard work, and they must realize this fact. Otherwise no amount of nagging will build a fire under the lazy sales rep.

Occasionally an apparently lazy person who has drifted into careless work habits because management has failed to communicate what was expected can be shaken by an ultimatum to perform or else. More frequently, once a person's work habits have been ruined it is difficult to restructure them.

Alcoholism.   One of the most difficult personal problems sales managers encounter is the sales person with a drinking problem. Unfortunately, some sales jobs are conducive to drinking by constantly putting the reps in social situations in which it is expected. Such jobs are terrible risks for those who cannot handle alcohol.

Alcoholic sales representatives cannot be tolerated. Not only will their work habits be affected but the quality of the work they do will suffer. Moreover, few things are more offensive to customers than doing business with an inebriated sales person. One problem is that the true alcoholic can disguise addiction for a long time, while it becomes increasingly harmful to work performance and other aspects of life. It is not the purpose of this book to instruct on the early detection of alcoholism. A great deal has been written about this, and the information is readily available.

Experience indicates the best policy for the sales manager to follow in dealing with an alcoholic is firmness and no coddling. The president of one outstanding company knowingly hired an alcoholic who possessed great talent when sober. "I told him when I hired him that if I ever so much as saw him with a drink in his hand or heard of him

A day-to-day operating problem in the

MAJESTIC GLASS COMPANY (G)

A large customer demands extra service

Gilbert O'Connor, Majestic's sales representative for the Denver area, had written his boss, Clyde Brion, a long letter, the gist of which was the question, "How much service should I give a customer?" He mentioned several cases of unusual demands by his accounts. But most of the letter concerned the Duncan Drug Company, a manufacturer of pharmaceutical products of many varieties. This company was a regular Majestic customer of long standing. However, O'Connor reported that Majestic never obtained more than 35 percent of Duncan's annual purchases of bottles and jars.

Following an incident in which Duncan had received a shipment in which a high percentage of bottles were broken, Duncan had begun to demand that O'Connor be present on the receiving docks whenever a shipment from Majestic was unloaded. The breakage incident had not involved a Majestic shipment and was later traced to a railroad accident and agreeably settled by the railroad. Nevertheless, Duncan continued to require O'Connor's presence.

Duncan had frequently asked O'Connor to make special rush deliveries from warehouse stocks personally, in his car. Occasionally he had been requested to attend conferences with Duncan's merchandising staff, to give advice on available containers, or to help design a new bottle. When he had given such aid, Majestic did not always receive the order. The Duncan purchasing officer had demanded that O'Connor give him a copy of Majestic's Stock Specifications Manual, which contained technical production details, manufacturing costs, and discount schedules.

O'Connor said that he had not complained to Duncan about such requests for service, but he had more than once heard the remark, "You'll want to do this for us, because our business is important to you." Requests from Duncan interrupted his planned call schedule on other accounts, he said.

Brion knew that the Duncan Drug Company was among O'Connor's ten largest accounts in total dollar volume.

Question

What policy should Cylde Brion adopt to cover the type of situation existing with the Duncan Drug Company?

Note: See the introduction to this series of problems in Chapter 2 for the necessary background on the company, its market, and its competition.

taking a drink, he was fired. It's the only way to deal with the problem He's been sober ever since."

Firmness can be a painful policy. The most difficult case is the salesman who has been with the company for a long time and was once an outstanding producer. Nevertheless, the manager who allows a sales person to discredit the company, with continued drinking or in any other way, is not doing his job. One newly hired sales manager who complained to his superior about having to fire an older salesman who had become an alcoholic was told, "That's the reason we pay you what we do. If the job was easy, we wouldn't have to pay you so much."

Expense accounts.   The folklore of selling is full of tales of sales expense accounts and their fictional contents. They can be a problem, an expensive one.

It is assumed that management intends the sales force to submit honest expense accounts. Managers who use liberal expense practices as a sub rosa means for paying sales people have no one to blame but themselves when some rep becomes too imaginative with the expense account.

Expense account policies should be clearly set forth for sales people when they are hired. Companies that expect the sales force to be honest make it clear that cheating on an expense account is grounds for dismissal, and they back up that policy with action.

When the sales manager detects that some rep's expense accounts are not factual but wants to keep him, a review of the situation with the rep is in order. Some managers simply disallow expenses they feel are not in order. Others will go over the expense report with the rep, thus letting him know that his expense reports are being watched. One sales manager placed limits on a chronic offender, telling the rep not to spend more than $50 on telephone calls during the next month. When he filed a $200 telephone bill, he was fired.

Other personal problems.   Sales people suffer all the personal problems people manage to get themselves involved with—financial, family, health, and so on. By their nature, many sales jobs are not conducive to good family relationships. If the rep must travel extensively or must work evenings, the family can be tested. Some people have home situations that will not take such stresses. Sometimes the manager can help by giving them a territory that allows them to spend more time at home, but such instances are not common. More frequently, there is little the manager can do. A sales rep may ask the manager to talk with the spouse about the necessity to travel, but care should be taken not to become involved in other people's marital problems.

Many people find themselves in financial difficulty from time to time, because of hospital bills, poor money management, bad investments, court suits, or for other reasons. Some turn to their employers for help during such times. While the manager may be tempted to help out, such a policy can lead to other problems. It usually is a mistake to become an employee's creditor; it seldom works out well.

As a general rule, most firms expect their employees to be able to manage their personal lives. Most administrators do not want to become involved in the lives of their subordinates outside the office.

QUESTIONS AND PROBLEMS

1. How would a field supervisor determine why a certain rep was performing unsatisfactorily?

2. Bill Jolton, a salesman for a large national soap company, informs his immediate supervisor that he is quitting as of the end of the month. The supervisor is surprised to learn of this, since he had thought that Jolton was doing a good job and was happy with his work. He would like to keep Jolton with the firm, for he feels that he shows exceptional promise. How should the supervisor handle the situation?

3. How can a field supervisor assist a sales rep in making more calls per day?

4. How can the supervisor determine what is wrong with a rep's selling tactics?

5. A sales manager of a large metropolitan automobile dealership required his sales force of eight men to meet each morning at 9:00 for about 30 minutes in order to plan their activities for the day. During this meeting, he would ask each man to tell what he intended to accomplish that day. Were these meetings sound? What was the manager's thinking in establishing them?

6. One sales manager of a concern that sold on a nationwide basis with a sales force of 15 reps had the policy of spending one week each year with each sales person in the territory. What would this manager expect to accomplish during these visits? Do you believe this is a sound method for supervising these reps? Might there be a better way of accomplishing the same tasks?

7. George Hermann, one of the top salesmen with the Mountain Machine Company, was continually arguing with his direct supervisor. He had complained many times to the sales manager and had asked to be left alone. One day, he stopped in the sales manager's office and declared: "If you don't get that clown you call a supervisor off my back you can have my job. I'm not going to put up with any more of his suggestions, and that's final."

Hermann was consistently a top producer with the company, but the supervisor had told the sales manager that he could be doing an even better job if he would just listen to some advice. However, the supervisor maintained that Hermann was an arrogant, stubborn, conceited man who thought he knew everything about selling and was just completely uncooperative. While the sales manager knew that Hermann frequently did not obey orders in pushing certain items and doing certain things the home office requested, still overall his work was highly satisfactory. The sales manager felt that there was a personal antagonism between the two individuals, stemming from the time the supervisor had been promoted to his position over Hermann. The supervisor had been a successful salesman with the company before his promotion, but he had not been nearly so good a salesman as George Hermann. How should the sales manager handle the situation?

8. How many people can a field supervisor manage if he must spend one day each month with each rep and he spends approximately ten days each month traveling and performing other duties?

9. Should sales supervisors be given overrides (percentage commissions) on the sales of the sales people under them?

10. If overrides are not given, how can the sales manager best motivate the supervisors to do an excellent job?

11. How can the sales manager evaluate the effectiveness of the various supervisors?

12. Should the field supervisor be given the authority to discharge a subordinate?

13. With more women selling, what changes, if any, in supervisory techniques might be needed?

Case 13–1
LAWRENCE SCOTT
Supervising a pharmaceutical salesman

Lawrence Scott joined the field sales staff of Beckman Drug Products Company as a salesman early in 1975. He was a college graduate, having majored in physical education. Although extremely interested in athletics, he apparently never pursued a coaching or teaching career. Beckman was a large manufacturer of ethical (prescription) drugs and other pharmaceutical products. Scott's job was referred to in the industry as "detailing." As a detail man, he was, in effect, a missionary salesman. His task was to call on doctors in their offices, introduce and explain new products, remind them of existing products in the line, and leave product samples and other promotional materials.

Note: This case was written by Professor Charles L. Lapp, Washington University.

The hope was that the doctors would then prescribe for their patients, or otherwise use, Beckman products.

Scott was first interviewed by Edward Graham, Midwest division manager. Scott impressed Graham as an aggressive, hard-working book salesman who appeared anxious to gain prestige and higher earnings by entering the pharmaceutical industry. Graham decided to consider Scott for the Louisville territory, and immediately instituted a personnel check through the Personal Credit Investigating Company. Character references and former employers spoke well of Scott and reported nothing unfavorable. However, Personal Credit reported that Scott was employed by the post office in his home town, Freeport, following his graduation from high school in 1965. (His application for employment stated that he had graduated from high school in 1966 and made no mention of his employment by the Freeport post office.) The report stated that during February 1966, a quantity of mail was found on a creek bank near Freeport. The mail had never been delivered, although it had passed through the Freeport post office. On investigation, a postal inspector discovered that Scott had disposed of two bags of mail by throwing it into the creek. Scott claimed that he had a date that night and had thrown away the mail to avoid being late. Scott was discharged by the post office for this offense, but no charges were pressed by the authorities.

Graham decided to employ Scott, and arranged to train him in the technical aspect of the job and familiarize him with the reporting systems and other paper work necessary to carry out his functions as a medical service representative.

Scott's territorial performance apparently pleased Graham. About a year after joining the company, Graham wrote to Scott as follows:

March 21, 1976

I should like to commend you very highly on your splendid performance during the last half of 1975. You finished this half with 104.7 percent attainment of quota. What is even more impressive, Larry, you attained 106.8 percent of your quota in old products. Very nice work. I know you will do everything possible to retain or better this position next year. Best of luck to you.

Edward Graham

During the following months, other sales representatives quoted Graham as remarking on Scott's outstanding performance and as using Scott as an example of how a good detail man should perform. Scott received salary increases in July 1975, January 1976, and again in July 1976. Although this was considered unusual and was not in accordance with the company policy, Graham insisted and the exceptions to policy were made.

Scott seldom corresponded with the home office except for routine matters. The only knowledge the home office had of his performance was obtained through copies of memorandums from Graham to Scott.

During 1976 Beckman Drug Company had grown rapidly and had expanded its field staff considerably. By the end of the year, several new sales divisions were to be created. Scott received word from the home office in December that effective January 1, 1977, he would be responsible to Douglas Rathbone, the newly appointed Cincinnati division manager. Rathbone was highly regarded by the home office, and Harry Lane, his regional sales manager, considered him very capable.

Soon after his appointment to division manager, Rathbone went to Louisville to work with Scott and to get acquainted with him. As he was eager to get acquainted with all the men in his division as soon as possible, Rathbone spent only two days in this field visit with Scott. Following this trip, Rathbone reported to Lane as follows:

February 17, 1977

To: Mr. Harry Lane
From: Douglas Rathbone
Subject: Field visit with Lawrence Scott.

Detailing
  Not too strong here. Tries to cover too much in the allotted time. Didn't have calling cards with him.
Accounts
  Very good support and cooperation with direct retailers and wholesalers. They all liked him. He should know the names of more of the personnel in the stores.
Comments
  Makes an excellent appearance—Neat. Well groomed. Has a good general knowledge of his territory. He appears conscientious and a willing worker.
  Ambitious.

Doug Rathbone

About two months later, Rathbone again worked with Scott.

During a telephone conversation a week or two later, Rathbone expressed to Lane his disappointment in Scott's performance. At that time, Scott was trailing the division in sales, and Rathbone was disturbed. However, he intended to devote extra time in Louisville just as soon as he completed training of some new full-time salesmen plus a group of medical students he had employed for the summer.

April 23, 1977

To: Mr. Harry Lane
From: Douglas Rathbone
Subject: Field visit with Lawrence Scott.

Detailing
   Weak. His detailing lacks enthusiasm, and his delivery needs more
   modulation and variety. A dull and uninspiring detail.
Accounts
   Has good wholesaler support. Could stand improvement with some of
   the retailers.
Comments
   On the favorable side, the man has a nice appearance and is well
   groomed.
   He is also sales-minded.
   On the negative side is his manner of expressing himself in the
   physician's office. Definitely a candidate for a Dale Carnegie course
   or Toastmasters. He was so advised.
   His organization is just fair. His car and detail bag were poorly organized. We repacked his detail bag, and I advised him to organize his
   car better. The man has the basic qualifications but needs development
   to become a first-rate detail man.

                                          Doug Rathbone

   On June 4, Lane received an announcement from Scott that his wife
had delivered a baby girl, Louise, on May 29. Rathbone had been
traveling extensively during the month of May, and by early June he
was in the midst of training the summer student-salesmen. On Wednesday, June 6, he was in Centerville, a town located on Swan River
about 300 miles from Louisville. Centerville was a resort town, offering various types of amusements and sporting facilities. Rathbone
called Paul Norris, the local representative, to accompany him on an
afternoon appointment he had with the manager of the local wholesale
druggist.
   As Rathbone and Norris were driving toward the outskirts of town
at about 4 p.m., Rathbone thought he saw Scott on a miniature golf
course with an unidentified young woman. Scott appeared to be at-
tired in bathing trunks and an open shirt. As the two passed the golf
course, Rathbone requested Norris to drive around the block. On returning to the scene, both Norris and Rathbone ascertained that it was
Scott who was playing golf. They did not stop but continued on their
way to the wholesaler.
   As Rathbone drove home to Cincinnati that evening, his thoughts
were concentrated on Lawrence Scott.

Questions

1. What action should Douglas Rathbone now take?
2. After his field visit with Lawrence Scott in February 1977, what action, if any, should Rathbone have taken?
3. Evaluate the policies and procedures of Edward Graham in this case.

Case 13–2
PAUL CABOT
A depressed salesman

Paul Cabot had been an excellent sales engineer for many years with the Fraser-Mead Company. However, ever since his wife had been killed in an auto accident over a year ago, Paul had changed considerably. His effectiveness and productivity had declined to the point where he was creating some real problems for the company. Mr. Oscar Zoeller, the sales manager in the Food Processing Division of Fraser-Mead, realized he had to take some sort of action regarding Paul, before the situation deteriorated further.

Fraser-Mead Company was started over 70 years ago in California as a merger of two other firms. Originally, Fraser-Mead was an engineering-construction firm serving the mining industry with the engineering, construction, and installation of mining equipment. Through the years, Fraser-Mead had expanded into three additional major industries—power generating, food processing, and petroleum-petrochemicals. Consequently, the company's current organization consisted of four divisions, each serving one of these four major industry markets. There also were several staff departments, such as accounting-finance, legal, purchasing, and advertising–public relations. Exhibit 1 is a skeleton organization chart.

At the head of each industry division was a sales manager who reported to a vice president. The Food Processing Division was headed by Oscar Zoeller as sales manager and was composed of five departments—sugar, pet food, dehydration (corn, alfalfa, etc.), protein concentrate, and beverages. Each department marketed specialized equipment and engineering services. At the head of each of these departments was a chief sales engineer who reported to Zoeller. Paul Cabot was the chief sales engineer for the sugar department, and under his supervision were seven engineers.

Fraser-Mead was one of the largest engineering-construction companies in the United States, with sales of about $750 million last year.

EXHIBIT 1
Organization chart

FRASER-MEAD COMPANY

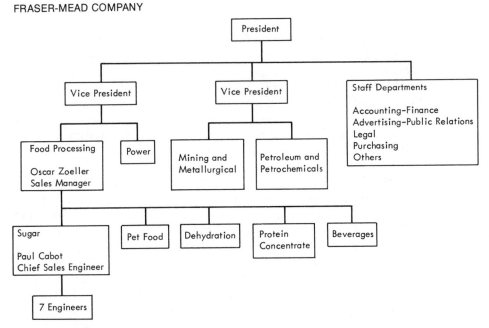

Sales in the Food Processing Division were $50 million, with the sugar equipment and services department contributing $8 million of this total. The sugar department, although contributing a relatively small share of Fraser-Mead's total volume, was a profitable operation. Last year it earned $1 million net income on its $8 million sales volume. During the past eight years, the profitable results in the sugar department had been due largely to the excellent performance of Paul Cabot.

The equipment and engineering services provided by the sugar department was designed specifically for each customer's needs. Engineering and design services were provided for both beet sugar factories and cane sugar refineries. Feasibility and marketing studies were conducted for customers interested in promoting new plants and processes in the sugar industry.

The producers of sugar (from sugar beets or sugar cane) constituted the sole market for the products and services of Fraser-Mead's sugar department. Most sugar producers are large firms, able to finance new production facilities. Competition from foreign sugar sources, with their lower labor costs, constantly forces U.S. producers to seek new production technology to enable them to reduce or substitute for their high labor costs. Consequently, there generally was a good market for the products and services of such suppliers as Fraser-Mead's sugar department.

For the past five years, Fraser-Mead's market share in sugar equipment and engineering services had held at about 70 percent, despite growing competition from foreign companies. These foreign firms currently had about 20 percent of the market. Their share had increased over the years at the expense of four small U.S. firms whose market share had been declining and now was about 10 percent. The European and Japanese competitors were large, well-financed, and well-managed. Long ago they had pushed the U.S. companies, including Fraser-Mead, out of the foreign markets. Zoeller forecast that within a few years they would push the four small U.S. firms out of the domestic sugar equipment and services business as well.

For the past 20 years, up to the time of his wife's death, Paul Cabot had done excellent work in every job he had held with Fraser-Mead. Rising slowly but steadily, he had been led by top management to believe that he would be promoted to the position of sales manager of the Food Processing Division when Zoeller retired in a few years. In his present position as chief sales engineer, Cabot, now 50 years old, was responsible for obtaining sales of sugar equipment and process engineering services, maintaining continual contact with all regular customers, making periodic calls on prospective customers, watching orders, checking delivery schedules, and coordinating the in-house work of the engineers under him. In sum, he was responsible for the performance of his department.

Both Zoeller and the vice president over him, Mr. Harry Binney, recognized that the sugar department had continued to hold its large share of the U.S. market primarily because of Cabot's excellent sales performance. Many of the customers had commented favorably on the service they had received from Cabot and his sugar department. They had been able to come up with several innovations which enabled the U.S. sugar producers to become more efficient and thus to stay competitive with foreign sugar producers. Cabot continuously had won for his firm the large, important contracts in the sugar industry. Within the company, he was respected by his superiors, subordinates, and fellow chief sales engineers who headed up the other four departments in the Food Processing Division.

The death of his wife had marked a turning point for Cabot. They had no children, so he was left with no family. Oscar Zoeller noticed that Paul seemed to be discouraged and demoralized. Zoeller could understand Paul's attitude for six months or so after his wife's death. However, the problem was that after almost a year Cabot had not improved his general outlook or his job performance. Naturally, Zoeller was concerned about the effect this would have on the sugar department's morale and sales volume. He talked the situation over with Vice President Binney, and they decided they would give Cabot another three months to readjust before they took any action. Zoeller would continue to encourage Cabot to restore his confidence and desire to work effectively, and would watch the performance of the department closely.

To Zoeller's disappointment, at the end of the three-month period Cabot was still depressed and was doing a generally substandard job of running the department and making sales. Also, Zoeller had been receiving complaints from several important customers about Cabot's indifferent and unenthusiastic attitude toward them on his last several calls. Zoeller had spoken to Cabot about these problems on several occasions, but Cabot had not offered any explanations. Zoeller decided to not force the issue. By now, sales in the sugar department were off by 40 percent from projected figures, and these sales were going to the foreign firms. Zoeller's discussions with several of the men under Cabot in the department yielded complaints about lack of leadership and the generally poor attitude in the department.

Finally an event occurred which convinced Zoeller that a decision in regard to Cabot could no longer be postponed. Fraser-Mead had the most know-how and experience in designing and installing pollution abatement equipment for sugar refineries. Because of recent local legislation, a Utah sugar company needed a new pollution control system to meet strict requirements in five of its plants. The total cost of the project was estimated to be over $4,000,000, and Fraser-Mead was almost certain to get the contract. However, the contract went to a German firm after Cabot showed up two hours late for a board meeting at the Utah sugar firm where Fraser-Mead's proposed plan was to be presented. Moreover, he appeared rather disinterested during the meeting.

Cabot offered no excuses and acted as if this was a minor incident. He seemed surprised when Zoeller roasted him on his conduct. Zoeller said, "Paul, I realize you've had a personal tragedy, and we are all deeply sorry for you, but it appears that you have continued to put forth little effort to bring your performance back up to its old standards."

Zoeller then met with Binney and recommended that a younger man from the sugar department replace Cabot. He felt that to keep Cabot in his present position any longer could result in a disastrous decline in Fraser-Mead's market share in the sugar industry. He worried that once Fraser-Mead's present customers started doing business with foreign firms, it might lose them permanently. Binney was willing to make the change provided the other chief sales engineers in the Food Processing Division were informed of the situation and were given a chance to express their opinions. He made this qualification because even though Cabot was hurting his own department's performance, he was still respected and well liked by the other chief sales engineers.

At the meeting with these sales engineers and the vice president, Zoeller proposed to move Cabot to the position of assistant purchasing agent. In this position he felt that Cabot could not hurt the company, and he would retain a job with Fraser-Mead, although it would mean a reduction in pay and authority. Zoeller and the vice president wanted to keep Cabot with the company because of his previously outstanding service. A liberal pension plan was available for employees at age 65, and they were hoping Cabot could take advantage of this by finishing his career in the purchasing department. Zoeller felt that a move to another department was preferable to a demotion within the sugar department.

The sales engineers did not agree to the proposed transfer. All of these men were long-time employees and had sympathy for Cabot. After all, Cabot had been an excellent employee for 20 years, and he had not purposely tried to hurt the sugar department's performance. They felt that no matter what the price involved, Cabot should be kept in his position as a reward for his long years of service, or at least should be given more time before a transfer was considered. They also believed that Cabot would protest the proposed change and wondered how it would affect Cabot's attitude. Zoeller felt that Cabot would accept the proposed transfer, though perhaps grudgingly, because he would be able to recognize and admit to his unsatisfactory performance since his wife's death.

The next day, when Zoeller told Cabot of the transfer decision, Cabot reacted strongly, claiming that it was an attempt to get rid of him. He said this was unbelievably rough treatment after he had devoted over 20 years of his life to the company. He claimed that it was like kicking a man when he was down, and under no circumstances would he accept the transfer. Zoeller would have to fire him first.

Question

1. What action should Oscar Zoeller now take regarding Paul Cabot?

14

Sales force morale

It takes two to speak the truth—one to speak and
another to hear.

THOREAU

The word *morale* is commonly used to designate the mental and emotional attitudes of an individual toward his environment. Major elements of this environment include the family, business associates, the employer, neighbors, and the community. When the attitudes are positive, the morale is said to be good, or high; when they are negative, morale is considered poor, or low.

Group morale involves a sense of common purpose, while individual morale is concerned with one person's state of psychological well-being. The sales manager must be concerned with both. Group morale may be healthy, but individuals in the group can harbor poor attitudes for a number of reasons. Everyone does not prosper, even in the best of situations, and everyone is not unhappy in the worst of them.

The group generally exerts a strong influence on the individual's morale. Good group morale can improve the attitudes of a member whose morale is sagging. In the same way, an individual with a positive outlook can affect the morale of the group.

One factor that limits the ability of the manager to work with the sales force as a whole is that in many instances no group actually exists. The sales people may be geographically distributed so that they have little contact with one another. Therefore, the sales executive generally must deal with sales people's attitudes on an individual basis.

Attitudes toward work are important for both economic and social reasons. From the economic standpoint, productivity is likely to be higher in groups whose members have relatively good morale. It does not always follow that high morale results in high productivity, however. A group may have a good attitude but poor results. Nevertheless,

353

productivity is usually higher for employees who have good mental attitudes toward their jobs.

From a social point of view, people who develop negative attitudes toward work can make life miserable not only for themselves but for those around them. Life is too short to be spent working in an unpleasant environment. The proposition that good morale should be created in the work environment for its sake alone certainly has merit. The social ramifications of poor morale are felt not only in the home that is, in the employees attitudes and relations with their families, but also throughout the entire community.

EFFECTS OF LOW SALES FORCE MORALE

A sales representative with a bad attitude toward the job and the company develops an antimanagement orientation. Such a person fights suggestions made by the manager and is critical of the company's policies and practices. For real or imagined reasons, such an individual regards the company as an adversary and attempts to retaliate against management suggestions.

The effects of such a manifestation of poor morale in a sales force are almost infinite in number and variation. However, they can be grouped into the following seven categories:

1. Unsatisfactory job performance.
2. Excessive turnover.
3. Increased expenses.
4. Effect on fellow employees.
5. Magnification of minor complaints.
6. Development of outside interests.
7. Incentive for unionization.

Unsatisfactory sales performance

Probably no job in an entire company is so directly dependent on good morale as is the selling task. No one with a poor attitude toward the job can sell effectively. Experienced sales managers know that when a sales rep's volume declines in relation to the rest of the sales force, the first place to look for trouble is in the individual. A rep's mental attitude is reflected throughout the sales presentation. A poor attitude can destroy the effectiveness of a sales presentation and result in lost sales.

One study of job attitudes and sales performance has suggested, however, that morale may not be significantly correlated with performance. While the study found sales performance to be associated with appliance salesmen's general vigor, feelings of personal worth on the job, and satisfaction with pay, it concluded that "Little evidence of statistical association between the various job satisfaction measures and sales performance was uncovered."[1]

This conclusion can help clarify what constitutes morale. While morale may be equated with job satisfaction, as in this study, that is only one of its many dimensions. The factors *satisfaction with pay, feelings of personal worth on the job,* and *general vigor* are also important components of morale. There is also the likelihood that a person's "general vigor" is a function of his morale, not vice versa. Indeed, it could be argued that morale and these other factors are interrelated. A person who has good job morale is apt to be more satisfied with the pay and have better feelings of self-worth.

Thus morale is not only the overall result of a complex mixture of forces, it can have a reciprocal relationship with the forces that affect it. The effect is seen often in sales work. A sales person has good morale and is relatively satisfied with the job and what it pays. Then something happens; perhaps management changes, or there are problems at home. Suddenly morale sags. Now the same job and pay are unsatisfactory.

While there may be no scientific proof that morale and sales performance are correlated, observation indicates it is a good working assumption for a sales manager to operate on.

Excessive turnover

One of the most widely recognized indexes for measuring the morale of a firm is the turnover of workers in the group. The theory underlying this criterion is that most people with poor mental attitudes toward their jobs become so dissatisfied with their situations that they seek employment elsewhere. Observation indicates that among sales people with high morale there is little turnover; contented reps do not quit. Thus the number of people quitting is a good measure of the state of morale in an organization.

Impact on expenses

Sales people who do not have a good attitude toward their employers seldom attempt to control their expenses. These reps may openly state that they intend to get everything they can from the com-

[1] James C. Cotham, III, "Job Attitudes and Sales Performance of Major Appliance Salesmen," *Journal of Marketing Research*, November 1968, pp. 370–75.

pany and only lightly disguise their intention to quit at some time. When poor morale not only lowers sales volume but also increases expenses, it puts a dual pressure on profits.

Effect on fellow employees

One person with a bad attitude can lower the morale of all those around him if he is forceful enough. There is no such thing as a perfect organization. People will always make mistakes, regardless of their standing in the firm. There is always some executive decision a malcontent can use as a basis for complaint.

Magnification of minor complaints

Sales people who have poor morale are apt to magnify minor complaints out of proportion to their importance. Things that normally would go unnoticed in an organization with good morale can become points of contention in other groups. For instance, inadequate office facilities might not be a cause for complaint in an organization with good morale, but they could be a source of annoyance in a firm where workers were generally dissatisfied.

Often the sales manager must handle a series of minor complaints instead of being able to deal with the real source of the irritations. Sales people who fail to perceive the real cause of their morale problems may seize on whatever is at hand to complain about. In sports, it has been observed that there are few problems on winning teams, but if they start to lose, complaints about all sorts of conditions are apt to be voiced.

Development of outside interests

When some people are placed in a situation in which they are frustrated and unhappy, they mentally withdraw from it. Such an employee in effect refuses to become emotionally involved with the organization. Some hold two jobs simultaneously; others use company time to seeking other work.

Unfortunately, however, many individuals with poor morale do not quit. For various economic and social reasons, they may go on working for years at a job they detest. Some of them cannot find an equally good job elsewhere. Others do not want to leave the location. Or, they wait out the situation in hopes that it will improve or certain executives whom they blame for their dissatisfaction may move elsewhere. Usually in such situations they develop outside interests—they look elsewhere for their satisfactions in life. They spend as little time as

A day-to-day operating problem in the

MAJESTIC GLASS COMPANY (H)

Moonlighting

While vacationing in Michigan, Clyde Brion, general sales manager for Majestic Glass Company, decided to buy a new car. One evening he visited an auto dealer's showroom and was surprised to be waited on by Paul Jenkins, a Majestic salesman. Jenkins recognized Brion, jovially called him by name, and tried to sell him a car.

Next day Brion went to the public warehouse where Jenkins had his office and asked him to explain why he was working for two employers. Paul Jenkins first tried to laugh off the matter. When he realized that Brion was serious, he stated that there was "no law against having two jobs." He said he knew of four other Majestic salesmen who had second jobs at night or on weekends, including one who played a guitar in a nightclub. Jenkins explained that his wife had been ill and he needed extra cash to meet medical bills. He said that he did not mix the two jobs, being careful to avoid mentioning cars during his calls on Majestic customers. But by "keeping his ears open" he had obtained some prospects among this group and had followed up and sold cars to them in the evening. He admitted that his wife did not know of his second job. She was told that he was making calls for Majestic at night. He would not have reported the second job to Brion, either, he said, if Brion had not discovered it.

Brion knew that Majestic had paid Jenkins about $16,000 in commissions last year. In sales volume, his territory ranked 13th among the 18 Majestic territories. He had nearly always drawn upon anticipated commissions, up to the established limit. Twice he had written to Brion, asking that the limit be raised temporarily.

Question

What, if anything, should Brion do about Jenkins' moonlighting?

Note: See the introduction to this series of problems in Chapter 2 for the necessary background on the company, its market, and its competition.

possible on the job and do just a minimum amount of work. They withdraw from their work group.

Incentive for unionization

One of the outgrowths of poor morale has been the development of labor unions. This was certainly the case in production, but it has also been true in some sales organizations. If the sales force comes to believe that management does not care about them, they will cease to care about management. Needing work, they do not quit, but they sometimes form their own organization—a union.

The genesis of sales people's unions has been quite uniform. They are created when a group of sales people come to the conclusion that they can no longer communicate with management and that management does not have their best interests at heart.

CAUSES OF LOW SALES FORCE MORALE

Any attempt to list the various reasons sales people may have for poor attitudes is bound to be incomplete. Like the effects of poor morale, the causes are numerous and varied. However, experience has shown that several common occurrences lead to poor morale. Through a study of these factors, the sales manager may be able to gain an insight into how workers are motivated.

Each person is unique, however, and it is a mistake to try to apply broad rules of thumb to a specific case. Instead, each individual must be studied separately before any understanding can be achieved.

Poor morale in the sales force can be created in two broad areas— work relationships and personal affairs.

Work-related reasons for poor morale

The sales manager should become acquainted with the various work-related reasons for poor morale first. They are his direct concern and responsibility. Moreover, he has more control over them than over personal factors that affect morale. Characteristics of the work environment that can lead to poor morale are discussed in this section.

Inadequate channels of communication. The problem of communication is of crucial importance to many aspects of sales management. When channels of communication are absent or faulty, neither management nor the sales force knows what the other thinks.

The lack of communication is more than a lack of contact; it is also a lack of understanding. Although this seems absurdly simple, probably no greater problem exists in American industry today. How many sales people really know what management is trying to do and the reasons behind its actions? That is the essence of downward communication. How many executives really know what their employees think and feel about various things? That is the essence of upward communication. Morale is affected by both.

Of course, there are instances in which sales force morale would suffer if the reps knew what management was really thinking. One management had plans for eliminating its sales force in favor of using sales agents. Had the salesmen known of those intentions, the operation would have come apart at the seams.

An important facet of communication is to relay management's expectations to the sales force. A sales person may be placed in a territory to sell merchandise, and may do well. Only when he is passed over for a promotion does he find out that management was also interested in how well he performed other tasks, such as placing displays and doing sales promotional work. He had been neglecting these tasks in favor of sales activity. Such a breakdown in the communications system may mean a sales rep will never find out why he is not getting anywhere in the company. Morale is found to suffer in such circumstances.

The sales rep in the field faces many problems which can result in grievances and troubles. The rep may be realistic enough to know that management can do nothing about many of these troubles, but still will want management to know they exist. Direct action on many complaints may not be expected, but the opportunity to express them to someone in authority is still valued. Some employees take drastic steps to gain upward communication, such as deliberately violating company policy in order to gain a hearing. Others resign in order to communicate the fact that management is ignoring complaints.

In production management, one of the major tools used to counteract poor morale caused by lack of communication was the establishment of workers' grievance committees. Through this machinery, the employees could make sure their complaints were known to the firm. Many authorities believe the rise of unions was largely caused by the breakdown of upward communications. Employees had no way of communicating their desires to top management. They were completely blocked by first- and second-level supervisors who tended to view any complaints of employees as personal criticisms that reflected on their own abilities. The supervisors wanted management to think that all was operating smoothly in the ranks. The union mechanism made it possible for employees to bypass the chain of command and go directly to top executives in the organization and have their grievances heard. Because the union business manager has entry to offices that the employee finds closed, the employees in effect hired the union business manager to do the griping for them.

Some sales managers form grievance committees to ensure the sales people will have every opportunity to be heard. However, these committees alone are not the answer to communication problems. Upward communication consists of much more than hearing grievances. It is a matter of knowing what the sales people are doing, thinking, and feeling. This can be accomplished only through individual personal contact. Person-to-person communications is one of the major reasons morale is usually far better in a small sales force than in a large one.

Although personal contact greatly facilitates good communications, it does not ensure them. It is possible for two people to hold a face-to-face conversation and yet fail to communicate with each other. This occurs when one, or both, of the parties is so intent on what he or she is saying that no attention is paid to the other's message. Good communication requires an understanding receiver as well as a good sender.

Understanding is a function of how well a message is stated and explained and how earnestly the receiver attempts to comprehend it. An employee always understands management's policies and practices better when a clear explanation for them has been given. Communications are hindered when the parties are unable or unwilling to state their cases accurately and logically. Frequently, semantic problems hinder good communications. Both the sales person and the manager may agree that the job requires incentive pay, but what each party actually means by *incentive* can vary tremendously. The sales manager may mean that the reps should be on a straight commission plan, while they mean that they should be given a relatively small bonus in addition to a substantial salary. The administrator must be careful to use specific terms with exact meaning so that misinterpretation is minimized.

The establishment of good communications with the sales force is no easy task. The sales manager must constantly seek an understanding with the sales force through personal contact and full, specific explanations of policies and practices. In addition, the manager must genuinely try to determine and understand the sales reps' position.

Unsatisfactory status in the organization.   Many people are motivated by high status; they cannot tolerate being inconsequential in an organization. It is frequently said that such individuals prefer to be big frogs in a little pond rather than little frogs in a big one.

Status is frequently measured by many seemingly trivial things. Some employees measure their status in the organization by the location and furnishings of their office, the number of people under them, or various privileges they are allowed, such as eating in the executive lunchroom or having their name on a parking place.

The sales manager informally determines the status of the various sales people in the organization by the way he treats them. If he consistently seeks out certain reps for advice in managerial matters, these reps are, in effect, elevated to higher positions in the organization. People who are not so consulted can become dissatisfied with their apparently inferior status.

The general treatment accorded reps by home-office personnel also can be a status symbol. Some firms treat the sales force the same way as maintenance personnel; they are just some more employees. Others have acquired the ability to make their sales people feel important. They let sales people know they consider their services so valuable that the rest of the company would be unable to operate without them.

Unfair treatment.   Probably the quickest way to ruin sales people's morale is to give them good reason to feel that management is treating them unfairly. The unfair treatment may be only in the sales person's imagination, but it will still affect morale adversely. Imagined grievances are usually the result of poor communications. The rep does not know the facts in the matter and has formed an opinion on the basis of rumor or just by guessing.

However, sales people often do have real grievances against management for obviously unfair treatment. Such conditions must be remedied when discovered, but it is far better that they never arise in the first place. The sales manager must be careful to treat all reps fairly and not to discriminate against any of them. For instance, a salesman for one large business machines manufacturer had learned that once the sales volume in his territory had achieved a certain level, the company would split the territory in half, thereby automatically reducing his volume. Since he was paid a straight commission, his earnings would be directly affected. In other words, his reward for a job well done was to have his income cut in half. Since the man was too old to get a comparable job, he was retaining his present one, but his attitude was not good. The company certainly was not realizing everything it could from his territory. He found a level of sales volume that the company was happy with but that did not penalize him. Similar situations commonly occur.

Poor working conditions

The physical environment in which the sales person is required to work can be a source of discontent. Since many sales reps primarily work outside the home office, their working conditions consist largely of the automobile they travel in and the style of living the company's expense account allows them to maintain. Usually this presents no problem, since most firms allow their sales people to drive good automobiles and provide satisfactory expense accounts.

Problems do arise in the management of inside sales representatives, however, such as automobile sales reps and those who sell out of an office. They need satisfactory desk space and a pleasant, clean place in which to talk with prospects.

Lack of confidence in ability of the manager or the organization. A big cause of poor morale in the sales force, and one which is difficult to remedy, is lack of confidence in the manager's ability or in the organization. If the sales person does not feel the leaders are able to do a good job of managing, a poor attitude will result. Most sales people realize that their productiveness and their future welfare depend to some degree at least on the abilities and talents of their superiors. When they lose confidence in management, they cannot avoid a poor attitude toward the company and the job.

This is the area that we will refer to in another section as the integration of interests. It is maintained that building morale is basically a process of integrating the interests of the individual with those of the firm. Employees who lack confidence in the leadership of the firm have found that their interests do not coincide with those of the firm or its executives. Once this has happened for a considerable number of employees, a rather substantial shake-up in the organization may be needed to recapture their confidence.

One real estate organization had a manager who, in the opinion of all of its agents, simply did not have any ability to sell or to manage. Behind his back, the agents laughed at him, and they all were looking for other jobs. Their morale was extremely poor, since they were convinced that this firm would not succeed under its present sales manager, and they had better look for another position if they were going to achieve their goals. The owner of the firm recognized that the manager was not being effective and undertook an investigation. The result was employment of a new manager, who quickly captured the confidence of the sales force by his obvious grasp of the situation. They felt he really knew what he was talking about, and his plans were very practical. Morale was restored in a matter of a week.

At times the lack of confidence is not in the sales manager but in the organization. Sales people may respect the manager but feel he is being retarded by inept leadership. Sometimes this lack of confidence stems from poor products or marketing policies decided by management.

One manufacturer of vacuum cleaners maintained a door-to-door sales force exclusively. The firm did not sell through retail stores or do any advertising. The reps were faced with the task of calling cold on customers. Not 1 out of 100 housewives called on recognized the brand name of the vacuum cleaner, since they had not seen it advertised and had never seen such a unit in retail stores. This made a normally difficult sale even more difficult. The sales reps were distressed over the company's policy on advertising. Every time two or more of them met, this was the first gripe they exchanged. Finally the firm was forced to alter its marketing policy and institute an advertising program just to get its brand name recognized.

Top management must remember that the sales force is vitally concerned with its marketing decisions, and if they appear to be unwise, morale will be adversely affected. This points up the necessity of explaining to the sales force the reason for making marketing decisions that may appear questionable.

Lack of recognition.   Near the top of most lists of factors that cause poor morale is insufficient recognition for performance. Most people, when they feel they have done a job well, like to be recognized for it. This is an emotional problem, but nevertheless a very real one. Bestowing recognition on deserving individuals is one of the main tools a good sales manager can use to build better relations with the sales force.

Recognition is important to the individual because it is tangible evidence that management appreciates his efforts. It indicates gratitude for the person's dedication to the company's affairs. Yet, despite its low cost, gratitude remains one of the scarcest human emotions. This may be why it is one of the most valued.

Poor compensation plans.   The matter of pay level was discussed in Chapters 10 and 11, on compensation. If sales people do not feel they are getting paid in proportion to the importance of the job they are doing, their attitude toward the company probably will be bad. Sales people are in continual contact with reps who work for other firms, and they are in a good position to know what is being paid for similar jobs. If the comparison is continually unfavorable, they may come to believe they are working for a low-paying concern and would do better elsewhere.

It is difficult for the sales manager to instill a good attitude among the sales force when their pay is not commensurate with their activities. Further, the firm risks lowering morale if the compensation plan fails to be fair, offer some security and incentive, and otherwise meet the characteristics of a sound plan discussed earlier.

A person's pay is loaded with other connotations. It is a status symbol which tells other people a great deal, and also tells the individual what the boss really thinks of him. As tangible recognition and spendable gratitude, pay is far more than just money.

Nature of the job.   In sales work, the job and the individual must be matched. Any person who feels unproductive or noncreative in a job will have poor morale. One major problem in managing a door-to-door selling organization is that many people do not feel right doing it. One organization selling encyclopedias door to door had worked up a prepared sales presentation that was largely untruthful. The sales reps were instructed how to get in the door through the use of deceit and misleading statements. After a short period, many reps found they could not maintain their self-respect and dignity while living such a constant lie.

A sales manager of a business machines company described his early days in selling when he was working for a furnace company. He said that although the position paid handsomely he had to get out of it because of the nature of the job. A salesman would approach a housewife and say he was inspecting furnaces and for a small sum of money he would clean hers. Instead of cleaning the furnace, he took it apart and left the parts on the floor. If the homeowner wanted the furnace put back together again, the company had to be hired for an expensive furnace repair job. The Federal Trade Commission has since specifically prohibited this practice. In such situations, good sales force morale is almost impossible.

Lack of security.   An individual who must be concerned with future welfare and employment possibilities cannot operate at anywhere near a normal level of productivity. No one who has not been afraid of losing a job can appreciate the fears and emotional stress that go with such a feeling. The manager who can alleviate these fears does much to establish good morale for the operation.

Ironically, people who do not care for security—and there are many such individuals—may not make the best sales representatives for a firm. They usually believe that their best security is their own ability, and without doubt they are right. Since they have this ability, however, they often leave other sales organizations to form their own enterprises, such as manufacturers' representatives or brokers. These reps are usually too good for the typical sales organization to keep. If they do stay, they may be so independent that they present managerial problems. It takes a most skillful and understanding executive to manage such highly talented people.

Dissatisfaction with promotions.   Promotions can have serious repercussions for morale. For every opening in the executive hierarchy, there are always several people who feel they should be the ones to get it. Many of them have valid cases. Administrators often face the dilemma that one promotion is to be given, and there are several equally qualified individuals from whom to choose. Such situations can create poor attitudes among previously good employees.

No individual who is doing a good job can be other than disappointed at not receiving a promotion to which he feels he was entitled. This problem has no easy solution, and many times it has no solution whatsoever. Some of these good people quit when a promotion is not forthcoming. Many times nothing can be done, since there simply is no room for them in the executive level.

The best procedure for a sales manager to follow when there are several good candidates for a promotion is to explain in complete detail the basis on which the promoted person was chosen. He must point out to the other prospects that not enough openings were available to promote everyone qualified and emphasize that it is not a matter to be taken personally. Sometimes the sales manager softens such blows by giving others a reward, such as an extra bonus or a raise, to show that he considers them equally valuable and wants to keep them.

The situation is even worse when the sales force generally believes the wrong candidate has been promoted. Without question, promotion of an individual others consider undeserving has a bad effect on morale. The promotion of an undeserving person also creates problems when she or he attempts to exercise managerial authority over former peers.

Severance of personnel.   Another major source of morale trouble is the severance of personnel. Many administrators cannot face up to the task of firing someone or laying off personnel when necessary. The sales manager who does not approach this problem correctly can ruin the morale of the entire organization. Others will easily identify with the discharged individual and regard his treatment as unfair, even though ample cause may exist.

In some companies salesmen are seldom fired but instead encouraged to quit. There is a distinct difference. A sales manager can take many actions to cause a person to want to resign. Indeed, when you hear some woeful tale of a sales rep who is being treated terribly, you may be hearing a story of how one manager has chosen to fire an unsatisfactory employee. If management is treating some rep badly, perhaps it is trying to tell him something or encourage him to do something.

Poor territories.   The allocation of territories is another source of poor morale in the sales force. Although from a theoretical viewpoint it is highly desirable to equate the territories of all the sales people, this is a practical impossibility in most cases. Some people must be given better territories than others. Areas that require relatively more travel, for example, usually are not regarded with favor by most reps.

Sometimes the sales manager uses territory allocation as a means of promoting people. However, this can create other problems. Territorial changes directly affect the sales reps' welfare. Moreover, the company's best interests may not be served by changing a person's territory. Production may suffer for some time until the rep can establish the rapport with new customers that made him successful in his former district.

Problems with sales quotas, report requirements, and restrictions.   Sales quotas cause their share of morale troubles. Reps who do not believe their quotas are fair or based on a logical analysis of their markets will have poor attitudes toward their work. The sales quota often has a direct bearing on the rep's compensation and can be as important as the commission rate.

Reports and paper work can be troublesome if the sales manager refuses to be realistic about them. Paper work should be kept to a minimum. If the sales people come to regard it as merely red tape and a symbol of administrative bungling, their morale is certainly not helped.

Restrictions placed on sales reps by home-office regulations can be a source of considerable irritation. When the home office restricts their actions by credit regulations, sales emphasis, or indirect management of their time, the reps must understand the reasons. Morale is better if they agree with the restrictions or at least are willing to comply with them.

One women's apparel manufacturer was constantly urging its reps to open up new accounts. Yet top management restricted the acceptance of new dealers by requiring that the stores had to have been in business for five years, have a top credit rating, and not be carrying certain other lines of apparel. Few qualified new dealers could be found, yet management would not review its unrealistic restrictions. This was a frustrating situation for the reps.

Handling of older sales people

The handling of older sales people has plagued many managers and has a direct bearing on the morale of all sales representatives in the firm. Today, allowances are often made for older sales reps. Most of them do not expect to make the earnings they once did. Frequently they accept a reduction of territory or work load in exchange for the assurance that they will not be retired.

There is considerable evidence to support the older salesman's place in most sales organizations. While he cannot cover the territory he once did, many times his selling efficiency and profitability can match those of any other person in the organization. One older salesman of women's apparel has been calling on his trade for so long and has such a large group of friends among retailers that he does not have to do the traveling that younger people in the same organization must do. When he wants to cover the state of Oklahoma, for example, he

A day-to-day operating problem in the

MAJESTIC GLASS COMPANY (I)

Company retirement policy: Mandatory at age 65

When he reached his 65th birthday, Herman Millard was retired from the Majestic Glass Company, despite his protests. He was the first sales rep to be retired under a companywide policy which provided for payment of about $600 per month to retired employees having Millard's length of employment with the firm.

Millard had been Clyde Brion's best sales representative. He had spent many years in the Milwaukee area, which was an important territory for Majestic because of the concentration in that city of a substantial segment of the brewing industry, an important user of bottles.

In attempting to avoid retirement, Millard had pointed out that he was in excellent health and had served the company faithfully. He was responsible for the support of a large family, could not live on $600 per month, and knew no trade other than the glass container business. He showed Brion a letter from the president of one of the Milwaukee breweries expressing a personal friendship for Millard and urging Majestic to keep him on the sales force. Brion told Millard he was sorry, but the company's retirement policies applied to everyone, including himself.

Within six months after Millard's retirement, it was reported that he had been appointed manager of the Milwaukee sales office of the Corona Glass Company, one of Majestic's closest rivals for brewery business. Millard was selling to some of the same buyers he had formerly called upon for Majestic.

On checking his sales personnel records, Brion noted that three more salesmen would reach age 65 within the next seven years.

Question

What should Clyde Brion do regarding this retirement situation and the problems it causes?

Note: See the introduction to this series of problems in Chapter 2 for the necessary background on the company, its market, and its competition.

merely obtains a suite of rooms in a hotel in Oklahoma City and calls all his dealers by telephone. The dealers go to Oklahoma City to view his line, thereby eliminating the need for him to travel to all the little towns in the state. Younger reps of the same company have not been able to master this wonderful method of selling, since they do not have the necessary rapport with their customers. The older salesman is highly efficient, since his expenses are at a minimum and he wastes very little time.

Personal reasons for poor morale

For many conditions which can cause poor morale in the sales force, the sales manager has little, if any, responsibility. Nevertheless, these nonbusiness factors can play an important part in determining the attitude brought by employees to the job. About the most effective control the manager has over these factors is the selection program. Most personal problems can be handled only by the individual, so the sales manager must pick a recruit who is likely to be able to take care of his or her personal life in a satisfactory manner.

Several trouble spots in personal lives which affect job attitudes are discussed below. However, they certainly do not constitute an exhaustive list of all the personal problems an individual can have.

Domestic difficulties. It has become almost axiomatic in the field of business administration today that an administrator does not hire one person but an entire family. An important factor in the selection decision frequently is the family situation. It has been proven that the right spouse can be important to success in selling, but the wrong one can ruin an otherwise good sales rep.

People having troubles at home cannot devote proper attention to the job. Since it is usually unwise for the sales manager to enter directly into a domestic situation, he can only hire people who seem to be reasonably compatible with their families. However, it is impossible to completely anticipate domestic problems. When one does arise, about the best the sales manager can do is to give the employee some time to get it straightened out.

The sales manager of a large building products company that pioneered the hiring of women as marketing representatives related his experience with family matters:

> I now have a new problem. One of our women requested that she be given a new sales territory in San Francisco because her husband has been transferred there. We did not need anyone in San Francisco, but she made such a fuss that we made a job for her there. Now I have a man who has requested a transfer to Los Angeles because his wife has been transferred there. We don't need him in Los Angeles, but he means

business. If we don't move him, I'm sure we've got a lawsuit on our hands.

Financial problems.   Anyone in financial difficulties is worried and distracted and likely to acquire selling habits that are detrimental to his long-run success. The sales person with financial problems may push too hard to make extra income or may cheat on his expense account. Executives seldom want to hire people who have a record of being unable to manage their own finances. There are many signs, such as being heavily in debt or having few liquid assets.

Careful selection will not avoid the problem, however, since many financially sound people can fall into difficulties after they have been hired. Unexpected illness in the family, an accident, and other unforeseen events can cause major drains on a bank account. Sometimes it is necessary for the manager to offer financial help, but this can have poor consequences. It should be attempted only for an exceptionally good sales rep whom the company wants to salvage.

Poor health.   It is hard for an individual in poor health to have a good attitude toward the job. Most employers hire only people in good health, but health is not a permanent condition, and people do get sick. All the sales manager can do to protect the health of the sales force is to make certain that they live prudently while on the road and take good care of themselves. A lot can be done to educate sales people on the importance of good health.

Sometimes the company can transfer a chronically ill sales person to an office position or some other job within the firm. Considerable goodwill is thereby created. Not only is the sick individual grateful, but the other reps are comforted by the knowledge that the company will take care of them in similar circumstances.

DETERMINING THE CAUSE OF POOR MORALE

The sales manager may know that sales force morale is not good but may not know the reasons for it. Four basic actions can help uncover the true cause of the discontent.

1. An outlet for complaints.   First, the sales manager must offer sales people an outlet for their complaints. From such opinions he may gather that some common factor is bothering them and may be able to act on it. Sometimes it is advisable to conduct informal question sessions under social conditions. Often a sales rep who will not complain while in the work environment will say what is bothering him at a cocktail party or a ball game.

Whatever a rep tells the manager, it should never be belittled or dismissed as trivial. Although the complaint may seem silly, it is probably serious to the employee. If the sales manager does not listen understandingly and then do something about valid complaints, the reps will soon learn that talking with him gains them nothing. After hearing what a sales rep has to say, it usually is a mistake to make a snap judgment on the matter without an investigation. By checking each sincere complaint, the manager will not overlook something that needs attention.

2. *Opinion and attitude surveys.* A second method used to determine the facts about conditions that affect morale is to conduct opinion and attitude surveys among employees. Often a firm hires an independent consulting agency to conduct the studies. Such surveys do have *some* validity if properly done. However, employees often are reluctant to expose their real attitudes, even to a supposedly independent interviewer.

Another limitation on this method is that many times the sales people do not know the *real* reasons for their attitudes. All they know is that they are not happy with things, and frequently they will give surface reasons for this attitude. These surface complaints may not be the real cause for their basic dissatisfaction. For example, employees often say that low pay is their complaint against the company, when that is not the real issue. It is quite common to find people who blame the compensation plan when what they are really saying is: "I am not being paid enough money for what I have been putting up with." So the sales manager must not take all the complaints at face value. Many are only outcroppings of a deeper seated problem that lies unrecognized.

3. *The exit interview.* A widely heralded tool for uncovering trouble areas in an organization is the exit interview. Its proponents maintain that the departing employee will open up and tell the employer the real reason for leaving and his true attitudes toward the company.

This point of view is probably not correct. Most employees know that they need a recommendation from past employers in order to get future jobs. Particularly, most sales people have enough social intelligence to know that it is never wise to tell an individual the truth about his own shortcomings. What salesman in his right mind is going to tell the sales manager that the real reason for his leaving is that he thinks the manager is incompetent? In most exit interviews, in fact, the interviewer is given some surface excuse which is widely accepted as a valid reason for leaving an employer. Such reasons as a better job, more pay, returning to school, or a change in climate are stated frequently.

This does not mean that exit interviews should be discontinued, for if properly handled they can provide some insight. If the interviewer does not accept the surface reason the employee gives for leaving, the real reasons may be discovered by probing. It depends on the rapport the interviewer can establish with the departing employee and how much confidence the worker has that any revelations made will not adversely affect future recommendations. One firm conducts exit interviews several months after the employee leaves. The theory is that this gives the employee time to evaluate what went wrong in the firm and also time to get whatever recommendations he needs from the firm. One practical difficulty is that frequently the people have moved to another area and are unavailable for interviewing.

4. *Close relationships with subordinates.* Some sales executives cultivate a few close relationships with subordinates which can be used to learn what is going on in the ranks. The administrator who uses this technique must be careful not to ruin the informants' relationships with the other sales people. If the sales force learns that one of their number is being used in effect as a spy, his effectiveness is immediately curtailed.

THE MORALE-BUILDING PROCESS

This chapter has discussed the effects of poor morale and the factors that cause it. Little has been said of how the sales manager can constructively affect the morale of the sales force. It could be done by avoiding the situations discussed above, but there are several other ways to build a good attitude among sales force members.

Building morale in the work environment depends on showing people that they can achieve their personal objectives in life by working for the organization. This is known as the *process of integrating interests.* It is founded on the principle that every person wants certain things out of life; each has a set of objectives and goals. If the person is convinced he can achieve these goals through working for a given organization, his morale while with that group will be excellent. Should he become convinced that he cannot achieve his personal objectives, either his morale will be severely damaged or, in all probability, he will look for another job.

In using this morale-building theory, the sales manager must recognize the *theory of the self-concept* and its governing influence on the behavior of individuals. The theory states that each person has a concept of what he or she is and would like to be. The individual is constantly striving to come closer to this concept of the person he would like to be. If an action by management is interpreted by the individual to have a favorable impact on him—that is, if he thinks it will allow him to move closer to his desired concept—the influence on his morale is favorable. Should management make a decision that moves the person further from his goal, his morale will be adversely affected.

Suppose that the sales people in a firm generally regard themselves to be extremely well off in relationship to most other members of society. If management should decide to furnish them with low-priced, unequipped compact automobiles, they would be moved away from their self-concept. They would probably prefer to drive their own cars rather than have inferior transportation furnished. Yet the same managerial decision about automobiles could have a beneficial effect on the morale of sales people who hold different concepts of themselves. If the sales force consisted mainly of people who did not complete high school and were merely sales clerks, they would consider any car furnished by management an upgrading of their status, and their morale would thereby be improved. Naturally, all people do not have the same self-concept. Nevertheless, in any sales force the selection process usually ensures that people of like backgrounds and personalities will be employed. This results in some degree of uniformity in their goals.

The process of integrating the interests of the person and the organization begins at the time of hiring. It is folly to hire anyone for whom the company cannot provide a successful work experience. The sales manager must make a frank analysis of exactly what the firm is able to furnish its people. He should not hire those who cannot use what the company has to offer.

If the firm is of a size and nature that it has no promotional opportunities for its sales reps, the manager is making a mistake in looking for management-type individuals. If a person whose self-concept requires eventual promotion into top management were hired by such a firm, his morale would gradually decline as it became obvious that the firm held no promise of advancement. Similarly, many firms have nothing but money to offer. Their jobs are not desirable, and there is little prestige or glamor connected with them. In such circumstances, the manager is unwise to hire people who are not primarily motivated by money but instead are looking for prestige positions.

It is almost impossible for the manager to alter the individual's self-concept to conform with what the company has to offer. This can be done only by the individual, and it is an extremely painful process at best. Consequently, about the only control the administrator has over the integration-of-interests aspect of morale is either to hire individuals who conform with what the company has to offer or to change what the company has to offer to conform with what the person wants.

Changing the company to conform with what the sales people want is not all unheard of. If what they want is prestige on the job, possibly the firm can create more prestige for them. Giving reps the title of manufacturer's representative or district manager may be in part the answer to such desires for prestige.

QUESTIONS AND PROBLEMS

1. A branch manager of a large, nationally known appliance manufacturer, in talking about getting good salesmen, said: "There's no problem in getting salesmen. Salesmen are things. You buy them like you buy merchandise. You put them on straight commission, and they either cut the mustard or get out. After you've been through a few hundred of them, you will have your good sales force." Comment on this philosophy, bearing in mind that this manager's branch has been over quota each year he has managed it, and prior to that time it was a sick operation.

2. The Pittsburgh branch of a large plywood company had been having trouble in keeping its managers. In the past year, there had been three managerial changes. The present manager, who had been on the job less than a week, said: "I really don't know what the troubles of the previous managers have been, for I haven't had time to find out with all the work connected with moving in from Memphis. I understand the last man had some trouble adjusting to Pittsburgh. I believe he had been transferred up from the home office in Atlanta." Comment on this situation.

3. Under what conditions should the sales manager attempt to help a subordinate financially? When should help be refused?

4. How can the sales manager encourage a person to resign?

5. How can the manager integrate the interest of the individual and the organization?

6. How can the sales manager determine the morale of the organization?

7. Can someone work successfully for a person he or she dislikes?

8. Managers are continually told to listen to their people and to be sensitive to the signals they emit. But managers continue to listen without hearing a thing. What does it mean to *listen?*

9. What are some of the methods the sales manager can use to determine the state of a recruit's morale before hiring him?

10. How can the manager give the sales force more status within the organization?

Case 14–1

RON MORGAN
Outstanding salesman bypassed for promotion

Within a few weeks after he received his initial field training, Ron Morgan made his presence felt in the Springfield territory. He was a dynamic young man of 24 years who grasped product information exceedingly well and appeared to have a convincing manner in conveying his thoughts to the physicians on whom he called.

Enthusiasm was second nature to Ron. Hours and long trips never bothered him. He thought nothing of working Saturdays and often spent evenings visiting with interns and residents in many of the hospitals he called on.

In January 1975, Ron was employed as a salesman by the Ludlow Laboratories, a national manufacturer of ethical drugs, pharmaceuticals, and proprietary (nonprescription) medicines. In general, his job was that of a detail man, calling on physicians and pharmacists to promote existing products and to introduce and explain new products. As a detail man, Ron's job was *not* to solicit orders; instead, his task was to persuade (a) physicians to prescribe Ludlow products and (b) pharmacists to order Ludlow products from drug wholesalers.

Prior to his employment by Ludlow, Ron worked as an assembly man in his uncle's plant, which manufactured components for air conditioners. His uncle had developed a prosperous and growing business over the years and had offered him a permanent job after his graduation from college in June 1974. He felt that he wanted to succeed on his own merits without the benefit of family connections, although he knew that his uncle's business offered him security and rapid progress.

At the end of his first year with Ludlow Laboratories, Ron had exceeded all expectations of Victor Sherwood, his district manager. Sherwood was convinced that he had hired a real gem, and he hoped Morgan would continue to be a top producer. He was top man in his district and third man in the country at the end of 1975.

Vic Sherwood praised Ron on his accomplishments but was careful not to overencourage him. Vic realized that Ron was ambitious but young, and it sometimes puzzled him just how he could keep him productive over the next few years. There was no doubt in his mind that Morgan had potential for growth in the organization, but Ludlow management was not inclined to promoting salesmen until they had at least five to eight years' experience in the field, carrying a bag.

Note: This case was prepared by Professor Charles L. Lapp, Washington University

The year 1976 was another record-breaking one for Morgan. He again led his district and was top man in the country. Although he never pressed the issue, on occasion Morgan did speak to Sherwood about the future. Sherwood tried to be noncommital without evading the issue, and he assured Morgan that patience would bring rewards.

The early months of 1977 were a period of rough competition for Ludlow. One of their major products was competing with a new, dramatically different, and superior compound developed and marketed by a leading manufacturer. While sales were slipping badly in many territories throughout the country, Ron was holding his own and was meeting 1976 sales figures.

In June 1977, Stanley Hoffman, Ludlow sales manager, resigned. On July 1, the president of the company announced the appointment of Victor Sherwood as sales manager. One of the first problems that faced Sherwood was the appointment of a successor as regional director. He naturally thought of Morgan, but because of his youth and relatively short experience in the field, he gave more serious consideration to Jim Bradley, a salesman who had joined Ludlow nine years before. Bradley was 36 years old, had had a very successful career with Ludlow, and was highly respected by his fellow salesmen.

When Morgan arrived home on the evening of August 1, he opened his mail as soon as he arrived. His wife noticed him turn white as he read of Jim Bradley's appointment to the position of Northeast District manager.

Sales volume in the Springfield territory showed a noticeable drop during the next several months. By the end of the year, Morgan's sales position was nearer the bottom than the top of his district. Sherwood was well aware of this performance. During what appeared to be an unplanned visit to Springfield early in 1978, Vic telephoned one evening, asking Ron to meet him at the hotel the next morning. Ordinarily, when Sherwood would call him on arriving in town the evening before a meeting, Ron would immediately drive downtown and return home with Vic. Not this time.

The next day, Sherwood made a number of calls with Morgan and noticed a discouraged, almost demoralized attitude. Late in the afternoon, he asked Ron if he and his wife, Ruth, would join him for dinner. Ron said he would, but his wife wasn't feeling well. After a couple of cocktails, Sherwood brought up the subject of Morgan's sales performance since the previous September. Ron had little to offer in explanation, but he did admit that the disappointment of not being selected for the job of district manager had an effect on his performance.

Following his visit with Ron, Vic wrote to him (see Exhibit 1) restating parts of his conversation during dinner a few nights before. Vic also reported to Jim Bradley the results of his day in the field with

EXHIBIT 1

LUDLOW LABORATORIES   INTEROFFICE MEMO

To: Mr. Ron Morgan   Date: January 29, 1978
From: Victor Sherwood   Copies: Mr. Bradley
Subject: Territorial operation

During my visit to Springfield a few days ago, we had the opportunity to discuss together various phases of your territorial performance covering the past several months. As I mentioned to you then, Ron, I have been extremely disappointed in your sales picture and in your daily call average of only four physicians.

Quite frankly, Ron, this situation cannot continue! Although economic conditions may control sales figures to some extent, the very least we can expect is a definite improvement and upward turn in physician calls. I cannot justify any excuse for one, two, or three physician calls, repeatedly day after day. Certainly you must be concerned about this matter, but it appears to me that little effort has been extended on your part to improve your territorial performance.

As you are aware, we are striving to attain an overall average of 7 physician calls per day, plus other calls to total 13. We are very close to that average, and several representatives are surpassing it with little or no difficulty.

I suggest you give this entire matter serious thought during the next few days, Ron, and then let me know how you plan to improve your sales and increase physician coverage in your territory in the future.

I will await your reply.

Best regards,

Vic

VIC SHERWOOD

EXHIBIT 2

LUDLOW LABORATORIES   INTEROFFICE MEMO

To: Mr. Jim Bradley   Date: January 29, 1978
From: Victor Sherwood   Copies:
Subject: Personnel report—Mr. Ron Morgan

During my field visit this week with Mr. Morgan, I once again had the opportunity to discuss and completely review with him his territorial performance covering the past several months.

I pointed out to Ron that he has never had a better opportunity than now to prove his true value to Ludlow. If he were to pull himself out of his present position and work his territory up to where it would place him among the top territories by the end of the year, he could prove to us that he has the potential we believe he has. I also mentioned the possibility of a salary increase in July as an expression of our sincerity and confidence in his abilities. He honestly does not want to be considered for an increase at this time, because in his own words he "doesn't deserve one." He further stated that when his territory was showing progress he was adequately compensated in salary increases and would not consider it proper to receive an increase this July.

It is only natural that the thought comes to mind there may be a possibility that Ron will leave Ludlow to join his uncle's company. On discussing this subject with him, this move appears unlikely—but could still be possible through family pressure. It appears as though Ron would not be especially happy working under his brother-in-law, a vice president. The only way that Ron would consider going with this firm would be if his uncle does not retire as he plans so he might in some way lean on him for guidance.

It is my hope that Ron is sincere in his desire to pull his territory up during the next six months and that he will continue to work for Ludlow Laboratories.

Vic Sherwood

VIC SHERWOOD

Morgan (see Exhibit 2). At this point, Sherwood wondered just what he and Bradley could do to reinstill in Morgan what appeared to be his lost enthusiasm, drive, and ambition.

Questions

1. At this point, how should Victor Sherwood or Jim Bradley handle Ron Morgan?
2. What administrative mistakes did Sherwood make in this case?
3. Should Morgan, instead of Jim Bradley, have been promoted to the district manager's position?

Case 14–2

BANCROFT RESTAURANT SUPPLY COMPANY
Returning a rehired salesman to his former territory

For several years Henry Rockwell had been an outstanding salesman for the Bancroft Restaurant Supply Company. Six months previously, he had resigned from the Bancroft Company to go into the restaurant business for himself. Five months later he sold the restaurant and returned to the Bancroft Company, filling a vacancy in the Denver, Colorado, sales territory. Now Rockwell has approached his sales manager, Roger Baum, with the request that he be given back his former territory which covered the northern half of Bancroft's market. Baum is uncertain as to how he should respond to Rockwell's request.

With offices and a warehouse in Denver, the Bancroft Company was a regional wholesaler of restaurant equipment and supplies. The company's market covered Colorado, New Mexico, Wyoming, and the western part of Oklahoma, Kansas, and Nebraska. Last year the company's sales volume was approximately $4.7 million. For the past several years, Bancroft's sales volume had been increasing about 10 percent a year.

The Bancroft Company's product line consisted of about 4,000 items which were used by restaurants, bars, hospital food-serving departments, and the eating-drinking facilities in country clubs. The product assortment included such articles as glasses, china, silverware, serving equipment, cooking utensils, cookware, paper disposables, and bar equipment. Bancroft also contracted for restaurant operations; they would furnish an entire restaurant, including tables, furniture, and all the food preparation and serving equipment.

A total of 19 salesmen were employed by Bancroft. Fifteen of these people, each with his own geographic territory, sold restaurant supplies—the china, glasses, silverware, cooking utensils, etc.—as separate from equipment products such as furniture. Two other salesmen were employed in contract sales. One of these contract territories was the northern half of the market—northern Colorado, western Nebraska, and Wyoming. This was Henry Rockwell's former territory. The territory of the other contract salesman included New Mexico, southern Colorado, western Kansas, and the panhandle of Oklahoma. There were also two full-time inside salesmen in the Denver home office. These men sold to walk-in and telephone order customers. About one half of the salesmen had college educations, and the other half had high-school educations and considerable sales experience.

The compensation plan was essentially a straight commission for the 15 supplies salesmen and the two contract salesmen. The inside salesmen were paid a salary plus a small commission based on the gross margin of the products they sold. The 15 supplies salesmen received a commission of 35 percent of the gross margin on all sales that they themselves made. On any orders from a salesman's customers, where the customer came as a walk-in to the main office or else telephoned in his order, the salesman's commission dropped to 15 percent of the gross margin. The two contract salesmen each earned a commission of 5 percent of the total amount of the contract order—that is, 5 percent on sales volume. While a contract sale could be quite lucrative for the salesman, it often took a considerable period of time to set up and complete a contract sale.

The average income for a territorial supplies salesman was about $17,000 a year. A very experienced contract salesman could earn twice that amount of money. However, until contract salesmen had accumulated about five years experience, they usually made from $2,000 to $3,000 less than the territorial supplies salesmen.

Rockwell had been a superior contract salesman in Bancroft's northern territory prior to resigning. He was 48 years old, a high school graduate, with 25 years of selling experience. Rockwell's sales manager, Roger Baum, said "Henry has an almost magic sales ability, and our contract sales have suffered since he left us."

Baum had hired Ronald Lorillard to fill the position vacated by Rockwell. Lorillard was 24 years old and a recent college graduate. Baum believed that Lorillard was a very bright, alert young man who had excellent potential to become a fine salesman in contract restaurant sales. He apparently really liked the northern Colorado–Wyoming–western Nebraska territory. In fact, he said that the availability of this territory was one strong motivation for his seeking out and accepting the job with Bancroft after he graduated from college.

During the six months that Lorillard had been a contract salesman in Henry Rockwell's former territory, he had made a major effort to build up customer confidence in himself and his restaurant planning ability. His sales for the six-month period were $85,000, approximately one quarter of the sales Rockwell would have made during the same period of time. Lorillard earned 5 percent commission, or $4,250, on his sales. However, Baum felt that he had the potential to earn $35,000 per year by the end of his fifth year with Bancroft. Because the average commission income for a territorial salesman was $17,000, Lorillard anticipated considerably more future income by retaining the northern contract sales position.

Baum estimated that the company would get about $1.6 million more in sales over a 5-year period by returning Rockwell to his old territory. However, Lorillard threatened to quit if he was forced to give up the contract sales job and transfer to the job of a supplies salesman in the Denver metropolitan area. Baum also realized that he thus far had invested about $3,400 in training Lorillard for the contract sales position.

Baum did not want to lose either of the two salesmen. He saw considerable potential in Lorillard, but Rockwell's sales ability already had been proven. Baum also knew he had to make a decision pretty soon.

Question

1. Should Henry Rockwell be given his former contract sales territory?

Case 14-3
ATLANTIC DRUG COMPANY
Building morale

"They warned me that I was walking into a real mess, but I had no idea it could be this bad," Stan Wood complained to his friend Al Berkes, sales manager of another firm. Two months previously, Stan had accepted the sales managership of the Atlantic Drug Company, a drug wholesaler in the Richmond, Va. trading area. The sales force of 11 men sold the firm's thousands of items directly to retail drug outlets. The salesmen were paid a straight salary which averaged $14,000 a year in 1977. A fixed expense account of $150 a month was designed to cover their auto expenses.

Each man was assigned a fixed route of accounts upon which to call. The accounts were divided into three categories—A, B, C—depending upon their market potential. A accounts were to be called upon twice weekly, B accounts each week, and C accounts every two weeks. A salesman's normal routine was to leave home about 8:45 in the morning for the first of about 12 calls. After making the planned calls for the day, the salesman reported to the office to hand in orders, plan the next day, do their paper work, and meet with the sales manager if necessary. Normally, the men started drifting into the office about 3:00, and all would be in by 4:30.

Wood continued his tale of woe to Berkes. "I recall the first time I met with them as a group. It was after work on that first day I was there. They just sat there glumly saying nothing as I was trying to give them a pep talk and lay out some plans I had for a social get-together with them and their families. I tried to get them to appoint a committee to plan the affairs, but I couldn't get any takers."

"You may have been rushing things a bit," Berkes observed.

"Perhaps," said Wood. "But there's more. In order to get a feel for how the operation was working, I have been visiting various important accounts to find out what they think of us and our service. I work the calls into my schedule whenever I have some time to do so. Well, last week one of the druggists casually told me after I had introduced myself that Charlie—that's our salesman who calls upon him—had warned him that I might call upon him to check up on him. From what the druggist said I gathered that the salesmen thought I was playing private detective to get the goods on them."

"Why didn't you travel with the salesman to call upon the account?" asked Berkes.

"Exactly to keep them from thinking that I was checking up on them. I just wanted to get the feel of our customers, our market. I wanted to be able to put some faces on the names of our customers," Wood explained. "Besides, I've never thought much of traveling with the reps. They just put on an act and you don't find out too much."

"You might find out what kind of an act they think is important. And it is sometimes interesting to watch the relationships between the salesman and the customers. I worry when the customers don't recognize our guy," Berkes said.

Wood nodded and continued, "Despite everything I was able to put together a fairly good picture of our situation, and it isn't good. Our customers don't seem to have much of a relationship with our salesmen. They don't really know them. They have an image of the company as a bad place to work. Our men are viewed as zombies, listless order-takers. One woman told me, 'I really like Paul. He comes in here quietly, doesn't bother anyone, picks up the want book to write the order, and then slips out.' Now that is some salesman! Why don't we just phone them for their want book orders?"

"Why don't you?"

"They call us, so there is no need for it," Wood answered. He continued, "And you know, I have yet to find a customer who has been called upon before 10 o'clock."

"I know, the stores don't open before then," Berkes laughed.

"You can laugh. I'm crying. Then I find out that several of the men are moonlighting by working in some of the drug stores they are calling upon. Boy, that poses some real problems in conflict of interest. I'm about to clean the lot of them out and start fresh. These guys are ruined beyond salvage."

"Have you talked this situation out with them yet?," asked Berkes.

"They won't talk," said Wood. "They just sit there and make some low noises."

"Stan, I just can't believe you. People will talk if you know how to let them. I bet they are dying to tell you all sorts of things. And I bet you won't like hearing what they have to say. But if you want to make it in that job, you had better find a way of getting them to open up to you. They call it communication and you need a bunch of it, fellow."

Wood did not like what Berkes said, but he was too good a friend and too good a sales manager to ignore.

"But I guess I don't know how. What should I do, Al?" Wood asked his friend.

Question

1. What should Al Berkes tell Stan Wood?

15

Motivating the sales force

People are as lazy as they dare be, and some people are mighty daring.

MARK TWAIN

Behavioral theorists claim that people generally want to work. Sales managers are apt to comment, "Perhaps, but not very hard." There are managers who believe that motivating people to work is the crux of the managerial task. They spend considerable time and thought trying to figure out how to motivate sluggish employees to do their jobs properly. Sometimes they can, sometimes they cannot. There are no magic motivators that will invariably stir sales people into effective action. But management does have several ways to establish an environment in which the individual is likely to become motivated to work hard and effectively.

There is a difference between working hard and working effectively, or productively. Just working hard does not guarantee results; countless people who work hard each day have little to show for it. There are other people who are highly productive yet do little actual work. The manager cannot adopt the idea that the only key to productivity is getting people to work hard—in sales work, to make lots of calls. Yet it must be acknowledged that many sales people fail because they will not work hard and do not make the calls that are needed.

Before we consider the various techniques managers use to motivate sales people, an introduction to basic motivational theory may help you improve your understanding of why people do the things they do.

SELF-CONCEPT THEORY

Perhaps the best and most comprehensive theory of human behavior developed to date relates people's actions to drives evolving from strong desires to fulfill the ideal concepts they have developed of themselves. The self-concept theory is both a simple explanation of human behavior and a most complex one, depending upon the depth of understanding desired. On the simple level the theory proposes that each of us, through our experiences, has developed ideas or concepts of who we are and what we can and cannot do, and the type of person we are. These thoughts we hold ourselves—things we believe as true—are called our *real self-concept.*

In addition to these real concepts we hold, we have developed thoughts about who we would like to be, what we want to be able to do, and the type of person we want to become. This is called our *ideal self-concept.*

These two self-concepts are internalized. They are our own personal business, and we do not always want others to know about them. Instead, we develop a separate, but overlapping, set of thoughts about what other people think of us—what *we* think other people really think of us. We call this our *real other-concept.* In conjunction with this concept we develop ideas of what we *want* others to think of us. These thoughts of how we want other people to see us are called our *ideal other-concept.*

Both of these *others* are generalized, but in actual life we also develop several specific *other-concepts.* We want our children to see us one way and our boss to see us another. A man's parson views him differently than his bookmaker does. For the sales person, these specific *others* can vary even among customers. When the sales representative calls on an old friend who is a small dealer in a rural community, he seeks to project one image, or self-concept. When calling on the purchasing agent for a large corporation a different image may be projected—a different *ideal other* is sought. We want different people to see us differently.

Success as a sales representative depends in part on an ability to perceive the correct image to be projected and then projecting it.

Hierarchy of concepts

Some of our self-concepts are quite general, and others are more specific. If they are arrayed as in Figure 15–1, each of the person's concepts can be identified in progressively more specific detail.

FIGURE 15–1
Levels of self-concept abstraction

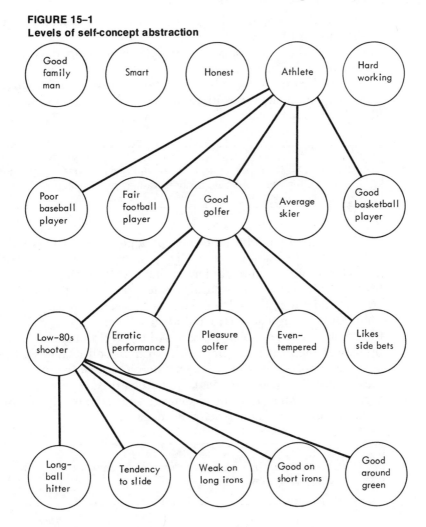

The self-concept and motivation

The relation between these various self-concepts and motivation can be explained with a series of principles and comments on them.

Principle no. 1.   A person will do things that he thinks will move his real self-concept or real other-concept closer to his ideal concepts.

The *ideals* are goals. The *reals* are where the person now is. The whole idea of life is to move closer to one's *ideals*. Suppose one of a sales rep's ideal self-concept is that he is a prosperous, successful executive. If the sales manager offers that rep the title of district manager and a luxury car for achieving a certain level of productivity, the rep will be motivated to work for the rewards. They would help move him closer to his ideals.

> *Principle no. 2.* A person will reject all behavior that he thinks will move his real concepts away from his ideal concepts.

This principle involves the concept of perceived risk. People reject risks to their real self-concepts. They strongly prefer the status quo over accepting some new behavior that may move them further away from their ideals. Suppose a new sales manager decides that to increase production, the sales force should make more calls in the evening. A salesman whose real and ideal self-concepts focus around the idea that he is a good family man will try to reject such a suggestion by management. It is incompatible with his self-image. Or the manager may urge a saleswoman to use more pressure in closing. But she views herself as a professional, low-pressure sales consultant, not a high-pressure huckster. The manager's suggestions will likely be rejected unless she changes her self-image.

> *Principle no. 3.* Many of a person's self-concepts are in conflict with one another.

Suppose a married woman has the ideal self-concepts that she is a successful career woman but also a good wife and mother. There will be many instances in which these two ideals will come into conflict. The sales manager may offer her a promotion that will involve more travel and time away from home. If she accepts, her role as homemaker will be jeopardized. When such conflicts are resolved internally the strongest force wins out, but not without creating guilt.

Most adult behavior involves conflicts and thus creates guilt. Every decision involves a consideration of tradeoffs. If you do one thing, you cannot do something else.

Principle no. 4.   People want to minimize the guilt involved in their behavior.

It is indeed a clever manager who learns the delicate art of removing guilt from the sales rep's behavior. If the saleswoman who disdained the use of high-pressure closing tactics were shown to her satisfaction that such closes would not only make her far more money but also would simplify the customer's buying process, these results might lessen her resistance to strong closes. The manager tries to lessen guilt by pointing out the positive virtues of the desired behavior. Sometimes a positive action can be taken to alleviate the guilt.

The salesman in the Northwest for a women's garment manufacturer had to be on the road for several weeks at a time. This caused serious problems for him at home. The manager solved the problem by sometimes allowing the wife to accompany the rep at the company's expense.

Principle no. 5.   Success is achieving one's ideal concepts, so that the real and ideal concepts became essentially the same.

Although a person's ideal concepts do not remain static throughout life, still they are fairly stable, particularly as one ages. As the individual's real concepts approach the ideal concepts, great personal satisfaction is realized. People who achieve their ideal concepts are generally pleased with themselves and with their situation. Their morale is usually excellent. Consequently, their behavior becomes stable. They tenaciously continue to do the things that they have been doing. To do otherwise would likely move them away from the ideal concepts that have been giving them so much satisfaction.

Using the self-concept in motivating sales people

In sales work, motivation begins in the selection process. The sales manager should not hire people for jobs in which they cannot achieve success.

In a healthy, productive relationship between employer and employee, the worker must believe he is achieving success by working for the manager. If a sales person begins to think that he is not coming closer to his ideals by serving the company, his behavior will move further from management's goals.

It is important to tell the applicant exactly what the job has to offer. Then what the applicant evidently seeks in life should be compared with what is offered. If the job cannot furnish success to the individual, neither his time nor management's efforts should be wasted by hiring him.

Throughout the selection process management must try to determine the individual's self-concepts. If a sales career is incompatible with the individual's self-concepts, success is unlikely. Only people who can be motivated to produce in the job and who want what it can furnish should be here. A person who does not want what the job has to offer will not be motivated and will be difficult to control.

STIMULATING SALES ACTIVITY

While many of the managerial tools used by sales administrators provide strong motivation, in some instances they are insufficient and additional incentives are required. Most sales executives agree that a sound compensation plan is by far the strongest force that can be used to motivate sales people. Also, they agree that selection, training, field supervision, establishment of equitable quotas, and other actions all play an important role in stimulating sales performance. However, this chapter covers special stimulation techniques not discussed elsewhere—conventions, contests, and honor awards.

CONVENTIONS AND MEETINGS

Meetings and conventions are a vital part of the sales world. The daily activity boards at most hotels will attest to the large number of sales meetings taking place every day. Some companies hold small meetings for local or regional sales forces while others sponsor national conventions for the entire sales force. There are industrywide conferences and trade shows. Meetings can be the bane of the manager's existence because they take up so much time and effort; and they are costly.

Yet that there must be good reasons for such meetings, despite the often-heard protests. There are many good meetings at which much work is done which can only be done in this manner.

Purpose

The three basic purposes of a convention are inspiration, training, and communication. Some meetings have no purpose other than to stimulate the sales force to work harder. However, many also include considerable training material, such as new-product information, help on current sales problems, and other information sales people can use to help them do a better job in the current market situation. Several of the specific purposes that can be included under the basic training function of a convention are:

- To introduce new products or product modifications.
- To explain a forthcoming advertising campaign.
- To provide training in selling techniques.
- To make announcements of company policies on pricing, channels of distribution, organization, and personnel.
- To gain rapport between the sales force and management.

Most successful meetings are for training rather than inspiration. Inspirational messages certainly have a place in any convention. However, a meeting based entirely on them will probably fail rather miserably. Many people resent having to attend a glorified pep talk.

Disadvantages

Holding a sales convention has several disadvantages. First, the sales people are taken from their work, which may cause a loss of sales volume. Second, conventions are expensive to conduct. Not only must the company stand the cost of bringing the reps to the convention and sustaining them while they are there, but the expenses of renting hotel accommodations and meeting room space and of providing for entertainment are considerable. The cost factor alone has caused many concerns to curtail the number of meetings.

Third, the sales reps sometimes regard a convention merely as a company-paid vacation and conduct themselves accordingly. It may be difficult for people attending a sales conference in the West Indies to feel that its primary purpose is to work. Experienced sales managers have proven this need not be the case. Fruitful meetings can be held anywhere if they are handled properly and it is made clear that work comes before play. At a sales meeting held on the island of St. Martin in the West Indies, they worked from nine to noon each day, took the afternoon off to play, and met again in the late evening. That meeting cost no more than the one the following year, which was held in New York City for "economy."

One disadvantage of conventions is that the reps get too little aid on problems peculiar to their own situation. Everything at the convention is usually handled on a group basis, with no provision for personal counseling. Special sessions for counseling or informal counseling during social activity periods can overcome the disadvantage.

Relative merits of national and regional meetings

Whether to hold one national meeting or several regional ones depends largely upon the logistics of the situation and the main purposes of the meeting. The question is moot for firms with only a few sales people—less than 20 or 30. They can get together in one meeting fairly easily, and splitting such a small group into two groups unnecessarily doubles management's time and costs. Some groups can be too small for good cross-fertilization of ideas.

Regional meetings are used when the manager of a relatively large sales force wants to meet with the sales force in smaller groups— usually no more than 30 reps—in order to work more closely with each person. Regional meetings are best for training purposes or real work sessions. The travel costs and time of the sales people are minimized. Also, while top management is usually available for one national meeting, a series of meetings makes it difficult for them to attend.

National meetings are frequently held for inspirational purposes, usually focused around the introduction of new products. In recent years, technological developments have made possible some imaginative programs that try to take advantage of the strengths of both national and regional meetings while minimizing the weaknesses of each. Closed-circuit TV has made it possible to bring the national program to the reps in the field without having to travel the circuit. General Electric equipped a large airplane as a flying convention meeting room. The company took its national show out to the representatives and dealers in the field, who would come to the airport much as they would to a downtown hotel.

Planning and conducting a convention

Four basic aspects must be fully planned if a convention is to be a success:

The time and place must be established

The objective and theme or subjects must be determined

The program must be developed in detail.

Arrangements must be made for space, meals, transportation, and other administrative details.

If not properly handled, these can cause much inconvenience to those in attendance.

Time and place. The sales manager should try to time the convention when it will interfere least with selling activities. The industry may have certain periods of the year, such as Christmas season or summer, during which business is slack. Next, the sales manager must choose the city in which the convention will be held. Although other factors are involved, this is basically a matter of executive preference. Some prefer to hold it in the city where the home office is located. This minimizes the amount of executive time that must be allocated to the meeting, and many sales people can profitably acquire more exposure to the home office and production facilities. However, other executives do not want the sales force to disturb home-office routine, or the office may be located in a city which is not ideal for conventions. Basically, most of these decisions come down to the question of whether to hold the convention in some major city, such as New York, Chicago, or San Francisco, or to hold it in some vacation resort. Much can be said in favor of both, but the decision usually depends on the objective of the meeting. There is probably a trend away from holding conventions in large cities. Many managers have found the more tranquil life in resort areas conducive to morale and learning.

Sometimes the sales manager finds it expedient to have the sales people combine the convention with a family vacation, and the reps are encouraged to bring their families. This may lessen their demands on management for longer vacations during critical times. It also makes the families more favorably inclined toward the company and the spouses' jobs—an important consideration.

Theme. Conventions should have some basic theme. Considerable showmanship is involved in the conduct of a convention, and a good show should have a plot. The sales manager can usually determine the theme only after analyzing what the major purpose is in holding the convention. There should be no doubt among the sales force about the basic purpose of the meetings, and the theme is one way by which this message can be carried to them. For instance, one firm introducing a new product into its well-established product family used as a theme the birth of a baby. Salesmen received birth announcements inviting them to come and see the new addition to the family. The entire convention was conducted in a manner that carried out this idea. The salesmen were given masks at the door and the new product was in a crib on a stage decorated as if it were a nursery.

Program. The program must be planned in complete detail. Both the time spent in meetings and the periods for recreation should be accounted for in the planning process. The person responsible for developing the program must obtain the proper speakers or other leaders for the various meetings, and the topics for each meeting must be chosen. All these things must be decided in advance and stated in a printed program so that everyone can see ahead of time exactly what they will be doing at each session. This can be not only time-consuming but also demanding. Meaningful programs do not occur by turning the speakers loose to talk about whatever they want. They need to be given considerable guidance on what is wanted. Much liaison work is needed with each program participant. Moreover, some materials have to be prepared and distributed.

Physical facilities.   Physical facilities are of considerable importance to the success of a convention. Rooms of proper size, ventilation, and accommodations are essential to ensure attention to the proceedings. Meals and entertainment must be provided, and care must be taken that all participants are suitably lodged.

Common mistakes made.   Several errors are often made by those who plan and conduct conventions and meetings. Probably the most serious is to select speakers who are boring or not qualified to discuss the assigned topic. Frequently, sales organizations find it advisable to hire outside experts with proven speaking abilities to deliver the key speeches. This is particularly recommended when the proper personnel are not available within the organization.

Another frequent error is to allow the participants in a convention to go home without tangible evidence of what has been achieved. It is usually wise to place in their hands copies of the material presented at the convention. If the major purpose of the meeting is to introduce new products, for example, the reps should be furnished with written data about these items.

Surprisingly, lack of planning and preparation frequently ruin meetings. For some reason, possibly an enlarged ego, some managers try to walk unprepared into a sales meeting, relying solely on their extemporaneous skills. Sometimes this works, but not often. People resent giving their time to someone who has refused to take the time to prepare for them.

CONTESTS

Contests are frequently used to provide special incentives for sales people. Of the 434 questionnaires returned by members of Sales and Marketing Executives—International, 74.4 percent reported use of sales contests.[1] And a *Sales Management* survey indicated that 66

---

[1] Albert Haring and Malcolm L. Morris, *Contests, Prizes, Awards for Sales Motivation* (New York: Sales and Marketing Executives—International, 1968), p. 18.

percent of the firms used contests.[2] Despite its many faults and draw-backs, the sales contest is widely used as a tool in sales management.

Purpose

All contests should have a definite purpose—broad or specific. It is senseless to hold a contest just for the sake of playing a game. The sales manager may want a contest for the broad purpose of stimulating over-all activity. Other broad objectives may be to increase profits or to improve the firm's market position. But as a general rule, such broad purposes should be avoided. The manager should rely on basic incen-tive programs to achieve such broad objectives. Contests are best used to reach highly selective goals.

There can be many specific reasons for conducting a contest. Table 15–1 presents the results of the Haring-Morris survey, which posed the question: "What are the objectives of your special-incen-tive programs for your own sales force?" The managers reported that the main objective of their contests was to increase total sales volume. But to accomplish this overall objective, the contests had to be aimed as specific objectives that result in increased volume. The objectives are *factors* that lead to increased total volume. The theory is that if these factors are improved, greater volume will follow. Therefore, finding new customers was the most important reason given for holding contests. This leads to increased sales, but the man-ager significantly is telling the sales reps exactly how to go about getting this additional volume instead of just giving them the general mandate to increase sales.

Most contest objectives reported in the survey can be grouped into a few categories. Several of the purposes are basically the same—getting new customers. For instance, the objective of getting better territorial coverage essentially comes down to contacting new custom-ers in the territory. Another common classification of objectives is to concentrate sales attention on certain products. The classifications "promote special items," "introduce new products," "ease an unfa-vorable inventory position," and "get a better balance of sales" all refer to concentrating attention on the sales of given products. When the objectives are totaled, it can be seen that the majority of companies think the most important one is to get additional sales volume by some special emphasis, either on products or on customers. Use of contests for the purposes of lowering selling expenses or giving better service was distinctly in the minority.

---

[2] "What's Wrong with Sales Contests," *Sales Management,* September 10, 1967, pp. 34–35.

TABLE 15–1
Objectives of special-incentive programs for the sales force

	Respondents reporting use		Considered most important	
	Number	Percent	Number	Percent
Total	323	100.0%	323	100.0%
Increase overall sales	276	85.4%	217	67.2%
Find new customers	209	64.7	133	41.2
Promote special items	142	44.0	70	21.7
Obtain greater volume per call...........	135	41.8	89	27.6
Overcome seasonal sales slump	131	40.6	66	20.4
Introduce a new product, line or service ..	119	36.8	51	15.8
Get better territory coverage	103	31.9	58	18.0
Stop or slow a sales decline	92	28.5	33	10.2
Get better balance of sales	86	26.6	36	11.1
Get renewal of business with former customers............................	79	24.5	29	9.0
Develop new sales skills	76	23.5	23	7.1
Ease an unfavorable inventory position....	66	20.4	27	8.4
Improve sales service to customers	62	19.2	24	7.4
Sell higher quality products	54	16.7	24	7.4
Build better product displays	39	12.1	17	5.3
Do self-training	38	11.8	14	4.3
Lower selling costs	33	10.2	13	4.0
Reduce selling time.....................	14	4.3	7	2.2
Get better sales reports	12	3.7	2	0.6
Other	21	6.5	17	5.3

Source: Albert Haring and Malcolm L. Morris, Contests, Prizes, Awards for Sales Motivation (New York: Sales and Marketing Executives—International, 1968), p. 25.

The specific reasons for holding a contest should be placed in writing and kept before the manager at all times during the planning stage of the contest. This will help ensure that the design of the contest does not include factors that have no bearing on its original purpose. If the purpose of a contest is to gain new accounts, the sales manager may be tempted to insert an additional objective such as increased sales volume or lower expenses. However, each additional aim detracts attention from the major goal, thereby lessening the probability of achieving any objective.

Advantages of contests

In some situations when sales people feel they are in competition with one another, a contest can serve to stimulate their interest in doing a good job. Frequently, it can add zest to an otherwise dull situation. Many sales people obtain a great deal of psychological satisfaction from winning or placing high in a contest, regardless of the prizes offered. Most individuals like to win just for the sake of winning, despite the size of the stakes. A penny ante poker player may get as much satisfaction out of winning as does a big gambler.

Contests can be made as cheap or expensive as management desires. Many of the best ones may cost only a few dollars. The sales manager may promise to buy a steak dinner for the first person who meets a quota, for example. Contests can be used to cover short-run situations in which management does not want to make any permanent alterations in its other stimulation tools. It was pointed out that it is a mistake to keep altering the compensation plan to meet every new situation. Hence the contest can frequently serve in place of such a change.

Some of the most effective contests a manager can use are short, inexpensive, specific goal creations. At one Monday morning sales meeting, the sales manager of a large Chrysler dealership said, "I have two tickets to a Lakers' playoff game for every car sold today." At the end of the day, the sales records showed that a considerable amount of business had been conducted. The key is to use as bait something that the sales people really want and tie it to immediate sales action.

Objections to contests

Many sales managers do not operate sales contests and can offer several valid objections. One of the major drawbacks is that once contests are initiated they cannot be easily discontinued. In fact, organizations that use contests seem to find it necessary to use them more and more.

One sales executive said, "Creating sales incentive programs is like drug addiction. Try it a few times and you're hooked, and whether or not any real benefits are forthcoming, you've got to keep the contests going." Another sales manager said, "It's hard to say what benefits we get out of them. But if we stopped, we'd be in trouble. Our salesmen take them for granted."[3] Once the sales people realize that they can get something over and above their regular compensation for doing their jobs, they tend to work less effectively unless they are given extra awards. In objecting to contests, the administrator simply asks, "Why should we pay someone a second time for doing his job?" If the compensation plan is properly designed, it should be paying the sales force for doing the jobs the average sales contest seems to encourage—that is, obtaining new accounts and performing a balanced selling job. If sales contests are being used to bolster a faulty compensation plan, management is in error and should be giving its attention to remedying these faults.

[3] "The Sales Incentive," *Sales Management*, September 21, 1962, p. 41.

A day-to-day operating problem in the

MAJESTIC GLASS COMPANY (J)

Sales contests

For many years a sales contest had been conducted among the sales force during the slack selling months in late summer. All sales representatives were entered, and they were awarded points after an analysis of orders submitted during the contest period as follows:

    1 point for each $100 of sales.
    2 additional points for each $100 of sales to new accounts.
    100 additional points for each 1 percent improvement in total sales over the salesman's record in the preceding year's contest.
    1 additional point for each $100 of sales of special products.

Special products were hard-to-sell items that usually had high profit potential but low turnover. The list of special products varied from year to year and was announced by Clyde Brion, the general sales manager, prior to the start of each year's contest.

The sales rep having the most points at the end of the contest was declared winner. Second, third, fourth, and fifth places were also designated. All five winners were given merchandise prizes, such as color TV sets, golf clubs, ladies' furs, or camping equipment.

Morgan Ivey, Majestic's Seattle sales representative for seven years, had never won a prize. In discussing his contest performance with Brion he said: "I've given up—a lot of the fellows have. We can't win." When Brion pressed him to explain why, he found that Ivey had no objection to the contest rules or scoring. He believed, however, that the sales manager was unfairly helping some of the sales people during the contest period but not others.

"I happen to know," Ivey said, "that last July you sent Elton Boggess in Cincinnati a complete sales plan for a big order he got from a new distillery in his territory. Result—he won third place. I didn't get any help like that!"

It was Brion's practice to contribute to Majestic's sales whenever and wherever he could. The amount of his assistance varied, from merely sending a sales person a newpaper clipping that suggested a possible new prospect, all the way to visiting customers himself to participate in sales negotiations. These efforts were admittedly spotty. The sales representative in the territory affected always received full commissions and contest points, regardless of Brion's help.

> "It really isn't fair," Ivey continued, "that a salesman should get a full commission on a sale you helped him make. But I doubt if anything can be done about that. We do think, however, that you and the rest of the home-office staff should keep hands off during the contest period."
>
> *Question*
>
> Should Clyde Brion and other home-office staff keep hands off during a contest?
>
> Note: See the introduction to this series of problems in Chapter 2 for the necessary background on the company, its market, and its competition.

Frequently, sales contests lead to undesirable selling methods, such as overstocking, overselling, and various pressure tactics. In the short run these tactics may enable the sales person to win the contest, but in the long run may cause trouble. This is not an objection of contests per se, however, only of poorly designed ones. Nevertheless, this potential danger exists in all contests, and care must be taken to be sure that such activities do not upset the overall sales strategy of the firm.

Many executives object to contests on the grounds that they create morale problems. In any sizable sales force, inequities are bound to occur and must be negotiated. The mere fact that somebody must lose may create a morale problem regardless of what the sales manager can do. Since morale is of such great importance, some managers wonder why they should assume avoidable risks.

Some administrators object to contests on the grounds that they are so time-consuming that other activities tend to be neglected. Since a contest is only an appendix to the overall sales operation, it is a mistake to get so involved in its operation that other managerial activities as supervision, control, and training are neglected. Also, the sales person is tempted to neglect activities not connected with the contest. An individual who has determined to achieve the top award will focus attention on those factors that lead to that goal and will neglect any work that does not contribute toward it. For instance, certain servicing obligations are constantly required of the sales person, yet these are seldom placed in a contest design plan. During a contest a salesman may ignore all servicing activities, to the detriment of his long-run success.

Some sales administrators consider contests to be childish and nothing more than games designed to pacify immature people. They feel that their sales people will react in the same way and that management will appear ridiculous if it tries to stimulate them with this type of activity. This may be a valid objection in certain situations. A few managers are fortunate enough to have a sales force which is mature and would look down on any attempt at this type of stimulation. In such situations very little stimulation from contests is required, since the reps are able and perform their duties satisfactorily without additional prodding. However, this describes a small portion of the sales forces in the United States. Often, sales people appreciate and enjoy contest games.

One of the biggest objections to sales contests is that, almost inevitably, a decline in sales occurs afterward; the sales force cannot keep up the high level of activity. Many questions have been raised about the long-run benefits of a contest. Obviously, if the contest has achieved wider distribution and new dealerships, a long-run benefit should occur. But if the contest has been focused mainly on sales volume, its long-range value can be questioned. The absence of a permanent accomplishment is not necessarily bad. Many contests are designed for short-run purposes such as selling out an overstocked inventory. The postcontest decline in sales usually occurs because the contest merely borrows sales volume from the future. It does not increase total sales over a long period of time but merely changes the time when an order is submitted. This problem of decline is a serious one for which no satisfactory answer generally applicable to all situations has ever been developed.

Planning and conducting contests

If a contest is to be successful it must be planned, and the following tasks must be completed in advance:

- A relevant theme must be developed.
- The opportunity to win should be equalized for all participants.
- The length of the contest must be established.
- The contest must be adequately promoted.
- A fair scoring system must be established.
- Proper awards must be selected.

Planning. A good sales contest requires at least one month of planning time. Planning covers a multitude of activities. The administration of a sales contest is a matter of considerable detail, and these details are extremely important to its success. Such things as the scoring system, the prizes, and the theme all must be carefully worked out to ensure that they achieve the specific objectives established for the contest.[4]

Theme. A sales contest must have a theme, even though it is strictly a sales theme. Many contests are built around a sport currently in season. Other examples of themes are military campaigns, a search for gold, or something to do with earth satellites and outer space. Some themes have a direct bearing on the basic philosophy underlying the contest. One firm adopted a poker theme in which each salesman was allowed to draw one card from a deck for each 100 points he had earned in the contest each week. From these cards, each salesman attempted to make the best possible poker hand. The man who had the high hand won the prize for the week. This inserted a considerable element of luck into the contest, since the man who drew the most cards would not always have the highest hand. He just had the best chance of winning. This was a deliberate decision on management's part to allow all salesmen to have an opportunity to win each week, thus minimizing the chances that the good reps would monopolize the prizes and discourage the others.

Opportunity to win. The sales manager should provide each person with a chance to win a prize. If the average or poor sales reps learn that the top producers are the ones who win all the prizes, they will tacitly withdraw from competition, and the contest will serve little purpose for the organization as a whole.

Opportunity to win may be equalized in four ways. First is the use of quotas; 70 percent of sales executives surveyed reported using this technique.[5] Through the use of quotas, allowances can be made for differences in territories and selling abilities. The rep who makes the greatest improvement relative to the others is the winner. In this way, even the poorest sales person has a chance to win. One criticism of this technique is that the person who has been doing a poor job actually has a better chance of winning than the good sales rep does, because the poorer seller has more room for improvement. Quotas must be soundly and accurately established for this equalizing technique to work properly. Sales people who feel that their quotas have been set unfairly or unrealistically probably do not compete vigorously in a contest. The trend is away from quotas and toward one of the other methods because the difficulties with quotas are being recognized.

In the second method of equalizing opportunity to win, sales reps are paired off so that they can compete against others of the same general ability. A third system is to have the reps compete against their own previous records. This is very similar to the quota technique and is

---

[4] Haring and Morris, *Contests, Prizes, Awards for Sales Motivation*, p. 52.

[5] Ibid., p. 7.

subject to the same criticisms. Finally, the sales manager may assemble teams or groups in which good and poor salesmen are combined. Then the groups compete against one another. In this way, an average or poor producer can be a member of a winning team.

Length of contest.   Contests seldom run longer than three months; most often, the duration is one month.[6] If a contest runs too long, the participants may lose interest and become bored. This is especially apt to happen to those who see no chance at all of winning. For them, it is better to end the contest as soon as possible and hope they will be inspired when the next one starts.

Promotion.   The success of a contest depends largely on how well the contest is promoted to the sales force. An outstanding example was a contest conducted by the Sheaffer Pen Company. The contest was introduced at a convention in Fort Madison, Iowa, the company's home office. A professionally staged musical comedy about the life and problems of a Sheaffer Pen salesman was climaxed in the final act, when a new Cadillac was driven onto the stage. Such a car was to be the first prize in each of the company's five regions. The salesmen had no previous knowledge of this contest; in fact, the company had never before conducted one. The sales manager explained the details of the contest, but the promotion did not end at that point. Each week thereafter each salesman was mailed some reminder to whet his interest in winning the prize. One week, the local Cadillac dealer in each rep's home town contacted contestants to take their orders for color and other equipment. Another week, a facsimile of the automobile title was sent to each man. One mailing included a key to the automobile. Another mailing was a special run of the Fort Madison newspaper with a headline that stated the salesman had won a Cadillac. Each salesman's name was put in the headline of the newspaper sent to him.

Scoring systems.   An objective scoring system is important to the success of a contest. If the reps feel that it is not being fairly scored, considerable ill will can result. Sometimes it is difficult to be completely impartial. What appears to be an objective system really has some subjective factors underlying it. On the surface it would appear that a sales quota is an objective basis for scoring, but the methods by which the quotas are established may be completely subjective. If so, any scoring system based on this quota is in reality subjective, and the sales people have good reason to be displeased with it.

Even when quotas are established on a relatively unbiased basis, considerable dispute can arise, since market analysis is not an exact research tool. A bias existing in most market figures favors sales

---

[6] Ibid.

people who operate in rapidly growing territories and discriminates against those in other areas.

Most scientifically established quotas are set on benchmark data that, at best, are a year or two old. These data provide the sales people in rapidly growing areas with a distinct edge, because their potential market is much greater than the sales manager realizes. Quotas established on such indexes as population or number of economic institutions in an area do not reflect the higher consumption patterns in growing regions. Sheaffer Pen encountered this problem in the contest described above. In the region that included California and the Southwest, a rapidly growing area, the second-place winner had more points than any of the first-place winners in the other four regions. He was greatly distressed and threatened to quit because, in his mind, he had done a better selling job than the winners of the Cadillacs in the other four regions, yet his prize was of much less value. This man should have realized that he was selling in an area of such rapid growth that it was much easier for him to get points by obtaining new dealerships, and so forth, than it was for sales reps in some eastern territories. His performance was actually not so much a reflection of his ability as it was of the territory where he was selling. Unfortunately, this may also be true of most other contests.

Awards. Basically, two types of awards are given in sales contests—merchandise or cash. In addition, other awards, such as trips, vacations, and honors of various types, are used frequently. The current thinking on the subject leans toward giving merchandise rather than cash. The theory is that, first, cash is quickly spent and then forgotten, whereas the winner keeps the merchandise, continually takes pride in it, and gains prestige for having won it. Furthermore, management usually can buy the merchandise at less than retail price. For the same amount of money, a firm can give a prize in merchandise that is worth more than if it were given in cash. Suppose a company wants to give $500 to the contest winner. That same $500 invested in merchandise can probably buy some item worth from $750 to as much as $1,000 at retail. Consequently, the sales person may place a higher monetary value on the award if it is in merchandise than if it is cash.

Although trips and vacations are currently popular as awards, they do pose certain problems for the winner. Many times, the family situation is such that it is impossible for the sales people to get away to take a trip. Or they may not want to go on a vacation at the required time or to the specified place. Even though problems may arise, such noncash awards as vacations or merchandise are popular because they frequently represent something the person would like to have but would never feel free to buy. The rep who really wants to go to Hawaii or

Bermuda, but may never feel able to afford it, would probably work hard to win such a trip.

Cash does have benefits. It has a universal attraction, whereas a given noncash award may not appeal to the entire group. The winner can then spend it to yield the most utility. He may be able to pay a large hospital bill with a cash award, for example, but he could not do this if the prize were a new hi-fi set. Also, the winner may be able to keep the cash himself, whereas many merchandise prizes go to the family; this may or may not lessen the incentive of some people to compete vigorously in the contest.

Another aspect of the award problem is that the manager must decide what percentage of the sales force is to win prizes. Prevailing opinion on this subject is widely divergent. The philosophy that everyone should be a winner in a contest, and only the value of the awards should be varied, is not unusual. This is sound managerial practice, but it is a mistake to operate a contest on an all-or-nothing basis, with one big prize going to the winner and the others getting nothing. In most contests, it soon becomes apparent where a person stands. Once a person has fallen so far behind that he realizes he cannot possibly win, he withdraws from competition, and the purpose of the contest is defeated. The more prizes that can be given, the more assurance the sales manager has of maximum participation.

RECOGNITION AND HONOR AWARDS

One of the fundamental principles of good human relations is to give full recognition to individuals who deserve commendation. It is really difficult to give too much recognition to anyone. This is particularly true in reference to sales people, whose personalities often require considerable praise to keep up their morale. Approximately 67 percent of the sales managers responding to the Sales and Marketing Executives survey said that they used honor awards to recognize their salesmen for doing a good job. The nature of the awards and evaluation of their use by respondents is shown in Table 15–2.

The recognition method for stimulating the activities has much to recommend it. It can be used on a continual basis, and it is difficult to overdo. If the recognition system is properly administered, no ill will will be created. To ensure this, the manager must make certain that everyone gets recognized frequently. For example, one company published a monthly sales bulletin in which each salesman in the United States had his sales reported in comparison with his quota, thereby allowing everyone to see just how he stood in comparison with all the other sales people.

TABLE 15–2
Use of honor awards and recognition for sales force

				Ranking by respondents				
	Method	Rating	Total 249	1	2	3	4	5
1.	Titles—"Salesman of the Month," etc.	100	195	92	37	29	18	19
2.	Trophies	67	168	26	45	31	34	32
3.	Congratulations from high-ranking officials	66	176	31	31	34	37	43
4.	Recognition for wives of successful salesmen—flowers, medals, etc.	66	160	31	40	32	27	30
5.	Membership in honorary clubs or organizations	58	129	40	27	22	21	19
6.	Recognition in house publications	55	155	11	29	43	41	31
7.	Pins and rings	34	83	15	19	22	13	14
8.	Certificates, diplomas, etc.	28	100	3	9	20	34	34

Source: Haring and Morris, *Contests, Prizes, Awards for Sales Motivation*, p. 66.

TABLE 15–3
Methods doing most to stimulate average sales person to improve usual or normal performance

				Ranking by respondents				
	Method	Rating	Total 282	1	2	3	4	5
1.	Basic compensation plan	100	243	168	25	22	13	11
2.	Sales contests	62	225	31	52	57	45	26
3.	Bonus payments	47	175	31	54	38	0	1
4.	Honor awards and recognition	37	153	17	27	31	38	24
5.	Friendly, informal relations between salesmen and their immediate supervisors	30	141	9	24	21	39	37
6.	Scientific planning of quotas and territories to assure equal recognition for equal effort expended	25	104	8	23	25	13	24
7.	Fringe benefits	20	99	0	24	23	23	19
8.	Profit sharing plan	19	71	7	15	20	14	13
9.	Vacations with pay	14	71	5	5	14	18	18
10.	Performance of salesmen's positions if performance is satisfactory	6	42	0	4	9	6	12
11.	Suggestion systems	4	27	0	4	2	6	11
12.	Complaint procedures	1	11	0	0	1	1	3
13.	Other	5	17	6	3	2	1	4

Source: Haring and Morris, *Contests, Prizes, Awards For Sales Motivation*, p. 69.

CONCLUSION

To provide a picture of the overall stimulation problem, Table 15–3 presents a summary of actual practices in industry reported in the Sales and Marketing Executives survey in answer to the question: "Which methods will do the most to stimulate the average salesman to do a better job?" Most sales managers agree that the compensation plan is by far the best method. However, it should be recognized that several other classifications, such as bonus payments, vacations with pay, profit sharing, and fringe benefits, could be considered part of the compensation plan. Next in order of importance in actual use are sales contests. However, the classification "friendly informal relations between salesmen and their immediate superiors" ranks almost as high. We believe it should rank far above contests.

QUESTIONS AND PROBLEMS

1. How can a person's self-concept be determined during the selection process?
2. What behavior can be expected from an individual whose real self-concept is far removed from his ideal self-concept and is moving farther away from it each month?
3. How would an administrator locate interesting speakers for sales meetings?
4. Should conventions be held in resort areas or in large central cities?
5. Make up a list of dos and don'ts for managing a sales convention.
6. How can a sales manager design a sales contest that would overcome the tendency for a decline in activity on its termination?
7. How can a manager design a contest to prevent overstocking of dealers or stealing of volume from future periods?
8. What is the best method for equating the chances of everyone to win a contest?
9. In what way would the type of compensation plan in use by a firm affect its use of special incentives?
10. In what circumstances would cash prizes for contests be more advisable than merchandise?

Case 15 –1

POWERTECHNICS
Motivating sales engineers

Mr. Ernest Oaks, sales manager for Powertechnics, had not been impressed with the enthusiasm and vigor with which his sales force had been applying themselves to the tasks at hand. Too many engineers had been coming in late in the morning and going home in the middle of the afternoon. Requests for information from good prospective customers were not being followed up promptly. Negotiations with customers seemed to drag on far too long. The breaking point came when a sales engineer reported that he had failed to get a large contract from an appliance manufacturer. To Mr. Oaks's thinking, the engineer should have been downhearted about his loss, but he wasn't. It did not seem to make any difference to him.

Powertechnics was a large manufacturer of electrical motors of sizes up to 1 horsepower. The firm was noted for its excellent engineering on extremely small electrical motors. It was represented in the field by 65 electrical engineers who called directly on manufacturers of equipment using small electrical motors.

The sales engineers were paid a straight salary, with all expenses reimbursed by the company. The salaries were reviewed each year to reward meritorious performance. In practice, these salary reviews were routine adjustments for cost-of-living increases, plus an increment to reflect the rep's continued tenure with the company. Thus salaries reflected seniority more than anything else.

Management felt that the nature of the sales job precluded paying the engineers an incentive for getting business. Each rep performed much nonselling work, and several reps were usually involved in any substantial sale. Moreover, it might take several years of effort before a sales engineer would be able to get Powertechnic's motors into some large manufacturer's products.

Nevertheless, Mr. Oaks strongly felt that much of what he was seeing resulted from a lack of incentive pay. He proposed to change it. Hereafter, all money that would normally go into salary increases would be put into an incentive fund for use in proding the reps to great effort. The fund for the coming year would be about $100,000.

Mr. Oaks proposed to use those funds in a variety of ways to stimulate activity. He had in mind such things as:

- Giving a $200 bonus for every contract the sales engineer produced.
- Paying $20 for every prospect information lead procured from the firm's advertising.

- Giving $200 each week to the sales engineer who, in Oaks's opinion, had been hustling the most.
- Giving tickets to sporting events as rewards for any meritorious effort observed by Oaks.

As Oaks put it, "I want $100,000 to spread around among the people I see who deserve it."

Question

1. What should Ernest Oaks do in this situation?

Case 15–2
LARA LEE DESIGNS
Work or play?

It was to be Jane Cookson's first national sales meeting since she had been hired as national sales manager of Lara Lee Designs, manufacturers and distributors of costume jewelry.

The line was sold directly to large retailing chains and department stores through the efforts of 41 sales representatives who handled it exclusively. Since Lara Lee products were well accepted by the market, the reps' earnings were high. The average rep made $43,000 in 1977 from the 5 percent commission. The reps paid their own expenses.

In the late winter each year, the company had held a national sales meeting in Palm Springs, California, at which the designs for the coming season were introduced. Other work was also done at the meeting to improve the sales force's performance. Normally, these meetings lasted for five days. The sales reps (all of whom, except three, were men) met in the mornings, played golf in the afternoon, and played young in the evening. A good time was had by most, and the semiannual meetings were eagerly looked forward to by the sales force.

Jane Cookson had studied the records of the previous meetings and thought little of them. "They are an expensive bash at the company's expense. Those guys go out there and drink it up for five days. We sell costume jewelry, not golf clubs," she told Lara Lee, the company's founder.

"What do you propose to do about it?" Lara Lee asked. Cookson replied, "This year we will meet here in Providence for two days, during which we will work their tails off. Then if they want to go play golf, they can catch the next plane for Miami or wherever."

"You know that they do pay their own way to the meetings. We only pay for our costs and the parties we throw for them," Lee said. Cookson nodded and went on to lay out the detailed plan for the two-day sales meeting. Lee said little during the presentation, but suggested that Jane should seek some reviews of her plan by some of the key sales reps.

That afternoon the New York sales rep was in the office so Cookson laid out the whole plan to him. He laughed and said, "That looks great if you like being alone. There's no way you're going to get this crowd to Providence in January. They've been working hard and want to play a bit. You are asking for a lot of trouble with this plan."

Jane countered, "What are the women supposed to do while you guys are playing golf and boozing it up?" She did not like the rep's answer, which was, "Well, that's their problem. They could take up golf and join the gang."

Jane was even more convinced that she had to break up this semi-annual ritual. She proceeded with her plans. When Lara Lee heard of Jane's plans, she was uneasy about them. She wondered what, if anything, she should do.

Question

1. What should Lara Lee do?

Part three

SALES PLANNING

16

Forecasting market demand

Always count the house.
BILLY ROSE

Planning sales force activities begins with a consideration of market potentials and sales forecasting. All plans should be based upon some estimate of the sales volume the firm is likely to realize during a planning period. The sales forecast is the basis of all planning and budgeting.

In establishing sales territories, the sales manager must consider the amount of potential business that exists in each area. Sales quotas that are not based on the potential market available are usually meaningless in evaluating the relative performance of sales representatives. Market analysis techniques are just as important in the administration of the sales force as in planning products, pricing, promotion, and channels of distribution.

DEFINITION OF TERMS

Before explaining quantitative market analysis it is necessary to define some of the terms that will be used. These terms are frequently used interchangeably and in careless fashion. As much as possible the definitions of the American Marketing Association will be followed, although varying interpretations may be made.[1]

---

[1] Committee on Definitions, *Marketing Definitions: A Glossary of Marketing Terms* (Chicago: American Marketing Association, 1960), pp. 15, 20.

411

> *Market potential.*   The expected sales of a commodity, a group of commodities, or a service for an entire industry in a market during a stated period.

> *Sales potential.*   The share of a market potential which a company expects to achieve.

The portion of the total expected sales of an industry which the managers of a firm expect that firm to get is its Sales Potential. By means of marketing research a firm may establish a market potential for the industry of which it is a part. One or more sales forecasts should enable management to determine a sales potential for the firm. From this may be derived the sales budget and a sales quota for the entire company or any part of it.

> *Sales forecast.*   An estimate of dollar or unit sales for a specified future period under a proposed marketing plan or program. The forecast may be for a specified item of merchandise or for an entire line; it may be for a market as a whole or for any portion thereof.

Two sets of factors are involved in making a sales forecast for a firm: (1) forces outside the control of the firm that are likely to influence its sales, and (2) changes in the marketing methods or practices of the firm that are likely to affect its sales.

In the course of planning future activities, the management of a firm may make several sales forecasts, each consisting of an estimate of probable sales if a given marketing plan is adopted or a given set of outside forces prevails. The estimated effects on sales of a number of marketing plans may be compared in the process of arriving at the market program that, in the opinion of management, is best designed to promote the welfare of the firm.

> *Sales quota.*   A sales goal assigned to a marketing unit for use in the management of sales efforts. It applies to a specified period and may be expressed in dollars or in physical units.

A quota may be used in checking the efficiency, stimulating the efforts, or fixing the payment of individual salesmen or groups of salesmen or other personnel engaged in sales work.

A quota may be set for a salesman, a territory, a branch house, or for the company as a whole. It may be different from the sales figure set up in the sales budget. Since it is a managerial device, it is not an immutable figure arrived at by exact statistical formulas, but may be set up with an eye to its psychological effects upon sales personnel. Two sales people, working in territories of identical potentials, may be assigned different quotas because of variation in their sales efforts due to differences in their characters or personalities.

The following two definitions are used frequently in our discussion, though no definitions for them were included in the American Marketing Association's report.

> *Market factor.* A market factor is some reality existent in the market that causes demand for a product. For instance, the market factor behind the demand for dwelling units may be the number of new families formed each year.

> *Market index.* A market index is a mathematical expression of one or more market factors that underlie the demand for a given product. In analyzing the demand for medical service, for example, a market index may be composed of two market factors— population and effective buying income. Frequently, a market factor or index is broken down by geographic areas so that territorial potentials, quotas, or forecasts can be established.

NEED FOR CONSUMER ANALYSIS

Determining the market factors underlying the demand for a product requires a penetrating analysis of consumers and their buying habits. A distinction must be made between the person who actually *buys* the product and the individual who *uses* the product. The market factor usually depends on the individual *for whom the product is intended.* Although women buy a large proportion of men's shirts, still the market potential for men's shirts is determined by the number of men, not by the number of women.

The starting point in any customer analysis is to determine who will use the product and to identify all possible characteristics of the users.

Are they household consumers, industrial users, or both? If they are ultimate household consumers, for example, the seller wants to classify them further by age, sex, marital status, area of residence, income, occupation, religion, education, and possibly several other bases. A manufacturer considered introducing a line of earrings for women with pierced ears. In addition to determining the usual market factors, he had the problem of establishing how many women had pierced ears. This was no easy task, because it was discovered that the incidence of pierced ears was not uniform throughout the population by income groups or geographical regions.

Another aspect of consumer analysis is to determine how rapidly the product in question is used. Many items are consumed daily or weekly, while others may be purchased only once every 10 or 20 years. This rate of usage must be known if the market potential for a period of time is to be calculated.

Suppose there are 60 million homes in the United States and the owners replace the furnace every 20 years. Then the market potential for replacement sales would be roughly 3 million units a year. However, if a firm that made only one type of home heating unit was soliciting a segment of the market that purchased such a unit every 10 years, its market potential would be considerably different.

It is usually important to determine exactly what causes the actual purchase. Many products are purchased as a result of some special event. When people get married they usually buy furniture, appliances, dwelling units, clothes, and many other products. Manufacturers of these products frequently use the marriage rate as the basis for estimating the size of their markets. A manufacturer of baby furniture may base its entire market analysis on births, for these are the events that cause the demand for these products. The establishment of a new business precipitates the demand for numerous items of supplies and equipment.

For certain products that are bought on several occasions or in various amounts during a given period, the analyst must determine the *quantities* the consumers buy. This is particularly important in such things as food, clothing, and most of the convenience goods on the market. It is simply not enough to know who buys and how frequently. Management also must know how much they buy during the period.

DETERMINATION AND USE OF MARKET FACTORS

No analysis of potentials is better than the validity of the market factors on which it is based. If the market factor is not really the cause of demand, or if it includes too many impurities that do not directly affect the potential demand for the product, then the resulting market potential cannot be accurate. Each product has its own characteristics. Many are relatively easy to work with, while others are extremely complex. Analyzing the potential market for an aluminum playpen for babies would be easy compared to evaluating the market for an aluminum ingot producer. Market analysis is more complex if the product is sold to many markets and its demand is caused by numerous factors.

A complete list of possible market factors would be impossible to compile because it would have to encompass every quantitative and qualitative factor existent in society. However, several commonly used market factors can be helpful in a large number of instances. Most of these are widely used, not so much because they precisely measure what the analyst is seeking but because they are the only statistics available. One of the constant disappointments to a researcher is to always be limited by the data available. Often the researcher is forced to accept some substitute measure instead of the exact information wanted.

Unquestionably, good market analysts are familiar with available statistical sources. They know what data are accessible and where to get them. Moreover, they should be perceptive observers of the socio-economic scene, because everything that happens in society affects the demand for things in some way. In a consumers' society, every time someone does anything it creates a demand for something. Thus good market analysis studies the things people do and what they need to do them.

BASIC TECHNIQUES FOR DERIVING POTENTIALS

Although the usual procedure is first to determine the market potential for the commodity and then estimate the portion of that amount that will go to a given brand, it is often more expedient to calculate directly the sales potential for an item. In some cases the market potential and the sales potential may be identical. If a product is truly unique and has no direct competition, the market potential and the sales potential are the same as long as the firm maintains its monopoly. The market potential for electric power in an area is usually identical with the sales potential of the firm that holds the franchise to sell in that region. In other cases, the sales potential may be such an insignificant portion of the market potential that it is useless to deal with the larger figure. The sales potential must be computed directly. One small manufacturer of cotton dresses determined its sales potential from the results of a few test markets. The total market potential for cotton dresses was so large that reference to it was futile in attempting to evaluate the potential sales of this one firm. Its share of the market depended entirely on how well the styles were received each season.

The techniques used for forecasting the demand for either consumer or industrial products are the same. It cannot be said that one market is more complicated to evaluate than another, since it depends entirely on the product. Some industrial products are relatively easy to work with because their end users may be few and identifiable. Other industrial items may go to such diverse markets and are used in such varied ways that their market analysis is most difficult. We have avoided using industrial illustrations in favor of consumer goods because the nature of the market for the consumer article is easier to understand.

The four fundamental techniques for determining market and sales potentials for a product are market factor derivation, correlation analysis, survey of buyer intentions, and test markets. In addition, a new technique, biofeedback, is emerging.

Market factor derivation

The market factor derivation method for determining the size of a potential market begins with the market factor. By eliminating various segments of the market, an estimate of the number of people who would purchase the product is finally derived.

A manufacturer of baby playpens discovered over the years that he sold 16 playpens for every 1,000 births in the United States. Using births as a market factor, he directly computed his sales forecast as follows:

> Estimated number of births, 1978: 3,300,000
> Rate of sale: 16 per 1,000
> Sales forecast for 1978: 52,800 playpens

An independent supermarket operator in Nashville, Tennessee, computed his sales potential by using as his market factor *Sales Marketing & Management's* estimate of food sales ($375,039,000) in that city.[2] He did not sell to the entire area but appealed only to a region in which about 15 percent of the population resided. So he estimated his market potential to be about $56 million. Since three other large supermarkets plus some smaller stores competed in that

---

[2] "Survey of Buying Power," *Sales & Marketing Management,* October 25, 1976, p. 58.

same area, he set 20 percent as his probable share of the market. Therefore, his sales potential was $11 million for the year.

Nashville food sales	$375,039,000
Times: Percent of market covered	× .15
Company market potential	$ 56,255,850
Times: Market share	× .20
Sales potential	$ 11,251,170

This market factor derivation technique for determining market and sales potentials has several advantages. First, the face validity of the method is high—that is, individuals can follow the logic of it without a knowledge of statistics or marketing research. The method is usually founded on some valid statistics that have relatively little error. This is in direct contrast to two methods described later—the survey of buyer intentions and the test-market methods—in which the basic foundations of the processes can be criticized. Another favorable aspect of this technique is that it is relatively simple, requires little statistical analysis, and is relatively inexpensive to use. The wise market analyst usually starts with this technique and goes to others only when forced to in order to get an acceptable figure.

The major weakness of the method is that frequently the bases on which segments of the total are eliminated are only estimates. No accurate data may exist for determining what portion of the total figures will be in the market for the product.

Correlation analysis

The correlation analysis method for deriving market potentials is closely related to the market factor method except for the mathematical processes utilized. In correlation analysis, the variation of the market factor is correlated with variation in demand for the product under study, and a resulting mathematical relationship is evolved. This method can be used only when a sales history of either the industry or the firm is available, because correlation is merely a mathematical analysis of the relationship between the variations in different series of data. If the sales history is for the industry, the resultant estimating equation will give the market potential. But, if the sales history is for the firm, the estimating equation will yield the sales potential.

One of the major virtues of this method is that its final result is a seemingly accurate estimating equation. Into this equation the executive may insert an estimate of the market factor and obtain an apparently precise estimate of the product's demand. However, great care must be taken in using this technique. Unlike many fields in which a correlation of ±.50 or ±.60 is considered highly significant, in market analysis a coefficient of ±.90 or better is frequently needed to obtain a useful working estimating equation.

Probably the biggest drawback to correlation analysis is that the average sales manager does not understand what is being done and therefore tends to regard its results with a degree of suspicion. This is particularly true in cases that require multiple correlation and various curvilinear measures of relationship. Although the market analyst may thoroughly understand the procedure, other executives must accept the results strictly on faith. Another limitation to the use of correlation analysis is that few organizations have competent statistical personnel available, and few sales managers are able to compute a coefficient of correlation.

Surveys of buyer intentions

The survey of buyer intentions technique for determining potentials consists of contacting potential customers and questioning them with the hope of determining whether or not they would purchase the product at the price asked.

One businessman contemplating the production of an aluminum playpen for babies used this technique. The playpen was to be made exactly like the ordinary wooden playpens on the market, except that aluminum tubing would be used instead of the wooden bars. Since the cost of the unit would be higher than the wooden units, he wanted to know, first, how many people would buy such a product if it were placed on the market at the retail price of $29.95, and second, what the consumers thought such a product should sell for.

A survey was conducted through personal interviews with 240 mothers of infants. The results showed that 170 of the 240 (approximately 71 percent) would be interested in such a product. However, they indicated that the price would have to be $19.95 to capture that size market. The average (mean) price quoted was $22.50, but this price would eliminate half of the respondents who showed interest in the product. At the retail price of $29.95, only ten women said they would be interested in purchasing the product. Although it is extremely doubtful that all ten of these women would buy the product if it were placed on the market, still, using that figure only about 4 percent of the market would be interested in it at $29.95.

Since the survey indicated that only about one third of all child-bearing families purchase playpens at all, this would indicate that the total market potential for aluminum playpens would not be more than approximately 50,000 units at best. This figure was derived by dividing the total number of births per year, 4 million, by 3 and taking 4 percent of the result. Actually this rough calculation glosses over some of the other factors that existed in the situation. However, it served the purpose because it showed the manufacturer that market interest in the playpen was sufficient to warrant further investigation. He had established previously that he would be satisfied if he sold only 5,000 units a year, and this seemed possible on the basis of the survey.

One motion-picture exhibiting chain wanted to know the potential market for a closed-circuit system for showing first-run movies on television screens in the home. Interviews were conducted with a selected sample of families in the particular city where the service was to be inaugurated. The results indicated that, ultimately, about 50 percent of the market would be interested in such a system. However, the responses on the interviews led the investigators to believe that initially only about 10 percent of the market would subscribe to the system. The remaining 40 percent would wait to see the results of the system before committing themselves. On the basis of this survey, the movie exhibitor decided that sufficient market potential was available in that city to warrant operations.

One major disadvantage of this method lies in its cost and time-consuming execution. For the sales manager who must quickly get some idea of the market potential of a product, the survey method is not suitable. One businessman spent $1,500 for a small survey consisting of 24 depth interviews. His problem was of such a narrow nature and so limited in scope that these 24 interviews were all that were needed. Even so, the project took three months to complete. For the manufacturer who intends to distribute on a national basis, consumer surveys can easily run into the thousands of dollars and take three to six months for completion.

It is generally recognized that surveys of buying intentions are hazardous undertakings. It is easy for the respondent to say that he or she would buy a certain product, but the acid test is whether or not the person is willing to spend money to back up those stated intentions. Such surveys are widely used in industry today.

Often, a survey is the only practical way to estimate the size of a market. The motion-picture exhibitor in the example had no other way to approach the problem, since no data were available on which to base any correlation analysis or market factor derivation. Often, the survey method is employed to determine the various percentages used in a market factor derivation.

Test markets

Although they take considerable time and money, test markets are probably the most accurate method available for estimating the sales potential for certain products. The reason is that a test market actually requires the buyers to spend their money, and this is the acid test of most marketing situations. All the other methods discussed require at some time or another in the calculation some estimate of what share of the market the product will achieve. Frequently, these estimates are merely guesses. The test market eliminates this guessing. Many factors are involved in the careful control of the test-market situation, and it is not within the scope of this book to discuss the detailed administration of market testing. It is assumed that management has properly controlled the conditions surrounding the test market. However, this is no easy task.

The International Minerals and Chemical Company, manufacturer of a brand of monosodium glutemate called Ac'cent, used a test market to estimate the size of Ac'cent's consumer market. The product had been selling successfully to food processors and institutional markets for some time, but had not been sold to housewives. There was considerable uncertainty over how the product would be received by the consumer. It was impossible to use any of the other methods and still obtain an intelligent estimate of the market size, so the firm chose to undertake a market test of the situation.

For a period of three months, the product was distributed and promoted in Peoria, Illinois, under conditions approximating those that would be employed in other areas should the product be nationally marketed. After the test period, the company determined that a total of 37 percent of the families in Peoria had tried the product. Of the 37 percent that had tried Ac'cent, only 25 percent of them had purchased the product a second time. In other words, about 9 percent of the total number of families in Peoria were repeat purchasers of its product. It was estimated that the average users consumed the product at the rate of one-half pound per year. Applying these results to the national scene, it was then estimated that the sales potential for Ac'cent was approximately 1.8 million pounds per year to the consumer market. This figure was obtained by using 40 million families as a basic market factor, taking 9 percent of that as the number of repeat buyers of the product, and then multiplying the answer (3.6 million) times the half pound of usage per family. This placed the consumer market in its proper perspective, since the firm had been selling considerably more than that to the industrial market. It was obvious that although a substantial market existed for Ac'cent at the consumer level, it was still no bonanza. While it is granted that a three-month test period unduly restricts the chances for the product to gain a wider market by word-of-mouth advertising, many factors in a test situation bias the results in the other direction.

The one obvious advantage of the test market technique is that it directly results in a sales potential for products under consideration. It is unfortunate, however, that the test market requires a considerable amount of effort and time before its results are known. Many products that require extensive investment in fixed assets before any output is developed cannot be evaluated by this method, since most of the risks have been taken before the answers are known. The test market is used mainly when a relatively small number of units can be produced at a minimum cost, so that the size of the market can be estimated before any sizable amount of money is invested in one venture. Test markets may provide poor evaluations of products that require time to gain market acceptance or have a low rate of consumption.

Biofeedback

Some experimental and rather innovative forecasting techniques are being developed by a few researchers. Biofeedback is one such method which seems to hold promise for a few selected applications.

One forecaster in Dallas, Texas, has had great success at forecasting the sale of individual phonograph records, previously an almost impossible task. The music is played to people in a laboratory who are connected to various biofeedback instruments, and the investigator thus determines their biological reactions to it. The assumption that mental processes are somehow reflected biologically has been well established in the psychological literature. A researcher compares the biological reactions of the sample who listen to the new music with benchmark data on the reactions of people who were measured listening to other music whose sales volume is known. From these results the researcher develops a sales forecast index by which the appeal of the new record can be compared to that of previous records.

This technique is in its infancy. It holds great promise for the forecasting of sales of new products and those with strong fashion factors.

TERRITORIAL POTENTIALS

After the total sales potential has been determined, the sales manager usually wants to divide it among the various territorial divisions in order to allocate selling efforts properly and to evaluate the relative performance of each district. The usual method for accomplishing this is to use some pertinent market factor or index broken down by small areas.

Various data such as population, retail and wholesale sales, births, industrial activity, and, in general, most of the data included in the national census are available by counties. *Sales & Marketing Management's* annual "Survey of Buying Power" is primarily designed to aid the executive in allocating activities among areas. Data are furnished on each county and many cities in North America. Most managers find some appropriate figure which can be used to apportion the sales potentials.

One manufacturer of women's ready-to-wear whose total sales potential had been set at $25 million for 1977 divided it among territories as shown in Table 16–1. For convenience of illustration, the territories have been slightly regrouped to coincide with the census divisions.

TABLE 16–1

Division of sales potential among territories using retail sales as a market index

Territory	Percentage of total retail sales*	Territorial sales potential $25M × Col. 1 ÷ 100
New England	5.5	$ 1,375,000
Middle Atlantic	15.3	3,825,000
East North Central	19.0	4,750,000
West North Central	7.4	1,850,000
South Atlantic	16.2	4,050,000
East South Central	6.0	1,500,000
West South Central	11.0	2,750,000
Mountain	5.0	1,250,000
Pacific	14.6	3,650,000
	100.0	$25,000,000

*From "Survey of Buying Power," *Sales & Marketing Management*, October 25, 1976.

SALES FORECASTING

Nature and importance of the sales forecast

After the market or sales potential for the product is established, management can make a sales forecast. This is an essential step in sales planning. While the sales forecast and the sales potential may be identical in some circumstances, a firm's sales forecast may be less than its sales potential for several reasons. The company's production facilities may not allow it to realize its full potential volume; the concern may not have the distribution organization with which to sell to all of its potential market; or for profit reasons or financial limitations the firm may decide to forego the full realization of its potential sales. Thus, the sales executive should differentiate between sales potential and actual forecast of sales.

The sales forecast is the foundation of all planning and budgeting. From it production, personnel, finance, and all other departments plan their work and determine their requirements for the coming period. If the forecast is in error, so will the plans based on it be. If it is unduly optimistic, the organization can suffer great losses because of overexpenditures of funds in anticipation of revenues that are not forthcoming. If the sales forecast is too low, the firm may not be prepared to sell what the market requires, thus foregoing profits and presenting its competitors with additional sales and an opportunity to gain market share.

Sales forecasting periods

Sales forecasts are commonly made for periods of three months, six months, or one year. For purposes of this discussion, forecasts for periods of less than a year will be considered short term, those for a year will be treated as the normal sales forecast or the fiscal period forecast, and estimates for longer periods will be considered long term. In actual practice, the traditional yearly forecast becomes a short-term one as it is modified every month or so as experience indicates.

The sales forecasting period usually coincides with the firm's fiscal period, since it is used as a basis for planning fiscal operations. When the forecast depends to a great extent on *estimates* and indexes of future business activities compiled on a yearly basis, it usually is desirable to align the forecasting period correspondingly.

The decision of whether the forecast should be made for periods of less than a year usually depends on the nature of business in which the firm is engaged. In many lines of endeavor, activity is so volatile that any estimate of sales beyond a few months is highly questionable, because it may be impossible to look intelligently that far into the future.

Some firms find that their conversion cycle of operations is considerably shorter than a year and prefer to forecast for that cycle. In the apparel trades, normally there are four conversion cycles per year. The firms produce goods for one season and then completely sell out those goods before starting the next season's work. They are concerned only with the coming season's activity, since they are buying goods and labor for that period only.

In operations where a high degree of accuracy is mandatory in the forecast, a short time period often is advisable, since greater accuracy usually can be obtained. It is usually easier to forecast for the coming month than for the coming year.

Many firms prepare more than one forecast. In addition to the fiscal period estimate on which the entire budgeting procedure is based, they also undertake monthly or quarterly forecasts to get closer control over operations. Should these short-run estimates indicate considerable divergence between the fiscal forecast and the actual level of activity, revisions would be made in the annual forecast and its resulting budgetary allotments.

Long-run sales estimates are usually undertaken for purposes of planning capital expenditures. It is not unusual to find that top management wants to know something about the long-run outlook for sales before it undertakes any plant expansion. While these composites are frequently called sales forecasts, in reality they more closely resemble sales potentials. That is, they usually measure only the market opportunity for the firm's products, and do not take into consideration the impact of the marketing programs.

Factors influencing probable sales volume

The sales forecast must take into consideration many factors other than quantitative statistics. The forecaster must analyze four major areas:

Conditions within the company.

Conditions within the industry.

Conditions in the market for output.

General business conditions.

Conditions within the company.   Any changes in the price structure, channels of distribution, promotional plans, products, or other internal marketing policies may influence future sales, and the forecaster must estimate the quantitative extent of this influence. It maybe known, for example, that the firm soon will have to raise prices. Although this action would reduce unit volume, total dollar volume might go up or down, depending on the product's price elasticity. Therefore, it is impossible to formulate a realistic sales forecast without taking into consideration the future price of the product. If the firm had plans for widening the distribution of its products or otherwise altering its channels of distribution, such an action would have an influence on future sales.

There may be plans for altering the advertising program or the selling organization. If advertising expenditures are to be increased and a new campaign is being undertaken, the sales manager may have a good reason for believing that the sales forecast should be increased. If additional salesmen are to be put into the field, that also probably will result in increased sales volume.

Additions to the product line or product changes also have a direct bearing on future sales. If the company has recently redesigned its products or has added some new items, the sales forecast should take into consideration these changed conditions.

Conditions within the industry. A firm obtains its sales volume from total industry sales. Therefore, any change within the industry has a direct impact on the firm. If competitive conditions within the industry change through either a variation in the number of firms competing or a change in their activities, such as advertising, selling, or product design, the future sales volume of the company will be affected. New producers in an industry may mean that whatever volume they gain must come from existing companies. Thus, the sales forecast may have to be revised downward. If it is known that a competitor is planning to redesign its line of products, the possibility that it may obtain a larger share of the market during the coming period must be considered. There also must be some regard for change in competitors' price policies. Since price is an important factor directly affecting the distribution of markets among firms, a survey of price policies can be extremely critical.

Changed market conditions. If basic demand factors are in a slump, the future sales of the firm will be affected. The firm's manager must be aware of any basic changes in the primary demand for the industry's output. Such changes may not be apparent by market analysis based on the past rather than on the future. An analysis of future market conditions is particularly important if the concern sells to relatively few industries.

Mor Flo, a manufacturer of solar water heaters, saw its sales potential suddenly multiply several fold when the nation suffered shortages of natural gas. And, as the price of gasoline soared, the sales potentials for the makers of compact cars expanded significantly.

General business conditions. A major influencing factor in future sales development is the general state of the economy. Basically, many of the methods of sales forecasting are simply reflections of overall opinion or calculation of what the general business activity of the economy will be during the coming period. The sales executive must be a competent predictor of future business conditions in order to be an able sales forecaster. This involves much more than just being familiar with the various indicators of economic activity. It requires considerable understanding of the workings of the economy and a determination to keep abreast of current economic developments.

Needless to say, each forecaster develops favorite indexes to indicate the economic climate. The indicators most frequently used by business forecasters are listed below. Naturally, the group of indexes that *lead* general business conditions pose the greatest interest. Those that *lag* are of little use. A leading index is one whose movement upward or downward precedes—leads—the movement of the factor one is attempting to predict. Examples are:

Leading indexes

Business failures
Common stock price index, Dow-Jones
New orders, durable-goods manufacturing industries, value
Residential building contracts (floor space)
Commerical and industrial building contracts (floor space)
Average workweek, manufacturing
New business incorporations
Index of spot market prices, basic commodities

Simultaneous indexes

Employment in nonagricultural establishments
Unemployment
Bank debits outside New York City
Freight carloadings
Industrial production index (including utilities)
Wholesale price index, excluding farm produce and foods
Corporate profits after taxes
Gross national product, current dollars

Lagging indexes

Personal income
Sales by retail stores
Consumer installment debt (end of month)
Manufacturers' inventories, book value (end of month)
Bank interest rates on business loans (last month of quarter)

Risks in forecasting

Forecasting is subject to some risks the sales manager must understand in order to function efficiently. It is a mistake for a person to use a tool that has limitations of which he is unaware. Placing a 4,000-pound car on a jack designed to hold 3,000 pounds will always be unsatisfactory.

Sales forecasting suffers from the same general drawbacks that plague the computation of market and sales potentials. The degree of accuracy sometimes leaves much to be desired. One study indicated that the average company's sales forecast deviated more than 5 percent from actual results. (See Figure 16–1.) It takes time, money, and qualified personnel to execute a forecast properly. However, sales forecast-

FIGURE 16-1
Average deviation between sales forecast and actual sales volume

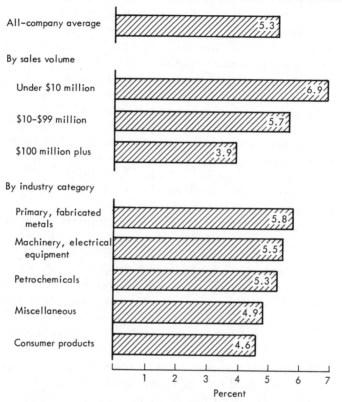

Average deviation between sales forecast and
actual results

Source: "Sales Forecasting: Is 5% Error Good Enough?" *Sales Management,* December 15, 1967, p. 43.

ing is also hampered by some additional factors that are not so directly applicable to potentials, although these limitations can be applied to all planning activities.

Growth elements. One of the problems in forecasting is to anticipate growth rates. There is considerable uncertainty over whether the present rate of growth will continue or begin to level off. The question is whether a turning point will occur in the coming period. Usually, the sales administrator simply estimates a given amount of growth and inserts that decision into the sales forecast.

The most common mistake made in this regard is the forecasting of sales for a product whose sales have grown rapidly for several years.

There is a tendency for the forecaster to assume that the product's growth rate will continue, but experience indicates that growth rates usually plateau—the rate of growth decreases with time.

Sales history. Most of the techniques of sales forecasting depend on the existence of a sales history for their base, and without this history forecasting is hazardous. Sales forecasting for a new product is risky because without past sales to use as a benchmark, it is difficult to determine what share of the market it will capture.

However, the existence of a long sales history can lead to a false sense of security. It is not unknown for products with a long, stable sales history to suddenly have their sales patterns altered drastically. For decades the sales of Bon Ami were as dependable as anyone could want; it was a household staple. Then suddenly it was pushed out of the market by new products. The past does not automatically predict the future.

Fashion. A fashion element in the firm's products inserts considerble risk into any prediction of future sales. They depend entirely on how well the market receives the style the firm plans to sell. The experience of most industries has been that if the style catches on and becomes fashion, all forecasts were too conservative, and if the style proves unpopular, all forecasts were too optimistic. It is difficult to predict whether or not a given style will prove acceptable to the consumer. Unfortunately for the market analyst, fashion is becoming increasingly important in many industries.

Psychological factors. If psychological factors are important in the demand for a product, the manager faces a rather sizable forecasting problem. Measuring the psychological attitude of the market is difficult. This factor is fleeting in nature and can upset the prediction in times of economic stress. Almost overnight, consumer psychology can change from confidence to apprehensiveness about the future. A war scare could immediately cause a tremendous jump in the demand for tires and new automobiles, for example.

Methods of sales forecasting

Any of the following basic methods may be used to forecast the future sales of a product:
- Executive opinion.
- Sales force composite.
- Users' expectations.
- Projection of trends.
- Analysis of market factors.

The sales manager is not faced with the choice of which method to use so much as he must determine in which one to place the most faith. Some sales executives may use several methods in an attempt to get a good picture of the situation. The theory is that if they should all convey approximately the same results, more confidence could be placed in the findings. However, if widely divergent estimates are obtained, a deeper investigation of the situation is needed. Since the sales forecast is so important, most managers consider the multiple-method approach to be sound policy.

Executive opinion. The executive opinion method of forecasting sales is the oldest and simplest technique known. It consists of obtaining the views of top executives regarding their beliefs about future sales. These executive opinions may or may not be supported by facts. Some administrators may have used certain methods of forecasting to arrive at their opinions. Others may have formed their estimates largely by observation and intuition.

The major advantages cited for this technique are that it is quick and easy to do. The disadvantages attributed to it are more numerous and considerably more potent. First, many businessmen consider it to be a highly unscientific method of operating, since it is little more than a premeditated practice of group guessing. Most of the opinions brought into the conference are based not on fact but, on personal feelings about future business conditions.

Second, it is unwise to bring into the sales forecasting system anyone who is not closely associated with sales activity. What would a production manager, for example, know about future sales? The jury of executive opinion may waste the time of executives who have no business being involved in the process.

Another disadvantage is that any breakdown of the sales forecast by products, customers, or other marketing units for operating and controlling purposes is difficult to make if the sales estimate has not been compiled from basic market statistics.

Some managers claim that executive opinion should be used in the absence of external or internal data on which to base the forecast. It may be the only feasible means of forecasting sales. This is another way of saying that use of the executive opinion method is better than no sales forecast at all. This may be so, but it is rather unlikely that no internal or external data would be available.

Nevertheless, executive opinion remains the method used by most small- and medium-sized companies. Usually the boss and the sales manager get together, study all the factors known to them, and come up with their guess as to what sales will be for the coming year.

The Delphi technique. A highly publicized technique developed at Rand Corporation for predicting the future, called the Delphi technique, is little more than a jury of expert opinion. In administering a Delphi forecast a panel of "experts" is selected. Then each expert is asked to make a prediction on some matter. The resulting range of forecasts is then fed back to the experts. Then they are asked once again to make another prediction on the same matter, with the knowledge of what all the other experts have reported. This process is repeated until the experts arrive at some consensus of opinion.

This technique could well be used in sales forecasting.

Sales force composite.   The sales force composite approach begins by collecting from each sales person an estimate of the future sales of various products in his territory. Usually the sales reps are provided with appropriate forms to aid them in making their estimates. These estimates may be made in consultation with some sales executive or compiled without assistance.

The total sales forecast for the firm is a composite of the individual forecasts of each sales person. If all sales people do not forecast their sales accurately, it is not likely that their individual errors will cancel out and allow an accurate forecast to evolve. It is more likely that some common bias will cause errors in one direction. Any such bias is magnified many times over in the final forecast.

In certain situations, however, this method of forecasting sales can be accurate. It can be used most fruitfully when the sales force consists of high-caliber sales reps who are competent to do this type of work. The nature of the market also plays an important role in their forecasting ability. If they sell to relatively few accounts, they probably can furnish more reliable forecasts than if they are selling to many small customers.

General Electric uses this technique for forecasting the sales of its various industrial products. The salesmen are required to complete a form on the available business from key-market customers. They frequently get together with customers and go over their needs for the various products sold by General Electric, which are itemized on the order blank. Not only does the form require the rep to make an estimate of the total available business—the market potential—but an estimate must be made of GE's share of that business.

Considerable work is involved in the completion of such forms. This is definitely a nonselling activity, and care must be taken that it does not intrude on the sales person's time to such an extent that his selling effectiveness is impaired.

The Conference Board has summarized the advantages and disadvantages of this method as follows:[3]

---

[3] The Conference Board, *Forecasting Sales*, Studies in Business Policy, No. 106 (New York, 1964), p. 21.

Advantages

1. Uses specialized knowledge of men closest to the market.
2. Places responsibility for forecast in the hands of those who must produce the results.
3. Gives sales force greater confidence in quotas developed from forecasts.
4. Tends to give results greater stability and accuracy because of the magnitude of the sample.
5. Lends itself to the easy development of product, territory, customer, or salesmen breakdowns.

Disadvantages

1. Salesmen are poor estimators, being either too optimistic or too pessimistic as conditions warrant.
2. If estimates are used as a basis for setting quotas, salesmen are inclined to understate the demand in order to make the goal easier to achieve.
3. Salesmen are often unaware of broad economic patterns which are shaping future sales and are thus incapable of forecasting trends for extended periods.
4. Method requires an extensive expenditure of time by executives and sales force.

Users' expectations.   Some industrial concerns forecast sales by asking their customers for information on expected purchases for the forthcoming period. This technique is limited to those situations in which relatively few, well-identified potential customers are in the picture. In such situations, the product being sold may be so unique that no other information is available on which to base a sales forecast. A manufacturer of small, four-cycle engines sold to power lawn mower manufacturers found this method to be the best forecasting technique. A maker of garden tractors sold exclusively to mail-order houses forecast solely on the basis of its customers' announced buying plans.

Users can be contacted by telephone, mail, or in person, but far more satisfying results have been obtained by personally interviewing responsible members of the customer's management.

The Conference Board summarized the advantages and disadvantages of this method[4] by listing them as follows:

Advantages

1. Bases forecast on information obtained direct from product users, whose buying actions will actually determine sales.
2. Gives forecaster a subjective feel of the market and of the thinking behind users' buying intentions.

---

[4] Ibid., p. 31.

3. Bypasses published or other indirect sources, enabling the inquiring company to obtain its information in the form and detail required.
4. Offers a possible way of making a forecast where other methods may be inadequate or impossible to use—e.g., forecasting demand for a new industrial product for which no previous sales record is available.

Disadvantages

1. Is difficult to employ in markets where users are numerous or not easily located.
2. Depends on the judgment and cooperation of product users, some of whom may be ill-informed or uncooperative.
3. Bases forecast on expectations, which are subject to subsequent change.
4. Requires considerable expenditure of time and manpower.

Projection of trends. The projection of past sales trends can be used for making both long-term and short-run forecasts. No discussion of estimating general business conditions through the use of trend analysis is undertaken here because it is felt that such procedures are not sound. Throughout this discussion, the word *cycle* has been studiously avoided, since it connotes a regularity in future business activity that simply does not exist. Future business activity is determined by various economic and social factors and political decisions being made at present, and it is illogical to forecast sales on the basis of cyclical trend analysis. The experience of our economy in the past 20 years should be more than sufficient to demonstrate the risks of predicting by a trend analysis any estimate of sales for a given year.

The short-run forecasting technique based on adjusting present sales behavior by a seasonal index is little more than a mathematical formula to determine what the present sales picture means when projected into the future for a month or so. It is successful because over a period of a few months few economic events can affect its accuracy to a significant degree. Unfortunately, such extremely short-run forecasts are not too useful for the fiscal planning activities most firms find necessary. It is definitely unwise to attempt a yearly sales forecast on the basis of seasonal behavior. However, for monthly or quarterly forecasts it has proved to be accurate in many instances.

Analysis of market factors. As noted previously, future sales depend on the future behavior of the factors that determine the product's demand. From a scientific point of view, the most valid method for approaching the problem of forecasting sales is by estimation of the behavior of the market factors that underlie demand for the product. Once the forecast of market factors is made, it can be mathematically translated into sales volume. There are two basic procedures for making this translation, direct derivation and correlation analysis, both of which were discussed in the section on market potentials.

EXAMPLES OF APPLICATION OF FORECASTING METHODS

In this section, the use of several methods for forecasting sales will be applied to various problems, for illustrative purposes.

Long-run projection of trend

The sales history for Richard D. Irwin, Inc., from 1964 to 1973 and the calculations for extrapolating that trend to 1974 are shown in Table 16–2. The resulting trend line is shown in Figure 16–2. Note how well the line fits the past sales history. Using the least squares method for forecasting a sales trend, it would be estimated that the sales for Richard D. Irwin, Inc., for 1974 would be $15.2 million.

TABLE 16–2
Sales forecasting, long-run extrapolation of sales by least squares

RICHARD D. IRWIN, INC.

Year	X (times)	Sales (in millions)
1964	−9	$ 4.8
1965	−7	5.8
1966	−5	6.9
1967	−3	8.1
1968	−1	8.6
1969	1	9.9
1970	3	11.6
1971	5	11.6
1972	7	12.7
1973	9	14.7
1974	11	

$$N = 10$$
$$\Sigma Y = 94.7$$
$$\Sigma XY = 172.7$$
$$\Sigma X^2 = 330.$$

$$a = \frac{\Sigma Y}{N} = \frac{94.7}{10} = 9.47$$

$$b = \frac{\Sigma XY}{\Sigma X^2} = \frac{171.8}{330} = 0.52$$

$$Y = 9.47 + 0.52\,(X)$$

Forecast for 1974 would be:
$$9.47 + 0.52\,(11) = \$15.2 \text{ million.}$$

FIGURE 16–2
Projection of sales trend by least squares method, 1964–1974

RICHARD D. IRWIN, INC.

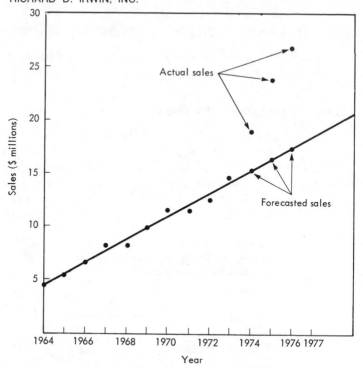

The major fear that haunts the forecaster using such trend projections is that at some time in the future the trend will change. Seldom
can a company maintain such a constant growth pattern. The usual
experience is that the growth of the firm will taper off sometime, but
the forecaster is never certain when that plateau will start to form.

A pleasant development, but also embarrassing to the forecaster,
occurred for Richard D. Irwin Inc. Sales in 1974, 1975, and 1976 were
$19 million, $24 million, and $29 million, respectively. Suddenly, the
past sales history no longer forecast the future. A new relationship
seemed to exist. So it is with using history to forecast the future; relationships can break down at any time. Solid forecasting requires an
appraisal of the behavior of the critical market factors that determine
the firm's demand.

Short-run projection of trend

The monthly distribution of sales as a percentage of the total annual
sales for a men's apparel retail store is shown in Table 16–3, along with

TABLE 16–3
Short-run extrapolation of sales

MEN'S RETAIL APPAREL STORE

Month's sales as a percentage of annual sales based on 10 years' experience		1977 sales	1978 forecast ($364,000 annual sales)
January	6.4%		$23,000
February	4.8		17,000
March	6.1		22,000
April	6.9		
May	7.1		
June	5.0		
July	5.7		
August	9.2		
September	12.2		
October	10.5	$37,000	
November	12.1	43,000	
December	14.0	51,000	
	100.0%		

the calculations for extrapolating sales for the next three months' operations.

The October sales of $37,000 would indicate an annual rate of sales of $352,000 ($37,000/0.105); November sales would indicate an annual rate of $355,000 ($43,000/0.121); and the December rate of sales would be $364,000 a year ($51,000/0.14). If the sales for the last three months are totaled and divided by the sum of the percentages for those months ($131,000/0.37), an average annual rate of sales of $354,000 is obtained. At this point the forecaster must do some subjective evaluation of those months' sales to select which base might be best to use to forecast the coming months' sales. If there is good reason to believe that the annual rate of sales is increasing as the data indicate, the forecaster might decide that the most valid annual rate would be the one for December ($364,000). Perhaps a venturesome forecaster might even project that increasing annual rate of sales and base the January or even the first-quarter forecast on some annual rate even larger than the one for December. It is just a matter of judgment.

If, for some reason, the forecaster felt that the December rate of sales was not typical or not what could be expected in January or the first quarter of the year, he might decide to use the average rate of sales for the last quarter of the year. The forecaster who makes such judgments looks at such minute things as the weather, the actual number of selling days each month (one or two more selling days per month make a big difference in the month's sales), or any other irregular factor that might have affected sales.

Assume that no such undue irregular factors were perceptible in this instance. Using the December rate of sales of $364,000, the forecast for January would be about $23,300 ($364,000 × 0.064 = $23,296). The sales forecast for the first quarter would be about $63,000 ($364,000 × 0.173 = $62,972).

It is important to understand the premises upon which such forecasting is based. First, it is assumed that a fairly reliable seasonal index is available. The method cannot be used if such an index cannot be developed. Second, it is assumed that the annual rate of sales will not change drastically in the short run. This is usually a fairly valid assumption, but there are times when it may prove to be false. Sudden turns in world events or domestic crises may jolt sales one way or the other, but such developments may invalidate all forecasts.

Market factor derivation method

Direct market factor derivations take many routes; some are short and direct, while others are circuitous. It depends on the situation.

We will examine a short derivation first. A patio door manufacturer had determined that sales were directly related to the number of new dwelling units built. Research had shown that the firm sold 7.2 doors for every 1,000 dwelling units started each year. Thus, if the housing experts predicted 2 million units would be built in a coming year, the manufacturer multiplied its 7.2 market participation factor times 2,000 to estimate sales for that year as 14,400 doors. Such short derivations are not at all uncommon when a product's usage is a function of something that can be counted. The consumption of many products is proportional to such things as the number of houses either being built or in existence, the number of automobiles, or the number of people having some demand-affecting characteristic.

Let's use the automobile as the basis of an example of a somewhat more complicated derivation. Suppose Mohawk Tire Company wants to forecast its sales volume for the coming year. It knows that in the areas in which it has distribution, it has a 3 percent share of the replacement market. While excellent data are available on the total number of tires sold in the United States by all tire manufacturers, they are not easily available for selected sections of the country. However, an estimate could be developed from the number of automobiles in each area, a statistic easily ascertained. Several approaches could be used to determine this, such as use of the following formula:

$$\text{Sales forecast} = \frac{\text{No. of autos in Mohawk territory}}{\text{Total no. of autos in U.S.}} \times \frac{\text{Total no. of replacement tires sold in U.S.}}{} \times 0.03$$

Or the forecaster might prefer to build up a forecast along the lines in Figure 16–3. Such derivations are simply a matter of logic. Start with the basic market factor, then operate on it with whatever other factors are relevant to the situation. Logic can be tricky. For example, the subtraction of new-car tire miles might be overlooked or mishandled. Mohawk does not sell tires to the car manufacturers, so this share

FIGURE 16–3
Sales Forecast

MOHAWK TIRE COMPANY

Total autos in Mohawk distribution areas	40,000,000
Times: Average miles driven in year	× 10,000
Equals: Total auto miles in area	400,000,000,000
Times: Four	× 4
Equals: Tire miles driven in area	1,600,000,000,000
Minus: Tire miles by new cars	−200,000,000,000
Equals: Replacement tire miles	1,400,000,000,000
Divided by: Average mileage per tire	÷ 20,000
Equals: Number of replacement tires	70,000,000
Times: Percent of market share	× .03
Equals: Mohawk sales forecast	2,100,000

Note: All figures are hypothetical.

of the market must be excluded from the company's forecast. However, new cars on the road for an average of only six months rather than the full year, so that must be allowed for in their mileage. One bit of logic is missing from the above example, for the sake of simplicity—the spare tire. When a new car owner has to replace the original set of tires, only three tires are needed, not four. Such an adjustment to the figures could be made.

Correlation analysis

Certainly correlation analysis ranks as the most powerful analytical tool available to the forecaster because it determines in a fairly precise way the mathematical relationships between series of data. In sales forecasting, one series, the dependent variable, is the sales of the product or firm being studied. The other series may be any one or several market factors the forecaster feels affect sales.

The widespread usage of the computer has caused a rather significant change in this section of the book. Previously a rather lengthy correlation analysis was illustrated, complete with the computations of the correlations and estimating equations. Such methods are now outdated by the computer. The packaged programs available for computer usage make the computation of complex multiple correlations simple. Moreover, business students are now being exposed to correlation and regression techniques in the quantitative courses they must take.

SOME GUIDING PRINCIPLES FOR FORECASTING

A number of principles on which to base market demand forecasting are discussed in this section.[5]

Minimize the number of market factors

In market analysis, simplicity has great virtue. The larger the number of market factors on which an analysis is based, the more difficult it is to determine exactly what it is that affects the demand for a product. Often the inclusion of many factors in a market index only results in the duplication of a few basic forces. One drug manufacturer computed a market index from the following factors: (1) number of drugstores, (2) population, (3) number of physicians, (4) income, (5) number of hospital beds, and (6) number of people older than 65. Actually, this market index essentially was based on two things— population and income. Several of the supposed market factors were merely surface indicators of these two basic forces. The number of physicians in an area is a reflection of the population and income of that area. Similarly, the number of drugstores and the number of hospital beds usually are largely dependent on population.

Use sound logic

Sound logic is the basis of all good market analysis. In determining and using market factors, essentially all that is required of a market analyst is a keen, logical mind that can trace back and isolate the exact forces that cause the consumption of the product under study. If the logic is faulty, so will the results of the analysis be. To be logical, the analyst must have a fundamentally sound background in economics and marketing theory. It is axiomatic that a good marketing researcher must be first of all a good marketing specialist. One who does not

---

[5] For a collection of illustrative cases on the development of industrial market potentials, see The Conference Board, *Appraising the Market for New Industrial Products,* Studies in Business Policy, No. 123 (New York, 1967).

really understand the marketing process usually will be weak in reasoning out what factors cause the demand for a particular product. Just being a competent statistician is insufficient. The true art is in being able to discern what statistics to collect and use, and this requires marketing acumen.

Use more than one method

The experienced market analyst uses as many of the analysis techniques as possible in order to check one against another. The forecaster usually begins with the market factor derivation method, using several different factors as checks against one another. Then if a correlation analysis is possible, its results are compared with answers obtained previously. If consumer surveys are available that may throw some light on the subject, figures from them are used to check the previous results.

The market analyst can have a bit more confidence in the results if all the estimates of the market potential reasonably agree with one another than if they vary widely. If wide variation occurs in the estimates, more research is needed to validate the work. If there is considerable uncertainty in the estimates, test markets may be undertaken to determine the product's potentialities more accurately.

It is just good research technique to try all the available ways. While exploring the various avenues leading to estimates of the potential, the investigator also gains a better comprehension of the situation. This will greatly facilitate future forecasts for the product.

Use the minimum-maximum technique

Sound research strategy dictates the use of both minimum and maximum estimates in all computations in order to obtain the range of possible variation that can occur when a product is placed on the market. The analyst should work up one set of estimates which assume the worst possible developments in each of the calculations. In doing this, he or she computes the lowest probable potential market for the product. At the same time, he should make an estimate of what the market potential would be should all things be favorable. He also may prepare other estimates, each based on varying assumptions between the two extremes.

Often the researcher constructs graphs to show precisely how a variation in each factor alters the final market potential figure. This helps managers to form their own conclusions about possible courses of action. Of course, it is considerably more work, but it is highly effective in getting a feel of the product's potential market. This technique combined with a break-even analysis shows where in the range of the potentials the company must operate if the venture is to be profitable.

Some firms have developed mathematical models of their sales operations. The various factors that affect their sales volume are incorporated in a formula which is then programmed for computer use. Then the firm's executives can vary each factor at will to determine its probable effect on sales. Such models help the manager gain an overall understanding of the factors that affect the firms sales volume.

Consider each product as different

Companies that market several different products usually find it necessary to undertake a separate analysis for each item or line of products. In its industrial division, General Electric estimates a separate potential figure for each of its lines of products. On its form for estimating such figures, the first five products mentioned are: general-purpose component motor, specialty component motor, specialty transformer, gear motor and transmission components, and small integral motor. The company breaks down its market analysis into these small segments because each is affected by different market factors. Obviously, this can become an exceedingly tedious job for a concern with thousands of products. Large firms of necessity often have large marketing research staffs.

Become familiar with sources of information

No one can be a truly competent marketing researcher without a thorough knowledge of the information available. The analyst must be familiar with all the data available from governmental agencies, standard reference works, universities, private research concerns, trade associations, and general literature.

Understand mathematics and statistics

The determination of market and sales potentials is no work for the statistically and mathematically uninformed. Anyone who makes market analyses should be qualified to handle with facility any statistical problems that may arise. A sales manager should be sufficiently acquainted with statistical techniques to recognize any serious errors in the material presented. The executive with little knowledge of statistics is at the mercy of a faulty statistician and often is unable to perceive discrepancies or errors.

One manufacturer considered making stoves for use on boats. A brief analysis clearly indicated that these stoves would be used only on boats with enclosed cabins. The market analyst assigned the job of determining the market potential for this boat stove came up with a rather substantial figure for the total number of boats in the United States. With such a sizable market potential, the manufacturer went into production. When sales results were disappointing, an investigation showed that the figure for the number of boats included everything from an 8-foot flat-bottom rowboat to sea-going yachts.

Competent statisticians examine every number carefully to determine exactly what it represents. Definitions and explanations of statistical data are extremely important in all research work. Because it did not appreciate these facts, the stove company executives innocently accepted without question what their market analyst told them.

Another example of this failure to understand statistical theory happened recently to a group of businessmen who planned to develop a large suburban shopping center. They wanted to know the average income of the families residing in the trading area of the proposed center. A consultant hired to undertake the survey determined that the average income per family was quite high. With a high average-income clientele, the stores in the shopping center catered to upper-income tastes. The development was a failure until the merchants became aware of the real situation. The average income quoted to the businessmen was meaningless. In statistical theory, an average is a symbol used to represent the central tendency of a group of figures. However, if no central tendency exists, the average is a meaningless figure. For instance, the average of a U distribution describes very little. In the shopping center case, the distribution of income was exceedingly bimodal. There was a very large group of low-income families with incomes of around $10,000 to $12,000, and relatively few families with exceedingly high incomes. These high incomes managed to offset the low incomes of most of the other families, so that on balance it appeared as if a rather substantial income existed throughout the area when really the opposite was so. The vast majority of the families in the area had modest living standards. In this case, the mode would have been the proper statistical measure of central tendency.

LIMITATIONS OF QUANTITATIVE MARKET ANALYSIS

Quantitative marketing research has four basic limitations: accuracy, time, costs, and personnel. The sales executive must be aware of these and be willing to live with them in order to use market analysis successfully as a sales planning tool.

Accuracy

Marketing research does not produce results with perfect accuracy. Many times even the best figures contain considerable error. However, this does not mean that these figures are not valuable. One of the most difficult things for students of marketing research to grasp is that estimates can vary 10 or 20 percent from reality and still have value. Many sales estimators would be delighted to be able to predict within 10 percent accuracy.

In seeking a yes or no decision, a sales executive often can get a worthwhile answer from marketing research even though the study contains a large degree of error. Engineers for a manufacturer thinking of making a carpet sweeper found that for the operation to break even at the anticipated price, the firm would have to sell 500,000 units a year. Marketing research estimated that 1.8 million units per year was the size of the total market for carpet sweepers. Further investigation indicated that one manufacturer already had a strong hold on the market—70 percent of it. The remainder of the carpet sweeper companies each had about 5 percent of the market. Since this manufacturer would need more than 20 percent of the market to break even on the venture, it was a poor risk. Nothing in the product or the situation justified a belief that it could do any better than the other producers in the field. Even if the estimate of the market potential was 100 percent in error, the venture still would not be a good investment.

Many times all that can be done in market research is to make an estimate—some people prefer to call them guesstimates. All marketing researchers have been forced to do this at some time or another, particularly in the research usually conducted for the marketing of new products. A qualified guess is often better than no guess at all.

Time

Good research takes time. Often, it cannot be accomplished in a day or a week, and many times it will take months before results can be given with any degree of assurance. The sales executive who must have answers quickly is handicapped. About all that can be done when time is short is to use a market factor derivation or a correlation analysis. As noted above, these can be based on subjective judgment rather than a sound analysis of the consumer.

Costs

Good research costs money—lots of money. Inexpensive research is usually poor research. The sales manager who is not prepared to spend some money is usually disappointed in what he buys.

Personnel

As indicated throughout the chapter, it takes highly able individuals to do good research. As in any activity, some practitioners are charlatans or incompetents. The sales executive who is thinking of hiring a researcher must take great care that he or she is fully qualified for the work. Unfortunately, such individuals are scarce. Many people who go into marketing research have only minimum qualifications. Far more than a knowledge of how to interview people is needed to make a good market researcher.

QUESTIONS AND PROBLEMS

1. Indicate what market factor or factors you would use to estimate the market potentials for each of the following products.
   a. Jostin's class rings.
   b. Flintkote asphalt roof shingles.
   c. First Flight golf clubs
   d. Scotts grass seed.
   e. Rose Marie women's swimsuits.
   f. Mohawk carpeting.
   g. Head skis.
   h. Collins Radio defense electronics.

2. After one year of market testing, the manufacturer of a new food product had sold 4,800 packages in the test city of Louisville, Kentucky. What would be the estimated national market for this product?

3. An automobile manufacturer expected to sell in the coming period 1.2 million new automobiles in the United States. What would be the expected sales for each state?

4. Under what conditions must price levels be forecasted before a sales forecast can be formulated?

5. How would a sales manager locate and hire a fully qualified marketing analyst?

6. What are some of the pitfalls in conducting test markets?

7. What market factors would a large lumber company use to predict construction activity?

8. A study was made of all the articles appearing in Fortune magazine since its inception which contained forecasts of future events. It was discovered that in most instances the forecasts were far too conservative. Change and growth have been far more rapid than forecasters want to admit. Why is this so?

9. Seeburg Company has introduced a stereo phonographic system in which the user merely dials a number to play any one of 50 records stored inside. It sells for about $900. How would a market analyst go about estimating its market potential?

10. One major state university has developed a model for predicting the sales potential for any given restaurant location. It has programmed this model for a computer and offers the service to prospective restaurant owners. What factors do you think are in that model?

11. Why is the executive opinion method of forecasting widely used, and why does it frequently give usable results?

12. Should salesmen be paid a substantial bonus for correctly forecasting their sales volume for a coming period?

13. What forecasting methods are most appropriate for use in estimating the probable sales of a new product?

14. What are some of the most frequent reasons a sales forecast is substantially lower than the sales actually realized? Which step in the forecasting procedures contains the greatest likelihood of errors?

Case 16–1

CORTINA SPORTS, INC.
Sales forecasting in the ski equipment industry

Perry Cahners, president of Cortina Sports, Inc., would describe the ski equipment industry as a volatile business at best. "One year a recession kills you," he has said. "The next year in the same recession, business goes up 12 to 15 percent. If it isn't the European and American manufacturers overproducing and dumping their products on the market, then it is too little (or too much) snow. One year our sales doubled when we had forecasted a 50 percent increase. The next year our sales declined 15 percent when we had predicted a 25 percent increase. All in all, our sales forecasting stinks, and I just don't know what to do about it."

In a little more than decade, Cortina Sports, Inc. had evolved from a small New England plastics manufacturer to become one of the premier names in the manufacturing and marketing of ski boots. The main offices and manufacturing plant were located in New England. In addition, the company had an assembly plant in Canada (Toronto) and was negotiating to open plants in Japan and Europe.

The company's net sales had increased each year for the past decade, but profits had not kept pace. Losses had been incurred during five of those years. For the past two years a primary goal of Cortina's management had been to strengthen the company's financial position. Its short-term debt was refinanced, and arrangements were made for long-term financing.

Cortina Sports began under another name in 1959, originally engaging in the extrusion and molding of various plastic products. Then in the 1960s one of the company's engineers started to develop a molded, flexible epoxy (plastic) ski boot. At that time most ski boots were made of stitched leather. The development of Cortina's ski boot covered a period of several years, because only part-time attention was devoted to the project. The company's main business continued to be in other plastic molding and extrusion work. Finally, after some years of research, experimentation, personal tests by Cortina executives, and ski tests by ski instructors, the Cortina boot finally was introduced to the market in 1970.

The executives were so convinced they had a real winner that they decided to concentrate all the company's efforts on producing and marketing molded, flexible epoxy ski boots. Consequently, the firm changed its name to Cortina Sports and discontinued its other manufacturing.

In the mid–1970s Cortina's management decided to expand the company's sporting goods product line, not only to reduce the risks inherent in marketing only one product but also to capitalize on the company's network of retailers. By adding other sporting goods, Cortina could use its existing sales force and dealer structure. So over a period of years, the company had added, either by its own production or by outside purchase, product lines of skis, ice skates, tennis rackets, and ski sweaters. However, during this time ski boots remained the company's major product and the backbone of the business.

Essentially, a plastic ski boot contains two elements—an outer shell and an inner lining. Some brands of boots have one piece outer shells. In others, like Cortina, the outer shell is molded in two parts. There are varying degrees of stiffness among the many brands and models of ski boots. The most popular inner lining is a "flow" type in which a plastic substance flows within the boot's inner lining to conform to the shape of the wearer's foot and ankle. Cortina, and some other firms, also produced a foam lining which entailed the injection of a plastic foam and required custom fitting. Plastic boots are very durable, lasting about three times as long as leather boots.

All in all, the Cortina executives believed that their boot had several distinctive features which made it demonstrably superior to competitive products. Cortina marketed five basic models of ski boots. Each was priced in the high end of the price range for that type of boot. One model was designed for the budget-minded beginning skier. A second was for beginning and intermediate recreational skiers. The third model was intended for advanced and expert recreational skiers. The Competition model was for racers and other real experts. The fifth model was a distinctive boot designed especially for women.

The ski industry had enjoyed unprecedented growth during the 1960s—a growth rate substantially in excess of that for U.S. industry as a whole. Although it had continued to grow during the 1970s, it had been at a slower rate. In some parts of the country during the early 1970s, the industry declined because of poor snow conditions and the economic recession. Nevertheless, Cahners was optimistic about the long-run prospects for the industry as a whole throughout the United States.

Cortina faced stiff competition in its ski boot line. There were several brands produced by both American and European firms. One of the economic problems in the ski industry was the periodic overproduction by these producers, with severe price cuts resulting.

One factor helping Cortina's market position had been the performance of racers wearing Cortina boots in international competition. During the 1970s several major races were won in both men's and women's competition by skiers wearing Cortina boots. Even the winners of the World Cup competition in some years had been wearers of Cortina boots. Cahners believed that this reputation in competitive racing helped increase the popularity of the Cortina brand among recreational skiers. Cortina had outpaced the ski industry's overall growth rate for several years. Cahners was hoping that the fine name and performance Cortina had achieved in ski boots would help to sell the other products the company was adding to the line.

Cortina had 12 sales reps selling directly to over 800 retail outlets in the United States and Canada. These retailers included specialty ski shops, sporting goods stores, and department stores in the major metropolitan areas and all major ski resort areas. The sales people were paid a straight commission. They worked under the direction of the general sales manager, Joseph Hester. In addition to direct selling, the sales job also included such activities as supplying promotional materials to dealers, training their retail sales people, and helping the dealers with their advertising programs. Cortina did not have any special arrangements with its dealers regarding territorial or product limitations. Virtually all of Cortina's dealers also sold competitive products.

In the market decline of the early 1970s, many ski retailers suffered heavy financial losses, and several were forced out of business. Since that time, Cortina and other ski equipment producers had paid special attention to credit ratings when selecting retail dealers. In addition, Cortina was careful about selling to discount sporting goods stores, preferring *not* to sell to those that held frequent big sales at drastically cut prices. The specialty ski shops were Cortina's major retail outlet, and the company did not want to alienate those dealers by selling to the discounters who greatly underpriced the specialty shops.

The sales history for Cortina ski boots for the period 1971–77 is shown in Exhibits 1 and 2. Sales started out at a modest level for the first three years and then boomed in 1974 and 1975. They declined some in 1977 from a peak in 1976, although the company's total sales were up in 1977 over 1976.

EXHIBIT 1
Forecasted versus actual sales of ski boots, in units, 1971–1977

CORTINA SPORTS, INC.

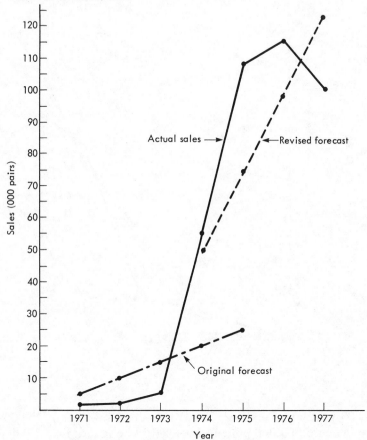

Cortina's management had been forecasting its ski boot sales since 1971. These unit and dollar forecasts also are shown in Exhibits 1 and 2. Management's forecasting record was poor, especially since 1973. And it was exactly this poor forecasting performance which was bothering Cahners so much. He noted that the original 1974 forecast called for sales of 20,000 pairs of boots—an increase of 5,000 pairs, or

EXHIBIT 2
Forecasted versus actual sales of ski boots, in dollars, 1971–1977
CORTINA SPORTS, INC.

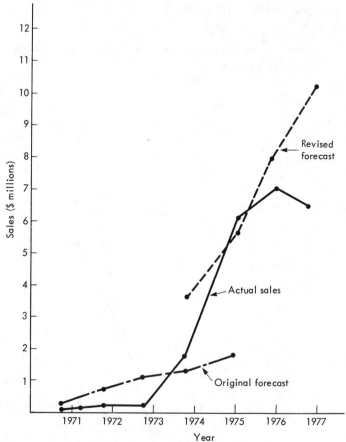

33 percent, over 1973. The 1974 actual sales were 55,000 pairs—an increase of 1,000 percent over 1973's actual sales of 5,000 pairs.

The original forecast for 1973 and especially for 1974 was so far off that starting in 1974 a revised forecast was prepared each year. Even though the revised forecast predicted sales at a much higher level than the original estimates, the revised forecast also proved to contain a huge margin of error. 1975 sales doubled those for 1974 (110,000 over 55,000 pairs), when the forecast predicted a 50 percent increase (75,000 over 50,000 pairs). Sales declined about 15 percent in 1977, when the forecast called for a 25 percent increase.

In preparing these sales forecasts, Hester, the general sales manager, used two forecasting methods. He took the projected estimates supplied by the salesmen (sales force composite method) and then adjusted these totals in light of his own market estimates (executive opinion method). Hester argued that this was the most reliable forecasting approach in the highly volatile ski industry.

Hester was well aware that his forecasting record left much to be desired. In answer to criticisms from Cahners and other executives, he pointed out several factors which contributed to the industry's volatile and unpredictable performance. First, overproduction in the ski equipment end of the business occurred on the heels of the general industry boom in the 1960s. Second, just about the time the market for skis and boots was saturated, three things occurred to further destroy forecasting accuracy. One was poor snow conditions in some of the major ski areas. Then an economic recession hit the country, and finally, the unanticipated durability of plastic ski boots had an impact. These new boots were so well made and so durable that they lasted about three times as long as the leather boots, but this factor had been overlooked in forecasting.

The net result of this overproduction and market saturation was a wave of unanticipated drastic price-cutting by many producers, plus the dumping of European boots in American markets at loss-level prices. Many manufacturers and retailers of skis and boots suffered heavy financial losses.

Through these years, however, Cortina did manage to post an excellent sales performance in numbers of pairs of boots sold. However, because its forecast usually was so far off, management frequently found itself in a financial bind. The company would be heavily undercommitted or overcommitted financially because actual revenues were so different from budgeted figures. Cortina also suffered financially (as did all the manufacturers) when retailers went broke or were delinquent in paying their bills. During some years, Cortina's accounts receivable were dangerously high.

As a consequence of all of this, Cahners realized that somehow the company had to develop more accuracy in its sales forecasts. "Whatever the reasons, and however volatile the industry conditions are," Cahners said, "there simply has to be a better way for us to forecast. Look at the results so far."

John Baxter, the chief financial officer, proposed that the company use some form of market factor analysis as its basis of forecasting—perhaps the direct derivation method, or even the more formal correlation analysis. He was not certain, however, whether Cortina had a long enough sales history in ski boots to make correlation analysis a valid method. Cahners thought that the company might rely more heavily on consumer surveys and users' expectations. Hester said he doubted whether they could get accurate or reliable data from these methods of analysis.

Question

1. What method of sales forecasting should Cortina use for its ski boot sales?

Case 16–2
TERRI LEE, INC.
Sales forecasting in the apparel industry

The management of Terri Lee, Inc., had become increasingly disenchanted with its sales forecasting system. Its accuracy had not been everything that management had hoped for. In the previous three years, the forecast had been in error as follows:

	Forecast (in millions)	Actual Sales (in millions)
1974	$ 96	$ 88
1975	98	105
1976	111	122

Mr. Richard Thomas, director of sales, was asked by the company's board of directors to develop a more accurate system.

Company background

Founded in 1938, Terri Lee had expanded until it was a leader in many segments of the high-quality women's sportswear industry. Its increasing sales volume had resulted in a more than proportional increase in its net profits. Thomas, a Harvard MBA, had assumed his job in 1975. Prior to joining Terri Lee, he had been an assistant merchandising manager for one of New York's largest department stores. Terri Lee's 73 salesmen operated out of 17 offices located in the principal cities of the United States.

Product information

Terri Lee manufactured and distributed high-quality women's sportswear, among which were a complete line of slacks, knit sweaters and skirts, coordinated pants suits, and full-length formal party wear. Slacks and knit sweaters contributed more than half of the concern's sales volume and profit.

A differential advantage of considerable importance was developed in 1961 when the company patented a durable press process, also known as permanent press, which was an extension of the highly publicized wash-and-wear finishes developed in 1958. Permanent press is a shape-setting process that sets creases to stay creased and flat areas to stay flat. Under two processes, postcure and precure, the fabric is impregnated by heat-sensitive chemicals and intense heat is applied to activate the chemicals. Terri Lee was the first firm to patent the process, but others followed in its wake.

The textile and apparel manufacturers were operating at about 96 percent of capacity in 1976. Knitting, one of Terri Lee's main areas of interest, had been one of the fastest growing segments of the industry. Traditional methods of weaving and knitting were being replaced by more elaborate fabric-forming methods.

Terri Lee's main competitors were White Stag, Jantzen, Bobbie Brooks, Koret of California, and Jonathan Logan. The company's share of its relevant markets had been about 16 percent and was increasing slightly. Jantzen, the leader, was only about 4 percent larger in sales.

The total value of all knit fabric shipments in 1976 was $2.1 billion, which included all types of knit products for men, women, and children. No specific data were available for the exact markets to which Terri Lee sold. Derivation of market share was difficult because of the noncommonality of product lines between competitors.

Problem background

The company was experiencing difficulty in determining its sales forecast. The forecasts were sales force composites. Each salesman would be asked to evaluate each of his accounts to determine what it would probably sell during the next year by product lines, then total them for submission to the sales department. Analysis of the forecasts, compared to actual sales results, disclosed that the salesmen seldom could accurately forecast what product lines would sell in which stores. In total, their forecasts were more accurate than their individual forecasts of how much of one product any one store would sell.

The piece-goods manufacturers from whom Terri Lee purchased its fabrics were approaching capacity production. Increased productive capacities by the piece-goods manufacturers were not anticipated because it was widely believed in the industry that the consumer demand for knit fabrics was a matter of fashion, and fashion would change as it always had previously. The industry had a bitter history of overexpanding in the face of high demand, only to encounter financial difficulties when this demand slackened. Moreover, most manufacturers were undercapitalized. Other alternative piece-goods manufacturers lacked the technical proficiency to deal with the patented fabric process, and their quality of workmanship did not meet Terri Lee's standards.

The profitable growth within the permanent press industry was reflected in the outstanding growth of Terri Lee. For several years Thomas had been proposing the construction of a company-owned knitting mill that would allow the company better control over the scheduling and delivery of the highly volatile fashion fabrics.

If 1977 sales exceeded $135 million, a knitting mill owned and operated by the company would be profitable. Sales of less than that amount would not allow economic operation of a company knitting mill.

The previous inaccuracies of the sales force composite forecasts made Thomas wonder just how much confidence he could place in them as a basis for making a decision to build the $10 million knitting mill. He decided to use the talents of Richard Day and Thomas Waters, two newly hired MBA graduates who had majored in statistics. Day and Waters were each asked to submit a separate sales forecast for the company for 1977. Exhibits 1 and 2 present the sales forecasts prepared by each man.

EXHIBIT 1
Annual sales forecast for 1977, prepared by R. Day
TERRI LEE, INC.

Annual sales for Terri Lee over the period 1960–76 have shown a tremendous growth rate. Figure 1–A clearly demonstrates that sales during this period have not grown in a linear progression. The rapidly increasing rate of growth indicates that some nonlinear function best describes Terri Lee's sales.

Plotting sales on semilogarithmic paper yields a straight line. Thus the sales function is logarithmic, as shown in Figure 1–B.

The derivation of the sales forecast for 1977 shall be based on a projection technique using a logarithmic straight-line equation.

The general form of the logarithmic straight line, or exponential curve, is:

$$Y = ab^x$$

However, the more common form of the equation, after taking the logarithm of the equation is:

$$\log Y = (\log a) + x(\log b)$$

EXHIBIT 1 *(continued)*

FIGURE 1–A
Annual sales, 1960–1976

TERRI LEE, INC.

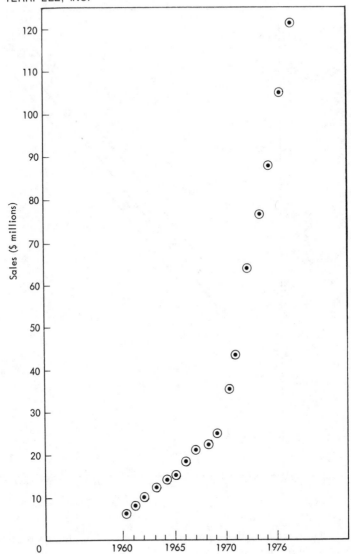

EXHIBIT 1 *(continued)*
FIGURE 1–B
Annual sales, 1960–1976

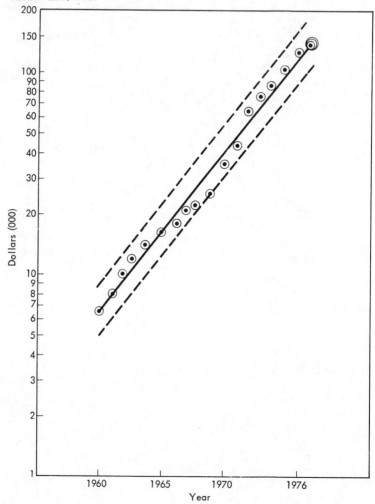

TERRI LEE, INC.

Derivation of the equations for (log a) and (log b) by the least squares procedure yields:

$$(\log a) = \text{Sum of } (\log Y) / n$$

where $n =$ number of data years, and

$$(\log b) = \text{Sum of } (x \log Y) / \text{Sum of } (x^2)$$

as long as Sum $(x) = 0$.

EXHIBIT 1 *(continued)*

Substitution of Terri Lee sales data from Table 1–A into the above equations produces:

$$(\log a) = 75.3808/17$$
$$= 4.4341$$

and

$$(\log b) = 32.4671/408$$
$$= 0.0795$$

Thus, the general form of the exponential curve for our data is:

$$Y = 4.4341 + (x)0.0795.$$

TABLE 1–A
Exponential sales forecast data, 1960–1976 (sales in thousands)
TERRI LEE, INC.

Year	Net sales = Y	Log Y	x	x(log Y)	x²
1960	$ 6,317	3.8005	−8	−30.4040	64
1961	7,828	3.8936	−7	−27.1852	49
1962	10,015	4.0065	−6	−24.0390	36
1963	12,391	4.0831	−5	−20.4155	25
1964	14,360	4.1571	−4	−16.6284	16
1965	15,810	4.1983	−3	−12.5949	9
1966	17,618	4.2459	−2	− 8.4918	4
1967	20,824	4.3185	−1	− 4.3185	1
1968	22,342	4.3491	0	0.0000	0
1969	25,014	4.3981	1	4.3981	1
1970	35,721	4.5529	2	9.1058	4
1971	44,068	4.6441	3	13.9323	9
1972	63,920	4.8056	4	19.3024	16
1973	75,763	4.8794	5	24.3970	25
1974	87,599	4.9424	6	29.6544	36
1975	105,167	5.0212	7	35.1484	49
1976	121,500	5.0845	8	40.6760	64
(1977)*	(139,600)	(5.1496)	(9)		
Totals		75.3808	0	+176.6144	408
				−144.1473	
				+ 32.4671	

* Quantities in parentheses derived and excluded from totals.

EXHIBIT 1 *(concluded)*

Substitution of positive and negative 8 for the values of x will yield the expected trend values for 1960 and 1976. This will also permit a graphical check of the fit of our trend equation.

Thus:

$$x = -8 \ (1960)$$
$$\log Y = \quad 4.4341 + (-8)(0.0795)$$
$$= \quad 4.4341 - 0.6360$$
$$\log Y = \quad 3.7981$$
$$Y = \quad \$6,270,000$$

and

$$x = +8 \ (1976)$$
$$\log Y = \quad 4.4341 + (+8)(0.0795)$$
$$= \quad 4.4341 + 0.6360$$
$$\log Y = \quad 5.0701$$
$$Y = \quad \$117,500$$

Plotting the two trend values on Figure 2 produces the projective base from which the 1977 sales forecast can be derived.

Thus:

$$x = +9 \ (1977)$$
$$\log Y = \quad 4.4341 + (+9)(0.0795)$$
$$= \quad 4.4341 + 0.7155$$
$$\log Y = \quad 5.1496$$
$$Y = \quad \$139,600$$

The projected trend value for 1976 would have been $117,500,000. Actual sales amounted to $121,500,000, or a variance of less than 3 percent of total sales.

Also illustrated in Figure 1–B are extreme bands of confidence levels which are relatively narrow for the exponential curve logarithmically drawn.

Graphically, as well as mathematically, the projected Terri Lee sales forecast for 1977 is:

$$\$139,600,000$$

EXHIBIT 2
Terri Lee annual sales forecast for 1977, prepared by T. Waters

Terri Lee, a leader in permanent press ladies' knitwear, is experiencing a phenomenal growth rate. The annual sales increase has been relatively constant, indicating that some *linear* relationship might describe the sales record. An exact form of the general straight-line equation can be derived to indicate the average annual net sales of Terri Lee.

The general form of the straight-line equation is $Y = a + b \ (x)$ where a is the intercept; b is the slope of the line, or as applied to this problem, the

EXHIBIT 2 *(continued)*

average annual *rate* of increase; and x is the year that the trend value of sales, Y, is desired to be known.

From the least squares derivation, the values of a and b are:

$$a = \text{Sum of } (Y)/n$$
$$b = \text{Sum of } (xY)/\text{Sum of } (x^2)$$

TABLE 2-A
Annual net sales data, 1971–76

TERRI LEE, INC.

Year	Net sales (000s)
1971	44,068
1972	63,920
1973	75,763
1974	87,599
1975	105,167
1976	121,500

These equations are valid only for an arbitrary time scale which sums out to zero.

From the data in Table 2–B the exact values of a and b can be derived. Thus:

$$a = 498,017/6$$
$$= 83,003$$

and

$$b = 326,626/28$$
$$= 11,666$$

Thus, the general form of the straight-line equation for our data is:

$$Y_T = 83,003 + 11,666 \ (x).$$

Substitution of values of negative and positive 3 will yield the trend values for 1971 and 1976. This will also allow a graphical check of our trend line. Now:

$$Y \ (1971) = 83,003 + 11,666(-3)$$
$$= 83,003 - 34,998$$
$$= 48,005$$

and

$$Y \ (1976) = 83,003 + 11,666(+3)$$
$$= 83,003 + 34,998$$
$$= 118,001$$

EXHIBIT 2 *(continued)*

FIGURE 2–A
Annual sales, 1971–1976

TERRI LEE, INC.

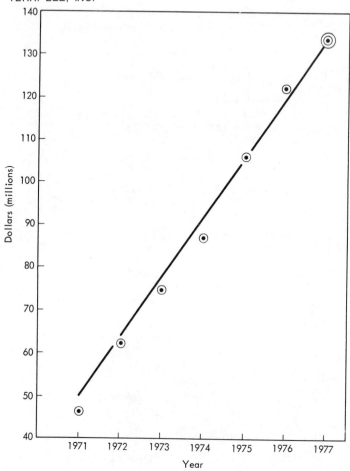

Plotting these values on Figure 2-A shows that the trend lines fit the data from which it was computed.

By the substitution of positive 4 for a value, which corresponds to 1977 on our arbitrary time scale, we may extrapolate the desired 1977 sales forecast: Thus:

$$Y\ (1977) = \ 83{,}003 + 11{,}666(+4)$$
$$= \ 83{,}003 + 46{,}664$$
$$= 129{,}667$$

or $129,667,000.

EXHIBIT 2 *(concluded)*

TABLE 2–B
Straight-line sales forecast, 1971–76

TERRI LEE, INC.

Year	Net sales = y	X	Xy	X²
1971	$ 44,068	−3	−132,204	9
1972	63,920	−2	−127,840	4
1973	75,763	−1	− 75,763	1
1974	87,599	+1	87,599	1
1975	105,167	+2	210,334	4
1976	121,500	+3	364,500	9
			+662,433	
			−335,807	
Total	$498,017	0	+326,626	28

Questions

1. In which of the forecasts would you place the most confidence?
2. Explain why the forecasts differ.
3. What advice would you give Mr. Thomas concerning his sales forecasting? And how about building the knitting mill?

17

Sales department budgeting

That what we plan we build.
PHOEBE CARY

Once the market has been evaluated and a sales forecast has been formulated, the next step in sales planning is to prepare budgets for the sales department and all other segments of the enterprise. As noted in Chapter 16, the sales forecast should be used as the basis of all planning and budgeting.

A budget is simply a tool, a financial plan, which an administrator uses to plan for profits by anticipating the revenues and expenditure of funds. By adopting various budgetary procedures, management hopes to guide the operations of the organization to a predetermined end—a given level of profit on a certain volume of operations. Without a budget, management could never be certain whether operations were going successfully. Executives would not know if the goals of the firm were being met until the final accounting had been made for the fiscal period. Then it would be too late to revise the plan or provide remedies.

BENEFITS OF BUDGETING

Budgeting serves numerous functions for the firm. Some of these are discussed in this section.

Provides control of expense-revenue ratio

An important goal in operating a business is to maintain the desired relationship between expenditures and income. The objective of a business is to buy revenues at a reasonable cost, and the budget clearly shows what this cost should be. If sales of $5 million are forecast for the coming period, management can establish how much the firm can afford to pay for that revenue. If the company wants a profit of 10 percent on sales, then $4.5 million can be paid out to "buy" the $5 million in revenue. Part of the $4.5 million would go to the production and administrative departments, and another portion would be available to operate the sales department. Thus the sales executive has a definite sum to use in selling the merchandise. In this way, the budget restricts the sales executives from spending more than their share of the funds available for the purchase of revenues. Hence the budget helps to prevent expenses from getting out of control and keeps them in proper alignment with sales.

Acts as a coordinating mechanism

Budgeting is the best way to plan, control, and coordinate the activities of the various segments of an enterprise. Production must be coordinated with sales. It is folly to produce more or less merchandise than can be sold. A budget serves quite well as a coordinating tool. With a budget based on a sales forecast, the production manager can plan output closely so that the necessary goods will be available when required. But until the sales department tells production its anticipated needs, there is no way of knowing how much to produce.

Budgeting also allows the financial executive to plan for coming needs. Without some established forecast of what the organization will be selling and what it will be spending for materials, labor, and marketing expenses, the financial executive has no way of knowing how much money will be required during periods of the conversion cycle. The sales budget allows the controller to judge how much money the firm will require to finance accounts receivable, inventory, and various overhead expenses. The production budget allows him to predict the expenditures for purchases of raw materials and labor. Without accurate budgets, the firm would be forced to carry more money than is necessary for efficient operation. If excess capital were not carried, the company frequently might be required to undertake emergency financing.

Provides a standard of performance

The budget serves not only as a plan of action but also as a standard of performance for the various departments. Once the budget is established, the departments can begin organizing to realize that plan. If the budget has been based on a sound analysis of potential markets and competition, the organization will be encouraged to realize its full potential. Otherwise, the departments might not know what they could or should be achieving. This is of special importance to sales people because it is through a detailed breakdown of the sales budget among products, territories, and customers that they are notified of what management expects of them.

Serves as an evaluation tool

Any goal, once established, becomes a tool for evaluation of performance. If the organization meets its goals, management can consider the performance successful. Hence, the sales department budgets become tools by which the department's performance is evaluated. If the sales manager is able to meet the sales goals set forth in the budget at the costs allotted for obtaining that volume, he has strong evidence to demonstrate his success as an executive. The manager who is unable to meet budgetary requirements is usually less well regarded. Failure to keep to the budget indicates one of two things. Since the sales manager usually establishes the sales budgets, he is either a poor budgetary officer or a bad sales manager.

BUDGETS FOR SALES DEPARTMENT ACTIVITIES

The marketing and sales executive has the responsibility for formulating four basic budgets: the sales budget, the selling-expense budget, the advertising budget, and the sales department administrative budget.

It would not be inaccurate to say that success in large organizations depends upon skills in developing and managing budgets in such a way that the manager is made to look proficient. In management folklore the managers who are considered to be skilled are the ones who sell more than is expected of them at a cost less than budget. One young publishing executive rose rapidly in the organization when attention was directed to him because he literally was the only one who was meeting his budgets. Though his personal ways irritated many superiors, he was promoted over better liked men who had poor budgetary performances. The administrator who fails to meet budgets is clearly evident and must endure many uncomfortable moments with superiors.

The sales budget

The sales budget is the revenue or unit volume anticipated from sales of the various products. This is the key budget. It is the basis of all operating activities not only in the sales department but also in the production and finance areas. The validity of the entire budgetary process depends on the accuracy of this one sales budget. If it is in error, all others will also be in error.

An example of a sales budget is presented in Figure 17–1. Management must estimate the sales of each product, and many times separate forecasts must be made for each class of customer and each territorial division. Budgets for territories and classes of customers usually are of interest only to sales executives. Other departments typically need only the sales budget for product divisions.

The sales budget calls for extreme detail. Every single product sold by the firm must be accounted for, since it must be either purchased from outside or produced within the organization. It does little good to tell production planners that $100,000 worth of small parts will be needed. They must be told specifically what small parts will be sold in what quantities and at what time.

The selling-expense budget

The selling-expense budget anticipates the various expenditures for personal-selling activities. These are the salaries, commissions, and expenses for the sales force. This is not a difficult budget to develop. If the sales people are on a straight commission, the amount of the revenue allotted will be determined by the commission rate. Experience rather clearly indicates how much money must be set aside for expenses. If they are paid a salary, the process is merely compiling the amounts, taking into consideration any raises or promotions to be made during the coming period. Any plans for sales force expansion also should be anticipated in this budget.

The advertising budget

Several methods are widely used to determine the funds appropriated for advertising. Many firms allocate for advertising a certain percentage of anticipated sales. The advertising budget may be established by the amount of funds available or by the task advertising is supposed to accomplish. The decision on the method to be used is ordinarily a matter of executive judgment.

Once the total amount of advertising money has been agreed on, the funds must be allocated to time periods, media to be used, products to be promoted, areas where the promotions will occur, markets to be stimulated, or any other meaningful marketing cleavage.

The administrative budget

Besides having direct control over management of the sales force, the typical sales executive is also an office manager. Ordinarily, there

FIGURE 17–1
Sales budget, 1977 (all figures in units except last column)
COLORADO SKI COMPANY

PRODUCTS	CUSTOMER A*	CUSTOMER B†	TOTAL	CUSTOMER A	CUSTOM B
SALESMAN--		JOE			GUS
Skis:					
Ski #45	1 400	1 140	2 540	1 360	1 12
Ski #60	390	260	650	240	21
Ski #80	210	420	630	190	29
Total Skis	2 000	1 820	3 820	1 790	1 62
Ski Accessories:					
Ski Poles #100	400	600	1 000	300	40
Ski Poles #200	300	400	700	200	30
Boots #30	80	180	260	10	4
Boots #50	50	140	190	20	5
Boots #70	30	100	130	20	7
Laces	1 200	3 200	4 400	1 750	2 00
Bindings	250	300	550	200	27
Safety Straps	300	900	1 200	100	50
Wax	4 800	7 500	12 300	4 600	5 60
Mittens #3	1 200	2 400	3 600	800	1 40
Mittens #5	1 400	1 800	3 200	900	1 00
Goggles #1	1 500	2 800	4 300	750	1 50
Ski Pants:					
Pants #10 Men's	1 100	800	1 900	800	60
Pants #10 Women's	1 400	1 500	2 900	950	80
Pants #20 Men's	900	1 100	2 000	610	75
Pants #20 Women's	1 500	1 100	2 600	800	97
Total Pants	4 900	4 500	9 400	3 160	3 12
Parkas:					
Parkas #8	2 500	1 700	4 200	1 800	1 20
Parkas #15	3 200	2 200	5 400	900	1 00
Total Parkas	5 700	3 900	9 600	2 700	2 20

* Sporting goods stores.
† Specialty ski shop.

are sales department secretaries and office workers; the total staff can be large. Under the sales manager there may be several assistant sales managers, a marketing research staff, an advertising manager, a credit manager, several sales supervisors, and sales trainers. Budgetary provisions must be made for the salaries of these individuals as well as for such sales office operating expenses as suppliers, rent, heat, power and light, office equipment, and general overhead burden.

URE 17-1 *(continued)*

TAL	PETE CUSTOMER A	PETE CUSTOMER B	TOTAL	TOTALS CUSTOMER A	TOTALS CUSTOMER B	TOTAL	DOLLAR VOLUME $
2 480	1 290	1 080	2 370	4 050	3 340	7 390	169 970
450	260	140	400	890	610	1 500	45 000
480	220	180	400	620	890	1 510	60 600
3 410	1 770	1 400	3 170	5 560	4 840	10 400	275 570
700	150	250	400	850	1 250	2 100	8 400
500	100	200	300	600	900	1 500	7 500
50	20	30	50	110	250	360	5 400
70	20	50	70	90	240	330	8 250
90	20	50	70	70	220	290	10 150
3 750	800	1 200	2 000	3 750	6 400	10 150	3 140
470	75	110	185	525	680	1 205	9 640
600	50	300	350	450	1 700	2 150	700
0 200	3 000	3 700	6 700	12 400	16 800	29 200	14 940
2 200	700	1 300	2 000	2 700	5 100	7 800	11 700
1 900	600	800	1 400	2 900	3 600	6 500	16 250
2 250	650	1 500	2 150	2 900	5 800	8 700	17 400
							113 470
1 400	500	400	900	2 400	1 800	4 200	42 000
1 750	700	600	1 300	3 050	2 900	5 950	59 500
1 360	450	500	950	1 960	2 350	4 310	86 200
1 770	540	600	1 140	2 840	2 670	5 510	110 200
6 280	2 190	2 100	4 290	10 250	9 720	19 970	297 900
3 000	1 200	800	2 000	5 500	3 700	9 200	73 600
3 750	1 600	1 000	2 600	7 100	4 650	11 750	176 250
6 750	2 800	1 800	4 600	12 600	8 350	20 950	249 850
						TOTAL DOLLAR VOLUME	936 790

The task of preparing these administrative budgets is usually a matter of compiling estimates of what will be required to operate the sales office for the coming period. Usually such estimates are based on past performance. If previous budget allotments were satisfactory, the budget-making executive will use them again unless an anticipated increase or decrease in business activity is likely to affect the expenditure of funds in a particular category.

THE BUDGETING PROCESS FOR THE FIRM

The entire budgeting process of the organization is a complex, detailed procedure. The *Corporate Treasurer's and Controller's Handbook* lists 19 separate budgets and discusses them at some length.[1] They are:

1. Sales budgets.
2. Cost-of-sales budgets.
3. Inventory increase or decrease budgets.
4. Production budgets.
5. Direct material budgets.
6. Direct labor budgets.
7. Machine-hour budgets.
8. Direct, indirect labor budgets.
9. Utility budgets.
10. Indirect supplies budget.
11. General factory overhead budgets.
12. Selling expense budgets.
13. Advertising expense budgets.
14. Administrative expense budgets.
15. Other operating income and expense budgets.
16. Nonoperating income and expense budgets.
17. Profit and loss budgets.
18. Capital expenditures budgets.
19. Cash budgets.

For convenience in discussion here, budgets are grouped as follows: sales department budgets, financial planning budgets (such as cash and profit and loss budgets), production budgets, and general administrative and overhead expense budgets. Figure 17–2 shows the flow of information from one budget to another.

It can be seen that everything starts with the sales budget described above. From it, data flow in five directions. The sales budget provides the basis for establishing the various sales department budgets, such as advertising, selling expenses, and sales office expenses. Sales budget figures also flow directly to the production department. Here the total production budget is established, and from that the various materials and labor budgets are determined.

Anticipated-sales figures from the sales budget also are given to the financial officer for preparation of the cash and the profit and loss budgets. The cash budget is a tool by which the financial officer determines how many dollars will be flowing into and out of the firm

---

[1] Lillian Doris (ed.), *Corporate Treasurer's and Controller's Encyclopedia*, rev. 1975 (New York: Prentice-Hall, Inc., 1975), p. 106.

FIGURE 17–2
Flow of information from sales budget to other budgets

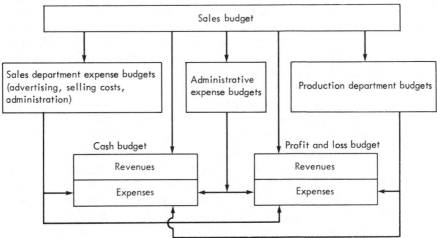

each month. The need for this budget arises because of the discrepancy in time between the expenditure and receipt of funds. It is necessary to lay out money for materials, labor, advertising, and selling expenses many months prior to selling the merchandise. Then after sales of the goods, it may be several months before the cash is received. It is the duty of the financial officer to ensure that the firm has sufficient cash to enable it to finance the lag between the expenditure and receipt of funds.

The financial officer also uses the anticipated net sales figure as the beginning of profit and loss budget. The budgets for sales department expenses, production, and general administrative expenses all flow into the profit and loss and cash budgets to determine the expected costs of operation. Thus, all budgets are summarized in the profit and loss and cash budgets. Errors in the sales department budgets have a twofold effect on the financial plan. First, the revenues will not be correct. Second, expenses will be out of line because the sales budget determined production and administrative expenses.

FLEXIBILITY IN BUDGETING

One classification of budgets divides them into two categories—flexible and inflexible. In an inflexible budget, once the figures are established they are not varied. For instance, once $100,000 has been allotted to advertising, that figure will not be altered. In a flexible budget, even though a figure has been established for a certain expenditure, it can be altered to meet changing conditions.

The decision of whether to use flexible or inflexible budgets normally has been dependent on the accuracy of the sales forecast. One authority states that an inflexible budget can be used only if the sales forecast (hence, the sales budget) is within a 5 percent range of accuracy. If the accuracy of the company's forecast is outside that range, a flexible budget is recommended.[2]

In practice, such a differentiation is unwise. It is tantamount to saying that once an executive makes up his mind he should not change it, regardless of what happens. Even if the sales forecast is accurate to the nth degree, an astute sales manager still wants a flexible budget. For example, it seems unsound to establish an advertising budget and then stick by it in face of anything. Even though the firm is meeting all sales goals, changing conditions in the field may require alteration of the advertising program or promotional mix. It may be necessary to add more sales people in order to continue the fine performance.

One of the major troubles with an inflexible budget is that it tends to become a master rather than a servant. Once a certain allotment is designated for a purpose, the executive tends to regard it as sacred and will spend the funds regardless of need. This perverts the purpose of the budget system.

There is always some unexpected need. It is impossible to foresee accurately everything for which money will be needed. Boilers burst; equipment wears out; a star salesman demands more money, or he will go to work for a competitor; a Federal Trade Commission investigation means hiring more legal help; or a good territory suddenly sours for want of promotional effort. The manager needs an emergency fund from which to meet such unexpected events. A budget system that prevents the manager from spending money where it is needed is a most dangerous tool because it can result in not doing the things that must be done and doing other things that are not so important but are budgeted. Some budgets do just that when they tie the executive's hands with inflexible figures.

BUDGET PERIODS

The three major periods for which budgets are commonly created are yearly, semiannually, and quarterly. Some firms prepare budgets for all three periods; others prefer to operate on an annual basis, thereby reducing the amount of paper work required. The length of

---

[2] Ibid., pp. 106–7.

the budget period is closely associated with its flexibility. Firms that use a three-month period have a much more flexible system than those that use an annual budget.

The quarterly budget forces an executive to reappraise the firm's position four times a year, thereby decreasing the likelihood that operations will get out of control. Many companies find a quarterly system advisable because that is roughly their conversion cycle of operations. Garmentmakers usually have four conversion cycles per year. That is, they put out four different lines of goods, one for each season, and find it convenient to budget for each selling season. The main advantage of a short planning period is that it is more likely to be accurate. The shorter the forecasting period, the less likelihood there is that the estimate will be disturbed by unforeseen developments.

In arriving at a decision on the period to be used by a firm, closeness of control must be balanced with the costs of compiling the budgets. The same period need not be used by all departments. The advertising budget may be on a quarterly basis, even though the selling-expense and sales office budgets are on an annual basis. However, any alterations in one budget will force changes in all others affected by the first one.

THE BUDGET-MAKING PROCEDURE

The first step in establishing a budget is to determine the sales forecast. Then each administrative unit must estimate the funds it will require to operate at the projected rate of activity. This is usually accomplished by the tedious task of (1) surveying each of the activities the unit must perform, (2) determining just how many individuals will be required to accomplish the job, and (3) figuring what materials and supplies will be required for them to do it properly.

In a large organization, the chief sales executive, for example, may request that separate budgets be prepared and submitted by the managers of each administrative unit in the sales department, such as marketing research, sales statistics, and the various sales territories. The executive then audits these budgets to determine if any changes are needed to fit into the overall sales program. Any necessary modifications should be made, of course, only after a conference between the sales manager and the department head involved. It may be that factors unknown to the sales manager justify the original figure.

Once the sales department budgets are compiled into one major budget, it is forwarded to the financial executive, who disseminates the information to the other departments. The due dates on various budgets must be staggered if the budgeting program is to be a success.

The budget from the marketing research department must be completed before the due date of the total sales department budget so that the sales executive will have sufficient time to compile and study the figures. In a similar manner, the sales department budget must be in the hands of the financial officer before final preparation of the production budget, since the production budget is completely dependent on the sales budget. The job of compiling all the budgets into the overall cash and profit and loss budgets can be done only after all other work on the plans of the organization has been completed.

The budgeting process involves considerable detail and time-consuming paper work. Obviously, the more complex and detailed the budget, the more time is required for preparation. There is always a point where additional information in the budget is unwarranted in light of the additional costs incurred, as compared with benefits to be realized from it.

Line-item budgeting versus program budgeting

There are two basic approaches to apportioning funds among the organizational units. The first, and oldest, is the line-item budget, in which funds are allocated in considerable detail to each identifiable cost center. Under such a line-item system, the sales department might have budget amounts for such items as:

office supplies	legal expenses
postage	telephone
taxes	recruiting costs
wages	consulting fees
insurance	equipment
travel	power
entertainment	automobile costs
research	

Each item would have to be forecasted and accounted for in minute detail.

To avoid some of the problems with line-item budgeting, program budgeting was developed. In this plan, the administrative head of each program is budgeted a lump sum sufficient to carry out the unit's mission. Then the manager uses this amount in whatever way seems most advantageous. Thus program budgeting provides for considerable flexibility. Moreover, it eliminates the need to play games to get money for things that are needed but for which there are no funds left in the budget. A scant recruiting budget, for example, may be bolstered by calling such costs entertainment and paying for them from that budget. Such diversions might negate the purpose of line-item budgeting.

Zero-based budgeting

A recent development called zero-based budgeting has been adopted in a few organizations as an answer to one problem posed by traditional budgeting procedures. Traditionally, a firm budgets for the coming period by adjusting the previous period's budgeted amounts. This history-based approach perpetuates certain practices past their reason for existence.

Under zero-based budgeting, each period starts from scratch. The administrator must justify each dollar requested. Thus each existing program is forced to prove its requirements before new funding is provided. In theory this sounds wise and prudent, but in practice it is a terrible waste of administrative time. The manager must spend too much time proving to other people the department's need for funds. Such internal paper generation is inefficient. One sales manager said of the plan, "If I have to prove to my boss each year that the sales department needs funds on which to operate, I'm going to get a new boss, a smarter one."

REASONS SOME FIRMS DO NOT USE BUDGETS

Budgeting is by no means a universal business practice; some firms operate without benefit of any formal budgeting process. Some of these are successful in their activities and feel no real need for adoption of a budget system. The reasons given for not wanting to use a budgeting system are varied. Some of them are quite valid, and others are actually the result of unwise budgeting procedures.

Unreliable sales forecasts

Unless a fairly reliable sales forecast is available, a meaningful budget is almost impossible. Without an accurate estimate of anticipated sales for the budgeting period, the administrator would be creating a work of fiction rather than a realistic plan of operation.

Time requirements

Some executives feel that the budget procedure takes more time than it is worth. They point out that a budget makes no money in itself, but it definitely costs money to create. They usually operate on the idea that the company can fill whatever sales orders are received, and they always try to keep their costs at a minimum. No doubt this is a valid point in a business where little anticipation of events is necessary in order to satisfy either sales or expense demands. If a firm is so situated that it can immediately meet any new demand for its goods or services, and if its incidence of expenses is regular and unaffected by sales volume, probably the executive is basically right in contending that the budget takes more time than it is worth. However, this describes a relatively small segment of the business world.

Admittedly there are some large organizations whose budget systems are so complicated and demanding that far too much time is spent on them. Such situations are not only frustrating but costly. One symptom of such an organization is that people must spend so much of their time on internal operating affairs that their efforts to reach the organization's goals are significantly retarded.

Revenue lag

One of the problems of budgets is that they commit the firm to expenditures before the actual revenue develops. Thus losses will result if sales drop substantially during the period. The longer the budgetary period, the greater are the chances for this to happen. Suppose a firm forecasts $10 million in sales volume for the coming year. With this anticipated level of activity, it decides to spend $2 million in advertising its products. If some unforeseen situation, such as a strike, stronger competition, or a sudden economic reversal occurs, the sales forecast will prove to be too high. If the firm already has contracted to spend the $2 million, the operations for the period probably will result in a loss.

Inflexibility

Budgets are capable of inserting a considerable degree of inflexibility into the sales picture, if the sales executive is not in continual contact with developments in the field and has not provided for unanticipated occurrences. An inflexible budget can prevent a firm from taking advantage of market opportunities that may come its way. Suppose that after a budget is established, the sales manager discovers a considerable market opportunity for a certain new product. If he has not had the foresight to anticipate such developments, he may encounter considerable difficulty in locating funds with which to do the necessary marketing research and technical development for such a product. Or a changed competitive position in a market may require the firm to increase its advertising expenditures. If the sales manager has not anticipated the possibilities of such developments and provided for them in the sales department budget, it may be difficult to find sufficient funds to accomplish the needed promotional activity.

Unforeseen situations almost always occur, and no one can be sure what they will be or how much money they will require. This weakness can almost preclude the use of a budget if the nature of the business is such that the unanticipated is commonplace. All budgets are predicted on the fundamental predictability of revenues and expenses. The more regular and foreseeable they are, the more useful the budgets are to the administrator.

Size of firm

Some administrators think their firms are too small to have any meaningful grouping of sales and costs. They maintain that their operations are of such a limited nature that it is ridiculous for them to budget for any one activity such as advertising. They claim that about the best they could do in a budget would be to allot money for total administrative expenses and for total selling expenses, and such a budget would be virtually meaningless.

This may or may not be true, depending on the situation. Even a broad budget classification, such as total selling expense, can be of assistance to a small concern that wants to keep costs in line with sales volume. Actually, the problem is that the small firm has a more difficult time developing a reliable sales forecast and estimating its expenses.

Reduced incentives

In some cases, the budget tends to become a goal that, once reached, reduces the incentive of the organization to improve its performance. Once a sales budget has been established and all activities of the enterprise have been focused on achieving that performance, the organization may have difficulty going beyond that goal. This is logical because a sound budget allots only enough money to each expense category to enable the organization to reach its goal.

The argument that budgets reduce incentive is basically not an objection to budgeting in itself. Instead, it is an indication that the firm is unable to forecast sales goals accurately. If they are set too low, the firm may lose market opportunities.

Waste

Another criticism leveled against budgets is that they lead to waste, because the various departments feel it is necessary to spend budgeted funds regardless of need. The criticism of waste is essentially a reflection of a weakness caused by inflexibility in budgeting. Frequently administrative officers plead with their departments to spend all the funds in a certain budget before the end of the period, so the surplus will not revert to a general fund and the amount will not be reduced in the next budget.

Sometimes budgeting can lead to perennial attempts to increase the funds each period. A budget discussion might go as follows. "Last year we were given $500 for supplies. Let's ask for $800 this year, and maybe they will give us $600." The budget should be established on a basis of need for funds to do a job, but it has degenerated into competition to get more money.

Waste in budgeting can also occur when funds are allotted to one budget and then allowed to be transferred to others at the whim of a department head. Executives often find it easier to get funds for one budget than for another. Therefore, they ask for more than is needed in the easy-to-get areas and then later they transfer the surplus to other uses.

Many of these problems are caused by dividing the budgets into too many categories. The more classifications that are made, the more chances there are that excess funds will be granted in any one. The real solution to this problem is not in the mechanics of the budget but rather in indoctrinating the organization with the correct philosophy. It can be disastrous if department heads regard a budget as something to be beaten rather than as a tool designed to help them do their jobs better. Once they develop the attitude that the budgeting process is a game between them and the budget officer to see which one can outwit the other, the entire process becomes questionable.

Unfortunately, the well-intentioned administrator who tries to carry out budget responsibilities in good faith frequently falls victim to the budget games played by peers. Superiors often are unable to recognize the budget tricks being played on them. It is not uncommon for some administrator to be referred to as "good with a budget." This means they are able to gain control over more than their fair share of funds by negotiating and operational tactics.

Some managers feel that budgets cause waste when they are too ample and unwise economy when they are too strict. They believe there is little likelihood the right amount will be budgeted in any one category, and one error does not offset another; rather, they compound one another. They are probably right; it is impossible to budget each expense classification accurately. Each item will be either over or under the theoretical right amount. In this respect, the budget is a compounding of a lot of little mistakes that do not offset one another.

This is a classic case of chasing pennies down an alley while the dollars roll down the streets. It is much better to make many small mistakes than a few big ones. Granted that a budget usually contains many small errors and possibly several medium-sized ones, it still prevents the manager from making a tremendous error in expenditures.

The recognition that one error in budgeting does not offset another should warn an executive not to compile the budget carelessly, under the philosophy that all will balance out satisfactorily in the end.

Conservatism

Critics of budgeting sometimes maintain that budgets almost inevitably tend to be ultraconservative, thereby preventing the organization from reaching its full potential. These critics claim that the people responsible for preparing a budget are influenced basically by the belief that they are going to be judged by the plan. Therefore, almost inevitably they understate their department's capabilities so that the actual performance will make them appear in a favorable light. Few people set their goals higher than they believe they can reach, because the results could make them appear incompetent. Thus most budgets underestimate performance capabilities and overestimate the funds required to accomplish the job.

These executives claim that, in effect, the budgetary process is one of planned mediocrity. They maintain that maximum business efficiency and effectiveness will never be attained if the organization must abide by a budget. Striving for maximum sales, regardless of forecasts, and spending only those funds that seem necessary to achieve that volume is proposed as an alternative.

The charge of conservatism has just enough truth to make it difficult to refute. Possibly the only argument that can be made is that it may be better to make such errors deliberately and with considered judgment than to run the risk of unknowingly making very grave errors. This criticism drives to the heart of the administrator's basic philosophy: Is he a businessman or a gambler? The gambler will be antagonistic toward all budgets, since they restrict his freedom of operation. The true businessman does not want to assume the risks the gambler willingly incurs. He prefers to work steadily, making a planned profit and minimizing all the risks society forces him to underwrite. The budget is the tool of the conservative executive who wants to know something more about what lies ahead and wants to plan his activities. He grants the critics of budgeting many points, but he answers them all by saying that a slightly faulty plan is better than no plan at all.

Conclusion

The criticisms that some administrators levy against budgets can be condensed into two main categories. First, some sincerely feel that they cannot make reliable forecasts on which a meaningful budget could be based. Their firms are often in industries where forecasting is indeed perilous, but it should be pointed out to these people that many firms faced with similar situations are able to use budgets. Often what these administrators really mean is that they are unwilling to do the research necessary to form accurate forecasts. Granted that under many conditions a workable sales forecast is difficult to derive, it is not impossible.

Second, and more important, the use of the budget is usually a matter of business philosophy. Many administrators are so inclined that they cannot use a budget. They would be unwilling to abide by it even if some of their staff members were to convince them that the organization required one. Many executives who operate successfully without the benefits of a budget would rebel at being forced to adopt it as a planning tool. In many cases, they receive a high degree of psychological satisfaction from being able to operate their businesses successfully through their own ingenuity and insight. To them, business is a game similar. However, the economy quickly weeds out those executives who are poor players, while those who are successful in their gambles remain convinced of the basic soundness of their operating policies.

Many of the imputed criticisms of the budgeting procedure are not faults of budgeting but instead indicate administrative weaknesses. Evidence is provided by the executive who: (1) allows the budget to become his master or to restrict him, (2) budgets in too much detail and spends too much time doing it, (3) is unable to forecast sales volume accurately, or (4) is too conservative in the establishment of goals and too generous in the allotment of funds. In essence, executives who either refuse to budget or who claim that budgets are not adaptable for them are saying, in effect, that as business administrators they are incapable of planning their activities.

Budgets can be as simple or as complex as desired. Even the simplest ones can be of great value in planning; it is a mistake to believe that a budget must be considerably detailed. Even if the administrator merely plans some range of sales volume and sets aside certain amounts of money for total production costs and for total selling costs, this can greatly assist in planning activities. In fact, many organizations err in their planning by budgeting in too much detail, thereby obscuring the overall picture.

One expert maintained that most budget problems are, in reality, human relations problems. He projected the following principles:

1. If budget plans and decisions are made by higher management, their lower-level managers cannot be expected to consider budget control their responsibility.
2. If each level of management punishes the next lower level for over-

spending, then each level will add contingencies to its estimates, inflating the total budget.

3. If management uses underspending this year as justification for cutting back budgets next year, it should not be surprised if the result is simply an increase in the lower managers' spending abilities.[3]

QUESTIONS AND PROBLEMS

1. Can a very small firm use budgets?
2. How can a manager build flexibility into the budgeting process in order to provide for unexpected events?
3. How can an executive keep subordinates from wasting funds in overly generous budgets?
4. How can an executive avoid having subordinates ask for more funds than are needed?
5. Can budgets be developed without an accurate sales forecast?
6. If total expenses must be reduced by 10 percent, should an across-the-board cut or a selective reduction be used? If selective, how should the selection be made?
7. One executive claimed that if the department failed to spend its funds during one budget period it should be allowed to keep them and still get its regular allotments. Do you agree?
8. One sale manager commented, "Zero-based budgeting is a fraud . . . a gimmick dreamed up by some accountant to get attention. There is no way in the world management can ignore the past costs of operation. If it cost us $500,000 last year to produce $5 million in sales, and we want $6 million in sales this coming year, then the past budget has to affect the future budget." Comment.
9. A sales executive observed, "Perhaps line-item budgeting is overly detailed and leads to many inflexibilities, but if you think I am about to turn over a lump sum of money to a project manager to spend as he or she desires, you're badly mistaken. If they go off the deep end and blow the dough unwisely, all I can do is fire them, even though the company has been badly damaged." Comment on this thought.
10. "Budgeting is a bunch of bureaucratic baloney dreamed up and supported by administrators who prefer to shuffle papers rather than go out into the streets to sell something." Comment on this statement by a highly successful sales woman.

---

[3] Charles L. Hughes, "Why Budgets Go Wrong," *Personnel*, May–June 1965, pp. 19–26.

Case 17–1

SPRING PARK DEVELOPMENT COMPANY
Cutting the budget

Eleanor Allan, president of the Spring Park Development Company, studied the worksheets on her desk, which had been furnished by the firm's controller. The verdict was clear. Expenses had to be reduced quickly. The 1977 sales forecast had been overly optimistic. Anticipated sales were projected for 1977 at $6.5 million. As of July 1, the actual sales volume of $1.8 million, when projected on an annual rate, indicated that 1977 sales volume would more likely be around $5 million, 23 percent below budget.

Operating expenses for 1977 had been budgeted for $5.5 million, as shown in Exhibit 1. The board of directors had instructed Allan to reduce expenses to no more than $4.5 million. Therefore she called for the firm's accountant and asked for a detailed breakdown of each budget category into hard and soft classifications. She felt that in each budget account there were costs which could or should not be cut, and these should be identified before any budget cutting could take place. The budget reductions would have to come from the so-called soft expenditures.

EXHIBIT 1
Operating expenses

SPRING PARK DEVELOPMENT CO.

Salaries	$1,500,000
Commissions	390,000
Advertising	1,650,000
Entertainment	100,000
Occupancy	75,000
Overhead	600,000
Automotive	55,000
Travel	180,000
Engineering	315,000
Office expenses	225,000
Employee benefits	200,000
Contingency	210,000
Total	$5,500,000

The accountant suggested that while this approach seemed wise and proper, in practice it would prove fruitless. All the soft expenditures had been ruthlessly weeded out at the time the budget was formulated. He insisted that in the end she would just have to cut the budget 18 percent across the board and let it go at that.

Allan disagreed. "We will examine each budget separately this afternoon," she said. "Have the figures here at 2."

Then, she began considering the nature of each budget category. She knew that the salary budget could only be reduced by letting some people go. Salaries could not be cut without a severe impact on morale, and she wanted to avoid that.

She wondered about the rest of the budget amounts. How much could come out of them without hurting operations, thus lowering sales even more.

Questions

1. Give a capsule evaluation of the likelihood of reducing each budget amount significantly.
2. What do you think the new budget amounts will be?

Case 17–2
HALE COMPANY
Supporting a budget request

Mr. John Dee, sales manager for Hale Company, had been called by Mr. Weir, controller, to explain his budget requests for the coming year. In particular, Dee was asked to justify his request for large salary increases for the salesmen.

He had asked for an average salary of $18,000 a year for all salesmen. The company had been paying an average of $12,000 a year. Dee was persuaded that Hale Company's salary structure was woefully low. Six of the ten salesmen had resigned during the preceding two years to accept better paying positions with competitive firms. Each was adamant that his only reason for leaving was that he could make more money elsewhere.

Dee thought that competitors were paying their salesmen on the average of about $16,000 a year. He had proposed the $18,000 figure because he wanted to maintain a policy of paying higher than average wages. Moreover, he felt he would have to pay higher salaries in order to rectify the damages done by the previous policy and to attract the type of men he needed.

Hale Company manufactured a wide line of plastic sheets and tubes which were sold in various forms and specifications to other manufacturers for their operations. The company's salesmen were located in the large industrial cities of the nation.

Dee had experienced great difficulty in replacing the men who had resigned. Not only did the beginning salary offered discourage the number of applicants for the jobs, but their quality was not what he wanted. He was not happy with the men he had been forced to hire. Top management had made it clear that the vacancies were to be filled with the best men immediately available no matter how good that "best" might be. The company could not tolerate having one of its territories without a representative for long, as each man was responsible for so much potential volume.

Dee's request had caused quite a stir in top management when Weir had informed them of it, because the company policy had been to pay below-market wages for all employees. The plastics business was highly competitive, and the company competed on the basis of price. Thus it was of the utmost importance that the firm keep its costs as low as possible. Since wage costs were the largest single element in the firm's cost structure, wages were carefully controlled.

The board of directors had instructed Weir to inform Dee that he was to appear at the next board meeting to substantiate his request. Shortly after Weir's phone call to Dee, the sales manager received another call from a friend in the top echelons who was most sympathetic to the idea of paying higher salaries. He was warned not to come into the meeting with "jawbone" arguments, or he would be crucified. The board was ready to spike his movement at its inception. He was told to bring in hard, incontestable facts for which he had proof in hand.

Question

1. Prepare John Dee's presentation to the board of directors.

18

Sales territories and routing

It is a bad plan that admits of no modification.
SYRUS

Establishing sales territories is another part of sales management's planning job, along with determining market and sales potentials, making sales forecasts, and preparing budgets. Territories make it possible to bring the other aspects of planning down to a regional basis. Ordinarily, it is not practical to plan, direct, and control sales people's activities without establishing sales districts. A company's total market usually is too large to be managed efficiently without them.

> A sales territory is:
> A number of present and potential customers,
> located within a geographical area, and
> assigned to a sales person, branch, or middleman (retailer or wholesaler).

In this definition, the key word is *customer* rather than *geographical*. To understand the concept of a sales territory, we must recognize that a market is made up of people, not places—people with money to spend and the willingness to spend it. A market is measured by people times their purchasing power rather than in square miles. Geographical factors should be considered only to the following extent:

- The customers who constitute a territory should be located in the same general area to facilitate effective coverage by the sales force.

481

- Geographical boundary lines should be drawn around the groups of customers to facilitate quantitative identification of a territory and control by management.

REASONS FOR ESTABLISHING SALES TERRITORIES

To ensure proper coverage of potential market. Under a sound territorial arrangement, the sales reps are more apt to cultivate their regions thoroughly than if they are allowed to sell in any area or to any type of customer. The areas should not be so large that anyone must spend an undue amount of time traveling. However, the sales potential should not be so great that the rep only skims the cream off the market.

To increase sales people's interest and effectiveness. The delineation of territories is likely to encourage responsible managerial attitudes in the sales force. When sales representatives have their own territories, they are virtually in business for themselves. They can take pride in their accomplishments and, at the same time, be more aware of their obligations. They realize that on matters controllable by the field sales force, they alone are responsible for the results in their districts.

Setting territories defines a sales job more concretely. It is more effective to say, "You are assigned the seven counties that constitute this trading area," than it is to say, "Your job is to go out and sell." Furthermore, restricting sales representatives geographically may sharpen their sales abilities. They may route themselves more carefully, plan the frequency of calls, and generally be more aware of their own inefficiencies.

To control and evaluate sales force activities. Restricting a sales representative to a given territory gives management an effective control device. A list of customers can be given to a rep, along with suggestions or instructions on the frequency of calls for each account. A territorial structure also can be a great help to management in its evaluation of sales people's effectiveness. Their actual performance can be measured against territorial potential or territorial quotas.

To facilitate performance of other sales and marketing management functions. Analyzing sales and cost data can be more meaningful if the task is done on a territorial basis rather than for the market as a whole. Marketing research can be used more effectively to set realistic quotas and to prepare sales and expense budgets. Sales people may be instructed to distribute point-of-purchase advertising materials, get dealers to engage in vertical cooperative advertising, or perform other work related to advertising. The results of all these activities usually are more effective if the work can be assigned and controlled on a territorial rather than a total market basis.

To reduce selling costs.   If management is careful in designing the territories and in routing the sales force, it is possible to reduce selling costs considerably. No overlapping territories, with the waste of duplication, will occur. When reps are restricted to one area, they probably spend less time and money traveling than if they are allowed to go anywhere in the total market to look for business. If less time is spent in traveling, an increase in effective selling time, with its related advantages, should result.

To improve customer relations.   Carefully established territories can do much to improve the quality of service the sales people can give to their accounts. A sales person routed properly, can call on accounts regularly, and they will learn to look forward to the visit. Regularity in sales calls is especially important if a staple, repeat-order type of product is being sold. If the regular sales person is not there, the order can just as easily be given to a competitor.

REASONS FOR NOT ESTABLISHING SALES TERRITORIES

Formal territories may not be needed in a small company with a few people selling only in a local market. In this case, management can undoubtedly plan and control sales operations without the aid of districts, and still achieve many of the specific objectives outlined in the preceding section. Territories generally become more necessary as a company's markets and sales force increase in size.

New territories may not be needed immediately in a company which has a well-established territorial structure in one part of the nation but which wants to expand geographically. Management should wait until it has more information about realistic sales expectations in the new market.

The absence of territories may be justified when personal friendships or acquaintances play a large part in the market transaction. This is one reason automobile dealers and commodity and security brokers usually do not district their sales forces. Highly specialized sales engineers also are not often confined within territorial boundaries. But they may serve in troubleshooting assignments or be called in to help close a difficult sale.

PROCEDURE FOR ESTABLISHING TERRITORIES

The ideal goal in territorial design is to have all districts equal in both sales potential and the sales representatives' work load. When sales potentials are equal, it is easier to evaluate and compare sales rep's performance. Also, equal opportunities reduce disputes between management and the sales force and tend generally to improve workers' morale. To achieve both objectives is an ideal, usually unattainable, goal, but this should not deter an executive from constantly striving to reach it.

In many organizations where territories have existed for some time, no planned approach to their establishment has been made. Usually they were established arbitrarily by assigning each person a few states or cities. Little attention was paid to market potential, customary flow of trade, or competition. Then, the districts were allowed to grow indiscriminately. Frequently new ones were added and old ones revised in an unsatisfactory fashion, often on the basis of expediency.

Changing market conditions put continuing pressure on companies to study and adjust their territories. Although different procedures may be used to design the districts, basically a company's territorial structure is influenced by the potential business in the firm's market and by the work load required of its sales force.[1] One plan for establishing territories includes the following five steps.

1. Select a base or control unit for territorial boundaries.
2. Analyze sales people's work loads.
3. Determine basic territories, considering sales potential and call patterns.
4. Establish a route plan for the sales force. (This step is optional.)
5. Conduct territorial sales and cost studies on a continuing basis. (This step is discussed in Chapters 20 and 21.)

Determine basic control unit for territorial boundaries

When establishing territories, the first step is to select a geographical control unit to serve as a territorial base. Commonly used units are states, counties, cities, metropolitan areas, and trading areas. A typical territory may comprise several individual units. One person's district may consist of four trading areas; another's may be three states. It is preferable that the unit be small, for at least two reasons. First, a small unit will aid management in realizing one of the basic values of territories—the geographic pinpointing of potential. Second, the use of small control units makes it easier for management to adjust the territories. If an organization wants to add a little to one person's dis-

---

[1] For a mathematical model and a heuristic-solution procedure for realigning sales territories, see Leonard M. Lodish, "Sales Territory Alignment to Maximize Profit," *Journal of Marketing Research*, February 1975, pp. 30–36; and L. M. Lodish, "'Vaguely Right' Approach to Sales Force Allocations," *Harvard Business Review*, January–February 1974, pp. 119–24.

trict and reduce another's, a county unit facilitates the adjustment better than a state unit.

In the past it was customary for firms to use some political unit (state, county, or city) as a base and to draw territorial lines to coincide with political boundaries. These units afforded a base that was easily understood by both management and the sales force. Furthermore, much government census data and other market information are available for political units.

Today, political units, particularly counties, are still used extensively as a basis for territorial boundaries simply because of the availability of these market data. However, a marked change has occurred in their manner of use. Other market factors are recognized, such as customer buying habits and normal patterns of trade flow. A territory may be based on a unit of a trading area, and the boundaries are drawn to coincide with county lines only so that data may be accumulated for a given trading area. Counties are grouped into trading areas or metropolitan areas as a basis of territories rather than being grouped by states.

States.   Many companies still use a *state* as their control unit in establishing territorial boundaries, and for some conditions this unit may be satisfactory. Territories may be built around states if a firm has a small sales force covering a national market in a selective rather than an intensive manner. A luggage manufacturer on the West Coast who sells directly to a limited number of selected retail accounts has used the state unit with apparent success.

Territorial systems built around states are simple, inexpensive, and convenient. However, for most companies states do not serve well as bases for territories, because in their buying habits customers often are oblivious to a state line as a trade boundary. An Oregon-Washington boundary ignores the fact that many consumers and retailers in southern Washington buy in Portland. Trade from Alton and East St. Louis, Illinois, gravitates to St. Louis, Missouri, rather than to any city in Illinois. Usually a state is an area too large for management to control and evaluate sales operations adequately.

Counties.   For companies which realize the drawbacks to the state unit but which prefer to use a political subdivision as a territorial base, the *county* may be the answer. There are almost 3,100 counties, as against 50 states. Working with smaller control units gives management a better chance to design territories that are equal in potential and to pinpoint problem areas. Many kinds of statistical market data (population, retail and wholesale sales, income, employment, and manufacturing information) are available from several sources on a county basis—the smallest geographical unit for which these data typically are available.

About the only serious drawback to the county unit is that for a limited number of companies it still is too large. A manufacturer or a wholesaler may want to assign several reps to cover one county because the potential is far too much for one person to handle. For certain firms this situation may prevail in such counties as Los Angeles, Cook (Chicago), Wayne (Detroit), or Cuyahoga (Cleveland). It then becomes necessary to divide the city into a series of territories, and some control unit smaller than a county is needed.

Cities and metropolitan areas.   In the past, such firms as wholesalers of food, drugs, and tobacco often used a *city* as a control unit for territorial boundaries because most of the market lay within urban limits. In fact, in many instances even the city was too large, and several sales reps were used within a single city. Then some subcity unit was needed, and business made use of precincts, wards, census tracts, or even city blocks. While it is possible to establish homogeneous territories with reasonably comparable potentials and work loads, it is difficult to get much statistical market data for geographical units smaller than a county or city.

Many companies have found that a significant share of their market has shifted to suburban and satellite cities outside the major central city. These firms have been aided tremendously by the delineation of *standard metropolitan areas*. The federal Bureau of the Budget has established boundaries for about 265 of these areas. By definition, a standard metropolitan area is a county or group of contiguous counties that contains at least one city of over 50,000 population, or two contiguous cities with a combined population over 50,000, the smaller city having at least 15,000 population. The minimum total area population is 100,000. Cities of over 50,000 within 20 miles of each other are included in the same area, and the region's title is hyphenated—for example, San Francisco–Oakland or Tampa–St. Petersburg. The bulk of the workers in each city must be nonagricultural employees, and the counties must be economically and socially integrated with the central county of the area. An area may cross a state line.

A standard metropolitan area is essentially urban in character and usually is smaller than the trading areas around the hub of a city. Because a standard metropolitan area is defined in terms of counties, the same vast amount of statistical data is available. Although small in total land area, the standard metropolitan areas account for a substantial majority of the nation's population and buying power. Thus, they constitute lush, concentrated markets for many consumer and industrial products.

The 300 standard and potential metropolitan areas as defined by *Sales & Marketing Management* accounted for the following percentages of the national totals in 1976: population, 75; effective buying income, 80; retail sales, 79.[2] Because of this highly concentrated market potential, some firms assign territories that consist of a number of metropolitan areas. They encourage their sales people to work only in the metropolitan area and to skip the region outside or between the areas.

Trading areas. A popular territorial base, especially for firms that sell to or through wholesalers or retailers, is the *trading area*. This control unit is a geographical region that consists of a central city, which dominates the market, plus the surrounding area whose trade normally flows to the hub city. Thus, a trading area is based on consumer buying habits and normal trading patterns. A trading area usually ignores all political boundaries, although its boundaries are drawn arbitrarily to coincide with county lines so that the census and other market data may be used.

The concept of a trading area is used in general terms as a base for territories. Actually, however, a trading area must be thought of in terms of a specific product. A retail trading area exists for drugs or furniture, or a wholesale trading area may exist for groceries or dry goods. There is no such thing as a Denver trading area. Rather, there is a Denver wholesale trading area for jewelry or furniture.

Theoretically, no customer in a given trading area would go outside the boundaries to buy merchandise, nor would a buyer from outside enter the trading area just to purchase a product. However, from a practical standpoint, trading areas are not that sharply defined. Frequently, considerable overlapping occurs, particularly in the more densely populated sections of the country. A shadow or twilight zone, rather than distinct lines, divides the two regions. Buyers located in this zone may patronize outlets in either or both areas.

Use of a trading area as a territorial base for the sale of a given product has several advantages. These areas are based on economic considerations, not political ones. They are realistic in that they represent patterns of trade; they are based on customer buying habits. They should facilitate sales planning and control. For instance, there is little danger that after a manufacturer's sales rep does considerable missionary work with retailers, they will buy the product from a wholesaler in another rep's territory. The only time a problem may arise is when trading areas overlap. A manufacturer's sales person operating in the Chicago wholesale trading area for large home appliances may call on two retailers in Springfield, Illinois. He may be successful in getting both of them to place orders for his line of merchandise. One retailer gives an order to a Chicago wholesaler, and the rep gets credit. However, the other dealer does business with a St. Louis wholesaler, so

---

[2] "Survey of Buying Power," *Sales Marketing & Management,* July 25, 1977.

another sales person gets the credit, even though the Chicago rep is responsible for the sale.

Probably the major drawback to the use of trading areas as territorial bases is the difficulty in defining them for a given product. Areas differ considerably in size and shape, depending on such factors as the nature of the product, topographical conditions, the highway network, the number and size of potential customers, the channel of distribution used, and the level of distribution (wholesale or retail).

A company may have to develop its own trading area map, and considerable effort and expense may be involved. However, several organizations have prepared trading area maps covering various types of products. Rand-McNally, for example, publishes a trading-area map of the United States showing 494 basic trading areas and 50 major trading areas. In most large cities the major newspapers and other private firms prepare market information maps from which trading areas may be delineated.

Analyze sales people's work loads

Because territorial design depends basically on the company's sales potential and the work loads of its sales force, it is most important that management identify and measure the factors that influence these work loads. Two companies, each selling in markets of comparable potential and geographical size, may have quite different territorial structures simply because of a difference in the sales reps' work loads and the resultant call patterns set by management.

Nature of the job. A sales rep's call patterns are influenced by the nature of the job. A rep who does selling only can make more calls per day and therefore cover a larger territory than the rep who must do a considerable amount of missionary work along with selling. In markets with very strong competition and a concentration of large profitable accounts, management may feel it desirable to have two sales people to cover each account. One may call periodically to do straight selling, while the other takes care of any necessary missionary work. If the total job is split between two people they each can cover a larger territory.

Nature of the product. The nature of the product also can have an effect on a sales person's call pattern. A staple, convenience good with a rapid rate of turnover may require more frequent calls by sales reps than would an industrial product with very limited repeat-sale business. Therefore, a representative who sells this industrial product can handle more accounts than can the person who sells the convenience good. Often, the nature of the product has a considerable bearing on the number of outlets or the number of customers. A rep who sells a specialty good purchased by one or two outlets in a city can cover a larger territory than the rep who sells a convenience good purchased by every grocery store and drugstore. Even though the convenience good is probably sold through a wholesaler, it may still be necessary for the sales person to call on the retail accounts to do missionary work.

Channel of distribution used.   The channel of distribution a company uses has a great deal of influence on the number of accounts found in a typical 100-square-mile area. Firms that sell to wholesalers do not have as many accounts in a trading area as do companies that sell direct to retailers. And neither of these two types has as many accounts within a given area as do organizations that sell direct to the consumer on a door-to-door basis.

Stage of market development.   When entering a new market, a company's territories typically are larger than in markets where the firm is well entrenched. This situation occurs even though the market potential is comparable to the old and new regions. A large geographical district is needed initially to yield an adequate volume of business for the sales representative to make a decent income and, at the same time, show a satisfactory ratio between sales and expenses.

Intensity of market coverage.   If a firm wants mass distribution, smaller territories will be required than if it follows a selective or exclusive distribution policy. It is also possible for a firm to eliminate a number of its unprofitable accounts but not reduce the size of territories. Instead, it encourages sales reps to devote more time to the remaining accounts, in an attempt to develop additional business. A firm that wants to increase its share of a market may have to reduce the size of its territories. The sales force will then have more time to concentrate on present accounts and to develop business with firms that buy from competitors.

Competition.   No general statement can be made about the net effect competition has on the size of the territory. If management's decision is to make an all-out effort to meet and beat competition, then territorial borders probably will be contracted. Sales people will be instructed to intensify their efforts by increasing the frequency of call and the length of time spent with each account. On the other hand, competition may be so fierce, or the territorial markets so overdeveloped, that the company is not going to make much profit in the district. Therefore, the decision may be to expand the geographical limits of the district, or to merge it with an adjacent one and have the sales rep cover the broader area in an extensive fashion. The rep would call only on selective accounts, thus tending to skim the cream from the market rather than attempting any intensive coverage.

Ability of sales person.   Even though two districts may be reasonably equal in sales potential and work load, adjustments may be needed because of the variation in the ability of the sales people who cover the two regions. The physical condition of the reps may be an important barrier, because some regions require more traveling and generally drain a person physically more than others do. Certainly the age of the rep is a controlling factor. Although they often are better sales people than the younger ones, the older representatives may not be able to cover a large territory.

Ethnic factors.   A company may adjust its territorial boundaries in large cities because of the market concentration of certain racial, national, or religious groups. One part of the city may have a heavy concentration of people of one nationality. The retailers also may be predominantly of the same origin, and use of the group's mother language may be widespread in the area. A firm that sells to these retailers may alter its territorial boundaries so that the particular nationality group comprises one district. Then the sales person assigned to that region not only will be the same nationality, but also will speak the language. In the city of Chicago, a concern that sells to retail businesses may establish separate territories in some parts of the city to cater to the black, Italian, Polish, and Jewish markets. The person who covers each of those districts is from the corresponding ethnic group, and where necessary can speak the foreign language.

Determine basic territories

The third general step in designing sales districts is to establish a fundamental territory based on statistical measures. This step can be accomplished by using either the buildup or the breakdown method. Under the *buildup* procedure, territories are formed by combining small geographical areas based on the control unit selected. The *breakdown* system involves division of the whole market into segments. The buildup method is particularly adapted for manufacturers of consumer products or for companies that want intensive distribution. The breakdown method is more popular among manufacturers of industrial products or organizations that want selective distribution.

Buildup method.   Several variations are possible in the procedure used to establish territories by building up from the basic control unit. Usually, however, these variations depend fundamentally on some type of customer analysis, as well as study of the sales people's call patterns. A suggested procedure is outlined in the following paragraphs.

1. *Determine number, location, and size of customers.*   Management first should determine the number, location, and size of both present and prospective customers within each selected control unit. Size is measured in terms of potential purchases of the seller's product. An analysis of sales records, including sales people's call reports, should establish the location of present customers in each trading area

or other control unit. Prospective customers can be identified with the aid of company sales reps plus outside sources such as trade directories (e.g., Thomas' Register), publishers of mailing lists (e.g., R. H. Donnelley Corporation), subscription lists from trade journals, trade association offices, classified telephone directories, or credit rating firms (e.g., Dun & Bradstreet, Inc.).

Once the customers are identified, management should make an assessment of the potential business that may be expected from each account. For these estimates, a company may refer to some of the same sources used to build customer lists. Of course, a company should be able to estimate with reasonable accuracy the potential business that could be done with present customers.

After an estimate has been made of the volume of business that may be expected from each present and prospective customer, management can classify these accounts into several categories, based on their potential profitability to the seller. This step furnishes some of the necessary background for a determination of the sales people's call patterns.

2. *Determine desirable call patterns.* Following the customer analysis, management should establish desirable call patterns in each territorial control unit. This means determining the number of calls to be made in a day, and the frequency with which each account should be visited.

The *number of calls* that can be made effectively in one day depends, in turn, on several factors. One is the average length of time required for a call. This is influenced by the number of people to be seen in each account, the amount of missionary work to be done, and the interruptions. Quantitative data about the average length of time for each call may be gathered from sales people, a time and duty analysis, or an analysis of call reports. Another factor that influences the number of daily calls is the amount of travel time between customers.

The *call frequency* is influenced by the nature of the product, customer buying habits, the nature of competition, potential business done with an account, the cost of calling on a customer, and the method of distribution.

As they affect the frequency of call, these factors fall into two general categories. One group affects to the same extent all the accounts within a territorial control unit. As an example, the nature of the product and the method of distribution fall in the first category. Based only on these two factors, call frequency may be set at one a week for a grocery wholesaler calling on retail grocery stores. The second group of factors—examples are size of account and cost of calling on an account—affect each account differently and therefore necessitate different call frequencies.

Management may group its accounts into three categories—A, B, and C—according to the amount of business expected from each. Group A accounts are called on each time a sales person goes through a territory, Group B's are visited every other trip, and group C's only on every third trip. A rep presumably could call on twice as many customers in class B as in class A, because the call frequency in B is only one half that in A.

3. *Determine number of accounts to assign each sales person.* By relating the average *number* of daily calls and the average *frequency* of calls for each class of accounts, management can tentatively determine the number of customers that can be handled by each sales rep. This step of determining the number of accounts to assign ordinarily must be done on an individual territorial basis because of the differences among territories.

To illustrate the process of assigning accounts to the sales force, we shall use a relatively uncomplicated situation. It is based on the assumption that one person can average 6 calls a day (30 a week), and his average frequency of call is monthly. We also assume that each customer is called on with the same frequency. Then each sales rep can call on approximately 120 customers. In a second situation, the same conditions prevail, except that some customers should be called on semimonthly, others monthly, and others bimonthly. The average frequency still is about once a month, and therefore a sales person can handle 120 customers, the same number as in the first example.

In a third situation, management may want to refine its analysis by classifying customers in three divisions, A, B, and C, based on a profit analysis of accounts. Class A accounts are the most profitable and are called on semimonthly. Class B accounts are visited monthly, and class C accounts bimonthly. Table 18–1 shows the number of calls per year for each class of account, assuming a certain number of accounts in each of two trading areas. If a sales person can average 6 calls a day (which equal 30 calls per week, or 1,500 per year) in trading areas X

TABLE 18–1
Example of call frequency for different customer classes

Customer class	Call frequency	Trading area X		Trading area Y	
		No. of accounts	No. of calls per year	No. of accounts	No. of calls per year
A	2 per month	10	240	5	120
B	1 per month	25	300	15	180
C	1 every 2 months	15	90	60	360
		50	630	75	660

and Y, then either trading area will take slightly over 40 percent of a rep's time. Both areas require about the same number of calls, even though Y has 50 percent more accounts than X. The reason for this is that Y has far more small, unprofitable accounts that require a call only every other month.

As shown in Table 18–1, a sales person could cover trading areas X and Y and still have room for accounts that called for a total of about 210 calls a year $(1,500 - [630 + 660] = 210)$. A sales person could cover any number of customers who, in total, required 1,500 calls a year. For example, one rep could cover 125 accounts if they were divided this way: A, 25; B, 50; C, 50. He could handle 165 customers if they were grouped: A, 15; B, 40; C, 110. Or, he could call on only 80 if 50 were good accounts (class A), 20 were B accounts, and 10 were in class C. Obviously, any *increase* in the average number of daily calls, or any *decrease* in the call frequency, will increase the number of customers any one sales person can cover.

4. *Draw territorial boundary lines.* The final stage in the buildup method is to accumulate enough contiguous territorial control units so that the number of accounts included therein constitutes an adequate potential and a reasonable work load for one sales person. Ordinarily, a common statistical formula cannot be developed for all territories because of differences in call patterns, number of potential accounts, and other influences. A company has a choice of places from which to start the grouping. On a national scale, a firm that groups contiguous trading areas into territories may start in Maine and work south to Florida, then go back to Ohio and again work south to the Gulf of Mexico. Another firm, using county control units, may start each territory with a county that includes a major city, and then complete a given region by fanning out in all directions until the necessary number of contiguous counties are included. Other organizations group counties or trading areas around a central unit which includes a branch office or plant.

To illustrate the grouping of territorial control units into sales districts, we can use the example of the sales person who averages 6 calls a day with a monthly call frequency and is able to cover 120 accounts. For simplicity's sake, assume that each control unit has 24 customers. To give this person a full work load, the territory assigned would be composed of five control units. In another situation, there may not be a perfectly even distribution of customers among the control units. The rep who can call on 120 customers may have them divided among five units, as follows: area A, 15; area B, 30; area C, 25; area D, 40; area E, 10.

When a company does not use the same call frequency for all customers, a slightly different approach must be taken. Management cannot work merely on the basis of *number* of accounts, as in the preceding examples. Rather, the *importance* of the accounts must be considered. Quantitatively the importance is reflected in the number of *calls* needed to cover the trading area. In a previous example, it was assumed that a rep can make 1,500 calls a year. Trading area X requires 630 calls for adequate coverage, and trading area Y takes 660. Trading area Z is contiguous to X and Y. If Z can be covered with approximately 210 calls, then these three trading areas can constitute one person's territory (630 + 660 + 210 = 1,500). This territory may have a total of 140 customers. An adjacent territory may include four trading areas and 190 customers. But because they are not such large accounts, they still can be adequately covered with 1,500 calls and are assigned to one person.

Often, unless a company splits a trading area, it is unable to group contiguous trading areas or other control units into statistically reasonable territories. In the above case of trading areas X and Y, which together require 1,290 calls, no trading area may be contiguous to X and Y that can be covered with approximately 210 calls—the number needed to give the sales rep normal load of 1,500 visits per year. A good rule of thumb in these cases is not to split the control unit. Statistical data may not be available for partial units, so territorial planning and control would be more difficult. Rather than split a control unit, the call frequency for some accounts may be increased or the number of daily calls reduced, so the sales person can intensify efforts in a smaller geographic region. In the opposite situation, the size of the total territory may be *increased* by cutting the call frequency or raising the number of daily calls.

In the examples to this point, it has been assumed that the selected territorial control unit is small enough so that a sales person's district includes at least one, and usually more, of these control units. However, it is possible that in some part of the market the basic unit may be too large in potential or in work load for one person to cover. If two or more reps are needed to cover a control unit, in those areas management should use a smaller basic unit. For example, a firm that uses the county unit may find it adequate in all but 8 or 10 counties in the country. In those 8 or 10, a smaller unit is needed. But the procedure for determining the number of customers, call pattern, and so on is essentially the same as outlined above.

Breakdown method.   The other major method used to establish the basic statistical territories is the breakdown method. As noted above, it is often used by firms that want exclusive distribution or that sell some types of industrial products.

1. *Determine sales potential.*   The first step in the breakdown method is to determine what sales volume the company can expect in

its entire market and in each territorial control unit (county, trading area, and so on). To obtain regional potentials, first the *industrywide* potentials in the total market where the company operates is estimated. Then the firm can calculate its potential in its total market and in each territorial control unit.

2. *Determine volume expected from each sales person.*   Next, management must establish how much each sales representative must sell in order to have a profitable business. A study of past sales experience should help in this matter, and a cost analysis often is used as an aid.

3. *Determine number of territories needed.*   The third step is to divide the total sales potential by the volume needed from each person. The answer is the number of territories a company must establish. For instance, if the total potential is $20 million and the average volume per person is $500,000, then the business needs 40 sales reps.

4. *Tentatively establish territories.*   The final stage in the statistical phase of the breakdown method is to divide the entire market so that each sales rep has about the same potential. In the company with 40 sales people, each would be assigned an area comprising about 2.5 percent of the company's total sales potential. Potential has already been established for each of the basic territorial control units, so management needs to assign a sales person enough contiguous units so that he has 2.5 percent of the total potential. The boundaries of each territory should coincide with the borders of the control units. As in the buildup method, control units should not be split between two people, even if that means a slightly different potential for each one.

5. *Modify basic territories.*   Up to this point in the breakdown procedure, the company's sales potential has been the controlling factor in designing the territories. Now, management should modify these tentatively established districts in light of the work-load requirements set for the sales people. Such factors as the nature of the product, the stage of market development, and other considerations may influence the work loads and call patterns and, consequently, the territorial boundaries.

ROUTING THE SALES FORCE

After sales territories have been carefully established, management can turn its attention to the possibility of routing the sales people within their respective districts. *Routing* is the managerial activity that establishes a formal pattern for sales reps to follow as they go through their territories. This pattern usually is reflected on a map or list that shows the order in which each segment of the territory is to be covered. Although routing is referred to as a managerial activity, this does not imply that it is done only at some executive level. Often, a firm asks its sales people, as part of the job of managing their work, to prepare their own route schedules.

Routing is an optional step in sales planning. For reasons discussed later, many firms omit the activity entirely. However, other concerns believe that the job of districting the sales force is not completed until a route plan is designed to ensure systematic coverage of the territories.

Reasons for routing by management

Managerial routing of the sales force can be expected to reduce travel expenses by ensuring an orderly, thorough coverage of the market. A large percentage of a typical sales person's time is spent outside a customer's establishment. Studies indicate that it is not at all unusual for a rep to spend one third of the daily working hours in traveling. At that rate, for a total of four months out of a year the sales representative is not even inside a customer's office.

Proponents of management's handling of the routing activity believe the typical sales person is unable to do the job satisfactorily. They feel that sales people will look for the easiest, most pleasant way to do their job, although this may not be the most effective way. Left to their own routing devices, they will backtrack and crisscross in a territory in order to be home several nights a week. Some companies have pinpointed the problem by showing the percentage of potential sales realized from each account. Around a rep's home base can be drawn a circle whose radius is about the distance he can travel in one day and still get home at night. On either side of the circle's edge is an area bounded by several minutes of travel time. Within this area, actual sales are far below potential. This is the marginal area that a rep can cover and still get home at night. Beyond this marginal region, the rep is resigned to being gone overnight, so he concentrates on selling and turns in a creditable performance.

Objections to routing

Many sales executives feel that routing reduces people's initiative and straitjackets them in an inflexible plan of territorial coverage. They believe the sales rep in the field is in the best position to decide in what order the accounts should be visited. Market conditions often are so fluid that it would be a mistake for a company to set up a route plan and prevent a sales person from making expedient changes to meet some situation. High-caliber representatives usually do not need to be routed and may resent it if the plan is forced on them.

Factors conducive to routing

Before deciding to route its sales force, management should consider the nature of the product and the job. If the call frequencies are regular and if the job activities at each customer's location are reasonably routine, it is easier to plan a person's route than it is if the visits are irregular. Sales people for drug, grocery, tobacco, or hardware wholesalers also can be routed without serious difficulty. In fact, to attempt an irregular call pattern with a given customer can result in loss of the account. A drug retailer, for instance, plans his buying on the basis of a sales rep's call, say, every Tuesday morning. If this retailer cannot depend on the wholesale sales rep's call regularity, the buyer may seek another source of supply.

Procedure for establishing a routing plan

If management has done a thorough job in designing its territories, most of the research needed in setting a routing plan has been completed. The present and prospective accounts can be spotted on a map of the territory. The daily call rate has been determined, along with the desired call frequency for each account. With all this information available, the actual establishment of routes is reasonably mechanical. Some of the commonly used route patterns are circular, straight line, cloverleaf, and hopscotch.[3] When call frequencies differ among the accounts, management may employ a skip-stop routing pattern. On one trip the sales person may visit every account, but on the next trip he may call on only a third of the accounts—the most profitable third.

The problem of routing salesmen effectively is another sales operational area that is ideal for computer application. In a given sales person's territory, management knows the number of cities, the number of accounts, and the location of these accounts. Call frequencies can be set for each account. A number of computer models have been designed to help management determine the one route through a territory which will minimize either total travel time or travel cost.[4]

---

[3] In a hopscotch pattern, a salesman starts one trip at the furthest point, say north, of his home and works back toward home; on the next trip, he goes to the most distant point in another direction and works toward home. See Theodore H. Biggs, "Salesmen's Routing Plans," in The Conference Board, *Allocating Field Sales Resources*, Experiences in Marketing Management, No. 23 (New York, 1970), pp. 68–72.

[4] See William Lazer, Richard T. Hise, and Jay A. Smith, "Computer Routing: Putting Salesmen in Their Place," *Sales Management*, March 15, 1970, p. 29.

REVISING SALES TERRITORIES

When a firm first starts in business, ordinarily sales territories are not carefully designed. Instead, each person may be assigned a vaguely defined part of the market. Through the years, these territories continue to develop indiscriminately, until finally the executives realize they no longer can ignore the situation. Some territorial revision is imperative. Or management may have done an accurate job of districting its sales force at some time in the past. As market conditions or other controlling factors change, however, a territorial structure can easily become outdated.

Is problem in territorial design?

Revising territorial boundaries is a very difficult job. If possible, it should be done infrequently, and then only for major reasons and after a thorough study. Before making any boundary adjustments, management must be certain that the danger signals are the result of a poor territorial design and not because of poor administration in other areas. The fault may lie in the compensation plan, inadequate supervision, or a poor quota system.

Indications of need for adjustment

Frequently, sales potential outgrows a territory, and as a result the sales person is cream skimming rather than intensively covering his district. When out-of-date measures of potential are used, a territory can become too large for one person to cover effectively, and the performance results from this district can be quite misleading. In a fast-growing region, for instance, one sales person's volume may have increased 100 percent over a period of years—the largest increase of any rep in the firm. Management praises him highly and holds him up as the model of a good sales rep. Actually, he may have been doing a very poor job, because the territorial potential increased 200 or 300 percent. The company really was losing its former share of market, because the districts were not reduced in size in order to encourage more thorough coverage.

On the other end of the scale, territories may need revising because they are too small. The mistake may have been made when they were first set up, or changing market conditions may have caused the situation.

Overlapping territories are a form of structural weakness that should be corrected. This problem generally stems from previous boundary revisions. To illustrate, salesman Carter originally had as his territory

A day-to-day operating problem in the

MAJESTIC GLASS COMPANY (K)

Splitting a high-potential territory

Majestic's Milwaukee territory was one of the smallest in area, because of the concentration in that city of a substantial segment of the brewing industry, an important user of bottles. Herman Millard, who perhaps was Majestic's best salesman, was awarded this territory after a long apprenticeship in territories with smaller potential.

Recently, increased competition for the beer container business had been felt, particularly from manufacturers of metal cans, which Majestic did not produce. To keep the brewers' business, Clyde Brion, general sales manager, believed it necessary to intensify sales efforts in Milwaukee. He wanted to maintain almost continuous contact with customers' executives at several levels of management. As a temporary measure, Mr. Brion went to Milwaukee to assist Millard, but he allowed Millard full commissions on all sales that either of them made.

Because he had other duties, Mr. Brion could not stay in Milwaukee indefinitely. He believed that his assistance to Millard was resented by Majestic sales people in other territories. Therefore he proposed to Millard that another sales person be hired and given a fraction—perhaps one third—of the Milwaukee territory.

To this proposal Millard objected strenuously, saying, "I earned my right to this territory, and now you want to take it away from me!"

Question

Should the Milwaukee territory be split?

If so, how should Clyde Brion handle Herman Millard's objections?

Note: See the introduction to this series of problems in Chapter 2 for the necessary background on the company, its market, and its competition.

the three West Coast states—California, Oregon, and Washington. As the potential grew in this territory, it was divided into two districts. Carter kept California, and a new rep, McNeil, was assigned Washington and Oregon. However, Carter also was allowed to keep a given number of preferred accounts in what is now McNeil's territory. The reason given for this decision was that Carter had spent much time in developing the accounts, the customers liked him, and they might switch to a competitor if Carter did not call on them. Rather than create a possibly serious morale problem with a good sales rep (Carter), management allowed the overlap to develop in the territories. By avoiding a morale problem, which probably could have been handled easily by a good administrator, the company planted the seeds for even greater morale problems as time went by. Eventually, McNeil will chafe under the arrangement. Also, higher cost and selling inefficiencies generally result from overlapping territories.

Territorial adjustments are necessary when claim jumping is practiced. It may be that management has established territories with definite boundaries, but has tolerated, or in some cases even encouraged, having a person in one district go outside its borders and sell in another's district. On the face of it, the practice seems unsound. If each territory has an adequate potential, and one sales rep jumps another's claim, then the first one obviously is not satisfactorily developing his own area. On the other hand, if one person has done a thorough job in his own region and still has the time or need to go into the next district, some adjustment is needed because the first territory is too small. The increasing costs, inefficiencies, and friction among the reps that can develop when one cuts into another's region should be obvious.

Effect of revision on sales force

Most people dislike change, partially because they cannot forecast the consequences. Management may hesitate to make obviously needed adjustments in territorial boundaries for fear of hurting sales force morale. In fact, many of the territorial problems—overlapping districts, for instance—are a result of management's trying to avoid friction in the past.

A morale problem is particularly apt to arise when a sales person's territory is reduced in size. He is suspicious that management is attempting to curtail his earnings, and he is reluctant to lose accounts he has cultivated over a period of time. Certainly, it should be helpful for management to get sales people's suggestions periodically during the revision procedure.

When a sales person's territory is cut, it is also almost automatic that his income (along with his morale) will drop unless management makes some compensation adjustments. If the job of redistricting has been done properly, the reduced territory ultimately offers a better volume opportunity and the chance to cover the area more intensively. Until the sales rep can fully develop the smaller territory, however, he probably will need some special compensation help during the transition period. It is a practice among many firms to make *no* adjustment whatsoever in a person's pay but instead to try to sell him on the idea that the intensive development of his remaining territory will quickly bring his income to its former level, or higher. Understandably, it usually is quite difficult to get the rep to accept this line of reasoning. Consequently, his morale and perhaps also his loyalty to the firm will very likely decline.

Another procedure frequently employed is to guarantee the sales person his previous level of income during a definitely stated adjustment period. While this approach may allay a sales person's immediate fears, it also may well lull him into a false sense of security. He may continue to put off the time when he must exert the necessary effort to reach his former level of sales in the new, smaller region. Then, when the guarantee period expires he is suddenly jolted by the sharp decrease in earnings level.

QUESTIONS AND PROBLEMS

1. What companies might logically use states as control units for territorial boundaries?

2. For the following industries, in which trading area is your school located?
   a. Wholesale food.
   b. Wholesale sporting goods.
   c. Wholesale jewelry.
   d. Retail furs.
   e. Retail high-fashion women's ready-to-wear.

3. What control unit would you recommend in establishing sales territories for the following companies? Support your recommendation.
   a. Manufacturer of men's shoes.
   b. Food broker.
   c. Appliance wholesaler.
   d. Manufacturer of textile machinery.
   e. Manufacturer of outboard motors.
   f. Lumber wholesaler.

4. The text discussed several qualitative factors that may affect a territory's sales potential and thus necessitate a change in the statistically determined boundaries. How can variations in competition, or ability of the

sales force, each be reflected in square miles, trading areas, or other geographical measurements of territories?

5. What are some of the signals indicating that a company's territorial structure may need revising?

6. Assume that a territory's potential has increased to the point where the district should be realigned to form two territories. Properly developed, each of the two new units should bring an income equal to what was earned previously in the one large district. Should management assign to one of the new districts the same sales person who formerly had the combined territory, or should the rep be transferred to an entirely different area before the division is attempted?

7. Sales people typically are prohibited from going outside their territorial boundaries in search of business. Sometimes, however, a customer located in one district will voluntarily seek out a sales rep or branch office located in another district. Perhaps this customer can realize a price advantage by buying outside his home area. What should be the position of the seller in these situations? Should he reject such business? Should he insist the order be placed in the territory where the customer is located? If the order is placed in the foreign territory, should the sales person in the customer's home territory be given any commission or other credit?

8. If a company has several branches and insists that each of its suppliers send the same sales person to all branches, what problems are involved in such a situation? What course of action do you recommend for firms that sell to the company in question?

9. In the process of redistricting, many firms do not allow a sales person to keep any of his former accounts if they are outside his new district. One hardware wholesaler realigned his territories and then found he faced the loss of some good customers because they said they would do business only with the wholesaler's salesman who had been calling on them for years. Should the wholesaler make an exception and allow this salesman to keep these accounts outside his new district, and thus have overlapping territories? Is the loss of these good accounts the only other alternative?

10. Since it is impossible to equate territories perfectly, should the manager use them to provide promotions for good people? For example, should the best reps be given the choice areas?

11. "Routing is a managerial device for planning, controlling, and conducting the activities of the sales force." Explain the function of routing in relation to each of these concepts.

12. *a.* Under what conditions is a firm most apt to establish route plans for its sales force?

    b. What type of sales job lends itself least to formal routing patterns for the sales force?

Case 18–1

GLORAMA JEWELRY COMPANY
Splitting territory of well-established salesman

Philip Caine, the general sales manager for the Glorama Jewelry Company, was increasingly concerned over his company's position in the Texas–eastern New Mexico market. In this sales territory he felt that the company was not achieving its objective of acquiring new customers. He was beginning to realize that the territory had simply grown too large for one salesman to cover, and it was time to split that territory in some way. Caine realized he had a delicate situation on his hands, because the salesman in that territory, Michael Stern, had been with the company for 30 years and was influential in the firm's success and status.

The Glorama Jewelry Company was a family-owned wholesaler of costume jewelry located in Chicago. The company was started in 1940 by Werner Spivak, an immigrant from eastern Europe. The current top management consisted of the founder's son and son-in-law, Frank Spivak and Eric Jenkins, who acted as president and vice president, respectively. In expanding the sales force through the years, Werner Spivak had hired only men who were hard workers, aggressive, personable, willing to work on straight commission, and who did not mind travelling 46 weeks out of the year.

With this type of sales force and management philosophy, Glorama grew and prospered in a fiercely competitive business. Currently the company had 32 salesmen who covered all mainland states except in New England. The firm was in excellent financial condition. Last year's sales were $15 million, and net profits ran 10 percent of sales. To continue its rate of growth and level of performance, management planned to increase Glorama's territorial coverage by opening new accounts and building up the existing ones.

Glorama carried a wide assortment of costume jewelry products which were purchased from hundreds of manufacturers. All products were sold under the Glorama brand name to retailers. The typical markup on these products was 50 percent of the retail price (100 percent of Glorama's selling price to retailers). The products ranged in retail prices from $1 to $30. About 50 percent of Glorama's volume was in items which retailed for $2 to $3, and over 75 percent was in the $2–$15 retail price range. With the introduction of jewelry into men's fashions, Glorama had recently added a small assortment of men's jewelry items. Since the costume jewelry business was extremely faddish and seasonal, the profit and volume contribution of each item varied from season to season, as well as from year to year. Over the years, however, pierced earrings and necklaces had contributed the most to both volume and profit. Other major product groups were rings, bracelets, and pins.

The costume jewelry industry closely resembles perfect competition, in that there are hundreds of small manufacturing suppliers and hundreds of wholesalers. Yet no two of these distributors are exactly alike in the styles and mix of products they carry. Since many wholesalers buy from the same supplier, Glorama was in direct competition with other distributors who carried the same product. Glorama had several competitive advantages, however. For example, their large size and stable financial condition enabled them to carry a large selection of styles with an adequate back-up inventory stock. Also, since they were centrally located, they could ship to most of their customers within a reasonable period of time. Furthermore, some of their salesmen participated directly in the buying process, so they could quickly and accurately reflect their customers' wants and ideas.

On the other hand, the very factor of Glorama's large size in relation to most of its competitors did present some competitive limitations. These smaller firms located throughout the nation could deliver an order in some locations sooner than Glorama. Retailers sometimes wanted to purchase from a more specialized line, thereby overlooking Glorama. Many competitors also had easier lines of credit and later payment dates than Glorama. Competitors would also ship smaller quantities of merchandise.

Generally speaking, Glorama salesmen would sell to any retailer who was interested in carrying costume jewelry. However, the salesmen did have to be cautious about selecting and selling to stores located close together in a city. By selling the same type and price range of products to two closely located stores, a salesman ran the risk of alienating and thus losing both accounts.

Currently, the percentage distribution of Glorama's total sales volume by type of retail store was as follows:

Type of store	Percent of sales
Discount	30%
Department	15
Chain	15
Drug	15
Dress	10
Gift	5
Jewelry	5
Miscellaneous (men's stores and trading-stamp company)	5
Total	100%

The two salesmen who had the highest volume and most profitable territories in the Glorama company were both located in Texas. Together they generated about 22 percent of the company's total sales volume. Currently there were ten other firms which were considered to be strong competitors in that region. The no. 2 salesman was Michael Stern, who lived in Dallas, Texas. His territory was the largest in the company. It covered north, east, central and west Texas, as well as eastern New Mexico.

Mike Stern had been with the Glorama firm for 30 years. Early in his career with the company, Mike moved to Texas and started to develop a territory previously untapped by Glorama. Since then he has continued to be the only sales representative the company has ever had in the Texas–New Mexico territory. Initially his main accounts were jewelry and drug stores. Then as department stores, discount stores, and other types of retailers began to carry inexpensive jewelry, Stern expanded his customer list. Over the years he built a sizable clientele to the point where his straight commission earnings (12 percent of sales) for the past several years had been well in excess of $100,000 a year.

Over the past 30 years Mike Stern had become very well known and liked by his customers, as well as his competitors. His instinct and knowledge of future trends in costume jewelry had helped establish excellent rapport and trust with his customers. In many instances, he had gone beyond the call of duty in servicing his customers. For example, if a certain product did not sell, he would personally pick up the "dog" from the customer and return it to the company.

Philip Caine, the Glorama sales manager, said that "Mike is a man of his word and will not push anything he does not believe in. In a dog-eat-dog industry such as ours, where most salesmen want to make a quick buck, Mike is genuinely concerned with providing his customers with the goods and services they want."

In addition to his field-selling activities, Mike Stern also was influential in getting management to establish some written policy and procedure guidelines for the sales force. He sometimes helped in the buying process by indicating what styles he thought would be good sellers in the future. He even had made several large purchases from suppliers who had been overlooked by the regular purchasing executives. Also, when a new sales person was hired, Stern usually was assigned the responsibility for on-the-job training.

For the past ten years, Stern had devoted most of his time to his larger key accounts. Although he serviced large towns of more than 75,000 people, over 60 percent of his business was in towns of less than 75,000 people. This meant that many cities in Stern's territory were not being covered to their full potential.

Currently, Stern had 500 active accounts in his territory. He called on 300 of these customers on a regular basis four times a year. The other 200 accounts came to him when he showed his entire line at jewelry trade shows in Dallas. These showings were held during eight weeks of the year. In addition, many accounts called in an open order to Stern. This meant that Stern used his own judgment in sending his customers merchandise that they did not select personally. In recent years, Stern's volume of open orders had increased tremendously, causing him additional paper work at night and on weekends.

Of the 300 accounts which Mike Stern called on regularly, over 200 were located more than 200 miles away from his home in Dallas. This meant he spent four nights a week away from home when he was on the road. It was not uncommon for him to spend two to three weeks away from home when he traveled to west Texas and New Mexico. At the age of 54, Mike was hoping to slow down by traveling less and spending more time in the Dallas area.

Since his sales volume to existing accounts had been increasing each year and was now over $1 million, Mike really had not spent much time developing new customers. This was exactly the situation which had been worrying Philip Caine. In the highly competitive costume jewelry industry, Caine realized that Glorama could not afford to ignore the underdeveloped potential in a growth market like Texas and New Mexico.

He realized that the "textbook" answer was simply to split Stern's territory. He could leave Stern with the area nearer to Dallas, and add a new salesman (or transfer an existing sales person) to the newly established west Texas–eastern New Mexico territory. However, in view of Stern's long and valued associations with both Glorama and its customers, Caine was not sure about what he should do in this situation. He realized that, if Stern were sufficiently dissatisfied with any new arrangement, he might resign and go to work for one of Glorama's competitors, taking about 75 percent of his sales volume with him.

Caine discussed this problem with both Frank Spivak and Eric Jenkins, and also to some extent with Stern. Several alternatives were proposed in the course of these discussions. One idea was to form a separate territory consisting of eastern New Mexico and the El Paso metropolitan area of west Texas. This new territory, which accounted for 18 percent of Stern's present sales volume, would be assigned to another salesman. To compensate Stern for his loss, he would be paid an override commission of 2.5 percent of the sales in this new territory for a period of three years. A related suggestion was to pay Stern an override starting next year at 2.5 percent and declining each year to a level of 0.5 percent by the time he retires in ten years.

Jenkins proposed that the company leave well enough alone—that is, they should do no territorial restructuring but simply encourage Stern to continue increasing his sales by servicing his existing accounts. Frank Spivak brought up the idea of adding another sales person to cover the same geographical area now covered by Stern. *However,* the new person would call only on potential accounts not now serviced by Stern. That is, Stern would keep, and be limited to, his present list of customers. The new sales rep would be free to develop all other potential customers.

One of the executives set forth a rather unusual alternative—let Stern hire an assistant sales rep and put this new person on Stern's payroll rather than the company's. Stern's compensation level was considered to be high enough to support an assistant. The plan was for Stern to pay his assistant a guaranteed draw of $250 a week ($13,000 a year), or a 10 percent commission on the assistant's sales volume, whichever was greater. On these same sales the company would still pay Stern his 12 percent commission. After a training period, the junior sales rep would be given his own line and assigned to call on specific accounts. Eventually, Stern would assign to the assistant a part of Stern's outlying areas for complete coverage.

Question

1. How should Michael Stern's territory be restructured in order to get better coverage of existing and potential customers?

Case 18–2
SAKO IMPORTING COMPANY
Adjustments in sales territories

The Sako Importing Company was established in 1969 to distribute Japanese-made electronic equipment and components throughout the United States. The company was run by two partners, one of whom chose everything west of the Mississippi River as his sales territory and the other partner everything east of the Mississippi. This arrangement lasted for only a year because the firm's business prospered to such an extent that it became necessary to hire more personnel.

In 1970, the partners assumed managerial roles and hired five sales people. One of the partners, Bill Sachs managed the office and the sales force, while Jack Konen, the other partner, handled all the tech-

EXHIBIT 1
Sales territories
SAKO IMPORTING COMPANY

nical liaison work between the manufacturers and the customers. The territories of the five sales people are shown in Exhibit 1. In the following two years the business continued to expand.

In 1972, each of the five sales reps was promoted to manager of his region and was instructed to divide his area into five new territories and to hire sales people to staff them. The resulting 25 territories are shown in Exhibit 2. And still the business continued to grow.

By 1977 it became apparent that three of the regions—the Northeast, the Pacific Coast, and the Southeast—desperately required more sales reps. The partners disagreed on how the new territories should be divided. Sachs wanted to take this opportunity to revise all the territories because he felt that there were many unfortunate circumstances causing the sales force considerable inconvenience. While Konen agreed that the existing design of the territories left something to be desired, nevertheless he felt that the advantages which might be gained by a total revision would be overcome by the expenses and dissatisfactions involved in moving the sales people around. Moreover, he believed that an even more serious loss would be sustained from altering long-standing. sales person–customer relationships. The value of sales people increased significantly as the number

EXHIBIT 2
Revised sales territories
SAKO IMPORTING COMPANY

of times they called upon one customer increased. As customers grew to know and trust the sales rep, sales became easier. Many times the customer would give the company business solely on the basis of such relationships. Konen wondered how many such relationships would be disrupted by a total territorial revision.

Konen proposed that each regional manager be instructed to develop a plan for revising the territories in his region, keeping in mind that he should try to minimize the amount of transferring of sales reps and the number of significant accounts that would have to be assigned to another sales person.

Sachs felt that the whole plan should be revised, and the sooner the better. "Let's bite the bullet now. It'll hurt less than when we will be forced to do it later."

Konen countered, "I don't think it is really all that important. There's certainly no pressure from either the sales force or our customers for such a change."

Sachs replied, "Of course not! We're the ones who are paying for these territories. They are too expensive to cover, and we're not getting the coverage that we could be getting."

The partners were not sure how they were going to resolve their differences of opinion. They had a policy of always agreeing on something before doing anything—no agreement, no action.

Questions

1. If you were called upon by the partners to arbitrate their differences, what recommendations would you make?
2. What errors do you see in their present territorial assignments?

19

Sales quotas

You cannot put the same shoe on every foot.
SYRUS

Up to this point in our sales planning activities, presumably we have prepared a sales forecast and a sales budget. Also, we have established the sales territories. Now it is time to translate the results of these planning activities into work assignments in the form of sales quotas for our sales force or other marketing units.

> A sales quota is a sales performance goal.
> It is assigned to a marketing unit—a sales person, branch, middleman, or customer.
> It aids in the planning, control, and evaluation of sales activities.
> Typically, the goal is established in terms of sales volume, although other bases such as gross margin, expenses, or activities can be used.

PURPOSES OF SALES QUOTAS

Some of the reasons sales quotas are often used are discussed in this section.

To indicate strong or weak spots in the selling structure

When accurate quotas are established for each territory, management can determine the strength of territorial development on the basis of whether or not the quota is being reached. If the actual sales are under the quota, immediately management is warned that something may be amiss in that district. By the same token, if the sales total significantly exceeds the predetermined standards, the reasons for this type of variance should also be analyzed. Failure to meet a quota tells management that something has gone wrong. Of course, it does not tell *why* the failure has occurred. It may be that competition is stronger than expected, the sales people have not done a good selling job, or the potential was overestimated. Any one of a legion of factors may account for failure to reach a quota. The more detailed the goal, the easier it is to determine the reason for not meeting that goal. A company can pinpoint its problem areas better if quotas are set for each trading area, product line, or customer classification.

To furnish a goal and incentive for the sales force

In business as in any other walk of life, individuals usually perform better if their activities are guided by standards and goals. It is not enough to say to a sales person, "We expect you to do a good selling job." It is much more meaningful to express this expectation in the concrete form of a quota, consisting of a given dollar sales volume or number of new accounts to be acquired during the next month. Without a standard of measurement, a football team cannot tell whether it made a first down, golfers cannot tell whether they shot par, and sales reps cannot be certain their performance is satisfactory.

To control sales people's activities

A corollary to the preceding point is that quotas enable management to direct the activities of the sales force more effectively than would otherwise be possible. Through the use of the appropriate type of quota, executives can encourage a given activity such as selling high-margin items, collecting past due accounts, or getting orders from new customers. The sales reps are not in a position to know which area of activity should be stressed unless management informs them. Left to their own devices, they may do a fine job, but in some area that does not interest management.

To evaluate productivity of sales people

Quotas provide management with a yardstick for measuring the general productivity and effectiveness of sales representatives. By comparing a rep's actual results with his quota, management can evaluate that person's performance. Quota performance also provides guidance for field supervisors by indicating areas of activity where the sales force needs help. Decisions on whether to give sales people promotions or raises in salary often are based in large part on their performance in relation to their quota.

To improve effectiveness of compensation plans

A quota structure can play a significant part in a sales compensation system. Quotas can be used to furnish incentives to sales people who are paid on a straight salary. A sales rep knows, too, that a creditable performance in meeting assigned quotas will reflect favorably on him or her when it is time for a salary review. Quotas also are fundamental to many plans involving commission payments. For instance, a company may pay a salary plus commission after a sales quota is reached.

Inequities in territorial potential may cause inequities in compensation unless a quota system is established. In one territory, a person may get a $400 monthly salary plus a 5 percent commission on sales over a quota of $5,000. In a district that presents a small potential and a more difficult selling job, the sales rep may have the same arrangement, except that the commission starts when the rep reaches a quota of only $3,000 each month. Compensation plans in which a bonus is an element often incorporate quotas into the structure. A bonus may be paid, for example, when a person's sales reach 10 percent over quota.

To control and reduce selling expense

Expense control and reduction often can be stimulated by the use of expense quotas alone, without tying them to the compensation plan. Some companies gear payments for the sales people's expenses to a quota. For instance, a business may pay all the expenses of a sales rep up to 8 percent of sales. Other companies may set an expense quota and let the sales people know their effectiveness is being judged in part by how well they meet this goal.

To evaluate sales contest results

Sales quotas are used frequently in conjunction with sales contests. Sales people rarely have equal opportunities in a contest unless some adjustment is made to compensate for variation in territorial potentials and work loads. By employing the common denominator of a quota, management can assure each participant a reasonably equal chance of winning, provided the quota has been set accurately.

To allocate advertising expenditures

Management can use quotas as an aid in allocating the advertising budget. Some companies correlate advertising expenditures and quotas in the various districts. For instance, if the quota in territory A is 7 percent of the sales quotas for all districts, then 7 percent of the advertising budget would also be appropriated for territory A. If product A has a sales quota that is three times as much as the one for product B, the advertising budget for A would be triple that for B.

TYPES OF QUOTAS

The most frequently used types of sales quotas are those based on:

1. Sales volume.
2. Gross margin or net profit.
3. Expenses.
4. Activities.
5. Some combination among these four.

The type of quota management selects depends on several considerations, including the nature of the product and the market, and the specific objective the quota will help to achieve. If the company wants to correct an unbalanced inventory situation, for instance, a volume quota set by product lines may be used to move the surplus stocks of the given items. A firm that sells industrial products to a few large accounts can set a volume quota for each customer more easily than can an organization that sells convenience goods to many outlets. If management wants to develop a new territory for long-range benefits, an activity quota probably is called for in preference to a volume or expense quota.

Sales volume quotas

Undoubtedly the most widely used type of sales quota is one based on sales volume. A volume quota may be established for a geographical area, a product line, a customer, a time period, or for any combination of these bases. If a volume quota is used, the smaller the marketing unit for which the goal is set, the more effective is the quota as a tool for managerial control. Instead of setting a quota for an entire region, it is better to have one for each territory. Ordinarily, it is more effective to set a monthly or quarterly quota than an annual one.

Volume goals are used because they are simple to understand and easy to calculate. Many sales managers still are essentially volume conscious and regard sales people's sales volume as the only real measure of their worth to the company. However, sales volume alone does not tell the full story of a rep's productivity and effectiveness. It does not indicate the profit generated by the person's efforts, nor does it measure the extent to which a fully balanced sales job has been accomplished. In fact, volume quotas discourage balanced activities by the sales force in that volume is stressed, to the detriment of nonselling activities. Sometimes the profit factor can be introduced into a volume quota by establishing separate quotas for products grouped on the basis of their gross margin.

When using volume quotas, management must decide whether to express them in dollars or units of the product sold. The dollar base is probably the more frequently used of the two. It is particularly good if the firm sells a wide variety of items, as does a wholesale hardware, drug, or grocery sales company. Using dollars as the base also enables management to relate volume quotas to other measures, such as expenses or compensation, by means of ratios.

If a product line consists of relatively few items and they carry high unit prices, a quota may well be expressed in units. Even when a company sells a large number of products, it may be feasible to group them into a few broad lines and set unit quotas for each line. For example, an appliance manufacturer may set unit goals for small appliances in one group, white goods (refrigerators, ranges, washers) as a second group, and electronic products (radio, television) as a third line. Unit quotas also have an advantage in that they need not be recomputed every time the price changes on an item. Therefore, products whose prices fluctuate frequently often lend themselves nicely to unit quotas.

Profit quotas

Many companies set quotas based on gross margin or net profit. These goals may be established on many of the same bases as a volume quota. For instance, a gross margin quota may be set for a sales person, a branch, or a group of products. The preference some companies show for profit instead of volume quotas is a reflection of management's recognition of the importance of profit as compared with volume.

High-volume operators are not necessarily the best sales reps for company interests. Easy-to-sell items may be low-margin items. Unless some control is placed on these reps, they may be in the position of decreasing company profits every time they increase their volume. They are emphasizing the sales of profitless items or sales to profitless customers.

Note, however, that a volume quota may work essentially toward the same end as a gross margin quota. This happens when management properly sets a volume quota for each product line in such a way as to encourage the sales of high-margin items and give little credit for low-margin goods.

One significant drawback to gross margin or net profit quotas is the increased clerical and administrative expense involved. Another weakness is the possibility that friction may arise between management and the reps because the sales force members may not understand the derivation of their quotas or may not be able to compute their progress, and they therefore become suspicious. A final limitation— particularly true of a net profit quota—is that the goal is based on too many factors over which the sales representatives do not have complete control. A compromise approach is to base the quota on a sales rep's contribution to profit. Contribution to profit (or contribution margin) is the amount left after deducting a sales person's direct expenses (the ones he has control over) from his gross margin. The remainder is the amount the rep is contributing to cover the overhead (fixed) costs.

Expense quotas

Some companies attempt to encourage a profit consciousness by establishing a quota based on the rep's travel and other expenses. Often, the expense quota is related to volume, to the compensation plan, or to both. A sales representative may be given an expense quota equal to 4 percent of his sales. That is, his direct expenses, such as travel, entertainment, food, and lodging, must not exceed 4 percent of his net sales volume. In another example, a person may get a $200 bonus if his expenses drop to a given level.

Granted that expense quotas probably encourage a sales person to be more aware of costs and profits than do volume goals. Nevertheless, it seems that an expense quota is a negative approach to the problem. A rep's attention is devoted to cutting expenses rather than to boosting the sales of profitable products.

Activity quotas

One way to decrease the overemphasis on sales volume is to establish a quota based on activities. Management may select from such tasks as daily calls, prospective customers called on, orders from new accounts, product demonstrations made, and displays built. An activity quota properly established and controlled can do much toward stimulating a fully balanced sales job and is particularly valuable for use with missionary sales. Probably the principal difficulties in administering an activity quota are, first, to determine whether the activity actually was performed and, second, to find out how effectively it was done.

Combination quotas

Companies that are not satisfied with any single type of quota may combine two or more types. As an example, a firm may want to establish a quota based on three activities, plus gross margin in one product line and sales volume in another. The results for one rep may come out as follows for the January–March quarter:

	Quota	Actual	Percent of quota attained
Sales volume, product line A	$20,000	$22,000	110
Gross margin, product line B.........	$30,000	$25,000	83
Product demonstrations made	120	135	113
Orders from new accounts	45	50	111
Window displays obtained	20	19	95

Average = 102.4%

The sales person in this example reached a little over 102 percent of his combined quota. The five components were weighted equally, but management may want to assign more value to some elements than others.

A combination quota is an attempt to enjoy the strong points of the several individual types, but frequently this plan is limited by its complexity. Moreover, a sales rep may overemphasize one element in the quota plan. In the above illustration, for example, the rep may reach 200 percent of the quota for product demonstrations and do virtually nothing in securing orders from new accounts.

PROCEDURE FOR SETTING A SALES VOLUME QUOTA

The volume quota is selected to illustrate the quota-setting procedures because it is the most commonly used type, but essentially the same procedure can be used for the other types. Fundamentally, three general approaches may be used to set volume quotas:

1. Quotas are set in conjunction with the determination of territorial potentials.
2. Quotas are set in relation to the company's sales forecast or market potential estimate for the total market. Territorial estimates have not been prepared.
3. Quotas are set independently of any consideration of sales or market potentials.

When territorial potentials have been determined

Quotas related directly to potentials. One common practice in quota setting is to relate them directly to the territorial sales potentials.

Chapter 16 discussed the methods used to determine sales forecasts and to establish territorial sales potentials (the share of the estimated total industry sales that the company expects to realize in a given territory). The companywide sales forecast for many firms óften is built by piecing together estimates calculated for each territory. In the course of computing territorial forecasts, management considers several factors, such as past sales, competition, and changing market conditions. It also takes into consideration any projected changes in pricing, product policies, or promotional policies.

Thus if the territorial sales potentials or forecasts have already been determined, and the quotas are to be related to these measures, the job of quota setting is largely completed. For instance, if the sales potential in territory A is $300,000, or 4 percent of the total company potential, then management may assign this amount as a quota for the sales person who covers that territory. The total of all territorial quotas then would equal the company sales forecasts. The general reasoning in support of this practice is that the territorial potentials were accurately determined because proper allowance was made for all modifying factors.

Reasons for adjusting potential-based quotas. Companies frequently prefer to use the estimate of territorial potentials only as a starting point for the determination of a volume quota. These figures are then adjusted in order to arrive at a quota for the person who covers the territory.

1. *Human factors.* Several of the reasons for adjusting territorial potentials are based on the human factor in quota setting. In one instance, a quota may have to be adjusted downward from the potential figure because an older salesman is covering the district. He may have been with the company for years and have done a fine job, but as he approaches retirement age his physical limitations prevent him from performing as he once did. Obviously, it is not good human relations to discharge him. Nor will it help his morale to give him a quota that is impossible for him to reach, however realistic it may be in relation to sales potential. In part the problem may be solved by reducing the size of his territory and then equating his quota to the potential in the curtailed area.

Another territory may be covered by a weak sales person. In one case, the regional potential was $400,000 in a year, but the sales were only $300,000. This had been the pattern for the previous several years. Executives had carefully studied the problem and were convinced that failure to meet the quota was due to the sales person's poor performance and no other reason. Therefore, steps were to be taken to upgrade the rep's effectiveness by more training and supervision. However, management ordinarily should not try to remove a large deficit in one quota period. In fact, it may take two or more quota periods for weak producers to reach the point where their quota can be set at the equivalent of the territorial potential.

A situation requiring careful handling occurs when management has not used up-to-date figures for its sales potential. The goal may have been set at $200,000 for several years, for example, because five years previously a study indicated this was a reasonable estimate of potential. Since then, the potential has grown, until today it is $350,000. Management finally studies the market, updates the figures, and realizes the sales person's quota should be increased 75 percent to make it accurate. The question is whether a quota should be raised 75 percent in one year. Granted that the potential is present, management may have a morale problem if the new quota is set at $350,000, even if an explanation is offered to the rep. It may be better to use two or three quota periods to raise the goal to the desired level. From then on, management should keep its potential up to date so the problem does not recur.

2. *Psychological factors.* Some sales managers feel that the goal should be set just a little higher than the expected potential. Management recognizes that it is human nature to relax a bit after a goal has been reached. Therefore, the quota is set a bit high just in case some reps can do better than was expected. Other managers set all quotas a shade above potential as a precautionary measure.

As an illustration, assume that the quotas are equal to potentials. One person may have reached only 90 percent of his goal, while another sold 102 percent—an average of 96 percent between them. The second person did what was required, and there was no adequate incentive to strain further. However, if all quotas had been set at 110 percent of potential, the first person still would have attained only 90 percent, but the other might have hit 110 percent or more. The average then would have been at least the desired 100 percent.

In setting a quota above an expected limit just for psychological purposes, management must take care lest the goal be set so high that it is unrealistic. A quota that is too far above potential can actually discourage the sales force. They soon will see it is unattainable, and their morale and sales performance may suffer. The ideal psychological quota is one which is a bit above the potential but still such that a person can meet it and, if possible, even exceed it by working effectively.

3. *Compensation.* Some companies relate their quotas basically to the sales potential but adjust them to allow for the compensation plan. In such a case the company is really using both the quota and the compensation systems to stimulate the sales force. As an example, one organization may set its quotas at 90 percent of potential. Then one

bonus is paid if the quota is met and an additional bonus if the sales reach 100 percent over the quota, at which point the sales would approximate the potential.

When only total market estimates are available

Some companies prepare a total sales forecast for their entire market or estimate the market and sales potential for the market as a whole. In either case no territorial breakdown is available. If these firms want to set volume quotas for sales people or branches, the first step is to estimate the sales that can reasonably be expected in each geographical area. For instance, the total sales forecast may be allocated among districts in the same proportion as past territorial sales were to total sales in the company. Or the territorial divisions of market potentials (industrywide sales) may be adopted by the individual company. However, usually the best method for apportioning the total sales estimate among territories is to employ some market index that reflects those market factors that have a reasonably proven relationship to sales of the company's product.

Once the territorial potentials are established, the procedure for quota setting follows a pattern similar to the one discussed in the preceding section. The same qualitative factors that may influence a company to adjust a quota based on territorial potentials are present in this case.

When potentials are not directly considered

A company that does not wish to set its sales quotas in relation to territorial potentials has these alternatives:

Quotas may be set strictly on the basis of past sales.

Quotas may be determined by executive judgment alone.

Quotas may be related to the compensation plan.

The sales people may set their own quotas.

Past sales alone. In some organizations, the byword is "Beat last year's figures." As a result, sales volume quotas are based strictly on the preceding year's sales or on an average of sales over a period of several years. In some instances, this method of quota setting is used when no sales forecast has been made. Each sales person's quota is set at an arbitrary percentage increase over sales in some past period. In other companies, a sales forecast is made. As an example, if management forecasts that sales companywide will increase 5 percent next year, each marketing unit is assigned a volume quota 5 percent higher than the unit's sales for the year.

About the only merits in this method of quota setting are simplicity and low cost of computation and administration. If the procedure is to be followed, at least an average sales figure for the past several years should be used as a base instead of only the previous year's sales. Employing an average reflects a trend and also tends to decrease the effects of years in which sales were abnormally high or low.

While past sales are frequently recommended as one of the important factors to be considered when forecasting sales and determining territorial potentials and quotas, certainly a quota-setting method based on past performance alone is subject to severe and inherent limitations. To set a rep's quota at 5 percent over his sales for the preceding year simply because the company's total sales forecast calls for a 5 percent increase ignores possible changes in the sales potential in his territory. General business conditions this year may be depressed in the rep's district, or a strong competitor may have entered that territory, thus cutting the sales potential. Or new potential customers may have come into the district, thus boosting the potential volume.

Basing quotas on previous year's sales may not uncover ineffective performance in a given territory. A person may have had sales of $100,000 last year, and his quota is increased 5 percent for this year. He may even reach the goal of $105,000. However, the potential in the district may be $200,000. The representative may perform poorly for years without management's recognition that a problem exists. Quotas set on past sales also ignore the percentage of sales potential already achieved. Assume the sales potential in each of two territories is $200,000, and one person's volume was $150,000 last year while the other's was $210,000. It is not realistic to expect each to increase his sales the same percentage over last year's figures.

Executive judgment.   In setting quotas for sales reps, some companies rely entirely on what they refer to as executive judgment but may more precisely be called hunches or guesswork. As with past sales, executive judgment is usually an indispensable ingredient in a sound procedure for setting quotas, but to use it alone is certainly not recommended. Even though the administrator may be very experienced, too many risks are involved in relying solely on this factor without heed to quantitative, objective market measures.

Quotas related to compensation.   Earlier in this chapter we maintained the idea of relating compensation to volume quotas based on potential. Quotas may also be used in compensation plans but without any relation to potential. As a case in point, a company may prefer to pay its sales representatives by straight commission. However, in this organization management realizes that a salary plus commission plan is more palatable to the reps. Therefore, the combination plan is adopted, with a salary of $600 per month and a commission of 6 percent on all sales over $10,000 a month. By using the quota, management in effect achieves its preference for a straight commission because none is paid until the salary is recouped (6 percent of $10,000 equals $600).

Sales people set own quotas.   Some companies place the quota problem in the laps of the sales representatives and let them set their own performance goals. The rationale for this move is that the sales people are closer to their territories than management is and thus can do a better job. Factors that may not be considered in statistically set quotas still may be recognized by the sales people in the field. Also, setting their own quotas allows the reps to reflect their individual abilities. Finally, if sales reps make the decisions about their own goals they will be more cooperative, have higher morale, and strive more to attain the quota.

From a practical standpoint, however, this method leaves much to be desired. The field representatives are not in as good a position to set quotas as management is. Sales people do not have access to the necessary information, nor do they have adequate training to do an accurate job of quota selling. Also, since sales people often tend to be optimistic about their capabilities and the opportunities in their districts, they may set unrealistically high quotas. Then as the period goes on and it becomes evident that they cannot reach the goal, a serious morale problem may develop.[1]

ADMINISTRATION OF SALES QUOTAS

Usually the sales department is responsible for establishing the sales quota, and no approval of a higher executive is needed. Within the sales organization, the task may rest with any of several executives, depending on the size of the company, the degree of centralization, and the method used to determine the quotas. The chief sales executive may be responsible for setting the total company quota, but the individual breakdown may be delegated down through the regional and district managers. Or territorial sales potentials may be given to the district managers, and they set the sales people's quotas.

Attributes of a good quota plan

Several characteristics of a well-designed quota structure have been alluded to earlier in the chapter. Many are the same attributes

---

[1] See Thomas R. Wotruba and Michael L. Thurlow, "Sales Force Participation in Quota Setting and Sales Forecasts," *Journal of Marketing*, April 1976, pp. 11–16.

found in good compensation plans, territorial designs, and other aspects of sales management.

Realistic attainability. If a quota is to do its intended job of spurring the sales force to the efforts management wants, the goal must be realistically attainable. If it is too far out of reach, the sales people will lose their incentive as soon as they realize the cause is hopeless.

Objective accuracy. Regardless of what type of quota is being used, it should be related to potentials. Executive judgment is also required, but it should not be the sole factor in the decision. If the sales force is to have faith in the performance goal, they must be convinced it was set impartially and based on factual market research.

Ease of understanding and administering. A quota must be simple and easy for both management and the sales force to understand. A complex plan probably will cause friction and make the sales force resentful and suspicious. Also, from management's point of view, the system should be economical to administer.

Flexibility. No quota ordinarily is a good one unless there is adequate flexibility in its operation. Particularly if the quota period is as long as a year, management may have to make adjustments because of changes in market conditions. At the same time, unlimited flexibility should be avoided, since this may result in confusion and destroy the ease with which the system is understood.

Fairness. A good quota plan will be fair to the people involved. As much as possible, the work load imposed by quotas should be comparable, but this does not mean that quotas must be equal for all people. Differences in potential, competition, and sales representatives' abilities typically do exist.

Typical administrative weaknesses

Companies that do not use sales quotas may justify their position by citing various limitations in a sales quota system. Generally speaking, however, these are not limitations that are *inherent* in the system. Instead they are *administrative* weaknesses that reflect management's failure to put into practice the characteristics of a good quota plan.

Probably the major criticisms against quotas is that it is difficult or even impossible to set them accurately. This point may be justified in some cases. Perhaps a company is selling a new type of product for which very little marketing information is available, or a concern is selling a product wherein several quota periods elapse before the sale is consummated. It is granted that executive judgment must be used in setting most quotas, and the tasks performed vary among the sales reps in the territories. However, just because a company cannot set a goal that is 100 percent statistically correct is no reason for management to abandon the entire project. The company may have an expense control system, a compensation plan, and a territorial structure—all founded on something less than perfection. The executives cannot say they will have no compensation plan because they cannot establish one that is entirely accurate and fair to the sales force.

Other companies admittedly could set quotas with reasonable accuracy, but they prefer not to for at least two reasons. First, the job would incur more clerical and administrative expense than the executives want to spend. Second, they fear that the resultant plan may be too complex for practical usage. This line of reasoning again seems to indicate administrative ineffectiveness rather than basic limitations to quota plans. It is true that to set a quota properly may take considerable marketing research, and this can be expensive. However, the benefits to be gained ordinarily far outweigh the cost.

In other instances quotas are not used because management claims they lead to high-pressure selling and generally emphasize some activities at the expense of others. These criticisms may well be justified if a sales volume quota is used alone. Or, the compensation and quota plans may be so linked as to encourage a high volume of sales, irrespective of the gross margin. A quota also may well overstress a given selling or nonselling activity. However, these are indications of planning or operating weaknesses and are not inherent disadvantages of quotas.

While it may be a fine idea to use quotas in such a way that they help the poorer sales people develop properly, it is not sound administrative policy to have this developmental effort done at the expense of the better sales representatives. That is, the good sales reps should not have their quotas boosted just to balance out the lower-than-average goals set for those who are less able.

Obtaining the sales force's acceptance of a quota plan

A final essential ingredient in a well-planned and well-operated quota system is to obtain its wholehearted acceptance by the sales force. Sales people often are suspicious of quotas, either because the purposes are not apparent or because there are questions about the factors underlying the plan. They must be convinced that the quota is intelligently computed and that it possesses the attributes of a good quota plan. The purposes of the quota should be explained to the sales force. The bases on which the quota are set and the methods used in the process can also be discussed. When the final product is ready for formal installation, the sales force will probably be more inclined to accept it if they have had a hand in its development. Aside from the human relations aspect of the situation, management also stands to gain by soliciting ideas from sales people because they may introduce considerations that had escaped its notice.

Sales reps should be kept informed about their progress toward meeting the performance goal. Conferences and correspondence with the reps often are necessary. The sales force also needs some incentive to reach the goal. This may come from a bonus for achieving the quota or from some other direct link with the compensation plan. Management can make it clear that quota performance is reflected in periodic merit rating, salary review, or considerations for promotion.

QUESTIONS AND PROBLEMS

1. What types of quotas do you recommend for the sales jobs described in Figures 4–1 and 4–2 (in Chapter 4)?

2. Is it necessary to establish territories before setting quotas? Can sales quotas be set without a sales forecast, sales budget, or determination of territorial sales potentials?

3. Cite some specific instances when management may have good reasons for not using sales quotas. What are the reasons in each case?

4. What factors influence the type of quota used?

5. Should branch managers be assigned a quota? If so, what type should be used? Answer the same two questions for a sales supervisor.

6. "The use of quotas, or need for them, is an indication of an administrative weakness in some other area of sales force management. For instance, if the firm had a well-designed compensation plan which offered adequate incentive to the sales force, there would be no need for quotas." Comment on this opinion.

7. "The higher the caliber of a sales force, the less there is a need for a quota system." Do you agree?

8. Should quotas be used in each of the following cases? If so, what type do you recommend, and what should be the length of the quota period?
   a. Missionary or promotional sales rep for a manufacturer of candy bars.
   b. Sales person selling electronic computers.
   c. Sales person for manufacturer of industrial, central installation-type heating and air-conditioning units.
   d. Sales person for manufacturer of room air conditioners for home or industry.
   e. Door-to-door selling of sterling silver.

9. When establishing volume quotas for the sales force, many executives believe in setting the individual goals so that they total something *more* than the company's sales forecast. That is, an extra amount is added for psychological purposes. Yet, when these same executives prepare various budgets they often tend to be conservative, and they base their estimates on a total sales volume that is somewhat *less* than the firm's sales

forecast. How do you account for this apparent inconsistency in executive reasoning?

10. A luggage manufacturer uses volume quotas for its sales force.

    a. What effective measures may this firm take to encourage its sales people to do nonselling tasks such as prospecting for new accounts or setting up dealer displays?

    b. How can the customers be protected against overstocking, high-pressure selling, and other similar activities by this manufacturer's sales force?

11. Should quotas be tied in with the compensation plan?

12. One wearing apparel manufacturer established volume quotas for its sales representatives. The 1977 quota was 20 percent higher than in 1976. The sales force seemed perfectly happy with the new quota and generally was meeting it. Reps were paid a straight 5 percent commission on net sales. Under what conditions would this type of quota work?

Case 19–1
THE DORSETT DOOR COMPANY
Setting sales quotas

Donald Stone, sales manager for the Dorsett Door Company of St. Louis, Mo., had set aside the day for developing sales quotas for his five sales reps for the coming year. Considerable unhappiness and dissatisfaction had resulted the previous year from the quotas, which were considered by the reps to be unfair.

The Dorsett Door Company manufactured and sold heavy-duty steel doors used in commercial and industrial buildings. The doors were sold to distributors from whom contractors bought supplies.

The previous quotas had been set on the basis of the preceding year's sales volume. Each rep's sales for the year were increased to allow for price increases and increases in commercial building activity. The reps were paid a salary plus a substantial bonus for sales over quota. For as many years as the reps could remember there always had been a good bonus for everyone. Last year was the exception. Construction activity had dropped unexpectedly, and this had hurt door sales significantly. It had not been a Merry Christmas. While Don had felt like giving the men an extra bonus just to placate them, as a matter of management policy, he was not allowed to.

The philosophy of the management was to set quotas as accurately as possible for each rep and pay a salary for reaching that quota. For all sales over quota the rep would receive a 5 percent commission as a bonus. The bonus was paid at the end of each year.

First, Don intended to develop monthly quotas, in spite of management's belief that it was impossible to do this in a meaningful way. He thought the incentive compensation should be paid each month, not once a year.

Next, he wanted to get away from basing the quotas on the rep's previous sales. He wanted some external market factor on which to base them.

Third, he felt that it was good policy to see to it that every sales rep received something as a bonus if a reasonably good job had been done. He thought it damaging to morale for any rep to come up empty-handed at bonus time.

As he sat down to the task at hand, he could not help but recall some of the various thoughts that had been offered him by other members of management with whom he had consulted on this matter.

The accountant was brusque. "Who needs quotas? We don't. Just pay them a straight commission on sales and be done with it."

The production manager doubted if it would be possible to forecast sales accurately in their business. "It is just too uncertain. You're going to have to base your quotas on something besides a sales forecast."

The president asked, "Why are you here? I hired you because you were supposed to know about such things. Now go and know about them." Stone had made a bad mistake asking the president for direction.

Don sat at the desk staring at a pad of paper for an hour but nothing appeared on it. He did not know what to do.

Question

1.   Give Don Stone some specific advice on what to do.

Case 19–2
SOME QUOTA INCIDENTS

WE DON'T WANT ANY QUOTAS

The management of Ceramic Cooling Tower Company (see Case 9–2) had never established any sales quotas for its sales force of 52 sales reps who worked under five regional sales managers. The firm's sales volume of about $10 million was unsatisfactory to top management. Sales for the coming year were budgeted for $15 million.

At a meeting of the regional sales managers in the home office during which the next year's marketing program was presented, the sales manager asked the regional managers if sales quotas should be set for the sales reps. They overwhelmingly claimed that to do so would be a bad mistake.

Comment on this situation.

HOLDING UP THE ORDERS

The management of the McCoy Company established monthly sales quotas for each of its reps. The quotas were set on the basis of market research information about the sales potential in each rep's territory. The sales force was paid a substantial salary plus a 5 percent commission on all sales over quota for the month.

The sales manager had noted over the previous two years that most of the reps sold over quota about every other month. One day in early March, he saw in a report on the previous month's sales that not one sales rep came anywhere near selling his quota. Yet he recalled that in January they all had gone substantially over quota. He investigated past records and found this to be a pattern. He could not understand it because February should have been a good month for the McCoy Company. Something was going on, and he had to find out what it was.

One of his sales reps was rather famous for liking to talk, particularly when properly primed. The sales manager took him out for a friendly social outing. The rep let the cat out of the bag. "What kind of fools do you take us for? Why should we turn in orders in February when we know that there isn't much chance of going over quota. Even the days in the month are against us. So in January we really get busy and load up the customers so they won't need any in February. Then at the end of the month we wait a few days and put their orders in on March. We want to get as much sales volume in under the 5 percent commission as possible."

Evaluate the situation and make a recommendation.

MY TERRITORY IS DIFFERENT

Jim Frank had never met quota in his seven years with the High Line Furniture Company. His territory was West Virginia and western Virginia. The company sold expensive upholstered furniture directly to furniture stores.

The quotas were set on the basis of the retail furniture sales in the territory. Assume that 0.5 percent of the nation's retail furniture sales were made in a territory, according to *Sales & Marketing Management's* "Survey of Buying Power." Then the sales rep's quota was set at 0.5 percent of the company sales forecast. The firm's sales forecasts were set on a conservative basis. Most sales reps more than met their quotas.

Each year when Jim would be criticized for his failure to meet quota, he would claim that his territory was different. Everyone would laugh, as the sales manager shook his head.

Evaluate the situation.

LET'S NEGOTIATE

Tom Murray had been to a three-day session in New York held by a famous trade association. The subject was sales quotas. The experts told Murray that for sales quotas to be most effective they should be set this way: the sales manager should sit down with the sales person and go over all pertinent data to arrive at a mutually agreeable sales quota. In that way the sales representative at the end of the quota period would have no excuse for not meeting it—he had helped set it.

Murray came back from New York all set to put into practice his new-found technique. He had his assistant sales manager assemble all of the relevant data for each sales rep so that it would be ready to use in the conferences. Then he called in Henry Baxter, who had sold $650,000 worth of goods the previous year.

"As I see it, Henry, you should do about $750,000 this next year," Murray said in opening the negotiations.

"No way! I'll be lucky to sell half a million."

"What are you talking about? You did $650,000 last year."

"Blind luck. Stumbled into some big windfall sales."

And so it went for four hours. Henry would not agree on anything over $500,000 and Murray would not come down below $700,000. Each used selected arguments and data to support his position.

Finally Henry said, "Look! You asked me in here for my opinion. You have it. Now do what you want with it."

Those experts in New York didn't tell Murray how to handle Henry.

What went wrong with Murray's tactic? What does he do now?

Part four

SALES ANALYSIS AND EVALUATION

20

Analysis of sales volume

Economic distress will teach men . . . that
fact-finding is more effective than fault-finding.
CARL BECKER

Up to this point, the major parts of the book (after the introductory section) have been devoted to sales planning and sales operations. The next logical step in the management of a sales force is to analyze and evaluate the results of the field selling effort.

The managerial functions of planning, operating, and evaluating are related in a continuous fashion, as shown in Figure 20–1. Plans are made; they are put into operation by the organization; the results are evaluated. Then new plans are prepared, based on the evaluation findings.

Planning and evaluation are especially interdependent activities. Evaluation logically both follows and precedes planning. Evaluation *follows* the planning and operations of the current period of company activity. Planning sets forth what *should be* done, and evaluation shows what *really was* done. Without an evaluation, management cannot tell (a) whether its plan has worked, (b) to what degree it has been successful, or (c) what the reasons are for its success or failure. Then evaluation *precedes* the planning for the next period's operations.

INTRODUCTION TO SALES ANALYSIS

Sales analysis is a loosely used term. Here it is defined to include *all* analyses of sales force activities and other sales operations. It is the broad term that covers the (1) analysis of sales volume—the topic of this chapter, (2) marketing cost analysis and return on investment—the

533

FIGURE 20–1
**Interrelationship of planning, operations,
and evaluation**

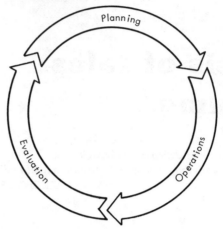

topics of Chapter 21, and (3) various analytical measures used to evaluate a sales person's performance—the topic of Chapter 22.

The marketing audit: A total evaluation program

The essence of a total evaluation program is embodied in the concept of a marketing audit.[1] An audit is a review and evaluation of some activity. Therefore, a *marketing audit* is a systematic, comprehensive, periodic review and evaluation of the marketing function in an organization—its marketing goals, policies, and performance. This audit includes an appraisal of the organization, personnel, and procedures employed to implement the policies and reach the goals.[2]

To qualify as a complete marketing audit, any appraisal must include *all* the marketing areas referred to in the definition—goals, policies, performance, organization, personnel, and procedure. A fragmented evaluation of some marketing activities may be useful, but it is not a marketing audit. It is only one part of such an audit.

A complete marketing audit is a very extensive project which provides something of an ideal for management to work toward. It is expensive, time-consuming, and difficult. But the rewards from a mar-

---

[1] See *Analyzing and Improving Marketing Performance: "Marketing Audits" in Theory and Practice*, Management Report 32 (New York: American Management Association, 1959), especially Abraham Schuchman, "The Marketing Audit: Its Nature, Purposes, and Problems," pp. 11–19, and Alfred R. Oxenfeldt, "The Marketing Audit as a Total Evaluation Program," pp. 25–36.

[2] Adapted from Oxenfeldt, "Marketing Audit as a Total Evaluation Program," p. 26.

keting audit can also be great. Management can identify its problem areas in marketing. By reviewing its policies and strategies, the firm is likely to keep abreast of its changing marketing environment. Successes also can be analyzed, so the company can capitalize on its strong points. The audit can spot lack of coordination in the marketing program, outdated strategies, or unrealistic goals.

Traditionally, an audit has suggested an after-the-fact review. In marketing, the use of an audit is broadened to include an evaluation of the effects of alternatives *before* a decision is reached. Thus the audit becomes an aid in decision making. Further, an audit should anticipate future situations as well as review past ones. In this way, an audit is intended for "prognosis as well as diagnosis. . . . It is the practice of preventive as well as curative marketing medicine."[3]

The evaluation process

The evaluation process—whether it is a complete marketing audit or only an appraisal of individual components of the marketing program—is essentially a three-stage task. Management's job is to:

1. Find out *what* happened—get the facts; compare actual results with budgeted goals to determine the variations.
2. Find out *why* it happened—determine what specific factors in the marketing program accounted for the variations.
3. Decide what to do about it—plan the next period's program and activities so as to improve on unsatisfactory conditions and capitalize on favorable ones.

Sales analysis and its components

Because of the time, cost, and difficulty involved in a full-blown marketing audit, sometimes it is more reasonable to evaluate the separate components of the marketing mix. With respect to field-selling efforts, such an approach to evaluation would involve an appraisal of sales volume results, related marketing expenses, and the performance of individual sales people.

While some overlapping does occur, the various types of sales analyses are sufficiently independent so that management can conduct one or two without the need to do all of them. One company may decide to analyze its sales volume but not its marketing costs. Another firm may study various ratios involving sales force activities without making any detailed sales or cost analyses.

---

[3] Schuchman, "Marketing Audit," p. 14.

An *analysis of sales volume* is a careful study of a company's records as summarized in the net sales section of its profit and loss statement. It is a study of the dollar and possibly the unit sales volume detailed by product lines, territories, key accounts, general classes of customers, and other categories. An analysis of sales may be expanded to include a corresponding study of cost of goods sold. The result is an analysis of its gross margin, also detailed by such segments as products or territories. A *marketing cost analysis* continues from the analysis of sales. It is a study made of the various marketing expenses in order to determine the profitability of various segments in the organization and also the efficiency with which the several activities are performed.

In a general sense, the two types of analyses are component parts of a detailed study of a company's operating statement. The sales analysis is a review of the statement through the net sales and possibly through the gross margin section. The marketing cost analysis starts where the analysis of sales ends and continues to the end of the operating statement.

The study of sales volume or marketing costs involves problems of analysis, not bookkeeping or accounting. However, the ease with which the sales analyst does the work, and even the success of it, depends to a great extent on the care and detail with which the accounting department has established account classifications.

Relation of sales analysis to sales control

Many writers and business executives refer to the topic under discussion in this chapter as *sales control* or *control of the sales operations*. We do not use any such label because we believe it is a misleading and unrealistic use of the term *control*. Control is not an isolated managerial function. It permeates virtually all other managerial activities. For example, management controls its sales force by means of the compensation plan, quota system, territorial structure, and expense payment plan. Control also is exercised through the training program, sales contests, supervision, and other devices.

Relation of sales analysis to sales force management

Should the topic of sales analysis be included in a book whose scope is limited to the management of a sales force? Generally, sales analysis is considered within the realm of marketing management, but not as the responsibility of the manager of the sales force. Nevertheless, sales analysis is tied to control of the sales force. If a sales analysis study uncovers territories where net sales have been consistently under the potential, the responsibility to correct the weakness may fall to a branch manager working with the reps in that district. Or, sales analysis may show that one product line is doing well in net sales but shows up poorly in a net profit analysis. To correct the situation, management may train the reps to sell this product more profitably (through larger orders, for example). In an extreme case it may be necessary to adjust the sales commission rate for this product.

SALES ANALYSIS AND MISDIRECTED MARKETING EFFORT

An overall sales analysis, particularly the analyses of net sales and marketing costs, is one step that may be taken to correct the misdirected marketing effort which exists in many companies today.

Nature of misdirected marketing effort: The 80–20 principle

A company does not enjoy the same rate of net profit on every sale. In most firms a large proportion of the orders, customers, territories, or products account for a small share of the profits. This relationship between selling units and profits has been characterized as the 80–20 principle. That is, 80 percent of the orders, customers, territories, or products contributes only 20 percent of the sales or profit. Conversely, the other 20 percent of these selling units accounts for 80 percent of the volume or profit. The 80–20 figure is used to epitomize the misplacement of marketing efforts. Actually, of course, the percentage split varies from one situation to another.

The basic reason for the 80–20 situation is that some misdirected efforts are found in most marketing programs. *Marketing efforts and costs follow the number of territories, customers, or products rather than their actual or potential sales volume or profit.* A firm may have one sales person and one branch office in each territory, with all the attendant expense, regardless of the volume obtained from these districts. For every order received, the seller must process a purchase order, invoice, and check, and approximately the same order-filling and shipping expense is involved whether the order is for $10 or $1,000. In most companies, if marketing efforts were to be matched with results, much of the marketing cost would be credited with only a small part of the total sales and profits.

Reasons for misdirected effort: The iceberg principle

Many executives are unaware of the misdirected marketing effort in their firms. They do not know what percentage of total sales and profits comes from a given product line or customer group. Frequently, executives cannot uncover their misdirection of effort because they lack sufficiently detailed information. The analogy of an iceberg in an open sea has been used to illustrate this situation. Only a small part of an iceberg is visible above the surface of the water, and the submerged 90 percent is the dangerous part. The figures representing total sales or total costs on an operating statement are like the visible part of an iceberg. The detailed figures representing sales, costs, and other performance measures for each territory or product correspond to the important submerged segment.

Total sales or costs on an operating statement are too general for a marketing executive interested in sales analysis. In fact, the total figures are often inconclusive and misleading. More than one company has shown satisfactory overall sales and profit figures, but when these totals were subdivided by territory or products, serious weaknesses were discovered. A manufacturer of rubber products showed an overall annual increase of 12 percent in sales and 9 percent in net profit on one of its product lines one year. But when management analyzed these figures more closely, it found that the sales change within each territory ranged from an increase of 19 percent to a decrease of 3 percent. In some territories, profits increased as much as 14 percent, and in others they were down 20 percent. This is a practical example of the iceberg principle.

The reason for the imbalance of marketing efforts and results is that, historically, management has measured the success of a marketing program by the criterion of sales volume. This attitude is typified in the countless companies that use sales volume quotas and compensate their sales people by commission on sales volume. Most sales reps find it difficult to forego business from a customer, even though the account is a losing proposition. This drive for volume is also evidenced by the fact that many companies employ a mass distribution policy, when a more selective distribution policy might be more profitable.

There is a more fundamental reason for misplaced marketing effort. Sales executives must make decisions even though their knowledge of the exact nature of marketing costs is inadequate. In other words, management lacks: (1) knowledge of the disproportionate spread of marketing effort, and (2) reliable standards for determining (a) what should have been spent on marketing, and (b) what results should have been obtained from these expenditures.

As an example, a sales executive really does not know exactly how much to spend on sales training, marketing research, or sales supervision. A firm that manufactures several lines of products has no real standards for determining the level or method of compensation for the sales force. What is even more troublesome, after some money has been spent, management has no yardstick to determine whether the results of these expenditures are satisfactory. If a firm adds 10 missionary sales people or employs field supervisors where none existed before, the executives ordinarily cannot say what should be the increase in volume or profit. Nor can they compare the value of two expenditures. If $100,000 is spent on a contest for the sales force, no one can say how much additional volume this expenditure will bring, as compared with spending the same amount on advertising.

PROBLEMS INVOLVED IN ANALYSIS OF SALES VOLUME

Lack of adequately detailed information

Sales administrators who want to analyze sales volume may find that adequately detailed data are lacking. The sales department works largely with figures supplied by the accounting department, and these records rarely are sufficiently itemized for the needs of sales managers. Often, a company will have one account for gross sales and another one for sales returns and allowances, with no further breakdown. Facts on net sales by product line, groups of customers, or other classifications usually are not readily available. Before a worthwhile analysis can be made in most companies, a system must be established to supply the sales department with the necessary facts.

The possible classifications of sales data and the combinations of these breakdowns have almost no limit. Some of the more widely used subdivisions for reporting and analyzing sales are the following:

1. Sales territories.
2. Sales people. If each representative has a district, an analysis of sales volume by territories also serves for individual sales reps.
3. Products. Reports may be in dollars and/or physical units for individual products or lines of products.
4. Customers. Management may classify the volume by the individual customers, key accounts, industrial groups of customers, or channels of distribution.
5. Size of order.

Any of this information may be reported monthly, quarterly, or for some other period of time.

The job of analyzing sales volume—or any other phase of sales analysis, for that matter—will be much easier if the company uses electronic data processing equipment in its information retrieval system. The raw data are gathered faster and more easily, and the data processing equipment allows management to do much more in the way of cross-classification and other analyses than would otherwise be economically feasible.

Sales volume analysis usually insufficient

An analysis of a company's sales volume alone usually does not furnish enough information to the sales department. Furthermore, what data are produced may be misleading. A study may show, for example, that the dollar *volume* of product A is 20 percent greater than the sales of product B. Yet, if the company were to determine the gross margin or net profit of the two products, management would find that B's dollar *profit* is 10 percent higher than A's. Granted that a full-scale sales and cost study is ideal, a good marketing cost analysis usually is difficult and costly. Further, while an analysis of volume alone has its limitations, it is far better than no analysis at all.

The sales executives may compromise between a volume analysis and a full-scale distribution cost study by expanding volume analysis to include the cost of the merchandise sold. Thus they end up with a gross margin analysis by territories, products, or customer groups with relatively little additional expense.

BASES FOR ANALYZING SALES VOLUME

Total sales volume

A reasonable place to begin an analysis of sales is with the total volume—the combined sales of all products in all territories for all customers. This is the most readily available figure and the one that will give the overall picture of how the company is faring. However, the *trend* in sales is usually far more important to administrators than is the volume for any given year. They are interested in two trends— the trend of the company's sales over a period of years, and the trend of the company's share of the total industry market.

A study of total sales volume is probably the easiest to make of all types of analyses. The only data needed are the total sales figure for the company over the past several years and the annual industry sales in the geographic market covered by the firm. Then the company's share of the market can be determined.

Table 20-1 shows the sort of information developed in a total volume analysis for a hypothetical firm, the Colorado Ski Company. The concern carries two basic product lines—ski equipment (skis and accessories) and a limited line of ski clothes (ski pants and parkas). The company manufactures some of these items, and others are purchased

TABLE 20-1
Information used in analysis of total sales volume

COLORADO SKI COMPANY

Year	Company volume (in millions)	Industry volume (in millions)	Company's share of market
1977	$4.5	$60	7.5%
1976	4.2	65	6.4
1975	3.9	60	6.5
1974	3.4	52	6.5
1973	3.5	50	7.0
1972	3.2	39	8.2
1971	3.3	40	8.3
1970	3.2	36	8.9
1969	3.0	30	10.0
1968	2.5	25	10.0

from outside sources but are sold under Colorado Ski's brand. The firm sells to two classes of customers—sporting goods stores and specialty ski shops—in some of the major ski markets in the nation. Annual sales in 1977 were $4.5 million. An analysis of the company's volume shows that its sales have generally increased each year since 1968, with the exception of 1972 and 1974. So far, the picture is encouraging. However, a different light is shed on the situation when the industry's figures are brought into the picture. The industry's sales also have increased since 1968, and at a significantly more rapid rate than Colorado's volume. As a result, the company's share of the market has steadily declined. Looking at the ten-year picture, management finds that its sales have increased 80 percent but its share of the market has declined 25 percent.

After Colorado Ski Company's management has uncovered the facts as shown in Table 20-1, the next step is to determine, if possible, the reasons for the company's decline from its former market position. Obviously, competition has outdistanced Colorado Ski. The administration must ascertain whether this result stems from specific weaknesses in the firm's operations or from particular strengths in the competitors'.

The possible weaknesses in Colorado Ski's operation are almost limitless. Something may be wrong with the product itself—its styling, construction, or color. Some aspects of the pricing structure may be the problem. The weakness may lie in some phase of advertising, such as the choice of media or the advertisements themselves. Then the entire area of sales force management can be examined in the search for an explanation of Colorado Ski's decline in market position.

On the other hand, it may be that all of Colorado Ski's operations are as good as they ever were, but the competitors have shown marked improvement. Possibly there are more competitors, or some of these firms may have made significant improvements in their product, advertising, or personal selling effectiveness.

If a company's total sales are *declining*, it is particularly important that management determine the trend of the industry's sales. If the industry's volume is increasing, then, again, there are weaknesses in the company's operations, strengths in the competition, or a combination of both factors. However, if the industry's volume is also decreasing, apparently the demand for the given line of products is declining. Different policies will be needed if the reason for the decline in sales lies in company weaknesses or competitors' strengths, rather than in a shift in consumer demand for the product.

Sales by territories

An analysis of total sales volume usually can be done easily and inexpensively. However, its value to management ordinarily is limited, because it tells so little about the details of a firm's marketing progress. The iceberg principle is at work; only the aggregate picture emerges and the separate parts remain submerged. As a step toward uncovering these parts, it is a common practice to analyze sales by territories. Frequently, some version of the 80–20 principle is operating in that the bulk of the volume comes from a small percentage of the sales regions. Management ordinarily is interested in locating districts strong or weak in relation to potential. This is a step toward determining whether the company is receiving efficient use of its investment in branches, sales force, advertising, and other territorial items. Also, an administrator must find out *which* territories are weak before he can be determined *why* they are weak.

One reasonably simple, inexpensive procedure for analyzing sales volume by territories follows these four steps:

1. Select a market index that indicates with reasonable accuracy what percentage of total sales should be obtained from each sales territory. For example, one firm may find it can establish standards for territorial sales performance by using retail sales as an index. If 10 percent of the total national retail sales were in the midwestern district, then 10 percent of the company's sales should also come from that district. Or if the firm sells in only eight southeastern states, then the total retail sales in the eight-state area would be equated to 100 percent. If 22 percent of the eight-state total retail sales were tallied in Alabama, then 22 percent of the sales in the

company should also come from Alabama. Other firms may find that a market index, such as wired homes, automobile registrations, or *Sales & Marketing Management's* "Buying Power Index," is related to their sales. (Market indexes and their use in determining territorial sales and market potentials were explained in Chapter 16.)

2. Determine the company's actual total sales in dollars or units during the period being studied.
3. Multiply the territorial index by the total sales figure to determine the goal or standard of performance in each district.
4. Compare actual regional sales with the regional goals to see how much variation has occurred.

An example of this procedure is developed in Table 20–2. The five territories that comprise the Western Division of the Colorado Ski Company are being analyzed. Incidentally, it makes no difference whether this firm sells in a national or in a regional market. Nor does it matter whether these five territories represent all or only part of Colorado Ski's total market. The approach used in Table 20–2 would serve any of these conditions.

TABLE 20–2
Analysis of territorial sales volume in five-territory Western Division
COLORADO SKI COMPANY

Territory	Market index (percent)	Sales goals	Actual sales	Performance percentage	Dollar variation
A...........	26.7	$ 600,000	$ 450,000	75	−$150,000
B	22.7	510,000	615,000	121	+ 105,000
C	15.0	338,000	414,000	122	+ 76,000
D	19.8	445,000	426,000	96	− 19,000
E...........	15.8	357,000	345,000	97	− 12,000
	100.0	$2,250,000	$2,250,000		

In the Western Division, Colorado Ski's total sales were $2,250,000, distributed among five territories as shown in the column headed "Actual Sales". Sales were $450,000 in territory A, $615,000 in territory B, and so forth. By applying a pertinent market index to the Western Division's total sales, management finds that 26.7 percent, or $600,000, of the total sales in the five territory market *should* have been made in Territory A. The goal in Territory B was 22.7 percent, or $510,000. In C, the goal was 15 percent, or $338,000, and so on.

A performance percentage is computed by dividing actual sales by the territorial standard as determined by applying the market index. A rating of 100 percent in the district means that the area turned in its predetermined share of the company's business. In Table 20–2 it may be seen that territories B and C did much better than was expected. Districts E and D were a shade below par, and A fell considerably short of expectations. In terms of dollars, A was $150,000 under what it should have been, while B's sales were $76,000 over the goal.

It is not enough to study the *percentage* by which an area's sales are over or under the goals. The more important measure usually is the *dollar volume*. It is possible that the district may be only a few percentage points under par. However, because the territorial potential is very large, these few percentage points may represent a significant sum of money—many more dollars than in a small territory that is far below par percentagewise.

The market segments that are below par—their actual performance does not reach the standard or anticipated results—may be called *soft spots*. In sales management, the *soft-spot principle* is that an administrator reaps the largest possible gain by working with the weakest segments of the organization. In line with this principle, a sales manager in the Colorado Ski Company should devote most of his attention to territory A, because it has the greatest room for improvement. By the same token, it is doubtful that even considerable executive attention could improve B and C very much. Already they are far above their goals. Probably the main benefit from a study of B and C would be a determination of why they apparently are so successful, and whether this information can be used to improve A.

Once the administrator has ascertained which territories are strong and which are weak, the next problem is to determine the reason for the relative performances. Territory A may be doing poorly because competition is particularly effective, or because some aspects of Colorado Ski's operation are especially weak. Management also may want to find why such variation in territorial potential exists. Territory E is supposed to bring in only 15 percent of the total, while A's goal is 26.7 percent. If all five districts were equal in potential, each should contribute 20 percent of the total volume.

Assuming that *industry* volume figures for each territory are obtainable with reasonable effort, another procedure may be used for a territorial sales analysis. Industry's sales are distributed on a percentage basis among a company's territories by dividing the dollar sales of a district by the industry's total sales. Thus industry percentages are established in each district. Then, the percentage of the company's sales in each district is compared with these industry percentages. A sales manager may find, for example, that 15 percent of the industry's sales are made in territory A and 10 percent in B, while 12 percent of the company's sales are in A and 20 percent in B. Thus, the company is doing far better than the industry average in B, but the firm is below average in A.

Sales by products

The 80–20 and the iceberg principles apply to products as well as to territories in many companies. Very often, most of the products in a company's line account for a small percentage of total volume or profit: Conversely, a few products may bring most of the volume. Also, there is no relation between volume and profit. Products that account for a large proportion of the volume may or may not contribute a corresponding percentage of the net profits.

Several types of volume analyses by product lines may be very helpful to management. The first is simply a summary of present and past total sales divided into individual products or groups of products, whichever is more practical. An appliance manufacturer may want to study the sales trend for each individual product. A hardware wholesaler, however, would be content to group thousands of products into divisions such as housewares, plumbing goods, toys, sporting goods, electrical equipment, paints, and so on. This type of examination shows the percentage of total volume contributed by each product or product group. By preparing such an analysis to cover a period of years, an organization can determine the trend in sales by products.

If *industry* figures are available for each product line, they may provide a yardstick with which a company can measure its own sales performance by products. For example, if the sales of product A are decreasing in one firm, its management need not be so concerned if over the same period the industry's sales have decreased at about the same rate. If product A accounts for only 5 percent of a company's volume, while the remainder is divided equally among three other products, management can appraise the situation better if industry figures are used as a comparison. It may be that product A accounts for only 3 percent of the industry's sales. Thus, even though the executives in the company may decide that they are doing a reasonably good job with product A, they also realize from a study of industry sales that A's potential is very small in comparison to the other three. Therefore it is doubtful that the company will expend much promotional effort to increase the sales of A unless it should happen to be an extremely high-profit item.

A further refinement of volume analysis by products is to study the sales of each product line in each territory. In this way, management determines not only which products are relatively strong or weak in volume, but also in what parts of the geographical market these conditions exist. Product A's total sales may be up 10 percent over last year, but in the southwestern region A's volume is down 14 percent. Another example is a company with four product lines. About 20 percent of the volume in each of three lines is sold in the Pacific Coast division, but this area accounts for only 5 percent of the volume in the fourth line. Once these facts are known, an administrator can try to determine the reasons for the variations and then take necessary corrective steps. In this example, it may be that the fourth line faces strong regional competition on the Pacific Coast. Or perhaps the product is just generally underconsumed, and the industry as a whole does poorly in that area.

A slightly different approach to the problem of volume analysis by product lines in each territory is to adopt one of the general methods suggested for territorial analysis. This involves the use of market indexes to determine how the company's total volume in each of the districts would be distributed among the product lines if each product reached its goal (or performance standard) in sales.

An analysis of sales by product lines also can be used to further refine the territorial analysis discussed in the preceding section and thus to further pinpoint the problem areas. Study of Table 20–2 shows that territory A was 25 percent *under* par, while B and C were 21 percent and 22 percent *above* par, respectively. By investigating the product sales in these districts, management can further isolate the reason for the variations from the expected norms.

Table 20–3 gives an example for the Colorado Ski Company. The appropriate market indexes were applied to the company's actual total volume of $2,250,000 in the Western Division to establish targets by products in each of the five western territories.[4] For instance, if the Western Division's sales had been distributed in relation to potential, sales in territory A would have been $600,000, with skis contributing $264,000, ski accessories accounting for $45,000, and so forth.

In the territorial analysis illustrated in Table 20–2, it was found that the company was short of its sales goal in region A by $150,000, or 25 percent. However, the shortage was not distributed equally among all four products. Further analysis by product lines exposes more of the submerged part of the iceberg. We now can see that the sales of ski pants and parkas were the primary sources of these shortages. The company failed to reach its target by $90,000 and $75,000, respec-

---

[4] Ideally, a separate index should be used for each product or line of products. To use the same index on all items means that the percentage share of the national market set as a target in the territory is the same for all products. In Table 20–2, 26.7 percent of the company's total Western Division sales should have been contributed by territory A. If the same index is used for all four products, then 26.7 percent of the sales of each product should be obtained from territory A. Such situations are unusual. Ordinarily, a company selling many different products should not expect that a given territory would contribute for each product the same percentage of the total sales of that product.

TABLE 20–3
Analysis of product sales performance in two territories

COLORADO SKI COMPANY

Product	Territory A (in thousands)			Territory B (in thousands)		
	Goal	Actual	Variation	Goal	Actual	Variation
Skis...............	$264	$285	+$ 21	$218	$270	+$ 52
Accessories	45	39	− 6	37	60	+ 23
Pants	150	60	− 90	135	180	+ 45
Parkas	141	66	− 75	120	105	− 15
Total	$600	$450	−$150	$510	$615	+$105

tively, for those two products. Sales of skis actually were $21,000 over the performance standard.

In territory B, even though the district as a whole was $105,000 over par, the product sales analysis shows considerable variations from the target figures. Volume in skis, ski accessories, and ski pants was satisfactory, but sales of parkas fell $15,000 (about 12.5 percent) short of the goal.

Let's assume that the sales volume has now been analyzed in detail by products and the soft spots have been identified. The next problem is to determine what policies should be adopted by the company. This is particularly needed with respect to low-volume products and goods whose sales have fallen short of the expected goal. Based on the findings in Table 20–3, ski pants and parkas in territory A and parkas in territory B seem to be soft spots, and thus should offer the best opportunity for improvement. There is not so much room for an increase when sales of a product have reached or surpassed a target figure.

A different situation prevails for low-volume products. Management's initial thought may be to drop these products, but before taking such a drastic step, other considerations should be taken into account. A cost analysis will aid in these decisions. If the product is a losing proposition for the company, this would be a strong point in favor of dropping the item. In some cases, however, a low-volume product must be kept whether or not it is profitable. It may be needed to round out a line, or customers may expect the company to carry the item.

A significant factor that can guide management in this problem is the industrywide situation for the low-volume product. If the item accounts for a very small percentage of the total industry's volume, the company would not seem to be in a weak position. At the same time, if the general consumption of the product is very limited, it is doubtful that the company would promote it aggressively. The only reason to do so would be if management has forecast a significant upward trend in volume or profit on the item.

If an analysis of industry sales showed that a low-volume product for the company enjoyed high-volume sales in the industry, the company obviously is in difficulty. Management must determine why the firm's product is doing so poorly. After uncovering the reason for the poor showing, it then must decide whether to make a competitive fight, go along as at present, or simply drop the item from the line. Several factors influence this decision.

Sales by customer classifications

A company is even more apt to find the 80–20 principle in operation when sales are analyzed by customer groups rather than by territory or product. It is not at all unusual to find that a small percentage of customer accounts for a major share of total volume. Typically, a firm sells to many accounts on a marginal or even unprofitable basis.

A firm can analyze its volume by customer groups in several possible ways. It may classify accounts on an *industry* basis. An oil company may group its customers into industry divisions, such as service stations, marine, farm, transportation, industrial, and governmental agencies. Another basis of classification is by *channels of distribution*. A sporting goods manufacturer may group its accounts by sporting goods wholesalers, department stores, and discount houses. A third classification is on the basis of *accounts* or just the key accounts. Any of these three groups may be cross-classified. An oil company may want to analyze its sales to key accounts in the service station industry groups, for example.

Furthermore, any of these customer classifications may, and usually should, be analyzed for each territory and for each line of products. In one company, it may be that sales to wholesalers are satisfactory on an overall basis. However, in line with the iceberg principle, sales to wholesalers are particularly poor in one territory. Management will not be aware of this situation until a careful analysis of sales is made. An oil company may assume that a given customer–industry group that accounts for 10 percent of total sales also contributes about 10 percent of the volume of each product line. An analysis may show that this industry accounts for 18 percent of the volume in product A but only 5 percent in product B.

Any customer analysis should be made for several periods of time so that significant trends will be uncovered. The trend analysis should show dollars and percentage relationships for each group studied. For instance, sales to department stores may be increasing *dollarwise* but dropping sharply as a *percentage* of total. Management must then determine whether the department store volume is satisfactory, or whether a shift in emphasis to discount houses is a better alternative, and so on.

USE OF COMPUTERS IN SALES ANALYSIS

Surveys indicate that the most meaningful application of the computer in marketing and sales force management is in the area of sales analysis. This is understandable. Companies typically are faced with iceberg and 80–20 situations in their total sales volume, and marketing effort is likely to be misdirected if management is unaware of the sales performance of specific product lines or individual territories in relation to potentials. Detailed sales analyses are needed as a basis of planning, operating, and evaluating by top management and middle management in a sales department. The computer can process swiftly and economically the masses of data used in a sales analysis. As a marketing executive in the Univac Division of the Sperry-Rand Corporation put it, "You no longer have to wait for the present to become past history to learn from its lessons. With the computer, you're on to your mistakes much faster."[5]

Done by hand, a sales analysis in a large firm ordinarily cannot be done quickly enough to be of much use, or at a low enough cost to be of much economic value. With a computer, sales can be analyzed in just about any detail desired by management.

In the air freight division of American Airlines, for example, early in the day the vice president can tell (1) which salesmen in Boston are behind quota, (2) that the volume of electronic parts shipped out of Dallas is declining, and (3) that a sudden spurt in shipments of TV sets from San Francisco to Cincinnati has put that air route 20 percent ahead of forecast. With these fresh facts, the vice president can act immediately: (1) the Boston sales manager is asked whether the sales territories are too large or the salesmen are having other problems, (2) Dallas is asked whether other industries' shipments can take up the slack, and (3) San Francisco is queried as to whether the TV business is a one-shot deal or is likely to be a recurring situation.[6]

Another air freight marketing executive at American Airlines explained that sales analysis has a prominent role in the company's computer operations because "air freight is a time-perishable product. If a plane takes off with unsold space, we never get another crack at the

---

[5] Thayer C. Taylor, *The Computer in Marketing*, rev. ed. (New York: Sales Management, Inc., 1970), p. 95.

[6] Ibid., p. 92.

sale." As this executive sees it: "The computer lets you focus the analysis where you want—by salesman, product, account, type of business. As a result, you're giving the salesman meaningful, accurate, up-to-date information. This helps him to deliver a consistently improving level of sales performance."[7]

In the Grocery Products Division of General Mills every territorial sales executive receives, at the start of the day, a detailed teletype report on what happened in his area the day before—orders placed, sales volume, cumulative totals by brand, percentage of estimated sales achieved to date in the period, and comparable progress percentages at the same time last year.[8] Management uses the computer to analyze its problem products each month to determine their current profitability against the operating target, trends in profitability, and so on.

One problem sometimes occurs as a direct result of the computer's data processing capacities. Sales people and field sales managers in many firms are inundated with computer reports to the point where they often are completely ignored or used in far less than optimal fashion. Management needs to do two things in these cases—condense and highlight the data, and show the sales force and field sales executives how to use the data in the reports.

QUESTIONS AND PROBLEMS

1. What is the relationship between a marketing audit and each of the following?
   a. Sales volume analysis.
   b. Job analysis.
   c. Sales forecasting and setting sales quotas.
2. Is it necessary for a firm to have a well-developed sales *planning* program before any tasks of analysis and evaluation can be conducted effectively?
3. What is the difference between control of sales people and control of sales operations?
4. How do the iceberg and 80–20 principles work together?
5. If the sales volume in a firm is increasing each year by a satisfactory percentage, is there any purpose in the firm's going to the expense of a volume analysis?
6. As a result of a sales volume analysis, many firms have eliminated some of their products or customers. Yet in several of these cases the sales volume has *increased* after the market cutback. How do you account for this result?

---

[7] Ibid., p. 94.

[8] Ibid., p. 97.

7. A territorial volume analysis indicated that a firm's sales had increased at about a 10 percent rate for the past three years in a given district. Is this conclusive evidence that the company's performance is satisfactory as far as sales volume is concerned in the given territory?

8. A company with 15 territories found that product A accounted for 40 to 50 percent of the sales in 13 of the districts, but this product brought in only about 20 percent of the volume in the remaining 2 territories. What factors might account for the relatively low standing of product A in the two territories?

9. Is it possible for a product, territory, or class of customer to be far below par but still not deserve much executive attention? Give examples.

10. Should sales people be furnished with complete statistics, not only on their own performances but on the performance of other sales people as well?

11. If a company made a *territorial* volume analysis and found some subpar territories, how might these facts affect the following activities as related to sales people?

   a. Supervision.   *c.* Training.
   b. Compensation.   *d.* Stimulation.

12. If a firm analyzed its sales volume by *customer classes,* how might the results affect the supervision, compensation, training, and stimulation of the sales force?

Case 20–1
STURDI-WEAR CLOTHING COMPANY
Analysis of sales volume

The Sturdi-Wear Company was founded in January, 1959. The owners of the firm were experienced in the manufacture and sale of men's and boys' clothing. Mr. Sam Smith, president, had been the production manager for an old-line clothing company prior to his present venture. His partner and vice president, Mr. John Adams, had been an outstanding salesman and was associated with the same firm as Smith. Sturdi-Wear was successful primarily for two reasons. Mr. Smith was able to produce quality clothing at competitive prices, and Mr. Adams was successful in transfering the business of a nucleus of his old customers to the new firm. Particularly pertinent was a contract negotiated in 1970 with two of the leading chain department stores headquartered in Chicago. The firm had been selling to these chain organizations for the past three years.

Note: Case prepared by Professor Donald W. Scotton, Cleveland State University. Reproduced with permission.

The firm manufactured and sold men's and boys' suits, sports coats, and slacks. These items were manufactured for the low-price market but were of good quality and style. Mr. Adams had an unusual ability to select the styles and patterns most desired by the market.

This firm had restricted distribution to the states of Indiana, Illinois, Iowa, and Missouri. The owners believed that there was sufficient opportunity for sales within the four-state area to absorb the maximum output of the plant. In addition, the plant was located centrally so that close contact with the accounts was possible, reorder shipments could be received by the accounts within four days from the date of order, and transportation costs were relatively small.

The firm employed six salesmen who were assigned as follows: (1) two men covered the Chicago area, which consisted of Cook, DuPage, and Kane counties; (2) one salesman traveled the remaining portion of Illinois; and (3) the other three salesmen were assigned one state each consisting of Indiana, Iowa, and Missouri. The three-county Chicago area was divided between the two salesmen working there so that one was responsible for all activity within the Chicago city limits, and the other traveled the other sections of Cook County and all of DuPage and Kane counties.

The salesmen sold directly to large retail accounts and to wholesalers to obtain coverage of smaller retail outlets. The Chicago salesman was responsible also for servicing the two chain organizations mentioned above. Although chain accounts were solicited, the salesmen had not been successful in obtaining others.

Sturdi-Wear sales for the year 1959 were $2 million and increased approximately at the rate of $2 million per year until 1969. The 1969 sales were $20 million. Sales from 1970 through 1972 were:

Year	Chain sales	Non-chain sales	Total sales
1970	$1,000,000	$21,000,000	$22,000,000
1971	2,000,000	22,000,000	24,000,000
1972	2,600,000	17,400,000	20,000,000

The management of the firm was concerned about the decline in sales between 1971 and 1972 and decided that an analysis of sales might be helpful. Although the owners knew a great deal about their customers, they recognized that continuous study of sales segments might be necessary.

Mr. William Brown was hired in January, 1973, to fill the newly created position of marketing analyst. The owners were aware that it would take some time to install a satisfactory system of market analysis and control and suggested that Mr. Brown review 1972 sales first. It was hoped that this analysis would serve as a beginning point in understanding the problem and possibly reveal some areas for further study and correction of weaknesses.

Mr. Brown selected counties as geographical control units. He experimented with various general indexes and found that a coefficient of correlation of .95 existed between his firm's *total* sales and the *Sales & Marketing Management* magazine's Buying Power Index. He believed that some geographic segment analysis within each of the states would be valuable. Thirty counties were selected at random to discover the correlation between county sales of his firm and the Buying Power Index. This testing demonstrated that the general index was not sufficiently correlated to the firm's sales at the *county* level. So he made a statistical study of market factors affecting the sales of the firm's products. It was found that an index consisting of population (weighted 1), effective buying income (weighted 2), and total retail sales (weighted 3) had a coefficient of correlation of .92 when related to county sales of Sturdi-Wear products. On the basis of these findings it was decided that the sales analysis of the four states would be made using the *Sales & Marketing Management's general index* and that the *specific index* would be employed in the analysis of county sales.

In preparing 1972 sales for analysis, it was noted that billings were:

Illinois	$12,600,000
Indiana	2,000,000
Iowa	1,600,000
Missouri	3,800,000
Total	$20,000,000

Because the Illinois sales were large, it was decided that this area should be analyzed further. In addition, it was believed that the sales to the chain store organizations should be examined as a possible influence on the other states. Finally, Mr. Adams suggested that Chicago area sales were of sufficient magnitude that they should be examined separately from the Illinois state totals.

To facilitate the analysis, the following information was gathered:

1. Chain-store sales were made at Chicago in the amount of $2,600,000. The chains reported that the goods represented by these sales were shipped and sold in their stores as follows: Illinois, 40 percent; Indiana, 30 percent; Iowa, 20 percent; and Missouri, 10 percent.
2. The chain groups indicated that all the Illinois sales of Sturdi-Wear clothes were made as follows:

Cook County	70%
DuPage County	20
Kane County	10
Total	100%

3. Other sales in the Chicago area, which included Cook, DuPage, and Kane counties, consisted of $4 million to large independent retail stores in Cook County and $4 million to wholesalers.
4. The Chicago area wholesalers reported that the Sturdi-Wear sales to retailers were distributed (at manufacturer's sale price) as follows:

Cook County	$2,400,000
DuPage County	1,000,000
Kane County	600,000
Total	$4,000,000

The sales analysis computations were presented in Exhibits 1 through 5 by Mr. Brown. Mr. Adams and Mr. Smith were interested in the findings, but they expressed doubt as to the adequacy of the analysis. Specifically, they suggested that a more comprehensive analysis follow this first effort. In addition, they requested that a plan be drawn for interpreting the results and taking corrective action.

Questions

1. Appraise the job of sales volume analysis performed by William Brown.
2. What conclusions can be drawn from the results of the sales volume analysis?

EXHIBIT 1
Sales & Marketing Management "Buying Power Index" and related variables, by state, 1972

State	Population (000)	Effective buying income (000)	Retail sales (000)	SMBP index	State % of index total
Illinois	11,285.7	$48,946,224	$25,891,375	5.9207	48.88%
Indiana	5,314.3	19,587,623	11,504,622	2.5235	20.83
Iowa	2,894.6	10,672,932	6,854,337	1.4144	11.68
Missouri	4,802.1	16,947,895	10,707,150	2.2543	18.61
Total	24,296.7	$96,154,674	$54,957,484	12.1129	100.00%

Source: "Survey of Buying Power" *Sales & Marketing Management* (annual issue), July 23, 1973.

EXHIBIT 2
Efficiency index by states, 1972

	Buying power index	Sales		Excess or deficit $(000)	Efficiency index
Outlets by state		Actual (000)	Par (000)		
Illinois					
Chain		$ 1,040			
Wholesale and retail		10,000			
Total	48.88	11,040	$ 9,776	1,264	112.93
Indiana					
Chain		780			
Wholesale and retail		2,000			
Total	20.83	2,780	4,166	−1,386	66.98
Iowa					
Chain		520			
Wholesale and retail		1,600			
Total	11.68	2,120	2,336	−216	90.71
Missouri					
Chain		260			
Wholesale and retail		3,800			
Total	18.61	4,060	3,722	338	109.08
Totals	100.00	$20,000	$20,000	-0-	

EXHIBIT 3
Specific index variables for Illinois counties, 1972

Illinois counties	Population		Effective buying income		Retail sales	
	(000)	Percent of 4-state total	(000)	Percent of 4-state total	(000)	Percent of 4-state total
Cook	5,572.7	22.93	$26,074,695	27.16	$12,791,370	23.25
DuPage	511.9	2.11	2,729,985	2.84	1,500,933	2.73
Kane	252.1	1.04	1,099,223	1.15	697,587	1.27
All others	4,949.0	20.37	19,042,311	19.83	10,901,485	19.82
Total	11,285.7	46.45	$48,946,214	50.98	$25,891,375	47.07

Source: "Survey of Buying Power" *Sales & Marketing Management* (annual issue), July 23, 1973.

EXHIBIT 4
Specific index computation for Illinois counties, 1972

Illinois counties	Population* +	Effective buying income†+	Retail sales‡ ÷ 6	= Specific index
Cook	1 (22.93) +	2 (27.16) +	3 (23.25) ÷ 6	24.50
DuPage	1 (2.11) +	2 (2.84) +	3 (2.73) ÷ 6	2.66
Kane	1 (1.04) +	2 (1.15) +	3 (1.27) ÷ 6	1.19
All others	1 (20.37) +	2 (19.83) +	3 (19.82) ÷ 6	19.91

* Population weighted 1.
† EBI weighted 2.
‡ Retail sales weighted 3.

EXHIBIT 5
Efficiency index of Illinois counties, 1972 (based upon the specific index)

		Sales			
Outlets by county	Specific index	Actual $(000)	Par $(000)	Excess or deficit $(000)	Efficiency index
Cook					
Chain		728			
Wholesale		2,400			
Retail		4,000			
Total	24.50	7,128	4,900	2,228	145.47
DuPage					
Chain		208			
Wholesale		1,000			
Retail					
Total	2.66	1,208	532	676	225.19
Kane					
Chain		104			
Wholesale		600			
Retail					
Total	1.19	704	238	466	295.80
All others					
Total	19.91	2,000	3,982	−1,982	50.22

21

Marketing cost analysis

*Business prophets tell us what should happen—but
business profits tell us what did happen.*

EARL WILSON

While an analysis of sales volume is useful, it tells us nothing about
the *profitability* of territories, products, customer groups, or other
sales control units. To determine the profitability of any of these control units, we need a marketing or distribution cost analysis of the
segment. (The terms *marketing cost analysis* and *distribution cost
analysis* are used synonymously in this chapter.) Sales executives are
particularly interested in the findings from a marketing cost analysis,
because this information can significantly affect the management of a
sales force. The discovery of an unprofitable territory may suggest the
need for a shift in territorial boundaries or a different call schedule.
The discovery of unprofitable products may result in a change in the
commission rate paid for sales of those items.

The purpose of this chapter is to discuss some of the objectives of
marketing cost analysis, its major uses as a tool in the management of
sales force operations, and examples of marketing policy decisions that
may be based on the studies. Our treatment of marketing cost analysis
will be in the nature of a survey, with very little attention being devoted to accounting and statistical techniques and procedures.

NATURE AND SCOPE OF MARKETING COST ANALYSIS

A marketing cost analysis is a detailed analysis of a firm's distribution costs. It is made in order to discover unprofitable segments and
inefficiently performed functions of the company's marketing program.

It goes beyond a volume analysis to determine the profitability of various aspects of the marketing operation. Thus it becomes an important part of an overall sales analysis.

Various sales department budgets frequently are an integral part of cost analyses. Management often wants to establish standards of performance (budgets) for some selling expenses, and then study the causes of variation between the actual and budgeted expense. Once the facts of the situation are known, management is in a better position to take intelligent action to improve the situation.

Relation between marketing cost analysis and the accounting system

Marketing cost analysis is somewhat different in purpose and scope from the usual accounting system in a firm. Accounting is concerned largely with maintaining a complete *historical* record of those company events that in any way have a financial flavor. Thus the system feeds to management a story of merchandise sales, materials purchased, equipment depreciation, salaries paid, and all other activities involving financial considerations. Marketing cost analysis is a managerial tool designed more for use in the planning and control of *future* operations in a firm. Of course, an analysis of past financial events often serves as a guide for future operations.

A distribution cost study usually is not a part of the regular accounting system in a company. It takes up where the accounting system stops. A study of costs is largely analytical and statistical in nature and is not concerned with the routine accounting practices. The accounting system is operated perpetually, and each transaction is recorded. The cost analysis often is performed on a sporadic or sampling basis. The profitability of certain products may be studied in 25 percent of the territories for six months out of a year. Or, an analysis of size of orders may be made in only half the districts from January through April.

In a marketing cost study, regular accounting records provide virtually all the data. Therefore, to do a thorough cost analysis, it is imperative that there be a detailed system of account classification. For instance, one account for salesmen's commissions is not at all sufficient to analyze the commissions paid on sales of a given product to selected customers in a territory.

Marketing cost analysis compared with production cost accounting

Marketing cost analysis and production cost accounting are intended to serve as tools for controlling costs in their respective areas.

Also, each is employed most effectively when the production or marketing activities are subdivided in sufficient detail so that carefully pinpointed analyses can be made. Beyond these general similarities, the two concepts have marked differences.

First, in production cost accounting the costs ordinarily are computed only for the units of the *product*, because knowledge of this single relationship is usually adequate for managerial control of production expenses. For marketing costs, the situation is quite different. Sales administrators are not satisfied with knowing only the costs of selling each product. They also want to know the distribution expenses for territories, customer groups, order sizes, and other performance evaluation measures, or for any combination of these control units.

Marketing cost analysis is less exact than production cost accounting, because the bulk of production costs can usually be attributed to machines or people whose work can be closely supervised. On the other hand, many marketing costs are incurred by sales people who are not under constant direct supervision and whose jobs are *not* totally routine. It is not feasible to conduct a time and motion study of a sales person's activities in order to determine the exact time and cost of various phases of the sales job.

There is another significant difference. In controlling production costs, management is concerned with the effect of volume on costs. In the control of distribution costs, management's attention is directed toward the effect of costs on volume.

> Cost-volume relationship in production and in marketing:
>
> In production: Costs are a function of volume.
>
> In marketing: Volume is a function of costs.

Production managers are striving to reach the optimum point of output. So they study what happens to unit production costs when the volume of output increases or decreases by some given percentage. If the company is operating in the decreasing stage of its production cost curve, production managers know that their costs can be cut by increasing output. Also, they usually know the exact quantitative relationship between an increase in output and a decrease in costs.

The sales administrator, on the other hand, wants to know what the effect on volume will be if a given cost is changed. For example, what change in volume would occur if two sales people were added to the eight now operating in the Dallas district? Or, what would be the effect on sales volume if one field supervisor were added to the staff of each branch? Or, what volume increase can be expected by increasing the advertising budget 70 percent in the Chicago district? Sales executives typically cannot determine answers to these questions with nearly the degree of accuracy that production managers can. In other words, management is much less certain about the effects of marketing costs on volume than about the effects of volume on production costs.

PROBLEMS INVOLVED IN MARKETING COST ANALYSIS

Marketing cost analysis projects can be expensive in time, money, and manpower. To minimize this expense and still retain the benefits of such analyses, a company may conduct a cost analysis on a time-sampling basis. Thus costs may be analyzed by sales territories for the July–September quarter, or a customer-group analysis may be conducted from October through December.

Another major problem is to get adequately detailed data in a form that is useful to management. Some of the aspects of this problem are discussed in this section.

Bases for cost classification

Accounting ledger costs versus activity-group costs. In typical accounting records, the expenses are classified according to the immediate object of the expenditure. Ledger accounts may be found for such marketing expenses as sales salaries, sales commissions, branch office rent, supplies, cost of advertising space or time, and loss from bad debts. For purposes of a marketing cost analysis, sales executives usually must regroup these expenses into various activity classifications. All the expenses related to a given marketing function, such as warehousing or advertising, are grouped together.

The problem in separating costs into activity groups is twofold. First, a decision must be made on the categories to be established. Second, many expenses listed in accounting records cut across several activity groups. Consequently it is necessary to *allocate* a given ledger account among the appropriate activities. For instance, the ledger account for office supplies must be allocated to each activity group (such as direct selling, advertising, and shipping) that incurs this expense.

Each firm should decide on a list of the major activities that are relevant to its marketing program. A retail chain ordinarily performs activities that are different from those carried on by a manufacturer of electric generators. A typical list, however, usually includes many of the following groups of expenses:

1. Direct selling expenses: sales force compensation and travel expenses, and all costs connected with branch sales offices.
2. Advertising and sales promotion expenses.
3. Transportation and shipping expenses.
4. Warehousing expenses.
5. Credit and collections expenses: losses from bad debts and all expenses related to the credit office.
6. Financial, clerical, and handling expenses: costs of processing purchase orders, billing, receiving payment, interest on investment in accounts receivable, and finished goods inventories.
7. Marketing administrative expenses: all costs of central sales offices and sales and marketing executives.
8. Marketing's share of general administrative expenses: compensation and travel expense of the president and other general executives in the company, and the expense of equipping and maintaining executive offices.

Direct or separable versus indirect or common expenses. Direct (or separable) costs are those that are incurred in connection with a single unit of sales operations. Therefore they can readily be apportioned in total to a specific marketing unit, whether it is a territory, product, or customer group. If the company were to drop a given territory or product, all direct expenses tied to that marketing unit would, by definition, be eliminated. Indirect (or common) costs are those that cannot be related directly to specific products, territories, or other market segments, because they are incurred by more than one segment. In general, most distribution costs are totally or partially indirect.

Whether a given cost is classed as common or separable depends on the market segment being analyzed. The cost never remains permanently in one or the other category. Assume that each sales person in a company has a separate territory, is paid a straight salary, and sells the entire line of products. Sales force salaries would be a direct or separable expense if the cost analysis were being made by territories. But the salary expense would be an indirect or common cost if the cost were being studied for each product. Sales force travel expenses would be a *direct* territorial cost but an *indirect* product cost.

The term *overhead costs* frequently is used to describe a body of expenses that cannot be separated out and identified solely with individual product lines, territories, or other market segments. Sometimes, overhead costs are referred to as fixed costs. However, it is preferable to think of these items as *indirect* rather than fixed expenses. They are not fixed in the sense that management is unable to influence them. Instead, they are fixed only in the sense that they are not directly allocable among territories, product lines, or some other group of market segments. The point is that these costs cannot be attached solely to individual market units.

Difficulty of allocating costs

A major problem in a marketing cost analysis is that of allocating the various distribution costs to individual territories, products, or whatever segment of the market is being studied. Actually, the problem of prorating arises at two levels—when accounting ledger expenses are being allocated to activity groups, and when the resultant activity costs are apportioned to the separate territories, products, or customers.

A direct or separable cost can be apportioned in its entirety to the marketing segment being analyzed; this phase of allocation is reasonably simple. For example, assume that a territorial cost analysis is being made and each sales person has his own territory. Then all his expenses—salary, commission, travel, supplies, and so on—can be prorated directly to his district. Some of the advertising expense, such as the cost of advertisements in local newspapers and the expense of point-of-purchase advertising materials, can be charged directly to a territory.

However, the majority of costs are common rather than separable, and the real allocation problems occur in connection with these expenses. For some costs, the basis of allocation may be the same regardless of the type of analysis made. Billing expenses are often allocated on the basis of number of invoice lines in a territory, product, or customer cost analysis. The basis for allocation also can be influenced to a great extent by the type of analysis, however. Consider sales force salaries as an example. In a territorial cost study, these salaries may be allocated directly to the district where the people work. In a product cost analysis, the expense probably is prorated on the basis of the proportionate amount of working hours that a rep spends with each product. In a cost analysis by customer classes, the salaries may be apportioned in relation to the number of sales calls on each customer group.

Another situation that makes cost allocation a difficult problem is that often it is not possible to use the same allocation basis for all component parts of a given activity cost group. In a product cost analysis, sales force commissions, sales force salaries, and sales force travel expenses each may require a separate allocation basis, even though all three items are part of the direct selling function. Commissions on net sales may be apportioned directly to each product line. Salaries may be prorated according to the sales people's time spent with each line. And some other basis may be used to apportion the travel expenses.

The last big allocation problem mentioned here concerns costs that are *totally indirect*. Many expenses carry some degree of direct relationship to the territory, products, or other marketing units being analyzed. In billing, shipping, and advertising expenses, if a company were to eliminate 10 percent of its territories the chances are that these costs would decrease. However, other items, such as sales administrative or general administrative expenses, have no direct relationship whatsoever to the marketing unit being analyzed. The fundamental question about costs of this nature is whether they should be allocated at all, and if so, what should be the basis.

Many administrators question whether it is reasonably possible to allocate totally indirect costs. Consider the problem of allocating the general sales manager's expense to territories. Part of the year he travels in these districts. The costs of his transportation, food, and lodging while he is on the road probably can be allocated directly to the territory involved. However, how should his salary and the expenses of his office be apportioned among sales districts? If he spends a month in territory A and two months in B, then presumably one twelfth of these expenses may be allocated to A and one sixth to B. At the same time, this method may be unfair to territory A, because during his month's stay there he spent much time on telephone calls involving unforeseen difficulties in territory F. Moreover, how would the company apportion the expenses incurred while he is in the home office and not dealing with the affairs of any one particular territory?

In another example, consider the problem of allocating sales people's salaries and travel expenses among the products they sell. To allocate in proportion to the volume sold ignores the fact that all products are not equally easy to sell. Short of a time and duty analysis, it may be impossible for management to get an accurate basis for apportioning sales force salaries and other expenses.

The following three methods are frequently used to allocate indirect costs. Each reflects a different philosophy, and each has obvious drawbacks.

1.   Divide the costs equally among all territories, products, or whatever market segments are being analyzed. This method is often applied to administrative expenses. The method is easy, but at the same time it is patently inaccurate and usually unfair to some segments.

2.   Allocate the costs in proportion to the sales volume obtained from each territory (or product or customer group). This method often is used for many costs such as billing, order filling, and accounting, as well as for the sales and general administrative costs. The underlying philosophy is that the burden should be applied where it can best be borne. A high-volume territory would be charged with a larger share of the indirect expenses than would a small-volume district. Again, this system is simple, but it also can be highly inaccurate. It tells management

very little about the profitability of the market segment. What is even worse, the results of such a method of allocation can be very misleading.

3. Prorate (allocate) the common (indirect) costs in the same proportion as the total separable (direct) costs. If product A had been charged with $200,000 out of a total of $800,000 direct expenses, this product would also be charged with 25 percent of the total indirect costs.

The contribution-margin versus full-cost controversy

In a marketing cost analysis, two ways of handling the allocation of indirect expenses are the contribution-margin (also called contribution-to-overhead) method, and the full-cost method. A real controversy exists regarding which of these two approaches is the better one for managerial control purposes.

In the *contribution-margin* approach, only the direct expenses are allocated to each marketing unit (territory, product) being analyzed. These are the costs which presumably would be eliminated if the corresponding marketing unit were eliminated. After deducting these direct costs from the gross margin, the remainder is the amount which that unit is contributing to cover total overhead (indirect expenses). In the *full-cost* approach, all expenses—direct and indirect—are allocated among the marketing units under study. For any given marketing unit, these two methods may be summarized as follow:

Contribution-margin approach	*Full-cost approach*
Sales	Sales
− *Cost of goods sold*	− *Cost of goods sold*
= Gross margin	= Gross margin
− *Direct expenses*	− *Direct expenses*
= Contribution margin (the amount available to cover total overhead expenses plus a profit).	− *Indirect expenses*
	= Net profit

An example of the contribution-margin approach is shown in Table 21–1. The net sales, cost of goods sold, and gross margin are shown for each of the three geographic divisions in the Colorado Ski Company (a hypothetical firm introduced in Chapter 20). Then, the direct (escapable) operating costs of the Colorado Ski Company are allocated among the three divisions, and each division's contribution to the remaining $363,000 of indirect (overhead) costs is shown. The Eastern Division, for instance, incurred $207,500 in escapable costs, contributing $192,500 to the overhead expenses and net profit. If the Midwestern Division were eliminated, presumably the company would save $122,000 in direct expenses. However, the division's $78,000 contribution to overhead would then have to be absorbed by the remaining two regions, assuming the indirect costs still totaled $363,000.

TABLE 21–1
Income and expense statement, by geographic divisions, 1977
(using contribution-margin approach)

COLORADO SKI COMPANY

	Total	Eastern	Mid-western	Western
Net sales	$4,500,000	$1,500,000	$750,000	$2,250,000
Less cost of goods sold	3,150,000	1,100,000	550,000	1,500,000
Gross margin	$1,350,000	$ 400,000	$200,000	$ 750,000
Less direct operating expenses:				
Direct selling	$ 514,500	$ 150,000	$ 94,500	$ 270,000
Advertising and sales promotion	125,000	42,000	18,000	65,000
Transportation and shipping	12,000	4,000	3,000	5,000
Warehousing	10,000	3,000	2,500	4,500
Credits and collections	12,000	4,500	1,500	6,000
Financial and clerical	13,500	4,000	2,500	7,000
Total Direct Expenses	$ 687,000	$ 207,500	$122,000	$ 357,500
Contribution margin	$ 663,000	$ 192,500	$ 78,000	$ 392,500
Less indirect operating expenses:				
Direct selling	$ 120,000			
Advertising and sales promotion	73,000			
Transportation and shipping	18,000			
Warehousing	21,500			
Credits and collections	10,500			
Financial and clerical	24,000			
Marketing administrative	70,500			
General administrative	25,500			
Total Indirect Expenses	$ 363,000			
Net Profit before Income Taxes	$ 300,000			

Table 21–2 illustrates the full-cost approach to cost allocation. An alternative procedure is shown in Table 21–3, where the contribution margin and the full-cost approaches are combined. First, the direct expenses are allocated to determine each division's contribution to overhead. Then the allocation of indirect costs is shown separately, to arrive finally at a net profit figure for each region.

There is considerable argument over the relative merits of the contribution-margin and full-cost methods. Proponents of the full-cost approach contend that the purpose of a marketing cost study is to determine the net profitability of the units being studied. They feel that the contribution-margin approach does not fulfill this purpose.

Contribution-margin supporters contend that it is not reasonably possible to make an accurate apportionment of indirect costs among market segments. Furthermore, items such as administrative costs are

TABLE 21-2
Income and expense statement, by geographic divisions, 1977 (using the full-cost approach)
COLORADO SKI COMPANY

	Total	Eastern	Mid-western	Western
Net sales	$4,500,000	$1,500,000	$750,000	$2,250,000
Less cost of goods sold	3,150,000	1,100,000	550,000	1,500,000
Gross margin	$1,350,000	$ 400,000	$200,000	$ 750,000
Less operating expenses:				
Direct selling	$ 634,500	$ 185,000	$114,500	$ 335,000
Advertising and sales promotion	198,000	72,000	30,000	96,000
Transportation and shipping	30,000	11,500	7,500	11,000
Warehousing	31,500	13,000	8,000	10,500
Credits and collections	22,500	7,000	4,000	11,500
Financial and clerical	37,500	12,000	10,500	15,000
Marketing administrative	70,500	23,500	11,750	35,250
General administrative	25,500	8,500	4,250	12,750
Total Operating Expenses	$1,050,000	$ 332,500	$190,500	$ 527,000
Net Profit before Income Taxes	$ 300,000	$ 67,500	$ 9,500	$ 223,000

not all related to any one territory or product, and therefore the unit should not bear any of these costs. These advocates also point out that a full-cost analysis may show that a product or territory has a net loss, whereas this unit may be contributing something to overhead. Some executives might recommend that the losing department be eliminated, overlooking the fact that the unit's contribution to overhead would then have to be borne by other units. Under the contribution-margin approach, there would be no question about keeping this unit as long as no better alternative could be discovered.

Actually, both approaches have a place in marketing cost analysis. The full-cost method is especially suited for the systematic reporting of historical costs as a basis for future marketing planning. Full cost allocation also is useful in making long-range studies of the profitability of various market segments and in establishing *long-range* policies on product lines, channels of distribution, pricing structures, and promotional programs.

The contribution-margin approach is especially useful as an aid to decision making in marketing situations that involve *short-run* considerations. Where cost responsibility is directly assignable to particular market segments (as in the contribution margin approach), management also has an effective tool for controlling and evaluating the efforts of the sales force.

TABLE 21–3
Income and expense statement, by geographic divisions, 1977 (combining the full-cost and contribution-margin approachs)

COLORADO SKI COMPANY

	Total	Eastern	Mid-western	Western
Net sales................................	$4,500,000	$1,500,000	$750,000	$2,250,000
Less cost of goods sold................	3,150,000	1,100,000	550,000	1,500,000
Gross margin	$1,350,000	$ 400,000	$200,000	$ 750,000
Less direct operating expenses:				
Direct selling........................	$ 514,500	$ 150,000	$ 94,500	$ 270,000
Advertising and sales promotion.......	125,000	42,000	18,000	65,000
Transportation and shipping	12,000	4,000	3,000	5,000
Warehousing	10,000	3,000	2,500	4,500
Credits and collections	12,000	4,500	1,500	6,000
Financial and clerical	13,500	4,000	2,500	7,000
Total Direct Expenses.............	$ 687,000	$ 207,500	$122,000	$ 357,500
Contribution margin	$ 663,000	$ 192,500	$ 78,000	$ 392,500
Less indirect operating expenses:				
Direct selling........................	$ 120,000	$ 35,000	$ 20,000	$ 65,000
Advertising and sales promotion.......	73,000	30,000	12,000	31,000
Transportation and shipping	18,000	7,500	4,500	6,000
Warehousing	21,500	10,000	5,500	6,000
Credits and collections	10,500	2,500	2,500	5,500
Financial and clerical	24,000	9,000	8,000	8,000
Marketing administrative	70,500	23,500	11,750	35,250
General administrative	25,500	8,500	4,250	12,750
Total Indirect Expenses	$ 363,000	$ 125,000	$ 68,500	$ 169,500
Net Profit before Income Taxes	$ 300,000	$ 67,500	$ 9,500	$ 223,000

TYPES OF MARKETING COST ANALYSIS

A company's marketing costs may be analyzed in three ways:

1. As they appear in the ledger accounts and on the profit and loss statement.
2. After they are grouped into functional (also called activity) classifications.
3. After they have been allocated to territories, products, or other marketing units.

Analysis of ledger expenses

The simplest and least expensive marketing cost analysis is to study "object-of-expenditure" costs as they are recorded in the company's accounting ledgers. The procedure is simply to take from the ledger accounts the totals for each cost item (sales force salaries, branch office rent, office supplies), and then analyze these figures in some detail. Totals for this period can be compared with similar figures for past periods to determine trends. We can compare actual expenses with budgeted expense goals. We can analyze each expense as a percentage of net sales. When trade associations disseminate cost information, a company can compare its figures with the industry's averages. In some cases, the trade association data are classified by geographic region or by size of firm as measured by annual sales volume. Then, management in one firm can compare its totals with those for other companies of similar size and geographic location.

An analysis of ledger cost items is of limited value because it provides only general information. A study of these costs may show that telephone and telegraph expense incurred last year in a firm's marketing operations was up absolutely and as a percentage of sales over the average of the preceding three-year period. Or a company may note that sales compensation costs are 4.7 percent of sales, whereas the industry's average for firms of similar size is 6.1 percent. Findings of this nature are of some help in guiding management and allowing executives to control the sales force. However, a much more detailed analysis is needed to pinpoint the reasons for trends observed in the company's costs and variations from industry norms.

Analysis of activity expenses

An analysis of ledger costs alone usually does not provide a sufficient degree of managerial control. Such an analysis provides inadequate information about the costs of direct selling, advertising, and the other major activities in a company's marketing program. For more effective cost control, management should analyze its marketing costs after the ledger expenses have been classified into groups representing these marketing activities.

The procedure is to select the appropriate activity groups, and then allocate each ledger expense among those activities. A useful tool in this analysis is an expense distribution sheet such as the one pictured in Table 21–4. All the ledger costs are listed vertically in the left-hand column, and the activity groups are listed at the top of the columns going across the sheet.

The next step is to take the ledger expenses one by one and distribute their totals among the activities. Some expenses are easy to apportion because they are direct expenses, and the entire amount can be allocated to one activity. In Table 21–4, advertising salaries of $37,500 were allocated entirely to advertising and sales promotion. Sales force

TABLE 21–4
Expense distribution sheet showing distribution of ledger cost items to activity groups, 1977

COLORADO SKI COMPANY

						Activity cost groups			
Ledger expenses	Totals	Direct selling	Advertising and promotion	Transportation and shipping	Warehousing	Credits and collections	Financial and clerical	Marketing administrative	General administrative
Sales force commissions	$ 390,000	$390,000							
Sales force salaries	150,000	150,000							
Sales force travel	57,000	57,000							
Office supplies	18,000	3,000	$ 2,550	$ 1,950	$ 1,500	$ 1,500	$ 5,250	$ 900	$ 1,350
Media space and time	150,000		150,000						
Advertising salaries	37,500		37,500						
Administrative salaries	150,000	24,000		10,500	10,500	9,000	21,000	60,000	15,000
Rent	24,000		2,250	4,800	5,250	2,880	2,820	3,150	2,850
Taxes	19,500	2,550	1,200	3,450	3,750	1,575	1,575	2,775	2,625
Heat and light	9,750		1,200	2,025	2,025	1,275	1,275	975	975
Insurance	13,800	2,025	675	3,450	4,050	600	1,725	675	600
Telephone, telegraph	9,000	4,200	675	525	150	870	630	1,050	900
Bad debts	3,000					3,000			
Depreciation	12,000	1,200	750	2,550	3,300	600	2,400	750	450
Miscellaneous	6,450	525	1,200	750	975	1,200	825	225	750
Totals	$1,050,000	$634,500	$198,000	$30,000	$31,500	$22,500	$37,500	$70,500	$25,500

travel expenses of $57,000 were apportioned in their entirety to direct selling.

Other expenses are indirect. Thus their allocation requires considerable executive judgment because they must be apportioned among several activity groups. The main problem for each indirect expense is to select a basis for its allocation. For example, rent may be distributed on the basis of square feet used for each activity. In the Colorado Ski Company example, of the total floor space on which rent was paid, about 20 percent was in the shipping department and another 12 percent was in the credit department. Consequently, $4,800 of rent expense (20 percent of $24,000) was allocated to the transportation activity, and $2,880 (12 percent of $24,000) was charged to credits and collections. Office supplies and telephone and telegraph bills may be audited to determine their distribution among the activities.

After all individual ledger expenses are allocated, the columns are totaled, and the resultant figures are the activity expenses. In Table 21–4 the expenses totaled $1,050,000. The total for direct selling alone was $634,000, the full cost of the advertising and sales promotion activity was $198,000, and so on.

From this type of analysis, the total cost of each activity can be determined rather accurately. Through a periodic study of activity costs, management can observe cost trends and take whatever control measures seem necessary. Moreover, a study of an expense distribution sheet each year shows not only which *ledger* costs have increased or decreased but which *activities* were responsible for these changes. An analysis of activity expenses also provides an excellent starting point from which management can analyze its marketing costs by territories, products, or other marketing units.

Analysis of activity costs by marketing units

The third and most beneficial type of marketing cost analysis is a study of the costs and profitability of each segment of the market. Common practice in this type of analysis is to divide the market by territories, products, customer groups, or order sizes. Cost analysis by market segment will enable management to pinpoint trouble spots or areas of satisfactory performance much more effectively than can be done with an analysis of either ledger account expenses or total activity costs. Neither a ledger account nor an activity-group analysis will shed much light on the *profitability of various segments* of the marketing system in a company. The iceberg principle suggests that unless a more detailed analysis is made, management may be unaware of the strong and weak market segments.

A complete marketing cost analysis by sales territories or some other market unit involves the same three-step evaluation procedure outlined in the preceding chapter. That is, we determine what happened, why it happened, and what we are going to do about the situation.

To determine *what happened*, the procedure in a cost analysis by market units is quite similar to the method used to analyze activity

TABLE 21–5
Bases of allocating functional cost groups to sales territories and to product groups

Functional cost group	Basis of allocation	
	To sales territories	To product group
Selling—direct costs: sales salaries, incentive compensation, travel, and other expenses	Direct	Selling time devoted to each product, as shown by special sales call reports or other special studies
Selling—indirect costs; field sales office expense, sales administration expense, sales personnel training, marketing research, new product development, sales statistics	Equal charge for each salesperson	In proportion to direct selling time or time records by projects
Advertising: media costs such as TV, radio, billboards, newspaper, magazine; advertising production costs; advertising department salaries	Direct; or analysis of media circulation records	Direct; or analysis of space and time by media; other costs in proportion to media costs
Sales promotion: consumer promotions such as coupons, premiums, etc.; trade promotions such as price allowances, point-of-purchase displays, cooperative advertising, etc.	Direct; or analysis of source records	Direct; or analysis of source records
Transportation: railroad, truck, barge, etc.; payments to carriers for delivery of finished goods from plants to warehouses and from warehouses to customers; traffic department costs	Applicable rates times tonnages	Applicable rates times tonnages
Storage and shipping: rent or equivalent costs for storage of inventories in warehouses; insurance and taxes on finished goods inventories; labor and equipment for physical handling, loading, and so on	Number of shipping units	Warehouse space occupied by average inventory; number of shipping units
Order processing: preparation of customer invoices; freight accounting; credit and collection; handling cash receipts; provision for bad debts; salaries, supplies, space, and equipment costs	Number of order lines	Number of order lines

Source: Adapted from Charles H. Sevin, *Marketing Productivity Analysis* (New York: McGraw-Hill Book Co., 1965), pp. 13–15.

expenses. Each component of each activity cost is allocated to each territory, or whatever marketing units are being studied. By combining a sales volume analysis with a marketing cost analysis, a profit and loss statement may be prepared for each territory, product, or class of customer.

To determine what happened in the geographic divisions of the Colorado Ski Company, as an example, we would go through the following four steps:

1. Determine the gross margin for each region. The net sales and the cost of sales in each area should be reasonably easy to uncover in the regular accounting records. It is also possible that the company regularly conducts an analysis of sales volume or gross profit. If so, this step has already been completed in a cost analysis.

2. List all the activity expenses and their component parts. For example, list direct selling and its parts—sales force salaries, travel expenses, telephone charges, office supplies, and so on.

3. Allocate each part of each activity cost among the three geographic divisions. Table 21-5 lists examples of some reasonable bases for allocating groups of functional (activity) costs among sales territories and among product groups. (Remember that some component parts of a given activity cost total may require separate allocation bases. Also, some of these components may be direct expenses, while others are indirect costs.) Only *direct* costs may be allocated to each district (contribution-margin approach), or *all* costs may be apportioned (full-cost approach), as explained earlier and as illustrated in Tables 21-1, 21-2, and 21-3.

4. Assuming that the contribution-margin approach is employed, subtract the total direct expenses for each region from the gross margin to obtain the region's contribution to overhead. If the full-cost approach is used, the total operating expenses for each division can be subtracted from its gross margin to arrive at the net profit for that division.

USE OF FINDINGS FROM COST ANALYSIS

So far in our discussion of marketing cost analysis, we have been dealing generally with the first stage in the evaluation process. That is, we have been finding out *what happened*. To conclude this section, now let's look at some examples of how management might use the combined findings from both a sales volume and marketing cost analyses.

Territorial decisions

Once management knows the net profit (or contribution to overhead) and the sales volume of the territories in relation to their potential, then the executives may decide to adjust territorial boundaries to bring them in line with their current potential. Possibly the district is too small. That is, the potential volume is not adequate to support the expense of covering the territory. Or it may be too large, so that the sales person may be spending too much time and expense in traveling.

Management also may consider a change in selling methods or channels in an unprofitable area. Possibly mail or telephone selling should be used instead of incurring the full expense of personal-selling visits. A company that sells directly to retailers or industrial users may consider using wholesaling middlemen instead.

A weak territory sometimes can be made profitable by an increase in the appropriation for advertising and sales promotion. Possibly, the sales people are not getting adequate support in this respect. A company's competition may have strengthened so much through the years that management must be resigned to a smaller share of the market than was formerly held. The problems in poor territories may lie with the activities of the sales people. They may need closer supervision, or too large a percentage of their sales may be in low-margin items. There is also the possibility that they simply are a poor sales rep.

As a last resort, it may be necessary to abandon a territory entirely, not even using the facilities provided by mail, telephone, or middlemen. Possibly the potential once present no longer exists. However, before dropping a territory from its market, a company should consider the cost repercussions. The territory presumably has been carrying some share of indirect, inescapable expenses, such as marketing and general administrative costs. If the district is abandoned, these expenses must be absorbed by the remaining areas.

Products

When a cost analysis by products shows differences in the relative profitability of each line of products, the executives should try to determine the reasons for the differences. It may be that the variations in profit rates stem from typical order sizes, packaging requirements, or other factors that are fairly firmly set and offer management little opportunity for improvement. On the other hand, administrative action on low-profit items may be taken to correct the situation. A firm may be able to simplify its line by eliminating some models or colors for which there is little call. This will reduce the costs of storage and inventory. Also, simplification makes it possible for the sales force to concentrate on fewer items and probably increases the sales of the remaining products.

Sometimes the profitability of a product can be increased by redesigning or repackaging the item. Packaging the product in multiple rather than single units may increase the average order size and thus cut the unit costs of order filling, shipping, and packaging. Another possibility is to alter (increase or decrease, as the case may be) the amount of advertising and other promotional help appropriated for the product. Possibly, a change in the sales force compensation plan is needed to increase the sales of profitable items or discourage the sales of low-margin goods.

It is not always possible to drop a low-volume item from the line, nor can a company always drop an item even though it shows an irreducible net loss. The product may be necessary to round out a line, and the customers expect the seller to carry it.

Classes of customers and size of order

Another major type of cost study is based on some classification of customers. They may be grouped by *channels of distribution*. For example, a manufacturer who sells to wholesalers, large retailers, and other manufacturers may use those three classifications to group its accounts for a cost analysis. Another possible classification is based on the *major industry groupings of customers*. A glass container manufacturer may sell to food processors, breweries, soft drink bottlers, and dairies. This producer can classify each account in one of those four categories and then make a distribution cost analysis of each of the four classes.

Marketing costs can then be allocated to each of the customer groups. Following the 80–20 principle, ordinarily the bulk of the volume and profit comes from a small percentage of customers who constitute the large purchasers. The average total purchases of the majority of customers are small. As a group, they ordinarily account for a small percentage of the total volume and profits.

Small-order problem.   Management should also consider a cost analysis by *size of order*. The firm can determine its break-even point by size of order. A common situation plaguing many companies is the *small-order problem*, wherein a significant percentage of orders taken are so small that they result in a loss to the company. Many costs, such as direct selling, billing, and accounting, often are the same for each order, whether it is for $10 or $10,000.

A cost analysis by customer groups is closely related to an analysis by order size. Frequently, a customer class that returns a below-average profit also presents a small-order problem. Large-volume purchasers sometimes build up their volume by giving the seller many small individual orders. Management should review both their customer and order-size analyses before making policy decisions in these areas.

Accounts that are small-order problems or are otherwise losing propositions require careful consideration. At first blush, it might seem that customers who are sold at a loss should be eliminated, and orders below the break-even point should not be accepted. Actually this is a hasty conclusion. An administrator first should determine *why* the accounts are unprofitable and *why* the average orders are small. Then, he should consider the many possible ways these situations could be improved.

Any of several reasons may account for the small orders or the unprofitableness of a customer. An account'may buy a large amount in total over a period of a year, but it buys the products for several suppliers. Thus, it represents only a small customer to each of these suppliers. Or take the case of a company that buys a large amount in total and buys it all from one supplier. This firm still can present a small-order problem if it purchases frequently and on a hand-to-mouth basis, so that the average order is small. In other situations accounts may be small but growing, and the seller caters to them in hope of future benefits. A small-order problem also is caused by a customer who is now small and, as far as can be projected reasonably into the future, will remain small.

Sometimes the accounting method used in figuring marketing costs can be the difference between a profitable or unprofitable small-order customer. If costs are computed on an average basis, a given account may show up as a loss for the seller. But if only marginal costs were allocated to this account, it would be a profitable one. An illustration is a small store located across the street from a large department store. A manufacturer's sales rep calls on the large, profitable account. When only the additional (or marginal) costs are determined for making a brief call on the small store across the street, a different profit figure may result for the specific customer than when an average cost is applied to all accounts.

A multitude of practical suggestions is available for increasing the average size of an order or for reducing the distribution costs of small orders. A short list of these suggestions follows.

1. Management may be able to educate the customer who is buying from several different suppliers. The seller may be able to point out to the account the obvious advantages of concentrating its purchases with one supplier.

2. For the customer who purchases a large total quanity but does it on a hand-to-mouth basis with frequent small orders, management again has an educational task on its hands. The sales reps should point out that by ordering, say, once a month instead of once a week the customer will eliminate all its handling, billing, and accounting expenses connected with three of the four orders. The buyer will write one check and one purchase order instead of four. There will be one bill to process and one shipment to put into inventory instead of four, and so on.

3. The company may have to educate its salesforce as well as its customers. In fact, it may be necessary to change the compensation plan to discourage acceptance of smaller orders. Or—a more positive approach—it may be necessary to offer some type of bonus or special premium for large orders.

4. Direct mail or telephone selling may be substituted for sales calls on unprofitable or small-order accounts. Or the sales reps may continue to call on these accounts, but on a less frequent basis.

5. An account may be shifted altogether to a wholesaler or some other type of middleman, rather than dealing directly, even on a mail or telephone basis.

6. A firm may drop its mass-distribution policy and adopt a selective one. Several firms that have adopted this policy have found that their total sales actually increased. The sales people were able to spend more time with the profitable accounts and were thus able to do a better selling job.

7. A seller may establish a minimum-sized order.

8. The pricing structure may be changed in order to pass part of the extra costs on to the buyer in the form of a minimum dollar charge or a service charge. Or the freight charge may be shifted to the buyer, or a higher price may be attached to the orders. Obviously the company that changes its pricing structure must make certain that the new policies do not violate the Robinson-Patman Act (restricting price discrimination) or any other form of pricing legislation.

9. The cost of handling orders can be reduced by such things as more efficient packaging and net pricing. For example, a firm may adopt by decimal packaging, where the units are packed in boxes of 10, 100, or 1,000, thus simplifying the accounting and other record keeping.

RETURN ON INVESTMENT

Return on investment (ROI) is another important measurement tool that management can use in evaluating sales performance and in making marketing decisions. An appropriate formula for measuring return on investment is as follows:

$$\text{ROI} = \frac{\text{Net profit}}{\text{Sales}} \times \frac{\text{Sales}}{\text{Investment (i.e., total assets employed)}}$$

The first fraction expresses the rate of profit on sales, and the second fraction indicates the number of times the total investment (assets employed) was turned over. By multiplying the rate of profit on sales times the investment turnover, the return on investment is determined.

The ROI concept is particularly useful for evaluating the performance of a territorial sales manager or some other segment of the field sales organization.[1] The factors in the equation would be modified to make them appropriate for the organizational segments being analyzed. If management is evaluating territorial performance, for instance, sales volume in each district presumably is readily available. For the profit figure, management can determine the contribution margin in each territory. That is, from a given territory's sales, we deduct the cost of goods sold and all operating expenses directly chargeable to (i.e., controllable by) that district. The investment (assets employed) in the territory consists of the average accounts receivable and inventory carried to serve that district. In equation form; this is:

$$\text{ROI} = \frac{\text{Contribution margin}}{\text{Territorial sales}} \times \frac{\text{Territorial sales}}{\text{Average accounts receivable} + \text{inventory}}$$

Territorial managers can improve their return on investment by influencing sales volume, contribution margin, or district investment. Thus, the ROI concept can serve field sales managers as a useful decision-making aid when they are considering the addition of new customers or products in their regions. In effect, return on investment is an analytical tool that facilitates the delegation of profit responsibility to territorial sales managers.

QUESTIONS AND PROBLEMS

1. Explain the similarities and differences between marketing cost analysis and production cost accounting.

---

[1] See Michael Schiff, "The Use of ROI in Sales Management," *Journal of Marketing*, July 1963, pp. 70–73; J. S. Schiff and Michael Schiff, "New Sales Management Tool: ROAM (Return on Assets Managed)," *Harvard Business Review*, July–August 1967, pp. 59–66.

2. Is an analysis of expenses as recorded in a company's accounting ledgers better than no cost analysis at all? What specific policies or operating plans may stem from an analysis of ledger expenses alone?

3. A national manufacturer of roofing and siding materials has 40 sales people, who have their own territories and sell all three of the firm's product lines. They sell primarily to wholesalers and large retailers in the lumber and building materials field. The company wants to make a *territorial analysis* of marketing costs. What bases do you recommend it should use to allocate each of the following costs?
   a. Sales force salaries.
   b. Sales force travel expenses.
   c. Sales force commissions paid on gross margin.
   d. Salaries and expenses of three regional sales managers.
   e. Sales training expenses.
   f. Television advertising (local and national).
   g. Newspaper advertising
   h. Billing.
   i. Shipping from three regional factories.
   j. Marketing research.
   k. General sales manager's salary and office expenses.
   l. Advertising overhead.
   m. Credit losses and markdowns on returned goods.

4. The company in the proceding problem wants to analyze its marketing cost by *product lines*. Suggest appropriate bases for allocating the above-listed cost items to the three product groups.

5. What is meant by unprofitable business' or an "unprofitable sale"? Explain in detail. Should a company accept unprofitable business? If so, under what possible conditions?

6. What supporting points could be brought out by the proponents of each side in the full-cost versus contribution-margin controversy over allocation of indirect marketing costs? Which of the two concepts do you advocate? Why?

7. In an analysis of expenses grouped by activities, a manufacturer noted that last year the firm's direct selling expenses (sales force compensation, travel expenses, branch office expenses, etc.) increased significantly over the preceding year. Is this trend necessarily an indication of weaknesses or inefficiencies in the management of the sales force?

8. Each of the following firms made a territorial cost analysis and discovered it had some districts that were showing a net loss. What actions involving the sales force do you recommend each company might take to improve its situation?
   a. Hardware wholesaler, covering six southeastern states.
   b. Regional manufacturer of cereals and dog food.
   c. Paint and varnish manufacturer.
   d. National business machines manufacturer.

9. What actions involving its sales force can each of the following firms take if they discover unprofitable products in their lines?

   a. Distributor of electrical goods.
   b. Flower seed producer.
   c. Manufacturer of small power tools.
10. "Large-annual-volume customers never present a small-order problem, while low-annual-volume customers always create small-order problems." Do you agree?
11. Under what conditions should a firm completely discontinue selling to a small-order account?
12. To determine return on investment, we multiply two fractions: Net profit/Sales and Sales/Investment. Why can't we cancel out the sales factor in each equation and simply divide net profit by investment?
13. Explain how the ROI concept may be used to evaluate the profit performance of a territorial sales manager.

Case 21–1
THE WHITING CORPORATION
Analyzing sales by product line and by sales office

The Whiting Corporation sells custom-designed heavy industrial equipment such as electric furnaces, overhead cranes, cupolas, and chemical-processing apparatus in the U.S. market through 12 geographically dispersed sales offices. The staff of each sales office includes a district sales manager, an average of two sales engineers, and clerical help. Most company sales are made directly to ultimate users. A few products, however, are sold to distributors for later resale to users.

The company regularly seeks to relate sales effort and sales results both for the sales offices and for major product lines. Basic information needed for this purpose comes from call reports and cost accounting records.

Weekly call reports, submitted by the field sales force, show how much time goes into selling as against nonselling activities. Also, for selling time, there is a breakdown among various product groups. (See Exhibit 1.)

In the column headed "Product" on the extreme right of the weekly call report, the sales people indicate the product or products discussed during a sales call. Then, at the end of the day they estimate their total selling time and the division of it among the various products they

Note: This case is adapted from The Conference Board, *Sales Analysis*, Studies in Business Policy, No. 113 (New York, 1965), pp. 44–48.

have discussed in their calls. The balance of the time spent on the job is divided between office, travel, and start-up and service.

When the completed reports are routed to company headquarters, the accounting department can conveniently segregáte time spent in selling and in other activities for all salesmen and then for their respective sales offices. It also can easily allocate direct-sales expenses among product groups, as well as tabulate the total number of calls attributable to each product group. When more than one product group is discussed in a single call, each group is credited with an equal share of the call. For example, if two product groups are discussed, each gets one half; if three, each gets one third.

Standard accounting records serve as the source of data for dollar product sales, the rent, clerical, and utilities costs of operating sales offices, and direct-selling expenses (sales force salaries, commissions, and expenses).

EXHIBIT 1
WHITING CORPORATION

WHITING CORPORATION
R-2597 R 6/1/61

WEEKLY CALL REPORT

CLOCK NUMBER	WEEK ENDING	SALESMAN

DATE	TOWN STATE	COMPANY CALLED ON	MEN INTERVIEWED AND TITLE	PRODUCT

INSTRUCTIONS

RECORD ALL PERSONAL CALLS DURING EACH WEEK.

MAIL TO HARVEY NOT LATER THAN MONDAY.

USE EXTRA SHEETS IF NECESSARY. ALLOCATE TOTAL TIME OF WORKING DAY REGARDLESS OF HOURS IN BEHALF OF EACH PRODUCT.

YOUR TIME ESTIMATES ARE USED TO ALLOCATE YOUR SALARY AND EXPENSES TO PRODUCT.

PRINT NAMES-GIVE INITIALS & TITLES

USE THESE ABBREVIATIONS

CRANE	C
LADLES	L
CUPOLAS	CU
ELEC. FRNC	EF
SWENSON	SW
TRANSPT	T
TRAMBEAM	TB
TRACKMOBILE	TM
PRESSUREGRIP	P

	BREAKDOWN IN HOURS					PRODUCT BREAKDOWN IN HOURS									
	OFFICE	TRAVEL	SELLING	START UP & SERVICE	TOTAL	C	L	CU	EF	SW	T	TB	TM	P	TOTAL
SUN															
MON															
TUE															
WED															
THU															
FRI															
SAT															
TOTALS															

EXHIBIT 2

Cumulative quarterly report of sales

WHITING CORPORATION

						Total calls for 6 months ended 10/31/63					New orders for period	Cost of depart-ment for period	Cost per call	New orders per call
Office	Pres-sure grip	Crane	Ladles, furnaces, etc.	Cupolas & acces-sories	Elec-tric fur-niture	Swen-son	Trans-porta-tion	Tram-beam	Track-mobile	Total				
70. California sales rep ...	2	17	—	1	6	81	10	1	—	118	$ 356,979	$ 13,505	$114.45	$3,025
72. Cleveland	6	74	17	25	19	32	18	2	6	199	65,988	8,543	42.93	332
73. Seattle	—	25	1	—	13	135	1	6	7	188	119,227	16,484	87.68	634
74. Charlotte	23	292	11	18	12	120	15	42	28	561	172,178	31,372	55.92	307
75. Minneapolis sales rep	—	97	8	22	12	74	8	5	8	234	210,426	10,784	46.09	899
76. Chicago	9	434	121	116	96	205	35	29	5	1,050	965,385	45,087	42.94	919
77. Cincinnati	1	136	75	112	42	90	6	18	5	485	364,883	21,152	43.61	752
78. Detroit	22	41	6	57	18	2	—	10	5	161	863,426	20,530	127.52	5,363
79. New York (domestic)	2	402	58	71	52	252	39	10	15	901	2,252,138	74,809	83.03	2,500
82. Pittsburgh	26	143	70	16	38	109	30	4	8	444	945,160	34,758	78.28	2,129
83. St. Louis	18	217	24	50	12	120	27	109	24	601	621,423	23,307	38.78	1,034
84. Houston sales rep	1	70	18	14	12	40	11	5	5	176	177,330	10,748	61.07	1,008
Subtotal	110	1,948	409	502	332	1,260	200	241	116	5,118	$7,114,543	$311,079	$ 60.78	$1,390
80. New York (export)	1	164	43	34	32	111	132	22	63	602	561,738	42,375	70.39	933
Total	111	2,112	452	536	364	1,371	332	263	179	5,720	$7,676,281	$353,454	$ 61.79	$1,342

To prepare the various sales reports required by Whiting's management, data from the weekly call reports and cost accounting records are punched into cards, which are subsequently run through an electronic data processing machine.

The principal sales reports prepared regularly for management are cumulative quarterly analyses, annual summaries, and year-by-year trend studies of sales calls, orders, sales revenue, and sales expenses.

Every three months a sales report covering the fiscal year to date is issued (Exhibit 2). In this report, the total number of calls are cross-tabulated by product group and district sales office. Then, for each one of the offices the following information is given:

The dollar value of orders booked during the period.

The cost of operating the district sales office.

The average cost of each sales call.

The average dollar value of orders booked as the result of each call.

The first of two annual sales summaries issued relates sales calls to dollar sales and sales expenses. This report shows the number of calls by sales offices for each of five product classifications, together with key sales and expense figures.

Exhibit 3, an example of this report, covers a fiscal year in which 11,838 total calls were made, resulting in total sales of $12,283,000. Dividing the second figure by the first yields the amount of business per call—in this case, $1,037. The report also presents similar information for each of five product classifications.

The total cost of maintaining all 12 district offices for the year covered in this report was $658,937. Dividing the 11,838 calls into this figure gives an average call cost of $55.70.

The other annual summary (see Exhibit 4) focuses on the relationships among total sales calls, large orders, and dollar sales volume for the five major product classifications. It shows that a total of 1,060 orders with a value of $24,841,000 resulted from 15,298 calls. Dividing the first figure into the third and then into the second discloses that the average order had a value of $23,437 and required 14.4 calls to obtain.

Exhibit 4 also shows that there was a wide variation among product classifications. For instance, the average transportation order was $12,994, resulting from an average of 18.7 calls, while the average process equipment order was $53,392 and required 23.6 calls.

The company regularly studies several year-to-year trends, including sales revenues, calls, and dollar value of sales per call for each product classification; the average number of calls per sales person per working day; the average cost of a single call; and district-office selling costs as a percentage of total dollar sales.

EXHIBIT 3
Annual report of sales calls, dollar sales, and sales office expenses (summary of call reports—5/1/62 to 4/30/63)

WHITING CORPORATION

Office	Cranes	Foundry products	Trans-portation	Swenson process	Distributor products	Total
Charlotte	436	95	61	263	302	1,157
Chicago	1,057	956	57	426	138	2,634
Cincinnati	292	487	19	182	53	1,033
Cleveland	232	266	73	102	28	701
Detroit	65	297	2	5	62	431
Houston	161	65	24	119	33	402
Los Angeles	79	20	20	130	19	268
Minneapolis	185	135	29	130	42	521
New York domestic, incl. Boston and Philadelphia	996	388	79	646	118	2,227
Pittsburgh	407	232	86	232	57	1,014
St. Louis, including Kansas City	605	189	40	148	191	1,173
Seattle	34	15	12	203	13	277
Total Sales Calls, All Offices	4,549	3,145	502	2,586	1,056	11,838
Offices (12 Months; 000)	$5,125	$2,081	$ 613	$3,861	$ 569	$12,283
Sales/Call	$1,126	$ 661	$1,223	$1,493	$ 539	$ 1,037
Office Expense all Offices, 12 months	$658,937					
Cost per call	$ 55.70					

Because of great differences among principal product lines in the average size of an order and in the number of calls required to obtain an order, it is essential, Whiting says, for information about sales results to be broken out on a product-line basis. And with scattered sales offices, sales figures on an office-by-office basis are likewise necessary. The company believes that its sales analysis procedure meets both these needs adequately.

Question

1. Evaluate the company's program for analyzing its sales by product line and sales office.

EXHIBIT 4
Annual report of total sales calls, large orders, and dollar sales volume by product classification (total no. of large orders; only orders in excess of $2,000 counted)

WHITING CORPORATION

	Cranes	Foundry	Trans-portation	Process	Resale	Total
May..............	19	17	7	9	33	85
June	9	18	4	5	42	78
July..............	15	12	0	7	50	84
August	15	16	1	7	49	88
September	9	13	3	12	35	72
October	23	20	2	19	48	112
November	20	12	4	10	29	75
December	10	14	5	10	25	64
January	20	9	3	8	62	102
February	26	18	3	12	40	99
March...........	31	13	3	11	31	89
April	20	20	8	12	52	112
Total	217	182	43	122	496	1,060
Total calls	3,990	3,103	806	2,874	4,525	15,298
Sales (000)*	$ 8,551	$ 3,779	$ 558	$ 6,513	$ 5,440	$24,841
Calls/Order	18.4	17.1	18.7	23.6	9.1	14.4
$/Order	$39,408	$20,764	$12,994	$53,392	$10,969	$23,437

* Includes repair orders.

Case 21–2
APEX ABRASIVES, INC.
Marketing cost analysis

Apex Abrasives, Inc., was a manufacturer of abrasive products consisting of paper sheets, cloth sheets, paper rolls, belts, and disks. The principal backing materials used were paper and cloth, which were coated with a variety of abrasives.

Initially, Apex Abrasives sold these abrasive products to the automotive and industrial markets. Sales were made through jobbers and direct to users. The automobile market consisted of sales through automotive jobbers to repaint and repair shops throughout the country. The industrial market consisted of sales direct and through jobbers to industrial plants of all types.

The sales organization of Apex Abrasives consisted of one sales

Note: Case prepared by Professor Michael Schiff, New York University. Reproduced with permission.

manager who supervised seven divisional sales managers who in turn supervised the field sales force. Field sales people were divided into two categories: automotive and industrial. There was a further subdivision of the automotive group into senior reps and promotional sales reps. The promotional sales force was used to develop the automotive market by selling Apex Abrasives for new jobbers to repaint and repair shops. Promotional sales people took orders which they in turn passed on to the jobbers for shipment to the repaint shops.

Apex Abrasives engaged in a heavy research program during the first ten years of its existence. The company's policy had been to spend approximately 1½ percent of sales on product research. As a result, they were able to improve product quality and develop new products which, combined with an aggressive sales organization, enabled them to rapidly attain the position of second largest abrasives manufacturer in the country.

In 1969, after an intensive market survey, Apex Abrasives decided to enter the consumer field. The consumer field consisted of retail sales of sandpaper, emery cloth, and disks for home workshops through various retail outlets, principally hardware stores. To reach this market, Apex established a separate consumer products sales force which sold to various types of jobbers and directly to large retailers. A new position of sales manager for consumer marketing was established. But the sales people reported to the same divisional managers as did the automotive sales and the industrial sales force.

Apex felt that it was desirable to enter the consumer market for the following reasons:

1. The products sold would be similar to those already manufactured; the principal difference would be in the packaging of the product.
2. The market survey indicated that there was a potential market of $20,000,000 a year for abrasives sold to consumers.
3. It was apparent that a higher gross profit could be obtained on consumer sales than prevailed in the automotive and industrial markets.
4. It was felt that Apex Abrasives would be less subject to the swings in the business cycle if it could develop a consumer franchise.
5. It was expected that there would be a substantial boost given to the automotive and industrial lines if Apex Abrasives developed a well-known brand name through national advertising.

It was realized that it would be necessary to plow back most of the profits from the consumer line into advertising and selling expense for several years in order to develop a strong consumer franchise and attain at least 50 percent of the potential market. As a result, since 1969

Apex Abrasives had been computing their annual advertising and sales promotion budget by deducting direct selling expenses from gross profit obtained from sales to the consumer market. The balance then represented the amount available for consumer advertising during the following year.

At a meeting of the executive committee of Apex Abrasives, held early in 1978, the sales manager of the industrial and automotive division made a proposal to change the field-selling organization. He stated that he felt it necessary to have separate divisional sales managers for the industrial and automotive markets. At the present time (see organization chart, Exhibit 1), division managers supervised sales

EXHIBIT 1
Organization chart

APEX ABRASIVES, INC.

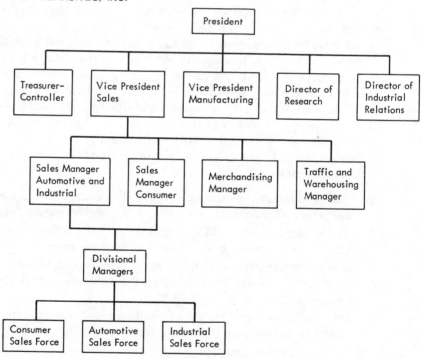

people selling in all three markets. The sales manager stated that he felt automotive and industrial sales were suffering from the divided attention the division manager gave them. He also stated that he felt it would be necessary to add at least ten additional industrial sales people in view of increasing competition in the market. He presented figures which indicated that Apex Abrasives had at the present time 35 percent of the potential industrial market, but in 1974 Apex Abrasives had had 39 percent of the industrial market. He further questioned the advisability of continuing the company's previous policy of spending so heavily for consumer advertising at the expense of the needed strengthening of the industrial market organization.

In response to this, the sales manager for consumer products stated that, despite the fact that at the present time Apex Abrasives had only 25 percent of the consumer market, encouraging progress had been shown. He believed that to let up on sales promotional efforts at this point would jeopardize the investment the company had been making in brand advertising during the past several years. In this he was supported by the merchandising director, who agreed that it would be unwise to cut advertising expenditures until Apex Abrasives had obtained at least 50 percent of the potential retail market.

The president of Apex Abrasives said that he would like to have an analysis of the problem prepared by the treasurer. He stated that he felt that expenses had increased substantially in areas related to selling activity, particularly in the number of clerical employees that appeared to have been necessary to add since taking on the consumer line.

The statement of profit and loss for Apex Abrasives is shown in Exhibit 2. This served as a starting point in the analysis undertaken by

EXHIBIT 2
Statement of profit and loss for year ending December 31, 1977
APEX ABRASIVES, INC.

	Amount	Percent of net sales
Sales:		
Civilian	$16,283,700	86.7
Less: Cash discount	293,107	1.6
	$15,990,593	85.1
U.S. government	2,806,298	14.9
Net sales	$18,796,891	100.0
Manufacturing cost	12,607,473	67.1
Gross profit	$ 6,189,418	32.9
Operating expenses:		
Selling	$ 1,282,599	6.8
Merchandising	1,575,856	8.4
Research	285,208	1.5
Shipping, warehousing and transportation	976,205	5.2
Accounting and general administrative	509,325	2.7
Provision for doubtful accounts	14,306	0.1
Total operating expenses	$ 4,643,499	24.7
Net profit	$ 1,545,919	8.2

the treasurer. A review of the classification of the operating expenses shown in the statement revealed that these expenses included sub-classifications as follows:

1. *Selling.* Field selling expenses (sales force salaries, commissions, travel, payroll costs, dealers' commissions). Divisional sales management expenses (managers' salaries, commissions, clerical salaries, travel, supplies, postage, telephone and telegraph, occupancy costs, payroll costs). Home office selling expenses (executive salaries, bonuses, clerical salaries, travel, professional services, supplies, telephone and telegraph, occupancy costs, sales meetings, shows, price lists and exhibits, samples, payroll costs).

2. *Merchandising.* Advertising expenses (consumer space, consumer art and mechanical, consumer radio and television, trade space, trade art and mechanical, point of sale displays, direct mail). Merchandising expenses (executive salaries, bonuses, clerical salaries, supplies, telephone and telegraph, payroll costs). Of a total of $1,575,856 expended for merchandising, $1,256,500 is directly attributable to consumer sales. Of this latter amount, $1,233,105 represents direct advertising expense (space, radio, television, and point-of-sale displays).

3. *Research.* Salaries, travel, supply, telephone and telegraph, occupancy costs, payroll costs, depreciation of equipment.

4. *Warehouse and shipping.* Salaries of executives and clerical, wages, shipping clerks, travel supply, telephone and telegraph, depreciation of handling equipment, occupancy costs, payroll costs, freight, parcel post, express.

5. *Accounting and general administrative.* Salaries of executives and clerical, bonuses, postage, supply, travel, telephone and telegraph, professional services, occupancy costs, payroll costs.

6. *Provision for doubtful accounts.* Estimate of expected losses on accounts receivable.

The initial approach suggested by the treasurer resulted in a report showing sales made by each line (Exhibit 3). The gross profit for each line was readily ascertained, since an extensive cost accounting system was used to control manufacturing operations. Next a percentage was derived showing the relationship between total distribution cost ($4,643,499) and net sales ($18,796,891). This came to 24.7 percent. This distribution cost percentage was then applied to the sales of each line and an allocation of distribution cost was achieved. The resulting profit for each line was then derived and expressed as a percentage of sales.

When this report was submitted, objections were raised by the sales manager—industrial and automotive. Treating every line as if the rela-

EXHIBIT 3
Sales, gross profit, and allocated distribution cost for year ending December 31, 1977

APEX ABRASIVES, INC.

	(1) Net sales	(2) Gross profit	(3) Allocated distribution cost	(4) (2 – 3) Net profit or loss before taxes	(5) (4/1) Net profit per- cent
Consumer	$ 3,581,633	$1,655,450	$ 884,790	$ 770,660	21.52
Automotive	3,130,610	1,038,149	773,372	264,777	8.46
Industrial	8,296,969	2,843,166	2,049,646	793,520	9.56
Home office and U.S. government	3,787,679	652,653	935,691	(283,038)	(7.47)
Totals	$18,796,891	$6,189,418	$4,643,499	$1,545,919	8.22

tive cost of distribution was similar ignored the facts in the case. Certainly the costs of selling the consumer market were higher than in the automotive and industrial markets. The mere fact that almost all merchandising costs were incurred for the consumer line was sufficient evidence, apart from the known differences in marketing the various lines.

The treasurer attempted to prepare a more extensive analysis. This time the component costs of each of the distribution functions were studied (selling, merchandising, research, and so on). These costs were separated into two classes based on their behavior relative to sales volume—fixed and variable costs. Only the variable costs were then allocated to product lines. The results are shown in Exhibit 4. Significant variations in profit contributions to fixed costs and profit are indicated. The consumer line shows a negative contribution of $250,234, or 6.99 percent of sales.

Questions

1. Determine the relative profitability of the four markets—consumer, industrial, automotive, and home office—U.S. government.
2. Evaluate the advertising policy for the consumer line.
3. Appraise the organizational structure used for the field sales function.

EXHIBIT 4
Sales, gross profit, and margins after variable costs for year ending December 31, 1977
APEX ABRASIVES, INC.

	Total		Consumer		Automotive		Industrial		Home office and U.S. government	
	Amount	Per-cent	Amount	Per-cent	Amount	Per-cent	Amount	Per-cent	Amount	Per-cent
Net sales	$18,796,891	100.00	$3,581,633	100.00	$3,130,610	100.00	$8,296,969	100.00	$3,787,679	100.00
Manufacturing cost	12,607,473	67.07	1,926,183	53.78	2,092,461	66.84	5,453,803	65.73	3,135,026	82.77
	$ 6,189,418	32.93	$1,655,450	46.22	$1,038,149	33.16	$2,843,166	34.27	$ 652,653	17.23
Direct distribution cost:										
Selling	$ 1,043,152	5.55	$ 456,601	12.75	$ 228,920	7.31	$ 352,228	4.25	$ 5,403	.14
Merchandising	1,454,604	7.74	1,256,500	35.08	69,431	2.22	110,612	1.33	18,061	.48
Research	285,208	1.52	54,475	1.52	47,630	1.52	126,347	1.52	56,756	1.50
Shipping, warehousing, and transportation	695,764	3.70	114,806	3.21	61,754	1.97	425,211	5.13	93,993	2.48
Accounting and administrative	62,324	0.33	16,017	0.45	12,216	0.39	31,100	0.37	2,991	0.08
Provision doubtful accounts	14,306	0.08	7,285	0.20	1,860	0.06	5,161	0.06		
	$ 3,555,358	18.92	$1,905,684	53.21	$ 421,811	13.47	$1,050,659	12.66	$ 177,204	4.68
Contribution to indirect expense and profit	$ 2,634,060	14.01	$ (250,234)	(6.99)	$ 616,338	19.69	$1,792,507	21.61	$ 475,449	12.55
Fixed distribution cost:										
Selling	$ 239,447									
Merchandising	121,252									
Shipping, warehousing, and transportation	280,441									
Accounting and administrative	447,001									
	$ 1,088,141									
Net profit before taxes	$ 1,545,919									

22

Evaluating sales force performance

The yardstick for measuring men is other men.
ANON.

In considering evaluation of the firm's selling effort, the preceding two chapters have emphasized the performance of the *total* sales force. In this chapter, attention is devoted primarily to appraising the productivity and effectiveness of the *individual sales people*. After examining the nature and purposes of this managerial activity, we will outline a complete program for evaluating sales performance. The last section of the chapter is a case example of how one firm interpreted the performance data it had assembled.

NATURE AND IMPORTANCE OF PERFORMANCE EVALUATION

The task of appraising the performance of an individual sales person is basically a part of the managerial function of evaluation. In effect, it is part of a marketing audit. Management is comparing the results of a person's efforts against the goals set for that person. The general purpose, of course, is to see what has happened in the period immediately past and then use this as a basis for planning for future periods.

Concept of evaluation and development

The evaluation activity takes on an added dimension viewed from the perspective of evaluation *and development* of individual sales people. Within this richer context, management is engaged in a counseling activity rather than solely a cold statistical analysis. Certainly management wants to measure past performance against standards to identify strengths and weaknesses in the firm's marketing system, par-

591

ticularly as a basis for future planning. But this activity is optimized only if it also is brought to the personal level of the sales person. It should serve as a basis for the person's self-development and as a basis for a sound company program for the guidance and development of sales personnel.

Sometimes management reduces the effectiveness of its evaluation and developmental counseling effort by confusing it with other tasks in sales force management, particularly with supervision or training. A more effective job of evaluation can be accomplished when this task is pinpointed as a separate managerial function.

Importance of performance evaluation

A statistical evaluation of sales force performance is a major tool for improving sales performance and for lowering marketing costs. Management can identify the outstanding sales producers and then study their sales techniques with an eye toward having the other sales people adopt them. It also can show high-cost performers how to reduce their selling costs.

Thus a good performance review can be a major aid in other sales force management tasks. Effective personal guidance is a significant factor in improving a rep's efficiency, and a valid evaluation system is the basis for this counseling. Promotions and pay increases can be based on objective performance data rather than on favoritism, subjective observations, or opinions. Weaknesses in field selling efforts, once identified, may be forestalled in the future by incorporating corrective measures in training programs. Performance evaluations may uncover the need for improvements in the compensation plan. The existing plan may be resulting in too much effort on low-margin items or inadequate attention to nonselling (missionary) activities. Sales supervision especially is helped by an analysis of performance. It is difficult to effectively supervise someone unless the supervisor knows *what* the person is doing correctly or incorrectly and *why* he is doing it. If a rep's sales volume is unsatisfactory, for instance, a performance review will show it. Moreover, the evaluation probably will identify the cause—whether the rep has a low daily call rate, is not working enough days per month, is calling on the wrong prospects, is having trouble with the sales presentation, and so on.

An effective procedure for appraising the work of an individual could be called morale insurance. Any person who knows what he is expected to do, and has some benchmarks for measuring accomplishments, feels more secure. In Chapter 14 we stressed that *recognition* has an important bearing on the morale of the sales force. A performance evaluation should ensure that those reps who deserve favorable recognition receive it, and those who deserve criticism also are appropriately handled. The sales person with the highest sales volume is not necessarily the best one and may not even be doing a good all-around job. To reward this person on the basis of sales volume alone, without knowing the full story, can hurt morale of others in the sales force. Similarly, morale is lowered when a rep is criticized for low volume, when the contributing factor was low territorial potential or unusually stiff competition. A performance appraisal system should forestall such situations.

By evaluating the sales people's achievements, management helps them discover their own strengths and weaknesses. This should motivate them to raise their levels of performance. Like most people, sales people seldom can be objectively introspective or make an effective self-evaluation. A salesman may know he is doing something wrong, as witness his output. But he is unable to determine the reasons for his poor productivity, either because he lacks the objective yardsticks by which to compare his performance with that of other salesmen, or because he is unable to see himself as others see him.

Difficulties involved in evaluating performance

Many firms seem to lack an effective, complete procedure for evaluating the performance of their sales people. Undoubtedly, the time, people, and expense requirements necessary to do a satisfactory job account in part for this. Other difficulties, however, also are encountered in the evaluation task.

First, many of the bases used in evaluations are approximations at best. The measure of a sales person's effectiveness in training his customers sales reps or his ability to prospect for new accounts can only be estimated. Even factors such as days worked, miles traveled, calls made, or expenses incurred may contain a degree of error, either intentional or unintentional.

Many of the duties assigned to sales people cannot be measured objectively, and some tasks are difficult to evaluate even on a subjective basis. A manufacturer's representative is supposed to service the firm's accounts with dealers and distributors; a wholesaler's sales rep is told to avoid high-pressure selling; all sales people are supposed to build goodwill with customers. Even if the company has close field supervision of the sales force, these tasks can be evaluated only subjectively. And, if management does not closely supervise the sales people in the field, the measurement of results from some of these duties may be virtually impossible.

By the same token, however, management sometimes does not recognize that many tasks of a seemingly subjective nature can actually be quantified. A sales person's tendency to high-pressure or oversell customers, for instance, can be measured by tallying the number and sales volume in canceled orders, the number of lost accounts, and the rate of reorders, as well as by the more subjective factor of customer complaints.

The wide variety of conditions under which sales reps work makes it difficult for management to compare the productivity and effectiveness of the people involved. There is no satisfactory method for equating territorial differences in potential, competition, or working conditions. It is difficult to compare the performance of city sales people with country sales people for example. Even if the districts are equal in potential, they are not comparable in area, customer size, or on other bases.

Sometimes performance evaluation is difficult because the results of a sales person's efforts may not be evident for some time. A district's improved position may show up only after a rep has been working there for a year or more.

When a joint effort between two or more people is involved in making a sale or in servicing a customer, it usually is difficult to assess individual credit for results. Whether two sales people are involved, or a sales person plus an executive (supervisor, branch manager, product manager), individual contributions are hard to measure.

In the phase of performance evaluation that involves subjective appraisal, management runs the risk that the sales rep with an attractive personality may be overvalued in relation to less spectacular associates. Similarly, the sales rep who works out of the home office or under the frequent observation of the evaluators is more likely to get a high rating on subjective points, unless the rating executives are aware of the distinction.

Importance of a good job description

In the task of sales force evaluation and development, as we have observed so many other sales force management activities, a good, detailed job description is of critical importance. Unless the evaluators can work from the reference point of a statement about what a sales person is supposed to do, they are not in a very good position to determine *whether* he did the job or *how effectively* he did it. Moreover, much of the merit in discussing the evaluation with the sales person is diminished if the evaluator and the sales rep are not communicating from the same frame of reference—the person's tasks as outlined in the job description.

PROGRAM FOR EVALUATING PERFORMANCE

This section suggests a procedural system for evaluating sales force performance. The program is a complete one; but it is also expensive and time-consuming. A firm probably would not participate in the entire program unless it is using some kind of electronic data processing equipment.[1]

Establish some basic policies

Preliminary to the actual evaluation, management should set some ground rules. One question that calls for a decision is: Who is to participate in the evaluation? Several executives normally are involved. The most likely one is the sales person's immediate superior. Perhaps this is a field supervisor, a district manager, or a branch manager. The boss of the immediate supervisor is also quite likely to be involved. Certainly, the sales person being evaluated should participate actively, usually with some form of self-evaluation. The personnel department may take part in the appraisal procedure, although its role probably is one of staff support—preparing forms, gathering data to help set performance standards, and so on.

Another needed policy decision concerns the frequency of evaluation. For a *complete* evaluation of a sales person's total performance, probably once a year (or twice, at the outside) is enough, in light of the time and costs required. Many firms combine an annual performance evaluation with a compensation review. Some form of appraisal is usually being conducted continuously as an inherent part of sales training or sales supervision. Also, as a special project and on a nonrecurring basis, management may evaluate the performance of some one aspect of the sales rep's job—the advertising displays they set up or their use of selling aids during sales calls, for example.

The role of self-evaluation by sales reps should be clearly understood by the sales reps as well as by the executives involved in the appraisal system. What evaluation data will be given to the sales people? What evaluation forms will they be asked to fill out? In what manner will they communicate their opinions and self-ratings to management? What appeal procedures are available?

Select bases for evaluation

One key to a successful evaluation program is to appraise a sales rep's performance on as many different bases as possible. To do otherwise is to run the risk of being misled. Let's assume that we are rating a sales-

---

[1] For a comprehensive, practical treatment of the problem of evaluating salesmen's performance, with much of the material extensively illustrated, see Wayland A. Tonning, *How to Measure and Evaluate Salesmen's Performance* (Englewood Cliffs, N.J.: Prentice-Hall, Inc., 1964). Also, for an analytical approach to the problems of evaluating performance in sales territories and establishing benchmarks for future sales territory performance, see James C. Cotham III and David W. Cravens, "Improving Measurement of Salesman Performance," *Business Horizons*, June 1969, pp. 79–83.

man on the basis of the ratio of his selling expenses to his sales volume. If this percentage is very low compared to the average for the entire sales force, he probably will be commended. Yet, he actually may have achieved that low expense ratio by failing to prospect for new accounts or by otherwise covering his territory inadequately. Knowing the average number of daily calls he made, even in relation to the average call rate for the entire sales force, does not help us very much. By measuring his ratio of orders per call (his batting average) we learn a little more, but we still can be misled. Each additional piece of information—his sales volume, plus his average order size, plus his gross margin, and so on— helps to give a clearer picture of the salesman's performance. Both quantitative and qualitative factors should be used as bases for a performance appraisal.

Quantitative bases. The quantitative factors that can be used as evaluation bases fall into two categories—input (or effort) factors and output (or results) factors. Productivity is a concept that involves the relationship between the two—output results as measured by sales volume, gross margin, and so on, and input effort as indicated by call rate, expenses incurred, nonselling activities, and others.

In a performance evaluation, the importance of output factors is readily recognized. Sometimes, however, the value of input effort factors is underestimated. They usually are critical in locating trouble spots. If a sales person's output performance (average order size, gross margin, and so on) is unsatisfactory, very often the cause lies in the way the various input factors over which the rep has control are handled.

A list of some *output* factors that ordinarily are useful as evaluation bases would include:

1. Sales volume.
   a. In dollars and in units.
   b. By products and customers (or customer groups).
   c. By mail, telephone, and personal sales calls.
2. Sales volume as a percentage of:
   a. Quota.
   b. Market potential (i.e., market share).
3. Gross margin by product line, customer group, and order size.
4. Orders.
   a. Number of orders.
   b. Average size (dollar volume) or order.
   c. Batting average (orders ÷ calls).
   d. Number of canceled orders.
5. Accounts.
   a. Percentage of accounts sold.

    b. Number of new accounts.
    c. Number of lost accounts.
    d. Number of accounts with overdue payment.

Some *input* factors that may be used as bases for evaluation are:

1. Calls per day (call rate).
2. Days worked.
3. Selling time versus nonselling time.
4. Direct selling expense:
    a. In total.
    b. As percentage of sales volume.
    c. As percentage of quota.
5. Nonselling activities:
    a. Advertising displays set up.
    b. Letters written to prospects.
    c. Telephone calls made to prospects.
    d. Number of meetings held with dealers and/or distributors.
    e. Number of service calls made.
    f. Collections made.
    g. Number of customer complaints received.

As evaluation bases, these output and input factors fall into two categories. One group consists of factors measured individually—sales volume, number of orders, daily call rate, or displays set up, for example. The other category includes ratios involving almost any two of the individual variables—such as expenses/sales, orders/call, or average order size.

Qualitative bases. It would be nice if the entire evaluation could be based only on quantitative factors, thus minimizing the subjectivity and personal biases of the evaluators. Unfortunately, this cannot be done. Too many factors—all of a qualitative nature—must be reckoned with because they directly influence a sales person's performance. These qualitative factors can cover a wide gamut.

1. Personal efforts of the sales reps.
    a. Management of their time.
    b. Planning and preparation for calls.
    c. Quality of sales presentations.
    d. Ability to handle objections and to close sales.
2. Knowledge of:
    a. Product.
    b. Company and company policies.
    c. Competitor's products and strategies.
    d. Customers.
3. Customer relations.

4. Personal appearance and health.
5. Personality and attitudinal factors. Some examples are:
    a. Cooperativeness.
    b. Resourcefulness.
    c. Acceptance of responsibility.
    d. Ability to analyze logically and make decisions.

Sources of information.   When deciding on which factors to use as bases for a performance evaluation, management should select only those for which data are available, at a reasonable cost. The four main sources of information are company records, the sales reps themselves, field sales managers, and customers.

Company records are the main source for data on most of the quantitative *output* factors. By studying sales invoices, customers' orders, credit department records, and accounting records, management can discover a great deal about sales peoples' volume, gross margin, average order size, market share, and so on. Most firms probably fall far short of making optimum use of their records for evaluation purposes. One reason for this shortcoming is that the information as recorded is not in usable form for a performance evaluating. It may be too expensive and time-consuming to tabulate and present the data in usable form. However, an increasing number of companies are using electronic data processing equipment as an aid in collecting, analyzing, and storing data in a form useful for evaluation purposes.

Reports submitted by the sales force are an important source, particularly for performance *input* factors. The regular use of call reports, activity reports, and expense reports can provide the necessary data on the sales people's work. Call reports can furnish the details of each visit to each customer, including problems that arose, customers' buying plans and potential, products presented, sales made, and so on. Daily or weekly activity reports summarize the rep's work with present, new, and potential accounts. These reports also can furnish territorial market information on competitors' advertising and pricing, customers' credit standings, and so on. Expense account reports tell management something about the number of miles traveled, days worked, customers entertained, and nights away from home. Analyses of the expense data may indicate to management the reasons for the performance level of a given sales rep. Perhaps he is not entertaining the appropriate customers or is not spending enough time with customers in the far reaches of his district.

The Achilles' heel in using sales people's reports as a source of evaluation data is that the information is only as good as the accuracy, completeness, and punctuality of the reps' reporting efforts.

Typically, far less than optimum use is made of the information the sales force submits. Often, much of the reported information is never used, or the data are used in a negative fashion to criticize and police the sales force. The effective use of reports can be a solid foundation in a performance evaluation. Certainly, the reps are more likely to cooperate in making reports if they see that their reported information is used in a positive fashion to help them do a better selling job. It is helpful if the information from sales reports can be fed into an electronic data processing system.

As a rule, sales supervisors and other sales executives regularly spend some time in traveling with the sales reps in the field. The managers observe the reps during sales calls on customers, noting customers' reactions, and engaging in work sessions with the reps away from the customers' offices. These executives, then, can make an eyewitness appraisal of a sales person's performance with customers. They also can evaluate the individual's self-management abilities—his ability, for instance, to plan his work and work his plan. These field reports also may be the best source of information pertaining to several of the qualitative evaluation bases mentioned earlier.

As a source of evaluation information, the customers can be used in one of two ways. The more common method is to gather information submitted by customers on a voluntary, informal basis. Unfortunately, this usually takes the form of complaints, because customers rarely take the time to report commendatory performance by salesmen. A less widely used approach is to actively solicit opinions from customers on some kind of regular basis. Both the sales force and the customers are quite likely to resent this approach, however.

Set performance standards

Management's next step in developing a procedure for performance appraisal is to set standards for the evaluation bases. Standards usually can be set for any of the quantitative factors. Qualitative factors, by their nature, present a different problem. The standards serve as a bench mark, or a par for the course, against which the sales people's performance can be measured. Also, they let a sales person know what is expected of him, and in this way they serve as a guide to him in planning his work.

Setting standards is one of the most difficult phases of performance evaluation. They must be equitable and reasonable, or the sales people may lose interest in their work and confidence in the management. As a result, there will be a decline in their morale. The problem is similar to the task of setting quotas, discussed in Chapter 19. If the standards are too high or too low, the resulting interpretations will be worthless or even harmful, in that management can be misled.

Standards for many of the output factors can be tied to company goals for territories, product lines, or customer groups. Such performance measures as sales volume, gross margin, or market share probably have already been set, as we discussed in the chapters on sales potentials, forecasting, and quotas.

It is somewhat more difficult to set performance standards for the effort (input) factors. A careful time and duty analysis of sales jobs should give management some basis for knowing what is satisfactory performance for daily call rates, travel time, displays arranged, and other factors. Another approach is to use executive judgment based on the personal observations made by those who work with the sales people in the field.

It is also possible to determine for any given factor (daily call rate, for instance) the average performance for the sales force or the average for the best third, middle third, and bottom third of the group. Determining performance averages may be a step toward establishing standards, but averages have two limitations. First, an average is simply a measure of central tendency. It indicates nothing about the quality of performance—whether it is good or bad. Second, average-based standards fail to consider performance variations due to differences in territorial market opportunities, personal abilities, competitive activity, and so on.

To measure the efficiency of a company's selling effort, management must balance the output against the input. Consequently, a firm should develop standards for such output/input ratios as sales volume/call, orders/call, gross margin/order, and sales volume/expenses.

Absolute standards.   The approach described above is a relative one for measuring an individual's performance against standards set by other people's performances. There is a countertheory which applies absolute standards to each sales person's efforts. Some sales managers say, "I don't care how you compare with other people. If you do the job I expect of you, we will get along fine. If not, your job is in jeopardy."

Suppose a firm is willing to pay only 3 percent of sales for selling costs. If a sales person's combination earnings and expenses the coming year are expected to be $30,000, he or she must sell $1 million worth of goods to meet this standard.

The absolute standard is born from the economics of the situation. Such standards circumvent many of the problems involved in measuring a person against other people. Standards set by a subpar sales force may make a number of the sales people look good, when in reality they are not paying their way. There is no escape from the ultimate standard of the profitability of each sales person's performance.

Compare performance with standards

The next step in the performance evaluation procedure is to interpret the accumulated information. This step involves comparison of an individuals' performance—both efforts and results—with the predetermined standards.

Problem of data comparability. A key point to consider is the problem of comparability of the various data on performance. Ideally, a sales person should be judged only on factors over which he has control. Consequently, management should identify the uncontrollable factors that affect sales performance and then, where appropriate, take these factors into consideration when appraising an individual's performance.[2]

The sales potential in a territory, especially in relation to its size and the number of customers, is a good example of these factors. In a large territory with many small, scattered customers, a sales person's expenses are likely to be higher than in a smaller district with fewer but larger volume accounts. Differences in competitive activity or physical conditions among territories must be considered when comparing performances. Usually, there are territorial variations in the amount of advertising, sales promotional support, or home-office technical service available to customers. These and several other factors tend to impair the comparability of performance data.[3]

Interpreting quantitative data. A few of the factors ordinarily used as bases for performance appraisal, and how they can be used by management, are discussed below.

1. Sales volume and market share. The first criterion most sales managers use for judging the relative performance of sales people is the sales volume they produce. Some executives believe that the one who sells the most merchandise is the best sales person, regardless of other considerations. Unfortunately, sales volume alone often is a poor indicator of a rep's worth to the company. Total volume alone tells us nothing about his contribution to profit or customer relations. It does little good to move huge volumes of merchandise at no profit.

Sales volume can be a useful indicator of performance, however, if it is analyzed in sufficient detail and with discretion. For evaluation

---

[2] See The Conference Board, *Measuring Salesmen's Performance,* Studies in Business Policy, No. 114 (New York, 1965), especially pp. 8–13; also see D. Maynard Phelps and J. Howard Westing, *Marketing Management,* 3d ed. (Homewood, Ill.: Richard D. Irwin, Inc., 1968), ch. 31.

[3] For a statistical technique which attempts to make more comparable the actual (raw) performance data of salesmen selling under dissimilar circumstances, see David W. Cravens, Robert B. Woodruff, and Joe C. Stamper, "An Analytical Approach for Evaluating Sales Territory Performance," *Journal of Marketing,* January 1972, pp. 31–37.

purposes, a rep's total volume may be studied by product line, by some form of customer grouping, or by order size. Even then, the volume figures are not very meaningful unless they can be related to some predetermined standard of acceptable performance, such as a volume quota for each product line or customer group.

Another important evaluation factor is the share of market obtained by each sales person. This figure is computed by dividing the rep's sales volume by the territorial market potential. Here again the data are more useful if share of market can be determined for each product line or customer group. The validity of a rep's market-share index is obviously dependent on the accuracy of the market potential figures for his territory.

When comparing market-share performance of one person with another, caution should be exercised simply because these figures may have limited comparability. Salesman A may get 20 percent of the market in his district, while salesman B captures only 10 percent of his market. Yet, B may be doing a better job. Competition may be far more severe in B's district, or the company may be furnishing A with considerably more advertising support.

2. *Gross profit.* In most firms, a sales manager is (or should be) more concerned with the amount of gross profit the sales people generate than with their dollar sales volume. Gross margin in dollars is a much better measure of a sales person's effectiveness because it gives some indication of his ability to sell the high-margin, profitable items. Since the prime objective of most businesses is to maximize profits over the long run, a person's direct contribution to profit is a logical yardstick for evaluating his performance.

Used with discretion, gross margin can be a significant basis for evaluation, especially when the company markets several different products with varying gross margins. Then, the rep who has generated a large sales volume mainly by selling low-margin items receives a lower evaluation than does the one whose smaller sales volume consists mainly of higher margin products. The second rep produces a higher gross margin percentage and, quite conceivably, a higher dollar gross margin.

Management can reflect its gross margin goals by setting volume quotas for each product line. In this way, the company can motivate the sales force to achieve a desirable balance of sales among the various lines. Then, even though the reps are later evaluated on the basis of sales volume, this evaluation will automatically also include gross margin considerations.

Gross margin is a particularly valid measure when the product sold involves a trade-in, and the sales person evaluates the unit trade-in. When the rep controls the price the product is sold for, it is easy to buy volume by quoting low prices or high trade-in values. In these situations, profit is a better measurement of the sales performance than volume.

As an evaluative yardstick, gross margin has some limitations. When selling expenses are ignored, there is no way of knowing how much it costs to generate gross margin. Thus, salesman A may have a higher dollar gross margin than salesman B. But A's selling expenses may be proportionately so much higher than B's that A actually shows a lower contribution margin. Furthermore, a sales person does not fully control the product mix represented in his total sales volume. Territorial market potential and intensity of competition vary from one district to another, and these factors can influence the sales of the various product lines.

3. *Number and size of orders.* Another measure of performance effectiveness is the number of orders and the average size of orders obtained by each sales rep. The average sale is computed by dividing a rep's total number of orders into his total sales volume. This calculation may be made for each class of customer to determine how the rep's average order varies among them. This analysis will disclose which reps are getting too many small, unprofitable orders, even though their total volume is satisfactory because of a few large orders. The analysis also may show that some reps find it difficult to obtain orders from certain classes of customers, although in total they make up for this deficiency by superior performance with the other accounts.

If a rep's order size is substantially below the company average, usually this means either he is not selling all the items in the product lines, or he is not suggesting sufficiently large quantities to customers. To determine the reason for the low average sale, the distribution of sales among products can be examined. If the volume in each line is proportionately the same as the company's total experience, it probably would be concluded that the rep is letting customers go with trial or token orders when the potential is much larger. Perhaps the accounts are simply smaller than average; this can be determined by a bit of investigation.

4. *Calls per day—call rate.* A key factor in sales performance is the number of calls made. A sales person ordinarily cannot sell merchandise without calling on customers; generally, the more calls, the more sales. Salesman A makes three calls a day, but the company average is four among salesmen who work under reasonably comparable conditions. If management can raise A's call rate up to the company average of four, his sales *should* increase about 33 percent because he will be making 33 percent more calls over a period of time.

For evaluation purposes, a sales person's daily (or weekly) call rate can be measured against the company average or some other predetermined standard for this activity. However, discretion must be exercised in interpreting a rep's call rate. Its significance is limited by the comparability of conditions under which the various sales people work. Their call rates are influenced by the number of miles they must travel and by the number of customers per square mile in the territory.

If management can reasonably adjust for the variation in customer density, then the call rate data can be useful. Usually, in a given business a certain desired call rate yields the best results. If the rep falls below this rate, his sales decline because he is not seeing enough prospects. If he calls on too many prospects, his sales may also decline, since he probably does not spend sufficient time with each one to get the job done.

When a sales person's call rate is below average, a supervisor's field investigation usually can uncover the causes. It may be that the rep is not getting into the field early enough in the morning or is quitting too early in the afternoon. Too much time may be spent talking with each customer. Or he may be losing too much time waiting to see prospects.

5. *Batting average.* A sales person's batting average is calculated by dividing the number of orders he gets by the number of calls he makes (*o/c*). The number of calls made is equivalent to times at bat; the number of orders written is equivalent to the hits made. As a performance index, the batting average discloses ability to locate and call on good prospects and ability to close a sale. A sales person's batting average should be computed for each class of customers called on. Often, a rep varies in ability to close a sale with different types of customers. A sales person may get orders rather easily from large department stores, for example, but have difficulty when selling to small merchants.

Analysis of a sales rep's call rate in relation to his order rate can be quite meaningful. If the call rate is above average but the number of orders is below normal, perhaps the rep is not spending enough time with each customer. If the call rate and batting average are both above standard but the average order is small, a field supervisor may work with the sales person to show how to make fewer but more productive calls. The idea is to raise the size of the average order by spending more time and talking about more products with each account. This is another way performance evaluation can pinpoint strengths and weaknesses and aid in field supervision and training.

6. *Direct selling expenses.* Direct selling expense is the sum of travel expenses, other business expenses, and compensation (salary, commission, bonus) for each sales person. These total expenses may be expressed as a percentage of sales, and the expense-to-sales ratios for the various sales people can be compared. Or management can compute for each sales person the cost per call or per order by dividing total

expenses by the number of calls made or the number of orders obtained.

In a performance evaluation, these various cost indexes may indicate the relative efficiency of the sales people in the field. However, these ratios must be interpreted carefully and in detail. An expense-to-sales ratio, for instance, may be above average because the sales person: (1) is doing a poor job; (2) is working in a marginal territory; (3) is in a new territory doing a lot of prospecting and building a solid base for the future; or (3) the territory covers far more square miles than the average district. A rep with a low batting average usually has a high cost per order. Similarly, the one who makes few calls per day has a high ratio of costs per call.

7. *Routing efficiency.* Dividing the miles traveled by the number of calls made gives the average miles per call. This will be either an indication of the density of the sales rep's territory or a measure of his routing efficiency. If a group of sales people all have approximately the same size and density of territories, then miles per call is a significant figure for indicating each one's routing efficiency. If five sales people selling for an office machines firm in a metropolitan area vary considerably in the number of miles traveled per call, then the sales manager may have reason to control the routing of those who are out of line in this respect.

8. *Days worked.* The number of days each sales person worked in the period under analysis is a critical statistic, because it is one of the major determining factors of all performance. The one who works the most days should be making the most calls, taking the most orders, spending the most money, and making the most sales. If certain individuals are not working enough days in the month, that alone may explain their poor sales performance.

Basic performance equations. The quantitative evaluation of a sales rep's performance can utilize either of the following equations:

$$\text{Sales} = \text{Days worked} \times \frac{\text{Calls}}{\text{Days worked}} \times \frac{\text{Orders}}{\text{Calls}} \times \frac{\text{Sales}}{\text{Orders}}$$

Sales = Days worked × Call rate × Batting average × Average order

If the sales volume for a representative is unsatisfactory, the basic cause must rest in one or more of these four factors. An analysis (such as that done in Figure 22–1 below) can help focus the manager's attention to the trouble spot so additional detailed investigation can pinpoint the rep's exact difficulties.

Bear in mind that the main purpose of this analysis is to help the person become more productive and therefore more successful. It is a training tool, not a disciplinary one. The manager cannot help a person

FIGURE 22-1
Evaluation of sales representatives' performance
Colorado Ski Company

Sales representative: Product line:	Joe Jackson			Bud Olson			Pete Burns			Total		
	Equipment	Clothing	Total	Equipment	Clothing	Total	Equipment	Clothing	Total	Equipment	Clothing	Total
Total sales	220000	360000	600000	110000	230000	340000	120000	140000	260000	470000	750000	1000000
Sporting goods stores	160000	220000	380000	80000	160000	240000	50000	80000	130000	290000	460000	750000
Ski shops	80000	140000	220000	30000	70000	100000	35000	60000	130000	180000	210000	450000
Calls made – Total			700			900			1100			2700
Sporting goods stores			300			500			500			1300
Ski shops			400			400			600			1400
Orders taken – Total			500			600			850			1950
Sporting goods stores			150			450			400			1000
Ski shops			350			150			450			950
Days worked			220			240			230			690
Expenses			24000			20000			18000			62000
Miles traveled			40000			15000			35000			140000
Market potential – Total	1000000	2000000	3000000	600000	1200000	1800000	600000	600000	1200000	3000000	2800000	6000000
Sporting goods stores	800000	1200000	2000000	400000	800000	1200000	360000	320000	680000	1560000	2320000	3880000
Ski shops	700000	800000	1000000	200000	400000	600000	240000	140000	520000	640000	1480000	2120000

	Sporting gd. stores	Ski shops	Total	Sporting gd. stores	Ski shops	Total	Sporting gd. stores	Ski shops	Total	Sporting gd. stores	Ski shops	Total
Average order	2533	629	1200	533	467	567	325	289	306	750	474	615
Batting average	.500	.875	.714	.900	.375	.667	.750	.800	.773	.769	.618	.722
Calls per day			3.18			3.55			4.8			3.9
Miles per call			86			50			32			52
Expense per sales $			4%			5.9%			6.9%			5.1%
Cost per call, excluding commission			$34.28			$22.22			$17.62			$20.96
Cost per order, including commission			$45.00			$33.84			$21.16			$31.78

	Equipment	Clothing	Total	Equipment	Clothing	Total	Equipment	Clothing	Total	Equipment	Clothing	Total
Percent of market – Total	24	18	20	18.3	19.2	18.9	20	23.4	21.7	21.3	19.3	20
Sporting goods stores	20	18.3	19	20	20.0	20	13.9	28.5	19.2	18.5	19.8	19.6
Ski shops	40	17.5	32	15	17.5	16.7	29.2	21.4	25.0	28.1	18.3	21.2

until specific difficulties are identified. It is pointless to provide the rep with more product training if his problem is laziness.

Evaluating qualitative factors. Lack of objectivity in evaluations is largely minimized when *quantitative* factors are used as bases in a performance evaluation. However, when the evaluation is based on *qualitative* factors, the personal, subjective element comes into full play. The evaluator assumes a key role at this point because the success of a qualitative evaluation depends in great measure on ability to be objective and completely impartial. Much of the information base for this phase of an evaluation comes from personal observations of the sales people and their activities in the field, as well as from customer feedback.

Merit rating forms are a helpful tool in this evaluation procedure. These forms permit the judgments of several evaluators to appear in a generally standardized manner. This uniformity aids in comparing one person with another. Rating forms also provide a written report for company records. More important, however, they should make an evaluator more thorough because his appraisals will be on record.

There is an almost limitless variety of evaluation forms. Each manager develops whatever form seems appropriate for the situation. Most such subjective forms suffer from three major defects.

First, there is the halo effect. Evaluators are biased one way or the other by a generalized, overall impression or image of the person being evaluated. If the manager just does not like the way a certain person dresses, that attitude will bias all aspects of the manager's evaluation of that person. Similarly, the manager who is impressed with a person's sales ability will be likely to rate highly other aspects of that person's performance.

Second, such rating forms generally overvalue inconsequential factors and undervalue the truly important ones. Teacher-rating forms commonly used in colleges today are an example. While the important aspect about a teacher's performance is whether or not the students learned what they were supposed to learn from the course, few rating forms probe that aspect of the classroom situation. Instead, they ask about how well organized the professor seemed to be, or the instructor's desk side manner, or several other attributes that may not have much to do with learning.

In a sales context, the manager should be interested in the sales person's ability to make money for the firm, not whether the individual is socially adept or impressively dressed. It is important in evaluation for the manager to keep in mind what is important and what is not. If it is not important, it should not be evaluated. The harm in doing so can be considerable, because few managers can ignore an unfavorable evaluation of any factor, whether or not it is relevant to sales performance. This aspect of evaluation is also subject to charges of discrimination in hiring and promotion.

The third defect with most subjective evaluation forms is that they force the evaluator to make judgments on some factors even though he or she has no valid basis for making them. Lacking valid information on the factor, the evaluator allows the halo effect to take over.

Discuss the evaluation with the sales person

After each sales person's performance has been evaluated, the results should be reviewed in a conference with the sales manager. This critically important discussion should be viewed as a counseling interview. The sales manager should explain the person's achievements on each evaluation factor and point out how the results compared with the standards. Then, the manager and the sales person together may try to determine the reasons for the performance variations above or below the standards. It is essential to discuss the managerial ratings on the qualitative factors and to compare them with the sales person's self-evaluation on these points. Based on their review of all the evaluation factors, the manager and the sales person then can establish some goals and an operating plan for the coming period.

The performance evaluation interview can be a very sensitive occasion. It is not easy to point out a person's shortcomings face to face. If the sales manager is not extremely tactful, the rep may resent this kind of interview. People dislike being criticized and may become quite defensive in this situation. Some sales executives resist evaluation interviews because they feel these discussions can only injure morale. The concern is real.

USING EVALUATION DATA: AN EXAMPLE

The case example in this section illustrates the computations, interpretation, and use of several quantitative evaluation factors, both input (efforts) and output (results).

The Colorado Ski Company distributes on a national basis four lines of products—skis, ski accessories, and a limited line of ski pants and-parkas. The company manufactures some of these products. Others are purchased from other firms, but are sold under the Colorado Ski Company's brand name. The products are sold to two basic classes of customers—sporting goods stores and specialty ski shops. The company uses its own sales force to reach these customers directly. The sales people are paid their travel expenses plus a straight commission of 5 percent on sales volume.

For purposes of a performance evaluation, the sales manager of the Colorado Ski Company has divided the products into two basic lines: skis and ski accessories (equipment) and (2) ski pants and parkas (clothing). The retailers' usual initial markup on all these products is 40 percent of the retail selling price. There are no significant variations among products in the gross margin percentages realized by the Colorado Ski Company.

The sales manager is especially interested in the performance of three of his salesmen: Joe, who sells in the Rocky Mountain region (a huge territory); Gus, who is selling in the Pacific Northwest; and Pete, who covers the New England market. Much of the quantitative performance data for these three salesmen is summarized in Figure 22–1. Based on an analysis of these data, the sales manager is trying to decide: (1) which of the three men did the best job, and (2) which particular points should be discussed with each man in an effort to improve his performance.

If the sales manager of the Colorado Ski Company were to look just at the sales production of these three men, he would have to conclude that Joe was best by far. He might even consider replacing Pete, since his volume looks weak in comparison. However, after comparing each man's volume against his market potential, it is evident that Pete sold a larger share of his market than either Joe or Gus did.

Joe's sales performance

Concentrating on evaluating Joe's performance, the sales manager could see that Joe had worked the fewest numbers of days (220), made the fewest calls (700), and took the fewest orders (500). He also had spent more money than the other men ($24,000) and had traveled far more miles (60,000). The sales manager can make some allowance for this because Joe's territory is the Rocky Mountain region, which is more sparsely settled than either Gus's or Pete's territory.

Joe's batting average (.714) is certainly adequate, and his average order ($1,200) is more than satisfactory. In fact, it is astonishingly high in comparison with the others ($567 and $306). The sales manager can justify this. The tremendous market potential ($3 million) in Joe's territory, in comparison with number of customers evidently located there, would naturally result in a high average sale. Assuming that Joe has done a satisfactory job of covering potential prospects, the market potential per dealer in the Rocky Mountain region evidently is far higher than in the other areas in the country. This would explain why he was able to take such large orders. Joe makes a little over three calls per day, which is relatively low in comparison to the others (3.55 and 4.8). However, it is not sufficiently out of line to cause any action to be taken, in light of his territory. The large number of miles per call is again indicative of the territory.

Considering expense per sales dollar, it would *appear* that Joe is the most efficient salesman, since he is spending only 4 percent of sales for expenses. The reps are being paid a straight commission of 5 percent of sales, which would bring Joe's total cost of selling to 9 percent. However, the sales manager can see that this low expense ratio is simply a function of his abnormally high sales, which, in turn, are a result of his large market potential.

Joe's cost per call ($34.28) and cost per order ($48) seem exceedingly high in comparison with those for the other reps. He worked 20 fewer days than Gus and 10 fewer days than Pete. Granted that he traveled 15,000 miles more than Gus, the cost of those miles at 15 cents a mile would be about $2,250, which leaves something to be explained. The sales manager probably should investigate Joe's expense accounts. Expenses are usually related to the number of days worked and miles traveled. They are not related directly to sales volume; it costs as much to take an order for $100 as one for $600. A large market potential that results in large sales can cause the expense-to-sales ratio to be misleading. Thus, Joe's high sales volume caused his expense ratio to appear low, when in reality he was spending too much money in making calls.

In analyzing Joe's selling effort with regard to products and customers, it became evident that he has a more difficult time getting orders from a sporting goods store (.500) than from a ski shop (.875), although his average sale to sporting goods stores ($2,533) is fantastically high. The sales manager may wonder if this is part of Joe's trouble on his batting average. Possibly in attempting to sell sporting goods stores so much merchandise he is simply scaring some of them away. However, the sales manager should be cautious here, since in total it is better that Joe continue to sell a high average order to sporting goods stores and settle for fewer orders than to bring both figures to average.

The sales manager may want to investigate the high average order to sporting goods stores. It may be that a few large discount sporting goods stores in the territory are placing huge orders with Joe. This may be no reflection at all on his ability to build up an order. Therefore, if his batting average could be raised in the sporting goods field, possibly no loss would occur at all to the average order, and the result would be higher sales volume. It would be something to investigate.

Another thing the sales manager may notice about Joe's performance is that he seems able to sell equipment (24 percent of potential) better than he sells clothing (18 percent of potential). He is well above average in his ability to sell skis, particularly to ski specialty shops (40 percent of potential), but he is below average in attention to clothing (17.5 percent). This may be just a reflection of his basic interest. He may prefer to talk about skis, bindings, and poles rather than about pants and parkas. Although this is understandable from a personality and interest standpoint, nevertheless the sales manager should make it a point to mention to Joe that he should be doing a bit better in his sales of clothing. It should be noted, however, that he is not sufficiently below par in any category to be unduly concerned.

Gus's sales performance

Probably the first thing the sales manager would note about Gus's sales performance is his apparent inability to sell to ski shops. He is closing only 37.5 percent of the calls he makes on them, whereas the company average is 67.8 percent. On the other hand, he has an extremely high batting average in getting orders from sporting goods stores (90 percent). The sales manager may conclude that Gus speaks the language of the nonskiing owner of a sporting goods store but does not communicate well with a ski expert. The sales manager may consider a conference with Gus to talk over the problems of the ski shop owner and how they differ from those of the sports shop. It may be that he is not sufficiently trained in the technical aspects of skiing to answer the questions and gain the confidence of the ski professional. Gus's expenses seem to be in line with the company average, and his calls per day probably would not be considered unsatisfactory. While he is not achieving par as far as a share of the market is concerned, the deviation is not significant enough to warrant any conference on the matter.

Pete's sales performance

Pete seems to do fairly well in getting orders from both sporting goods stores and ski shops, but his average order ($306) is significantly below the company average ($615). This indicates a problem area. The sales manager probably first wants to determine if these low average orders are a function of the size of Pete's customers or whether this truly reflects his inability to sell merchandise. That Pete made 1,100 calls with the smallest market potential indicates that his average customer is considerably smaller than those of the other reps. The sales manager may become alarmed at Pete's, relatively high expense of sales. However, he should realize that this is caused by the limited sales potential available to the man. Pete's cost per call and cost per order are the lowest of the three men, indicating that his expense accounts are not out of line with his efforts.

It should be obvious to the sales manager that Pete is working hard; he is making almost five calls per day. This factor helps to explain several of the others. His high call rate probably is the explanation for his low cost per call, and it explains the relatively large number of calls he makes. It also may explain why he is not selling so much per order. Perhaps he is not spending sufficient time with each customer. On the other hand, the number of miles per call (32) indicates that his territory is relatively dense, and this alone may be the reason he is able to make almost five calls per day. He does not have to spend as much time traveling between calls as do the other two men.

While a sales manager may at first seriously consider discharging Pete, a detailed analysis shows that he is doing as well as, if not better than, the other two men. His costs for efforts undertaken are lower. Also, he is achieving a larger percentage of the business available to him. It would seem that his only problem is having been assigned a territory of limited market potential.

The sales manager's decisions

In conclusion, the sales manager probably will undertake several different projects. First, he may try to get Joe to work a few more days in the year. It is understandable that this rep is tempted to do a little loafing, because he has an annual income of $30,000 and is leading the sales force in sales. However, Joe's territory has a tremendous sales potential. If he does not want to service it properly, the company can cut it in half, giving each rep a $1.5 million potential to work with. This would still result in two territories of larger potential than that worked by Pete. Also, the sales manager may investigate why Joe is not selling to more sporting goods stores.

With Gus, the sales manager probably will focus his entire attention on why ski shops are such an obstacle. Gus is not able to sell to ski shops with the facility of the others. The chances are he needs additional instruction on the technical aspects of skiing.

The sales manager may want to ask Pete why he does not sell more skis to sporting goods stores. That is about his only real weakness, outside of his low average order. Certainly, the sales manager would want to investigate the reasons for Pete's low average order. However, as previously noted, this may not be the result of poor selling ability.

QUESTIONS AND PROBLEMS

1. Explain how the evaluation of sales reps' performance is related to the sales training program; to supervision; to the compensation plan.

2. Why is an evaluation of sales performance such a difficult task?

3. List several quantitative factors frequently used as bases for performance evaluation. For each one, explain where a sales manager ordinarily can get the necessary data.

4. How can a sales manager determine the accuracy or truthfulness of the reports salesmen submit.

5. What are some of the qualitative factors frequently used as bases for a performance evaluation of sales people?

6. "In an evaluation of performance, many seemingly qualitative evaluation factors frequently can be measured in some quantitative fashion." Explain.

7. How can a sales manager determine the differences the reps encounter in the severity of competition in each territory?

8. Is there any way a sales executive can compare the effectiveness of a new sales rep with that of older, more experienced people?

9. What are some of the indexes a sales manager can use in evaluating the prospecting ability of his reps?

10. What are some of the indexes a sales manager can use to evaluate the degree to which each sales person is covering the assigned territory?

11. As sales manager for a baby food concern, you want to evaluate the ability of your reps to attain good shelf space in grocery stores. How would you do this?

12. How can a sales executive determine the ability of each rep to regain lost customers?

13. How can a sales manager determine whether any rep is using high-pressure selling tactics or other inadvisable techniques?

14. How can management increase its objectivity and minimize any biases when evaluating sales people on qualitative factors?

15. Should a salesman be shown the results of management's evaluation of him in comparison with other salesmen? In comparison with company norms?

Case 22-1

THE BORLAND COMPANY
Measuring dealer development

The executive committee of the Borland Company always opened its weekly Monday morning meeting with a few comments from the chairman of the board. Although no longer the firm's chief operating executive, Mary Weber was still its philosophical and inspirational leader. She also owned the company. Usually these comments were a few kind words designed to prod thinking and perhaps to stimulate action. Weber opened the meeting one week with the following statement:

> As you well know, we have built our business on a few simple propositions. One of these is that we strive to get the best dealers available for our goods, and then work with them to build up their sales of our merchandise. This development of our dealers is at the very heart of our success. I pray that we never lose sight of that truth.

Wade Baker, the vice president of marketing, could not get that thought from his mind throughout the meeting. He wholeheartedly believed in it. Yet he had on his desk a letter from a former dealer who was less than happy with the company. Wade wondered if the company's goal of dealer development was being realized.

Wade unburdened his uneasiness to the sales manager in a memo which asked:

> How well do our sales reps work with the dealers to develop the market for our goods?
> Who is the best at it?
> Who is the worst?

The sales manager, Mr. Samuel Lund, knew from past experience how to interpret the memo. It really said: "I want a report on the effectiveness of the sales reps in developing dealers." The sales department kept excellent data on the performance of the sales force, but nothing that directly measured dealer development.

Lund sat down to prepare a request to the manager of the computer center for a printout of the data he wanted. He also showed how he wanted the data processed in order to measure each of the sales rep's performance in developing good dealers.

Question

1. Write Samuel Lund's request to the computer center.

Part five

A FORWARD LOOK

23

Ethical and social responsibilities of sales executives

*I believe that every right implies a responsibility;
every opportunity, an obligation; every possession,
a duty.*

JOHN D. ROCKEFELLER, JR.

Since the mid-1960s, Americans have been turning sour on America—on its dreams, its promises, its leaders. Every major poll of public opinion has shown that. Now, in increasing numbers, Americans are focusing their new, European-style cynicism on the profits, prices, and policies of the country's largest corporations and on the workings of the entire economy.[1]

In our society, a combination of factors has generated an unfavorable attitude toward business, especially the larger companies. These factors include the soaring costs of energy, the pressures of inflation, economic recessions, consumer dissatisfaction with product performance, unrealized (but expected) social and economic gains by large segments of society, disclosures of bribery of foreign government officials by American firms, and many instances of bribery in domestic marketing.

Business is often criticized even by its strongest supporters. There is a popular argument that the giant corporations should be broken up.

---

[1] "America's Growing Antibusiness Mood," *Business Week*, June 17, 1972, p. 100; see also "Why Business Has a Black Eye," *U.S. News & World Report*, September 6, 1976, p. 22; and "The Embattled Businessman," *Newsweek*, February 16, 1976, p. 56.

People grossly overestimate corporate profits and favor a ceiling on them. They want industry to stop polluting and to clean up the environment. This wave of consumer discontent—popularly labeled *consumerism*—is not likely to abate. It has attracted too much political attention.

The main target of consumerism generally is the marketing activities in a firm and the function of marketing in the total economy. This is understandable because marketing usually is the part of a company's total program that is closest to the consumer. It is most visible and easiest to contact. Within a firm's marketing program, the area most likely to arouse consumer comment is promotion (personal selling and advertising). It is visible and in direct contact with the consumer, and its avowed goals are attracting attention and generating consumer action.

In response to this climate of criticism there is a growing interest, both among business executives and in some nonbusiness segments of society, in the idea of a *social audit* of a company's activities. In essence, a social audit is an evaluation of a firm's social and ethical policies, performances, and responsibilities. A social audit is designed to do the same job in social matters that an accounting audit performs in financial and economic areas.

As yet, unfortunately, there is much vagueness about the concept of a social audit. There is no general agreement on exactly *what* it is, precisely *what* should be conducted, or even *who* would do the job (a company itself or an outside agency). We speak of auditing a company's social responsibilities, but there is no consensus as to exactly what these responsibilities are in a given firm, or to what expense the firm should go in meeting them. Nevertheless, the increasing interest in the concept suggests that a social audit is an idea whose time has come.[2]

In the literature and discussions on the theme of social responsibilities of business leadership, much of the attention has been devoted to the societal performance of executives. Top management often may be aware of these responsibilities, but unfortunately some lower level executives may in practice be avoiding them. The purchasing agent may be placing undue pressure on a small supplier in order to get an extra low price, or the sales force may be using comparative prices in a misleading fashion.

---

[2] For some suggestions as to what should be included in a social audit and who should do this job, see Raymond A. Bauer and Dan H. Fenn, Jr., "What *Is* a Corporate Social Audit?" *Harvard Business Review*, January–February 1973, pp. 37–48; John J. Corson and George A. Steiner, *Measuring Business's Social Performance: The Corporate Social Audit* (New York: The Committee for Economic Development, 1975). The concept of a social audit for business was first suggested by Howard R. Bowen, *Social Responsibilities of the Businessman* (New York: Harper & Bros., 1953), pp. 155–56.

We believe that the various sales managers must share in the social responsibilities and ethical considerations of their companies. Consequently, in this chapter our discussion will center on two topics—the ethical problems facing sales managers, and the social responsibilities of sales managers and sales people.

BUSINESS ETHICS AND SALES MANAGEMENT

Webster's New Collegiate Dictionary defines ethics as the science of moral duty or the science of ideal human character. Ethics are moral principles or practices. They are professional standards of conduct. Thus, to act in an ethical fashion is to conform to some standard of moral behavior. Sales managers face the problem of translating this definition into some kind of a meaningful model that can serve as a workable guide in their daily administrative activities. In any given situation, they must be able to differentiate between what is ethical and unethical. They should forego the unethical, regardless of any possible short-run gain.

Some sales executives might question the idea of including a discussion of ethics in a book dealing with the practicalities of running a sales force. It is realistic and quite relevant, however, to connect the concepts of business ethics with the management of a sales force. If sales managers recognize their moral responsibilities as administrators, they are only operating in their own self-interest. The truth of the matter, however, seems to be that sales managers are not aware of the *practical* value of ethical conduct. Judging by their practices, too many still seem to believe in a caveat emptor philosophy when dealing with customers. That higher ethical standards are needed is evidenced by the continuing *increase* in governmental regulation of sales activities at local, state, and federal levels.

The pressure to compromise personal ethics

It is easy to be ethical when no hardship is involved—when you are winning and life is going good. Undoubtedly, most sales managers prefer to act ethically. The test comes when things are *not* going so good—when the competitive pressures build up. These pressures are not limited to sales management situations; they appear in all walks of life. Would you cheat on an exam in this course, if the alternative is to flunk the course? In professional football, if an offensive lineman cannot control his opponent on defense, should the offensive player resort to holding the defensive player (and hope that it goes undetected by the officials)? The alternative for the offensive lineman may be for his team to lose, or even worse, for him to lose his job.

Do business managers feel pressure to compromise their personal ethics for company goals? In many cases the answer is yes, even in firms that profess to be leaders in the campaign for business ethics. For example, surveys were conducted at Pitney-Bowes and Uniroyal, both of which stress ethical conduct as a management policy. A majority of executives in these firms reported that indeed they had experienced pressure to compromise their personal ethics to achieve corporate goals.[3]

These surveys also indicated that most managers believed that their peers would not refuse orders to sell off-standard and possibly dangerous products. An even larger majority said they personally would refuse to market such products, however. Most executives reported that they believe that young managers automatically go along with their superiors to show company loyalty.

Virtually all the surveyed executives believed it is unethical to turn in an incomplete report or to cheat on an expense account. An overwhelming majority supported a company code of ethics and the teaching of ethics in business schools. Almost all felt that business ethics, however imperfect, are as good as, or better than, the ethics in society at large.

The problem of determining ethical standards

It is easy to say that a sales executive should act in an ethical fashion, but it is far more difficult to put this axiom into practice. Sales managers as individuals usually have their own standards of conduct, which they believe to be ethical. And, usually they abide by these standards in the management of their sales forces. It is doubtful if many people, sales executives included, consciously commit unethical practices with any degree of regularity. Most of us believe we are acting ethically *by our own standards*. However, ethical standards are set by a group—by society—and not by the individual. Thus, the group evaluates the individual's judgment of what he or she thinks is ethical.

The problem is that the group (society) lacks commonly accepted standards of behavior. What is considered ethical conduct varies from one industry to another, from one company to another, and from one situation to another. The dictates of personal conscience are an individual matter, even among people with a common ethical tradition. Looking to the law or corporate policy for guidance leads only to more gray areas rather than to clearly defined, specific guidelines.

---

[3] "The Pressure to Compromise Personal Ethics," *Business Week*, January 31, 1977, p. 107. See also "How Clean Is Business?" *Newsweek*, September 1, 1975, p. 50.

The moral-ethical-legal framework presents special problems for sales executives, more than for most other managers. The rules for sales work are neither clearcut nor hard and fast. Entertaining customers in a gambling house, for example, may be either moral or immoral from an individual's point of view. This entertainment may be considered acceptable (ethical) or not depending upon the industry's practice. And, it may be legal or illegal depending upon whether it happened in Nevada or California.

As further examples of a sales executive's problem, consider these situations:[4]

1. A pen and pencil set may be a reasonable Christmas gift to give a $5,000-a-year customer. But is a $1,000 stereo set a gift or a bribe when given to a million-dollar customer?

2. It is acceptable practice and legally okay for a manufacturer to give a department store's sales clerks "push money" to promote the manufacturer's brand. But can this manufacturer rightfully give the head buyer a little something extra for first getting the product into the store?

3. It is customary for appliance manufacturers to reward their distributor-customers with an all-expense-paid incentive trip to the Bahamas. But is it acceptable for a pharmaceutical company to invite its doctor-"customers" to Jamaica for an all-expense-paid seminar?

The point is that sales executives have considerable latitude or discretion in the management of their activities—more so than do most other managers. As a result, the sales executives are more vulnerable regarding the ethical aspects of these activities.

An attempt at setting ethical guidelines

The problem of determining what is right and what is wrong is an extremely difficult one. Yet it is one that, to a degree, is soluble. It is not realistic for a sales manager to construct a two-column list of practices, one headed "ethical" and the other labeled "unethical." A better approach is to depend on time and conscious examples to point out the difference between acceptable and nonacceptable standards of performance. The same philosophy may be adopted as that followed in the writing and subsequent administration of Section 5 of the Federal Trade Commission Act. The act outlaws unfair competition but does not state what is meant by that term. The legislators wisely left the task of definition to the Commission and the courts. Thus through the years

---

[4] "It's Time to Repeal the Right to Do Wrong," *Sales & Marketing Management*, October 11, 1976, p. 40.

examples have been accumulated as the law has been administered and interpreted case by case.

As another approach to defining ethical practices, a sales executive may evaluate the ethical status of each proposed action by answering such questions as:

> Is this sound from a long-run point of view?
>
> Would I do this to a friend?
>
> Would I be willing to have this done to me? (The Golden Rule.)
>
> If other people learn of this act, what would be their reactions?

Arjay Miller, dean of Stanford University's Graduate School of Business and formerly president of the Ford Motor Company, suggested this guideline: "Do what you would feel comfortable explaining on television."[5]

One student of the subject proposed that marketing executives can develop some operational guidelines (although not universal answers) in areas of ethical considerations by borrowing approaches and insights from law and political theory.[6] Law administers justice by means of specific case decisions, and political theory traditionally deals with power and its regulation. James Patterson observed that the success of the Anglo-American constitutional experience is due much more to the structural limitations of checks and balances against potentially arbitrary public power than it is to the substantive, "thou shalt not" variety of limitations. In the realm of private business power, this structural limitations approach may well be used to ensure that business operates in a socially acceptable fashion. Market competition already acts as a structural limitation on private power. Other structures that restrain power include collective bargaining systems and dealers' councils in various industries. Perhaps too, a manufacturer could establish a customer review board to react to proposed marketing decisions.

A key consideration for sales executives is to take the *long-run* point of view regarding the ethics of a given situation. They should understand that ethical behavior not only is morally right but, over the long run, it is also realistically sound. Too many sales administrators are shortsighted and do not see the possible repercussions from many of their activities and attitudes. Whether or not the buyer was deceived or high-pressured may seem unimportant if only the sale is consummated. Management often does not recognize that such practices can

---

[5] As quoted in "More Concerns Issue Guidelines on Ethics in Payoffs Aftermath," *The Wall Street Journal*, March 16, 1976, p. 1.

[6] James M. Patterson, "What Are the Social and Ethical Responsibilities of Marketing Executives?" *Journal of Marketing*, July 1966, pp. 12–15.

lose customers or invite public regulation. Executives must consider the ultimate consequences of their acts. The brushmark of one immediate sale is unimportant when the entire canvas is examined. As Ohman said, ". . . the job is the life. *This* is what must be made meaningful. We cannot assume that the end of production justifies the means. What happens to people in the course of producing may be far more important than the end product."[7]

In the mid-1970s many executives were shaken by disclosures of such business practices as bribery of foreign officials by American firms, illegal donations to political campaigns, and large-scale bribery in domestic business affairs. Spurred by these revelations, many companies have developed written statements of ethical guidelines to be followed at all levels of management in the firm.[8] One example of such statements is the ten-point set of ethical guidelines designed specifically for sales force managers presented in Figure 23–1.

Writing a code of ethical conduct is not an easy task. The company may end up with a set of platitudes, for example. Each company should develop its own statement because, as one executive said: "Writing a code that would be universally accepted means you would end up with a motherhood sort of thing." Critics claim that such a statement usually is a public relations window dressing that covers up a bad situation and corrects nothing.

Nevertheless, there is growing agreement that these formal written statements are desirable. They lessen the chance that executives will knowingly or unknowingly get into trouble. They strengthen the company's hand in dealing with customers and government officials who invite bribes and other unethical actions. They strengthen the position of lower level executives in resisting pressures to compromise their personal ethics in order to get along in the firm.

There also is general agreement that effective enforcement of ethical codes is a major key to their success. The penalties should be severe, especially when top management is involved in the violations. Firing a few top executives, assessing stiff fines they must pay personally, or putting them in jail can be a strong deterrent to unethical action in a firm. Other executives may then think twice before engaging in such practices because "Everybody else is doing it," or "We must do it to make the sale," or "When in Rome, do as the Romans do."

---

[7] O. A. Ohman, " 'Skyhooks' (with Special Implications for Monday through Friday)," *Harvard Business Review*, May–June 1955, p. 37. This classic article was reprinted in *Harvard Business Review*, January–February 1970, pp. 4–8 ff.

[8] See "How Companies React to the Ethics Crisis," *Business Week*, February 9, 1976, p. 78; "More Concerns Issue Guidelines on Ethics in Payoffs Aftermath," *The Wall Street Journal*, March 13, 1976, p. 1.

FIGURE 23–1
Ten ways to keep your sales force on the straight and narrow

1. Get assurance from your board chairman and your president that they expect you to follow both the letter and the spirit of the law.
2. Develop and circulate a sales ethics policy. Seventy-five percent of the companies hit by the SEC in the foreign payoff scandals reported that they had no formal policies on commercial bribery.
3. Set the proper moral climate. One management consultant suggests that the marketing staffs most likely to commit bribery are in companies in which (a) new ideas are discouraged, (b) "the top person does everything himself," or (c) officers don't attend trade association meetings and feel that "nothing can be learned from the competition."
4. Set realistic sales goals. The salesman who is pressured by the need to meet an arbitrary, unfair quota is the one most likely to rationalize his way into a bribery or kickback scheme.
5. Institute controls when needed. For example, don't hesitate to keep close tabs on a salesman whose life-style exceeds his known income.
6. Encourage employees to call for help when they face an ethically troublesome sale.
7. Resist a prospectively shady deal. You'll sleep better.
8. Meet with your competition if payoffs are an industry problem. Thankfully, no antitrust law ever barred competitors from hammering out a code of ethics.
9. Blow the whistle when you must. Yes, it's the hardest of these suggestions to follow. A *Harvard Business Review* survey reports that four out of seven executives would rather cover up a bribery or price-fixing revelation than suffer the cost and conspicuousness of a prolonged legal battle. So, yes, you'll be bucking convention. You may also risk censure by your peers for "squealing" on the team or damaging the reputation of the company.
10. Keep your perspective. An anonymous author may have had bribery in mind when he said, "Following the path of least resistance is what makes men and rivers crooked."

Source: Reprinted by permission from *Sales and Marketing Management.* Copyright 1976.

Ethical situations facing sales managers

Ethical overtones are involved in many of the relationships sales managers have with their sales people, their companies, and their customers. A few of these situations are discussed here.

Relations with the sales force. A substantial portion of sales managers' ethical problems relates to their dealings with the sales force. Ethical considerations may be involved, for instance, when management splits a sales territory. Assume that the sales person has put a large amount of effective effort into building a territory into a highly profitable district. The rep may even have worked under a straight commission compensation plan and paid his own expenses. When management sees this sales person's relatively high earnings, an executive may decide there is too much territory and split it. Is this ethical? On the other hand, is it sound management *not* to split the district, if the sales executive believes the company is losing sales volume because of inadequate coverage of an overly large district?

In some companies, management takes over the very large, profitable accounts as house accounts. (These are customers who are sold directly by some executive, and the sales person in whose district the account is located usually receives no commission on the account.) Is this an ethical practice, particularly if the sales person spent much time and effort in developing the account to a profitable level? Yet, management may feel the account now is so important that the company cannot risk losing it. Thus, it receives executive handling.

Ethical questions often arise in connection with promotions, termination of employment, and giving references. When there is no likelihood that a certain sales representative will be promoted to a managerial position, should the rep be told this? If the sales manager knows that the rep is working in expectation of such a promotion, to tell him means to lose him. In another instance, when a managerial position is open in another region, a sales manager may be tempted to keep a star sales rep in his present territory, despite the rep's obvious qualifications and desire for promotion. And what is management's responsibility in giving references for a former sales person? If the rep was incompetent but a nice guy, an executive may be tempted to cover up for him. To what extent is this manager ethically bound to tell the truth, or to give details, about former employees?

Relations with the company. Changing jobs and handling expense accounts are just two situations that illustrate the ethical problems involved in a sales executive's relations with his own company. When changing positions, a manager may want to take customers with him to his new employer. These may be key accounts which he himself has been selling, but they also are quite important to his former employer. Ethical and legal questions may arise if he tries to move those customers to his new firm.

Many times a sales manager possesses information that could be highly useful to a competitor. Naturally, it is difficult to control the information a manager gives to a new employer, but there are limits beyond which such behavior is clearly unethical. One sales manager resigned to accept a similar position with a smaller competitor. He took with him material in his files, which included important marketing research information on the former firm's customers.

In dealing with sales expenses, it is quite clear that expense accounts should not be padded and the account policies set by top man-

A day-to-day operating problem in the

MAJESTIC GLASS COMPANY (L)

The letter of the law versus the spirit of the law. Or, is it ethical to accept this order?

While checking orders received from the sales force, Clyde Brion, general sales manager, noticed a very large sale of 26-ounce bottles, totaling $45,000, to the Florida Shores Marine Company, Palm Beach, Florida. Instructions were included in the order for special crating of the bottles. The Miami sales representative, Clarence Dutton, had written *New Customer* across the face of the order, thus claiming the additional 5 percent commission on orders from new customers. Curious, Brion wrote to Dutton asking for more information on the Florida Shores Marine Company, including an estimate of potential purchases from this account. Dutton replied in a registered letter, stating that the new customer was actually a small steamship line, and that the bottles were to be delivered to a rum manufacturer in Cuba. Because of the disruption of normal trade relations between the United States and Cuba, Dutton estimated that the account might well total $200,000 annually.

Question

Should Clyde Brion accept this order?

Note: See the introduction to this series of problems in Chapter 2 for the necessary background on the company, its market, and its competition.

agement should be followed. Ethical questions may arise, however, in the interpretation of these policies. Suppose that top management states it will pay only 12 cents a mile to sales reps or sales managers who use their personal automobiles for company business. Yet, the sales manager knows that actual expenses are 15 cents a mile at the minimum. He may be tempted to pad his mileage, and encourage the reps to do so, to make up the difference. He may justify this action on the basis that the money really is being spent for business purposes, and the spirit of the expense account is not being violated. Some of the ethical questions are: Should sales personnel manipulate expense accounts in order to protect themselves from the niggardly policies of top management, thereby recovering money honestly spent in the solicitation of business for the firm? Or should they attempt to get policies changed? Or, failing that, should they change employers rather than commit what they believe to be unethical acts?

Relations with customers.   Perhaps the most critical set of ethical questions facing sales managers is associated with customer relations. The major problem areas involve bribes, gifts, and entertainment.

1. *Bribes.*   Bribery in selling is an unpleasant fact of life that apparently has existed, in varying degrees, since time immemorial. However, bribery is not limited to selling. It exists in many other areas of social interaction. It can start with parents bribing their children: "If you are good kids today, we'll take you to the beach tomorrow," or, "If you get an A in those two courses, I'll buy you a new pair of skis."

Bribery is found in many (perhaps all) cultures and political systems. It is so implanted in many cultures that special slang words are used to designate it in various languages. In Latin America it is called the *mordida* (small bite). It is *dash* in West Africa and *baksheesh* in the Middle East. The French call it *pot de vin* (jug of wine), and in Italy there is *la bustarella* (the little envelope) left on a bureaucrat's desk to cut the red tape. In Chicago, they use "a little grease."

A complicating factor is that bribery is not a sharply demarcated activity. Sometimes the lines are blurred between a bribe, a gift to show appreciation, and a reasonable commission or reward for services rendered. The blatant bribes, payoffs, or kickbacks may be easy to spot. They are patently wrong. Unfortunately, today much bribery is done in a more sophisticated manner and is less easy to identify.

Bribery may involve a small fee for fixing a speeding ticket, or it may be a multimillion-dollar payoff to get a large government contract. In sales, the bribe offer may be initiated by the sales person, or the request may come from the buyer. Usually the buyer's request is stated in a veiled fashion, and the sales representative has to be perceptive to understand what is going on. During periods of product shortages, a buyer may offer an under-the-table payment to the sales person just to be allowed to buy the product.

Bribery in selling erupted as an international scandal in the mid–1970s. There were revelations of payoffs to foreign officials by American companies engaged in selling abroad. The resultant political sensitivity in the United States and in several foreign countries undoubtedly has done much to clean up a bad situation.[9] The furor also has served to spotlight bribery in domestic marketing and to discourage it there.

Undoubtedly, however, sales managers and sales people will continue to be put to the ethical test with respect to bribery. It would be naive to conclude that the recent scandals will mark the end of bribery in selling. In fact, in many foreign countries there is no way a company can hope to make sales without paying fees or commissions (often translate that as bribes) to agents in those countries.

Nevertheless, the scandals should strengthen the ethical resolve of sales executives with respect to bribery. They should not offer bribes. They should resist demands or suggestions for bribes from purchasing agents. They should encourage their sales people to do the same. If nothing else, sales executives should realize that the idea "Everyone else is doing it" is no longer a valid excuse. The penalties can be pretty stiff for proven takers or givers of bribes.

2. *Gifts.* The practice of sales executives and sales people giving gifts to their customers, especially at Christmas time, is time-honored in American business. The practice of gift-giving under some conditions also may be related to bribery. Today, perhaps more than ever before, the moral and ethical climate of gift-giving to customers is under careful scrutiny in many firms. The practice is being reviewed by both the givers and the receivers of gifts. Some firms put dollar limits on the business gifts they allow their employees to give or to receive. The Internal Revenue Service places a limit of $25 a year on the amount that may be deducted for business gifts to any one person. Other firms have stopped entirely the practice of giving Christmas gifts to customers. Some of these firms are offering instead to contribute (in amounts equal to their usual gifts) to their customers' favorite charities.

It is unfortunate that gift-giving to customers has become so complicated and so suspect in our society. A reasonably priced, tastefully selected gift can truly be an expression of appreciation and thanks to a customer for business. Today the problem lies largely in deciding what constitutes "reasonably priced" and "tastefully selected."

---

[9] See Thomas Griffith, "Payoff Is Not 'Accepted Practice,' " *Fortune,* August 1976, pp. 122–25 ff.; James D. Snyder, "Bribery in Selling: The Scandal Comes Home," *Sales and Marketing Management,* May 10, 1976, p. 35.

Fortunately, sales executives do have some time-tested guidelines to help them in avoiding gift-giving that is unethical or in bad taste. For example, a gift never should be given *before* a customer does business with a firm; it should not put the recipient under obligation to the giver. It may be all right to give a gift to a purchasing agents' children, but not to the agent's spouse. Inordinately expensive gifts or those with blatant advertising messages generally are in poor taste. A little common sense mixed with some social intelligence can go a long way toward keeping sales gift-giving within ethical boundaries.

3. *Entertainment.* Entertaining customers is a very common practice in selling today, but it, too, can pose ethical questions. A psychologist made the following suggestions for increasing the effectiveness of entertaining:

> Salesmen shouldn't be in too big a hurry to entertain. . . . As a general rule, it is far better to withhold the more lavish entertainment until after the first order, when it becomes a psychological "reward," and may help build a permanent relationship. On his early calls, the salesman may make it a point not to invite the prospect to lunch just when it seems he is going to do so. Then when the invitation comes, it may mean something. Of course, there are exceptions. If a buyer hints broadly that he wants to be taken to lunch to get away from the office for an hour or so, then the thing to do is to invite him on the spur of the moment. . . .
>
> Salesmen should be careful about doing actual selling during entertainment, especially at meals. Whenever feasible, it's better to talk about subjects other than business, giving the prospect the confidence that he is an enjoyable person.
>
> Salesmen ought to try to understand their own reasons for entertainment, especially at meals. They should ask themselves such searching questions as: Was I afraid I wouldn't make the sale otherwise? What would have happened on this if I had not taken the prospect to dinner?[10]

Although these points were stated many years ago, they still are quite pertinent today.

Over the years some useful generalizations have been developed which may guide sales representatives in their use of customer entertainment. Entertaining usually is done to develop long-term business relationships, rather than to get a one-time order. Ordinarily it is *not* a good idea to rely too heavily on entertaining. It is no substitute for a good product or the effective servicing of an account. If you try to buy business through entertaining, remember that some seller can always outbid you by entertaining more lavishly.

Good sales representatives usually learn to tailor their entertaining to the type of customer and potential value of the account. In fact,

---

[10] Daniel Brower, "A Psychologist Looks at Business Entertainment," *The American Salesman,* July 1960, pp. 90–96.

some customers do not want to be entertained for fear of being obligated, or because their companies do not permit it. Business entertainment is definitely a part of saleswork, and a large portion of the expense money often is devoted to it. If this money is spent unwisely on accounts with little potential, then a sales rep's time is wasted, and his selling costs will be out of line. Indeed, a contributing factor in sales people's success may be their ability to know who is the right person to entertain and what should be the nature of the entertainment.

WHAT IS SOCIAL RESPONSIBILITY?

A sales administrator has a tripartite responsibility. The first part is a revenue responsibility to the company. The administrator's function in this respect is to provide a satisfactory income over the long run by buying revenues at a reasonable cost in the marketplace. The second is a human responsibility to the sales force. In this sense his function is to provide a good working environment by proper management of the sales force and by adequate planning and control of sales operations. The sales administrator's responsibility to customers is to maximize their standard of living by delivering the desired products at the lowest reasonable cost. In all these relationships, *ethical* considerations quite frequently are viewed on a person-to-person basis.

The substance of *social responsibility* is much broader, however. It emphasizes an executive's institutional (company) actions and their effect on the entire social system. Without this broader viewpoint, personal and institutional acts tend to be separated. A sales executive can lead a model personal life but continue to justify his company's pollution of a river because there is no direct personal involvement. To him, river pollution is a public problem to be solved by governmental action. The concept of social responsibility requires him to consider his acts within the framework of the whole social system. Thus, the executive is held responsible for the effects these acts may have anywhere in that system.

> When a man's primary frame of reference is himself, he may be counted upon for antisocial behavior whenever his values conflict with those of society. If his values are limited primarily to a certain group or organization, he tends to become a partisan acting for that group. But, if he thinks in terms of a whole system, he begins to build societal values into his actions, even when they are for a certain organization. *This is the essence of social responsibility.* For the manager it means realizing that the business system does not exist alone and that a healthy business system cannot exist within a sick society.[11] (Italics added.)

---

[11] Quotation and adaptation of preceding paragraph from Keith Davis, "Understanding the Social Responsibility Puzzle," *Business Horizons*, Winter 1967, p. 46.

Reasons for the sales manager's responsibility to society

Sales managers should conduct their affairs in an efficient, ethical, and socially desirable manner in order to justify the privilege society has granted them to operate within a relatively free socioeconomic structure. No freedom or privilege that is worth much comes without a price. Just as our precious political freedoms sometimes have a high price, so also do our economic freedoms.

Minimize government intervention. If sales managers fail to perform in a socially desirable fashion, society will restrict their freedom of operation. Most of the governmental limitations placed on sales activities throughout the years have been the result of management's failure to live up to its social responsibilities. Once some form of governmental control is established, it is rarely removed. The wise course of action therefore is to understand and fulfill 'a social responsibility, thus minimizing any additional government intervention.

The power-responsibility equation. The concept that social power equals social responsibility may help to explain why business executives have a responsibility to society. Sales managers have a considerable amount of social power as they influence markets, speak out on matters of economic policy, and so on. The lessons of history suggest that the social responsibilities of businessmen arise from the amount of social power they have.

Today there are many practical applications of the idea of reasonably balanced power and responsibility in business. A management axiom holds that authority and responsibility should be matched, for example. If responsibility arises from power, then we may reason that the avoidance of social responsibility will lead to an erosion of social power. That is, "in the long run, those who do not use power in a manner which society considers responsible will tend to lose it."[12]

Sales department represents the company. Sales executives and their sales forces represent the company to the people. Some years ago, Procter & Gamble put this point nicely in an annual report: "When a Procter & Gamble salesman walks into a customer's place of business—whether he is calling on an individual store or keeping an appointment at the headquarters of a large group of stores—he not only represents Procter & Gamble, but in a very real sense, he is Procter & Gamble." Therefore, the way the public sees these people and their activities, is the way it will judge the concern. If a sales rep misrepresents a product or tries to use high-pressure selling techniques, any ill will incurred is reflected on the firm.

Ordinarily, people do not judge a concern by its office or plant workers because they rarely see these groups. In fact, the sales force

---

[12] Keith Davis and Robert L. Blomstrom, *Business and Society: Environment and Responsibility*, 3d ed. (New York: McGraw-Hill Book Co., 1975), p. 50. Also see Davis, "Five Propositions for Social Responsibility," *Business Horizons*, June 1975, pp. 19–24.

frequently is blamed for inefficiencies by office and production employees. If a product is defective or a bill is incorrect, the sales department bears the brunt of the customer's anger. Furthermore, the way the sales department handles the complaint can determine whether the customer will continue to patronize the organization.

Sales department represents our economy. In many instances, the system of enlightened self-interest and free enterprise is appraised by the public in light of the impression left by sales managers and their sales forces. Many people are strongly opposed to certain current marketing methods. Television commercials, advertisements in print media, door-to-door selling, and telephone soliciting often are the targets of consumer dissatisfaction. Often the critical reaction is: "There ought to be a law against such practices," or "This is what happens when business is allowed to go unrestrained."

In other words, the lack of social conscience in selling hurts not only the company involved but also the entire economic system. Hence, anything a sales administrator can do to develop a socially desirable sales operation will help to perpetuate our basic socioeconomic structure.

Positive action regarding social responsibilities

Earlier we noted that the public is losing its trust and confidence in business and its leaders. Active consumer groups, other advocacy organizations, and political reformers all are demanding change. Business must be more perceptive about these social and political trends. The early warning signs are there for management to see. If nothing else, management in one company should be learning from the mistakes made by other firms. It is becoming obvious that business must generate *substantive* change if it hopes to stem the movement toward further regulation. Merely *cosmetic* changes, coupled with doing business the same old way, simply will not be enough.[13]

Before sales executives (or any person, for that matter) can do much in the way of demonstrating social responsibility, they first must acknowledge that they have such an obligation. Many sales executives seem to believe their responsibility is solely to their companies and the stockholders. They must be aware that they also have responsibilities to society, or any further suggestions will fall on barren ground. There are several courses of action for those sales executives who are aware of and want to shoulder their social responsibilities.

---

[13] See Joseph Nolan, "Protect Your Public Image with Performance," *Harvard Business Review*, March–April, 1975, pp. 135–142; John F. Steiner, "The Business Response to Public Distrust," *Business Horizons*, April 1977, pp. 74–80.

Manage sales force effectively. A sales executive should manage the sales force in such a way that its business practices are approved by society. In a sense, the bulk of this book has been devoted to this one point—the intelligent and sound management of a sales force. Specific examples could be drawn from most chapters. A socially responsible sales administrator designs a compensation plan so that the best interests of the customer are considered. A sales quota should be set so that it is not necessary to high-pressure or overstock customers. Sales people should be properly selected and placed so that human resources are not wasted. The sales force should be to ensure a trained and supervised productive working group.

The *Sales Manager's Creed* (Figure 23–2) can serve as a good summary of a sales executive's social responsibilities and some practical ways to meet these obligations. This creed was developed several years ago by the Sales and Marketing Executives—International, and it continues to be relevant today. There are marked similarities in the spirit of the Creed and the ten-point program outlined in Figure 23–1, to stimulate ethical behavior in a sales force.

Sales executives also have another, perhaps broader set of responsibilities regarding sales people. Fundamentally, a sales manager is a manager of people. Thus, a sales manager should help sales people to realize their personal and professional goals. He should minimize, or try to offset, the disagreeable parts of their job. Too many people merely work for a living. They do not enjoy their jobs, as witness the TGIF (Thank God It's Friday) and the "Blue Monday" sentiments in our society. Many people count the hours until quitting time, the days until the weekend, and the weeks until vacation. A sales manager's goal should be to generate a working climate wherein sales people can derive some of life's satisfactions from the work they do. Perhaps this goal is too idealistic and is too much to expect but at least we can try in that direction.

Play a stronger role in the marketing planning process.[14] Top management in a company can help sales force managers perform in a more socially responsible manner by involving them in the marketing planning process to a greater extent than is typically the case. Sales managers' participation in the planning process is essential if the company's product and market plans are to reflect the customers' needs, and if the company is to get maximum commitment from the sales managers in executing these plans.

Field sales managers are responsible for achieving assigned performance levels. They will come closer to reaching these goals, and in

---

[14] This section is adapted from B. Charles Ames, "Build Marketing Strength into Industrial Selling," *Harvard Business Review*, January–February 1972, pp. 58–59.

FIGURE 23–2
Sales manager's creed

A CREED

I SUBSCRIBE TO THIS SALES MANAGER'S CREED, PREPARED BY THE NATIONAL FEDERATION OF SALES EXECUTIVES, WHICH I BELIEVE TO BE IN THE BEST INTERESTS OF AMERICAN BUSINESS:

All salesmen shall receive fair compensation during their initial or subsequent training periods.

While recognizing changes in compensation or territory to be functions of sales management, salesmen shall be consulted prior to establishing such changes and given reasonable notice of the effective date.

Earnings of commission or bonus salesmen shall be unlimited, unless otherwise specified at the time of their employment. Should basic changes in a business justify modifying this policy, all salesmen affected shall be advised of the fact a reasonable time prior to establishing such ceilings as become necessary.

When evaluating the ability of salesmen, conditions beyond their control, such as differences in the sales potentials of their territories, shall be given full consideration.

Salesmen shall be offered the same vacation, job or income security, and other employee benefits as are enjoyed by other employees in comparable positions in the same company.

The only "house" or "no commission" accounts shall be those clearly defined in advance of solicitation.

The paper work required of salesmen shall be held down to a minimum and its value clearly justified.

Salesmen's expense reimbursement policies shall be uniform, after taking all variations of conditions into consideration.

A sharp distinction shall be drawn between salesmen's earnings and expense allowance, and any system which affords salesmen either a substantial profit or loss on expense accounts, shall be corrected.

Salesmen shall be given either a contract, agreement, or letter covering those conditions of his employment which might otherwise be the basis for later misunderstandings.

If quotas are used—
(a) Salesmen should know how their figures have been determined, and
(b) The quotas shall be based on reliable seasoned personal evaluation of accurate and adequate criteria.

A salesman whose health or well being gives evidence of being prejudiced by the nervous tensions involved in his work, shall be given such relief as may be possible.

Pressure to achieve results shall be of a constructive nature, avoiding the use of "fear" psychology or threatened loss of employment.

No matter where a salesman may be located, he shall be provided with a simple means of stating his grievances, which shall be promptly considered and answered.

a socially responsible manner, if they are given a real voice in the development of the goals. Moreover, sales representatives are more likely to serve as marketing people—as territorial managers within the firm's marketing program—rather than operating as an independent sales and distribution system, if they have some voice in planning the marketing operations.

Interpret consumer demand.   A major responsibility of the sales executive is to determine what the consumers want and then supply products and services to satisfy these wants. It is *not* the consumers' responsibility to invent new products. Consumer demand for a product may be latent or dormant. That is, the demand is present but unrecognized by the consumer until a product appears on the scene to fulfill the want. For example, consumers seemed to get along well with standard transmissions, silk hosiery, and the old-fashioned paintbrush. However, when automatic transmissions, nylon hosiery, and roller paint applicators appeared on the market, they were eagerly accepted. Apparently, the demand was present even before the new products were marketed, but it was dormant.

If management refuses to accept the responsibility for interpreting consumer demand, the public will look elsewhere to have its wants satisfied. The institution they usually seek out in this case is some agency of the government. When private industry ignored consumer demand for electric power or irrigation water, the government developed power and water resources for the market. When private financial institutions failed to sell the necessary capital at a price investors were willing to pay, the government stepped in to satisfy the market demand for low-interest mortgage money.

Keep intelligently informed.   With easy access to television, radio, and the print media, sales executives can help themselves by reading on a wide variety of subjects. They should not be limited to business journals in their field. They owe it to themselves, to their companies, and to society to take advantage of this storehouse of knowledge. Some of the purposes for which sales executives may read are as follows.[15]

1. *For fun and amusement.*   Reading the comics in the daily newspaper or a joke book keeps alive our sense of humor. We can smile at other people's foibles and laugh at our own. Humor levels people and makes the encroachment of dictatorship difficult.

2. *For idle curiosity.*   A hurried glance at the newspaper can provide a glimpse of the actors on the stage of life. We keep up with

---

[15] For the idea and content of this list, we are indebted to Henry A. Burd, professor of marketing at the University of Washington until his retirement. See also B. J. Hodge and John W. Lee, "What Reading Will Do for the Executive," *Business Horizons*, August 1973, pp. 47–51.

the times superficially with this type of reading. It may be done over the breakfast table, on a commuter train, or at home in the evening. It also may be complemented by radio and television news reports and analyses.

3. *To keep up with their jobs.* Sales managers also may read for immediate practical purposes. This probably accounts for the bulk of the reading done by most sales executives. They may read periodicals of general business interest such as *Business Week, Fortune,* or *The Wall Street Journal* or journals of general marketing and sales interest, such as *Sales & Marketing Management* or *Industrial Marketing.* They usually will examine the trade journals in their own product field.

4. *To learn to write and speak better.* Careful reading, paying attention to the mechanics of expression, can help us improve our command of the language. To some extent, this overlaps several other types of reading. People may read trade journals to keep up with their jobs, for example, while at the same time they are conscious of the writing style and other aspects of expression.

5. *For a broader understanding of their living conditions.* This requires the reading of good magazines and books on economic, political, and social conditions.

6. *To learn to live more successfully.* This type of reading enters the realm of philosophy and religion. Consciously or unconsciously, we all have a philosophy of life. It may be sheer imitation, or it may be developed and modified by reading the Bible and other serious works.

7. *To satisfy a deep inner curiosity about the universe.* This involves reading about astronomy and the world of modern science, including the nuclear and space age.

8. *For appreciation.* Sales managers, however practical, want to read the world's masterpieces to enhance their appreciation of these classics.

Work closely with outside organizations. As part of their jobs, sales managers usually come in contact with various organizations outside the company. By working closely with these outside groups, sales managers frequently are helped in fulfilling their social responsibilities.

1. *Trade associations.* Sales executives who want to run a socially responsible sales operation often find their good intentions are thwarted by competitive conditions. Consequently, they may find their efforts will be more effective if they are handled on an industrywide scale through the coordinating efforts of a trade association. Usually, such agreements governing all firms in an industry are voluntary. Often the trade association provides the machinery for arbitrating any differences or grievances. The arbitrators may lack enforcing power, but their decisions usually carry considerable moral and ethical persuasion.

By working through their trade association, sales managers can also take advantage of the Trade Practice Conferences offered by the Federal Trade Commission (FTC). A trade association, working with representatives of the FTC, can draw up a set of trade practice rules relating to competitive conduct in the industry. Usually the rules are divided into Group I and Group II. Group I rules prohibit only those practices the FTC considers illegal under laws it administers. Group II rules are additional statements of ethical conduct which are not necessarily related to any law the Commission administers. The Trade Practice Conferences are entirely voluntary. The FTC simply offers an opportunity to define in a specific fashion what are considered fair or unfair competitive trade practices in a specific industry.

2. *Sales and Marketing Executives—International.* This organization has its headquarters in New York City and member clubs in virtually all large cities in the United States and in many foreign countries. It has done much to improve ethical standards in selling through its many practical programs for upgrading selling as a career. Education for better selling and sales management has been carried on through sales force workshops, executive development programs, and sponsorship of school courses in salesmanship. Findings from research studies sponsored by Sales and Marketing Executives—International have done much to improve the quality and character of sales leadership.

3. *Labor unions.* Sales managers whose sales forces are unionized have the responsibility of working as closely and harmoniously as possible with the union. The goal is not only to improve the material lot of the reps but also to upgrade the ethical standards followed in their work. A sales manager with a unionized sales force ordinarily is making a mistake if he tries to pretend the union is not really there. Although he may have fought vigorously against unionization, once the union is recognized as a bargaining agent he can gain little, and stands to lose much, by continuing to fight it.

4. *Better Business Bureaus.* A well-operated Better Business Bureau in a city can be a strong voice representing the consumer's interest. Sales managers should encourage the sales force to know the bureau and its operations. This is especially true of sales reps who sell directly to the consumer. At all times, the sales executive should cooperate with the local bureau in its efforts to maintain clean and fair competitive selling conditions in the community.

5. *Chambers of commerce.* A sales manager should be active in the local chamber of commerce, and a company should have a membership in as many of the communities as possible where it sells. Chambers are usually the voice of executives at the local, state, and even national level. A good sales manager has much to offer the chamber and, at the same time, has much to gain through active par-

ticipation. Chambers of commerce foster and support policies of general interest to sales managers. For example, many of the local and state laws affecting sales operations were started through efforts of some chambers of commerce.

Participate in community affairs. Every citizen has the social responsibility of participating in civic affairs to some extent. Sales managers should willingly accept the task of spearheading community projects such as a United Fund drive, a building expansion program in the local school district, or a "help keep our city clean" campaign. A manager who shirks this responsibility runs the risk of hurting the company's reputation, because to the public they *are* the company. Such neglect is also another small detriment for the socioeconomic system that makes their position possible.

Participate in politics. To the question, "Should marketing executives take part in politics?" it seems increasingly apparent that the answer generally is yes. Many marketing executives are coming to realize that such activity is desirable, if not mandatory, for the country's welfare. Top management more and more is encouraging people in the middle and lower executive echelons to engage in political affairs. Sales force managers particularly are in a good position to take part in politics at the state and local levels. Not only can this participation help to fulfill their responsibilities as citizens, but it also offers them a means of explaining the vital role of selling in our economy.

PUBLIC REGULATION AND SALES MANAGERS

Public regulation at any level of government—federal, state or local—probably touches a company more through its sales department than through any other phase of its operations. This does not imply that regulation of nonselling activities is unimportant. The Securities Exchange Commission affects corporate financing; the Taft-Hartley Act and minimum wage legislation influence several aspects of personnel and labor relations; various measures establish safety regulations for offices and factories; local zoning laws affect plant location, and so on. However, the various regulatory measures that affect areas of marketing, such as pricing, advertising, personal selling, packaging, labeling, and competition in general, seem to be more numerous and critical to the company's success.

Reasons for government intervention

A study of American business history will show rather clearly that regulatory government intervention typically comes about for one of two basic reasons. Either private industry is not able, or refuses, to accept its responsibility for acting in the best public interest, or special interest groups promote the legislation.[16]

Examples of governmental action resulting from private business's inability or refusal to meet its responsibilities include antitrust legislation, laws prohibiting unfair competition, and legal restrictions on advertising. Before the turn of the century, for example, society felt that the abuses engendered by monopolies were contrary to the public interest, so the Sherman Antitrust Act was passed in 1890. When private industry ignored its responsibilities in matters of labeling and selling food and drugs, so that adulterated products were sold and other items were deceptively labeled, the government intervened with the Pure Food and Drug Act (1906). As the years went by and shortsighted, antisocial businessmen found ways to circumvent this law, it was strengthened by amendments in 1938.

Early in the 20th century business practices had degenerated to the point where the Federal Trade Commission Act was passed in 1914 to restrict unfair competition. Through the ensuing years, the advertising done by many firms was misleading and deceptive. Industry self-policing was ineffective or not attempted. Once again the government stepped in, and the result was the Wheeler-Lea Amendment (1938) to the Federal Trade Commission Act.

Sometimes, a segment of private business seeks government intervention to support the self-interest of a limited group. Results of this action are found in the unfair sales practices acts, chain store taxes, laws restricting interstate trade, and municipal ordinances regulating door-to-door selling by firms not located in a given city.

Areas where public regulation touches sales executives

Four of the areas where sales executives are affected by the social control of business will be considered briefly: price discrimination, unfair competition, the Green River type of municipal ordinance, and "cooling-off" laws.

Price discrimination. The Clayton Antitrust Act (1914) and its Robinson-Patman Amendment (1936) are federal laws generally restricting price discrimination. A sales administrator, for example, can-

---

[16] Not all government intervention is of the *regulatory* type. In several instances, federal, state, or local governments offer aid on a voluntary basis to businesses in an effort to foster and preserve competition. For example, several states offer courses in distributive education, with federal support through the George-Dean Act. The Small Business Administration has published many marketing and sales aids for small businesses. Much of the statistical information used by firms in setting quotas and establishing territories comes from the Bureau of the Census of the U.S. Department of Commerce.

not allow members of his sales force to indiscriminately grant price concessions. Some customers may demand larger discounts than are normally allowed and threaten to take their business elsewhere if their demands are not met. If the seller grants the unusual discount, assuming no corresponding cost differential to justify the transaction, he (and the buyer) may be violating the Robinson-Patman Act.

In another situation, in order to make a sale it may be necessary for a seller to absorb some or all of the freight ordinarily paid by the buyer. Care must be taken to ensure that the move is made in good faith to meet an equally low price of a competitor. Price guarantees normally cannot be made to some customers without making the same guarantees to their competitors. If a firm wants to grant allowances to customers for such things as cooperative advertising or demonstrators, these attractions must be offered to all competing customers on a proportionately equal basis.

Unfair competition.   Unfair trade practices that may injure a competitor or the consumer are generally illegal under the Federal Trade Commission Act and its Wheeler-Lea Amendment. While no specific examples of unfair competition are spelled out in these laws, a large body of illustrations has been built up through the years as the Federal Trade Commission has administered these legislative acts. A few examples of unfair competition as they may relate to the sales force manager are as follows:

- Making false, deceptive, or disparaging statements about a competitor or his products.
- Bribing customers of an employer in order to acquire or hold an account.
- Representing as new products those that are rebuilt, secondhand, or seconds.
- Using bribery or espionage to learn the trade secrets of competitors.
- Making false or misleading claims about services that accompany the purchase of a product.
- Requiring customers to buy one product they really do not want or need in order to get another they do want. This form of tie-in selling is usually done when the product is in great demand and in short supply. (This is also a violation of the Clayton Act.)
- Misleading the customers into thinking they are getting a bargain, a reduced price, or some sort of free deal when such is not actually the case.

Green River ordinances. [17]   Many cities have ordinances restricting the activities of sales people who represent firms located outside the

[17] These legal measures derive their title from Green River, Wyoming, the location of one of the earliest of such acts.

city. These representatives may sell door to door, or they may call on retailers or other business establishments. Ostensibly, most of these laws were passed to protect local consumers and businesses from the fraudulent, high-pressure, and otherwise unethical selling practices of the outlanders. Actually the measures not only serve this purpose but also have the effect of insulating the local firms from external competition. Generally, these ordinances require the sales people to have a local license to do business in the town, and often it is difficult for representatives from some types of outside firms to get the necessary license. While the constitutionality of these laws is highly questionable, they nevertheless do serve as a deterrent to sales activity and generally are an effective form of public regulation that touches sales administrators and their sales forces.

"Cooling-off" laws.   To protect consumers against the sales activities—sometimes unethical—of door-to-door sales people, there has been considerable legislative action in recent years at the federal, state, and local levels. Much of this state legislation and FTC administrative rulings is of the "cooling-off" type. That is, the regulations provide for a cooling-off period (usually three days) during which the buyer of goods or services in a door-to-door sale may cancel the contract, return any merchandise, and obtain a full refund.[18]

The Federal Trade Commission rulings (1972) apply to all sales of $25 or more. They require the sales person to inform the customer orally and in writing about the opportunity to "say no to the company even after you've said yes to the sales person." By 1973, close to 40 states, as well as several cities, had passed widely various cooling-off laws. This poses real problems of compliance for national direct-selling companies, who may find themselves with more varieties of sales contracts than they have merchandise.[19]

Conclusion

Undoubtedly, the amount and severity of public regulation are increasing at all levels—federal, state, and local. The important question concerns the reactions of sales executives to this encroaching social control. Are they aware of the trend? Do they care about it? What can they do about it?

Most sales managers are probably concerned only indirectly and secondarily with the public interest. Instead, their attention is devoted to practices which will serve their short-run interests. They encourage

---

[18] For an analysis of the role of cooling-off legislation and its effectiveness in protecting consumers, particularly those with low incomes, see Orville C. Walker, Jr. and Neil M. Ford, "Can 'Cooling-off Laws' Really Protect the Consumer?" *Journal of Marketing*, April 1970, pp. 53–58.

[19] For summaries of the state laws, see "Cooling It, State by State," *Sales Management*, October 2, 1972, p. 16, and October 16, 1972, p. 32.

methods of operation by sales people that are very similar to those that have contributed to public regulation in the past. It is a bit discouraging to note how little sales administrators seem to have learned from history.

Sometimes, sales executives foster public regulation in another way. Outwardly they profess to be advocates of free competition. However, when they face strong but fair competition, they may run to their state or federal representatives to seek protection in the form of a tariff, a trade barrier, or some other type of regulation. In many cases, a sales manager's concept of fair competition means being able to beat a competitor, and it is unfair competition when the competitor wins. Sales executives must realize that it is not possible to regulate part of one segment of the economy and let the other part go unrestrained. Regulation begets more regulation.

QUESTIONS AND PROBLEMS

1. A sales manager is faced with the problem of whether to approve practices of his sales force that will result in profitable sales but also are slightly unethical. By sanctioning these practices the executive meets his responsibility to his company and its stockholders but fails in his social responsibilities. Is management's social responsibility thus incompatible with its responsibilities to its stockholders?

2. Discuss the problem of determining ethical standards, especially as your ideas may differ from those presented in this chapter.

3. Is ethical conduct always good for business in total, and unethical conduct always bad for business in total? Is your answer the same for the individual firm?

4. Are unethical practices always illegal? If not, cite specific examples of practices you feel are unethical but not outside the letter of the law. Are illegal practices always unethical?

5. Evaluate the consequences of outright firing of a sales person who has not performed adequately.

6. As sales manager, you have been asked to recommend someone for a job as sales manager with another, noncompetitive concern. You have several sales people who would be excellent for the position, but you would not like losing them. The other position would be a definite improvement for them, and they will never be able to do so well within your own concern. Would you tell them of the opening? Would you recommend them to the other firm?

7. As sales manager of a firm that makes printed electronic circuits, you have been requested to put on paper your policies on the entertainment of customers, the giving of gifts, and how you propose to handle bribery. State your policies in clear, specific terms so that all people concerned know exactly how you will handle each situation.

8. What are some implications in the power-responsibility equation with respect to a sales manager's responsibility to society?

9. Is it important that a sales manager have a degree of social responsibility higher than that of a production manager or an accountant in a firm?

10. *The Sales Manager's Creed* (Figure 23–2) was written over 30 years ago. Does it include any points you feel are now outdated and should be revised? Are there additional points you would add to the creed if it were to be rewritten today?

11. Should participation in community affairs be made part of the job description for a sales executive? If so, should this factor be considered when his compensation is being reviewed? Is your answer the same for a sales person on straight salary? On straight commission? Does the nature of the product sold have any bearing on your decision?

12. Discuss the question of whether sales managers and their reps should actively participate in politics.

13. In what ways are sales force managers affected by each of the following laws:
    a. Federal Trade Commission Act.
    b. Robinson-Patman Act.
    c. Green River ordinances.
    d. Cooling-off laws.

Case 23–1
DAVID BALLANTINE
Kickbacks

David Ballantine was the star salesman for The Dry Hole Supply Company of Oklahoma City. Year after year he was the top producer and thoroughly dominated his sales territory. He sold only one product—drilling mud. Mud is a chemical compound based on Bentonite that is used to lubricate the drilling bit as it rotates in the hole. It also serves as a vehicle for bringing up out of the hole the debris from the drilling. The compound is used in large quantities.

The "mud" industry is dominated by a few large concerns whose price policies are identical for the standard supply they are selling. Since all sellers quote the same price, competition is on the basis of service. Ballantine seemed to give the best service.

For his efforts, Ballantine received a commission of 6 percent of sales. His gross commissions in 1977 were $191,000. He paid all of his own expenses and had no specific territory. He could sell anywhere to anyone.

In 1977 the Dry Hole Supply Company was purchased by a group of Dallas business people from the estate of the company's founder who had passed away earlier that year. The new owners installed Don Calloway as general manager, with full authority to operate the highly profitable concern.

Calloway was most impressed with Ballantine's performance for the company. He quickly made Ballantine's acquaintance and socialized with him and his wife.

One of Calloway's first industry contacts was with the president of a competitive firm at a trade association meeting. As they were talking at a party, the other president asked, "Are you going to do anything about Dave Ballantine? The old man never would." Calloway looked puzzled and asked for an explanation. "You mean you don't know?" said the competitor. "That hot shot of yours has his big buyers in his pocket. There is no way anyone can sell against him. If we could get the goods on him, we'd have you guys in court."

Calloway felt it best not to react to that statement except to say, "I find that difficult to believe." He then sought other company. But the accusation stuck in his mind.

Upon returning to the home office, Calloway called the sales manager, Dan Metzger, into his office and related the incident. He asked, "Is there any truth in it?"

"I have no knowledge of any irregularities in Dave's selling tactics," Metzger replied.

"Now I am dead serious about this," Calloway said. "I don't want you to cover anything up."

"I repeat. I do not know of any illegal behavior by anyone on our sales force," was Metzger's emphatic answer. The meeting ended, but Calloway was not reassured. He wanted to know what problems he had inherited and decided to broach the matter directly by asking Ballantine about it directly.

At their next social outing, Calloway related accurately what had been said and asked Ballantine, "Any comments?"

Ballantine laughed and said, "Come on. What on earth are you doing talking to the competition, let alone listening to those worthless rascals? All you heard was sour grapes talking. If you go on listening to everything you hear in this industry, you're going to get into big trouble real quick. Man, I own this market, and it eats their guts out. They can't stand it and have tried everything in the book to get me fired. I'm going to tell you this just once and I don't want to hear anymore about it. There is going to be no end of wild tales you're going to hear about me and how I sell all that mud for you. Now if you can't live with those tales, then we had best part company right now because there will be no shortage of them. Just ask yourself what kind of story the guy who loses out to me on a big deal is going to cook up to justify his failure to his boss. All you're hearing is losers talking."

Calloway smiled and let the matter drop for five months. The issue was revived one day when a telephone call for Ballantine was routed to the general manager by mistake. Calloway heard gushing out of the phone a plea, "Dave, it's Billy Joe. I gotta have the dough today. I'm being pressed hard by the bank."

He asked, "Who is this?"

"You're not Dave." The phone went dead.

When Ballantine returned to the office, Calloway asked him who Billy Joe was. He replied that he was a big drilling contractor in the Permian basin. "He's one of our biggest customers."

Calloway then asked, "Then why would he be calling you here to give him money. Do we owe him something?"

Ballantine's face was frozen for a moment. Then he laughed, "Naw. I owe him a bundle from a poker game we were in out in Midland. He gave me a little time to raise the dough. He's a good ole boy."

"Dave, I think we need to talk about this. Do you really think that it is sound policy to play poker with your customers?"

"Depends on how good of a poker player you are."

"I'm serious," Calloway said.

"So am I," Ballantine fired back, suddenly changing character, "Listen, you Dallas dude. These guys buy from me because I'm a good ole poker playin', hard drinkin' buddy from way back."

Calloway was shocked by Ballantine's sudden change in behavior and speech. He had never seen this Dave, the oil field roustabout. He dropped the subject, but relations with Ballantine were never the same afterward.

The manager continued a quiet investigation of Ballantine's selling tactics. It developed that he was a big loser in poker games, and he seemed only to lose to his big customers. There it was. He was kicking back part of his commissions to the buyers in the guise of poker losings.

Calloway went to Dallas to meet with the owners to ask for their permission to order Ballantine to stop the practice. Calloway's sponsor in the firm, the man who had been largely responsible for his successful career, took him aside as the others left the room.

"Don, I think you've made a tactical blunder," he said. You should have taken the clue from your sales manager, who knew nothing about it. Your position would be much better if you knew nothing about it. Now it's your problem and you're trying to rope us in on it. We didn't hear you. Now, boy, you're in a heap of trouble. You evidently can't live with kickbacks and the potential troubles they pose, but you won't have your job long without Dave out there doing the dirty work for us. Why on earth do you think this company has been so successful over the years against all those big boys? Did you really think Dave could whip them so badly without something going on under the table?"

"If he goes over to a competitor, and he will if you go on with this, you'll be the laughing stock of the industry. Now you figure out what you want to do. If you want me to put you somewhere else, I have a little oil action going on over in Louisiana that needs some attention. Phone me before midnight and tell me what game we're going to play. But boy, just remember, I got a half million dollars in this action and so have each of those other fellows."

Questions

1. What should Don Calloway do?
2. Evaluate the ethical aspects of Dave Ballantine's behavior.

Case 23–2
MONARCH CHEMICAL COMPANY
Policy on giving Christmas gifts to customers

In November 1977, Mr. F. J. Vogel was hired by the Monarch Chemical Company to fill the position of sales manager. This was his first job in the chemical industry. His preceding position had been as sales manager for a small electric manufacturer. Two months after joining Monarch, Mr. Vogel received the following letter from Mr. A. R. Moreland, the director of purchasing for a large cable manufacturing company, which was an old and highly valued customer of the Monarch Chemical Company.

Dear Mr. Vogel:

I thank you and your company for the greeting you sent us for Christmas. We also wish you a prosperous new business year.

We take the gifts you sent to our purchasing agents as a token of your esteem. But I must ask you to discontinue this practice in the future. Our company recently decided on new purchasing policies. These policies do not allow our purchasing agents to accept gifts from suppliers. I am sure you will understand our situation.

I am looking forward to a continuation of the good business relations which traditionally exist between our companies.

> Yours sincerely,
> Arthur R. Moreland
> *Purchasing Director*

Vogel had no idea of Monarch's policies and practices concerning gift-giving. He therefore showed the letter to his assistant, Mr. Sprague. Sprague told him that Mr. Clyde Oberg, the former sales manager, had instituted the practice of sending wine as Christmas gifts to purchasing agents of customers, and in some instances also to members of the customers' engineering departments. The size of the gifts varied from 3 to 12 bottles, according to the sales volume of the account, the continuity of business relations, and many other factors. In practice, the number of recipients and the size of the gift were determined intuitively in agreement with the salesman who serviced the particular customer.

In today's business environment, Vogel felt that the practice of giving gifts to customers at Christmas or any other time was potentially an explosive issue, or at least a troublesome matter. Some business executives he knew considered gift-giving as a form of bribery. They believed that a sales person should sell a product on its merits—on its ability to satisfy a buyer's needs better than any competitive product could do the job. Other executives felt that gift-giving is a time-honored, respectable business practice which can become significant in a buyer-seller relationship, especially when many competitive products are essentially the same.

In any event, Vogel realized that he needed to have a clear-cut policy on gift-giving. With that goal in mind his first step was to understand the existing policy in his company and in the chemical industry.

Monarch was a medium-sized company located in New Jersey. The company manufactured a wide variety of chemical products for the industrial market. Its customer list included both large and small firms in a variety of industries located mainly in the eastern part of the United States. Monarch, for example, produced fibers for the textile industry, dyes for textile, paper, and leather goods manufacturers, pigments for paint manufacturers, and stabilizers for extruders of cable covers.

Monarch's major competitors were three of the largest chemical firms in the country, plus seven small- to medium-sized firms which marketed in the same general geographic area as did Monarch. The intensity of competition varied among the different products. Monarch's policy was to cultivate market niches which were not worthwhile for the big three competitors. But in the case of some products, such as the stabilizers for the extruders of cable mantles, Monarch competed directly with the large firms.

To distribute the products which were in competition with those made by Monarch, several of the competitive firms relied heavily on manufacturers' agents. A few of the competitors used their own sales forces for these products.

Monarch sold to about 900 accounts through a direct sales force of 11 people who were specialized by customer groups. They were compensated by a small salary plus a commission on net sales. They each had a limited expense account, under which limits were set for each major expense category. Entertainment, for example, was limited to $50 per customer per six-month period. Exceptions could be made, however, to most of the limits.

Vogel learned that Monarch's gift-giving practices at Christmastime had changed over the years, largely because there was no definite company policy covering this activity. For the past several years during Oberg's tenure as sales manager, the company had given good imported French or German wines. Oberg always claimed that wine was the perfect solution to the gift-giving problem. He had told his assistant that "most people enjoy drinking wine. And those who are not wine drinkers like having it around for visitors or for other occasions. The wine we send is of first quality. By ordering it in large quantities, we can get a good discount. And the sales people don't have to worry about what to give their customers for Christmas. They can spend their time more usefully in selling, rather than in Christmas shopping for presents for their customers."

The wine was ordered from a nearby wholesale importer who was a distant relative of Oberg's. Vogel found that the wine gifts had cost his company about $25,000, including packaging and mailing, for 9,000 bottles last year.

Because Vogel was new in the chemical industry, he decided to get his sales force's opinion on gift-giving. He also wanted to learn from them something about the gift-giving practices in the industry. He found that it was customary for firms to send Christmas gifts to their accounts. The gifts ranged from clocks, watches, gourmet food packages, liquor, and cigarettes to token gifts like calendars and pocket notebooks. In dollar value they ranged from under $1 to about $200.

When Vogel suggested the possibility of discontinuing the gift-giving, most of the sales reps opposed that idea quite strongly. They expressed their fear of losing business. They claimed that the manufacturers' agents who represented Monarch's competitors loomed as a special threat in this matter, because they typically gave very expensive gifts.

One salesman said he would like the opportunity to select the gifts which are given to his customers. Vogel also considered the idea of leaving it up to individual sales reps to buy and send gifts to their customers, but he would provide no company reimbursement for these expenditures.

After his investigation was completed, Vogel believed that the gift-giving issue boiled down to one question: Do gifts influence the buying decision of Monarch's customers? And he was not sure of the answer to that question. He also realized that if he did endorse gift-giving, then this move would raise some additional problems. For instance, what dollar value should be set for a gift? If it is too expensive, the gift might smack of bribery or ostentation. Low-cost items like a calendar might be ineffective or even create the negative impression that Monarch did not think highly of the customer.

Another issue was whether the gift selection should be centralized, which could make it inflexible and impersonal. Or, should the sales people pick their own gifts? This would personalize the activity but would also take valuable selling time. Finally, Vogel wondered whether the sales people should pay for the gifts themselves or the company should reimburse them. Since the emphasis in the compensation plan was on commission, it could be argued that the reps should pay for the gifts, because the gifts bring more business and thus increase commissions.

Questions

1. What policy should F. J. Vogel adopt with respect to gift-giving?
2. If you decide that gift-giving should be continued, then:
    a. What should be the approximate amount spent for each gift?
    b. Should the gift selection be centralized, or should the sales people select their own?
    c. Who should pay for the gifts—the company or the sales reps?

24

Careers in sales management

First say to yourself what you would be; and then do what you have to do.

EPICTETUS

The sales manager of an industrial fasteners company explained the satisfactions of his job as follows:

> I wasn't at all certain that I wanted to be sales manager when it was offered to me. After all, I was making real good money in the field, I liked the freedom and the customer contact, and I wasn't all that sure I would like managing men, let alone be able to do so. Now, as I look back, I can't understand my reluctance to go into management. Working with these men, building the organization, getting things done—I really get a kick out of it. For instance, take a green kid, turn him into a real producer, and you'll know what accomplishment feels like.

Unfortunately, the satisfactions provided by the sales manager's job are not widely known. This chapter will consider what a career in sales management offers in terms of advantages and disadvantages and will demonstrate what a sales manager must do to become successful.

In considering a career in sales management or any other field, you would be wise to examine carefully the attributes of the various careers open to you before casting your lot with any one of them. The cost in lost time, ineffectiveness, and unhappiness of selecting the wrong career is far too high. To help you decide if sales management is the right career for you, therefore, this field will be examined in some detail.

THE CHALLENGE

People of ability thrive on challenge. Jobs that do not utilize their capabilities to a significant degree quickly bore them. A key question you should ask about an anticipated career is: "Will it offer sufficient challenge to sustain my interest in doing a continually better job?" A sales manager's job has such a challenge.

For example, an old-line publishing company with $7 million sales volume was floundering badly. Its 1970 losses were going to be in excess of $2 million. A proven executive was hired from another publishing company. His experience was largely in the editorial side of the business, although he had started his career as a salesman and was widely known in the industry for his selling skills. He was given control over the firm's 40-man sales force with the mandate to remake it into a reasonably productive unit. While the company's average annual sales per sales person was $175,000, it was generally felt that a $300,000 average would be more in line with industry standards.

The new sales manager went into the field to work with each of the men for one day in order to evaluate their talents. He found most of them not only lacking sales skills but also lacking the desire and ability to develop them. He spotted 20 men he could use; the others were asked to find other employment. With overhead reduced, he set about molding his new crew into a hard-hitting sales force. They met for a week in Acapulco to mend fences and to put together a new sales plan; it worked. As the manager later explained, "I used to think that getting out a new book was a challenge, but it's nothing compared to turning a sick operation into a profitable one while giving 20 men more successful careers. It's the toughest job I've ever had, but it made me grow!"

The sales manager is in the front lines, where his performance is easily appraised by peers and superiors. While the abilities or contributions of a bookkeeper, personnel manager, or a design engineer maybe difficult to assess, the sales manager's effectiveness is quite evident. Such measurable indices as sales volume, selling expenses, turnover of the sales force, and percentage of market share are potent arguments either for or against the manager's performance. There is no place to hide.

THE WIDE VARIETY OF SALES MANAGEMENT POSITIONS

In most firms there is no such thing as *the* sales executive or *the* sales manager. The role of a manager in sales work can vary from top-management planner to little more than super sales person. The authority can range from that of a top manager to that of an office clerk. The sales force commanded may be large or small. Each sales managership is unique, and the aspiring executive should consider all such positions separately.

Principal classes of sales force executives

Chief sales force executive. Chapter 1 defined the duties of the chief marketing executive in charge of the entire marketing program for the firm. However, another type of administrator—the chief sales executive—is far more numerous. This is the administrator who has charge of the sales force. His exact role varies among companies, but usually he is given some responsibility for product, price, and distribution policies. The degree of authority over these decision areas varies, depending on the policies of the firm. If top management is marketing oriented, it will probably retain a great deal of authority over marketing policies. But if it has little interest or ability in the marketing field, it may rely heavily on their chief sales executive for guidance.

Assistant sales managers. Frequently, the chief sales force executive has under his direct command one or more assistants to aid him in executing the details of his plans. A subordinate to the chief sales executive who has direct line authority over the sales force usually is given the title of *assistant sales manager.* One who does not have direct authority over the people in the field is usually called *assistant to the sales manager.*

Usually the assistant sales manager works directly with sales force operating problems. The assistant *to* the sales manager may be given staff work, such as forecasting, budgeting, sales correspondence, marketing research, sales promotion, or other technical duties.

In larger organizations, several people may be employed in these capacities. One firm places an assistant sales manager over each of its five branches, though usually such expansions in the number of assistant sales managers follow either a product or territorial division.

Product sales managers. Many firms which distribute a wide line of products find it advisable to place the specific responsibility for a given product or group of products on one person. Usually, these people do not exercise line authority over the sales force but serve strictly in a staff capacity. Since they deal with product policy, pricing, and promotion of particular products, they have little contact with sales force management. Other companies segregate their sales forces on a product basis. At the head of each division is a product-operating executive who is responsible for managing those who sell one line of products. IBM has one group of sales managers for its typewriters, another for its computers, another for copiers, and one for supplies.

Territorial sales managers. A large concern may have a number of territorial sales executives—as many as three levels of them, each with responsibility for a specified geographical area. Often a firm is organized in regions, divisions, and districts. Management may divide the nation into five large regions, with a regional sales manager in charge of each. Each region may be divided into 5 to 12 divisions, depending on the circumstances, with a divisional sales manager in charge of each. Under each division head may be several districts, each with a district sales manager.

It is with these various types of territorial sales managers that this book has been most concerned. They usually are in direct line authority over the sales force, and they perform most sales management functions. In large organizations, most of the recruiting and selection of sales people is done by these territorial sales executives, who are also most directly concerned with their supervision, stimulation, training, pay, expenses, and control. Moreover, it is with this position that the college student should be most concerned, because it can be his or hers in the near future. A successful sales person will likely become some type of territorial sales manager.

Geographic coverage

The amount of territory the sales manager controls can vary from the whole world to a small city. The prospective sales executive can choose the size of area he prefers. A person who wants to minimize traveling should join an organization whose distribution is limited to a small geographic area. Many such opportunities exist in automobile dealerships, appliance distributorships, business machine branch organizations, office supply houses, insurance agencies, and local radio, television, and newspaper firms—in general, any retail or wholesale organization that serves a local trading area. Positions with small firms can be as desirable or challenging as those with companies that distribute nationally.

Sales managers of national concerns must travel more than those in local or regional organizations. The manager should look closely at what is at the top of the ladder before starting to climb it. One executive of an automobile manufacturer complained that he would not have started with the firm if he had realized that each promotion would entail more traveling. It was too late to do anything about it, because he could not walk away from the money. He was too high on the ladder to quit.

Geographic location

Sales management positions are located in every section of the country. Prospective sales executives can determine their living environment by getting a job in the area where they want to live. Of course this limits their bargaining power and choice of firms. It should be pointed out, however, that most sales management positions are located in larger cities and in the more densely populated areas of the country. This is to be expected because it is in these cities that corporations have their home offices, branches, and sales offices. This does not suggest that there are no firms with headquarters in small towns. The home offices of Maytag Company and W. A. Sheaffer Pen Company are both located in small towns in Iowa, for example.

Types of selling activities

The sales executive can also choose the type of selling activity to be administered. Each type of sales job requires a varying degree of pressure, different personal qualities, and varying efforts. The job of managing a door-to-door sales organization is different from the task of guiding individuals in selling large industrial installations to top executives. The task of managing a group of automobile salesmen is different from that of administering the activities of a manufacturer's sales force.

The sales job in each industry is unique and has its own characteristics and demands. In planning a sales management career you should give considerable thought to what you will be happiest selling. Experience indicates that there are great advantages to staying in one industry throughout a sales career. The person who jumps from one industry to another creates problems for himself. Much of his knowledge and many of his contacts would be of little value to him in a new industry.

THE LIFE OF A SALES EXECUTIVE

While it is true that each sales manager's job is unique, there are common elements which we can discuss.

Travel

Some traveling is required for the performance of any sales management job. However, the amount can vary from an occasional convention trip to an extensive amount of field work with the sales branches or with customers.

The amount of traveling sales managers do somewhat depends upon their attitudes toward it. Many enjoy being on the road. They seize every opportunity to get out of the office and into the field because they love it. One man enjoyed the road so much that he failed to spend sufficient time in his office doing the paper work. In the end his boss divided the job by hiring an inside man to take care of the office tasks, thus leaving the manager full time in the field.

Paper work

Inherent in modern management is the nuisance called paper work. No one relishes it, but "It goes with the territory." However, few people who are lax in handling the paper work connected with a job ever advance very far in management. Business systems rely heavily on documents for communicating information among the various units. A manager who neglects the paper work input to the company's information system places a burden, sometimes a difficult one, on other executives who must have the information.

What constitutes doing paper work properly? First, it should be done accurately and completely, not haphazardly. Second, it should be done on time; the manager who is habitually late getting things done seldom lasts long or goes very far. Finally, it is done discriminately; the talented manager learns when to create documents and when not to. Useless reports or memos are one mark of an inefficient administrator.

Conferences

Next to paper work, administrators seem to complain most about the seemingly endless conferences through which they must sit, some of which appear to be totally unnecessary. The conference is a favorite administrative communication and decision-making technique, but it is frequently overused in the name of participative management. Nevertheless, the capable administrator learns how to participate effectively in conferences. Methods have been developed for dealing with others in meetings and conferences.

Work with people

While all administrators must deal with people, this point is particularly true for sales managers. They have one more interface with people than do most of the other executives in the company: The sales manager also deals directly with customers.

If there is one common denominator among sales managers, it is that they must deal with people at all levels. In one day, the sales manager may hold conferences with both the sales force and the board of directors, or may contact both top executives and a customer's operating staff.

Sales

Most sales managers continue to sell to customers to some extent. Some retain certain key accounts upon whom they continue to call. Others go into the field for important sales. Few sales managers ever get very far away from selling—it is the name of the game.

Picking people—talented ones

We have stressed in this book that the sales manager's most important job is selecting sales personnel. The knack of picking winners is critical to the sales manager's own success.

Above all, they are managers

Many supersalesmen have failed as sales managers because they did not realize that, above all, they were expected to be managers in the full context of what management means. A manager *manages!* A manager leads a group to accomplish its mission. A manager gets things together and makes things happen. Responsibility is a key concept. The manager is *responsible* for what happens to the group.

One man whose tenure as sales manager was short seemed to consider his promotion to the position to be an honor recognizing his years of successful service. His concept of the job was badly distorted. He evidently thought that a manager spends a couple of hours in the morning in a paneled office, then retires to the golf course for an afternoon round. Meanwhile, the sales force would take care of itself. "Just let them alone and they'll get the job done!" was his managerial philosophy. It seldom happens that way, as you should realize after completing this text.

Life on the job

One of the major attractions of a sales manager's job is its lack of routine. Every day is a new experience, presenting new problems, different people to meet, and different activities to perform. The sales manager is not bound to a desk; indeed, the problem is just the reverse. It is difficult to find time for the necessary desk work.

THE REWARDS OF A SALES MANAGEMENT JOB

Reward systems are important in shaping the behavior of the people in an organization. In several direct and many subtle ways, how much people are paid and the way it is distributed determines what they will produce. The rewards awaiting the sales manager are an important consideration in your job choice.

Direct monetary rewards—The money

There are a few current studies of the earnings of the "average" sales manager which can give you an idea of how much you might earn in sales management. However, you should bear in mind that the idea of the average sales manager is difficult to pin down. The variations in the data are such that statistics on central tendencies are not very meaningful.

More significantly, inflation quickly makes such studies mostly interesting history. Five-year-old data on what sales managers earn will not be meaningful to you today.

The samples used for such studies also are almost always heavily biased toward big business. One such study which reported that the chief marketing executive earned $79,500 in 1975 was based on a sample size of 360 executives who worked for one of *Fortune* magazines 1,000 largest companies list. Moreover, some of these executives controlled the sales force, but many others had much broader responsibilities.[1]

Sales & Marketing Management magazine reported in 1976 that the average compensation for the 103 sales executives they surveyed was $89,938. However, these were sales executives of large companies whose earnings are reported publicly. Sales managers for smaller concerns make far less than that.[2] The article also cited other several studies of various sales managers in middle management which indicated that $25,000 was about what a district or branch sales manager could expect to make. However, it emphasized that industries and companies vary widely in how much they pay sales managers. The top reported total pay package of $258,466 was for the vice president of sales at Russ Togs.

The pay you can expect in sales management depends upon the industry and the company for whom you work. There are industries that notoriously underpay their people. Similarly, there are companies

---

[1] "Profile of a Chief Marketing Executive," (Chicago: Heidrick Struggles, Inc., 1976).

[2] "Marketing's Finest Hour: Payday," *Sales & Marketing Management*, October 11, 1976, p. 43.

that try to get a lot of mileage from the payroll dollar. Such managements claim they run a "tight ship." Their employees agree only on the word *tight*.

Another perspective on the matter of earnings was provided in an interview of J. W. Bauder of Bauder & Associates, an executive search concern. He began by emphasizing that earnings depends on the industry and the company. When pressed for some statistics, he said, "A national sales manager will make about $60,000 to $70,000. A regional sales manager will make about $50,000, with the district managers making about $40,000."

Indirect monetary payments

Little is known statistically about the extent of indirect monetary payments, such as company-paid insurance plans, pension systems, country club memberships, company-owned airplanes, and other company-furnished additions to a manager's standard of living. However, it has been well established that they are widely used. The importance of these indirect rewards should not be underestimated. There comes a point in a career when a high value may be placed on deferred compensation, such as stock option plans, pension plans, and insurance policies, which are nontaxable or are taxed at lower rates than ordinary income. A $1,000 country club membership would be worth about $2,000 if it were paid as regular compensation.

These considerations are of particular importance to the sales manager. It is easier to justify to the Internal Revenue Service that the sales manager needs such things as company-owned airplanes or a country club membership than it is to build the same case for the production manager. It is far more likely for the sales executive to be given these benefits than it is for any other executive on the same level in the organization.

WHAT IT TAKES TO BE A SUCCESSFUL SALES MANAGER

Education

Not too many years ago a sales manager needed only successful sales experience to qualify for the job. Today, perusal of the job specifications for a wide range of sales management positions indicates that applicants for these jobs should have college degrees. It is disheartening to be asked to counsel mature men with long, successful sales records whose careers are at a dead end for lack of a degree—not lack of talent, just the degree. It is usually impractical for them to return to school, so they remain stuck in their jobs.

Career advancement is easier if the proper credentials are acquired along the way. Career management calls for requisite training and certification. It is difficult to have to go through life explaining why you have failed to acquire the background considered necessary for a job you want.

Experience

Sales experience is necessary, but it is not necessary for you to be an outstanding sales producer to advance into sales managership. Nevertheless, you will have a brighter future as a sales manager if you have performed successfully in a selling job. Such a background provides several advantages.

First, the sales force will have more respect for you than if your sales experience has been limited or unimpressive. They will know that you have been in the field and know the problems they face each day. When you tell them to do something, they will have confidence that you know what you are talking about.

Second, sales experience enables you to be realistic in planning activities and in your supervision and control efforts. You are not likely to expect the impossible of the sales force, but you will be able to recognize a loafer when you see one.

Third, the customer contact provided by selling is valuable for any top policy-making executive. Knowing the problems of the customer is essential in developing sound marketing plans. Having personal acquaintances among the firm's customers is also helpful.

More important than sales experience, however, is managerial experience. If you have had no experience as a supervisor or in some other administrative position, it may be difficult for top management to determine whether you have executive talent.

"But how can I prove I have management skills if I am not given the opportunity to show them?" is a common complaint of sales reps who are continually passed over for promotion because they have had no managerial experience. The person who really has management talents, however, will find ways of showing them to the boss.

Development of administrative skills[3]

One member of the Young Presidents' Organization, when questioned about how he had developed his administrative skills, advanced this idea:

---

[3] This section is adapted from Richard H. Buskirk, *Your Career* (Boston: Cahners Books, 1976), p. 51.

After I got out of college and settled down into my first job, I made it a point to get involved in all sorts of community activities, any group that would take me. Little League, church, neighborhood, you name it and I joined it. I volunteered to do whatever it was that·had to be done. I found out that you can learn a great deal about how to get people to do what it is you want them to do—managing them, if you will—in just such activities.

At first I found I was terrible at it. I remember that first year. It was awful. Everything was messed up, nothing flowed right, and I couldn't organize my people. I didn't do a very good job of it, but with experience I learned the ropes. I learned how to organize projects, how to line up things, and how to get things done. I attribute a large part of my success in business to those early years in community activities where I learned to manage people.

That is the way one person developed administrative skills. He learned by doing. He projected himself into situations that required administrative skills and then was perceptive enough to learn them.

Another individual, the vice president of manufacturing for a large machine tool company, used another approach to develop administrative skills.

In my first years with the company I seized every opportunity I could to show some management skills. I remember that first year the boss wanted someone to organize the company picnic. I stepped forward and knocked myself out to make sure that was the best run picnic the company ever had. And it was! The boss never forgot that. For the next ten years he was continually reminding me of the great job I did on that picnic. Then there was the time we had all of the confusion when the workers struck. We were trying to keep the plant open to get out critical orders and run the place on a skeleton staff. I worked round the clock organizing that effort, and I think more than anything else that was responsible for getting me where I am now. The boss was really impressed with how I held things together during that strike.

A sales manager relates:

I always wanted to be in sales management and I spent a lot of time thinking about how I was ever going to prove to Mr. Howard (the boss) that I had management skills. One day he hired a new salesman and I saw an opportunity. I walked into his office and volunteered to help train the new man. He was so happy to get rid of the responsibility that he agreed. I really trained that young man, and he was immediately successful in the field. Time after time Mr. Howard would comment about how much he liked my ability to train new sales people. I think that's what was responsible for my promotion.

The moral of these stories seems clear: You must aggressively seize every opportunity to use administrative skills. You will only develop these talents if you use them. You will never be a manager if you duck the responsibility for making things happen.

A young junior engineer was able to develop his position rather admirably when he volunteered to open a liaison office for his company—an electronics manufacturing concern—at Las Cruces, New Mexico. This office would work closely with the people at White Sands Testing Station. He went to the city alone, set up shop, and successfully did business there. At the same time, he received his Ph.D. in electrical engineering at New Mexico State University. Now there was a developmental program that did wonders for a career.

Desire

Probably more than anything else, you must *want* to be a successful sales manager if you are to become one. Your desire must be sufficiently intense that you will apply yourself diligently to all the difficult tasks that lie ahead of you. Many otherwise successful sales people do not become sales managers simply because they have no desire to do so. If you really want to be a sales manager, you probably will have the opportunity at some point in your career.

WOMEN IN SELLING

One of the significant current trends in selling is the rapid influx of women into the sales field, both as sales people and managers. While their impact is now being felt in the field, the future is even more impressive. In the fall of 1976, of the 50 students in one of our sales management classes, 29 were women. Previously, a woman taking a sales management course was a rarity.

According to *Sales & Marketing Management*, manufacturing firms now employ 4,100 women sales managers.[4] One reason sales is an attractive field for career women is that it offers pay in proportion to results. According to the women sales managers interviewed, the biggest problem they faced with saleswomen is the reps' unwillingness to move to another area. Such immobility has limited somewhat the promotability of the successful sales woman. The woman who does not want to move would be wise to work for local concerns where a promotion would not mean a transfer.

Comments from some successful women executives interviewed by *Business Week* can provide a few insights into some of the problems women encounter in competing for positions in the business world.

---

[4] "Manage Sales? Yes, She Can," *Sales & Marketing Management* June 13, 1977, p. 33.

"Little boys learn to play on the same team with other boys they don't even like. Their relationships focus on achieving objectives. Little girls are very select about their friends. They emphasize the quality of the relationship with no set goal . . . and business organizations fit the male experience. To succeed as executives, women must resocialize themselves," said Dr. Anne Jardin of Simmons College in Boston.[5]

"Being a manager requires a tremendous amount of toughness. . . . I believe in team management. We all argue in my department. But it's my responsibility at some point to say yes or no," said Juliette Moran of GAF Corp.[6]

"I care about how men feel about women managers, but I'm not there to resocialize anyone. I'm paid to do a job that will affect sales and profits. If someone won't work with me for whatever reason, I will work around him, under him, over him, whatever is possible to move a project," said Diana Levine of Continental Air Lines.[7]

One woman felt that being a woman is more of an asset than a liability because her husband's salary freed her to take risks that a male breadwinner might duck.

It is clear that women are rapidly advancing in the field of selling and sales management. They will undoubtedly make whatever adjustments are required for success in the field.

CONCLUSION

A career in selling offers the college-trained person essentially four advantages:

- An opportunity to make relatively high earnings.
- Freedom of movement and control over one's time.
- Good mobility between firms.
- Extensive contact with people.

However, there are people for whom selling offers little. Some people are uncomfortable in the role of calling on people to ask them to buy something. There are those who are unable to accept a high rate of failure. Others do not like being rejected. The sales person is continually involved in interactions with people who feel socially superior to them. In contemplating a sales career, you should give considerable thought to how well you can deal with these pressures.

---

[5] "Up the Ladder, Finally," *Business Week*, November 24, 1975, p. 65.

[6] Ibid., p. 60.

[7] Ibid., p. 61.

While you will have little difficulty finding a sales job, getting one that meets your particular requirements is another thing. The really good sales jobs do not usually come looking for you. You must exert considerable effort finding them and then being hired.

QUESTIONS AND PROBLEMS

1. If you were applying for the job of president of a corporation and had been a sales manager for a competing organization, what statistics and factual data would you present to prove your abilities?
2. What aspects of the sales manager's job are distasteful to you?
3. Suppose that you wanted to become a sales manager. Formulate a detailed plan for realizing this goal.
4. How does the job of managing a door-to-door sales organization differ from that of administering the activities of people selling business machines to commercial organizations?
5. If you wanted to work as a sales manager in Miami, Florida, how should you go about achieving this goal?
6. The statement has been made that, in general, sales personnel are far more mobile than any other people at the same level in the organization. Why is this so?
7. How should an individual go about preparing to be a sales manager? What type of experience is best? Would a graduate degree be an aid?
8. While sales managers are usually relatively free to arrange their own schedules, many of them find it impossible to break away from their jobs and enjoy themselves. Why is it that some people seem to be able to do their jobs and spend relatively little time doing so, while others seem to become prisoners of their work?
9. If you were seriously considering the field of sales management as a lifetime career, what should you do in order to arrive at a final decision on the matter?
10. As the president of a small, recently established tool company making a new type of crescent wrench, how would you go about finding a topnotch sales manager?

Case 24–1
XEROX OR IBM?
Making a job change

The phone rang late one winter evening in 1977 in the home of an author who had just published a book on career management. The caller said, "You don't know me. My name is Cary Richards. I live in Orange County, California. I've just finished reading your book and had to call you to talk about a decision I have to make. I don't know what to do, and it's driving me crazy. Got a few minutes?"

"Sure," said the author. "It's your money. Besides it may make a good case for another book."

"Thanks. I have been selling copiers for Xerox for a year since I graduated from college. I've been pretty successful. Been right at the top of the producers each month. Now I have an offer from IBM to sell their new minicomputer line. If I accept the IBM offer it means starting all over again at the bottom and going to sales training school."

Richards was asked, "Well then, why are you even contemplating the offer?"

The reply was, "Because it looks to me like a lot better opportunity. Here at Xerox all I am going to do is sell copiers, and I'm not really acquiring that much knowledge doing it. But minicomputers are something else. If I acquire that knowledge I'll have a much broader perspective and much more potential than I do now. In the end I want to go up into management."

"Well, what are your chances of advancing into management with Xerox?" asked the author.

"I've talked it over with the manager, and he said that if I show managerial capabilities I will be promoted. And I already have one year in with Xerox," Richards replied.

The two men explored the matter in depth for more than 45 minutes over the long-distance lines. Clearly Richards was most undecided about what he should do. On the one hand the Xerox job was paying extremely well, and he was having considerable success with it despite his lack of advancement into management. On the other hand, it appeared that the selling of IBM minicomputers offered a greater potential. However, Richards was finding it difficult to accept the rather substantial reduction in pay that would result, as well as having to go back to the beginning of a career.

The conversation ended on an indefinite note, but the issues had been somewhat clarified.

Question

1. What should Cary Richards do?

Case 24–2
TODD ROGERS
It's a long, long trail

Todd Rogers had been graduated from a large midwestern university in 1946 after returning from Naval service in World War II. He majored in marketing, since he strongly desired a career in selling. After interviewing several of the nation's leading marketing organizations, he accepted the offer of National Corporation. This was a firm that was highly respected in the industry for its aggressive marketing policies and its fine sales training program.

Todd learned his lessons well under the guidance of one of the industry's finest sales managers. He rose rapidly in the ranks and, in 1955, was promoted to sales manager. In 1959 he was made president of a small subsidiary the National Corporation established to market a new line of products it had developed. Todd took the fledgling company and built it into a profitable small organization.

Unfortunately, Todd's personal life had not prospered as well. As president of the subsidiary, he was making only $40,000 a year. He felt that he not only needed more money than that, but he had earned it.

In the early 1960s Todd invested some money in a mobile home manufacturing company that was just being formed. While this company had much promise, a multitude of problems plagued it. Serious management deficiencies hampered its growth, and in turn this created serious financial problems. The investors had to keep putting more and more money into the new enterprise. Moreover, they called on Todd frequently for managerial help. Since by 1968 he had more than $100,000 invested in the mobile home enterprise, he felt he had to do everything possible to make it successful. Thus he spent increasingly more time with it and less time tending to the affairs of National Corporation.

The president of National Corporation was extremely fond of Todd and had supported his career almost from the beginning. He was aware of Todd's involvement with the other enterprise and did not approve of it. They had several friendly talks about the matter in which Todd was urged to get out.

The problem was he could not see any way out of it. There were no buyers, and the company was technically insolvent. One of the firm's big distributors had gone bankrupt while owing the manufacturer about $300,000. Things were bleak enough for Todd. Then his wife left, and his personal life crumbled.

Relationships with National's management deteriorated even though Todd's operation continued to be profitable. Finally, matters came to a head. Depending upon who was talking, Todd was either fired or resigned. No one was quite certain what precipitated the termination, but the result was final. Todd now could devote his full time to the affairs of the mobile home manufacturing company.

Even with much effort and borrowing, the company failed in 1973. However, after a successful suit against the distributor that owed the company money, Todd was able to pay the company's creditors and get his own money back.

In 1974 he remarried. His new wife strongly preferred to live in Knoxville, Tennessee, since her family and her children lived there. Todd felt bound to that location. Thus he accepted a sales job with Lake Company, a medium-sized but highly profitable firm that was attempting to enter the markets Todd had previously sold to for National.

Even though the scope of his activities was coast to coast, he was able to work from his Knoxville home. This job paid him $30,000 a year in salary plus a 1 percent override on the business he developed. He had by far the most successful record of any of the people who had been hired to develop this new entry into the market. However, internal politics in the home office, located in Toledo, Ohio, was weakening his position in the company. He sensed he was being frozen out of the firm. If he were to quit, he would lose the 1 percent override on all the business received from the distributors he had signed up. He decided to hang on for as long as he could.

Todd kept quiet and went about his way. Covertly, he was looking for a place to land. He became interested in a small Knoxville operation that was just getting ready to market a new method of distributing the same product Todd had been selling. There was doubt if this new method would work, but if it did, the profit potential was great.

Todd accepted the presidency of this new company, but it was kept secret in the industry. When the tests of the new idea were not favorable, Todd dropped the matter after a two-week tenure in the presidency. The investors in the new company had urged him to take their enterprise and build it up conventionally, as he had done previously with National's subsidiary. If he would do so, they would give him 50 percent of the business, with no investment on his part. He refused, saying, "I've done it once, and I don't feel like doing it again."

To hedge against his future departure from the Lake Company, Todd started working in a real estate development company in Knoxville. After six months moonlighting in real estate, however, he had little to show for his time and efforts.

In late 1977, he did not know what to do. He still had his position with the Lake Company, but things did not look too promising there. He had been cut back to half time with them, and several of his expense allowances had been discontinued.

As he put it to a friend, "Here I am, 53 years old. I've been to the top and can still produce. But I don't know what to do."

Questions

1. Evaluate Todd Rogers' career path.
2. What mistakes did he make?
3. What do you recommend he should do?

Case 24–3
THE STIRLING COMPANY
Selection of a sales manager

Paul Lang, vice president of marketing for the Stirling Company of Montclair, New Jersey, knew he had to make a decision on whom to select as managers of the company's 28-man sales force. Seven months previously the former sales manager had resigned to accept a vice presidency of sales for a larger competitor. During the previous few months, Lang had assumed direct control of the sales force, but he clearly saw that in doing so he was not only neglecting his other responsibilities but also was doing a poor job of managing the salesmen.

Lang's search for a new manager had narrowed down to two men, Ben Worth and Dale Rugg, both of whom were seemingly well qualified for the job.

The Stirling Company made and distributed a wide line of special-purpose fasteners used by metal fabricating companies. The salesmen worked closely with both the purchasing agents and the engineers in the customers' organizations. While there was some calling on potential new accounts, the bulk of the salesmen's time was spent working with established accounts in the Middle Atlantic states.

The sales manager was charged with the full responsibility for maintaining an effective field sales force. This included hiring, firing, training, supervising, compensation, controlling, and evaluating the salesmen. Moreover, he was responsibile for all the paper work connected with the sales department. At times he had to work closely with the salesmen in handling special accounts or particularly important orders. There were no field supervisors to help the men with their problems. A large portion of the sales manager's time was spent in meetings with other members of management in order to coordinate sales force activities with all other functions of the business. The manager had to work particularly closely with Lang.

Lang had taken the files on the two prospective managers home for the weekend to contemplate his decision. He had decided to announce his selection Monday morning.

As he reviewed Ben Worth's file, he fully realized that if Worth were not made sales manager, some repercussions might be felt. Ben was not only the company's best salesman but also was well regarded throughout the organization. He had sold for the company for 17 years and before that had worked in production for four years after graduation from high school. Worth, now 38 years old, had outsold all other salesmen for the past ten years and had always exceeded quotas by more than 20 percent, even in difficult times. Since the sales force was paid on a commission basis, Ben had become moderately wealthy. His average annual earnings over the past decade had been about $30,000; last year his earnings were $46,000.

Worth was married to an understanding woman of considerable charm. Their three children were in high school and, to Lang's knowledge, were outstanding youngsters. The Worths were extremely adept at entertaining and socializing with people. Hardly a week passed that they did not have some type of social event in their home.

Although Worth had not attended college, Lang knew he was intelligent and had acquired considerable business know-how. He had accumulated an impressive library of business books and had participated in many meaningful self-improvement programs.

Upon learning of the previous sales manager's resignation, Worth had come directly to Lang and requested the position. He outlined his achievements for the company and then gave a brief account of the goals that he would work toward as manager. Lang recalled acknowledging at the time that Worth was certainly a prime candidate for the job and that he could be assured he would be given every consideration. However, Lang had told Worth that the decision was not entirely his (Lang's) to make. The president had suggested that a thorough search be made in order to assure that the best man available was placed in the position. The president felt keenly that the company had prospered largely because of its excellent sales force, and he wanted to do nothing to jeopardize that success formula.

Privately, Lang had some reservations about making Worth sales manager, but he was hesitant to bring his thoughts into the open for fear of engendering animosities that would later haunt him. First, he was fearful that if he promoted Worth he would lose a good salesman and get a poor manager. He had seen it happen in other companies, and sales management literature was full of warnings that top salesmen might not make good sales managers. The two jobs required different skills. Second, Lang was worried that Worth find the sales manager's salary of $35,000 inadequate, despite his insistence that he would be more than happy with it. Third, he was afraid that because Worth preferred customer contact, he would not not stay in the office enough to do the required paper work. Finally, Lang was disturbed by Worth's relationships with the other men; he was well liked by everyone and was known as "a guy who would give you the shirt off his back." Would Worth be able to maintain discipline among his men?

Worth had forced Lang to make a selection soon by appearing in his office Friday morning to issue a rather strong ultimatum: He had been offered a sales managership with another company and had to give an answer within two weeks. Worth had made it clear that he did not want to leave, but he would do so to become a sales manager if he did not get the opportunity with the Stirling Company. Lang inwardly rebelled at this holdup play, but he realized that it was a fair tactic.

Lang proceeded to review his other leading candidate, Dale Rugg, with whom he had been acquainted for more than four years. They were both members of the New York Sales Executives Club and the Glen Ridge Country Club. Rugg was sales manager for an electronic instrumentation company and had developed an enviable reputation in the industry for building an outstanding sales force.

Rugg was 32 years old, married, had two young children, and was a graduate of the Florida State University School of Business. While he had a most agreeable disposition, all evidence indicated that he ran a tight ship. He demanded high performance and got it.

Lang had casually mentioned the job opening to Rugg one day at the club, on the off chance that he might know some outstanding person he could recommend for the job. Rugg had hesitated for a moment, then replied, "Let's have a drink. I think we should talk."

He then confided that his firm was about to be sold to a large conglomerate, and from what he had learned about it, he was somewhat less than enthralled about his potential bosses. "They are not my kind of people," he went on to say. "From what I know of you and your operation, I think I would like very much to be considered for the job."

Lang sat for two hours contemplating the pros and cons of going with each man. He was still undecided.

Question

1. Whom would you make sales manager?

Index

Index